Wyndham Lewis titles published by Black Sparrow Press

The Apes of God (novel) (1981)

Blast 1 (journal) (1981)

Blast 2 (journal) (1981)

The Complete Wild Body (stories) (1982)

Journey Into Barbary (travel) (1983)

Self Condemned (novel) (1983)

Snooty Baronet (novel) (1984)

Blast 3 (journal) (1984)

Rude Assignment (autobiography) (1984)

The Vulgar Streak (novel) (1985)

Rotting Hill (stories) (1986)

The Caliph's Design (essays) (1986)

Men Without Art (essays) (1987)

The Art of Being Ruled (philosophy) (1989)

Creatures of Habit & Creatures of Change: Essays on Art, Literature & Society 1914–1956 (essays) (1989)

Tarr: The 1918 Version (novel) (1990)

The Revenge for Love (novel) (1991)

Time and Western Man (philosophy) (1993)

Forthcoming:

The Enemy (3 volumes) (journal)

The Lion and the Fox (essays)

America and Cosmic Man (essays)

WYNDHAM LEWIS

TIME AND
WESTERN MAN

EDITED WITH AFTERWORD
AND NOTES BY
PAUL EDWARDS

BLACK SPARROW PRESS
SANTA ROSA ◀ 1993

ACKNOWLEDGMENTS

Cover illustration: "Figures in the Air" by Wyndham Lewis. Pencil, Pen and Ink, Watercolor, 1927. Michel 635.

The artwork by Wyndham Lewis facing the title page and at the foot of the last page of text are from the original London edition published in 1927.

Previously unpublished sections of *Time and Western Man* printed with the permission of the Poetry/Rare Books Collection, University Libraries, SUNY at Buffalo.

Previously unpublished drafts and correspondence printed by permission of the Department of Rare Books, Cornell University.

Letter by Wyndham Lewis to C. H. Prentice quoted by permission of Random House UK Limited.

Black Sparrow Press books are printed on acid-free paper.

LIBRARY OF CONGRESS CATALOGING-IN-PUBLICATION DATA

Lewis, Wyndham, 1882-1957.
    Time and western man / Wyndham Lewis ; edited by Paul Edwards.
      p.   cm.
    Includes bibliographical references and index.
    ISBN 0-87685-879-5 (cloth trade ed.) : $30.00 — ISBN 0-87685-880-9 (deluxe cloth ed.) : $35.00 — ISBN 0-87685-878-7 (paper ed.) : $17.50
    1. Time. 2. Literature, Modern—History and criticism. 3. History—Philosophy. 4. Spengler, Oswald, 1880-1936. Untergang des Abendlandes. 5. Civilization—History. I. Edwards, Paul, 1950-   II. Title.
BD638.L4   1993
115—dc20   93-1568
                                               CIP

EDITOR'S NOTE

TIME AND WESTERN MAN has been virtually unobtainable for many years, but it is one of Wyndham Lewis's major works, and no student of Lewis can afford to (or, having sampled it, would want to) ignore it. It is also indispensable for an understanding of the Modernist movement and the wider culture of the first half of this century, since (in the words of John Holloway) "for insight, for largeness of view, for synthesis (and analysis as well) of the thought contemporary with itself and also the whole European background of that thought, it is matchless among English books written this century."

The first objective of this edition has been simply to make *Time and Western Man* available in a clear, reliable text. Two chapters that Lewis dropped from the book at a fairly late stage are also published for the first time, in the Editorial Section. They contain a more extensive and detailed engagement with the ideas of Henri Bergson, in particular, than can be found in the book as published — and Lewis considered Bergson to be the fountainhead of the "Time-doctrines" that he was combating. They also provide fascinating insight into Lewis's own attempts to define positively the nature of our sense of the "real."

The remainder of the unusually large Editorial Section is intended to assist both the general reader and the specialist student in a number of ways. The Explanatory Notes give references for nearly all quotations, and attempt to provide a context for some of Lewis's discussions, in relation both to his own other works and to the writers and thinkers he discusses. The first part of the Afterword attempts a similar but broader contextualization more discursively. Part II of the Afterword gives a detailed account of the emergence and development of *Time and Western Man* from Lewis's projects for *The Man of the World, The Childermass* and *The Enemy*. A knowledge of this history is essential to an understanding of what the book really is. Though the account given here will seem too detailed for some, it is intended more as a stimulus for further research than as a definitive statement. The Table of Variants in the Textual Appendix performs a related function; it is not merely a dustbin full of misprints

and rejected readings (though these are indeed included). Many
passages from manuscripts and earlier drafts that the editor considers significant are given in the table, and it is hoped that these
will illuminate, by contrast with, the text that Lewis decided to
publish.

While the main body of this volume, therefore, presents *Time
and Western Man* as a self-contained book, uncluttered by any
editorial accretions, the Editorial Section tries to open the book
out, and to show how it may be regarded as the end-result of
Lewis's combined struggles with the compositional, intellectual,
economic, personal and cultural difficulties of shaping his work
into publishable form.

Note that within the Editorial Section all references to pages
of this edition are given in the form "page 267," while page
references to other books, etc., are in the more conventional form
of "p. 267."

Many people have helped me in producing this edition. A Small
Personal Research Grant awarded by the British Academy enabled
me to travel to the United States and study Lewis's manuscripts
and books at the Olin Library, Cornell University, the
Poetry/Rare Books Collection in SUNY at Buffalo, and the Harry
Ransom Humanities Research Center at the University of Texas.
I am most grateful to the staff of those institutions for the kind
and friendly help they gave me. Particular thanks to Michael
Basinski, Lucy Burgess, Lynne Farrington and Sue Murphy.
Michael Bott of the library of the University of Reading was
especially helpful in providing me with material from the Chatto
and Windus archive held there. I have probably spent most time
on research in Cambridge University Library, however, tracking down the quotations that Lewis for some reason neglected
to identify. My thanks to the staff of the library for all their
book-fetching.

David Peters Corbett let me consult a draft version of his notes
for *The Enemy*, No. 1, which saved me a lot of time in writing
my own notes for "The Revolutionary Simpleton." Peter Nicholls
and Ian Patterson have also helped with information for notes.
Thanks are also due to Peter Caracciolo, John Constable, Howard

Erskine-Hill, Mrs. Valerie Eliot, Geoff Gilbert (for pointing out that Lewis always dots his i's), Hugh Kenner, John Martin (for patience), and Alan Munton (for commenting on a draft of Part II of the Afterword). Thanks finally to Claire and her mother, for support and help with proofreading.

CONTENTS

Part II

Part III

EDITORIAL SECTION

AUTHOR'S PREFACE

THIS PREFACE IS ADDRESSED to the general reader. It has been my object, from the start, to secure an audience of people not usually attentive to abstract discussion, the general educated man or woman. Everyone, I am persuaded, must today fit themselves for thinking more clearly about the problems of everyday life, by accustoming themselves to think of the abstract things existing, more distinctly than ever before, behind such problems. Where everything is in question, and where all traditional values are repudiated, the everyday problems have become, necessarily, identical with the abstractions from which all concrete things in the first place come. And the everyday life is too much affected by the speculative activities that are renewing and transvaluing our world, for it to be able to survive in ignorance of those speculations. So everyone, I think, in one degree or another, has this alternative. Either he must be prepared to sink to the level of chronic tutelage and slavery, dependent for all he is to live by upon a world of ideas, and its manipulators, about which he knows nothing: or he must get hold as best he can of the abstract principles involved in the very "intellectual" machinery set up to control and change him.

"As best he can," I have said: and there is the difficulty. Everything in our life today conspires to thrust most people into prescribed tracks, in what can be called a sort of *trance of action*. Hurrying, without any significant reason, from spot to spot at the maximum speed obtainable, drugged in that mechanical activity, how is the typical individual of this epoch to do some detached thinking for himself? All his life is disposed with a view to banishing reflection. To be alone he finds terrifying. But even if that were not so, it would be difficult for him to secure the necessary seclusion for a contemplative "spell," in which he could bring himself "abreast of" the contemporary problems. His life thrusts new problems upon him in profusion and simultaneously withdraws all possibility of his getting the time to grasp them, it would seem. This is the inherent difficulty that the modern man must in some way overcome.

Whether as a clearing house for scientific theory, a "critical" tribunal, or a carefully organized deposit for inherited wisdom, of the great "questions left over" when science has done, the department labelled "Philosophy" in our modern intellectual economy is of immense practical importance. It is not merely a luxury for the idle or for the "very clever": in its widest interpretation, it is the department where everything ultimately comes up for judgment. Such an invention as wireless, for example, which, in the first years of its appearance, runs wild, left to its own devices, as it were, will certainly in the end be subjected to critical discipline, for the good of all of us. It is the philosophical intelligence, broadly, that reviews the claims of such a phenomenon of mechanical creation for survival, and fixes the terms.

But the function of Philosophy has a more positive side. Notions are manufactured or concocted in its laboratory that come out later into the concrete everyday world: there they assume shapes as definite as aeroplanes and crystal sets, though of another order. That is why the rough ascent into the region of the abstract, proposed by me in this essay, should be undertaken by all those aspiring to an enfranchised position, or willing to make the effort to retain it. If you balk this exacting adventure you must sink, as things are, into a condition that will be less than free.

The great technical inventions — wireless, the petrol-engine, the cinema — affect radically the life of everybody, no one can fail to observe; but mere notions, or philosophical theories, not incarnated in any physical discovery, are not so palpably influential. Yet the metaphysics of Relativity, the doctrine of "Behavior," of "Gestalt," of "Emergent Evolution," and so forth, have an even more intimate, and a more insidious, effect. People feel themselves being influenced, but their brain and not their crystal set is the sensitive receptive instrument. As the mechanism of the brain is not visible, the inventions of theoretic thought remain undefined for the Plain Man. Ideas, or systems of ideas, possess no doubt an organism, as much as a motor-car or wireless set: but their *techne*, or application, and their components, the stuff out of which they are manufactured, are facts that are in a sense too vague to be readily accessible, it is generally felt.

There is no way, however, of making this study so attractively simple that the most breathlessly busy of Plain Men can be induced to engage upon it with the guarantee that its essentials will be economically garaged in his head under half an hour. It is quite impossible to "pot" the thought that makes the world go round in such a way that anybody, after a fortnight's application for half an hour a day, will, for the rest of his life, recognize at a glance the true nature of any ideology that is sprung upon him. That cannot be done.

What I think can be done is this. The more intelligent of the student-youth, or the more intelligent of those people, of whom there are a fair number, who follow the transformations of the intellect, can have their attention directed first to certain manifestations of will or purpose in the life around them: and then they can be referred back to certain *ideas*, that are the origin of those *things*. Some art form — as with popular music — suddenly takes a new and unexpected turn. Jazz is such a mode. Purpose is betrayed in this event: but the average man marvels, and if he asks himself *Why?* seeking to account for this appearance, he always has the Zeitgeist to fall back on, if he has no other answer. Cross-word Puzzles, Community Singing, and so on, flower for him, for no reason. They are "Nature," Fate, Zeitgeist, not the work of man. He who is so prone to personalize everything, never sees a human activity expressing itself in these things, for some reason.

Of course the paths that lead from the metaphysical principle to the *event*, upon the plane of everyday occurrence, to the happenings of politics or of social fashion, are often very complexly disposed. Even if people are a little familiar with the ideational background, and thoroughly familiar with the concrete outcropping in fact and in "history," it is not always easy to demonstrate the uninterrupted liaison. But some kind of chart of these relations can be drawn up, so that the general reader can equate things that at first sight have little connection.

But, suppose that you advance such a statement as the following. "(1) Sacco and Vanzetti are executed under such and such circumstances. (2) That is owing to the over-emotional strain in the composition of Hegel, that made his mind an imperfect philosophic instrument. (3) The reason that that philosophic instrument exercised the influence it did was on account of the romanticism prevalent in the years succeeding the French Revolution. (4) Because it served the ends of this person and that," etc., etc. (I am not maintaining the truth of this particular assertion, but merely taking that concrete event for the purpose of topical illustration, and suggesting not too wild a liaison from that.) If

you said this the average person would be none the wiser, in the
first place because "Hegel" (whose philosophy is in any case a
very repulsively technical one) would mean nothing to him. But
the best way even to get people to learn something about
philosophy would be *to show it at work*. The "ideas" of Plato
can be shown at work. The philosophy of Hegel can be shown
at work in Herzen, Bakunin and Lenin. The theories of Darwin
can be shown at work all over the world. Nietzsche trumpets
from the balconies of the Chigi Palace. I could show you many
Bergsonians. Both Bonnot, the famous French chauffeur-gunman,
and T. E. Hulme, the philosopher, were Sorelists, disciples of
Georges Sorel, the roman catholic, pragmatist Marxian.

There, anyhow, is the best method of showing the Plain Man
a little philosophy. In the *Bourgeois Gentilhomme* M. Jourdain,
referring to his own casual words, exclaims in his famous question, "Ah, is this *Prose* then, that we all speak?" He was astounded
to find that what daily issued from his mouth was such an important thing as "Prose." In the same way he could have been
told that many of his actions were "Philosophy," in quite as true
a sense as all his words were "Prose." And today in any company of people, whether it be a "highbrow" tea party or café
gathering, a labour demonstration or a cabinet meeting, what
they are all doing and thinking is as truly "Philosophy," in one
form or another, and however indirectly, as M. Jourdain's speech
was "de la prose."

That is why I start my book with the concrete manifestations
of the "Time-mind." The best way to expound the time-
philosophy, I thought, was to show how it has acted upon Miss
Stein, or Mr. Joyce, Mr. D. H. Lawrence or Mr. Anderson.

Miss Stein writes in her *Explanation* of her recent literary
compositions:

There must be *time*. . . . This is the thing that is at present the most
troubling and if there is the time that is at present the most troublesome
the time-sense that is at present the most troubling is the thing that
makes the present the most troubling.

That gives an account (of course in an affected stammering form)
of what is in fact at the bottom of the whole "transitional" chaos.
He who understands fully what Miss Stein means by "time" in
this connection (not the Miss Stein that is the *faux-naïf* literary
performer, but the old pupil of James and follower of Bergson)

will possess the key to the "transitional" chaos, which he can then open at will, inform himself at his leisure of the true value of its highly-advertised interior, and then close it again, and lock it on the outside. The more people able to shut and lock that door the better. When enough have learnt how to do so, let us hope it will remain shut for good.

The body of this chaos, pumped full of "Time" in the metaphysical sense (this "Time" called the "mind of Space," and which is in fact the "mind" of this restless chaos), that body I have extended in this book, and dissected. I have especially laid bare for your inspection the clock-work of its "mind." And, that is the essential fact, *its mind is Time* (cf. Professor Alexander, *Space Time and Deity*). The full meaning of the metaphysical concept "Time," as understood and deified, in contempory philosophy, and imitated, in one form or another, in art, is what I have set out to explore.

So as I do not despise the hurried reader (and would catch him, if I could, upon the wing) I will make a few suggestions that I hope may be of assistance to him, in his haste. Had I written in such language as would have made my essay available for practically everybody, it could not have achieved its ends upon that plane of the "learned world" where it also had to act. On the other hand, I have gone out of my way to write a book that, with a little application, may be available to any averagely educated person.

What I hope to have done by opening my discussion of the great orthodoxy of "Time" by discussions of works of art, novels and pictures, is to have tempted the lazier or busier of my audience into taking *the critical step* over into the abstract region, there where ideas, and not people or events, have to be encountered. Once such an unwilling, or timid, person, or "hurried man," has been persuaded to grapple with *one* metaphysical ghost, and found he has succeeded in "laying" it, that is in laying it out, he will perhaps proceed, encouraged by his prowess, to engage in a series of such encounters. *L'appétit vient en mangeant*: in the end he will be led to enter this metaphysical world, it is to be hoped, as easily as he enters his club or his own bathroom. That has at all events been my idea or one of them. It has been my ambition to assist in the breeding of a race of transformed "hurried men," in the anglo-saxon world, who handle ideas as expertly as any other people, and whom, in consequence, it is less difficult to fool with transparently shoddy doctrines. In England and America we want a new learned minority as sharp as razors, as fond of discourse as a Greek, familiar enough with the abstract to be able to handle the concrete. In short we want a new race of philosophers, *instead* of "hurried men," speed-cranks, simpletons, or robots.

I would suggest to what is still "a hurried man," dismayed at the sight of all the hard work and intricate or "difficult" matter confronting him on the threshold of the second book of this essay, that he should start at p. 205, that is Book Two, Part I, Chapter 7. *Time upon the social plane and in philosophy*, the chapter is called.

In that chapter the question I set out to answer is this: Is the *time-mind*, the historic or chronological view of the world and of human life, to be found on the philosophic plane as well as upon the social and literary plane? On the latter I have shown it to exist, fairly conclusively, I think. But is there any parallel to this in the field of theoretic thought? If so (and there is no difficulty in demonstrating that there is, I claim), then surely there is likely to be some connection between the two. And, further, the operations by which these two parallel cults have stimulated and seconded each other, should be of considerable interest. They should provide us with a pattern by which all such inter-dependence could be gauged.

Upon p. 207 I quote Professor Alexander, where he says that it is "perhaps . . . Mr. Bergson in our day who has been the first philosopher to take Time seriously." He, indeed, Bergson, "finds in Time conceived as *durée* . . . the animating principle of the universe." And Professor Alexander associates Bergson with the mathematical physicists in this splendid work of giving Time, as a metaphysical conception, its just due.

At the present moment the special question of the exact relation of Time to Space has been forced into the front, because *Time has recently come into its full rights*, in science through the mathematical physicists, in philosophy also through Prof. Bergson . . . (*Space Time and Deity*, vol. i., p. 36.)

If the reader now turns from p. 207 to p. 220, he will find Dr. Wildon Carr, Bergson's british disciple, linking up Bergson and Croce, the most renowned living italian philosopher. They "reach," he tells us, "practically an identical concept." They reach this by different roads.

The "fundamental agreement . . . between the philosophy of Bergson and that of Croce" consists in the fact that both "focus attention" upon the *dynamical* aspect of reality.

Dynamical, as the most "hurried" of men is aware, means the bustle and rush of *action* — of Big Business, Armaments, Atlantic "hops," Wall Street, and Mussolini. A "dynamic personality" means, in journalism, an iron-jawed oil-king in an eight-cylinder car, ripping along a new motor-road, with a hundred-million-dollar deal in a new line of poison-gas bombs blazing in his super-brain, his eye aflame with the lust of battle — of those battles in which others fight and die. So there is no need to explain what "dynamical" means.

It is no "mere coincidence," says Dr. Wildon Carr, that Bergson and Croce reach the same conclusions. No. It "marks a tendency" in both these exalted thinkers "to emphasize the dynamic aspect of reality."

But how, in detail, do they differ, or rather agree, these two great and influential thinkers, only each with his own way of approach? Well, for Bergson "time is a material and not merely a formal element of the world" — Time is the very "stuff of things." Croce, on his side, does not talk about the abstraction "Time," but rather about "History." For Croce, "history is identical with philosophy."

As I am here engaged in showing the more breathless reader how to read the chapter I have indicated as a good one to start with, if, as is probable, he baulks the solid track I have laid down, and wishes for a short cut, I will go a few steps farther with him. Next he can turn to p. 211. There he will see a quotation from Bosanquet. For the italian "idealist" philosopher, such as Gentile, as much for the english "realist," such as Alexander,

in its basis and meaning reality is a history or an unending dialectical progress.

But this is what Dr. Wildon Carr has just asserted, in his summary of the doctrine of Croce. "*History* is identical with *philosophy*." All reality is history, tout court. So we now have in front of us a group of philosophers, gathered from various fields of thought. There is Alexander, Gentile, Bergson, Croce, Wildon Carr. In its very heart and at its very roots, for all of them, *reality* is "History," or reality is "time," which is the same thing, that is the capital fact, with all it implies, that has to be firmly grasped and understood.

But what is "Time"? That is a question that Spengler says no one should ever have been allowed to ask. But that the reader, nevertheless, disregarding Spengler, will next, I hope, press on to enquire. I would then refer him to p. 159. There he will obtain a little initial information upon that subject. He will anyhow read Bergson's account of what "Time" meant for the Hellene, in contrast to what it means for us. The chapter entitled "History as the Specific Art of the Time School" he might turn to next (p. 245). That would inform him what is intended by "history" in these discussions. And then if he wished to know how history is interpreted by a typical Time-mind, he could turn to the analysis of Spengler's *Decline of the West* (pp. 252–288). That is a very long and careful analysis: if he were not familiar with Spengler's book the reader would be constantly held up by references to things with which he was not familiar. So I would only refer him to that to suggest that he should read it here and there, with a view to gathering some further notions as to what "history," for Spengler or Croce, means.

As to my own position in this controversy, and the impulse that has brought me out to attack this formidable league, I cannot do better than reproduce more or less verbatim the preface that appeared at the head of "The Revolutionary Simpleton," when that appeared as an essay in my Review, *The Enemy*:

This essay is a comprehensive study of the "time"-notions which have now, in one form or another, gained an undisputed ascendancy in the intellectual world. In Book One the *time-mind*, as I have called it, is considered in its more concrete manifestations — as we find it, notably, in works of fiction, poetry, or painting. In Book Two the significance of all that type of belief and feeling which can conveniently be marshalled under the concept "Time," is examined in detail. How the "timelessness" of einsteinian physics, and the time-obsessed flux of Bergson, merge in each other; and how they have conspired to produce, upon the innocent plane of popularization, a sort of mystical time-cult, is shown. How history and biography, and more particularly autobiography, are, more truly than anything else, the proper expression of this *chronological* philosophy, is canvassed in the literary criticism of Book One and in the analysis of Spengler's "world-as-history" doctrine in Book Two.

As the object of this book is ultimately to contradict, and if possible defeat, these particular conceptions upon the popular, the concrete, plane, where they present themselves, as it is, in a rather misleading form, I have attempted to present my argument in the plainest manner that I could. With this end in view I have chosen to open the discussion among books such as those of Proust or Joyce, which have been widely read, and which are popularly accessible, and in which I consider that, with a very little attention, the *time-cult* can be observed in full operation. In this way I, at the outset, unmask the *will* that is behind the Time-philosophy, by displaying it in the heart of the representative ferment produced by it — in the full, instinctive indulgence and expansion of the artistic impulse, and imposing its values upon the impressionable material of life.

The main characteristic of the Time-mind from the outset has been a hostility to what it calls the "spatializing" process of a mind *not* a Time-mind. It is this "spatializing" capacity and instinct that it everywhere assails. In its place it would put the Time-view, the flux. It asks us to see everything *sub specie temporis*. It is the criticism of this view, the Time-view, from the position of the plastic or the visual intelligence, that I am submitting to the public in this book.

BOOK ONE

THE REVOLUTIONARY SIMPLETON

"It is in literature that the concrete outlook of humanity receives its expression. Accordingly, it is to literature that we must look, particularly in its more concrete forms, namely in poetry and drama, if we hope to discover the inward thoughts of a generation."

Science and the Modern World, *A. N. Whitehead*

CHAPTER ONE

SOME OF THE MEANINGS OF ROMANCE

AT THE CONFERENCE OF the Peace Society, on the eve of the Crimean War, John Bright reminded his audience of the title of their god, who was called the "Prince of Peace"; and he asked them: "Is this a reality? Or is your Christianity a romance? Is your profession a dream?" Christianity has been, for the European, strictly speaking, a *romance*. Also, of course, it has been an exceptionally bloody one, just as his socialism, in its turn, is proving.

Romance and reality, these are the two terms we most often employ to contrast what we regard as dream and truth respectively. The "romantic" approach to a thing is the unreal approach. John Bright used the word above in the sense of a lie. It is not, however, the calamitous snobberies waiting on Romance that concern us so much here. The attitude to "time" is the main subject of this essay, and Romance is a decisive factor in that attitude. That is why I am starting with a brief scrutiny of the romantic mind.

There is nothing that has a monopoly of "reality," nor a monopoly of "romance." Romance, even, is certainly real, existing not in the imperfect manner of a unicorn or of a golden mountain (though existing as highly mentalized fact certainly); and Reality can be, when it wishes, extremely romantic; if "romantic" you decide shall describe that which is full of the pungent illusion of life, and not consider it as the description, merely, of the unreal and impossible glamours of some super-existence.

That there could be anything "beautiful" about machinery, or anything "romantic" about industry, was never so much as entertained by the victorian mind. Wilde, I believe, was the first person to popularize the paradox that machinery could be beautiful. The conception of the romance of industry — indeed, the claim that nothing is so overwhelmingly romantic, looked at properly, that is from the point of view of the great monopolist, as is industry — marks the frontier between the Money-age in which we live, and the still aristocratic and feudal age that preceded it — when love and war were the typical "romances," what we still think of as the Romance-age proper. But the Money-age has created new values. It has incidentally bought the term Romance.

Even such a man as Fourier at the opening of the last century, was attacked with the sharpest disgust at the sight of the, at that time, novel pretension of Commerce to be *romantic*. In *The Art of Being Ruled* I have quoted a very interesting passage from his writings expressing his hatred of what he regarded as the decay of "poetry," or its transference to such things as soaps and boot-polishes. I will use some of it again here, as it shows how a vigorous and innovating mind, on the spot, when that great ideologic revolution was first occurring, could review the matter:

The philosophers, accustomed to reverence everything which comes in the name and under the sanction of commerce, will . . . consecrate their servile powers to celebrating its [the new order's] praises. . . . It is no longer to the Muses nor to their votaries, but to Traffic and its heroes, that Fame now consecrates her hundred voices. . . . The true grandeur of a nation, its only glory, according to the economists, is to sell to neighbouring nations more clothes and calicoes than we purchase of them. . . . The savants of the nineteenth century are those who explain to us the mysteries of the stock market. Poesy and the fine arts are disdained, and the Temple of Fame is open no longer except to those who tell us why sugars are "feeble," why soap is "firm." Since Philosophy has conceived a passion for Commerce, Polyhymnia decks the new science with flowers. The tenderest expressions have replaced the old language of the merchants, and it is now said, elegant phrase, that "sugars are languid" — that is, are falling; that "soaps are looking up" — that is, have advanced. Formerly . . . manoeuvres of monopoly . . . excited the indignation of writers; but now these schemes are a title to distinction, and fame announces them in a pindaric strain, saying: "A rapid and unexpected movement has suddenly taken place in soaps" — at which words we seem to see bars of soap leap from their boxes and wing their way to the clouds, while the speculators in soap hear their names resound through the whole land. . . . All those flowers of rhetoric contribute, doubtless, to the success of industry, which has found in the support of the philosophers the same kind of assistance they have extended to the people — namely, fine phrases, but no results.

The question may have sometimes occurred to people why what goes on in the bed or upon the battlefield should be more "romantic" than what happens in the bank. Romance is perhaps a word with a fatal absurdity inherent in it. Should we, however, transfer our term "romance" to the exclusive use of financial enterprise, we should be tripped up by the well-known conservatism peculiar to language. Chivalrous love was once a strange newcomer; but it coined the word "romance" for itself. There must have been a time even when war was strange, and ill-favoured. Some day, perhaps, it may become so again. But the word "romance" is haunted for ever by those activities. Language has to be destroyed before you transform ideas at all radically.

Sooner or later we shall have to discriminate between what is "romantic" for a person acquainted to some extent with the reality, and what is "romance" for a romantic, or a person who has not much grasp of present and actual things. The majority are "romantic," living as they do in a dream of non-existent things — for instance, the world of cheap art, education, and publicity, or else the feudal world of half their ordinary speech.

"Romantic" is very generally used to describe a "dreamer." Ruskin, we say, was such a man, for instance. One of his main doctrines illustrates this. He wished all machinery to be destroyed. Aside from the question of its desirability, we know this to have been irrealizable. The term "romantic" jumps onto our tongue, therefore, to describe a man capable of that aberration. A more sensible notion, more sweeping were it implemented, perhaps, but equally impracticable, would be this: *Let us destroy all the drums in the world* — kettledrums, side-drums, tom-toms, etc. — and arrange to hang any man discovered making one. Even to indulge in the "devil's tattoo" would become a criminal offence.

There you would have, it would be possible to contend, a tremendous innovation. It would banish at one stroke a great deal of gratuitous emotionalism. We should be well rid of that, you might believe. The time-honoured method of calling people to battle, to rut, to religious ecstasy, to every known delirium, would then not exist. Yet the individual advocating this measure we should call "romantic" — very romantic. It is not practicable. It is even ridiculous. It is reminiscent of the day-dream of the naïf prohibitionist. The same applies to dreams of banishing machinery.

In analysing "romance" the first definition required, perhaps, is to this effect: *the "romantic" is the opposite of the real.* Romance is a thing that is in some sense non-existent. For instance, "romance" is the reality of yesterday, or of tomorrow; or it is the reality of somewhere else.

Romance is the great traditional enemy of the Present. And the reason for the contemporary enmity to the mind of Greek Antiquity is because that mind was an "ahistorical" mind — without perspective. But that "yesterday" that was Rome, Jerusalem or

Athens is a great reality. So it is not a "romance" by any means. Similarly, if some political event of great magnitude is brewing today in Calcutta, let us say, capable of profoundly disturbing us all *here, tomorrow*; then, because Calcutta is not here, nor the event today's, it is not less "real" for that.

Again, sometimes dreams can be converted into realities. Your day-dream, supposing the requisite power is yours, may some day become a nice or disagreeable reality for your neighbour. His appeal to other facts, more reputably causal, will be useless. So much for a few of the traps that await the person essaying definitions of "romance." To circumscribe with distinct meaning such a word as "romance" is difficult.

Ezra Pound is, from any standpoint, a good person to whom to address yourself in such a difficulty. He is a poet; and he is a great authority on Romance. He has even been at the pains to write a book — *The Spirit of Romance* — for seekers after the truth, about Romance. To this I suggest we turn; and we shall find the following enlightenment:

"There is one sense in which the word Romance has a definite meaning — that is, when it is applied to the languages derived from the Latin"; and "Romance literature begins with a Provençal 'Alba,' supposedly of the tenth century." So much for the source of the term merely. As to its present meaning: "When England had a 'romantic school' it was said to join 'strangeness' with 'beauty' . . ." But, "speaking generally, the spells or equations of 'classic' art invoke the beauty of the normal, and spells of 'romantic' art are said to invoke the beauty of the unusual." Pound, however, "fears the pigeon-hole."

Generally speaking, as he says, the normal, the known and the visible, is what Romance is *not*. "Romance" is what is unusual, not normal, mysterious, not visible, perhaps not susceptible at all of visual treatment.

But Pound places his finger on a more important aspect of the matter when he writes (in the same book):

It is dawn at Jerusalem while midnight hovers above the Pillars of Hercules. All ages are contemporaneous. It is B.C., let us say, in Morocco. The Middle Ages are in Russia. The future stirs already in the minds of the few. This is especially true of literature, where the real time is independent of the apparent . . .

In the periodic images employed here, imbued with relativity sentiment, all "real time" (which also apparently includes "the future") is somewhere about, within the circle. There is no real "future" any more than there is a real "past." So, according to this way of looking at the matter, the "timeless" view, "romance" would consist in apparent absence, or in a seeming coyness on the part of time.

Men now dead will be the playfellows of your grandchildren, says Pound, and many ostensibly "alive" are really playing with Dante or Propertius, rather than with us; although Dante and Propertius, in their turn, were also "elsewhere" to a greater extent than was consistent with their temporal and spatial status.

The same "timeless" view is advocated by Spengler in his *Decline of the West*; indeed he expresses that standpoint so perfectly, by means of his "homology principle," as he calls it, that I will quote a passage which defines completely what we require:

The application of the "homology" principle to historical phenomena brings with it an entirely new connotation for the word "contemporary." I designate as contemporary two historical facts that occur in exactly the same — relative — positions in their respective Cultures . . . we might . . . describe Pythagoras as the contemporary of Descartes, Archytas of Laplace, Archimedes of Gauss. The Ionic and the Baroque, again, ran their course *contemporaneously*. Polygnotus pairs in time with Rembrandt, Polycletus with Bach. . . . Contemporary, too, are the building of Alexandria, of Baghdad and of Washington; classical coinage and our double-entry book-keeping; the first Tyrannis and the Fronde; Augustus and Shih-huang-ti; Hannibal and the World War.

Without further defining my position with regard to this "timeless" standpoint — a very common one for many years now, for Relativity fashion did not commence with Einstein's General Theory — a few of its implications can be pointed out. The circular, periodic imagery does knock out a good deal the sense of the "future." For, far enough back, it also is the "past." The idea of periodicity so used (of a spiral formation it usually is, with repetitions on higher planes) leaves, no doubt, some margin and variety to play with, but very little.

You have above, in the extract beginning "It is dawn at Jerusalem," an average example of the formula advanced on behalf of the "timeless" standpoint. Before leaving that subject (and still in touch with the psychology outlined above) the following observation is of great use. The profession of the "timeless" doctrine, in any average person, always seems to involve this contradiction: that he will be much more the slave of Time than anybody not so fanatically indoctrinated. An obsession with the temporal scale, a feverish regard for the niceties of fashion, a sick anxiety directed to questions of time and place (that is, of *fashion* and of *milieu*), appears to be the psychological concomitant of the possession of a time-theory that denies time its normal reality. The *fashionable* mind is par excellence the *time-denying* mind — that is the paradox.

This is, however, not so strange if you examine it. The less reality you attach to time as a unity, the less you are able instinctively to abstract it; the more important concrete, individual, or personal time becomes.

Bergsonian durée, or psychological time, is essentially the "time" of the true romantic. It is the same as in disbelief of the reality of life: the more absolute this disbelief is, as a formulated doctrine, the more the *sensation* of life (which we all experience impartially, whatever our philosophy) will assume a unique importance. Or we can add a third analogy, which will further clear up this obscure point in contemporary psychology. The less you are able to realize other people, the more your particular personality will obsess you, and the more dependent upon its reality you will be. The more you will insist on it with a certain frenzy. And the more "individualist" you are in this sense, the less "individualist" you will be in the ordinary political sense. You will have achieved a fanatical hegemony with your unique self-feeling.

Political "individualism" signifies the opposite of that. It expresses belief in the desirability of *many* individuals instead of *one*. Your "individualism" will be that mad one of the "one and only" self, a sort of instinctive solipsism in practice. It will cause you to be, therefore, the most dangerous of madmen, that kind that has no scruples where other people are concerned, because he has an imperfect belief in their existence. This rough preliminary note will, I hope, suffice to have made that point clearer.

We have now surveyed some of the principal conditions of the use of the expression "romance." What has emerged can be summarized as follows: The term arose in connection with roman dialects. It took with it, from the start, an implication of revolutionary unorthodoxy, of opposition to tradition. It was the speech of "the people," or of the roman colonials or rustics, who preferred to express what they had to say in a "living," not a "dead" language. Romance started as the opponent of tradition, as represented by the classical tongue.

In the modern "classic–romantic" opposition, Romantic is the warm, popular, picturesque expression, as contrasted with the formal calm of the Classical. There is no need to go through the usual questions of the Unities as opposed to disregard for classical construction. Those are the commonplaces of one of the oldest, and most closely canvassed, controversies in the world. The success of such a classification depends upon your examples, largely. If Racine is your "classic," and Shakespeare your "romantic," then "romantic," in that instance, wins the day. Between Pope and Marlowe the same thing happens, in my opinion. There are other cases in which "classicism" might score points. The fact is that the best West European art has never been able to be "classic," in the sense of achieving a great formal perfection. The nature of our semi-barbaric cultures has precluded that. So in that connection the "romantic" is the real thing, I believe, and not the imitation.

If in its origin the "classic–romantic" opposition possessed a political connotation — namely, the "classical" standing for the "old order," tradition and authority, the "romantic" for the new insurgent life of the popular imagination, the self-assertion of the populace; so today it still conforms to that political symbolism. The "classical" is the rational, aloof and aristocratical; the "romantic" is the popular, sensational and "cosmically" confused. That is the permanent political reference in these terms.

It is not in conformity with its position in this classic–romantic controversy, however, that the word "romantic" is generally used. Rather is it in opposition to positive science — not to the great traditional opponent of positive science, the classical ideal — that we find it employed. This gives it a rather unenviable and damaging sense. It conveys a negative — what would be thought of as the non-modern state of mind. Used in this way, it connotes the following characters. We say "romantic" when we wish to define something too emotionalized (according to our positivist standards), something opposed to the actual or the real: a self-indulgent habit of mind or a tendency to shut the eyes to what is unpleasant, in favour of things arbitrarily chosen for their flattering pleasantness. Or else we apply it to the effects of an egoism that bathes in the self-feeling to the exclusion of contradictory realities, including the Not-self; achieving what we see to be a false unity and optimism, regarding all the circumstances. It was that keen awareness of the Not-self, and the consequent conception of "righteousness," that Matthew Arnold pointed to (in his *Literature and Dogma*) as constituting the originality of the ancient jewish people. The deep "mentalism" and personal bias of such an intelligence as that of Proust is a "romantic" diagnostic, then. Yet "romance," as the opposite of the matter-of-fact, and as the frame of mind proper to very young people, comes in for a certain popularity. It depends in which connection you are using it.

CHAPTER TWO

THE PRINCIPLE OF ADVERTISEMENT AND ITS RELATION TO ROMANCE

ROMANCE, AS CURRENTLY used, then, denotes what is unreal or unlikely, or at all events not present, in contrast to what is *scientifically* true and accessible to the senses here and now. Or it is, in its purest expression, what partakes of the marvellous, the extreme, the unusual. That is why Advertisement (in a grotesque and inflated form) is a pure expression of the romantic mind. Indeed, there is nothing so "romantic" as Advertisement.

Advertisement is the apotheosis of the marvellous and the unusual; likewise of the scientifically untrue. The spirit of advertisement and boost lives and has its feverish being in a world of hyperbolic suggestion; it is also the trance or dream-world of the hypnotist. This world of the impossible does not pretend even to be real or exact. The jamesian psychology — more familiar to most Europeans as couéism — is its theoretic expression. What you can make people believe to be true, *is* true. (The american pragmatical test of any theorem is "What difference will its truth or falsehood make to *you*?")

Advertisement also implies in a very definite sense a certain attitude to Time. And the attitude proper to it is closely related to the particular time-philosophy we were considering above; namely, that philosophy that is at once "timeless" in theory, and very much concerned with Time in practice. Both that conscious philosophy, and the instinctive attitude of the advertising mind towards Time, could be described as a *Time-for-Time's-sake* belief. For both, Time is the permanent fact. Time for the bergsonian or relativist is fundamentally sensation; that is what Bergson's *durée* always conceals beneath its pretentious metaphysic. It is the glorification of the life-of-the-moment, with no reference beyond itself and no absolute or universal value; only so much value as is conveyed in the famous proverb, *Time is money*. It is the *argent comptant* of literal life, in an inflexibly fluid Time. And the ultimate significance of the philosophy of Time-for-Time's-sake (since Time is a meaningless thing in itself)

11

is Existence-for-Existence's sake. (This difficulty of the meaninglessness of Time, which becomes especially acute when it is your intention to erect Time into a god, as is the case with Professor Alexander, is dealt with at length by that philosopher.)

The world in which Advertisement dwells is a one-day world. It is necessarily a plane universe, without depth. Upon this Time lays down discontinuous entities, side by side; each day, each temporal entity, complete in itself, with no perspectives, no fundamental exterior reference at all. In this way the structure of human life is entirely transformed, where and in so far as this intensive technique gets a psychologic ascendancy. The average man is invited to slice his life into a series of one-day lives, regulated by the clock of fashion. The human being is no longer the unit. He becomes the containing frame for a generation or sequence of ephemerids, roughly organized into what he calls his "personality." Or the highly organized human mind finds its natural organic unity degraded into a worm-like extension, composed of a segmented, equally-distributed, accentless life. Each segment, each *fashion-day* (as the day of this new creature could be called) must be organically self-sufficing.

This account of the *fashion-day* of Advertisement may seem to contradict what is said elsewhere of the *organic* character of the time-philosophy. It will appear to negative the contrast between the Present of the classical mind, as opposed to the perspectives of the romantic, the time-mind, too. This misunderstanding will already have been partly averted. The reader's attention has been drawn to the paradox of the doctrinaire of "timelessness" more obsessed by Time, and the *fashion-day*, than is anybody else. For the further and complete dispersal of this possible difficulty, I must refer the reader to a subsequent section of my book. It can only finally be disposed of by a careful definition of the classical "Present," as opposed to the romantic "Present."

In the world of Advertisement, Coué-fashion, everything that happens today (or everything that is being advertised *here and now*) is better, bigger, brighter, more astonishing than anything that has ever existed before. (Dr. Coué actually was embarked upon his teaching, so he said, by noticing, and responding to, an advertisement.) The psychology that is required of the public to absorb this belief in the marvellous one and only—monist, unique, superlative, *exclusive*—fact (immediately obliterating all other beliefs and shutting the mind to anything that may happen elsewhere or tomorrow) is a very rudimentary one indeed. The best subject for such a séance would be a polyp, evidently. An individual looking, with his intellect, before and after, seeing far too much at a time for the requirements of the advertiser or hypnotist, is not at all the affair of Advertisement. For the essence of this living-in-the-moment and for-the-moment — of submission to a giant hyperbolic close-up of a moment — is, as we have indicated, to banish all *individual* continuity. You must, for a perfect response to this instantaneous suggestion, be *the perfect sensationalist* — what people picture to themselves, for instance, as the perfect American. Your personality must have been chopped down to an extremely low level of purely reactionary life. Otherwise you are of no use to the advertiser. If there were many like you, he would soon be put out of business.

The traditional yankee method of Advertisement suggests a credulity, a love of sensation and an absence of background in the submissive, hypnotized public, that could justly claim to be *unexampled*, and as beating anything ever heard of before in recorded history. But that method is now in universal use. It promises *monts et merveilles* every instant of the day. It has battered and deadened every superlative so much that superlatives no longer in themselves convey anything. All idea of a true value — of any scale except the pragmatic scale of hypnotism and hoax — is banished forever from the life of the great majority of people living in the heart of an advertising zone, such as any great modern city. They are now almost entirely incapable of anything except sensation; for to think is to be able to traverse the scale of values from the nadir to the zenith. The world of superlatives is a monotonous horizontal drumming on the top-note, from which an insistent, intoxicating time can be extracted, but nothing else. So Advertisement fulfils all the requirements of the general definition of "romance."

It is not altogether without point to refer this method to its origins in the competitive frenzy of finance, and of finance first become delirious as it saw its staggering opportunity in its operations in the New World. The marvellous american vitality enhanced this process, and may yet defeat it. For the decision, as to Europe and even the destiny of the White Race, rests with America, perhaps.

Just as the individual whose conscience is clear, and whose pockets are full, does not experience the need to overwhelm his neighbour with assurances of his honesty — indeed, if his pockets are sufficiently full, does not care much what his neighbour thinks; so such a system as that of Coué is not invented for people in robust health, but for the debilitated and ailing members of a ruined society. The optimism-to-order of "Every day and in every respect I grow better and better" is of the same kind as the political optimism-to-order of democratic politics.

The wholesale change-over of what was "public" into what, for the European, was private (the conditions obtaining in aryan civilization, what Maine calls the "ancient order of the aryan world," from the earliest tribal times, as a result of the "individualism" distinguishing our race), and *vice versa*, has been very much facilitated by the agency of Advertisement. Advertisement has functioned in the social and artistic or learned world rather as the engineer has in the factory. It has taught the public — as the engineer taught the producer — that as Advertisement-value nothing is refuse or waste. Indeed, the garbage is often more valuable than the commodity from which it proceeds. But this value is a money-value essentially, and functions imperfectly in its social application.

CHAPTER THREE

ROMANCE AND THE MORALIST MIND

BETWEEN ROMANCE AND the principle of Advertisement the liaison is clear enough, I hope, by now. On the other hand, for a reader unfamiliar with the time-philosophy of Bergson, the Relativists, Whitehead, Alexander and the other space-timeists, the psychology of the time-snob that I have outlined may be imperfectly defined; the relation between the advertising principle of competitive industry, and these time-philosophies, may still escape him. All that welter of thought and sensation which has recently culminated in Relativity Theory is the necessary background for even these preliminary remarks.

Perhaps an equally refractory conception would be that of the affiliation of Romance and of Morals — in the sense, it is understood, in which we may decide to accept these terms. But that is the next relationship I propose to examine. It seems to me a very important one indeed. There is nothing at all abstruse, at least, about the christian ethical code; especially that of the evangelical christian, of the "puritan" produced by the Reformation, and his descendants today. For its spirit and various ordinances are all to be found in the Old Testament. Our use of that primitive code, framed as it is for conditions totally different from ours, is symbolic of our incurably romantic outlook.

Our civilization is much more artificial than that of Greece or Rome; and the main cause for that is the christian ethic. Where Romance enters the sphere of morals is at the gate of sex; and nearly all the diabolism (helping itself to the traditional sadic and invert machinery), springing up so eagerly in a puritan soil, can be traced to a sex-root. It is even extremely easy in the modern West to *sexify* everything, in a way that would have been impossible in the greek world, for instance. To see this, you only have to consider the fact that the Athens of Socrates was notorious, as his dialogues witness, for what is (for us) the most obsessing sort of sex-cult. Yet it did not interfere at all with greek philosophy; life did not become the rival of thought, the life of the intellect and that of the senses co-existed harmoniously; and philosophic speculation, for the men who disputed with Socrates, was evidently as exciting as any of their other occupations. The dialogues of Plato have not an alexandrian effluvia of feminine scent; nor do they erect pointers on all the pathways of the mind, waving frantically back to the gonadal ecstasies of the commencement of life. They are as loftily detached from the particular delights in fashion with the Athenian as it is possible to be; the core of the mind was not invaded, or even touched, by the claims of that group of glands, in spite of the fact that the puppets who used to conduct the intellectual contests were often conventionally epicene. The psychological composition of the mind of such a philosopher as Socrates, or Democritus, showed no bias whatever such as you inevitably find in a Wilde or a Pater — that alexandrian enervation and softening of all the male chastity of thought.

In modern Western democracy thought usually, even, has to get started in a sex-centre. People are saturated with moral teaching and the artificialities of the legal or moralist mind to such a degree, that it is most difficult to make them think without first shocking them; or without, contrariwise, edifying them. Edification or outrage must precede thought; there is no escape generally from that law — the law of sensation, of extremism and of snobbery.

The attempt to escape will be made here. We shall aim to get behind morals, which is the same order of enterprise as getting behind Romance. And we can bear in mind, as regards the psychological aspect of our argument, that, generically, the romantic man is some sort of a moralist, simple or inverted. And he always, to that there is no exception, is an arch-snob. Snobbishness and the romantic disposition are commutative: to be "romantic about something" is to be "snobbish about something." Both imply superstitious excess, and capitulation of the reason.

When Revolution — that is simply the will to change and to spiritual transformation — ceases to be itself, and passes over more and more completely into its mere propaganda and advertisement department, it is apt, in the nature of things, to settle down in the neighbourhood of sex, and to make the moral disease its main lever. But Revolution in Europe and America must in the nature of things centre around "sex," owing principally to the over-sensitive "repressed" sex-psychology of the post-Reformation man. No Western revolution would be complete without its strident advertisement. In the pagan world the facts of sex had no undue importance. That they have derived entirely, as we have said, from the puritan consciousness. The whole bag of tricks of sex, simple and invert, reduces itself, on the physical side, to a very simple proposition. Chivalrous love, on the other hand, was a very abstruse and complicated religion (attached to the man-woman relationship). But at its intensest it ceased to be "sex" altogether. It was the christian counterpart of the idealistic boy-love of greek antiquity, complicated with mariolatry.

But in the power of "sex" as a lever in the modern european world (to which the success of Freud is witness) you are dealing with something quite different from that. It is necessary, if you are to understand it, to put out of your head all analogies with Antiquity, or with other periods. What you are confronted with, always, is *forbidden fruit*; that is what "sex" has meant persistently to the post-Reformation European. The delights of sex have been built round for us with menacing restrictions: and a situation has been created which a Greek or a Roman would with great difficulty have understood.

The result is that every licence where "sex" is concerned has been invested with the halo of an awful and thrilling lawlessness. If it were not for the superlative sweetness of lawlessness of a sex order, all lawlessness would lack its most exciting and hypnotic paradigm and principal advertisement. How this applies today is evident. If you are desirous of showing your "revolutionary" propensities, and it is a case of finding some law to break to prove your good-will and spirit, what better law than the dear old moral law, always there invitingly ready and eager to be broken? So it is that "sex" for the European is the ideal gateway to Revolution, that no one but a violent sex-snob can enter any more than a camel can go through the eye of a needle. And so it is that that will-to-change, or impulse to spiritual advance, which is the only sensible meaning of Revolution, is confused and defeated.

Any sex-licence at all has the revolutionary advantage of "lawlessness." But how much more is not this the case where some in itself insignificant eccentricity is in question. Blue infernal fire bursts up out of the ground, almost, for the superstitious puritanic mind (and in the West of Europe and America the evangelical, puritan spirit — the shadow of the genevan Bible — is strong yet) at the suggestion of one or other (there are only two) of the more sensational first-class sex-misdemeanours.

The levity and even lack of interest with which the Greeks

usually treated these things is so much more healthy, it is quite
evident, that it is a pity from any point of view that it should
not be expected of a "broad-minded" and "modernist" person as
a *sine quâ non* of modernity. If you believe that such things as
revolutionary propaganda of "original" vice are socially unde-
sirable, then all the more should you seek to apply to them the
chill of this moral indifferentism. For they would certainly wither
at the touch of it.

The most unlikely and incongruous things are dragged into
the emotionalism of "right" and "wrong," backed up by the sex-
impulse; a host of militant passions are let loose on both sides;
and in the ensuing tumult, the blood-and-thunder, brimstone and
blue fire, there is nothing that cannot instantly be submerged once
the business is started. The "mob of the senses," as Plato called
them, are let loose and our rational constructions founder.

So it is not *sex*, properly speaking and in its simple and natural
appeal, that is in question at all; it is the diabolics locked up in
the edifice of "morals" that is the arch-enemy of the artist. To
circumvent that ridiculous but formidable spirit is a necessary
but difficult enterprise.

There is no activity you can engage in that is not liable to be
trapped, pushed or misled into the moralist quagmire. As to artistic work of any kind, once it gets involved with that machinery,
for or against it, it is lost; for its particular values are entirely
engulfed in the sea of sensation — of "right" or of "wrong." Yet
the mind of the western public (and especially of the anglo-saxon
public) works in such a way that it is very difficult to convince
it that a man rebelling, perhaps, as a painter, against the degraded
standards of the Salon or Academy is not proposing some insidious attack also upon the stronghold of orthodox sex. The "I
told you so!" that must have arisen when the eccentric Bunthorne
poet, Wilde, was unexpectedly convicted of *vice*, must have been
universal. Yet, of course, Wilde was an inferior artist; that may
even have been one reason that decided him to add "sex" to what
was deficient as "art" — to heighten it and give it a sporting chance
to set the Thames on fire.

*Where any sex-nuisance is concerned, the greek indifference
is the best specific.* For with regard to anything which is likely
to obsess a society, it is of importance not to give it too much
advertisement. These few remarks may make it possible to understand a little better how "sex" of any sort, invert or direct, as an

ally, must be regarded by an artist, who is not a moralist. It also places the romantic and snobbish in its true light, where it is engaged in the diabolics of "sex." And it co-operates with the most intelligent tendencies in modern life, those directed to the rationalization of our automatic impulses.

CHAPTER FOUR

THE ROMANCE OF ACTION

BESIDE ADVERTISEMENT (as one of the bastards of Romance) can be set that instinct for the frantic and the excessive, for which it is difficult to find a compendious name. The prefix "super" — as in superman, or super-Dreadnought — gives the key to the state of mind involved. It is almost indistinguishable from Advertisement, in many ways, as a department of Romance.

Fatally and intimately connected with this is the gospel of *action*. This doctrine has, in the form of the romantic energetics of war, already made a living melodrama of the Western World. The last ten years of *action* has been so overcrowded with men-of-action of all dimensions, that they none of them have been able to act; and what has been *done* on this doctrinal but terribly real field-of-action, has brought us to our present state of inaction, in due course.

But the man-of-action (low-browed, steel-jawed, flint-eyed, stone-hearted) has been provided (whether in mockery or not is aside from what we wish now to prove) with a philosophy. And it is some form of that *Time-for-Time's-sake* philosophy we have already briefly considered. But this mechanical, functional creature would implicitly possess such a philosophy in any case; since the dream-quality of pure-action must leave him virtually a child, plunged from one discontinuous, self-sufficing unit of experience to another; always living in the moment, in moods of undiluted sensationalism; the ideal slave and instrument of any clever and far-seeing person — who, of course, is the *real* man-of-action; for it is never the frantic servant of this doctrine of *action* who ever does anything, at least of any use to himself.

The super-ism, or whatever you like to call it, with which we started is only the most exaggerated, fanatical, and definitely religious form of the doctrine of *action*. Mussolini is, of course, the most eminent exponent of both. As a politician he is only concerned with the *usefulness* of things, and so he cannot be justly criticized on account of them. What may be useful in one connection is often not appropriate in another, however. If you applied the conditions and standards required for the flowering of a Jack Dempsey to a Beethoven, say, you would be doing what is done in a more general and less defined sense on all hands at this moment, as a thousand different activities mystically coalesce in response to the religion of merging, or mesmeric engulfing.

Action (the dionysiac and dynamical) is highly specialist. But action is impossible without an *opposite* — "it takes two to make a quarrel." The dynamical — or what Nietzsche called the dionysiac, and which he professed — is a *relation*, a something that *happens*, between two or more opposites, when they meet in their pyrrhic encounters. The intellect works alone. But it is precisely this solitariness of thought, this prime condition for intellectual success, that is threatened by mystical mass-doctrines.

CHAPTER FIVE

ART MOVEMENTS AND THE MASS IDEA

THIS ESSAY HAS BEEN undertaken to examine the fundamental philosophic concept of the present age, namely, "Time," especially with regard to its influence upon the arts and upon the social world. Before coming to that eel-like concept itself, and attacking it in its home-waters (the philosophy of flux), it is my plan to show it powerfully operating in every department of "advanced" — that is the only significant — contemporary literature. I have chosen literature rather than the static or graphic arts, because in the nature of things such a concept has more leverage upon literature than upon them. That is, indeed, an important aspect of my argument. Still, even in the arts of painting, sculpture, and design, it has exercised, usually indirectly, some influence. And they are included in my survey.

A rigorous restatement is required, I have felt for some years, of the whole "revolutionary" position; nowhere more than in my peculiar province — art and literature. For me to undertake that statement must involve me also in a restatement of my personal position. This in its turn must bring me into conflict with the interests of several people with whose names mine has been fairly closely associated.

I have recently worked out, with great care, a system. The present essay is its philosophic elaboration. But before coming to a detailed criticism of the current interpretation of the concept "time," I am dealing with some of the concrete appearances of this compelling concept. If it is the good fortune of my critical system to be adopted or used by a certain number of people, it should make certain intellectual abuses, humbugs, and too-easy sensationalisms henceforth impossible. The arguments brought forward here, and the questions that will be constantly raised in my paper, or elsewhere, will have to be met. Where they are not met adequately, or are ignored, there will be a standing danger-spot in the defences of whoever attempts to evade them. For they are not idly-held opinions; but are a critical engine constructed from the material of directly observed fact of the most refractory description, sedulously submitted to repeated tests. The use of a "system" in the "systematic" at all is much resented. But it is my claim that this one is, and increasingly will become, an almost fool-proof system of detection where contemporary counterfeit, of the "revolutionary" kind, is concerned. It cannot, I think, be used as a destructive weapon by the irresponsible for things for which its machinery is not intended. But on the other hand, its activity may, on occasion, be reversed, so that it can be made to protect those things in whose interests its destructive ingenuity is set in motion.

In stepping directly into the world of art we shall fall upon a great deal of politics, too, as elsewhere, or the reflection of politics. To attempt to get rid of these politics, or shadow politics, is one of my reasons for undertaking this difficult analysis.

First of all, the same emotional tension, the same spurious glamour, in which no one believes, but which yet arrests belief from settling anywhere — extracting, as it were, the automatic reaction from it, without desiring, even, a more conscious, or deep-seated, response; the same straining merely to outwit and to capture a momentary attention, or to startle into credulity; the same optimistic air, suggestive of a bad conscience, or a vulgar self-congratulation; the same baldly-shining morning face; the same glittering or discreetly hooded eye of the fanatical advertiser, exists in the region of art or social life as elsewhere — only in social life it is their own personalities that people are advertising, while in art it is their own personally manufactured goods only. (In the case of the artist, his own personality plays the part of the refuse of the factory.) And these more blandly-lighted worlds are as full as the Business world, I believe fuller, of those people who seem especially built for such methods, so slickly does the glove fit. Yet who will say that the vulgar medium which the scientific salesman must use to succeed, in Western Democracy, does not, thrust into the social world, destroy its significance? The philosophy of "action" of trade is as barbarous as that of war.

But unlike social revolution, art is not dependent on fortuitous technical discoveries. It is a constant stronghold, rather, of the purest human consciousness; as such it has nothing to "revolt" against — except conditions where art does not exist, or where spurious and vulgar art triumphs. Modern industrial conditions brought about organized "revolutionary" ferment in the political sphere. They also rapidly reduced the never-very-secure pictorial and plastic standards of the European to a cipher. The present "revolution" in art is not a revolt against tradition at all. It is much more a concerted attempt, on a wider and subtler basis (provided by recent research and technical facilities), to revive a sense that had been almost totally lost, as the Salons and Academies witnessed.

The only art at the present time about which there is any reason to employ the word "revolutionary," or that sentimentalist cliché, "rebel," is either inferior and stupid, or else consciously political, art. For art is, in reality, one of the things that Revolutions are about, and cannot therefore itself be Revolution. Life as interpreted by the poet or philosopher is the objective of Revolutions, they are the substance of its Promised Land.

If, on the other hand, you wish to use "revolutionary" in the wider and more intelligent sense which I generally give it here, then there is a form of artistic expression that has attempted something definitely new; something that could not have come into existence in any age but this one. Art of that type is confined to a very small number of workers. And it is one of the tasks I have set myself here, to mark this off distinctly from the much greater mass of work which uses a very little of that newness to flavour something otherwise traditional enough, and which, if properly understood, is in no sense revolutionary; or else which looks novel because it is attempting to get back to standards or forms that are very ancient, and hence strange to the European.

London, for example, is periodically startled by some work in sculpture or painting which would have seemed a commonplace to Amenhotep III, or to a fifth-century Tartar Khan. It is probably much better than the average Royal Academy article; it could scarcely help being that. Yet one of the curious objections brought against works of that sort is that they are "asiatic." The trouble with them, if anything, is in reality the opposite to that — namely, that they are not asiatic enough. There is usually some germanic sentimentalism marring the conception — or some germanic brutality — which makes them inferior to the oriental masterpiece that has inspired them.

The first thing that would be noticed by anyone entering the art world for the first time would be that it was discriminated into "movements," rather than into individuals. It would be for the sake of *le mouvement*, for the advancement of "the group," not of the individual artist, that this or that was initiated. This becomes less pronounced as the decay of art, from a material point of view, advances, and the disillusionment deepens; but the movement or group idea is still sufficiently prevalent.

The effect of that form of organization, to start with, is, inevitably, to advertise the inferior artist at the expense of the better. Most inferior artists interpret such an arrangement as a good opportunity to combine against any of their number who displays conspicuous ability, and fix upon him obligations all to his personal disadvantage. Or else "the group" is more simply an organization of nothing but inferior artists, directed, sometimes by means of specific propaganda, against *the idea* of individual talent altogether; the suggestion being that only a great many cooks can make a really good broth; and the mastery of each individual must be of an unnoticeable, democratic order. The proof of this would naturally be in the eating. But as there is no public for such things today, these theorists are quite secure: it will never be put to the test.

Now no one, I suppose, will be found to contend that contemporary politics are not reflected in such "groups" and "movements" in art. We will assume that the resemblance is too striking to be passed over; that the "group," "movement," phenomenon in art is, where found, a political reflection, in its contemporary form.

But in art, as in anything else, all revolutionary impulse comes in the first place from the exceptional individual I have shown. No collectivity ever conceives, or, having done so, would ever be able to carry through, an insurrection or a reform of any intensity, or of any magnitude. That is always the work of individuals or minorities. It is invariably the man who is privileged and free, as Plato was, who initiates or proposes, and plans out, such further ambitious advances for our race. The rest follow.

Since writing *The Art of Being Ruled* (1925) I have somewhat modified my views with regard to what I then called "democracy." I should express myself differently today. I feel that I slighted too much the notion of "democracy" by using that term to mean too exclusively the present so-called democratic masses, hypnotized into a sort of hysterical imbecility by the mesmeric methods of Advertisement. But whatever can be said in favour of "democracy" of any description, it must always be charged against it, with great reason, that its political realization is invariably at the mercy of the hypnotist.

But no artist can ever love democracy or its doctrinaire and more primitive relative, communism. The emotionally-excited, closely-packed, heavily-standardized mass-units, acting in a blind, ecstatic unison, as though in response to the throbbing of some unseen music — of the sovietic or fourierist fancy — would be the last thing, according to me, for the free democratic West to aim at, *if* it were free, and *if* its democracy were of an intelligent order. Let us behave *as if* the West were free, and as if we were in the full enjoyment of an ideal democracy.

I prefer (I should say acting on this principle) the prose-movement — easy, uncontrolled and large — to the insistent, hypnotic rhythm, favoured by most fashionable political thought in the West. For me, there should be no adventitiously imposed *rhythm* for life in the rough. Life in the rough, or on the average, should be there in its natural grace, chaos and beauty; not cut down and arranged into a machine-made system. Its natural gait and movement it derives from its cosmic existence; and where too obsessing a human law — or time, or beat — gets imposed upon it, the life and beauty depart from it. *Musical-politics* — as the uplift politics of millennial doctrinaires can be termed — are, without any disguise, the politics of hypnotism, enregimentation, the sleep of the dance.

A unit looser and more accidental, moving more freely than the ubiquitous drum-throb allows, is to be preferred: "unemotional," as the American and Englishman is called usually; "individualist" as he is also called — not moving in perfect and meticulous unison with his neighbours, if even eccentric. The uniformity aimed at by the method of mass-suggestion is, as an ideal, only a counsel of desperation. Any man of intelligence must be instinctively against it. But in a more specialist connection, this uniformity is not very dear to the artist, either.

CHAPTER SIX

THE REVOLUTIONARY SIMPLETON

WE ARE NOW PREPARED to hail the figure in the title-rôle of Book One of this essay. Aside from the hack or small professional of "revolution," there is (and one of his habitats is the art world) *the revolutionary simpleton*. He is not the enthusiast of the will-to-change at its source, but only of its surface-effects, on the plane of vulgarization.

Almost all Tories are simpletons — the simpletons of what passes with them for "tradition," we could say (as is proved conclusively by the way in which they have defended themselves — how they hastily close all the stable doors long after the horses have all disappeared; also by their rare instinct for closing all the wrong doors, behind which there were never any horses). But the *revolutionary simpleton*, too, is a well-marked figure, found here and there. His characteristic gesture is the opposite to that of the Tory simpleton. He *opens* all doors, as it were — whether there is anything inside or not. He exclaims; he points excitedly to what he believes to be the herds of wild horses that are constantly pouring out of the doors flung dramatically open by him. We look where he points, and occasionally observe a moke or an old hack crawling forth. So he serves at least to advertise our terrestrial emptiness. Everything which is described as "radical" or "rebel," or which palpably can receive that label, and reach its destination, excites him, in rather the same way that "scarlet sin" and suggestions of Sodom or Lesbos, or worse, thrill the sex-snob, schoolboy, curate or spinster of stage tradition — the latter the authentic affinity of the revolutionary simpleton.

This personage is, in one word, a romantic — that is the essential diagnostic for his malady. He is sick for things he has never experienced, or which he is incapable of experiencing — as the schoolboy, or the curate or spinster of stage tradition, is sick for highly-flavoured, "wicked" or blood-curdling exploits and adventures. The revolutionary simpleton is a death-snob; though generally the most inoffensive and often engaging of people himself — the sort of man who would hurt a fly, and say *boo!*

27

very truculently, to a goose; mammock a butterfly; or, with motor gloves and a fencing casque, swing a small cat by the tail. Nothing but the thought of the great danger that so-called "revolutionary" art runs from this attractive simpleton would persuade me to open my lips about him, he is so nice, so pleasant.

I am not able to give you paradigmatically, in the concrete, this theophrastian booby. Generally he is obscure; he is an Everyman, necessarily an abstraction to some extent. Everyone is more Everyman now than in a less populous time, and in everybody now alive a proportion of "revolutionary simpleton" makes them a sort of feeble compass, dragged subtly to one centre. Their souls' form may be bent towards the West, they are nevertheless "carried towards the East"; and, become smooth and spherical to order, the destiny of all spheres overtakes them: they—

> Subject to foreign motions, lose their own.
> And being by others hurried every day
> Scarce in a year their natural form obey.

Some, however, are simpler than others, and at the same time have "revolutionary" written all over them. These are the authentic *revolutionary simpletons*. So though no outstanding, easily identified, person is supplied with this treatise by way of illustration, look round you, and Nature will make up for the deficiency; you will not have to look far to see some fool blossoming, in orthodox *red*.

With the revolutionary simpleton, where most people find a difficulty is in believing in his simplicity. But the simpleton does exist. I have known several quite guileless true-believers, often quite gifted people. But put before you the following kind of man, and you will have the pattern of what I am attempting to describe: one who is very much the creature of fashion, reverencing the fashionable fetish of the "group" or of any collectivity, with many excited genuflections and an air of cystic juvenile incontinence; a great crowd-snob, the portentous vociferous flunkey of any small crowd whatever, the richer the more afraid he is of them; regarding all creative work in opportunistic terms of a conformity to the fashions of this crowd or of that, the nearest to him at the moment—blind to the fact that all fashion is imposed on a crowd from somewhere without itself, in opposition to its habits, and belongs to it about as much as a hired fancy-dress; frightened and scandalized by the apparition of anybody who opposes any group or collectivity whatever; who believes snobbishly in any "minority," however large and flabby, provided it can satisfy him it is not a "majority," and who is always with the majority without being aware of it; his poor little easily "blowed" machine panting to be *there in time*, punctual at all the dates of fashion, remarked in the chattering van at all her functions; flying hatless and crimson when he hears an egg is to be broken, not particular as to whether it be an eagle's or a tom-tit's; very truculent but very sweet and obedient in fact; advancing any kitchen-maid's sickly gushed-out romance, provided she only calls her baby-boy her "bastard," and can be patronized (by himself and the reading-crowd he addresses) because she has never learnt how to spell, and so can be discovered, as you discover things in disused lofts or in gutters, or in that case in a scullery; advancing the fruit of the dead past as new, and when knowing what in the present is false, fearing to denounce it, because it is momentarily current, and he trembles at the shadow of the law; such a nice, simple, timid "revolutionary"-loving man is what you should have in mind. But the revolutionary simpleton is everywhere. It is important not to fix the mind on any particular figure. It is the *thing*, rather, incarnated on all hands, that it is my wish to bring to light.

CHAPTER SEVEN

THE RUSSIAN BALLET THE MOST PERFECT EXPRESSION OF THE HIGH-BOHEMIA

THE ART THAT I AM attacking here is the art of this High-Bohemia of the "revolutionary" rich of this time. That is the society the artistic expression of whose soul I have made it my task to analyse. That a glittering highly-intellectualist surface, and a deep, sagacious, rich though bleak sensuality make its characteristic productions appear, as art, a vast improvement on the fearful artlessness, ugliness, and stupidity that preceded it (what passed for art with the european bourgeois society of the nineteenth century), is true enough. That Marcel Proust (the classic expression up-to-date of this millionaire-outcast, all-caste, star-cast world, in the midst of which we live) is more intelligent, and possesses a more cultivated sensuality, a sharper brain, than his counterpart of the age of Tennyson, must be plain to everyone. But it is not with the intellectual abyss into which Europe fell in the last century that you must compare what we are considering. It is not the small, cold, smug sentimentalists that middle-class democracy threw up like a cheerless vomit to express itself for a hundred lamentable years, with which the typical works of our High-Bohemia should be matched.

All the works with which I shall deal in the course of this critical survey will not be the proper expressions of this world of "rebel" riches. But that the influence of its standards and its characteristic cults and predilections spreads, as an intellectual fashion or infection, far beyond what are its borders, should be remembered. People born outside it, and who have never passed much time in it, possibly, may still be spiritually of it.

As to the imitation of the old (always hand-in-hand with a strident claim to the "new") which characterizes this society, it may be said that what takes you to the old, or takes you, on the other hand, to what is there in the world around you, may be a principle of life or the reverse — the Black Man sees one tree and the White another, when both are looking at the same plant. In an attack on the snobbery of learning, Swift wrote as follows:

If it be necessary [he said] to take in the thoughts of others in order to draw forth [your] own, as dry pumps will not play till water is thrown into them; in that necessity, I would recommend some of the approved standard authors of antiquity for your perusal, as a poet and wit, because maggots being what you look for, as monkeys do for vermin in their keepers' heads, you will find they abound in good old authors, as in rich old cheese, not in the new. . . .

"Maggots being what you look for" — if that form of life, a low form but tasty, is what you look for — there is no need to go to the old cheese at all; for the new cheese has a very old and fruity air, and is completely full of maggots. You waste your time, really, in going back three thousand years.

A sort of neglected bride, her nuptials long overdue, Art remains waiting and watching, in the company of other disappointed entities — such as "the proletariat" — for the millennium, of course, which never comes. But as its once great sentimental part in the general revolutionary programme successively shrinks, it passes over, silently, but bag and baggage, to the same place to which "the proletariat" has gone — namely, to the volatile "revolutionary" millionaire-Bohemia.

That is probably the only millennium that either the artist or "the proletarian" will ever see. The artist, on account of the nature of his calling, is nearer to this ill-smelling pseudo-Paradise than are most "proletarians." If he is an artist with any taste he will find it difficult to believe, in contemplating this millionaire "revolutionary" Utopia, that it justifies its paradisal claim.

If there is one art-form more than another that is the faithful mirror of the High-Bohemia I have been describing, it is the Ballet created by Diaghileff, for the post-war world of Western Europe. In it you see the perfect expression of the society Proust has immortalized, and which today has come into its own, fully co-ordinated and provided with a philosophy. It is a *musical* society, essentially; so its theatre is a musical theatre. And the Russian Ballet is to that society what the theatre of Racine or Molière was to French Society in the gallic heyday. Only it is far more pleased with itself than was the society of *Les Précieuses Ridicules*, or *Le Misanthrope*. This might almost be said to be its peculiarity, as has already been pointed out, and as Benda also immediately noticed.

Mr. Diaghileff is a "revolutionary" impresario; that is to say, what he provides is designed to pass as the "latest" and most "revolutionary" fare possible. In Western Europe there is no other stage-performance so original and experimental as his Ballet.

Although invariably full of people, a very fashionable and wealthy audience, his performances are supposed, on account of their daring originality, not to pay. And everyone who has the interests of experimental art at heart is supposed to experience a fervent sympathy for those performances. For modern and experimental art there is no greater advertisement than that provided by Diaghileff's Ballets. And for the majority of educated people, their idea of the tendency of experimental art is a good deal derived from them. Therefore, Mr. Diaghileff has been in a position for some time to help or injure, according to his instincts, those interests. It is my opinion that he has injured them, and that he misrepresents entirely the dominant tendency, that that is most profoundly original and symptomatic of a "new birth," in the revolution in expression exploited by him.

So the "revolutionary" impresario Diaghileff can be convicted of deliberately manufacturing a bastard "revolutionary" article, to flatter the taste of his clientèle — the "revolutionary" High-Bohemia of the Ritzes and Rivieras. He can be said to have betrayed the principles of the so-called revolution in art (of which he has an intimate personal knowledge, and therefore his betrayal is the more flagrant) to the gilded "revolutionaries" of the post-war capitals: to have associated in the mind of the great Public the work of the finest artists of this time with the vulgar life of the war-gilded rabble: never to have seriously attempted what he was not sure would sell, and that yet all the time it has been understood that quite the opposite was happening, namely, that this idealist impresario was risking his neck, financially, every time his Ballet appeared, by his unpopular and revolutionary experiments. In that way he has used and degraded all the splendid material of artistic invention on which he could lay his hands to the level of *Gentlemen Prefer Blondes* (if you make the "blonde" a gentleman). He has given to that great impulse, which is essentially "chaste and masculine," a twist and colour entirely adventive to it.

With his high-brow loot from the Paris studios he has toured the world, surrounded by an epicene circus, appropriate, as it exists today, only to the representation of one phase of "revolution" — namely, "advanced" sex-revolution. On that particular head, whatever his intentions may be, the impression conveyed is that the epicene fashion which in many quarters has assumed the proportions of a fanatical cult, is being staged and insisted on. And, as though thirty or forty years ago that had not all been exploited to admiration, it is on that basis that this "newness" has found its culmination in a Nineties up-to-date. The Russian Ballet is the Nineties of Oscar Wilde and Beardsley staged for the High-Bohemia, evolved by the constellations of wars and revolutions of the past ten years.

If you turn to the earlier Russian Ballet, that is merely archaeological and romantic. Petroushka is a beautiful romantic ballet, possessing the advantage of music by Stravinsky; but as art it is of the same order as Gauguin; only where Gauguin went back to the primitive life of the South Seas, it goes back to the old times in Russia. Its charm is nostalgic, that of the Middle Ages, with orientalism thrown in.

All the earlier Russian Ballets consist of reconstructions of the Past and especially of barbaric times, principally russian or asiatic. The Ballet, thus, to start with, was a Scott novel, or a Tarzan of the Apes, in a sensuous, spectacular, choreographic form. It had nothing whatever to do with any artistic experiment specifically of the present period. And as to Diaghileff's more recent troupes, they reflect, as I have said, that phase of feminism expressed in the gilded Bohemia of the great capitals by the epicene fashion.

The Russian Ballet has stressed and advertised everything that the half-caste world of Riches and Revolution desires and imagines. It is therefore the most perfect illustration of what I mean in my analysis of the degradation of Revolution (cf. Appendix, p. 116), and the assimilation of that to the millionaire spirit.

If I were a woman and if I found an art springing up which founded itself upon and twisted everything into an interpretation of the world from the unique standpoint of my function as a woman, I should, if I were a little unassuming and distrustful of flattery, first ask myself why my sex was so strangely honoured and singled out for attention; and I should (with the same proviso again) condemn this one-sided and too specialized art-form. So whatever our sex-position may be, whether strongly polar, or of an intermediate nature, we must equally disclaim intellectual expressions that seek to found themselves upon sex, which is the most specialized thing about us, the most "artistic" thing, it is true, but the least promising as material for the finest art; and which is linked with interests that are too feverish and stupefying to guarantee a perfect aesthetic expression. Artistic expression is a dream-condition, and its interpretation must be kept clear of sex-analysis, or else the dreamer passes over immediately into waking life, and so we get no art, and are left with nothing but sex on our hands, and can no longer avail ourselves of the dream-condition.

THE PRINCIPAL "REVOLUTIONARY" TENDENCY TODAY THAT OF A RETURN TO EARLIER FORMS OF LIFE

THE GENERAL SUMMARY of this charge, citing the Russian Ballet first as best answering to all its requirements, is as follows. It is clear that we cannot go on forever making revolutions which are returns merely to some former period of history. Yet that is what most "revolutions" resolve themselves into. The little revolution of the Naughty Nineties was essentially archaeological and historical. Victorian England had piled up a scientific materialism, a mercantile spirit and a nonconformist humbug of such dimensions, that it was a target no artist-attack could miss. The "culture" gospel of Arnold and his war against the Philistine was responsible, of course, for the Naughty Nineties; it was that that infanted Wilde, Beardsley and Symons. It was a revolt that raised up against the "bourgeois" degeneracy of England the charms of the Eighteenth Century, the Restoration, or the Augustan Age, and more distantly the idealism of the Greek World. And the Russian Ballet, of the last un-russian phase, has revived the faded spirit of the Yellow Book, and given it a new dramatic life. Nothing new can be invented, it seemed to say, or, if invented, it could not be swallowed by the Publics degraded by the last phases of the democratic régime. So an old success had to be dug up and repeated. It has ended in a cynicism of a *What the Public Wants* description, where by "Public" is meant the moneyed throng of the "revolutionary" High-Bohemia.

The Fascist Revolution again, to revert to the political scene, is an imitation of antiquity. The fasces are the axes of the lictors; the roman salute is revived; and the Roman Empire is to be resuscitated, Mussolini continually announces. It is interesting to remember that it did not begin that way, but in an exclusive glorification of the Present. For *fascism* is an adaptation, or prolongation, only, of *futurism*. But however "revolutions" may begin, they always end in what Marinetti named *passéism*.

Feminism, to take another political movement, is a revolution that aims at reversing the respective positions of the sexes, and so *returning* to the supposed conditions of the primitive Matriarchate. It is indeed impossible to point to anyone of the many "revolutionary" movements of today that are not conscious returns to former, more primitive, conditions of society. "Communism" is, of course, an example of this.

All the most influential revolutions of sentiment or of ideologic formula today, in the world of science, sociology, psychology, are directed to some sort of *return to the Past.* The cult of the savage (and indirectly that of *the Child*) is a pointing backward to our human origins, either as individuals (when it takes the form of the child-cult) or as a race (when it takes the form of "the primitive").

Freud's teaching has resuscitated the animal past of the soul, following upon Darwin, and hatched a menagerie of animal, criminal and primitive "complexes" for the Western mind. All these approaches stress *the Past,* the primitive, all that is *not* the civilized Present. There is no revolutionary theory or movement that does not ultimately employ itself in bringing to life ghosts, and putting the Present to school with the Past.

But there is nothing so "new" and so startling as the Past, for most people. All the supreme novelties come from the most distant epochs; the more remote the more novel, of course. The "Future," it is true, contains *nothing* but potential novelties. But they are not yet in existence, and so cannot be educed. And the creative myths and dreams of the poets are no longer allowed. So what we generally name "the new" is the very old, or the fairly old. It is as well to point this out, and even to stress it, since it is an impressive fact not sufficiently recognized.

But where the "new" is dug up, pieced together, and given a new lease of life, it is customary to announce it as an absolutely novel creation. That is the rule today. And it is this bad rule or habit that it seems to me it would be a good thing if we could break. Let us call a spade a spade; let us call what the spade digs up old, very old; not new, very new. If we will not make use of our inventors, when it comes to the point, but only of our archaeologists, then do not let us call our discoveries "creative" or "new" (which they are not); but rather call them scholarship and archaeology — that is to say, the science of the *old* and the *primitive.* That would be more truthful, and it would prevent misunderstandings.

It is especially in art that this would prevent misunderstandings. Art is as much a "timeless" thing as technical invention is a creature of time. Its values are more static, as physically it is more static; in its greatest or most universal expression it is in another world from that of fashion. I am not therefore suggesting that where art is concerned other periods, races and countries should be banished. It is the "revolutionary" terminology and propagandist method, alone, that I am criticizing. But beyond that it is imperative to say as well that the perfectly novel inventive forces that contemporary science and technique suggest are not used in art; or when used are not recognized. If you happen to admire and enjoy the art of antiquity, as I do, you will welcome its exploitation. But there can be no object except a commercial one in advertising it as "new." And what really is new is obscured by that device. In that new creation I am supremely interested.

The "newness" obtained, again, as in the case of the Russian Ballet, by means of novelties that are not novelties (psychologically or formally), or by a mechanical collection of trivial surface-novelties, drawn from *The plane of vulgarization*, as the hybrid pseudo-"revolutionary" plane of the High-Bohemia could be called, are equally misnamed. And this sort of novelty, of necessity, takes on all the distorting modes of pseudo-Revolution, as affected by the Millionaire World; especially those centering round feminism and sex-revolt, to the confusion of the true revolutionary impulse.

These criticisms apply to all the phases of artistic expression I have subsequently to examine. Romance and scholarship plus advertisement, take the place of really new creative effort. Some quite ridiculous piece of the mildest "daring" in the world, or the tamest "experiment," is advertised as *an outrage*. And as an outrage it is accepted, on the word of the advertiser; though there is nothing there to disturb the pulse of a rabbit, and no more invention than is required to spell a word in an unusual way, or to paint a bird with a monkey's tail.

CHAPTER NINE

EZRA POUND, ETC.*

NEXT AFTER THE RUSSIAN Ballet I propose to range, for analysis, an old associate of mine, Ezra Pound. There are some obvious objections to this, chief among them the personal regard in which I hold him. Since the War I have seen little of Pound. Once towards the end of my long period of seclusion and work, hard-pressed, I turned to him for help, and found the same generous and graceful person there that I had always known; for a kinder heart never lurked beneath a portentous exterior than is to be found in Ezra Pound. Again, Pound is not a vulgar humbug even in those purely propagandist activities, where, to my mind, he certainly handles humbug, but quite innocently, I believe. Pound is — that is my belief — a genuine *naïf*. He is a sort of revolutionary simpleton!

But my present critical formulations must certainly bring me into conflict with many people whom Pound is pledged to support, or whom he is liable to support. For some time it has been patent to me that I could not reconcile the creative principles I have been developing with this sensationalist half-impresario, half-poet; whose mind can be best arrived at, perhaps, by thinking of what would happen if you could mix in exactly equal proportions Bergson-Marinetti-Mr. Heuffer (with a few preraphaelite "christian names" thrown in), Edward Fitzgerald and Buffalo Bill. At all events, Pound's name and mine have certain associations in people's minds. For the full success of my new enterprise it is necessary to dispel this impression.

I will start by giving the briefest possible account of how, in the past, we came to work together.

The periodical, *Blast* (the first number of which appeared in 1914 just before the outbreak of war, and the second in 1915 — the

---

* Since writing this chapter I have heard of the death, under tragic circumstances, of one of the people whose activities are examined here. But I have envisaged the *Q. Review* as essentially an activity of Pound; and whether it continue or not, it remains a portion of his history.

"war-number"), was, as its name implies, destructive in intention. What it aimed at destroying in England — the "academic" of the Royal Academy tradition — is now completely defunct. The freedom of expression, principally in the graphic and plastic arts, desired by it, is now attained, and can be indulged in by anybody who has the considerable private means required to be an "artist." So its object has been achieved. Though it is only about twelve years since that mass of propaganda was launched, in turning over the pages of *Blast* today it is hard to realize the bulk of the traditional resistance that its bulk was invented to overpower. How cowed these forces are today, or how transformed!

Ezra Pound attached himself to the Blast Group. That group was composed of people all very "extremist" in their views. In the matter of fine art, as distinct from literature, it was their policy to admit no artist disposed to technical compromise, as they regarded it. What struck them principally about Pound was that his fire-eating propagandist utterances were not accompanied by any very experimental efforts in his particular medium. His poetry, to the mind of the more fanatical of the group, was a series of pastiches of old french or old italian poetry, and could lay no claim to participate in the new burst of art in progress. Its novelty consisted largely in the distance it went *back*, not forward; in archaism, not in new creation. That was how they regarded Pound's literary contributions. But this certain discrepancy between what Pound said — what he supported and held up as an example — and what he did, was striking enough to impress itself on anybody.

My opposition to Marinetti, and the criticism of his "futurist" doctrines that I launched, Pound took a hand in, though really why I do not know; for my performances and those of my friends were just as opposed to Pound's antiquarian and romantic tendencies, his velvet-jacket and his blustering trouvère airs, as was the futurism of Marinetti. But these inconsequences were matched by many other disorders and absurdities in our publicist experiments — inseparable from things done just for the day, and regarded as of no more consequence than hand-bills, and possibly rockets or squibs. Pound supplied the Chinese Crackers, and a trayful of mild jokes, for our paper; also much ingenious support in the english and american press; and, of course, some nice quiet little poems — at least calculated to vex Signor Marinetti with their fine passéiste flavour.

Until quite recently I heard little of my old friend. Then I was informed that the good Ezra was breaking out in a new direction. He was giving up words — possibly frightened, I thought, by the widespread opposition to *words* of any sort — words, idle words, and their manipulators. He was taking to music — a less compromising activity. For in music the sounds *say* nothing. (M. Paul Valéry, like Ezra Pound, would prefer to believe that they *say* nothing in poetry either. But in spite of these musical dogmatists, *still they speak*. Pound shows his appreciation of this by turning to music.)

In the matter of revolutionary excitement there was indeed not much more to be got out of the plastic or graphic arts. Their purely "revolutionary" value exhausted after the war (which also eclipsed and luckily put an end to Marinetti's bellowings, besides killing off most of the "futurists"), their play-boys' place was taken by real, Red Revolution; just as Marinetti's post-nietzschean war-doctrine became War, *tout court*; and then Fascismo, which as Futurism in practice is the habit of mind and conditions of war applied to peace.

The Blast situation, on a meaner scale, repeats itself. Pound is there with a few gentle provençal airs, full of a delicate scholarship and "sense of the Past," the organizer of a musical disturbance. The real business is done by a young musician, Antheil, of a fiery accomplishment and infectious faith in the great future of jazz. (As I don't know the first word in musical composition I can say nothing about Antheil's work, except that what he has played to me I have got considerable pleasure from.) Not only a typical Pound-situation is thus set up, but (as I see it) a typical "revolutionary" situation of the bad type.

If Antheil is as interesting as I (quite ignorantly) believe him to be, and if he is really aiming at something *new*, the quality of Pound's championship, or his personal motives, would not concern us; though it is a question if his support is at any time more damaging or useful. But that is merely a practical question. It is *disturbance* that Pound requires; that is the form his parasitism takes. He is never happy if he is not sniffing the dust and glitter of *action* kicked up by other, more natively "active" men. With all his admirable flair for "genius" (in which he has described himself as "a specialist"), it leads him into the support of things that are at once absurd and confusing. He is not always so lucky as I believe him to be in his choice of Antheil. It is the *type* of man that Pound is, or partly is, and the *method* that he advocates, and practises, that sooner or later has to be repudiated by the artist.

Pound is, I believe, only pretending to be alive for form's sake. His effective work seems finished. The particular stimulation that Pound requires for what he does all comes from without; he is terribly dependent upon people and upon "atmosphere"; and, with a sensationalist of his type, in the nature of things little development is possible, his inspiration is of a precarious order, attached as it is to what he regards as his rôle, handed him by a shadow to whose authority he is extremely susceptible, a Public he despises, is afraid of, and serves. So he is easily isolated, his native resources nil.

It is said that Nature kills all lyrical poets young. Perhaps Pound believed that he had found a solution for that distressing situation. He may have become aware of an up-till-then undiscovered alternative for the lyrical poet. Just as Nature (very busy with other things at the moment), hearing a new lyric rising on the air from a quarter which she esteemed should have discontinued its issue of such youthful trifles, had turned with an obviously ugly intention towards the impertinent minstrel, lo! the utterance might change from the too literal howls and tenor-bursts of the tender passion, to a *romance sans paroles*, discreetly contrapuntal. "Lips, cheeks, eyes and the night goes." Nature is appeased. "Let the lyrical poet, the good Ezra, live, since he has become a mere musician," Nature might decide.

At all events, there is Pound (glad to be in the neighbourhood of a big drum) making music.

What made me finally decide that the time had arrived publicly to repudiate my association with Pound, was the following interview with him, appearing in the *Christian Science Monitor* two summers ago. Remembering his opposition, following me, to Marinetti and his "futurism" (to that intellectualist *commis* of Big Business — especially the armament line — and his ridiculous gospel), this interview is especially curious:

"It is possible to imagine music being taken out of the chamber, and entering social and industrial life so completely and so splendidly that the whole clamor of a great factory will be rhythmically regulated, and the workers work, not to a deafening din, but to a superb symphony. The factory manager would be a musical conductor on an immense scale, and each artisan would be an instrumentalist. You think perhaps that George Antheil and I are foolish visionaries, [etc.] . . ."

It was thus that Ezra Pound, American poet and musician, indicated the possibilities of a convergence of the lines of industrial and musical development. Revolutionary as the notion appears at first sight, it is extraordinarily suggestive. So a thousand men not only would be making material things, but in the process would be producing not a mere cacophony of confused noises, but a gigantic symphony in accordance with a score directed by a *chef d'orchestre* altogether surpassing the *chef d'orchestre* of the concert-room. An entire town might, in Pound's view, become the stage from which would arise the regulated harmony of industry.

Marinetti is rehabilitated by Ezra — music, provençal airs and ballads of Villon, as far as he personally is concerned, taking him paradoxically right to the great throbbing, singing heart of the great god, Industry. I should be tempted to think it had taken Ezra a decade to catch up Marinetti, if I were not sure that, from the start, the histrionics of the milanese prefascist were secretly much to his sensation-loving taste. I observe rather that he has not moved from where he was.

To turn from his musical enterprise to other schemes in which he has recently participated, I reach material about which I am more competent to speak. A vast publication appeared a year or so ago, which sallied forth under his banner. Not to burden posterity with an unnecessary name, I will call it the Q. *Review.*

This enterprise answers to all the requirements laid down, in connection with my criticism of the Ballet, for a typical production of the false "revolutionary" milieu of that Millionaire Bohemia that has absorbed and is degrading the revolutionary impulse of the West — the creative impulse, that is. It announces as surprisingly new what is old, or merely the dull wash of any time; as outrageous what might startle a secluded spinster charwoman, but no one else; as "daring" what does not display the dash of a tortoise. In fact, it is surprising with what completeness it fulfils these conditions, on an epic scale. The "revolutionary" enthusiast, whether a stupid or an intelligent one, will look in vain, in this colossal publication, for anything to satisfy his appetite, outside the fragments of work by Mr. Joyce and Miss Stein, now become the standbys of all "revolutionary" editors who are able to supply nothing revolutionary themselves. The editor freely flavours his barren sentimentalism with the early mannerisms of Miss Stein. That is the most violent thrill that you will get. Nothing of the roguishness even, or physical dislocation of Dada; no new technical attempt whatever enlivens those unhappy pages. But to make up for this striking absence of ordinary spirit, you will get all the big and noisy, six-foot advertisers' claims; all the "Greater than Shakespeares," the "Death to the Pasts," the announcement of this enterprise as that of an absolutely new era, with which you have long been familiar.

And there is Ezra Pound, as patron saint, at the heart of all this profuse and meaningless word-bath — full of his old love of the Past, plodding melodramatically through mediaeval Italy, and throwing in snatches of translation and paraphrase of the greek, or of any other language which is ancient or traditional enough. Meanwhile, the editor exclaims at the top of his voice: "Tradition is an unimportant fact. . . . To speak of continuing the great traditions today is to plead for the use of condemned bridges. . . . It is going to the scrap heap for advice on development." "It is the aim of the present writer to imagine that life has begun only today so far as culture and civilisation," etc. etc. How to reconcile what Mr. W-sh (the initial of the editor; posterity has to be protected) *says*, and what Pound, he and the rest of them, *do*, must be very difficult for the best-intentioned. If this ideal fool, W-sh, were a *little* shrewder and more intelligent, he might have spoilt what is a quite perfect give-away for himself and all his kind. As it is, he is worth quoting; for I dare say we shall never have such a fool as Mr. W-sh again to do some of our dirty work for us.

All the big words, then, without exception, are still there. Pound is enthroned as the master-poet of the absolutely *new* epoch; but all that was ever *new* or that showed any signs of wanting to evolve some formula never tried before, has evaporated. It is totally absent in the *Q. Review.* There never was anything *new* about Ezra, but there is now not the faintest flicker of "newness" in those with whom recently he has associated himself, always excepting Antheil, Joyce and Gertrude Stein. If your eye just fell on W-sh's editorials, you would turn to the rest of the paper, perhaps, with bated breath. "Great traditions — condemned bridges — scrap heap! Life has begun only today!" Turning to life, as exhibited in the contributions, you then would find, to your dismay, this sort of overwhelming literary innovation, both in manner and conception:

The protestant pastor was sane, so were the props of the protestant church who took the collection (all men) and the well-balanced fathers, brothers, husbands, brothers-in-law, judges, lawyers, doctors, architects, bank managers, bank clerks, farmers, waiters, gardeners, railway porters, [etc. etc.]

There was never any talk in the home about her being a painter; they had never known any such thing, but they would let her indulge in that low streak. Even her father's enthusiasm stopped short at that, and her mother was disdainful. Cissy said she should go, and saved money and sent it to her regularly. And there she found the *Atelier Carmen* (belonging to voluptuous Carmen), where the inspired master "corrected," and there she worked furiously with an eager group of American students.

You would be under the impression that you were reading a feuilleton in the *Daily Mirror*. There are forty closely printed pages of that. (For some reason the thirteen first pages are printed twice in different parts of the paper — so you get over fifty altogether.) Then there is this, from another, though very similar hand:

"I'll be American and try anything once, if it really isn't imposing on you, then," Miss Taylor answered as she left. Ni watched her as she walked away. He felt antagonistic in a way to her. She was too restrained, too insistent on balance and sense, he was sure. She must believe in taste and refinement. The calm English temperament put him off anyway, and he hated the cageiness of conventional minds of any race. Nevertheless, he was attracted, or curious about, Miss Taylor, beneath his antagonism, [etc.]

Damn it, there was no use. Virg and Margie might be feather-witted, but they were the kind of girls to be around with easily, and if he got amorous they didn't think it meant anything serious. Poor old Amy, whom no man but he bothered about on the campus, was apt to wish to believe that even an amiable attention meant marriage intentions in the offing. He supposed he had been rather abrupt with her, though, since coming back, and she had been decent about writing him letters, [etc. etc.]

There is a good deal of that as well; it is the handiwork of that literary wonder we will call Bud Macsalmon, announced by Wush to his readers as "one of the most astonishing writers since the fathers of English literature."

Here is the editor on this particular giant of his super-circus:

I can't wait [howls W-sh]. I can't wait *any* longer to say that Bud Macsalmon is one of the most astonishing writers since the fathers of English literature. If you care for Shakespeare, if you care for Dickens, if you care for Conrad, you will care more for Macsalmon. He is colossal without being dull. . . . He has the deep smile and the hidden laughter of Indian women pounding maize without caring at all who is to eat it. The world eats maize. The world eats bread. Very well. Pound maize. Somebody eat by and by. Everybody got to eat sooner or later. Pound maize. Macsalmon writes. He write a great deal, [etc., etc.]

He goes on to say of Bud and his friends that they are "the school that writes by instinct." And he illustrates this by quoting their spelling — they spell *tries* as *trys*, he exultantly points out. They are *true primitives*. All these primitives have had, like children, the same difficulty: they have not been able to spell! And yet how expressive their little faults of orthography can be! What a nice archaic feeling it gives one to see *tries* spelt *trys*! (Just like *Gentlemen Prefer Blondes*, as a matter of fact — only, of course, *much* higher-class stuff! else, of course, Shakespeare wouldn't have been mentioned — not in connection with *Gentlemen Prefer Blondes*!)

What is wrong with Ring W. Lardner, his publisher could ask Mr. W-sh, for "Shakespeare" honours, or the heavy-weight english literary belt? I will give a slice from the Lardner (he is a well-known American humorist, not appearing in the *Q. Review*. He is author of *Gullible's Travels*, etc.) You can compare it with Bud, and you will be able to judge on the spot if Lardner's chances would not be rosy if there were nothing but Bud there to stop him, for the literary world-title.

Before we started, Mother patted me on the back and told me to do my best, so we started in and I seen right off that I was in for it, as I hadn't pitched a shoe in sixteen years and didn't have my distance. And besides, the plating had wore off the shoes so that they was points right where they stuck into my thumb and I hadn't throwed more than two or three times when my thumb was raw and it pretty near killed me to hang on to the shoe, let alone pitch it.

Well, to make a long story short, I was just beginning to get my distance when I had to give up on account of my thumb, which I showed it to Hartsell and he seen I couldn't go on, as it was raw and bleeding. Even if I could have stood it to go on myself, Mother wouldn't of allowed it after she seen my thumb. So anyway I quit and Hartsell said the score was nineteen six, but I don't know what it was. Or don't care, neither.

That, from Mr. Lardner's latest book, will, I think you will agree, take some beating in its own class — the class, of course, of Wush's favourites. Lardner has the deep smile and hidden laughter of Indian women pounding maize. Also, if you like *Antony and Cleopatra*, you will like Lardner. He is colossal

without being dull — this is what he aims at and that is what he
achieves. If he does not spell properly, well, the Fathers of English
Literature couldn't either; and if he *can* spell, but *won't*, well,
then he's like a lot of other people. My money is on Lardner for
being read longer than his competitors, Wush's champions.
Besides he (Lardner) has the deep smile of Indian women *on purpose*, because it pays him to have that smile. He does not give
a hoot for that smile, I guess, aside from that. Lardner one can
respect. Mr. W-sh has a weakness for pidgin English too. But
the dialect of his predilection is the spurious child-language of
Miss Stein, cadenced and said twice over in the form of the hebrew
recitative. That is, as it were, his native tongue. I will quote a
few passages at random. Here he is writing about the greatest
genius that has ever lived (not Bud this time):

He never told me his thoughts. I never knew what was in his mind.
And *then came his book*, A HURRIED MAN, and that is why I am writing
and why I have told you all that I have because I want you to know how
one comes to know a great man not yet thirty years old and how one
is very close to a great pleasure and a great dignity without being aware.

"One" is also very close to Miss Stein, as will be perceived in
the way one expresses one's self — "and that is why I am writing
and why I have told you all that I have," etc. He is also, himself,
naturally, "a hurried man." You get the full flavour of the
breathless hurried confidential lisp of the little baby girl, rushing
to its mother's knee and pouring out coyly its winsome chatter,
do you not, with our Mr. W-sh? And yet soon this charm stolen
by that big rough hairy dark-browed Mr. W-sh, from some little
innocent, must wear out the most benevolent reader (for someone
must be benevolent where he is concerned, somebody must love
Wush, or he would not prattle in public in this way). "Told oo
all that me have, oo naughty mammie oo" is at all events the
type of his main line of writing. "Belly well. Pound maize.
Somebody eat by and by," is a side track.

The author of the *Hurried Man* is, along with "Bud" (the author
of *The Hasty Bunch*) and, as a third, the lady from whose work
I have already quoted, Wooshe's pick, the trio of his heart. So
he recommends to us one who is perhaps the "greatest" of the
"great." Here is a specimen of what is written by the author of
the *Hurried Man* (he is a poet and a little bitter, that is his note):

> I received from a friend
> a letter where

> was a portrait of yours
> cut from a paper;
> and was kinda nostalgic
> the way a man would be
> who'd left a barrel of rotting apples
> uneaten.

The daring of this takes your breath away, and the bitterness of the ending fair turns yer up: am I right? The very spirit of "revolution" breathes in every word of it.

Everything in this enormous *Review* of 350 pages was not so abominably foolish as W-sh, as might be expected. Hemingway, for instance, is an admirable writer, almost universally admired. But his impresario is not satisfied. He must be admired by Wush, as well; go through it he must, since he is there between the same covers with Wush. So Wush says:

> Hemingway is the shyest and proudest and sweetest-smelling storyteller of my reading.

What a horrible nosegay — for a really shy and proud man! Again he says:

> The genius of Hemingway's writing lies somewhere around his getting ready to write since some time back. The rest happened. Hemingway managed to get born in America and born with more sensitiveness than most young men in America.

So much for the Q. *Review.* Pound, Stein and Joyce I will deal with next, under a separate head. What a field for some Mencken is lying fallow, and it seems unsuspected, in the world of bastard "revolutionary" prose and verse. The laughable extravagance of some provincial american advertiser, evangelist or what not, is not more absurd, vulgar, and unnatural. But because the Wushes of this world fly the colours of "high art," are "poets" — *rebel* poets — are the intellectual élite, they are immune from critical notice. It would be an important service to art if some publicist like Mencken specialized in them for a season, and gave the lowbrows a turn to laugh, or vomit.

When a person, whatever his past services in the cause of art may be, reaches such a state of decay that he can support such enterprises as the Q. *Review,* it is time to cut loose, if you have been formerly in his company. The end with Pound cannot be long delayed. So it will be evident, I hope, already that my action as regards the estimable Ezra is by no means premature; that there was in fact not a moment to be lost.

CHAPTER TEN

TESTS FOR COUNTERFEIT IN THE ARTS

IN THE BEGINNING was the Word should rather be, *in the beginning was Time*, according to Miss Stein (as also according to Bergson, Prof. Alexander, Einstein, Whitehead, Minkowski, etc. etc.). And she is one of the most eminent writers of what I have described as our *musical society*; that is our time-society, the highly-intellectualized High-Bohemia.

"In the beginning there was the time in the composition that naturally was in the composition but time in the composition comes now and this is what is now troubling every one the time in the composition is now a part of distribution and equilibration."

In Miss Stein's composition there is above all *time*, she tells us as best she can. As best she can, as you see; for she is not able to tell us this or anything else clearly and simply; first of all because a time-obsession, it seems, interferes, so we are given to understand. The other reason is that she is not simple at all, although she writes usually so like a child — like a confused, stammering, rather "soft" (bloated, acromegalic, squinting and spectacled, one can figure it as) child. Miss Stein you might innocently suppose from her naïf stuttering to be, if not a child, simple, at least, in spite of maturity. But that is not so; though, strangely enough, she would like it to be thought that it is. That is only the old story of people wanting to be things they are not; or else, either as strategy or out of pure caprice, enjoying any disguise that reverses and contradicts the personality.

Composition as Explanation is a little pamphlet just published by the Hogarth Press. In it you have the announcement that "The time of the composition is the time of the composition." But simple as that sounds, it is only roguishness on the part of its authoress, all the while. That is her fun only. She is just pretending, with a face of solemn humbug, not to be able to get out the word; what this verbal inhibition results in is something *funny*, that will make you laugh. It is a form of clowning, in short; she will disarm and capture you by her absurdity.

But *Time*, you are told, is at the bottom of the matter; though that you could have guessed, since it has been so for a very long time, from the beginning of the present period; from the birth of Bergson, shall we say? (Bergson was supposed by all of us to be dead, but Relativity, oddly enough at first sight, has recently resuscitated him; for the *time-spacer* has turned out to be the old-timer, or timist, after all.)

Miss Stein announces her time-doctrine in character, as it were. She gives you an "explanation," and illustrations, side by side; but the explanation is done in the same way as the examples that follow it. A further "explanation" would be required of the "explanation," and so on. And in that little, perhaps unregarded, fact, we have, I believe, one of the clues to this writer's mind. It tells us that her mind is a sham, to some extent.

In doing her "explanation" of her compositions in the same manner as her compositions (examples of which she gives), she is definitely making-believe that it is impossible for her to write in any other way. She is making a claim, in fact, that suggests a lack of candour on her part; and she is making it with an air of exaggerated candour. Supposing that the following line represented a typical composition of yours:

FugfuggFFF-fewg:fugfug-Fug-fugue-fffffffuuuuuuG

Supposing, having become celebrated for that, you responded to a desire on the part of the public to know what you were driving at. Then the public would be justified in estimating your sincerity of a higher order if you sat down and tried to "explain" according to the canons of plain speech (no doubt employed by you in ordering your dinner, or telling the neighbouring newsagent to send you the *Herald*, *Tribune*, or *Daily Express* every morning), your verbal experiments, than if you affected to be unable to use that kind of speech at all.

Every painter who has experimented in abstract design, for example, has often been put into that situation; he must often have been asked the familiar question: "But do you really *see* things like that, Mr. So-and-So?" Were Miss Stein that painter, we know now what would happen. She would roll her eyes, squint, point in a frenzy at some object, and, of course, stammer hard. She would play up to the popular ignorance as to the processes by which her picture had been arrived at, in short. She would answer "in character," implying that she was cut off from the rest of the world entirely by an exclusive and peculiar sensibility. Yet

everyone knows who engages in experiments of any sort, verbal
or pictorial, that that is not at all the point of the matter. It is
a *deliberate* adjustment of things to some formula which
transforms what is treated into an organism, strange according
to the human norm, though it might appear normal enough to
the senses of some other animal. Normal speech, or normal vision, are not interfered with in the practitioner of these experiments, on the one hand; nor does what in the result has an
abnormal appearance arise *literally* in an abnormal experience,
or an experience without a normal, non-visionary, basis.

For these reasons Miss Stein's illustrations would have been
much more impressive if she had not pretended, to start with,
that, as to the explanation, she "could not do it in any other way."
In this fact, that "explanation" and "composition" are both done
in the same stuttering dialect, you have the proof that you are
in the presence of a *faux-naïf*, not the real article. Miss Stein's
merits elsewhere are not cancelled by this — people are often gifted
without being able to lay any claim to being "sincere," as we say.
But it is a little difficult to understand how she could be so stupid.
Her assumption that any advantage was to be gained by this
studied obscurity, where it was, after all, pointless, is that.
Perhaps, however, it was only conceit.

Should my ensuing remarks sting Miss Stein into a rejoinder,
then I think you would see something like the situation that would
be created if some beggar shamming blindness observed a person about to disappear with his offertory box. The "blind" under
such conditions would *see* at once, and rush after the robber.
It is the classic test case in the everyday world of everyday sham.
I am afraid, however, that Miss Stein is too cunning a stammerer
to be so easily unmasked. Miss Stein's stutter in her *explanation*
even of her other celebrated stutterings, is a proof, then, to my
mind, that she is a homologue of the false-blind; that, in some
measure, she is a sham.

Still, what we can retain from that little affected treatise, is
that *Time* is at the bottom of her mind, the treasured key to her
technical experiments. And so she is working in the strictest conformity with all the other "time"-doctrinaires, who have gathered
in such disciplined numbers, so fanatically disciplined, as though
to the beating of a ritualistic drum.

With a trick like Miss Stein's, everyone, I think, should have
to pay a fee for using it. It is quite certain that it would never

have occurred to most of those who use it more or less, like the editor of the Q., for instance, without the promptings of the jazz-sibyl. This habit of speech, like a stuttering infection, is very contagious. Mr. Joyce even has caught it, and, one of the most pedagogically careful of men, has thrown overboard a great deal of laboriously collected cargo, and romps along at the head of the fashionable literary world, hand in hand with Gertrude Stein, both outdoing all children in jolly quaintnesses.

The child-personality, the all-important base of this school that I am attacking, and all that the affecting of that personality, and of the language of childhood, implies, is of such decisive importance, that I will now, during some pages, provide a brief analysis of this sudden malady of childhood that has mysteriously overtaken all our world, from the hoariest veteran down to the veritable child.

CHAPTER ELEVEN

A BRIEF ACCOUNT OF THE CHILD-CULT

I SUPPOSE THAT THERE is no one who has not noticed, passim and without attentiveness, perhaps, in a hundred different forms, the prevalence of what now amounts to a cult of childhood, and of *the Child.* This irresponsible, Peterpannish psychology is the key to the Utopia of the "revolutionary" Rich; the people, namely, who have taken over, have degraded, and are enjoying the fruits of revolutionary scientific innovation — far from its creative ardours, cynically scornful of its idealisms, but creating out of its ferments, which they have pillaged, a breathless Millennium.

This subject has been so thoroughly analysed by me elsewhere that I do not propose to go into it again here. All that is necessary to say is that it is essential, if you wish to understand at all a great deal of contemporary art and thought, even the developments of positive science, not only to gather up all the dispersed manifestations of this strange fashion, but — having done so — to trace this impulse to its source in the terrible and generally hidden disturbances that have broken the back of our will in the Western countries, and have already forced us into the greatest catastrophes. Whether these great disturbances are for the ultimate good of mankind or not, no one can claim that they are pleasant, or that they do not paralyse and weaken the system they attack. Many complaints break out in consequence in the midst of our thinking; and the instinctive recoil of the stricken system makes it assume strange shapes.

What you have to ask yourself is why, exactly, a grown person should wish to be a child? — for to use the forms of infantile or immature life, to make an art of its technical imperfections, and to exploit its natural ignorance, is, in some sense, to wish to be a child.

That, to start with, it is connected with the cult of *the primitive* and the *savage*, is obvious. The same impulse that takes the romantic painter, Gauguin, to the South Sea paradise, takes a similarly romantic person of today to the Utopia of childhood, in the sense indicated above. Only the latter has the Heaven of

51

Childhood inside himself (it is a *time-paradise*); whereas Gauguin had to go a long way to reach Samoa. That is the advantage that *time-travel* has over *space-travel*.

That was really Proust's Utopia, too. And the great appeal of that author is partly because he shows a method for capturing and retaining that spirit — the *recherche du temps perdu* — and partly because he so feverishly expresses the will to that particular dream. As we read him, the "I" of his books is that small, naïf, Charlie Chaplin-like, luxuriously-indulged, sharp-witted, passionately snobbish, figure, a model for many variations bred thickly everywhere. But that is not the whole story; and rather than give an imperfect notion of what a little investigation will reveal, I will, having started the inquiry, leave it at this point, or refer the reader to that part of my recent book dealing with this subject.

How *the demented* also joins hands with the child, and the tricks, often very amusing, of the asylum patient, are exploited at the same time as the happy inaccuracies of the infant; how contemporary inverted-sex fashions are affiliated to the Child-cult; and in fact all the different factors in this intricate sensibility, being evolved notably by such writers as Miss Stein, will be found there. Not to seize the secret of these liaisons is totally to misunderstand the nature of what is occurring around you today.

CHAPTER TWELVE

"TIME"-CHILDREN. MISS GERTRUDE STEIN AND MISS ANITA LOOS

IN THE FEW EXTRACTS from a Review quoted on pages 43–44 and 45 we have in the *And then came A Hurried Man* specimen, this: "and that is why I am writing and why I have told you all that I have because I want you to know how one comes to know a great man," etc. I will take at random a passage from Miss Stein's *Three Lives*:

Melanctha Herbert had not made her life all simple like Rose Johnson. Melanctha had not found it easy with herself to make her wants and what she had agree. Melanctha Herbert was always losing what she had in wanting all the things she saw. Melanctha was always being left when she was not leaving others. Melanctha Herbert, [etc.]

Here is the opening of *Composition as Explanation*. Without any pricking of the ear, it is easy to isolate in these passages the Child, the naïf-motif:

There is singularly nothing that makes a difference a difference in beginning and in the middle and in ending except that each generation has something different at which they are all looking. By this I mean so simply that anybody knows it that composition is the difference which makes each and all of them then different from other generations and this is what makes everything different otherwise they are all alike and everybody knows it because everybody says it.

The "there is singularly nothing" is a jamesism, which with James was already a little over-naïf grace. "By this I mean so simply" or the concluding words are pure "child." It is in the same category as:

And I know and she knows and all the world knows
No girl need love unless she chose,

only Miss Stein does not say (as the poet who wrote the above lines implies) "now I am going to be a simple little thing, tossing my golden head in a Ring-o-ring-o-Roses."

I will now compare Miss Stein and Miss Loos. Here is a passage from *Gentlemen Prefer Blondes*, by Anita Loos:

Paris is devine. I mean Dorothy and I got to Paris yesterday, and it really is devine. Because the French are devine. Because when we were coming off the boat, and we were coming through the customs it was quite hot and it seemed to smell quite a lot and all the french gentlemen in the customs, were squealing quite a lot. So I looked around and I picked out a french gentleman who was really in a very gorgeous uniform, [etc.]

Here is a poem by Miss Gertrude Stein:

If you hear her snore
It is not before you love her
You love her so that to be her beau is very lovely
She is sweetly there and her curly hair is very lovely
She is my tender sweet and her little feet are stretched out well
    which is a treat and very lovely.

If you put the passage from *Gentlemen Prefer Blondes* into the free-verse form you will see the relationship still more closely:

Paris is devine.
I mean Dorothy and I got to Paris yesterday and it really is devine.
Because the French are devine.
Because when we were coming off the boat, and we were coming
    through the customs it was quite hot.
And it seemed to smell quite a lot.
And all the french gentlemen in the customs were squealing quite
    a lot.

Here is another passage from *Gentlemen Prefer Blondes*:

So while we were shopping in the afternoon I saw Louie get Dorothy off in a corner and whisper to her quite a lot. So then I saw Robert get her off in a corner and whisper to her quite a lot. So when we got back to the Ritz, Dorothy told me why they whispered to her. So it seems that when Louie whispered to Dorothy, [etc.]

The tricks are identical, and the reasons for them (in the last two instances) are identical. Everything is repeated over and over again. As Miss Stein says in her *Explanation*:

In my beginning it was a continuous present a beginning again and again and again and again, it was a series it was a list, [etc.]

This repetition which technically weds Miss Loos and Miss Stein is the "time-trouble," the "time-nuisance," as it were; though anyone who believed that it was such an unfortunate affair as all that for Miss Stein would be *bien naïf*. Here, in full-sail of affected naïveté, is Miss Stein complaining of this terrible sense that gives her and everybody else so much trouble, as a pretty girl may complain of her becomingly large hat on a windy day.

There must be *time*. . . . This is the thing that is at present the most troubling and if there is the time that is at present the most troublesome the time-sense that is at present the most troubling is the thing that makes the present the most troubling.

"*Composition is time*" — that is the secret according to Miss Stein. "In this way at present composition is time that is the reason that at present the time-sense in the composition is the composition," etc. It is in the repetition (the result of the troublesome time-sense, Miss Stein tells us, obsessing her, she can't help it) that the most obvious point of resemblance is to be found between Miss Stein and Miss Loos.

But the identity in all these tricks of manner is deeper than a simple technical imitation would explain. In the case of both the quotations from Miss Stein and from Miss Loos there are these two fundamental similarities. The passages are alike because (1) the person who is supposed to be writing is illiterate; and because (2) she or he is naïf, and engagingly childish. In the case of Miss Loos she has employed this method because she wished to obtain the breathless babble of the wide-eyed child, telling Mummie all about what has happened to her.

Let us take Ring W. Lardner again and see how he fits in. We will take his short story, *Some Like Them Cold*. This is how it opens (it is in letter-form):

Dear Miss Gillespie: How about our bet now as you bet me I would forget all about you the minute I hit the big town and would never write you a letter. Well, girlie, it looks like you lose so pay me. Seriously we will call all bets off as I am not the kind that bet on a sure thing and it sure was a sure thing that I would not forget a girlie like you and all that is worrying me is whether it may not be the other way round and you are wondering who this fresh guy is that is writing you this letter. I bet you are so will try and refresh your memory.

In all these cases, from Melanctha to Lardner's letter, the manner depends on the following essentials, postulated before the composition starts. The manner shall be that of a very simple, naïf person, suggesting extreme youth or at least the deepest inexperience; it shall be told with the breathlessness and monotony of the child; its charm shall be attached to a habit of never-varying, sing-song repetition; and (this is of great importance) the child shall be a *child of the people*, with the pathos of the illiterate added to the pathos of the child, the charm of both confounded. Humour is to be deliberately extracted from all this; that is to say that author and reader are both superior to the narrator.

Miss Gertrude Stein in her *Melanctha* is giving the life of a poor negress, not in the negress's own words, but in her own manner. Then the mannerism is intended to convey, with its ceaseless repetitions, the monstrous *bulk* and vegetable accumulation of human life in the mass, in its mechanical rotation. Creaking, groaning, and repeating itself in an insane iteration, it grows, flowers heavily, ages and dies. Its sodden lustreless heaping up of sheer meaningless material, composing the mortal career, is conveyed in the monotonous, imbecile, endlessly-repeated, lumbering words: Melanctha Herbert, for instance, the name of the principal figure. The tone, again, the words used, very roughly approximate to the subject.

Miss Anita Loos is engaged in the same literary game, and is employing the same method. Only her subject, or victim, is an american midinette, and the phases of her cheap gallantry, imbecile in its empty cunning, told in her naïf illiterate jargon, and in consequence supremely amusing to educated people in England and America, where, of course, it has achieved a similar success to that of the *Young Visiters*.

Miss Stein has a considerable reputation as a serious writer, of experimental type, but earnest intentions; therefore to compare her compositions with those of Miss Loos may still strike the well-informed reader as an extravagance. To see really how fundamentally alike they are you cannot do better than take a passage in her *Composition as Explanation* where she is speaking in the first person, giving an account of *herself* and her doings. The tone, as will be seen in the extract I am about to give, is almost identical with *Gentlemen Prefer Blondes*.

In beginning writing I wrote a book called *Three Lives* this was written in 1905. I wrote a negro story called Melanctha. In that there was a constant recurring and beginning there was a marked direction in the direction of being in the present although naturally I had been accustomed to past present and future, and why, because the composition forming around me was a prolonged present. A composition of a prolonged present is a natural composition in the world as it has been these thirty years it was more and more a prolonged present. I created then a prolonged present naturally I knew nothing of a continuous present but it came naturally to me to make one, it was simple it was clear to me and nobody knew why it was done like that, I did not myself although naturally to me it was natural.

After that I did a book called *The Making of Americans* it is a long book about a thousand pages.

. . .　　　. . .　　　. . .

Having naturally done this I naturally was a little troubled with it when I read it. I became then like the others who read it. . . . Then I said to myself this time it will be different and I began. I did not begin again I just began.

You will not have to listen very hard to catch, here, the accent of the little girl, telling how she wrote the curious pieces about which grown-ups made such a stir and to-do. "After that I did a book called *The Making of Americans* it is a long book about a thousand pages." It is pure *Gentlemen Prefer Blondes;* and the more emotional reader would exclaim automatically, "How sweet!" on reading it, completely bowled over by the punctuation, if nothing else.

There is all the craft of the Charlie Chaplin appeal, all those little dissimulated threads run cunningly to the great big silly heart of the innocent public, in this mannerism of Miss Stein and Miss Loos.

But this is only one aspect of her talent. Miss Stein is a sort of Epstein in words. Her puissant, heavy, churning temperament inspires respect. Or she is a ponderous romantic of the Conrad type; whereas Miss Loos is a lightly ballasted best-seller only, working on the same lines. In perspective the latter will appear as a small mercenary practitioner of the school of Stein, just as Arlen and Huxley are baser varieties of Marcel Proust, in the same tradition. It is not at all uninstructive to compare, making allowance for their respective scale and pretensions, these artists of varying calibre, but similar impulse and taste. (In the above illustration, I am not saying that Miss Stein is equal in importance to Proust; only that she is the limiting member of a certain class.)

So what Miss Loos does is this: she makes fun of the illiteracy, hypocrisy and business instinct of an uneducated american flapper-harlot for the benefit of the middle-class public who can spell, and who say "intriguing" and "divine," and who therefore are able to chuckle over the dish of bad grammar and naughtiness to their hearts' content; and Miss Loos arrives at this by affecting to be her victim ("told from the inside" method) by acting the part in her rôle of author.

CHAPTER THIRTEEN

THE PROSE-SONG OF GERTRUDE STEIN

MISS STEIN HAS certainly never had any unvirtuous and mercenary intentions of the kind besetting Miss Loos; she has never needed to be a best-seller, luckily for herself — had that been so, she would have opened our eyes, I suspect. But in her earlier books (from one of which I have quoted), she, too, *became* the people she wrote about, adopting their illiteracies and colloquialisms. The other main factor in her method resulted in her story taking the form of *a prose-song.*

It is in a thick, monotonous prose-song that Miss Stein characteristically expresses her fatigue, her energy, and the bitter fatalism of her nature. Her stories are very often long — all the longer, too, because everything has to be repeated half a dozen times over. In the end the most wearisome dirge it is possible to imagine results, as slab after slab of this heavy, insensitive, common prose-song churns and lumbers by.

To an Antheil tempest of jazz it is the entire body that responds, after all. The executant tires; its duration does not exceed ten minutes or so, consecutively. But it is *the tongue* — only the poor, worried, hard-worked tongue — inside the reader's head, or his laryngeal apparatus, that responds to the prose-song of Miss Stein.

At present I am referring to what I have read of Miss Stein at the *Three Lives* stage of her technical evolution. What is the matter with it is, probably, that it is so *dead.* Gertrude Stein's prose-song is a cold, black suet-pudding. We can represent it as a cold suet-roll of fabulously-reptilian length. Cut it at any point, it is the same thing; the same heavy, sticky, opaque mass all through, and all along. It is weighted, projected, with a sibylline urge. It is mournful and monstrous, composed of dead and inanimate material. It is all fat, without nerve. Or the evident vitality that informs it is vegetable rather than animal. Its life is a low-grade, if tenacious, one; of the sausage, by-the-yard, variety.

That is one aspect of the question, the technical one. There is another which has a certain reference to the political ideology I have been analysing. In adopting the simplicity, the illiterateness, of the mass-average of the Melancthas and Annas, Miss Stein gives proof of all the false "revolutionary," propagandist *plain-manism* of her time. The monstrous, desperate, soggy *lengths* of primitive mass-life, chopped off and presented to us as a never-ending prose-song, are undoubtedly intended as an epic contribution to the present mass-democracy. The texture of the language has to be jumbled, cheap, slangy and thick to suit. It must be written in a slovenly, straight-off fashion, so that is may appear to be more "real." Only the metre of an obsessing *time* has to be put into it. It has to be rhythmatized; and this proclivity both of Miss Stein, and of all the characteristic fashions of those for whom she writes, destroys the "reality" at least, giving to the life it patronizes the mechanical bias of its creator.

Next we will take up the fashionable child-factor as it is found in the work of Miss Stein, and in most art today, from Sir James Barrie to Charlie Chaplin. Her latest book, a vast one, I hear, I have not read. But many slighter, or at least shorter, more recent pieces, I know. In these, where she is not personifying a negress or some small american bourgeoise, but playing her own personal literary game (she may be described as the reverse of Patience sitting on a monument — she appears, that is, as a Monument sitting upon patience), this capable, colossal authoress relapses into the rôle and mental habits of childhood. Fact is thrown to the winds; the irresponsible, light-hearted madness of ignorance is wooed, and the full-fledged *Child* emerges. This child (often an idiot-child as it happens, but none the less sweet to itself for that) throws big, heavy words up and catches them; or letting them slip through its fingers, they break in pieces; and down it squats with a grunt, and begins sticking them together again. Else this far-too-intellectual infant chases the chosen word, like a moth, through many pages, worrying the delicate life out of it. The larynx and tongue of the reader meantime suffer acutely. Every word uttered threatens to obsess and stick to his tongue. Having come, wrongly spelt, wrongly pronounced, or wrongly according to usage, it refuses to move till it has been put right; yet will not come right in Miss Stein's hands.

It is in these occasional pieces that the *child-personality* of Miss Stein is discovered in its acutest form. But *the child* with her is always overshadowed by the imbecile. That is to say, that very clever, very resourceful Gertrude Stein is heavily indebted to the poor honest lunatic for her mannerisms. All the regions between the dull stupor of complete imbecility — which is splendidly portrayed in Picasso's pneumatic giantesses — and the relatively disciplined, alert, fixed condition, which is humanly regarded as the other pole to imbecility, she has thoroughly explored. The massive silence of the full idiot is, unfortunately, out of her reach, of course. In her capacity of writer, or wordknitter, she has to stop short of that, and leave it to her friend Picasso. For words, idle words, have one terrible limitation — they must represent human speech in some form. The silent canvas is their master there.

That, very briefly, is Miss Stein's rôle in the child-cult, and the kindred one (Freud-inspired or not) of *the demented.* She is herself a robust intelligence, a colossus among the practitioners of infancy; a huge, lowering, dogmatic Child. The point of her writing is best seen, perhaps, in less intelligent imitators or homologues. Even by taking a quite flimsy writer in the same movement (both on account of psychology and technique) like Miss Loos, you will be helped to that essential simplification.

My general objection, then, to the work of Miss Stein is that it is *dead.* My second objection is that it is *romantic.* As to the latter count, for all its force I feel it to be *unreal* in the same way that I feel Conrad or Zola to be, but without the rationale of the fictionist. It is the personal rhythm, the obvious bias, that of a peculiar rather than a universal nature, that produces this sensation. The dull frantic vitality of Zola is that of an inferior, a brutal, not a highly-organized, nature. The chocolate-cream richness of Conrad, the *romance* laid on with a shovel — best revealed where Mr. Hueffer helped him in the book specifically named *Romance* — all this excess, this tropical unreality, I find (of course, to some extent concealed in an elaborate intellectualist technique) in Miss Stein.

As to the quality of deadness, that can be matched most exactly by comparison with contemporary painting, even the best. In *The Caliph's Design* I have named this the *nature-mortist* school of painting.

In Miss Stein you get a temperament on the grand scale, as you do in Picasso; they both enjoy the colossal. But if you compare one of Picasso's giantesses (the first born about 1920, I believe) with a giant from the Sistine Ceiling, you will at once find that the Picasso figure is a beautifully executed, imposing, human *doll.* Its fixed imbecility of expression, its immense,

bloated, eunuchoid limbs, suggest the mental clinic immediately. They are all opaque fat, without nerve or muscle. The figures
of Michelangelo, on the other hand — the most supremely noble
and terrible creations of the dramatic genius of the West — are
creatures of an infectious life. Between the outstretched forefinger
of Adam and the finger of the hurrying Jehovah, there is an electric force in suspense of a magnitude that no vegetative imbecility,
however well done or however colossal, on one side and on the
other, would be able to convey.

The *weight*, then, that is characteristic of the work of Miss
Stein — like the sluggish weight of the figures, or the sultry op-
pressiveness of the chocolate-cream tropics in which they move,
of Conrad; or of the unintelligent, catastrophic heaviness of
Zola — is, to me, of a dead order of things. But this kind of doll-
like *deadness*, the torpid fatal *heaviness*, is so prevalent, in one
form or another, as to dominate in a peculiar way the productions of the present time. Now that we have enough of it to
generalize what was at first a sense only of the assembling of a
peculiar consciousness into a formularized mass, we can study
it as a very definite, clearly marked thing. It is the hall-mark of
a great school. Wherever a member of the school grows
ambitious — and in consequence colossal — he or she betrays this
essential *deadness*. The reasons, of a sociologic order, for this,
it is not my business, here, to analyse.

The inner meanings of the child-cult, again, as I have said, I
am not undertaking to recapitulate in this place. For a certain
restricted number of cases there is an explanation which suggests
itself, and which I have not so far advanced, but it only applies
to a few of the practitioners. Still it may be worth while to offer
it for what it is worth.

About fifteen years ago there was a fashion for child-art. But
it was the painting and writing of authentic children in the class-
room that was sought out and popularized. The possible explanation of the child-art of today, then, is this. It may be that some
of the present work of that description is what has been *left over*
from that period. The authentic children of that time — finding,
at that impressionable age, their childish ways so unexpectedly
appreciated — may have gone on ever since on the same road.
The personality of Miss Anita Loos, for instance, lends colour
to this theory. Here is an interview with her, on her arrival "at
London":

Anita staggers any one who sees her for the first time after reading her book. She is four-foot-something high, weighs a mere six stone, and has the fresh face, wide eyes, and unsophisticated voice of a child.

"That gel looks twelve," said the scene-shifter who saw her directing a rehearsal for her new play. He was right.

"I am really twenty-six now," she whispered to me, "but I started writing when I was thirteen, and I don't suppose I have really changed since."

This certainly seems a clue to the childish technical habits of Miss Loos. The "four-feet-something" of Miss Loos, again, may remind you of other tiny, but famous, personalities — the greatest of whom is Charlie Chaplin. And with a brief analysis of the causes of the triumphant success of that celebrated film-tramp, I will terminate this part of my scrutiny.

CHAPTER FOURTEEN

THE SECRET OF THE SUCCESS OF CHARLIE CHAPLIN

THE CHILDISH, PUNY stature of Chaplin—enabling him always to be the little David to the Goliath of some man chosen for his statuesque proportions—served him well. He was always the *little-fellow-put-upon*—the naïf, child-like individual, bullied by the massive brutes by whom he was surrounded, yet whom he invariably vanquished. The fact that the giants were always vanquished; that, like the heroes of Ossian, they rode forth to battle (against the Chaplins of this world), but that, like those distant celtic heroes, *they always fell*, never, of course, struck the Public as pathetic, too. For the pathos of the Public is of a sentimental and also a naïvely selfish order. It is *its own* pathos and triumphs that it wishes to hear about. It seldom rises to an understanding of other forms of pathos than that of the kind represented by Chaplin, and the indirect reference to "greatness" in a more general sense, conveyed by mere physical size, repels it.

In this pathos of *the small*—so magnificently exploited by Charlie Chaplin—the ordinary "revolutionary" motif for crowd-consumption is not far to seek. The Keystone giants by whom, in his early films, he was always confronted, who *oppressed, misunderstood* and *hunted* him, but whom he invariably overcame, were the symbols of authority and power. Chaplin is a great revolutionary propagandist. On the political side, the pity he awakens, and his peculiar appeal to the public, is that reserved for *the small man.*

But no one can have seen a Chaplin film without being conscious also of something else, quite different from mere smallness. There was something much more positive than scale alone, or absence of scale, being put across, you would feel. First, of course, was the feeling that you were in the presence of an unbounded optimism (for one so small, poor and lonely). The combination of light-heartedness and a sort of scurrilous cunning, that his irresponsible epileptic shuffle gives, is overpowering. It is Pippa that is passing. God is in His Heaven; all's well with the world (of Chaplins at all events). And, secondly, you would experience the utmost confidence in your little hero's winning all his battles. The happy-ending (for the militant child-man) was foreshadowed in the awkward and stupid, lurching bulk of the Keystone giants; in the flea-like adroitness of their terrible little antagonist. It was the little skiff of Drake against the Armada over again. In brief, your hero was not only small, but very capable and very confident. Throughout he bore a charmed life.

To the *smallness*, and to the *charmed life*, you now have to add the child-factor. Chaplin, the greatest screen artist, is *a child-man*, rather than merely *a small man*. That was his charm and the nature of his aesthetic appeal, as it were. His little doll-like face, his stuck-on toy moustache, his tiny wrists, his small body, are those of a child as much as is the "four-foot-something" body of Miss Loos. And without the public being conscious of it, no doubt, it was as a child that he went to its heart, which, as far as the popular audience is concerned, is maternal.

As to the sex-side of this psychology, it would be unscientific, if you like, to forget that the feminist revolution has been in progress all around the creative activities of this great clown, throughout his career. In Chaplin the simple woman would see clearly a symbol of her little Tommy — or little Charlie — giving that great, big arrogant, troublesome bully, Dad (even if her particular "man" was not a good specimen of the ruling-sex), a wallop. For the head of a crowd is like a pudding *en surprise*. Everything is put into it; it reacts to the spectacles that are presented to it partly under the direction of those spectacles, but mainly according to the directing synthesis of all that has fallen or been stuffed into it, coming from all that is going on around it.

That, I think, is the way in which Chaplin endeared himself to the great public of the mass-democracy. But he is certainly mistaken in supposing that that was also the secret of Napoleon's success.

Perhaps in the success of Charlie Chaplin we have the heart of the secret of the child-fashion. It is at least strange how many people answer to the Chaplin-Loos (wide-eyed naïf) standard. Even in physical stature it is strange how many have sprung up — or have *not* sprung up. And very many more lend their best energies to approximating as far as possible to this popular child-type.

I think it is an age to be small in, said an intelligent flea,
But I shall see!

And on the other hand, the rôle of the giant, or a rôle involving any greatness, is deservedly unpopular. Men fly from suggestions of greatness as though such things were tainted, as indeed they are proscribed. In their own bosoms they carefully stamp out all tell-tale traces of a suspect ambition.

I do not wish to be personal, but the subject is such a very significant one that that objection must be overridden. Picasso, then, is very small as well; with, however, a slightly napoleonic austerity lacking in Chaplin; though he has the same bright, darting, knowing eyes, the same appearance of microscopic competence. He is built on strictly infantile lines. I could name many more less-known people who answer to this description. Nature is certainly busy somewhere, and has been busy for a long time, turning these *eternal sucklings* out in the flesh, and not only in the spirit. What is Nature about? Why is she specializing in this manner? That is a question for the professional physiologist and psychologist. Those are, however, the facts; which anyone, with a few hours to spare, can observe for themselves. At that, for the present, I will leave the problem of the infant-cult.

CHAPTER FIFTEEN

A MAN IN LOVE WITH THE PAST

EZRA POUND DOES NOT share the child-cult at all with the people I have been considering. But this does not mean that he is unorthodox. He is very orthodox. He would be miserable if he thought he was not conforming to anything that claimed the majority of educated people as its adherents, or slaves. The fiats and orders-of-the-day of the latest encyclical of fashion never would find Ezra disrespectful. He has never desired, himself, to interfere in these mysterious dispensations, or to challenge the invariable worthiness of their origin. At the most, as one Sphinx to another, he may have ventured a wink, and a slight cough. Nor would it ever so much as pass through his mind to set the fashion himself. He receives; his is the receptive rôle; he is the *consumer*, as he would say. It is *we* who produce; we are the creators; Ezra battens upon us. And he is the most gentlemanly, discriminating parasite I have ever had, personally, nor would I desire a cleaner or sweeter (as Wush would say), if he ever wishes for a testimonial.

In the great Past there were creators, too; and there are few of them, from Sophocles to Cavalcanti, that Ezra has not pillaged. But I am sorry to say that I believe Ezra's effective life-work is over, as I have already remarked; for there are not many left, and of late he has steadily weakened.

But if anyone supposes from these remarks, or if they think I mean, that Ezra Pound is a nobody, he will be mistaken. Yet how he is a "somebody" is a little difficult to define. Pound is that curious thing, a person without a trace of originality of any sort. It is impossible even to imagine him being anyone in particular of all the people he has translated, interpreted, appreciated.

When he writes about living people of his acquaintance, as sometimes he has done, he shows himself possessed of a sort of conventional malice, perhaps, that says about them things that other people would say about them; but he never seems to have *seen* the individual at all. He sees people and things as other people would see them; there is no direct contact between Ezra and an individual person or thing. Ezra is a crowd; a little crowd. People are seen by him only as types. There is the "museum official," the "norman cocotte," and so on. *By himself* he would seem to have neither any convictions nor eyes in his head. There is nothing that he intuits well, certainly never originally. Yet when he can get into the skin of somebody else, of power and renown, a Propertius or an Arnaut Daniel, he becomes a lion or a lynx on the spot. This sort of parasitism is with him phenomenal.

Again, when he writes in person, as Pound, his phrases are invariably stagey and false, as well as insignificant. There is the strangest air of insincerity about his least purely personal utterance; the ring of the superbest conviction when he is the mouthpiece of a scald or of a jongleur.

The hosts of this great intellectual parasite, then, are legion; but in meeting Ezra you find yourself in the presence of a person who, if evidently not a source of life himself, has yet none of the unpleasant characteristics we associate with an organism dependent on others for its habitat and soil. He is such a "big bug" in his class, that he has some of the airs of his masters. If thoroughly conventional, as you would expect of a good servant—his mind moving in grooves that have been made for it by his social milieu—he is not without personality, of a considerable and very charming sort.

My way of accounting for these discrepancies is as follows:

If Ezra Pound as a living individual were less worthy and admirable, I am convinced he would be unable to enter into the renowned and noble creatures whom he has passed his time in entering, so cleanly as he does—so faultlessly in places that you could not tell which is Pound and which is them. They or their genius or something that is in their work to guard it, would detect the imposture, and would certainly prevent him from working through them, in the splendid way that he has, were there any vulgarity or sham in the essential Ezra.

His dedication to his task has been fanatical. In order to slip in and out, as he does, in order to want to do so, so often as he has, and in such a great variety of cases, it was necessary for him—for his proper dedication to these men-gods—to be a kind of intellectual eunuch. That is my idea.

So I like, respect, and, in a sense, reverence Ezra Pound; I have found him a true, disinterested and unspoilt individual. He has not effected this intimate entrance into everything that is noble and enchanting for nothing. He has really walked with Sophocles beside the Aegean; he has *seen* the Florence of Cavalcanti; there is almost nowhere in the Past that he has not visited; he has been a great *time-trotter*, as we could describe this new kind of tourist. And he is not unworthy, in himself, of these many privileges.

But where the Present is concerned it is a different matter. He is extremely untrustworthy where that is concerned. That is the penalty of his function, like that of the eunuch instanced above. When he tries to be up-to-date it is a very uncomfortable business. And because he is conventional, and so accepts counterfeit readily where no standard has been established, he is a danger as far as he exerts any contemporary influence. He should not be taken seriously as a living being at all. Life is not his true concern, his gifts are all turned in the other direction. "In his chosen or fated field he bows to no one," to use his words. But his field is purely that of *the dead*. As the *nature mortist*, or painter essentially of still-life, deals for preference with life-that-is-still, that has not much life, so Ezra for preference consorts with the dead, whose life is preserved for us in books and pictures. He has never loved anything living as he has loved the dead.

If this account of him is true, it is obvious how unfit he is to deal with living material at all. He has so much the habit of un-questioning obedience and self-effacement, that he cannot at all manage the unruly shape of things that are in-the-making, and which demand of him also some effort of a creative sort — ask him to set them limits, or direct them even. Ezra, in such a situation, is at his wits' end. He squints at them with an affectation of shrewdness, squares his shoulders, shouts something shrill and incoherent, but contributes nothing to the situation.

Before leaving Pound I feel it would be best to illustrate the foregoing observations a little. His best translations (the *Seafarer*, for instance) are classics. It is to his more mixed work that I will go for my extracts. First I will draw attention to a point in the less disintegrated of that mixed type of work, where the translation element predominates.

The reader is no doubt familiar with the word "terse" in its cant-ing sense. "He was rather *terse* with me," people say. This can be otherwise expressed, "He was *short* with me." "Terse" and "short" are ways of expressing the laconic manner of a person who is an-noyed, and in consequence uses few words, perhaps sarcastical-ly. (Brevity or conciseness is the original meaning of terse.)

Here is an example of a man being "terse" with another. Two doctors, Dr. Mann and Dr. Samuels, had a dispute as to whether a patient had fractured his collar-bone or not. In reporting their telephone conversation to a magistrate, Dr. Samuels said, "Dr. Mann replied, 'Tosh and nonsense.' " That was an extreme form of the explosive variéty of "terseness," of a conventional, professional type.

Now a kind of mock-bitter, sententious *terseness* characterizes most of Pound's semi-original verse, and even mars some of his translations. And then there is the "terseness" that enlivens his journalism, which must be distinguished from the other more fundamental "terseness" to which I am now drawing attention. In his journalism his "terseness" is of much the same order as Dr. Mann's; it is of a breezy and boisterous order. For example, such violent expressions as "bunk, junk, spoof, mush, slush, tosh, bosh," are favourites with him; and he remains convinced that such over-specifically *manly* epithets are universally effective, in spite of all proof to the contrary. But it is not that sort of "terseness" to which I wished to refer.

The other, more fundamental, "terseness" of Pound is also of a sententious and, by implication, "manly" order. It seems to me to make his better personal verse (as distinguished from his translations) very monotonous, and gives it all a rather stupid ring. It is not, of course, the nature of metre chosen to which I am referring, but the melodramatic, chopped, "bitter" tone suggested by the abrupt clipping and stopping to which he is addicted. It is the laconicism of the strong silent man. Were he a novelist, you would undoubtedly find the description "He broke off" repeatedly used. In his verse he is always "breaking off." And he "breaks off," indeed, as a rule, twice in every line.

> Cave of Nerea
> She like a great shell curved.
> And the boat drawn without sound
> Without odour of ship-work,
> Nor bird-cry, nor any noise of wave moving,
> Nor splash of porpoise, nor any noise of wave moving,
> Within her cave, Nerea,
> She like a great shell curved.

That actually seems to belong to the repetitive hypnotic method of Miss Stein and Miss Loos. "She like a great shell curved," and the "any noise of wave moving," both repeated, are in any case

swinburnian stage-properties. The whole passage with its abrupt
sententious pauses is unpleasantly reminiscent of the second-rate
actor accustomed to take heavy and emotional parts. Perhaps
in this next quotation it will be seen better what I mean:

> Now supine in burrow, half over-arched bramble,
> One eye for the sea, through that peek-hole,
> Gray light, with Athene.
> Zothar, and her elephants, the gold loin-cloth,
> The systrum, shaken, shaken,
>   the cohort of her dancers.
> And Aletha, by bend of the shore,
>   with her eyes seaward,
>   and in her hands sea-wrack
> Salt-bright . . .

How you are supposed to read this, of course, is with great stops
upon — *burrow, bramble, peek-hole, gray light, Athene, Zothar,
elephants, loin-cloth, systrum, shaken, dancers, Aletha, seaward,
sea-wrack, salt-bright.* The way the personnel of the poem are
arranged, sea-wrack in the hand of one, Aletha "with her eyes
seaward," the gold loin-cloth of another, etc., makes it all effectively like a spirited salon-picture, gold framed and romantically
"classical." It is full of "sentiment," as is the Cave of Nerea; it is
all made up of well-worn stage-properties; and it is composed
upon a series of histrionic pauses, intended to be thrilling and
probably beautiful.

These extracts are from Cantos XVIII–XIX, and made their appearance in the *Q. Review.* Here is a specimen of Pound's more
intimate verse (taken from the same place):

> And the answer to that is: Wa'al he had the ten thousand.
> And old Spinder, that put up the 1870 gothick memorial,
> He tried to pull me on Marx, and he told me
> About the "romance of his business"; . . . So I sez:
> Waal haow is it you're over here, right off the Champz Elyza?
> And how can yew be here? Why dont the fellers at home
> Take it all off you? . . .
> "Oh" he sez "I ain't had to rent any money...
> "It's a long time since I ain't had tew rent any money."

All Pound's comic reliefs speak the same tongue; they are all
jocose and conduct their heavy german-american horseplay in
the same personal argot of Pound. They can never have illumined
anything but the most half-hearted smile (however kindly) rather

at Pound than at them. Their thick facetiousness is of the rollicking slap-on-the-back order, suggesting another day and another scene to ours. If they were better done and less conventional in their broad unreality they would be welcome, like belated red-nosed comedians in the midst of a series of turns too strictly designed to meet the ultra-feminine drawing-room-entertainer taste, as a contrast. But they are not spirited enough to serve even that purpose. They are a caricature of Pound attempting to deal with real life — they are Pound at his worst.

If Pound had not a strain of absolutely authentic naïveté in him, had he possessed the sort of minor sociable qualities that make the trivial adjustments of the social world an open book to their possessor, he could not write in this clumsy and stupid way, when attempting to stage scenes from contemporary life. So though they represent Pound the artist at his worst, they show us, I believe, the true Pound, or that part that has not become incorporated in his best highly traditional poetry. And a simpleton is what we are left with. That natural and unvarnished, unassimilable, Pound, is the true child, which so many people in vain essay to be. But some inhibition has prevented him from getting that genuine naïf (which would have made him a poet) into his work. There, unfortunately, he always attitudinizes, frowns, struts, looks terribly knowing, "breaks off," shows off, puffs himself out, and so obscures the really simple, charming creature that he is.

CHAPTER SIXTEEN

AN ANALYSIS OF THE MIND OF JAMES JOYCE

1. THE WORK OF Mr. Joyce enters in various ways as a specimen into the critical scheme I am outlining. What I have to say will not aim at estimating his general contribution to contemporary letters. I prefer his writing to that of Miss Stein, that may as well be set down at once. It does not suffer from the obsessional afflatus that I have noticed in the latter. It has more elasticity and freedom; it is much less psychological, it is more physical. His vices of style, as I understand it, are due rather to his unorganized suscep- tibility to influences, and especially from the quarter I have been discussing (Miss Stein has influenced him, for instance), than to a native shortcoming.

I cannot see that any work of Joyce — except *Ulysses* — is very significant. It was about six or seven years ago that I first became acquainted with his writing. The *Portrait of the Artist* seemed to me a rather cold and priggish book. It was well done, like the *Dubliners*, which I have just read; and that was all, that I could discover. *Chamber Music* would certainly not have secured its author a place "among the english poets" — it would hardly even have set the Liffey on fire for five minutes. No writing of his before *Ulysses* would have given him anything but an honourable posi- tion as the inevitable naturalist-french-influenced member of the romantic Irish Revival — a Maupassant of Dublin, but without the sinister force of Flaubert's disciple.

Ulysses was in a sense a different thing altogether. How far that is an effect of a merely technical order, resulting from stylistic complications and intensified display, with a *Dubliners* basis un- changed, or, further, a question of scale, and mechanical heap- ing up of detail, I should have only partly to decide here. But it places him — on that point everyone is in agreement — very high in contemporary letters.

Its evident importance, its success, induced people to go out- side the contemporary field for their analogies; and, to start with, it may be as well to remove from our path a few of the un- necessary names at that time, in the first generous flush of praise,

73

injudiciously imported. Ireland, of course, furnished the most obvious comparisons.

So, to start with, Joyce is not a homologue of Swift. That is a strange mistake. There is very little of the specific power of that terrible personage, that *terribilità*, in the amiable author of *Ulysses*. Another writer with whom he has been compared, and whom he is peculiarly unlike, is Flaubert. But to mention all the authors with whom Joyce has been matched would take an appreciable time. So I will rather attempt to find his true affinities. The choice would lie, to my mind, somewhere between Robert Louis Stevenson and Laurence Sterne, if you imagine those writers transplanted into a heavily-freudianized milieu, and subjected to all the influences resulting in the rich, confused ferment of *Ulysses*.

Contact with any of his writing must, to begin with, show that we are not in the presence of a tragic writer, of the description of Dostoievsky or of Flaubert. He is genial and comic; a humorous writer of the traditional English School — in temper, at his best, very like Sterne. But he has the technical itch of the "sedulous ape" — the figure under which Stevenson (with peculiar modesty, it is true) revealed himself to his readers. The impression produced by his earlier books, merely as writing, is very like that of a page of Stevenson — not of Stevenson "apeing," but of the finished, a little too finished, article.

Ulysses, on the technical side, is an immense exercise in style, an orgy of "apeishness," decidedly "sedulous." It is an encyclopaedia of english literary technique, as well as a general-knowledge paper. The schoolmaster in Joyce is in great evidence throughout its pages.

Next, as to his position among the celebrated group of Irishmen contemporary with himself, or his immediate predecessors, that is now fairly well defined. What has distinguished all the famous irish literary figures of recent years, whether Wilde, Shaw or Yeats, has been the possession of what we call "personality." This really amounts to a vein of picturesqueness, an instinct for the value of the *person* in the picture, which dominates them, externally at all events. And they have probably always been led into making a freer use of this than would a Frenchman, for instance, of the same calibre, owing to the self-effacing, unassuming, over-plain habits of the english background, against which they have had to perform. Or it may have been that, as isolated adventurers — when they had passed from Ireland and descended into Piccadilly Circus, thenceforth watched by an Empire on which the sun never sets — they were as a matter of course mere *persons*, as contrasted with the new alien *crowds* they were amongst. This florid personal aplomb is, however, now expected of the Irishman by his english audience — although, owing to the political separation of the two countries, probably those times of genial interplay are passed.

Mr. Joyce is by no means without the "personal touch." But in a sense he is not the "personality" that Shaw or Yeats is, or that Wilde was. But that is in conformity with his rôle, which is a very different one from theirs. Joyce is the poet of the shabby-genteel, impoverished intellectualism of Dublin. His world is the small middle-class one, decorated with a little futile "culture," of the supper and dance-party in *The Dead*. Wilde, more brilliantly situated, was an extremely metropolitan personage, a man of the great social world, a great lion of the London drawing-room. Joyce is steeped in the sadness and the shabbiness of the pathetic gentility of the upper shopkeeping class, slumbering at the bottom of a neglected province; never far, in its snobbishly circumscribed despair, from the pawnshop and the "pub."

Shaw, again, escaped early from his provincial surroundings. Joyce resembles him in some striking particulars; but the more recent figure, this quiet, very positive, self-collected irish schoolmaster, with that well-known air of genteel decorum and *bienséance* of the irish middle-class, with his "if you pleases" and "no thank-yous," his ceremonious Mister-this and Mister-that, is remote from what must have been the strapping, dashing George Bernard Shaw of the shavian heyday. He is also quite unlike the romantic, aristocratical, magic-loving William Butler Yeats.

Shaw is much more a world-figure; but Joyce and Yeats are the prose and poetry respectively of the Ireland that culminated in the Rebellion. Yeats is the chivalrous embodiment of "celtic" romance, more of St. Brandon than of Ossian, with all the grand manners of a spiritual Past that cannot be obliterated, though it wear thin, and of a dispossessed and persecuted people. Joyce is the cold and stagnant reality at which that people had at last arrived in its civilized Reservation, with all the snobbish pathos of such a condition, the intense desire to keep-up-appearances at all costs, to be ladylike and gentlemanly, in spite of a beggared position — above which that yeatsian emanation floats.

But on the purely personal side, Joyce possesses a good deal of the intolerant arrogance of the dominie, veiled with an elaborate decency beneath the formal calm of the jesuit, left over as a handy property from his early years of catholic romance — of that irish variety that is so english that it seems stranger to a continental almost than its english protestant counterpart.

The Ireland that culminated in the Rebellion reached that event, however, in a very divided state. There was an artifical, pseudo-historical air about the Rebellion, as there was inevitably about the movement of "celtic" revival; it seemed to be forced and vamped up long after its poignant occasion had passed. As elsewhere in Europe, the fanatical "nationalist" consciousness invoked, seemed belated and unreal. Joyce was, I understand, against Sinn Fein. In his autobiographical books you obtain an unambiguous expression of his attitude in the matter. In the *Portrait of the Artist*, where the nationalist, Davin, is talking to him, Stephen (the author, of whom that is a self-portrait as a young man) says:

"My ancestors threw off their language and took another. They allowed a handful of foreigners to subject them. Do you fancy I am going to pay in my own life and person debts they made? What for?"
"For our freedom," said Davin.
"No honourable and sincere man," said Stephen, "has given up to you his life and his affections from the days of Tone to those of Parnell but you sold him to the enemy or failed him in need or reviled him and left him for another. And you invite me to be one of you. I'd see you damned first."

A little later Stephen remarks: "You talk to me of nationality, language, religion. I shall try to fly by those nets." So from the start the answer of Joyce to the militant nationalist was plain enough. And he showed himself in that a very shrewd realist indeed, beset as Irishmen have been for so long with every romantic temptation, always being invited by this interested party or that, to jump back into "history." So Joyce is neither of the militant "patriot" type, nor yet a historical romancer. In spite of that he is very "irish." He is ready enough, as a literary artist, to stand for Ireland, and has wrapped himself up in a gigantic cocoon of local colour in *Ulysses*.

It is at this point that we reach one of the fundamental questions of value brought out by his work. Although entertaining the most studied contempt for his compatriots — individually

and in the mass — whom he did not regard at all as exceptionally brilliant and sympathetic creatures (in a green historical
costume, with a fairy hovering near), but as average human
cattle with an irish accent instead of a scotch or welsh, it
will yet be insisted on that his irishness is an important feature
of his talent; and he certainly also does exploit his irishness and
theirs.

The appreciation of any author is, of course, largely composed
of adventitious sentiment. For his vogue to last, or ever to be
a serious one, he must have some unusual literary gift. With that
he reaches a considerable renown. But then people proceed to
admire him for something equally possessed by a quantity of other
people, or for reasons that have nothing to do with, or which
even contradict, his gifts. So Englishmen or Frenchmen who are
inclined to virulent "nationalism," and disposed to sentiment where
local colour is concerned, will admire Joyce for his alleged identity with what he detached himself from and even repudiated,
when it took the militant, Sinn Fein form. And Joyce, like a
shrewd sensible man, will no doubt encourage them. That,
however, will not at all help us to be clear about this very confused issue. Nor should we be very certain, if we left the matter
in that state, in our valuation of Joyce. We should find ourselves
substituting orthodox political reactions to the idea of fanatical
"nationalism" (which it is quite evident holds little reality for Joyce)
for direct reactions to what is in his work a considerable achievement of art.

2. Here, then, we reach one of the most obvious critical traps,
and at the same time one of the main things requiring a decisive
reply, in his work. What makes the question of capital importance is the problem set throughout the world today by the contradiction involved in (1) a universal promotion of "nationalism,"
which seems to take, even in great cosmopolitan states, an ever
more intolerant form, and (2) the disappearance of national
characteristics altogether as a consequence of technical progress.

Everywhere the peoples become more and more alike. Local
colours, which have endured in many places for two thousand
years, fade so quickly that already one uniform grey tint has
supervened. The astonishing advances in applied science and in
industrial technique made this inevitable. Simultaneously, and

in frenzied contradiction, is the artificially fostered nationalism rampant throughout the world since the War. So while *in reality* people become increasingly one nation (for the fact that they are fanatically "nationalist" does not prevent them from approximating more and more closely to the neighbours against whom, in their abstract rage, they turn), they *ideologically* grow more aggressively separatist, and conscious of "nationality."

The same process, of course, may be observed in "class-war." A Restoration courtier was very unlike the Restoration workman, as men go; whereas the contemporary magnate, in appearance, culture, manners and general tastes, is hardly to be distinguished from the average workman on his estate or in his factory. But the more social distinctions of a real order disappear, the more artificial "class-consciousness" asserts itself.

That sort of contradiction is paralleled throughout our life. There is no department that is exempt from the confusions of this strategy — which consists essentially in removing something necessary to life and putting an ideologic simulacrum where it was able to deceive the poor animal, who notices it in its usual place and feels that all is well, but which yet perplexes and does not satisfy him. The "sex-war" illustrates this as plainly as the "class-war." For example, the Y.M.C.A. meeting at Helsingfors (November 1926) starts a discussion on that stock subject with all religious bodies — the naughty thrill of which never diminishes — the "modern woman." So "short hair and short skirts were attacked," the *New York Herald* reports. But the objectors were overruled, it being decided, in the end, that "women are asserting their right to develop personality unhampered," by these means.

Leaving aside the comedy implicit in the mischievous journalese of the statement (namely, the highly-specialized nature of the "personality" to be "developed" by those methods), we can state the facts at stake in this way: according to the laws of specialization, the more a woman complicates her attire, the more she "develops her personality." The nude is a platonic abstraction. A thousand naked women on a beach, such as Borrow once saw, in Spain, would be a thousand abstractions, or one great palpitating abstraction, compared with the same number dressed in a "personal" way, and so more and more differentiated from each other. "Personality," therefore, is clearly the wrong word. Its sentimental use falsifies what is happening.

But it is the *abstraction*, of course, that is required, today, of every human being. To "develop the personality" is an alluring invitation, but it invariably covers some process that is guaranteed to strip a person bare of all "personality" in a fortnight. This does not seem to me necessarily a bad thing. I am only pointing out that this excellent result is obtained by fraud. So we must not take that fraud too seriously, however much we may applaud its aims.

But in the general arrangements made for our sex-life, there is this little contradiction also to be noted — that the otherwise popular notion of specialization of function (the key to the syndicalist doctrine) is taboo. The rationale of that taboo is that it is desired to turn people's minds away from sex altogether eventually. They are insidiously urged in a neuter direction. William Blake foresaw that development, with his prophet's eye, with a laudable equanimity. The anaesthetizing of the cruder desires and ambitions by closer disciplines is, after all, the only alternative to a rationalizing of impulses not excised. However that may be, "sex" is in the same category as that of the family; it can hardly survive as it is. The family costs too much; and "sex" is a very costly luxury, too. Its expensive ecstasies and personal adornments must go in the end. The supposed encouragement of them today is illusory.

The savage with only a loin-cloth is notoriously chaste, and even prudish, strange as at first that sounds. From every quarter of the world evidence of this is forthcoming. Havelock Ellis has collected its evidence in a pamphlet, with *Modesty among primitive people*, or some such title. The more clothes people have, and the colder the climate, the more "immoral" they become; that is now generally established, but not widely enough known to have an enlightening effect where what we are discussing is concerned: so attracted by the lure of the "immoral," everybody in the end will be induced to become more moral, simply-clothed, well-behaved and inexpensive.

So you obtain, up to date, in our feminized world, the following result: every woman is conscious of being a very daring and novel being, and "sex," and even sexishness, it is universally believed, is more prominent than ever before, because of the "short skirts," etc., discussed so acrimoniously at the Y.M.C.A. meeting, and which are thundered at by a thousand idiots to empty pews throughout the puritan world; and even the Pope chases "short skirts" from St. Peter's. Few people have yet perceived that not only is the present fashion in its effect more chaste (that a "comrade" or "chum" is hardly as intense a thing on principle as a "lover," to arrive at it by way of popular catchwords), but that the *intention* behind the fiats of fashion, leading to "short skirts," etc., is hardly to debauch the world. It is much rather intended to uniform and discipline it, to teach it to be neat and handy, *to induce it to dispense with that costly luxury, "personality," instead of to "develop" it, as it pretends;* to train people to be satisfied to be just like their neighbours, hat for hat, and button for button, and finally to be *active*, so that they can *work*. Skirts are short for work, not love. That is the principle to grasp beneath all the concentrated flattery directed upon the revolutionary amazon leading her sex to victory in a glorious "war" or social revolution. So the fashion is much more sensible than it affects to be, but also much less romantic.

This long excursion into the province of sex-politics has been justified, I think, by the light it throws upon the other questions belonging to the main stream of our present argument. I will now return to the contradiction subsisting between doctrinaire "nationalism," and the conditions of international uniformity created by scientific advance.

The adventitious stimulus given to the historic sense, the imposition of this little picturesque flourish or that, a patina like that manufactured for the faking of "antiques" (a good example is the "roman" veneer in fascist Italy), goes hand in hand and side by side with a world-hegemony, externally uniform and producing more every day a common culture.

It is headlong into this sheer delusion, which makes a nonsense of our continued civilized advance (unless you repudiate the idea of *advance*, and substitute that of mere fashionable *change*), that we are running, every time that we essay to found our view of things upon some harmonious and precise picture. We fall immediately into that trap of an abstraction coloured to look concrete, and placed where once there was something but where now there is nothing.

The romantic persons who go picking about in the Arran Islands, Shetlands, the Basque Provinces, or elsewhere, for genuine human "antiques," are today on a wild-goose chase; because the sphinx of the Past, in the person of some elder dug out of such remote neighbourhoods, will at length, when he has found his tongue, probably commence addressing them in the vernacular of the *Daily Mail*. For better or for worse, local colour is now a thin mixture; it does not inhere in what it embellishes, but is painted on, often with a clumsy insolence. It suits the political intelligence with its immemorial device, *divide et impera*, to encourage it, but its application to the conditions of mind and to the external nature of the machine-age becomes more and more fantastic.

There is nothing for it today, if you have an appetite for the beautiful, but *to create new beauty*. You can no longer nourish yourself upon the Past; its stock is exhausted, the Past is nowhere a reality. The only place where it is a reality is in *time*, not certainly in space. So the mental world of time offers a solution. More and more it is used as a compensating principle.

From this devastating alternative — the creation of new beauty — most people shrink in horror. "Create!" they exclaim. "As though it were not already difficult enough to live!" — But it is questionable if even bare life is possible, denuded of all meaning. And the meaning put into it by millennial politics of the current type is as unsubstantial as a mist on a Never-Never landscape.

How these remarks apply to what we are discussing will be obscured for some readers at first by the fact of the challenging novelty of the work in question. But the local colour, or locally-coloured material, that was scraped together into a big variegated heap to make *Ulysses*, is — doctrinally even more than in fact — the material of the Past. It is consciously the decay of a mournful province, with in addition the label of a twenty-year-old vintage, of a "lost time," to recommend it. The diffraction of this lump of local colour for the purposes of analysis will in the end isolate the time-quality, revealing the main motive of its collection.

3. Before turning to the more personal factors in the composition of *Ulysses*, I will briefly state what I have been approaching in the first phase of my analysis.

I regard *Ulysses* as a *time-book*; and by that I mean that it lays its emphasis upon, for choice manipulates, and in a doctrinaire manner, the self-conscious time-sense, that has now been erected into a universal philosophy. This it does beneath the spell of a similar creative impulse to that by which Proust worked. The classical unities of time and place are buried beneath its scale, however, and in this All-life-in-a-day scheme there is small place for them. Yet at the outset they are solemnly insisted on as a guiding principle to be fanatically observed. And certainly some barbarous version of the classical formula is at work throughout, like a conserted *daimon* attending the author, to keep him obsessionally faithful to the time-place, or space-time, programme.

The genteel-demotic, native subject-matter of Mr. Joyce assists him to a great deal of intense, sad, insipid, local colour. An early life-experience that had removed him from the small middle-class milieu would also have removed him from his local colour, and to a less extent from his time-factor. To this he adds the legendary clatter and bustle of Donnybrook Fair. Beyond that he is not above stealing a few fairies from Mr. Yeats, and then sending them in the company of Dr. Freud to ride a broomstick on the Brocken. Adventures of that order, in the middle of the book, take us still further from the ideal of the Unities, and both Space and Time temporarily evaporate. But on the whole the reader is conscious that he is beneath the intensive dictatorship of Space-time — the god of Professor Alexander and such a great number of people, in fact, that we can almost be said to be treading on holy ground when we compose ourselves to read a work dedicated to that deity, either in philosophy or fiction.

That Joyce and Proust are both dedicated to Time is generally appreciated, of course; Joyce is often compared to Proust on that score. Both Proust and Joyce exhibit, it is said, the exasperated time-sense of the contemporary man of the industrial age; which is undeniable, if the outward form of their respective work is alone considered. The ardent recapitulation of a dead thing — though so recently dead, and not on its own merits a very significant one — and as much the "local colour" as what may be called the *local time*, ally them. But having got so far, I should put in a qualification which would, I think, unexpectedly discriminate these two methods.

4. I will interject at this point a note on the subject of the temporal equivalent of "local colour," since I have had occasion to refer to it once or twice. I will not enter into the confusing discussion of which is space and which time in any given complex. I will suppose that there is some partly discrete quality which can come under the separate head of "time," and

so for certain purposes be something else than the "local colour."

This psychological time, or duration, this mood that is as fixed as the matter accompanying it, is as romantic and picturesque as is "local colour," and usually as shallow a thing as that. Some realization of this is essential. *We can posit a time-district, as it were, just as much as we can a place with its individual physical properties.* And neither the local colour, nor the local time of the *time-district,* is what is recorded *sub specie aeternitatis,* it is unnecessary to say.

Both may, however, become obsessions, and are so, I believe, today. But that is merely — that is my argument — because people are in process of being locked into both places *and* times. (This can be illustrated, where place is concerned, in the way that Signor Mussolini is locking the Italians into Italy, and refusing them passports for abroad.)

We are now sufficiently prepared and can educe the heart of this obscure organism that so overshadows contemporary thought, by showing its analogies. That the time-fanaticism is in some way connected with the nationalisms and the regionalisms which are politically so much in evidence, and so intensively cultivated, seems certain — since "time" is also to some extent a region, or it can be regarded in that light. We have spoken of a *time-district,* and that is exact. Professor Whitehead uses the significant phrase "mental climate." This is by no means a fanciful affiliation; for *time* and *place* are the closest neighbours, and what happens to one is likely to be shared by the other. And if that is so, the *time-mind* would be much the same as the geographic one, fanatically circumscribing this or that territorial unit with a superstitious exclusiveness, an aggressive nationalist romance. Has not time-romance, or a fierce partisanship on behalf of a *time,* a family likeness, at least, with similar partisanship on behalf of a *place*?

And then, too, the so much mocked and detested nonnationalist, universal mind (whose politics would be goethean, we can say, to place them, and whose highest tolerance would approximate to that best seen in the classical chinese intelligence) would have to be reckoned with — once the *time-mind* had been isolated by a thorough analysis, and its essential antagonisms exposed. These two types of mind would be found confronted, eternally hostile to each other, or at least eternally different — for the hostility would be more noticeable on the side of the partisan, the "time," mind, the mind of fashion, than on the side of the other. This is all that I shall say on this very interesting point, for the moment.

The philosophy of the space-timeist is identical with the old, and as many people had hoped, exploded, bergsonian philosophy of *psychological time* (or *durée*, as he called it). It is essential to grasp this continuity between the earlier flux of Bergson, with its Time-god, and the einsteinian flux, with its god, Space-time. Alexander, and his pupil Whitehead, are the best-known exponents, of philosophers writing in English, of these doctrines. It will not require a very close scrutiny of *Space Time and Deity*, for instance, and then of some characteristic book of Bergson's, to assure yourself that you are dealing with minds of the same stamp.

Temperamentally — emotionally, that is, and emotion is as important in philosophy as in other things — the earlier bergsonian, such as Péguy, for instance, and the relativist or space-timeist, are identical. The best testimony of this is the enthusiastic reception given by Bergson, the old time-philosopher, to Einstein, the later space-timeist. He recognized his god, Duration, cast into the imposing material of a physical theory, improved and amalgamated with Space, in a more insidious unity than he had been able to give to his paramount philosophic principle. Similarly the attitude of Whitehead, Alexander and so forth, where Bergson is concerned, is noticeably one of a considered respect, very different from the atmosphere of disrepute into which Bergson had fallen prior to the triumph of Relativity Theory. The so-called "Emergent" principle of Lloyd Morgan, adopted by Alexander and the rest, is our old friend "Creative Evolution," under another name, and with a few additional attributes. "Emergent Evolution" can for all practical purposes be regarded as synonymous with "Creative Evolution."

So from, say, the birth of Bergson to the present day, one vast orthodoxy has been in process of maturing in the world of science and philosophy. The material had already collected into a considerable patrimony by the time Bergson was ready to give it a philosophic form. The darwinian theory and all the background of nineteenth-century materialistic thought was already behind it. Under the characteristic headings Duration and Relativity the nineteenth-century mechanistic belief has now assumed a final form. It is there for any one to study at his leisure, and to take or leave. It will assume, from time to time, many new shapes, but it will certainly not change its essential nature again till its doomsday; for I believe that in it we have reached one of the poles of the human intelligence, the negative, as it were. So it is deeply rooted, very ancient, and quite defined.

In this part of my essay I am not developing my purely philosophic argument more fully than is necessary for the purposes of the literary criticism. I leave my attitude in the "time" discussion as an announcement of principle, merely. Students of the philosophies cited will be able at once to supply the outline of the position such an announcement involves. And the reader who is not conversant with those theories would not be much the wiser at the end of such brief analysis as I should be able to supply in this place. The plan I am following is to help the reader to an inductive understanding of the principle involved, in the course of this analysis of its literary and artistic expression. With Spengler the more technical region is reached. And after that the philosophical analysis is begun. I hope to have interested the reader sufficiently in the questions involved to take him with me into that.

5. The psychological history of the triumph of an idea is interesting to follow; and it is necessary to acquire some knowledge of those processes. To understand how ideas succeed you must first consider what that "success" implies, especially with reference to this particular age. You would have to ask yourself who those men are who profess them, the manner in which they get advertised, the degree of orthodoxy imposed, and by what means, at the moment. Then, behind that professional and immediate ring of supporters, the mass of people who blindly receive them on faith — as helpless, confronted with the imposing machinery of their popularization, as new-born children — they, too, would have to be studied, and their reactions registered.

Some such analysis of the domination achieved by an idea and how it ceases to be an idea, and becomes an *ideology*, as Napoleon called it, an instrument of popular government, has to be undertaken before you can hope to be in a position to meet on equal terms, without superstition, such prevalent intellectual fashions. If you are of that great majority who ask nothing better than to have intellectual fashions provided for them — with little handbooks describing which way up the idea (if a "difficult" one) should be worn, whether it should be worn with a flourish or a languish, with a simper or a pout, with fanatical intensity or an easy catholic grace — then you will have no use, it is needless to say, for such an arduous analytical discipline. It is only if you belong to that minority who care for ideas for their own sake, if you are philosophic in the truest sense, possessing a personal life that is not satisfied with the old-clothes shop, or its companion, the vast ready-made emporium, that this procedure will have any meaning for you.

The physical or philosophical theory in the ascendant at any moment is humbly and reverently picked up, in an abridged, and usually meaningless, form, by the majority of people. So it was with Darwin, so it is with Einstein. Apart from questions of expert qualification, few people are able to appreciate all that is involved in such theories. There is certainly never a question in their mind of "doubting" it. It is not a thing to doubt, but one that is either easy or impossible to understand, as the case may be. To repudiate it would be a still wilder presumption. It has to be "studied" in the few spare minutes that most people consider may be saved for such things from parties, golf, motoring and bridge, or the Russian Ballet. Then they will say in conversation, "It appears that there is no such thing as time"; or "Everything is relative, Einstein says. I always thought it was." (Relativity seldom involves much more than that to people.) More often than not the professors, who adopt and expound whatever theory has just succeeded, examine it as little. It *amuses* them; professors, like other people, have their amusements — their work is theirs. It is uncomfortable to be unorthodox, life is short, science is long, much longer than art; that is sufficient.

When such a dominant theory is *applied* in literature or in art, then, certainly, even less does anyone grasp the steps by which that theory has entered the mind of the author or artist; has either been welcomed at once as a friend and a brother, has taken up its abode there as a conqueror by main force, or else has seduced the sensitive little intelligence from the outside, from beneath the prudent casement from which the peeping-mind inside has watched, fascinated, the big romantic notion swelling invitingly; or has, on the other hand, as a matter of traffic and mutual profit, come to terms with a possible assistant or colleague. In short, any of the hundred ways and degrees in which assent is arrived at, and an intellectual monopoly or hegemony consummated, is even more arcane to the majority than is the theory itself.

Bergson and his time-philosophy exactly corresponds to Proust, the abstract for the other's concrete. There is so far no outstanding exponent in literature or art of einsteinian physics, for necessarily there is a certain interval, as things are, between the idea and the representation. But such a figure will no doubt occur; and further theorists of this great school will be accompanied by yet further artists, applying its philosophy to life. Or perhaps, since now the general outline of the cult is settled, and the changes within it will be incidental, largely, they may crop up simultaneously. Indeed, Proust and Joyce are examples to hand of how already it does not matter very much to what phase of the one great movement the interpreter belongs.

Without all the uniform pervasive growth of the time-philosophy starting from the little seed planted by Bergson, discredited, and now spreading more vigorously than ever, there would be no *Ulysses*, or there would be no *A la Recherche du Temps perdu*. There would be no "time-composition" of Miss Stein; no fugues in words. In short, Mr. Joyce is very strictly of the school of Bergson–Einstein, Stein–Proust. He is of the great time-school they represent. His book is a *time-book*, as I have said, in that sense. He has embraced the time-doctrine very completely. And it is as the critic of that doctrine and of that school that I have approached the analysis of his writings up to date. (I insert this last time-clause because there is no reason at all to suppose that he may not be influenced in turn by my criticism; and, indeed, I hope it may be so, for he would be a very valuable adherent.)

Yet that the time-sense is really exasperated in Joyce in the fashion that it is in Proust, Dada, Pound or Miss Stein, may be doubted. He has a very keen preoccupation with the Past, it is certain; he does lay things down side by side, carefully dated; and added to that, he has some rather loosely and romantically held notion of periodicity. But I believe what all these things amount to with him is this: as a careful, even meticulous, craftsman, with a long training of doctrinaire naturalism, the detail — the time-detail as much as anything else — assumes an exaggerated importance for him. And I am sure that he would be put to his trumps to say how he came by much of the time-machinery that he possesses. Until he was told, I dare say that he did not know he had it, even; for he is "an instinctive," like Pound, in that respect; there is not very much reflection going on at any time inside the head of Mr. James Joyce. That is indeed the characteristic condition of *the craftsman*, pure and simple.

And that is what Joyce is above all things, essentially the crafts-man. It is a thing more common, perhaps, in painting or the plastic arts than in literature. I do not mean by this that he works harder or more thoroughly than other people, but that he is not so much an inventive intelligence as an executant. He is certain-ly very "shoppy," and professional to a fault, though in the midst of the amateurism of the day it is a fault that can easily be forgiven.

What stimulates him is *ways of doing things*, and technical processes, and not *things to be done*. Between the various things to be done he shows a true craftsman's impartiality. He is become so much a writing-specialist that it matters very little to him *what* he writes, or what idea or world-view he expresses, so long as he is trying his hand at this manner and that, and displaying his enjoyable virtuosity. Strictly speaking, he has none at all, no special point of view, or none worth mentioning. It is such peo-ple that the creative intelligence fecundates and uses; and at pre-sent that intelligence is political, and its stimuli are masked ideologies. He is only a tool, an instrument, in short. That is why such a sensitive medium as Joyce, working in such a period, re-quires the attention of the independent critic.

So perhaps it is easy to see how, without much realizing what was happening, Joyce arrived where he did. We can regard it has a diathetic phenomenon partly — the craftsman is susceptible and unprotected. There are even slight, though not very grave, symptoms of disorder in his art. The painful preoccupation with the *exact* place of things in a room, for instance, could be mildly matched in his writing. The *things themselves* by which he is surrounded lose, for the hysterical subject, their importance, or even meaning. Their *position* absorbs all the attention of his mind. Some such uneasy pedantry, in a mild form, is likely to assail any conscientious craftsman — especially in an intensive "space-time" atmosphere, surrounded by fanatical space-timeists. The poor craftsman has never been in such peril as today, for it is a frantic hornpipe indeed that his obedient legs are compelled to execute. But otherwise Joyce, with his highly-developed *physical* basis, is essentially sane.

The method that underlies *Ulysses* is known as the "telling from the inside." As that description denotes, it is psychological. Carried out in the particular manner used in *Ulysses*, it lands the reader inside an Aladdin's cave of incredible bric-à-brac in which a dense mass of dead stuff is collected, from 1901 toothpaste, a bar or two of Sweet Rosie O'Grady, to pre-nordic architecture. An immense *nature-morte is the result*. This ensues from the method of confining the reader in a circumscribed psychological space into which several encyclopaedias have been emptied. It results from the constipation induced in the movement of the narrative.

The amount of *stuff* — unorganized brute material — that the more active principle of drama has to wade through, under the circumstances, slows it down to the pace at which, inevitably, the sluggish tide of the author's bric-à-brac passes the observer, at the saluting post, or in this case, the reader. It is a suffocating moeotic expanse of objects, all of them lifeless, the sewage of a Past twenty years old, all neatly arranged in a meticulous sequence. The newspaper in which Mr. Bloom's bloater is wrapped up, say, must press on to the cold body of the fish, reversed, the account of the bicycle accident that was reported on the fated day chosen for this Odyssey; or that at least is the idea.

At the end of a long reading of *Ulysses* you feel that it is the very nightmare of the naturalistic method that you have been experiencing. Much as you may cherish the merely physical enthusiasm that expresses itself in this stupendous outpouring of *matter*, or *stuff*, you wish, on the spot, to be transported to some more abstract region for a time, where the dates of the various toothpastes, the brewery and laundry receipts, the growing pile of punched 'bus-tickets, the growing holes in the baby's socks and the darn that repairs them, assume less importance. It is your impulse perhaps quickly to get your mind where there is nothing but air and rock, however inhospitable and featureless, and a little timeless, too. You will have had a glut, for the moment (if you have really persevered), of *matter*, procured you by the turning on of all this river of what now is rubbish, but which was not *then*, by the obsessional application of the naturalistic method associated with the exacerbated time-sense. And the fact that you were not in the open air, but closed up inside somebody else's head, will not make things any better. It will have been your catharsis of the objective accumulations that obstinately collect in even the most active mind.

Now in the graphic and plastic arts that stage of fanatic naturalism long ago has been passed. All the machinery appropriate to its production has long since been discarded, luckily for the pure creative impulse of the artist. The nineteenth-century naturalism of that obsessional, fanatical order is what you find on the one hand in *Ulysses*. On the other, you have a great variety of recent influences enabling Mr. Joyce to use it in the way that he did.

The effect of this rather fortunate confusion was highly stimulating to Joyce, who really got the maximum out of it, with an appetite that certainly will never be matched again for the actual *matter* revealed in his composition, or proved to have been lengthily secreted there. It is like a gigantic victorian quilt or antimacassar. Or it is the voluminous curtain that fell, belated (with the alarming momentum of a ton or two of personally organized rubbish), upon the victorian scene. So rich was its delivery, its pent-up outpouring so vehement, that it will remain, eternally cathartic, a monument like a record diarrhoea. No one who looks *at* it will ever want to look *behind* it. It is the sardonic catafalque of the victorian world.

Two opposite things were required for this result. Mr. Joyce could never have performed this particular feat if he had not been, in his make-up, extremely immobile; and yet, in contradiction to that, very open to new technical influences. It is the *craftsman* in Joyce that is progressive; but the *man* has not moved since his early days in Dublin. He is on that side a "young man" in some way embalmed. His technical adventures do not, apparently, stimulate him to think. On the contrary, what he thinks seems to be of a conventional and fixed order, as though perhaps not to embarrass the neighbouring evolution of his highly progressive and eclectic craftsmanship.

So he collected like a cistern in his youth the last stagnant pumpings of victorian anglo-irish life. This he held steadfastly intact for fifteen years or more — then when he was ripe, as it were, he discharged it, in a dense mass, to his eternal glory. That was *Ulysses*. Had the twenty-year-old Joyce of the *Dubliners* not remained almost miraculously intact, we should never have witnessed this peculiar spectacle.

That is, I believe, the true account of how this creative event occurred with Joyce; and, if that is so, it will be evident that we are in the presence of a very different phenomenon from Proust. Proust *returned* to the *temps perdu*. Joyce never left it. He discharged it as freshly as though the time he wrote about were still present, because it was *his* present. It rolled out with all the aplomb and vivacity of a contemporary experience, assisted in its slick discharge by the latest technical devices.

6. So though Joyce has written a time-book, he has done it, I believe, to some extent, by accident. Proust, on the contrary, was stimulated to all his efforts precisely by the thought of compassing a specifically time-creation — the *Recherche du Temps Perdu*. The unconscious artist has, in this case, the best of it, to my mind. Proust, on the other hand, romanticizes his Past, where Joyce (whose Present it is) does not.

To create new beauty, and to supply a new material, is the obvious affair of art of any kind today. But that is a statement that by itself would convey very little. Without stopping to unfold that now, I will summarize what I understand by its opposite. Its opposite is that that thrives upon the *time-philosophy* that it has invented for itself, or which has been imposed upon it or provided for it.

The inner meaning of the *time-philosophy*, from whatever standpoint you approach it, and however much you paste it over with confusing advertisements of "life," of "organism," is the doctrine of a mechanistic universe; periodic; timeless, or nothing but "time," whichever you prefer; and, above all, essentially *dead*. A certain *deadness*, a lack of nervous power, an aversion to anything suggesting animal vigour, characterizes all the art, as has already been pointed out, issuing from this philosophy. Or in the exact mixing in the space-timeist scheme of all the "matter" and all the "organism" together, you get to a sort of vegetable or vermiform *average*. It is very mechanical; and according to our human, aristocratic standards of highly-organized life, it is very dead.

The theoretic truth that the time-philosophy affirms is a mechanistic one. It is the conception of an aged intelligence, grown mechanical and living upon routine and memory, essentially; its tendency, in its characteristic working, is infallibly to transform the living into the machine, with a small, unascertained, but uninteresting margin of freedom. It is the fruit, of course, of the puritan mind, born in the nineteenth century upon the desolate principles promoted by the too-rapidly mechanized life of the European.

I will now turn to the scandalous element in *Ulysses*, its supposed obscenity. Actually it appears to me that the mind of Joyce is more chaste than most. Once you admit the licence that, at the start, Joyce set out to profit by, it is surprising how very little "sex" matter there is in his pages. What is there is largely either freudian echoes (they had to enter into it), or else it is horse-play of a schoolboy or public-house order. The motif of the house-drain is once and for all put in its place, and not mentioned again. It is the fault of the reader if that page or two dealing with it assume, in retrospect, proportions it has not, as a fact, in Joyce's pages. That passage can be regarded in the light of the reply of Antigonus to the poet Hermodorus, when the latter had described him as the son of the Sun.

I will next take up in turn a few further items of importance, expiscating them one by one. Joyce is not a moralist, but he has a great relish, on the other hand, for politics. Indeed, Lady Bolingbroke's remark about Pope, that he "played the politician about cabbages and turnips" (or as somebody else remarked, "he hardly drank tea without a stratagem"), could be applied to the author of *Ulysses* — the mere name suggests a romantic predilection for guile.

He could claim another affinity with Pope — namely, that although a witty writer, he is, as far as his private and personal legend is concerned, a man of one story. "One apothegm only stands upon record," Johnson writes of Pope; it was directed at Patrick. Joyce has one story to his credit, and it is at the expense of Yeats. As it is the general custom, even in the briefest account of Joyce, to tell this story, lest I should be regarded as imperfectly documented, I will give it here. When Joyce was about twenty years old he was very hard up, we are told, and he decided to go to Yeats and see if that gentleman would do anything to help him. He seems to have foreboded the result, and provided himself with a plan of action in the event of a rebuff. The appointed time arrived. As he entered the room, sure enough he read on the face of Mr. Yeats the determination *not* to help him. Thereupon he bore down on Yeats, bade him good morning, and immediately

inquired how old he was. On learning the extent of Yeats' senior-
ity, with a start of shocked surprise, he mournfully shook his
head, exclaimed, "I fear I have come too late! I can do nothing
to help you!" and, turning on his heel, left the apartment, the
tables neatly turned.

There is perhaps a sequel to that story, and, if so, it is to be
sought in the fact that Joyce himself has shown recently the
baselessness of its major implication. He has whitewashed, I think,
in one important respect that "scoundrel" that Mr. Shaw has
affirmed "every man over forty" to be, by displaying in his own
person, to this day, an undiminished ability to be influenced by
all sorts of people and things, from the jaunty epistolary style
of Ezra Pound to the "compositional" stammerings of Miss Stein.
Actually the further he advances the more susceptible to new
influences, of a technical order, he becomes. What gives *Ulysses*
the appearance of a merging of analects is a record of this. He
was rather unenterprising and stationary in his early years. The
Dubliners is written in one style, *Ulysses* in a hundred or so.

7. There are several other things that have to be noted as
characteristic of Joyce for a full understanding of a technique that
has grown into a very complex, overcharged façade. The craftsman, pure and simple, is at the bottom of his work. I have already
insisted upon that; and in that connection it almost appears, I
have said, that he has practised sabotage where his intellect was
concerned, in order to leave his craftsman's hand freer for its
stylistic exercises. That is a phenomenon very commonly met
with in the painter's craft. Daring or unusual speculation, or an
unwonted intensity of outlook, is not good for technical display,
that is certain, and they are seldom found together. The intellect
is in one sense the rival of the hand, and is apt to hamper rather
than assist it. It interferes, at all events, with its showing-off, and
affords no encouragement to the hand's "sedulous apeishness";
or so would say the hand.

The extreme conventionality of Joyce's mind and outlook is
perhaps due to this. In *Ulysses*, if you strip away the technical
complexities that envelop it, the surprises of style and unconven-
tional attitudes that prevail in it, the figures underneath are of
a remarkable simplicity, and of the most orthodoxly comic
outline. Indeed, it is not too much to say that they are, most of

them, walking clichés. So much is this the case, that your attention is inevitably drawn to the evident paradox that ensues; namely, that of an intelligence so alive to purely verbal clichés that it hunts them like fleas, with remarkable success, and yet that leaves the most gigantic ready-made and well-worn dummies enthroned everywhere, in the form of the actual personnel of the book.

A susceptibility to verbal clichés is, however, not at all the same thing as a susceptibility to such a cliché as is represented by a stage Jew (Bloom), a stage Irishman (Mulligan), or a stage Anglo-Saxon (Haines). Clichés of that description thrive in the soil of *Ulysses*. This paradox is an effect of the craftsman-mind which has been described above; that is my reading of the riddle. You could, if you wanted to, reverse the analytical process. The virtuosity would then be deduced from the fact of the resourceful presence of a highly critical intellect, but without much inventiveness, nor the gift of first-hand observation — thriving vicariously, in its critical exercises, upon the masters of the Past. That would be a description of what, in music, is a common phenomenon, namely, the interpretative artist, the supreme instrumentalist.

If you examine for a moment the figures presented to you in the opening of *Ulysses*, you will at once see what is meant by these remarks. The admirable writing will seduce you, perhaps, from attending too closely, at first, to the characterization. But what in fact you are given there, in the way of character, is the most conventional stuff in the world; and the dramatic situation for which they are provided is not even an original one, for it is the situation of *John Bull's Other Island*, picturesquely staged in a Martello-tower, with the author in the principal rôle.

Haines, the romantic Englishman, or "Sassenach," with the "pale eyes like the ocean wave that he rules," his extreme woodenness and deep sentimental, callous imbecility, his amateur-anthropologist note-gathering among the interesting irish natives; and in lively contrast to this dreary, finished "Saxon" butt (who always says what is expected of him), the jolly, attractive, Wild Irishman (Mulligan), who sees through, makes rings round, the ideally slow and stupid "creeping Saxon," while yet remaining "the servant" with "the cracked looking-glass" of Stephen's epigram — that is all pure *John Bull's Other Island*. Haines is a stage-"Saxon," Mulligan is a stage-Irishman; that on one side and the other of the Irish Channel such figures could be found is certain enough; but they are the material of broad comedy; not that of a subtle or average reality at all. They are the conventional reality of one satisfied with the excessive, unusual and ready-made; and they are juxtaposed here on the time-honoured shavian model.

But if they are clichés, Stephen Dedalus is a worse or a far more glaring one. He is the really wooden figure. He is "the poet" to an uncomfortable, a dismal, a ridiculous, even a pulverizing degree. His movements in the Martello-tower, his theatrical "bitterness," his cheerless, priggish stateliness, his gazings into the blue distance, his Irish Accent, his exquisite sensitiveness, his "pride" that is so crude as to be almost indecent, the incredible slowness with which he gets about from place to place, up the stairs, down the stairs, like a funereal stage-king; the time required for him to move his neck, how he raises his hand, passes it over his aching eyes, or his damp brow, even more wearily drops it, closes his dismal little shutters against his rollicking irish-type of a friend (in his capacity of a type-poet), and remains sententiously secluded, shut up in his own personal Martello-tower — a Martello-tower within a Martello-tower — until he consents to issue out, tempted by the opportunity of making a "bitter" — a very "bitter" — jest, to show up against the ideally idiotic background provided by Haines; all this has to be read to be believed — but read, of course, with a deaf ear to the really charming workmanship with which it is presented. *Written* on a level with its conception, and it would be as dull stuff as you could easily find.

The stage-directions with which the novelist in general pursues his craft are usually tell-tale, and *Ulysses* is no exception to that rule. The stage-directions for getting Stephen Dedalus, the irritating hero, about, sitting him down, giving accent to his voice, are all painfully enlightening.

This is how the hero of *Ulysses* first appears on page 2 of the book:

Stephen Dedalus stepped up, followed him [Mulligan] *wearily* halfway and sat down. . . .

He does almost everything "wearily." He "sits down" always before he has got far. He moves with such dignified and "weary" slowness, that he never gets further than *halfway* under any circumstances as compared with any other less dignified, less "weary," figure in the book — that is to say, any of the many figures introduced to show off his dismal supremacy. This is where (page 2) Stephen Dedalus first speaks:

". . . Tell me, Mulligan," Stephen said quietly.

In this *quiet* "Tell me, Mulligan" — (irish accent, please) — you have the soul of this small, pointless, oppressive character in its entirety. You wonder for some pages what can be the cause of this weighty inanition. There is perhaps some plausible reason for it, which will be revealed in the sequel. That would make things a little better. But nothing happens of that sort. You slowly find out what it is. *The hero is trying to be a gentleman!* That is the secret — nothing less, nothing more. The "artist as a young man" has "the real Oxford manner," you are informed; and you eventually realize that his oppressive mannerisms have been due in the first instance to an attempt to produce the impression of "an Oxford manner."

Let us, starting from the top of page 3, take a few of the clichés having a bearing on the point under consideration:

(1) Mulligan asks the hero for his handkerchief. "Stephen *suffered* him to pull out" the handkerchief, etc. The word *suffered* and the bathos of the gesture involved in the offering of the pocket, are characteristic.

(2) Buck Mulligan "turned abruptly *his great searching eyes* from the sea," etc. Great searching eyes! Oh, where were the great searching eyes of the author, from whom no verbal cliché may escape, when he wrote that?

(3) Mulligan to Stephen: "He [Haines] thinks you're not a gentleman." That is what Stephen Dedalus is pursued and obsessed by, the notion of "being a gentleman"; that is the secret, as has already been said, of most of the tiresome mannerisms that oppress a reader of *Ulysses* wherever Dedalus appears. (Compare "the Oxford manner," etc., above.)

(4) " 'Then what is it?' Buck Mulligan asked impatiently. . . . 'Cough it up.' Stephen freed his arm quietly" (page 7). Stephen does everything "quietly," whether he "quietly" touches Mulligan on the arm or "quietly" frees his own. He is a very quiet man indeed.

(5) On page 19 Mulligan has chanted a popular theological ditty. Haines says to Stephen: "We oughtn't to laugh, I suppose. He's rather blasphemous. I'm not a believer myself, that is to

say. Still his gaiety takes the harm out of it, somehow, doesn't it? What did he call it? Joseph the Joiner?"

This is a good example of the Saxon (*John Bull's Other Island* model) talking. Provided with such a foil, Stephen goes on replying "dryly," "quietly," or with "pained" superiority, to the end of the chapter. Such is your introduction in *Ulysses* to some of the principal characters.

It is unnecessary to quote any further; the reader by referring to the opening of *Ulysses*, can provide himself with as much more as he requires; these few extracts will enable anybody to get a more concrete idea of what is under discussion. It would be difficult, I think, to find a more lifeless, irritating, principal figure than the deplorable hero of the *Portrait of the Artist* and of *Ulysses.*

The method of the growth of these books may be partly responsible for it, the imperfect assimilation of the matter-of-fact naturalism of the *Dubliners* to the more complex *Ulysses*. But the fact remains that in the centre of the picture, this mean and ridiculous figure remains — attitudinizing, drooping, stalking slowly, "quietly" and "bitterly" from spot to spot, mouthing a little Latin, "bitterly" scoring off a regiment of conventional supers.

All you have got to do is to compare the frigid prig — hoping that his detestable affectations will be mistaken for "an Oxford manner," trusting that the "quiet" distinction of his deportment will reassure strangers on the burning question of whether he is a *gentleman* or not — with one of the principal heroes of the russian novels, and a spiritual gulf of some sort will become apparent between the ardent, simple and in some cases truly heroical figures on the one side, and the drooping, simpering, leering, "bitter" and misunderstood, spoilt-child conscious of its meanness and lack of energy, on the other, on that of Joyce.

The russian scene, which stood as a background for the great group of nineteenth-century russian writers, was mediaeval, it is true, and cast on more elemental lines than anything that has existed in the West since the days of Elizabeth. But the author of the *Dubliners* was alimenting himself from the French as much as were the last of the Russians, and Dublin as much as Moscow would be for a french contemporary of Flaubert a savage place. Historically the work of Joyce will probably be classed with books dealing with that last burst of heroical, pre-communist, european life.

What induced Joyce to place in the centre of his very large canvas this grotesque figure, Stephen Dedalus? Or having done so, to make it worse by contrasting it the whole time (as typifying "the ideal") with the gross "materialism" of the Jew, Bloom? Again, the answer to that, I believe, is that things *grew* in that way, quite outside of Joyce's control; and it is an effect, merely, of a confusion of method.

Joyce is fundamentally autobiographical, it must be recalled; not in the way that most writers to some extent are, but scrupulously and naturalistically so. Or at least that is how he started. The *Portrait of the Artist as a Young Man* was supposed to give you a neat, carefully-drawn picture of Joyce from babyhood upwards, in the result like an enlarged figure from the *Dubliners*. You get an accurate enough account, thereupon, of a physically-feeble, timid, pompous, ill-tempered, very conceited little boy. It is interesting, honest, even sometimes to naïveté — though not often that; but it is not promising material for anything but the small, neat naturalism of *Dubliners*. It seems as unlikely, in short, that this little fellow will grow into the protagonist of a battle between the mighty principles of Spirit and Matter, Good and Evil, or White and Black, as that the author of the little, neat, reasonable, unadventurous *Dubliners* would one day become the author of the big blustering *Ulysses*.

The effort to show Stephen Dedalus in a favourable, heightened light throughout, destroys the naturalism, and at the same time certainly fails to achieve the heroic. Yet the temper of *Ulysses* is to some extent an heroical one. So you are left with a neat little naturalist "hero," of the sort that swarms humorously in Chekov, tiptoeing to play his part in the fluid canvas of an ambitious *Ulysses*, unexpectedly expanding beneath his feet; urged by his author to rise to the occasion and live up to the rôle of the incarnation of the immaterial, and so be top-dog to Poldy Bloom. As it is, of course, the author, thinly disguised as a middle-aged Jew tout (Mr. Leopold Bloom), wins the reader's sympathy every time he appears; and he never is confronted with the less and less satisfactory Dedalus (in the beau rôle) without the latter losing trick after trick to his disreputable rival; and so, to the dismay of the conscientious reader, betraying the principles he represents. It is a sad affair, altogether, on that side.

Turning to Mr. Bloom, we find an unsatisfactory figure, too, but of an opposite sort and in a very different degree. He possesses all the recognized theatrical properties of "the Jew" up-to-date — he is more feminine than *la femme*, shares her couvade, the periodicity of her intimate existence is repeated mildly in his own; he counts the beer bottles stacked in a yard he is passing, computing with glee the profit to be extracted from that commerce; but such a Jew as Bloom, taken altogether, has never been seen outside the pages of Mr. Joyce's book. And he is not even a Jew most of the time, but his talented irish author.

In reality there is no Mr. Bloom at all, of course, except at certain moments. Usually the author, carelessly disguised beneath what other people have observed about Jews, or yet other people have believed that they have seen, is alone performing before us. There is no sign throughout the book that he has ever directly and intelligently observed any *individual* Jew. He has merely out of books and conversations collected facts, witticisms and generalizations about Jews, and wrapped up his own kindly person with these, till he has bloated himself into a thousand pages of heterogeneous, peculiarly unjewish, matter. So he has certainly contributed nothing to the literature of the Jew, for which task he is in any case quite unsuited.

This inability to observe directly, a habit of always looking at people through other people's eyes and not through his own, is deeply rooted with Joyce. Where a multitude of little details or some obvious idiosyncrasy are concerned, he may be said to be observant; but the secret of an *entire* organism escapes him. Not being observant where entire people (that is, people at all) are concerned, he depicts them conventionally always, under some general label. For it is in the fragmentation of a personality — by isolating some characteristic weakness, mood, or timeself — that you arrive at the mechanical and abstract, the opposite of the living. This, however, leaves him free to achieve with a mass of detail a superficial appearance of life; and also to exercise his imitative talents without check where the technical problem is concerned.

8. In the above account of the value of the figures to which the opening of *Ulysses* introduces us, I have given the direct impression received upon a fresh reading of it for the purposes of this essay. Had I undertaken to write a general criticism of the work of Joyce I should not have passed on this impression uncensored —

in its native sensational strength—but have modified it, by associating it with other impressions more favourable to the author. As it is, however, it is my object to obtain the necessary salience for an aspect of Joyce's mind that is of capital importance to what I have to say on the subject of the time-mind, as I have called it.

The radical conventionality of outlook implied throughout *Ulysses*, and exhibited in the treatment of the characters, isolated from their technical wrapping, has the following bearing upon what I have said elsewhere. This conventionality (which leaves, as it were, lay-figures underneath, upon which the technical trappings can be accumulated at leisure with complete disregard for the laws of life) is the sign that we are in the presence of a craftsman rather than a creator. That sort of effect is invariably the sign of the simple craftsman—an absence of meaning, an emptiness of philosophic content, a poverty of new and disturbing observation. The school of *nature-morte* painters in Paris, who made a fetish of Cézanne's apples; and indeed the *deadness* that has crept into all painting (so that whether it is people or things that are depicted, they all equally have the appearance of dead things or of dolls), is the phenomenon to which this other conventional deadness must be assimilated.

In *Ulysses* you have a deliberate display, on the grand scale, of technical virtuosity and literary scholarship. What is underneath this overcharged surface, few people, so far, have seriously inquired. In reality it is rather an apologuical than a real landscape; and the two main characters, Bloom and Dedalus, are lay-figures (the latter a sadly ill-chosen one) on which such a mass of dead stuff is hung, that if ever they had any organic life of their own, it would speedily have been overwhelmed in this torrent of matter, of *nature-morte*.

This torrent of matter is the einsteinian flux. Or (equally well) it is the duration-flux of Bergson—that is its philosophic character, at all events. (How the specifically "organic" and mental doctrine of the time-philosophy can result in a mechanism that is more mechanical than any other, I shall be considering later.) The method of doctrinaire naturalism, interpreted in that way, results in such a flux as you have in *Ulysses*, fatally. And into that flux it is you, the reader, that are plunged, or magnetically drawn by the attraction of so much matter as is represented by its thousand pages. That is also the strategy implied by its scale.

But the author, of course, plunges with you. He takes you inside his head, or, as it were, into a roomy diving-suit, and, once down in the middle of the stream, you remain the author, naturally, inside whose head you are, though you are sometimes supposed to be aware of one person, sometimes of another. Most of the time you are being Bloom or Dedalus, from the inside, and that is Joyce. Some figures for the moment bump against you, and you certainly perceive them with great distinctness — or rather some fragment of their dress or some mannerism; then they are gone. But, generally speaking, it is *you* who descend into the flux of *Ulysses*, and it is the author who absorbs you momentarily into himself for that experience. That is all that the "telling from the inside" amounts to. All the rest is literature, and dogma; or the dogma of time-literature.

I say, "naturalism intepreted this way" has that result, because there are so many varieties of naturalism. Some scientific naturalism does deal with things from the outside, indeed, and so achieves a very different effect — one of hardness, not of softness. But the method of *Ulysses* imposes a softness, flabbiness and vagueness everywhere in its bergsonian fluidity. It was in the company of that old magician, Sigmund Freud, that Joyce learnt the way into the Aladdin's cave where he manufactured his *Ulysses*; and the philosophic flux-stream has its source, too, in that magical cavern.

The claim to be employing the "impersonal" method of science in the presentment of the personnel of *Ulysses* can be entirely disregarded. If there were any definite and carefully demarcated personality — except in the case of Dedalus, or here and there where we see a casual person for a moment — it would be worth while examining that claim. But as there are no persons to speak of for the author to be "impersonal" about, that can at once be dismissed. *Ulysses* is a highly romantic self-portrait of the mature Joyce (disguised as a Jew) and of his adolescent self — of Bloom and Dedalus. Poldy Joyce, luckily for him, is a more genial fellow than Stephen Joyce — else the *Portrait of the Artist* stage would never have been passed by James.

Another thing that can be dismissed even more summarily is the claim that Bloom is a creation, a great *homme moyen sensuel* of fiction. That side of Bloom would never have existed had it not been for the Bouvard and Pécuchet of Flaubert, which very intense creation Joyce merely takes over, spins out, and translates into the relaxed medium of anglo-irish humour. Where Bloom is being Bouvard and Pécuchet, it is a translation, nothing more.

Nor really can the admirable Goya-like fantasia in the middle of the book, in which all the characters enjoy a free metaphysical existence (released from the last remnants of the nineteenth-century restraint of the doctrine of naturalism), be compared for original power of conception with the *Tentation*. As to the homeric framework, that is only an entertaining structural device or conceit.

9. In *The Art of Being Ruled* (chap. vi, part xii), I have analysed in passing one aspect of the "telling from the inside" method, where that method is based upon a flaubertian naturalism, and used by an english writer brought up in the anglo-saxon humorous tradition. There my remarks were called forth by the nature of the more general analysis I was at the time engaged upon, which included what I described as the "sort of gargantuan mental stutter" employed by Miss Stein, in the course of her exploitation of the processes of the demented. I shall now quote what is essential to my present purpose from that chapter relative to Mr. Joyce:

> . . . the repetition [used by Miss Stein] is also in the nature of a photograph of the unorganized word-dreaming of the mind when not concentrated for some logical functional purpose. Mr. Joyce employed this method with success (not so radically and rather differently) in *Ulysses*. The thought-stream or word-stream of his hero's mind was supposed to be photographed. The effect was not unlike the conversation of Mr. Jingle in *Pickwick*.

The reason why you get this Mr. Jingle effect is that, in *Ulysses*, a considerable degree of naturalism being aimed at, Mr. Joyce had not the freedom of movement possessed by the more ostensibly personal, semi-lyrical utterances of Miss Stein. He had to pretend that we were really surprising the private thought of a real and average human creature, Mr. Bloom. But the fact is that Mr. Bloom was abnormally *wordy*. He *thought in words*, not images, for our benefit, in a fashion as unreal, from the point of view of the strictest naturalist dogma, as a Hamlet soliloquy. And yet the *pretence* of naturalism involved Mr. Joyce in something less satisfying than Miss Stein's more direct and arbitrary arrangements.

For Mr. Joyce's use of Miss Stein's method the following passage will suffice (it is of the more genial, Mr. Jingle, order):

"Provost's house. The reverend Dr. Salmon: tinned salmon. Well tinned in there. Wouldn't live in it if they paid me. Hope they have liver and bacon today. Nature abhors a vacuum. . . . There he is: the brother. Image of him. Haunting face. Now that's a coincidence. Course hundreds of times you think of a person," [etc.]

"Feel better. Burgundy. Good pick-me-up. Who distilled first. Some chap in the blues. Dutch courage. That *Kilkenny People* in the national library: now I must."

Here is Mr. Jingle, from *Pickwick*:

"Rather short in the waist, ain't it? . . . Like a general postman's coat — queer coats those — made by contract — no measuring — mysterious dispensations of Providence — all the short men get the long coats — all the long men short ones.

"Come — . . . stopping at Crown — Crown at Muggleton — met a party — flannel jackets — white trousers — anchovy sandwiches — devilled kidneys — splendid fellows — glorious."

So by the devious route of a fashionable naturalist device — that usually described as "presenting the character from the *inside*" — and the influence exercised on him by Miss Stein's technique of picturesque dementia — Mr. Joyce reaches the half-demented *crank* figure of traditional english humour.

The clowning and horseplay of english humour play a very important part in the later work of Joyce. In *Ulysses* Rabelais is also put under contribution to reinforce this vein, though it is the manner of Rabelais that is parodied, and the matter of that unusually profound writer is not very much disturbed. Since *Ulysses* (but still in the manner of that book) Mr. Joyce has written a certain amount — the gathering material of a new book, which, altogether almost, employs the manner of Nash — though again somewhat varied with echoes of Urquhart's translations. He has fallen almost entirely into a literary horseplay on the one side, and Steinesque child-play on the other.

As to the Nash factor, when read in the original, the brilliant rattle of that Elizabethan's high-spirited ingenuity can in time grow tiresome, and is of a stupefying monotony. What Nash says, from start to finish, is nothing. The mind demands some special substance from a writer, for words open into the region of ideas; and the requirements of that region, where it is words you are using, must somehow be met. Chapman, Donne or Shakespeare, with as splendid a mastery of language, supply this demand, whereas Nash does not.

But Nash is a great prose-writer, one of the greatest as far as sheer execution is concerned, and in that over-ornate bustling field. Yet his emptiness has resulted in his work falling into neglect, which, if you read much of him, is not difficult to understand. His great appetite for words, their punning potentialities, along with a power of compressing them into pungent arabesques, is admirable enough to have made him more remembered than he is. But certainly some instinct in Posterity turned it away from this *too* physical, too merely high-spirited and muscular, verbal performer. He tired it like a child with his empty energy, I suppose.

Nash appears to be at present the chief source of Joyce's inspiration — associated with his old friend Rabelais, and some of the mannerisms of Miss Stein, those easiest assimilated without its showing. There is a further source now, it appears; he has evidently concluded that the epistolary style of Ezra Pound should not be born to blush unseen, but should be made a more public use of than Pound has done. So in it has gone with the rest.

I am not able to give parallel examples of Pound's epistolary style and those parts of Joyce's recent prose that derive from it; but a passage from Nash and one from a recent piece by Joyce I can. Here is Nash:

There was a herring, or there was not, for it was but a cropshin, one of the refuse sort of herrings, and this herring, or this cropshin, was sensed and thurified in the smoke, and had got him a suit of durance, that would last longer than one of Erra Pater's almanacks, or a constable's brown bill: only his head was in his tail, and that made his breath so strong, that no man could abide him. Well, he was a Triton of his time, and a sweet-singing calendar to the state, yet not beloved of the showery Pleiades or the Colossus of the sun: however, he thought himself another *Tumidus Antimachus,* as complete an Adelantado as he that is known by wearing a cloak of tuffed taffety eighteen years. [etc.]

Here is another piece from Nash, where Joyce and Nash meet on the common ground of Rabelais:

The posterior Italian and German cornugraphers stick not to applaud and canonize unnatural sodomitry, the strumpet errant, the gout, the ague, the dropsy, the sciatica, folly, drunkenness, and slovenry. The *galli gallinacei,* or cocking French, swarm every pissing while in their primmer editions, *imprimeda jour duy,* of the unspeakable healthful conducibleness of the *gomorrihan* great *poco,* a *poco,* their true

countryman every inch of him, the prescript laws of tennis or balonne
. . . the commodity of hoarseness, blear-eyes, scabbed-hams, thread-
bare clokes, poached-eggs and panados.

Here is the opening of an *Extract from Work in Progress*, by
James Joyce:

Shem is as short for Shemus as Jem is joky for Jacob. A few
toughnecks are still getatable who pretend that aboriginally he was of
respectable stemming (an inlaw to Mr. Bbyrdwood de Trop Blogg was
among his most distant connections) but every honest to goodness man
in the land today knows that his back life will not stand being written
about in black and white.

Again:

. . . a ladies tryon hosiery raffle at liberty, a sewerful of guineagold
wine and sickcylinder oysters worth a billion a bite, an entire
operahouse of enthusiastic noblewomen flinging every coronet-
crimsoned stitch they had off at his probscenium, one after the others,
when, egad, sir, he sang the topsquall in Deal Lil Shemlockup Yellin
(geewhiz, jew ear that far! soap ewer! juice like a boyd!) for fully five
minutes infinitely better than Barton Mc. Guckin with a scrumptious
cocked hat and three green trinity plumes on his head and a dean's
crozier that he won for falling first over the hurdles, madam, in the
odder hand, but what with the murky light, the botchy print, the tattered cover, the jigjagged page, the fumbling fingers, the foxtrotting
fleas, the lieabed lice, the scum on his tongue, the drop in his eye, the
lump in his throat, the drink in his pottle, the itch in his palm, the wail
of his wind, the grief from his breath, the fog of his brainfag, the tic
of his conscience, the height of his rage, the gush of his fundament,
the fire in his gorge, the tickle of his tail, the rats in his garret, the
hullabaloo and the dust in his ears since it took him a month to steal
a march, he was hardset to memorize more than a word a week.

The close similarity in every way of those characteristic
passages that I have quoted will be evident. In the first of the
extracts from Joyce, curiously enough, he reveals one of the main
preoccupations of the hero of *Ulysses*, namely, that arising from
the ravages of the gentleman-complex — the Is he or isn't he a
gentleman? — the phantom index-finger of the old shabby-genteel
typical query pursuing the author. In this instance, as he is not
writing about himself, we are given to understand that the figure
in question is *not*. His gargantuan villain-of-the-piece is not even
allowed to be very closely connected with the noble *de Trop
Bloggs*. But the implicit theme of the entire piece, what moves
Joyce to churn up the english tongue in a mock-elizabethan frenzy,

is the burning question still of his shabby-genteel boyhood, namely, To be a "toff," or not to be a "toff."

In the respectable, more secluded corners of the anglo-saxon world, everyone has at some time met keepers of tiny general-shops in provincial towns, char-ladies, faded old women in lodging-houses, and so on, whose main hold upon life appears to be the belief that they have seen better days; and that really, if everyone had their due, they, like their distant relatives, the *de Bloggs*, would be rolling in their Royces, and Ritzing it with the best. Because we do not usually associate this strange delusion with eminent authors, that is not a reason why, nevertheless, they should not be secretly haunted by it; especially if, as with Joyce, they issue from a similar shabby-gentility and provincial snobbishness. In spite of this necessary reflection it is always with a fresh astonishment that you come upon this faded, cheerless subject-matter.

But there is one thing that it will be well to note about this type of preoccupation, namely, that it is essentially the victorian poor or the country people or provincials, still victorian, who display that obsession, not the metropolitan poor of today, certainly. It was Thackeray's world, or the denizens of the books of Dickens, who felt in that manner; and whether for better or worse, no such intense and maundering shabby-genteel snobs are any more manufactured in urban England, and I doubt if they are even in Ireland. So in the emotive psychology of these burlesques, even, Joyce is strangely of another day or, on the principle of the time-philosophy, provincial. To read him where that emotion is in the ascendant is like listening to a contemporary of Meredith or Dickens (capering to the elizabethan hornpipe of Nash perhaps — as interpreted by Miss Stein).

10. The *Portrait of the Artist* is an extremely carefully written book; but it is not technically swept and tidied to the extent that is *Ulysses*. For instance, this passage from the opening of chapter ii would not have remained in the later book:

Every morning, therefore, uncle Charles *repaired* to his outhouse, but not before he had greased and *brushed scrupulously* his back hair, [etc.]

People *repair* to places in works of fiction of the humblest order or in newspaper articles; and *brushed scrupulously*, though harmless certainly, is a conjunction that the fastidious eye would reject, provided it had time to exercise its function. But elsewhere in the *Portrait of the Artist*, in the scene on the seashore with the bird-girl, for instance, the conventional emotion calls to itself and clothes itself with a conventional expression; which, however merely technically pruned, leaves a taste of well-used sentiment in the mind, definitely of the cliché order. The more full-blooded humour of *Ulysses* prevents that from happening so often.

It is in tracking this other sort of cliché — the cliché of feeling, of thought, and in a less detailed sense, of expression — that you will find everywhere beneath the surface in Joyce a conventional basis or framework. And until you get down to that framework or bed, you will not understand what is built over it, nor realize why, in a sense, it is so dead.

From this charge Joyce would probably attempt to escape by saying that with Dedalus he was dealing with a sentimental young man. But that unfortunately does not explain his strange fondness for his company, nor his groundless assumption that he will be liked by us. We do not find such a young man in Flaubert's *Education Sentimentale*, nor in any of the other modern masters of fiction. That is probably because they were in the truest sense less personal.

Into *Ulysses* a great many things have been mixed, however. You will find many traces in it of the influence of T. S. Eliot and of Pound's classical, romance, and anglo-saxon scholarly enthusiasms, not to be met with in earlier books. *The Enemy of the Stars*, a play written and published by me in 1914, obliterated by the War, turned up, I suspect, in Zurich, and was responsible for the manner here and there of Joyce's book. Then the viennese school of psychology made Molly Bloom mutter, "What are they always rooting about up there for, to see where they come from, I wonder?" or words to that effect. No Irish Molly — however much of an "eternal feminine" abstraction — would ever have soliloquized in that manner but for Sigmund Freud. Miss Stein can only be used — owing to the restrictions imposed by the naturalist method — when a character is half asleep, day-dreaming, its mind wandering, or, in short, in such circumstances as justify, naturalistically, the use of Miss Stein's technique. *Ulysses* is, however, able to come to an end as follows:

the jessamine and geraniums and cactuses and Gibraltar as a girl when I was a Flower girl of the mountain yes when I put the rose in my hair like the Andalusian girls used or shall I wear a red yes and how he kissed me under the Moorish wall and I thought well and as well his as another and then I asked him with my eyes to ask again yes and then he asked me would I yes to say yes my mountain flower and first I put my arms around him yes and drew him down to me so he could feel my breasts all perfume yes and his heart was going like mad and yes I said yes I will Yes.

That is the conclusion of *Ulysses*. This is Miss Stein (from *Saints in Seven*):

He comes again. Yes he comes again and what does he say he says do you know this do you refuse no more than you give. That is the way to spell it do you refuse no more than you give.

I have been gathering together all those factors in the mind of Joyce which make it, I am able to show, a good material for a predatory *time-philosophy*, bearing down upon it and claiming his pen as its natural servant. Social snobbery (for instance) suggests that he will probably be susceptible to merely fashionable hypnotisms; for more than any other thing it is the sign of the herd-mind. What Schopenhauer said of the jingo, that "if a man is proud of being 'a German,' 'a Frenchman,' or 'a Jew,' he must have very little else to be proud of," can equally well be applied to class. For one man that is proud of being a person, there are a hundred thousand who are compelled to content themselves with being vain about being somebody else, or a whole dense abstract mass of somebody elses—their nation, their class.

Joyce expresses the same idea as Pound in the quotation I have given (beginning, "It is dawn at Jerusalem") in the *Portrait of the Artist*:

Stephanos Dedalos! Bous Stephanoumenos! Bous Stephaneforos!
Their banter was not new to him. . . . Now, as never before, his strange name seemed to him a prophecy. So timeless seemed the grey warm air, so fluid and impersonal his own mood, that all ages were as one to him.

So we arrive at the concrete illustrations of that strange fact already noted—that an intense preoccupation with *time* or "duration" (the psychological aspect of time, that is) is wedded to the theory of "timelessness." It is, as it were, in its innate confusion in the heart of the reality, the substance and original of that peculiar paradox — that so long as *time* is the capital truth of your world it matters very little if you deny time's existence, like the einsteinian, or say there is nothing else at all, like Bergson; or whether space-time (with the accent on the *time*) is your god, like Alexander. For all practical purposes you are committed to the same world-view. *Practically* it will impose on you the same psychology; but further than that, if you wished to pursue it, you would find that the purely physical theory of Einstein is of such an order that, though it sets out to banish the mental factor altogether and to arrive at a purely physical truth, it nevertheless cannot prevent itself turning into a psychological or spiritual account of things, like Bergson's. For the mind of Einstein, like that of Bergson, or like that of Proust, is not a *physical* mind, as it could be called. It is psychologic; it is mental.

Beyond this rough preliminary statement it is not possible to go without much more elaboration, which I wish to avoid in this part of my essay. But a few further observations may be added to the foregoing, further to elucidate, upon this plane of discussion, the direction of my analysis, and its object as applied to the art-forms I have chosen to consider.

Most people have seen spirit-drawings — or drawings done, says the subject, under the influence of supernatural agencies. Whatever they may be like otherwise, they are generally characterized by a certain cloudiness, a misty uncertainty.

The processes of creative genius, however, are not so dissimilar to those of the spirit-draughtsman. A great artist falls into a trance of sorts when he creates, about that there is little doubt. The act of artistic creation is a trance or dream-state, but very different from that experienced by the entranced medium. A world of the most extreme and logically exacting physical definition is built up out of this susceptible condition in the case of the greatest art, in contrast to the cloudy phantasies of the spiritist.

It is a good deal as a pictorial and graphic artist that I approach these problems; and a method that does not secure that definition and logical integrity that, as a graphic artist, I require, I am, I admit, hostile to from the start. But no doubt what made me, to begin with, a painter, was some propensity for the exactly-defined and also, fanatically it may be, the physical or the concrete. And I do not think that you have to be a painter to possess such inclinations. Many painters, indeed, have no repugnance, it would appear, for the surging ecstatic featureless chaos which is being set up as an ideal, in place of the noble exactitude and harmonious proportion of the european, scientific, ideal — the specifically Western heaven.

What I am concerned with here, first of all, is not whether the great *time-philosophy* that overshadows all contemporary thought is viable as a system of abstract truth, but if in its application it helps or destroys our human arts. With that is involved, or course, the very fundamental question of whether we should set out to transcend our human condition (as formerly Nietzsche and then Bergson claimed that we should); or whether we should translate into human terms the whole of our datum. My standpoint is that we are creatures of a certain kind, with no indication that a radical change is imminent; and that the most pretentious of our present prophets is unable to do more than promise "an eternity of intoxication" to those who follow him into less physical, more "cosmic," regions; proposals made with at least equal eloquence by the contemporaries of Plato. On the other hand, politically it is urged that a-thousand-men is a better man than one, because he is less "conscious" and is bigger. It seems to me, on the contrary, that the smaller you are, the more remarkable. So as far as all that side of the argument is concerned — of ecstatic propaganda, of plunges into cosmic streams of flux or time, of miraculous baptisms, of the ritual of time-gods, and of breathless transformations — I have other views on the subject of attaining perfection. I prefer the chaste wisdom of the Chinese or the Greek, to that hot, tawny brand of superlative fanaticism coming from the parched deserts of the Ancient East, with its ineradicable abstractness. I am for the physical world.

CONCLUSION TO BOOK ONE

I HAVE ADVANCED throughout this essay a carefully constructed body of criticism against various contemporary literary and other modes of thought and methods of expression. I have chosen for discussion for the most part strongly established leaders, of mature talent; and have examined individual work in some detail. This hostile analysis in its entirety has been founded upon those wider considerations that I shall now at least adumbrate.

I will revert to a few of the instances chosen and once more pass them rapidly in review, in the light of this last and more general phase of my argument. Miss Stein I have dealt with at some length, but not because she seems to me a writer of any great importance; rather, living comfortably at the heart of things, and associated with all the main activities of the time, she is a rallying point that it was convenient to take. In her recent pieces her attack upon the logical architecture of words is in its result flat and literally meaningless, I think. Her attempt to use words as though they were sounds purely or "sound-symbols," or as though their symbolism could be distorted or suppressed sufficiently to allow of a "fugue" being made out of a few thousand of them, is a technical mistake, I believe. It is only doing what the musician has been doing for three centuries, but doing it poorly, because the instrument of speech on the one hand, and the verbal symbolism on the other, will not, in the case of words, yield such a purity of effect.

Again, Pound seems in somewhat the same difficulty as Miss Stein—lost halfway between one art and another. Pound's desertion of poetry for music may mean that music is really his native art; and having been misled early in life into the practice of an art in which he had nothing whatever to say, he is now painfully attempting to return to the more fluid abstract medium of musical composition. To put it another way, the form of life, the norm, which he represents, "has nothing to *say*"—reason is not its way of reaching its goal, but always sensation. A pure sensational expression is what it naturally clothes itself in; it is essentially hostile to the arts of the intellect. It can use them to admiration; but it is usually only in order to betray them to

111

sensation. And Miss Stein, like Pound, seems to have a hanker-
ing for an art which technically she does not possess.

The psychology of the different arts — of the visual, static arts,
of the art of pure sound, of literature with its apparatus of intellectual symbolism, and so on — has been attended to very little. It may be that as a painter I find it easier to be logical and,
at least in writing, to remain technically intact, and do not make
allowance enough for the itch, so often found in the writer, to
do a little painting in words, or to play the musician. I do not
propose to go into that question here. But for our present purposes let us imagine a person so complexly talented that he could
with equal effect express himself in musical composition, painting, sculpture or writing — Samuel Butler's ideal person. I think,
then, that we should find that that person's writing would show
little tendency to divest words of their symbolism, or to distort
them, nor to do imitational or "literary" music, nor to tell stories
in paint. The rather shallow "revolutionism" that consists in a
partial merging of two or more arts would be spared him. He
would achieve such a complete revolution every time he dropped from one of his accomplishments into the other, that he would
have no incentive to hybrid experiment. He would be the purest
possible artist in each of his arts. It is even quite possible to affirm
that no artist with only one art in which to express himself, can
keep that one art entirely intact and pure.

The powerful impressionism of *Ulysses*, constructed on the
most approved "time-" basis — that is, a basis of the fluid material
gushing of undisciplined life — I have chosen as in some ways the
most important creation so far issued from the "time" mint. The
approved "mental" method — dating from the publication of
Matière et Mémoire or of the earliest psycho-analytic tracts —
leads, as it is intended to lead, to a physical disintegration and
a formal confusion. A highly personal day-dream, culminating
in a phantasmagoria of the pure dream-order, is the result in
Ulysses. It is a masterpiece of romantic art: and its romance is
of the sort imposed by the "time" philosophy. Whimsically, but
like much romantic art, it is founded on a framework of classical
antiquity — about which its author is very romantic indeed.

But if I had to choose a book that would entirely fulfil all the
requirements, as a literary paradigm, for my criticism of the
"time"-motion school, it would not be to *Ulysses* that I should
go. I should go to another literary form altogether, namely,

history; and I should find in Spengler's *Decline of the West* my perfect model of what a time-book should be. Of that in the second part of this essay I provide an analysis.

Before closing this part of my essay I will examine for a moment one aspect of the literary problem that I have neglected; namely, the *politics of style*, as it might be called.

In literature it should always be recalled that what we read is the speech of some person or other, explicit or otherwise. There is a *style* and *tone* in any statement, in any collection of sentences. We can formulate this in the following way: *There is an organic norm to which every form of speech is related. A human individual, living a certain kind of life, to whom the words and style would be appropriate, is implied in all utterance.*

A great many writers today are affecting, by their style, to be children. What is implicit in much of the writing of Miss Stein, and, of course, of Miss Loos, is the proposition: "I am a child." Another thing that is also very prevalent is a choice of idiom, and of delivery, that is intended to reassure the reader of the mass-democracy that all is well, and that the writer is one of the crowd; a Plain-Man, just another humble cell in the vast democratic body like anybody else; not a detested "highbrow." This is so much the case that occasionally you meet in american papers the remark, in the review of a book, that so and so is "a gentleman writer." This evidently means that a certain absence of slavishness, of gleeful and propitiatory handrubbing, of slang, of a hundred tricks to put the Democracy at its ease, is absent from the work in question. This absence of what is expected of a writer has caused a shock of astonishment in the reviewer. He registers his surprise.

There are as many ways of expressing yourself as there are days in the year; there are all the varieties of stammer and maunder of the idiot, there is all the range of "quaint" naïveté of childhood; all the crabbed dialects of toil, the slang of a hundred different "sets" and occupations, the solecisms and parodies of the untaught; there is the pomp of the law and the polish of the aristocratic heyday of european letters. There is the style of the *code Napoléon*, which was Stendhal's model. And in any language there is that most lucid, most logical rendering of the symbols of speech which people employ when they wish to communicate anything as clearly as possible, and are very anxious to be understood. The latter is, after all, the best guarantee you can have that affectation and self-consciousness will be absent from the style in which you are to be addressed. There you get the minimum of fuss or of mannerism. When the mind is most active it is least personal, least mannered.

The psychology at the back of the various styles or modes we have been considering is to that extent political, therefore, in the sense that the *child-cult* is a political phenomenon, and without the child-cult men and women of letters would not be express-ing themselves in the language and with the peculiarities of in-fancy; and certainly "journalese" is, as much as the subject-matter of a newspaper report, contingent upon the "greatest happiness of the greatest number." It is a perfidious flattery of the multitude, though whether it is really appreciated, or indeed necessary at all, is open to question.

A seventeenth-century writer would express himself as a mat-ter of course as grandly as he could. He was not afraid of the "grand style," any more than a painter was; he was only con-cerned perhaps at not being grand enough. No figure was too high or too magnificent to accommodate his language. The Roman Senate was the sort of assembly he had in his mind's eye. A Cicero, an Aristides, an orator of the aristocratic roman or athenian caste, was the organ implicitly for which the words were destined. How does Milton write his *Areopagitica*? This is the way he addresses you — or the "civil and gentle greatness" of the Lords and Commons of England:

I might defend myself with ease, if any should accuse me of being new or insolent, did they but know how much better I find ye esteem it to imitate the old and elegant humanity of Greece than the barbaric pride of a Hunnish and Norwegian stateliness.

That is certainly "stately" enough, we should say; and we should acquit him of being "new and insolent"; and any Parliament to-day would be very surprised to be addressed in such "parliamen-tary" language. But it is a very curious question indeed to what extent the political atmosphere of the day must modify written speech, or even break it up altogether.

Can language hold out in any degree against politics, when politics are so extremely fluid, and, inevitably, so indifferent to the arts engendered in words? It would be a pity if we were prevented from communicating lucidly and grammatically with each other. There I must leave that question; its applications to the work I have been discussing will be immediately apparent.

For any intelligent European or American the point has certainly been reached where he has to summon whatever resolution he may possess and make a fundamental decision. He has to acquaint himself first of all with the theory of, and then decide what is to be his attitude towards, the time-cult, which is the master-concept of our day. This essay may, I hope, provide him with an adequate conspectus of the positions and source of the issues involved; and it has the initial advantage of not being an arbitrary or frivolous statement, nor one that can be represented as put forward just in order to be "contrary," since it embodies the practical reactions of a worker in one of the great intellectual fields, threatened by the ascendancy of such a cult.

APPENDIX TO BOOK ONE

1. TO BUILD UP A critical organism, composed of the most living material of observed fact, which could serve as an ally of new creative effort — something like an immense watch-dog trained to secure by its presence the fastness of the generally ill-protected theoretic man, guaranteed suitably to protect such minds as cared to avail themselves of it — that was the kind of thing I had in mind in starting to write my recent book, *The Art of Being Ruled.* The present volume will show more clearly, I think, at what ultimately I was aiming. Critical estimates in the field in which I am mainly interested, namely, art, literature and philosophy, it was with them that I was concerned.

In a period of such obsessing political controversy as the present, I believe that I am that strange animal, the individual without any "politics" at all. You will find neither the politics of Communism nor those of the militant Right here. How, then, can I include politics at all in my debate? you may ask. I can discuss them only on the ideal plane evidently. In a platonic commonwealth I should be a politician, for then politics would be identical with my deepest interests. Here they are not. Here I could not be a politician without ceasing to be other things which their profession would contradict.

So anyone reading my recent book as a politician would necessarily find it "inconclusive," as he would probably term it. It has been described as "a hostile analysis of contemporary society," which no doubt it is; but its "hostility" had no party-label. It had, if anything, the badge of an art, but not of any political party. But the obligation that obtains for everybody to contribute to the general intolerance, and to exercise his right to the most violent partisanship possible, is never foregone. Many opposite forms of militancy were scornful and offended by my unexpected unpartisan analysis of society.

Whether politicians or not, the affairs of art, literature or science cannot be treated by us as though hung somewhere in a state of enchantment, in the air. But there is more than that. If you want to know what is actually occurring *inside*, underneath, at the centre, at any given moment, art is a truer guide than "politics," more often than not. Its movements represent, in an

116

acuter form, a deeper emotional truth, though not discursively. *The Brothers Karamazov*, for example, is a more cogent document for the history of its period than any record of actual events. The parallel political displays, too, are only intended for the very simple as things are today; whereas the art-displays do often provide a little intelligent amusement.

So if art has a directer access to reality, is truer and less artificial and more like what it naturally grows out of, than are politics, it seems a pity that it should take its cue from them. The artist is relieved of that obligation of the practical man to lie. Why not retain this privilege to be one of the "truthful ones" of nietzschean myth?

Some of the adversaries of my recent book affected to think that I was aiming a blow at human freedom in its pages. On the contrary, I was setting in a clear light a group of trivial and meaningless liberties, which, in the pursuit of their small claims, obstructed freedom — in any sense in which that word is worth using. My criticism of "democracy," again, was of "democracy" as that is understood today; and it was based on the conviction that democracy is neither free, nor permits of freedom. If you must have it, however, it is better to organize unfreedom; so you get communism, another very elastic term, it appears.

About a year ago an essay by Mr. Haldane appeared on Gas-Warfare. It was an apology for the men of science engaged in the manufacture of poison-gas: the idea was that by their efforts they would make "the next war" of such a terrible nature that it would "end war." In *The Art of Being Ruled* one of my objects was to provide a substitute for Mr. Haldane's method. It had been triumphantly demonstrated, I showed, that these democratic masses could be governed without a hitch by suggestion and hypnotism — Press, Wireless, Cinema. So what need is there, that was my humane contention, to slaughter them? To that argument no answer was given, for there is no answer. The chemists and their employers are engaged in a quite gratuitous activity; that I consider I have shown.

In the endeavour to prove my humane thesis I was led to what appeared, it seems, a cynical acceptance of the processes I advocated — in preference, it was to be understood, to wholesale destruction of our kind. My book was described in one quarter as a "Bill of Hate" directed against mankind. What a strange misunderstanding! For Mr. Haldane's essay was everywhere received with gratitude, and I have seen no accusation brought against it of the sort with which mine was impugned.

I have somewhat modified my views since I wrote that book as to the best procedure for ensuring the true freedom of which I have just spoken. I now believe, for instance, that people should be compelled to be freer and more "individualistic" than they naturally desire to be, rather than that their native unfreedom and instinct towards slavery should be encouraged and organized. I believe they could with advantage be compelled to remain absolutely alone for several hours every day; and a week's solitary confinement, under pleasant conditions (say in mountain scenery), every two months, would be an excellent provision. That and other coercive measures of a similar kind, I think, would make them much better people. Perhaps this slight change of approach will be apparent in the present volume.

2. Today everybody without exception is revolutionary. Some know they are, and some do not; that is the only difference. Some, indeed very many people, actually believe that they are Tories, for instance. They really imagine that. As it is in nobody's interest, of consequence, to unseal their eyes, and let them know themselves for the humdrum conservative little revolutionaries they are, they remain undisturbed in that belief. So they stay locked in a close embrace with the dullest form of Revolution, convinced all the time that they are defending the great and hoary traditions of their race.

But again, many people who are aware that they are revolutionaries, yet have an imperfect notion as to what exactly they are engaged in. The following summary account may be of assistance to them.

Revolution is *first* a technical process; only *after that* is it a political creed or a series of creeds, and of adjunct heresies. The technical aspect of Revolution is of capital importance for a thorough understanding of it. The obsession of a mechanical *betterment*, proceeding without ceasing, is natural to industrial man; the "progress" of the engineer, the rapid changes and improvements of the technique of industry, make it natural for him to regard everything in terms of change and improvement, and to think that he can apply to himself or to other men the methods proper to machinery. I will quote at this point from my elaborate account of this phenomenon in my recent book: these words are Marx's:

Modern industry never looks upon and treats the existing form of a process as final. The technical basis of that industry is therefore revolutionary, while all earlier modes of production were essentially conservative. By means of machinery, chemical process, and other methods, it is continually causing changes, not only in the technical basis of production, but also in the functions of the labourer, and in the social combinations of the labour process . . . it . . . also revolutionizes the division of labour within the society and incessantly launches masses of capital and of workpeople from one branch of production to another.

The technical basis of production, the technique of industry, then, the engineer and his machine, is the true source of the inevitably "revolutionary" conditions subsisting today, apart from any political creed. It is the opportunist political mind that has seized on these highly favourable conditions, merely, to launch and to sustain a creed of political change, backfiring in a series of passionate revolts. So it is that everyone today, in everything, is committed to Revolution; all serious politics today are revolutionary, as all science is revolutionary.

But, to continue to quote, rather than rewrite these formulae:

There are two kinds of revolution — there is *permanent revolution*, and there is an impermanent, spurious, utilitarian variety. . . . A sorting out or analysis is necessary to protect as many people as have the sense to heed these nuances. A great deal of the experimental material of art and science, for instance, is independent of any destructive function. Reactionary malice or stupidity generally confuses it with the useful but not very savoury chemistry of the Apocalypse.

Will-to-change, induced by the rapid evolution of technique, is then what we call Revolution, and accept as a political dogma. Nature we attempt to control; but, regarding ourselves as an impulsive, non-automatic, rational being, a nature that issues from us, in the form of machinery, is of course above criticism or control. So it is that we get the good and the bad in natural science, our new "nature," merged in one confusing mass. But what we are attempting here is not a definition of Revolution that would be acceptable to a hard-worked, hard-headed, fanatical class-warrior, for whom Marx is Mahomet. This is a philosophic statement, not a specialist or technical one. What we have to bring out clearly is this: *Revolution, today, in its most general definition, is modern positive science, and the incessant and radical changes involved by that.* Without science there would be no Revolution, but only revolutions. Another thing to which it is necessary to draw attention is this: namely, the very small number of men responsible for this immense ferment. A distinguished contemporary man of science has just underlined this aspect of the matter as follows:

Everywhere the idea that the few thousand, at most, active creative workers in science can really be exercising any important influence on the destinies of great nations, and that, without these, and the ferment they have introduced, present civilization would probably not be different from that of previous epochs, has yet to receive due political recognition.

It will have to wait a long time for that, but the facts are demonstrably thus. Poincaré, in his *Science et Méthode*, says:

It is only necessary to open your eyes in order to see that the achievements of industry which have enriched so many practical persons would never have come to pass if those practical persons had been the only kind of men in the world; if they had not, that is, been preceded by disinterested madmen (*des fous désintéressés*) who died poor; who never gave a thought to what was useful; and who, all the same, had a different guide than mere caprice.

What I am trying to show by these remarks is that what we call Revolution, whose form is spectacular change of the technique of life, of ideas, is not the work of the majority of people, indeed is nothing at all to do with them; and, further, is even alien to their instincts, which are entirely conservative. From one century to the next they would remain stationary if left to themselves. And, again, all the up-to-date, "modernist" afflatus consists of catchwords, and is a system of parrot-cries, in the case of the crowd. Even so they are vulgarizations, of the coarsest description, of notions inaccessible to the majority in their original force and significance. The cheap, socially available simulacrum bears little resemblance to the original. And all the great inventions reach the crowd in the form of toys (crystal-sets, motor-cars), and it is as helpless children that, for the most part, it participates in these stirring events. (That it is as children, as resolute and doctrinaire Peter Pans indeed, that most people *wish* to live, is equally true; but that is not here the issue.)

That a very small number of inventive, creative men are responsible for the entire spectacular ferment of the modern world is then the fact. In the course of democratic vulgarization, the energy of these discoveries is watered-down and adapted to herd-consumption. As *fashion*—and politically or socially "revolution" is itself a fashion — we get the reflections of energies in their scope and ultimate implications unguessed at by the majority.

In an essay entitled *Creatures of Habit and Creatures of Change*, I have elaborated this aspect of the matter sufficiently, and will now quote this résumé:

In an attempt to get our minds clearer on this matter (namely, that of the reality of progress; and how the idea of progress is the rival and opposite of standardless change) it will be best to fix our attention on a spectacle with which we are all quite familiar. Let us take the spectacle of the alleged progress in social life from day to day, and decade to decade. And let us take sex as the most central and characteristic expression of it, the life-expression at its plainest. (This Belphégor could at least be the rebus of the Demolisher's and Excavator's trade.)

. . . The woman today says to herself, "My mother was not so free as I should like to be. I shall be more free than my mother." The daughter will be more "free" than she is, and so forth.

A constant source of simple-hearted amusement on the English Stage or in the newspapers — a theme that is of the nature of an institution — is the bewilderment of the petrified parent at the dashing slang of the child; her hands in her pockets, for instance, the Eton-cropped actress taking the juvenile lead will address her father as a Top or a Bean, and the suffocating laughter of the house from roof to pit will ensue. The very orchestra will smile. For this theatre is full of children, young and old, involved in the vast Punchesque joke of the "young idea." The rougher life reflected on the music-hall stage has for generations existed on the latchkey of the bibulous hubby who has been "at the club." Its equivalent on the more respectable stage is the latchkey of the young lady of eighteen. Her utterances of certain blood-curdling up-to-date tags (suggesting horrors of premature intimacy) are the stock-in-trade of those who cater for the widest english middle-class audience.

Here the "progress" implied is always a progress towards the shaking-off of parental control or inherited religious compulsion; and in a tremendously wise, cool, insouciant, slangy and rather wicked state of "modern" up-to-dateness, unashamed nakedness, sweet "scientific" reasonableness, removing all veils, fig-leaves and fusty obstructions, a weakest-go-to-the-wall, healthy, middle-class, animal Utopia is predicted. The modernist mother, with a perhaps ungraceful shoppiness, introduces her child of eight or ten to the chamber of horrors of sex with both pride and delight. The fact that she *herself* is the chamber of horrors out of which they have popped adds a piquancy to the demonstration.

So the only true "revolutionary" is in the melodramatic or political sense not a revolutionary at all. He is to be sought in those quarters where the shocks originate, with those who make

Revolution, in all its phases, possible; stimulating with subversive discoveries the rest of the world, and persuading it to *move* a little. The man-of-science could certainly exclaim, *I* am Revolution! If when it moves, it moves violently and clumsily and destroys itself, that is certainly its own doing and not his. But the change effected upon the social plane, with a wealth of cackling and portentous self-congratulation, is neither what interests the mind of Revolution, nor yet the political directorate, naturally. Neither it, nor the current doctrines of social reform or economic class-war, bear much relation, either in magnitude or intensity, to the forces released at the fountainhead.

The legislation, again, that is stimulated by scientific advance is, like the surface-movements of the social life, by no means always the true reflection of the thing from which it derives. Sir Henry Maine defined this very well, and I cannot do better than quote him:

> It is quite true that, if Progress be understood with its only intelligible meaning, that is, as the continued production of new ideas, scientific invention and scientific discovery are the great and perennial sources of these ideas. Every fresh conquest of Nature by man . . . generates a number of new ideas. . . . [But] experience shows that innovating legislation is connected not so much with science as with the scientific air which certain subjects, not capable of exact scientific treatment, from time to time assume.

Sir Henry Maine noticed, in short, at the time he wrote his *Popular Government*, that revolutionary legislation usually arose on the plane of vulgarization, where common things are coloured with Science; and not where Science is made, that is, where the impulse originates.

If we turn to art, we find that experiment in the arts, or *revolutionary* experiment, if that word is desired, has almost ceased since the War. By experiment I mean not only technical exercises and novel combinations, but also the essentially new and particular mind that must underlie, and should even precede, the new and particular form, to make it viable.

Very few people, it is probable, belong other than quite superficially to what is "new" in present life. It is very literally the word, "new," and the advertisement connected with it, rather than the thing itself, which attracts them. If you take a new popular art-form like jazz, it is doubtful if the majority of English people or Frenchmen, if they had never heard of it before, and

were offered it along with a dozen other forms — from the viennese waltz to the horn-pipe, breton gavotte, or sardana — would
choose it rather than the others. The same people would take
to any of the other forms just as readily, that is what I mean;
not that, once it is there, they do not enjoy it. A few musicians
and artists are more fundamentally attracted to it, and to similar
new forms (or new at all events to the European); but the dancing mass conforms, because jazz is there, being exclusively supplied to it, and because it has had the advertisement to start with
of a novel and experimental fashion in music.

It would be possible, of course, to go much farther than this,
and to say that the average European or American is fond of jazz,
for instance, because of its strangeness; that it is only as a sort
of *permanent novelty*, as it were, that such a musical form (so
out of key, or out of time, with the rest of his beliefs and habits,
inherited through many generations) can exist.

3. Whereas it is generally Industry that betrays and distorts
scientific invention in the course of its exploitation, it is usually
in the distorting medium of social life that artistic invention is
falsified. When a great creation or invention of art makes its appearance, usually a short sharp struggle ensues. The social
organism is put on its mettle. If it is impossible quite to overcome the work in question, it is (after the short sharp struggle)
accepted. Its canonization is the manner of its martyrdom. It is
at all events robbed of its effect by a verbal acquiescence and
a little crop of coarse imitations. Nothing really ugly or powerful, in most instances, has been at all disturbed.

All the revolutionary idealism of the European has by this time
suffered the same dilution, and, not canonization, but promotion to the status of an eminently respectable, millionaire article.
In the millionaire, and progressive middle-class, Atlantic World,
the general temper of revolutionary change has already been
thoroughly absorbed. This has very curious results. The phenomenon of the "revolutionary rich," of a gilded Bohemia whose
members disport themselves as though they were already in the
Millennium — as, indeed, as far as they are concerned, they are —
makes its appearance. I cannot here provide a substitute for the
very detailed analysis of these things that I have given elsewhere.
But I can briefly sketch the more salient features.

All the "smart-set" life of any Western capital today is a kind of Trianon existence, passed in the midst of a fabulous private luxury, the traditional "bohemian" manners of the poor artist borrowed — along with the term "bohemian" — to cover the glimpses the man-in-the-street may have of this excess. What was a picturesque necessity for the needy members of Mürger's sub-world of art, becomes a luxurious affectation for the super-world of irresponsible freedom of the revolutionary rich of today. Thus when some magnate in mufti (he is possibly a labour-member in "real" life, or he may be an armament magnifico) is observed with a brilliant party issuing from a Rolls-Royce, and making for one of those "quiet little bohemian restaurants" which are at least twice as expensive as the Ritz, it is not as a magnate or a "swell," at all, but as a mere "bohemian," that he is regarded by Mr. Citizen gaping at this lucky dog (an artist probably, thinks he, probably like one of those "artists" on the film, in a velvet jacket, palette in hand, in some semi-asiatic palace, the most expensive screen-star in America posing upon the sumptuous heavily-upholstered "throne"). And indeed Mr. Citizen would not be so entirely wrong; for any studio that is big enough to paint in is occupied by a millionaire, or by some member of this new tribe of debonair, millennial, bohemian magnates. What has happened to art and its practitioners it is unnecessary even to inquire.

This situation, which I have so hastily outlined, is, of course, a dream-come-true. It is a pity that some of the dreamers cannot return to witness it. It is (on a relatively small scale) the William Morris, tolstoyan, or other utopist dream of a millennium in which no one would have to work too much; and in which, above all, everyone would "have scope to develop his personality," everybody be a "genius" of some sort; in which everyone would be an "artist" — singing, painting, composing or writing, as the case might be, and in which a light-hearted "communism" should reign in the midst of an idyllic plenty. This has today been achieved by a section of the community, as I have indicated. In their political opinions these people are all, without exception, orthodoxly "revolutionary" or "radical." Several even have become militant socialists. Others are dramatists, others "great painters," or "great composers," many act or dance professionally, or are keepers of luxury-shops. Wistfully, but, oh, so bravely! they exclaim, Times have changed, we must all do something! And, of course, a great many people still possess the means required for such "little socialist experiments," as one of these pathetic people described what he was doing—for this thrilling type of idyllic *work*, the necessary capital to return to the Feudal Age as a romantic "craftsman," even if that return cannot be effected in the rôle of chatelain.

What results from this situation is, of course, that the audience, in the widest sense, becomes professional, or, worse, semi-professional (whatever may happen upon the stage), and the employer turns into a rival of his employee. The argument for "amateurism" of any kind is that "professionalism" is the drabbest, most mechanical and sordid affair; which, of course, is true; as it is true that most "professionals" are incompetent, untalented, hacks. But that is a one-sided argument; the assumption at this point always is that the amateur is a fresh, capricious and carefully-sheltered plant, and as such is relieved of the distorting necessities that dog the professional. So, romantically, *all* amateurs tend to become, for the sentimental utopian enthusiast of "amateurism," a kind of gifted eternal-child, their naïveté never blemished by that odious "power" that knowledge brings or by dark necessities of a bread-and-butter order. The truth is very different from that. Almost without exception the amateur in real life—not in utopian theory—is an imitation-professional. If he is not that, he is a *faux-naïf* of the most blood-curdling description. There are no more true naïfs among amateurs than among professionals.

But it is the results and not the causes that we are concerned with here. And the proof of that millennial pudding that we have eaten is there for everybody to observe, in the world of art at least. The merging of the spectator and the performer—for that is the technical definition of amateurism in its widest implication—can scarcely be expected in art or social life to have a more satisfactory upshot than the same process applied in politics or industry.

But as we look round us, and observe the rich bohemianism in which all social power is concentrated today, we should recognize that we are in the presence of an instalment of the millennium, in full-flower. That privilege should be made the fullest use of, and we should draw the necessary conclusions. Our opportunity for practical first-hand observation is a unique one.

BOOK TWO

AN ANALYSIS OF THE PHILOSOPHY OF TIME

*"But I marvel greatly that Socrates should have spoken with disparage-
ment of that body [the sun] and that he should have said that it resem-
bled a burning stone. . . . I could wish that I had such power of
language as should avail me to censure those who would fain extol the
worship of men above that of the sun . . . even if a man were as large
as our earth he would seem like one of the least stars. . . ."*

MSS. F. Institut de France, *Leonardo da Vinci*

*"Then overcome by the force of his teachings [those of Plotinus] he con-
ceived a hatred of his own body and of being human, and sailed to
Sicily . . . and 'avoided the path of men.' "*

Lives of the Philosophers, *Eunapius*

*"The same taunt is good for all who are devoted to philosophy. For
in fact such a student is not only unaware of what his next neighbour
is doing, but does not even know whether he is a man or some other
creature."*

Theaetetus, *Plato*

*"Con su mano serena
En mi cuello hería,
Y todos mis sentidos suspendía."*

St. John of the Cross

*". . . time is the medium of narration, as it is the medium of life. Both
are inextricably bound up with it, as inextricably as are bodies in space.
Similarly, time is the medium of music: music divides, measures, ar-
ticulates time, and can shorten it, yet enhance its value, both at once.
Thus music and narration are alike, in that they can only present
themselves as a flowing, as a succession in time, as one thing after
another; and both differ from the plastic arts, which are complete in
the present, and unrelated to time save as all bodies are, whereas
narration — like music — even if it should try to be completely present
at any given moment, would need time to do it in."*

The Magic Mountain, *Thomas Mann*

PREFACE TO BOOK TWO

Everywhere in the earlier part of this essay the liaison between the theoretic region and what happens upon the concrete plane of social life or in literary expression, has been stressed. In this second half of my essay we are to turn our attention to the pure theoretic field. There the concept Time reigns almost unchallenged as the master principle. I hope to lay bare, and offer for general inspection, the very fountain-head of those notions which, in their popular form, have such an overwhelming effect upon contemporary life.

The finest creations of art or of science, today as ever, only more so, reach the general public in a very indirect fashion. If that contact could be more direct it would be much more sanely "stimulating" — to use the favourite word of the present period, when everything is valued in terms of a drug destined for a debilitated organism. It is upon the essentially political middleman, the imitative self-styled "revolutionary," that I direct my main attack. It is he who pollutes on the way the prime issue of our thinking, and converts it into a "cultural" or "scientific" article, which is a masked engine of some form of political fraud, which betrays the thought of its originator. So it is that "revolution," in the true intellectual sense, and the only helpful one, miscarries. It is the man of *interpretative* intelligence at whose hands we all suffer. For the interpretation is usually political: whereas the original thought — such is my contention — is not political or merely practical at all, when it is of the highest order.

An important place is given in this analysis to Spengler's book, *The Decline of the West*. I give my reasons for this when I come to it. But the idea at the bottom of Spengler's book is that *all* manifestations of art, mathematics, biology, physics, are political. The Theory of Quanta, the Evolutionary theory of Darwin, the music of Wagner and Weber, a Dresden Shepherdess, El Greco and Einstein — all for him are inventions of a particular time, produced in response to a culture-spirit, and they have no validity except as chronological phenomena. They are events of *history* merely, like the Battle of the Boyne or the Rump Parliament. At bottom there is really no physics, no art, no philosophy,

only *politics* and *history*. I give in some detail my reasons for dis-
agreeing with that view of things. On the other hand, I agree that
politics do invade and pollute spheres where the plain man is not
taught to expect to find them. But when they are discovered
operating in the creations of science or of art, it is invariably some
inferior personality or thinker, you will find, who is responsible
for that, rather than the material in which he works. "Modern" or
"modernity" are the words that have come literally to stink: every
intelligent man today stops his nose and his ears when somebody
approaches him with them on his lips: but that is not, I argue, because what is peculiar to the modern age, or because the "new" in
itself is bad or disgusting, but simply because it is never allowed
to reach the public in anything but a ridiculous, distorted, and
often very poisonous form. The interpreter — not seldom the interpretative performer, where it is art or science — is to blame.

For the remainder of this preface to Book Two, I shall be engaged, mainly, in giving more precision to my personal position
in this critical analysis of Time-doctrine. The position from which
this essay is written is outwardly a "narrow" one. Any merit it
claims it founds if anything on a certain illiberality; for it had
to be sharp in order to penetrate, and so it had to be gathered
to a single point. I can perhaps give you the best idea of what
I think I am doing by quoting here a passage against myself, as
it were, from Caird, about the Cynic philosophy. I should be
sorry to give you the idea that I regard myself as a sort of Antisthenes, or on the other hand as a variety of his Megarian antagonist, Stilpo. Rather would I suggest to you such a position
as Socrates might occupy in a world of such people as the Cynics
and Megarians, with the inevitable extremism of a certain sort
that would most likely result. Still, in giving Caird's account of
the virtues and vices attendant upon the Cynic revolution, I shall
be furnishing you with a hint (against myself, as I say) that may
serve to enlighten you as to my intentions, unless you proceed
to apply it too literally.

The Cynic philosophy [Caird writes] was one of those beginnings
of progress which take the appearance of reaction. When some aspect
of thought or life has been for a long time unduly subordinated, or
has not yet been admitted to its rightful place, it not seldom finds expression in a representative individuality, who embodies it in his person and works it out in its most exclusive and one-sided form, with
an almost fanatical disregard of all other considerations — compensating

for the general neglect of it by treating it as the one thing needful. Such individuals produce their effect by the very disgust they create among the ordinary respectable members of the community. . . . Their criticism of the society to which they belong, and of all its institutions and modes of action and thought, attracts attention by the very violence and extravagance of the form in which they present it. And the neglected truth, or half-truth, which they thrust into exclusive prominence, gradually begins by their means to gain a hold of the minds of others, forces them to reconsider their cherished prejudices, and so leads to a real advance of thought. In this fashion the Cynic seems to have acted upon the ancient . . . world, as a disturbing, irritating challenge to it to vindicate itself — a challenge which was violently resented, but which awakened thought, and in time produced a modification, and even a transformation, of prevailing "opinions." (*The Evolution of Theology*, etc.)

Now I have supplied you with an analogy against myself for practical reasons, although it has no literal application, as I remarked above. I am doing a very different thing from what the Cynic was doing, and I am very differently placed. But certainly I am issuing a "challenge" to the community in which I live. I am "criticizing all its institutions and modes of action and of thought." I "create disgust," that I have proved, "among the ordinary respectable members of the community," that is to say among the established orthodoxy of the cults of "primitivist" so-called "revolution": what I say is "violently resented," and I very sincerely hope will "awaken thought." Finally, what I say is *one of those beginnings of progress which take the appearance of reaction.*" What I have written — and I call to witness my book, *The Lion and the Fox* — should prove me exceedingly remote from what is generally termed a "reactionary." But I am entirely sick to death, like a great host of other people, of many of the forms that "revolution" takes, in art, sociology, science and life: and I would, however modestly, hasten the day when "revolution" should become a more rigorous business, humanely and intellectually, if undertaken at all, and no longer be left only in the hands of people who do nothing but degrade and falsify it.

So let me return to my adumbration of this exclusive "one-sided" position that is mine, or that will be said to be mine. I will try next to give some compendious idea of the manner in which I regard the claims of *individuality*. First then, although it is true that a pig would be a strange pig who dreamt himself a cat, or a cat that allowed the psychology of the horse to overpower it,

and so forgot it was a cat, for this life, at least, a man still is
the most detached and eclectic of creatures. But if his life is centred
upon some deep-seated instinct or some faculty, he will find a
natural exclusiveness necessary to proper functioning. For our
only terra firma in a boiling and shifting world is, after all, our
"self." That must cohere for us to be capable at all of behaving
in any way but as mirror-images of alien realities, or as the most
helpless and lowest organisms, as worms or as sponges.

I have said to myself that I will fix my attention upon those
things that have most meaning for me. All that seems to me to
contradict or threaten those things I will do my best to modify
or to defeat, and whatever I see that favours and agrees with
those things I will support and do my best to strengthen. In consequence, I shall certainly be guilty of injustice, the heraclitean
"injustice of the opposites." But how can we evade our destiny
of being "an opposite," except by becoming some grey mixture,
that is in reality just nothing at all? Yet this fixation shall be upon
something fundamental, quite underneath the flux; and this will
in no way prevent my vitality from taking at one time one form,
at another another, provided, in spite of these occupations, on
the surface, of different units of experience, the range of my sensibility observe the first law of being, namely to maintain its identity; and that the shapes it chooses for experiment shall agree
with that dominant principle, and such shapes not be adopted
without rhyme or reason, at the dictate of fashion or some casual
interest, just because they happen to be there, in an eternal
mongrel itch to *mix*, in undirected concupiscence, with *everything*
that walks or crawls.

Yet how are you going about this fixation, you may ask; how
will you tell offhand what is essential and what is not, for the
composing of your definite pattern; and, even among essential
things, how do you propose to avoid the contradictory factors
of empirical life; since everyone includes, below the possibility
of change, dispositions that war with one another? Well, the way
I have gone about it is generally as follows. I have allowed these
contradictory things to struggle together, and the group that has
proved the most powerful I have fixed upon as my most essential ME. This decision has not, naturally, suppressed or banished
the contrary faction, almost equal in strength, indeed, and even
sometimes in the ascendant. And I am by no means above spend-
ing some of my time with this domestic Adversary. All I have

said to myself is that always, when it comes to the pinch, I will side and identify myself with the powerfullest Me, and in its interests I will work. And luckily in my case the two sides, or microcosmic "opposites," are so well matched, that the dominant one is never idle or without criticism. It has had to struggle for supremacy first with critical principles within, and so it has practised itself for its external encounters. This natural matching of opposites within saves a person so constituted from dogmatism and conceit. If I may venture to say so, it places him at the centre of the balance.

As to what this formally fixed "self" is, and how to describe it, I have already plainly indicated how I would go about that. From the outset I gave away the principle of my activity, and made no disguise of its partisan, even its specialist, character. So my philosophic position could almost be called an occupational one, except that my occupation is not one that I have received by accident or mechanically inherited, but is one that I chose as responding to an exceptional instinct or bias. So as the occupation is an art, and hence implies a definite set of faculties and predispositions (which, out of all the other things that it was free to me to occupy myself with, made me adopt that art as my occupation), it could perhaps more exactly be described as the expression of the instincts of a particular kind of man, rather than as an artist among men of other occupations. What philosophy is not that? — you could say, however, with truth. But the definiteness of those instincts, those of a plastic or graphic artist, make his responses to the philosophic tendencies around him more pointed than if he were a scholar mainly, or if he approached them from some political position, or as a professional of philosophic thought. For at least his partisanship from the start has its plain label, there is no ambiguity about where he gets his beliefs from: though there are artists and artists, and it is certainly true that many would take opposite views to those of the present writer.

But let me take an instance that will throw into more relief the rationale of the method I am explaining. Whatever the Marquis de Sade said about life or things in general, you could be in no doubt as to what his remarks would come back to in the end; you would know that they all would have the livery of the voluptuary, that they would all be hurrying on the business of some painful and elaborate pleasure of the senses, that they would be devising means to satisfy an overmastering impulse to feel acutely in the regions set aside for the spasms of sex. With as much definiteness as that, whatever I, for my part, say, can be traced back to an organ; but in my case it is *the eye*. It is in the service of the things of vision that my ideas are mobilized.

The significance of the concept "Time" in contemporary philosophy, and the results of its application to all the complex of life and artistic expression around us, is the main subject of this essay. But in the title, *Time and Western Man*, another notion is introduced, namely, "Western Man," and that notion stands in this case simply for the environment in the midst of which we have been scrutinizing, in Book One, the ravages of the doctrine of "Time." That spectacle leads us to believe that perhaps that doctrine may have a particularly unfortunate effect on specifically Western Civilization; though of course it might equally well be found to have a devastating effect upon the remnants of the immemorial civilizations of the East. But what at least I think can be shown is that the Time-doctrine is not, emotionally and psychologically, essentially Western; and so the Western scientific man cannot, really, be held responsible for it. But on the other hand, it could hardly have seen the light in the native atmosphere of the indian intelligence, for instance; it is not a philosophy that would have had much appeal for the true heirs of upaniṣadic thought. If we must place it, it would be in the mongrel westernized-orientalism of alexandrian mystical doctrine that we should see it first flowering, its highest flight "the flight of the Alone to the Alone"; via Bergson it has reached, philosophically, our distressed contemporary Western arena, contributing beyond doubt to our ever-deepening confusion of mind.

Western Man, as such, is of course the completest myth. The only question is whether we should not erect that myth into a reality, define it more (not *historically* so much as in conformity with the realities of the moment); and whether, in short, some such generalization would not serve our purposes better than the multiplicity of myths that swarm in our drifting chaos. "Western" does respond to something that the European is responsible for, for good or ill; but of course there is every sign that before long the great asiatic populations will have been turned into "Westerners" *pur sang*, and the factory hand of Wigan and

Hanchow "meet" long before the Trump of Doom, in a way that would have been quite inconceivable to Mr. Kipling when he wrote his famous imperial ballad, with its mystical "Eastern" and "Western" duality. We are told, for instance, that the jewish settler in Palestine is so very "Western" that the Arab can see no traces in him of that first-cousin who left the Ancient East after the exploits of Titus, and indeed regards him as a complete alien. So "Western" must be a very inclusive term; and the "Westerner" flirts incessantly with the Black Bottom of the Swanee River, with mahometanism, with the tobacco-coloured Samoans of Gauguin, and the Japanese of Lafcadio Hearn, and indeed with everything that is *opposite*, technically, to his own kind (so romantic is he), for which latter poor White trash he advertises the greatest contempt. So the task of fixing a "Western" norm would be anything but an easy matter. Still, perhaps the time has arrived (so familiar are we now with all that is strange and different) to turn back with a thrill of novelty to *ourselves*—even that, at last! The European, or generally the Western Man, should be almost ripe for the novel proceeding of flirting with his own kind, for a change.

"Thought turns to hope"; or it could be said that thought was in the nature of a promise. But it is not with such hopes, or thoughts, that we are concerned here. And the "Western" of our title is given no more definition than what naturally inheres in the something that still characterizes our Western environment, as opposed to others distinct in tradition and outlook.

But there are still a few difficulties that, before any further progress is attempted, should be cleared up. Very reasonably it has been objected, upon the evidence of the first and already published part of this essay, that this "occupational" standpoint of mine should not be a starting-point for criticism of things that do not fall within the sphere of that occupation: (very reasonably if that view of what I was doing—and to which perhaps my first uncompleted statement gave some colour—had been the correct one). It has been suggested, for instance, that as an artist I have tended to imply that mathematical physics should conform to the creative requirements of the arts in which I am exclusively interested: and that I should be better advised to ignore such things, and only attend to what happens in my own field. Now that I should be delighted to do if these different worlds of physics, philosophy, politics and art were (as, according to my view, they should be) rigidly separated. To receive blindly, or at the best confusedly, from regions outside his own, all kinds of notions and formulae, is what the "creative artist" generally does. Without knowing it, he receives into the central tissue of his work political or scientific notions which he proceeds to embody, if he is a novelist, in his characters, if he is a painter, or a poet, in his technique or emotional material, without in the least knowing what he is doing or why he is doing it. But my conception of the rôle of the creative artist is not merely to be a medium for ideas supplied him wholesale from elsewhere, which he incarnates automatically in a technique which (alone) it is his business to perfect. It is equally his business to know enough of the sources of his ideas, and ideology, to take steps to keep these ideas out, except such as he may require for his work. When the idea-monger comes to his door he should be able to tell what kind of notion he is buying, and know something of the process and rationale of its manufacture and distribution. But further than this, of course, it was as a critic, and not as a creative artist, that I was speaking in the first part of this essay. And as such it was certainly my business to know the origins of what I was examining in the works chosen for discussion.

In this part of my essay I am, however definitely passing over into the metaphysical field, following the tracks of all the ideas that find their way into the regions of artistic creation: and my objectionable task, as a perhaps over-conscientious critic, is to examine to the best of my ability their credentials.

I do not feel at all impelled to explain myself when I am examining a mere philosopher: he speaks my language, usually with less skill, but otherwise much the same as I do. But there is a certain feature of my proceedings that does, I think, require elucidation, for my argument will run more smoothly and free of interference if I forestall possible objections. I refer to my dealing with the physicist, or the ideas emanating from the physicist. Just as the practical engineer receives from the mathematician fresh knowledge, theoretically arrived at, that makes him rub his mere practical eyes, and just as these formulae are found to *work*, so the equations of the mathematical physicist are found often to be truth-telling in the same way: they take their rise in response to the difficulties met with in experiment, and, having met that case, they are perhaps found applicable to a whole system of new facts. Within a few years of the arrival of Einstein upon the european scene, the layman, I suppose, knows more about Relativity physics than any layman has ever known about the newtonian cosmology, either during Newton's lifetime or since. There is an enormous Relativity literature from which any one who cares can acquaint himself with the main bearings of these theories. Of course, the more ignorant people are with regard to the points at issue, the more likely they are to say that you must be a mathematician to discuss them at all. But, in point of fact, there is no more reason today why a person should refuse himself the right to use his wits, on the grounds that he is not a mathematician, than there was in the time of David Hume. If Hume, Hobbes, Berkeley or Locke, for instance, who were not mathematicians, had closed their minds to us, we should know far less about the world than we do today. It is a superstition to suppose that the instruments of research, as today developed, have excluded from participation in the general critical work of intellectual advance, the independent critical mind, for that mind is still the supreme instrument of research: and the history of thought amply proves that that instrument is not always mathematical, any more than it is always artistic. The criticism of the newtonian system made by Berkeley is in fact one of the main bases of mathematical thought today; and yet the newtonian system is the most gigantic mathematical achievement. In spite of that, it was built on assumptions that Berkeley, observing it independently and not as a mathematician, was able to detect and, in the interests of his God, finally to discredit.

These remarks are by no means preliminary to an announcement that it is my intention to cast my mere artist's eye, like an impertinent bird's, into the awful machinery of Relativity, and with an inspiration transcending disabilities of any description, pluck out the heart of that arcane fastness of logic. No. My remarks are merely directed to clearing the field of any of the more troublesome lookers-on or camera-men, who would perhaps attempt to prevent us from questioning the Sphinx, on the ground that we were using words instead of other symbols.

I have very little to do with Relativity physics, however, as it happens. I am only concerned with their *effects*; and I am in that, on the principle indeed of all the most approved and most recent scientific method, thoroughly justified. For it is now quite accepted that all we need deal with in anything is the *effect*— what, for instance, can be observed *to come out of* the atom— rather than what we should commonly describe as the "cause" of the disturbance. We are authorized, and indeed commanded, to remain sublimely indifferent to what "causes" what we can see and note, or indeed whether it has a "cause" at all. God, even, from being, as common-sense saw it, a Cause, has now become an Effect, when he is allowed a place at all in this curious picture. Instead of being the Cause of Causes, he is the Effect of Effects. So all we are allowed or invited to do is to invent a certain number of things that give the "effects" a properly non-causative aspect. A great many *effects*, a whole string of highly characteristic disturbances, *come out of* einsteinian physics, then. And those I am thoroughly competent to observe, and it is those with which I have set out to deal: the physics themselves can remain for us in the region at most of hypothesis, a vague *something* that produces, in the observable field of philosophy, a chain of *effects*, or of mysterious happenings. The cause, if a cause we must have, is einsteinian physics. But what *they* are, or if they exist at all, indeed, we shall be not only justified, but invited by the most approved scientific procedure, entirely to neglect.

In spite of this highly fortunate disposition of the contemporary mind, absolving us from going *inside*, as it were, the "reaction-mass," or the "atom" (or in this case the mathematical corpus producing the disturbances labelled "space-time"), indeed exacting that we should remain at the periphery and should merely jot down what *happens* — count, classify, describe and assess the *effects* — nevertheless a few brief remarks may be made on another aspect of the matter relating to the celebrated author and proximate cause of what we are about to observe. I have been taxed with identifying Einstein with Bergson, Alexander, Cassirer and the rest. This, in fact, I have not intended to do: for Harvey, in discovering the circulation of the blood, clearly could not be described as doing so with a view to showing us to be machines, or for any motives except those of pure scientific curiosity; and the physical investigations as to the structure of our universe which culminated in Einstein, were, for all anyone need suppose to the contrary, as innocent as that (or as the formulae for constructing an improved type of bridge or the formularies of an actuary) of any human *arrière-pensée*. Nor, further, were they necessarily at all metaphysical in origin. "It is not . . . metaphysical concepts (which even before this had brought time and space together) but the mathematical fact of the invariance of Maxwell's equations and the demonstration of the consequences of this fact by experiments in physics, which leads us to the new conception with its paradoxical consequences." Let us take that account of the matter; we can accept that without further trouble; and as the time-space or space-time solution is the capital one for us, in Einstein, that disposes of our wishing to associate Einstein with subsequent relativity-philosophy, or with the time-philosophy of Bergson, in any close or peculiar way: nor, if the subsequent or preceding philosophies are proved to possess some especial sociological or political colour (as Bosanquet or Benda thinks they have), need such impurities be ascribed to the mathematical physicists, of whom Einstein is the most famous.

But having said that, and made our position clear as regards the great mathematical innovators who have had such a vast influence in all contemporary thought, and in some ways such an invigorating one, the following considerations should be associated with that statement. First it is inconceivable (fully allowing for the natural detachment from mundane things of the mathematical intelligence as contrasted with the philosophic) that the mathematician working in such imaginative material as was Einstein, or Minkowski, so provocative of metaphysical stimulus, should not *be* to some extent metaphysical; or that their mathematical formulation of pictures of the world should not conceal, or be susceptible of, some metaphysical belief or meaning, of which they were quite conscious. It is mere superstition to suppose "a mathematician" to be a sort of divine machine. In any reasonable, and not romantic, account of the matter, we must suppose the mathematical physicist not entirely unaffected by neighbouring metaphysical thought. That Einstein, as much as Sorel or Proust, for instance, had not at least read the work of Bergson, and formed some opinion upon it, favourable or otherwise, is unlikely, to say the least. It would be just as unlikely as that Newton remained entirely uninfluenced by the english platonism by which he was surrounded. The newtonian conception of absolute space probably came to him while basking in the platonic airs of the *Enchiridion* of More, or the similar benignant atmospheres of Cudworth or Cumberland (and so, it is now believed, it would be indirectly derived from Philipon, an alexandrian whose importance Duhem and Wohlwill have lately brought to light). Is it, then, so unlikely that the *time* factor so powerfully transforming mathematical physics in our day had something to do with the metaphysical speculation preceding it, and all that growth of time-dimensional speculation with which most people are familiar: in other words, that *time* may have found its way into those systems by the same metaphysical road that *space* took to reach the mechanics of Newton? It does not seem at all impossible, though there is no occasion to insist upon such a possibility: indeed it will be one of our tasks here to make such an explanation otiose.

If I quote a passage from Einstein's Boswell, Moszkowski, some people might object that a person of such a low order of intelligence as he shows himself in one sense to be, deserves no notice. But it must be remembered that the type of criticism which these pages are designed to circumvent on the popular field is often of a far lower order of intelligence than that displayed by the man whom Einstein, after all, admitted to his intimacy. And at least Moszkowski, to put it no higher than that, is more intelligent than Spengler. In his book of gossip about his hero, Moszkowski has (*chap. V*) secured permission, on the occasion of his next visit to Einstein, to open a grand full-dress discussion upon "*discovery* in general." He prepares himself intellectually for this great occasion. "We are precluded from questioning Galileo personally about the foundations of Mechanics, or Columbus about the inner feelings of a navigator . . . [etc.] but a great discoverer lives among [us], [etc., etc.]" So he gets ready. "Before meeting him again I was overwhelmed with ideas that arose in me at the slightest echo of the word 'discovery' . . . the sum of [man's] discoveries . . . find their climax in the conceptions *civilization* and *philosophy*, just as they are partly conditioned by the philosophy of the time. We might be tempted to ask: which of these two precedes, which follows?" He comes to the conclusion that "they are intimately interwoven with one another, and are only different aspects of one and the same process." In short, he takes quite the same view of the matter as does Spengler. Then he goes on:

It seemed to me that even at this stage of my reflections I was somewhere near interpreting Einstein's intellectual achievement. For his principle of relativity is tantamount to a regulative world-principle that has left a mighty mark in the thought of our times. We have lived to see the death of absolutism: the relativity of the constituents of political power, and their mutability according to view-point and current tendencies, become manifest to us . . . the world was far enough advanced in its views for a final achievement of thought which would demolish the absolute also from the mathematico-physical aspect. This is how Einstein's discovery appeared as inevitable.

So there is no question about the way in which Einstein's Boswell regards his master's discoveries. He brings to them, perhaps, a peculiarly political eye: he sees them as a rooting out from the Cosmos, by means of a kind of mathematical guillotine, of the principle of *the Absolute*; rather as Heine regarded Kant — as a God-killer (Robespierre merely killed kings, whereas Kant destroyed a God, in the eyes of that witty but snobbish enthusiast).

History does not [continues Moszkowski] adapt itself to the time measures of politics and of journalism . . . but if we make our unit a hundred years, the connection between philosophies and great discoveries remains true. Whoever undertakes to explore the necessity of this connection cannot evade the fact that the lines of the result had been marked out in the region of pure thought. . . . Even the achievements of Copernicus would follow this general rule . . . it was the last consequence of the belief in the Sun Myth which had never been forsaken by man in spite of the violent efforts of the Church and of man himself to force the geocentric view. . . . [Copernicus'] discovery was the transformation of a myth into science.

Then he proceeds to discuss the parallel between Bergson and Planck:

. . . deep down in the consciousness of man there has always been an opposition to [the formula *Natura non facit saltus*], and when the french philosopher Henri Bergson set out to break up this line of continuity by metaphysical means in ascribing to human knowledge an intermittent, cinematographic character, he was proclaiming . . . what had lain latent in a new, but as yet incomplete, philosophy. Bergson made no new "discovery," he felt his way intuitively into a new field of knowledge and recognized that the time was ripe for the real discovery. This was actually presented to us in our day by the eminent physicist Max Planck . . . in the form of his "Quantum Theory." This is not to be taken as meaning that a revolutionary philosophy and a triumph of scientific research now become coincident. . . . [It] was probably not a case of the accidental coincidence of a new philosophical view with the results of reasoning from physical grounds, but a demand of time, exacting that the claims of a new principle of thought be recognized.

A very interesting discussion ensues when he gets to Einstein's house — or it would be interesting if Moszkowski expressed himself with less bombast and possessed the literary skill of Johnson's friend. Einstein appeared to put forth the view that the "discovery" rather discovered the "discoverer," or condescended to pop into his head, than that the discoverer himself *y était pour quelque chose.*

Really Moszkowski (although possessing all the peculiarities of a born "Boswell," perhaps of a not very high order even in his own class) is not such a blockhead as people would no doubt suggest, nor as his style would imply. What he has just said above shows that for him Relativity is not devoid of a *political* significance: and in his remarks on Bergson and Planck, he describes Bergson as "intuiting" what Planck subsequently "discovered," both impelled to these facts by the Zeitgeist. A few pages further on Einstein remarks: "the really valuable factor is *intuition!*" This appears to put Planck's invention or "discovery" on the same plane as Bergson's "intuition," only the latter was the first on the scene. The gist of Einstein's part in this dialogue is that there are certain things existing eternally which people come upon, indifferently "intuiting" or "discovering" them. Some of the "intuitions" don't come off, owing to the unfortunate prevalence of the negative instance, but some do, like Relativity, though all subject, Moszkowski energetically does *not* think, to Duhem's law of reversal, whereby *any* physical system can be knocked over, and can rely on *no* experiment, however "crucial."

Both these statements of Moszkowski's may be absurd; but they are made by a person not devoid of common-sense, at a time when he was in close association with the greatest physicist of the day, who apparently did not regard him as such a fool as all that. The opinion favoured here is that he exaggerated the political parallel between the destruction of the *Absolute* in Einstein's physical system, and the rise of bolshevism in the political world. It is fantastic to suppose that such a parallel could *absolutely* exist — though people in speaking of Newton's system are certainly in the habit of saying, for instance, that he conceived the sun as a monarch round whom the planets revolved, because in his day the political system contained a monarch at its centre (cf. Bertrand Russell: "In Newton's theory of the solar system, the sun seems like a monarch whose behests the planets have to obey. In Einstein's world there is more individualism and less government than in Newton's"). Sorel gives an analogous account of the effect of the spectacle of the stability of the kingship, as illustrated supremely by the Roi Soleil. These parallels between a construction of the "pure intellect" and a political system terrestrially circumscribing its author, must be admitted as real. It is only by fully accepting the evident fact that many men of science, or philosophers, are politicians, and their supposed "pure" theoretic mind in reality merely a very practical one, working in and through ideas as it would otherwise and more becomingly be working in soap, hair-oil or sanitary appliances, or at bookmaking or stockbroking, that we can show that *all* theory and all theoretic men are *not* involved in those proofs and arguments. The *historical* world of Spengler or of Moszkowski is a world of the second-rate. Is not any average volume of history a long account of the triumphs and disappointments of the secondrate, of kings, bootleggers, bishops and merchants? It is the *average* life of England, France and America today, for instance, only *past* and treated flatteringly as "history." What part does any truly great achievement of the mind play in those historical feuilletons? If Moszkowski's reading of Relativity could be shown by some competent person to be true, then immediately we should know that the Relativity physics we had been taught to admire was not an achievement of the first order, and that we had been taken in, however much amused in the process. For such an *ad hoc* universe as would result from a desire to "banish absolutism," or equally on the other hand to "establish absolutism," and impose terrestrial politics upon the stars, would indeed be scientifically a farce, however intelligent a one. But so many eminent men of science have accepted Einstein's theory, that Moszkowski, as far as Einstein is concerned, must be wrong. In the case of Einstein Mr. Bertrand Russell, I venture to think rightly, attaches less importance to the "relativism" which has provided the theory with its title (and it is after all the oldest feature of his system, relativity being a classical doctrine of idealism) than to the merging of Space and Time, which is the great novelty. Surely in that highly technical operation, one would have thought, there could be no reflection of political passions! With the Moszkowskis and Spenglers we reach the point at which the system of the mathematical physicist becomes suspect, in exactly the same way as for long now we have been accustomed to regard with suspicion the system of the philosopher. If there *is* something in the air of a time that influences even the processes of the secluded mind of the "pure mathematician," we should at least not turn a blind eye to it, but investigate it as we would anything else.

There are no doubt good and bad times: in the bad ones these influences may be more powerful. The immense influence exerted on our lives by these "discoveries" cannot leave us indifferent to the character of the instruments that are responsible for them — namely, the minds of the discoverers. But it is only the less fine instruments that can be influenced in that way and lend colour to spenglerism, that is our argument. This essay is among other things the assertion of a belief in the finest type of mind, which lifts the creative impulse into an absolute region free of spenglerian "history" or politics.

As to the plan according to which I have arranged my arguments, I have not left a general "summing-up" until the end, but attempted as I went along to introduce, as early as possible, and in connection with each particular phase of my arguments, the conclusions that must ensue from my evidence.

PART I

"But, let the consequences of such a belief be as dire as they may, one thing is certain; that the state of the facts, whatever it may be, will surely get found out, and no human prudence can long arrest the triumphal car of truth—no, not if the discovery were such as to drive every individual of our race to suicide!"

C. S. Peirce

"Classical man, according to Protagoras, was only the measure and not the creator of things, a view that unconsciously forgoes all conquest of Nature through the discovery and application of laws."

Decline of the West, *Spengler*

"The pilgrim fathers of the scientific imagination as it exists today, are the great tragedians of ancient Athens, Aeschylus, Sophocles, Euripides. Their vision of fate, remorseless and indifferent, urging a tragic incident to its inevitable issue, is the vision possessed by science. Fate in Greek Tragedy becomes the order of nature in modern thought."

Science and the Modern World, *A. N. Whitehead*

CHAPTER ONE

PROFESSOR ALEXANDER AND THE AGE OF TIME OR MOTION

IN THE FOLLOWING analysis of time-doctrine I shall direct attention to the *Space Time and Deity* of Professor Alexander more than to any other recently-published book. It is not comparable in importance, in this movement, to the books of Bergson, for instance. But it is the only exposition on a large scale of the time-doctrine in its "space-time" form in the english-speaking countries. As far as possible, again, I shall confine myself to a few books, rather than accumulate evidence on all hands. The reason for this is that, agreeing as they do, to an uncanny degree, in all fundamentals, and especially where the doctrine of the reality of time is concerned, this great school of philosophers give variety to their doctrine in detail. These modifications are as a rule ultimately unimportant, and would only confuse the reader. So far as possible I have confined myself to the teaching of the few most characteristic writers of the school.

I will begin with a passage from *Space Time and Deity*, which, if properly read, is capable of throwing a great deal of light at the start on our discussion. It will serve immediately to establish the attitude of the space-timeist to that for us all-important philosophic entity, the Hellenic World, and give the clue to the animosity always exhibited by the time-philosopher for it.

It is in fact the cardinal defect of universals as conceived by Plato or the Pythagoreans that they were changeless and immovable and eternal. *For not even the mind of Plato could be free from the habits of his age,* one of whose tendencies was to seek the highest ideals of perfection in gravity of action and statuesque repose rather than in restless motion. Hence to account for motion he had to look for another source which he found in soul. *It is claiming no great credit that for us universals should have from the beginning the form of motion,* should be not merely spatial but spatio-temporal.

In a footnote he quotes (as though further to underline the tendency that he represents) the famous impressionist sculptor, Auguste Rodin. For anyone familiar with the fluid photographs in commercially-produced marble of that artist—the plastic counterpart of Bergson (his sculpture contemporary with the doctrine of *élan vital*, and looking as though it had been done expressly to illustrate it), the calling of that witnesses will be of very great significance.

Rodin is today so remote from all the interests of contemporary artistic expression that it is impossible to be more completely forgotten. He is as remote as Pujol or Canova. To artists he means today nothing whatever; but not so with philosophers, looking for illustrations for their space-time flux. It is full of significance that a post-relativity book of philosophy should recall him at a highly characteristic juncture. It brings into relief at once the fact of the deep separation between the intellectual standards and ideas of the relativist flux-philosopher, and the plastic or graphic artist.

The influence of Bergson went down beneath the wave of formal enthusiasm that immediately preceded the War. In the arts that movement brought imagination back once more, banishing the naturalist dogmas that had obtained for fifty or sixty years. Impressionism was driven out and the great ideals of structure and of formal significance were restored, to painting and sculpture, at all events. Sensationalism seemed to have been superseded in Europe by a new and severer spirit, come from nowhere, as though by magic. The plastic and graphic arts were more immediately affected by this general movement than any other department of the intelligence.

It seemed, though, that that was the form things were to take in every kind of speculation. There was a very powerful reaction in France against all that Bergson represented. But the War and einsteinian physics have turned the scales once more. There is naturally no question of reinstating Bergson; there are plenty of others of the same sort, but with a more up-to-date equipment, without having recourse to him. Fundamentally all the tide of thought today, however broken up into the complexity of a confusing network of channels, is setting towards the pole of Sensation. But it carries with it as it goes a wreckage of disciplines and severities; so on the surface it has a more stable and imposing look than really belongs to its purely sensational impulsion.

No painter, sculptor or architect today dreams, however, of repudiating the great movement so triumphantly begun, and which has been responsible already for more art of the first order than has been seen in Europe since the Renaissance. That is an important feature of the present situation. But in this way the artist is rather strangely isolated; for he is like a detachment in a battle that has held its own, while all the rest of the line is disappearing in confusion. This situation is *physiological*, I believe, or ensues from the physiological fundamentals conditioning the graphic and plastic arts. Into that we need not enter here, but shall content ourselves with the facts this analysis is putting in evidence.

If you turn back to the quotation from Professor Alexander, you will find that I have italicized two passages. They seemed to me typical of the fluid standards that may be expected from the flux-philosopher, so accustomed to conjure with things that he hardly any longer cares whether what he says holds water or not, where πάντα ῥεῖ—knowing that he can "make anything of anything"; and, Time being in its mercurial Heaven, all is well with the world of the little space-timeist, wherever, or whenever, he be.

Yet the confusion in those italicized passages is so typical that it is worth dwelling upon it for a moment; although it is nothing to the muddle that reigns in the metaphysical heart of the argument, where a "formula for space-time" is being provided (in chap. ii of book ii) and Time is being described as the "mind of Space." The disorder at that point of the proceedings beggars description.

Then *"not even the mind of Plato could be free from the habits of his age,"* says Professor Alexander; and I suppose that we are right in assuming, as a consequence of that, *that not even the mind of Professor Alexander can be free from the habits of* his age. Even, since Professor Alexander's mind is probably not such a perfect and original instrument as Plato's, we could assume, without much risk, that the mind of Professor Alexander was far less free than that of Plato, and far more the slave of the "habits of his age."

The extreme naïveté of the second of the italicized passages is worth a great deal of argument to a lucky opponent. *"It is claiming no great credit,"* Professor Alexander says, *"that for us universals should have from the beginning the form of motion."*

Professor Alexander is almost too modest. "Do not thank me—thank 'the age,' for these superlative advantages of an excelling truth—one that seeks the highest ideal of human perfection in restless motion"! he says in effect. "*I* claim no credit for being able to tell you that universals should be regarded under the form of motion. I have the good fortune to be a philosopher of flux and movement, coming in the alexandrian wake of Bergson and hoisted on the tide of Einstein. Plato was not a flux-philosopher, but then Plato had not the good fortune to live in this age! Pity poor Plato! But it is not *I*, it is *the age*, that is superior to Plato!"

But since "not even the mind of Plato could be free from the habits of his age," and still less probably that of Professor Alexander from his, as we have already agreed, of what value is Professor Alexander's testimony as to the superiority of his age? — who would not inquire (unless so predisposed to believe everything and anything that they would let anything and everything pass, whatever nonsense it made).

The attitude of mind implied in this chance remark ("it is claiming no great credit," etc.) is deeply characteristic of the contemporary mind. People are so overwhelmed with the prestige of their instruments that they consider their personal judgment of scarcely any account. They assume a full consent to the one central doctrine whose dictation they, on their side, never question. But as everybody knows, and none better than Professor Alexander, the age of Plato swarmed with empirical, sensationalist philosophers, from Protagoras downwards. So how is it that poor Plato was not able to be "free from the habits of his age," but that they were? Around him were many men, highly articulate, from whom he could have learnt as well as he could from Bergson or Alexander. There were really, of course, a hundred ages all together, as there always are; there was no *one* age — far less, indeed, than there is at this moment.

And thus we arrive, through all this confusion, at the meaning of Professor Alexander. He wishes us to believe that the truth of Plato was merely the *one* truth of Plato's *one* age. Thereby he weakens the platonic truth, making it merely *historical*, or a *time-truth*. So he pits "age" against "age," on a kind of "nationalist" analogy. Every true time-patriot will agree at once that if it is a question of this age or the age of Plato, the here and now is right — my time-country right or wrong! And if you said to him that that "here and now" was as much an abstraction as is a modern "nation," he could call you a low-down inter-temporalist, a conshie in the glorious time-war, if he wanted to, and were not too courteous and sensible, in spite of philosophy.

So modestly retiring behind his "age" or time, Professor

Alexander assumes, it appears, almost without reflection, that there is nothing more to be said. The only answer to that attitude is the direct affirmative that as there was an age of Protagoras and an age of Plato co-existing, so there are today, strangely enough, at least as many people on the earth who are *not* of one mind with the time-doctrinaires, as there were in Plato's day persons not of one mind with Protagoras.

CHAPTER TWO

THE PHILOSOPHY OF THE INSTRUMENTS
OF RESEARCH

NEXT I WILL TAKE A FEW of the features of Professor Whitehead's book, *Science and the Modern World*, published in 1926. And I will start by using it further to clear up a point raised by my quotation from the *Space Time and Deity* of his colleague and co-space-timeist, Professor Alexander.

What Professor Whitehead's definition of an age or epoch would be he tells us in the historical analysis that occupies the greater part of his *Science and the Modern World*. It would be simply the condition of the instruments of experiment and research at the time in question. Galileo dropping his objects of various weights off the leaning tower at Pisa symbolizes one age or epoch. An instrument of far great precision than any known to Galileo — those employed by Michelson, for instance — brings about another epoch or age. That, with all that it entails of readjustment of our world-view and revolution in our habits, *is* the age.

The ideal basis for an epoch would certainly be the instruments of research, invented for the advancement of the common good; and certainly the impulse behind all "revolution" — the will, that is, to pass from one epoch to another and better (of course) — is the work of the man of science. But unfortunately the best-organized and most powerful minorities will a different thing to the common good; and the more irresponsible power they obtain, the more their chosen interpreters (who are not, however, the great and inventive minds, but rather the opportunist and interpretative) expound the discoveries of science in a sense vaguely favourable to that power.

It seems to me that *the total effect* of a discovery or of a scientific theory, metaphysically susceptible, in most cases, of several different interpretations, should be more insisted upon than it is. A discovery by itself is of no value at all, any more than the entire destructive apparatus of a modern army would be, deposited upon a planet where there was no life. Just as any discovery of pure science, again, finds its inevitable expansion in industry, not in *more* pure science, at least at once; so the much more practical and humanly-significant philosopher (of the type of which we are speaking) is lying in wait for the productions of science as much as is the industrialist. And there is no reason to suppose that the philosopher is invariably more scrupulous than his industrial contemporary. Science is for both a means to human ends.

In the *total effect* of a scientific discovery you must, then, consider what it comes to signify to men. As it is the work of men, what other meaning can it have? And how can it, except for the moment, isolate itself from their passions? The philosopher interprets it emotionally for men. That is his function.

So Whitehead's view would tend to underrate the rôle of the metaphysician — even the originating power, too, of such a mind as Berkeley's, reflected forward into scientific and mathematical discovery. Bergson discovered nothing; he interpreted science; and he gave it an extremely biassed interpretation, to say the least, of a highly alexandrian order, which (I mean the colouring, the interpretation) was immediately accepted.

Does nature imitate the creations of art, or does art imitate nature? is a hackneyed inquiry. Its form might be employed in connection with the same problem, posed by the relation between man's will and what he "discovers" in science. Is he not directed to some extent in that by what he *wants* to discover? Has he not often a blind eye for what he does not want; and does he not *always* interpret what has been discovered, by himself or other men, as he *wants* to understand it, or as somebody else requires him to?

Where opposite theories have existed and flourished, even, side by side, this question is not so relevant. But when, as today, an unusual orthodoxy of thought is in full operation, it is extremely relevant. And it is only because the enormous power of speculative thought on the common life of men is not realized, that this question receives so very little attention.

William James (one of the two great philosophers indicated by Whitehead as supremely significant, both opening an epoch) is extremely illuminating on this particular point. With a truly philosophic, or better say scientific, tolerance, James describes the personal and interested nature of all philosophy. Where, in his *Pluralistic Universe*, he is concluding his argument, he sets forth without any ambiguity the process by which pluralism, as much as monism, must succeed. The two "horns" — the pluralistic and monistic — make pragmatically different appeals to different individuals. These are his words:

Whatever I may say, each of you will be sure to take pluralism or leave it, just as your own sense of rationality moves and inclines. . . . This world *may*, in the last resort, be a block-universe; but on the other hand, it *may* be a universe only strung-along, not rounded in and closed. Reality *may* exist distributively just as it sensibly seems to, after all. On that possibility, I do insist.

One's general vision of the probable usually decides such alternatives. They illustrate what I once wrote of as the "will to believe." In some of my lectures at Harvard I have spoken of what I call the "faith-ladder," as something quite different from the *sorites* of the logic-books, yet seeming to have an analogous form. I think you will quickly recognize in yourselves, as I describe it, the mental process to which I give this name.

A conception of the world arises in you somehow, no matter how. Is it true or not? you ask.

It *might* be true somewhere, you say, for it is not self-contradictory.

It *may* be true, you continue, even here and now.

It is fit to be true, it would be *well if it were true*, it *ought* to be true, you presently feel.

It *must* be true, something persuasive in you whispers next; and then — as a final result —

It shall be *held for true*, you decide; it *shall* be as if true, for *you*.

And your acting thus may in certain special cases be a means of making it securely true in the end.

Not one step in this process is logical, yet it is the way in which monists and pluralists alike espouse and hold fast to their visions.

This analysis of the birth of a philosophy, arising in a kind of hypothesis of the will; this *als ob* behaviour of the mind as it chooses one "horn" or the other, presented to it at the start, of the initial dilemma, should be committed to memory by persons disposed to see in everything advanced in the name of science, and generally accepted, a fiat of Reason. Later on we shall be discussing this problem in detail. The tendency of James is to stress in everything the "pragmatical," and so to provide a bridge to the purely chronologic. But the element of truth in this attitude cannot safely be overlooked.

Professor Whitehead very justly describes Aristotle as the last great european philosopher without a theological axe to grind. After Aristotle came the alexandrian hellenizers, and the Western World ever since has produced dogmatic philosophic theologians or anti-theologists.

The secular sceptical spirit of Western democracy is capitulating to those emotional semi-religious forms that political cults are assuming. So once more we must expect dogmatists. And by "politics" today we must understand something very much wider than what was formerly meant by that. Very much more has been put into "politics" than the European of a hundred years ago would have considered appropriate to that term.

I do not think it is too optimistic to believe (if this ferment continues and if an empire of some kind results) that it will be more intelligent and less obscurantist than was Rome. The Galileos of the future may, of course, be muttering under their breath, "But all the same it moves!" (or — more likely — "But all the same it does *not* move!" according to the nature of their discoveries) just having signed their recantations. But I think that nothing indicates such a state of affairs, ultimately, as that. It seems unlikely that an orthodoxy of that order would supervene. In the first phases of the change-over, however, in which we exist, everything is subordinated to *action*: and certainly all the Galileos of today will be compelled to shout, "How fast, how incessantly, and how beautifully, everything *moves!*" whatever they may think to the contrary. For *movement* and *struggle* are ideas more favoured by the man-of-action than are repose and peace: and is not science a "doctrine of motion"? And if we said that this age is an "intensely active age" that would do quite as well as to say that it was "an intensely political" one.

But that sort of activity has become a cult; so politics do, installed in the heart of the cult of movement and action, affect us, I think, very much. No one, I suppose, would dispute that the calm of the sage of chinese antiquity, or of the yogi, or even of the greek stoic or cynic, is not typical of our Western civilization today; or that its *opposite*, "action," is almost exclusively typical of it. And I suppose that no one would deny that for the greatest achievements of the intellect, whether in art or in science, tranquillity and a stable order of things is required; that the artist or thinker is better off in a settled and well-policed state; that for the production of his work he is better off in a clean, quiet and peaceful workshop or laboratory, than he would be in the turmoil of a slum, or in the middle of a battlefield. That much is all, I take it, self-evident, and beyond dispute. And if you say the contrary, you are merely asserting, like a good little egalitarian, that people *should not be* philosophers, men-of-science, or artists — that they should give up all those vain things, and plunge into the centre of the flux of life — *live* and not think; that all that sort of life of the intellect has nothing to do with the social revolution. In that last contention, at least, you would be demonstrably wrong.

The political orthodoxy or new world-phase that is taking shape, whether for good or ill, has still immense forces to contend against and to manipulate. In the past, peoples the whole of whose mind has been bent to a practical end have not usually been very speculative or intellectually free. The man-of-action is not very speculative, usually, nor is he a "free intelligence" as a rule, but an extremely narrow, unreflective, functional person. The Roman has left little behind him compared with the Greek or the Chinese. So, on the same principle, how can an age, so bent on practical tasks as ours, be intellectually free or very speculative? It is only when a community is secure (and usually soon after, owing to its freedom and speculative licence, it begins to disintegrate, or else it takes a plunge or a series of plunges back into a self-defensive obscurantism) that it can become free and creative. And although there are great forces established in the world today, their power is very fluid and by no means secure; and they have no time for play.

Professor Whitehead says that an "age" is simply its *instruments of research*. And that is what the philosophy of our age is, too, as it exists today. And just as politics follows technique, a technique that is uniform throughout the world, and as it gets a considerable uniformity therefrom — for at any one time throughout the world there is only *one* type of perfected industrial technique — so philosophy tends to become more and more uniform, since the instruments of research on which it attends are in the same position to it as is the technique of industry to politics.

When I speak of an "orthodoxy of thought," therefore, or a philosophic orthodoxy, I refer to this strict uniformity that ensues from the scrupulous following of the datum provided by the instruments of research, by philosophy and by all speculative thought. And the identity of philosophy or of speculative thought with politics is largely owing to the fact that both depend more and more absolutely upon machines of greater and greater precision, on machines so wonderfully complex and powerful that they usurp to a great extent the functions of independent life. But philosophy and speculative thought is, further, an emotional interpretation, and not entirely a soulless imitation, of technical discovery.

This "philosophy by instruments of research," as it could be called, has the following disadvantage. It fixes the philosopher down to a kind of *absolute nature*. It is the *absolute of a moment*—a sort of *temporal* absolute—that is erected for him by this means. Any speculation outside this *latest fact*, as it were, is forbidden him. What the instrument—the latest instrument, the instrument operating at that particular moment—reveals to him, is the whole of nature. All the "problems of life"—those "problems left over" that are the subject of philosophy, as James said—are idle or outside his recognized scope. It also turns philosophers out very much on a pattern, as anyone can ascertain for themselves. There is only *one* philosopher at a time, really—where there is only *one* nature, seen through the eye of *one* instrument, at *one* time.

If in every period these rigid inducements to orthodoxy had been present, then the "World-as-history" of Spengler would be true. Each time or each "Culture" would be an absolute. But this has not been the case. Thanks to science, our age is probably the first *absolute* one in that sense.

CHAPTER THREE

SPATIALIZATION AND CONCRETENESS

BERGSON'S DOCTRINE of Time is the creative source of the time-philosophy. It is he more than any other single figure that is responsible for the main intellectual characteristics of the world we live in, and the implicit debt of almost all contemporary philosophy to him is immense. Whitehead makes no bones about his debt to Bergson. "Bergson," he says, "introduced into philosophy the organic conceptions of physiological science." And he refers some pages before that (p. 207) to his own doctrine as "the organic theory of nature which I have been tentatively putting forward."

He associates James, Descartes and St. Thomas Aquinas as the most outstanding figures in European Philosophy, the last marking the close of the classical period, of course. But then he corrects this presumably tentative classification as follows:

"In many ways neither Descartes nor James were the most characteristic philosophers of their respective epochs. I should be disposed to ascribe these positions to Locke and to Bergson respectively. . . ." It is then that he says that Bergson "introduced into philosophy the organic conceptions of physiological science." And the "organic theory of nature" is what he, Whitehead, professes. So there is no ambiguity at all where the Bergson–Whitehead relationship is concerned. Alexander is more circumspect, but his affiliations are even more implicit in his doctrine.

The position of Bergson for these philosophers can be still better defined, perhaps, by the following quotation: "Descartes," Whitehead says, "in his distinction between time and duration, and in his way of grounding time upon motion, and in his close relation between matter and extension, anticipates, as far as it was possible at his epoch, modern notions suggested by the doctrine of relativity, or by some aspects of Bergson's doctrine of the generation of things." For them it must be merely "some aspects of Bergson's doctrine," etc. But when Descartes is being assigned his great rôle of innovation, his distinction between time and

158

duration carries us to Bergson; and (as you see above) as "modern notions" the doctrine of relativity has to be bracketed with Bergson's flux.

By students of philosophy Bergson is still read, but by no one else. Even by these he is read as little as possible, I should imagine. Until I began my scrutiny of the contemporary time-philosophy I knew him very little. But I rapidly found that if you wished to trace the history of that movement, more and more you were led to sources in Bergson's psychological time-conception, and his doctrine of a "creative" flux — the physiological, organic, view of nature.

At the present stage I will not go very far into this. But I will quote a passage from Bergson, which, if the reader is not familiar with his writing, will give a hint at least of what my argument signifies where it relates to him. It is a passage indexed as "the apogee of the sensible object":

For the ancients, indeed, time is theoretically negligible, because the duration of a thing only manifests the degradation of its essence; it is with this motionless essence that science has to deal. Change being only the effort of a form toward its own realization, the realization is all that it concerns us to know. No doubt the realization is never complete; it is this that ancient philosophy expresses by saying that we do not perceive form without matter. But if we consider the changing object at a certain essential moment, at its apogee, we may say that there it just touches its intelligible form. This intelligible form, this ideal, and, so to speak, limiting form, our science seizes upon. And possessing in this the gold-piece, it holds eminently the small money, which we call becoming or change. This change is less than being. The knowledge that would take it for object, supposing such knowledge were possible, would be less than science.

But, for a science that places all the moments of time in the same rank, that admits no essential moment, no culminating point, no apogee, change is no longer a diminution of essence, duration is not a dilution of eternity.

Time, on the physical side, and apart from its discrimination, in the hands of Bergson, into mental time and mathematical time, is merely change or movement. An object (for ancient philosophy, in the account given above by Bergson) realizes itself, working up to a climax, then it disintegrates. It is its apogee or perfection that is *it*, for classical science. It is the rounded *thing* of common-sense.

Eternity is, for classical science, registered in those moments, or in those things. With this Bergson contrasts that other science that has no favoured moments, peaks, objects, or locations. An *egalitarian science*, as it were, is the science of his preference, which recognizes no "objects," that substitutes for them a cluster of "events" or of perspectives, which shade off into each other and into other objects, to infinity. Reality is where things run into each other, in that flux, not where they stand out in a discrete "concreteness."

The greater part of Professor Whitehead's analysis, in his *Science and the Modern World*, turns on what, as he starts by announcing, was the main objective of Bergson's criticism. Bergson had said that the intellect "spatialized" things. It was that "spatialization" that the doctrinaire of motion and of mental "time" attacked. It is that, too, that Whitehead is busy confuting; only, he acquits the intellect of this villainy, where Bergson pursues it with his hatred and abuse. For this exoneration Whitehead invents an argument which he calls the "Fallacy of Misplaced Concreteness." This phrase describes very well the compromise that it sets out to provide. He wishes to be concrete at once and yet not concrete. He wishes to use, subjugate, invest and possess the concrete, in the interests of the abstract: and when so clothed, in his full panoply of "concreteness," to deliver an attack upon another sort of "abstract" that he does not like. The analysis of the contemporary time-philosophy is so fanatically directed to disintegrate and to banish the bogey of "concreteness," that it would be impossible not to receive the impression of a peculiar hostility to "the concrete," in its most inclusive sense, in favour of something abstract and mental, even if that doctrine did not express itself so often in almost violent terms of our "spatializing" habits.

Behind all the various pictures or notions of the contemporary schools which we shall henceforth be examining — always simplifying those notions as far as that is possible, and avoiding such detail as, in such a comprehensive survey, would make our exposition increasingly intricate and perhaps meaningless to the general reader — there is a fundamental issue. Or rather, intricate as the overgrowth of theory and technical detail is, there is one issue more than another that is fundamental. It can be described as the problem of the "abstract" versus the "concrete" at the base of the various world-pictures to be discussed. For what I have called the time-school, time and change are the ultimate reality.

They are *the abstract school*, it could be said. And almost every contemporary philosopher of any prominence may, in the really important issues, be included in that great school (if we except the thomistic theologian, still vigorous, but, I do not think, to be classed as a serious speculative "opposition").

So, under whatever form it takes, the position we are attacking is the *abstract* one, as against the *concrete* of, say, such an "idealism" as that of Berkeley, Bradley or Bosanquet. I am afraid that stated in that way this will be without very much meaning to the general reader. If he attends to it at all, he will perhaps think that it is a strange thing that "absolute idealism" should stand for the *concrete*, the *non-abstract*, whereas contemporary thought, which is surely highly "realistic" and positivist, should stand for the *abstract* or the *non-concrete*. If I added, as is indeed the case, that such an extreme idealist doctrine as that of Berkeley, far more even than the sceptical idealism of Bradley, stood even fanatically for the *concrete*, as against the *abstract*, the reader who had not given much attention to philosophy would be completely mystified, no doubt, as indeed Berkeley foresaw would be the case when he first launched his doctrine. But that is a paradox that it is extremely important to lay hold of at the outset.

The particular tendencies to express which the term *phenomenalism* has been coined, or indeed all the various different types of effort to discover a scientific absolute — *something* that could be shown to be objective and self-existent, have resulted in the production of a new race of *things-in-themselves*, or noumena, which have all been invented to *physical ends*, to commence with, and are on the other hand exceedingly abstract and, according to the general use of the term, non-physical. The "physical" or "scientific object" of the time-science is very unlike anything, that is, that we customarily mean by "physical." The creation of these exceedingly abstract transcendent entities has observed universally the condition of a suppression of the traditional subject or mind. This absolute is a "creative" evolutionist object. The saying that "extremes meet" has been verified in these transactions: for the search for this hardest, firmest, coldest of philosopher's stones, has, on some sides, resulted in a volatilization which is at least the characteristic result, most people would say, of any teaching of "idealism." Thought or perception has tended to be entirely cut off from this new absolute. We, the

forlorn *subjects* of this objective drama, and all our phantasmagoria of quality and sense, are left suspended nowhere, high and
dry in a No Man's Land of "common-sense": or left turning in
our circular, many-coloured, primitively furnished, maze. The
reality has been pushed infinitely far away, and the severance
between it and us is complete. Both we and it have become
abstractions, while between us flourish phantasmally the scenes
of the visible world. There is nothing *concrete* left, either on one
side or on the other.

I shall leave the final elucidation of this rough statement until
the conclusion of my essay: but, as we go along, its meaning will,
I hope, gradually unfold itself in the most concrete manner possible. All that I suggest should be borne in mind is that, *with the
"realists" with whom we shall be dealing, their "real" is the opposite of the concrete.* And the position from which we are conducting this analysis — and which would come under some heading
of "idealism" — is in favour of a conception of reality that is as
concrete as theirs is abstract.

A useful figure under which to imagine this temporalizing process of "intensive abstraction" would be to consider it as an act
of bringing *the dead* to life. That is indeed the miracle that is
contemplated. It is still matter, a *materia prima*, what common-
sense regards as the "dead" setting for our organic life, about which
the main dispute is gathered. The "materialist" of Berkeley's time
believed firmly that *dead* nature, or matter, was *real*. The materialist of today is still obsessed with the wish to make this dead
matter *real*: only he is more subtle, and he knows very well that
it cannot be "real" if it remains "dead" and "matter." So he brings
it to life, by pumping it full of "time," until it is a quicksilver
beneath his hand. Having done this, he proceeds to attempt its
fixation, somehow and at some point, into an objective absolute:
and (seeing the ferment that has then resulted from the time-
treatment) that is no easy matter.

The kind of objection that has been brought against the first
draft of my essay (directed to establishing a new position contradicting the abstract, the "time," view) was that, as my statement then stood, I seemed to wish to deny to the scientist his
"scientific object"; and to wish him, in the teeth of his truth-telling
instruments, to attach himself to my "art object," as it might be
called, or to some form of the familiar thing of our perceptual
experience. But that was certainly not my meaning, though in

the brief preliminary statement I did, I feel, give some ground for that view.

I will clear up that difficulty a little before proceeding. As regards the series of pictures offered by any given "object" or "quality-group," or whatever you like to call it, those pictures have each *truths* and *uses* attached to them. As pictures, if you place them in a row, one beside the other, they differ beyond recognition. The "scientific object" which, in our perceptual world, is a chair, for example, bears no resemblance at all to a common or garden chair. Both thought and perception tend to be shorn away in favour of this most abstract of our series of entities. And the reality is to be sought at its unqualitied end. But, further, it is an *absolute* reality that is said to be discovered there, of an objective order, the equal of the perceiving mind. But this ultimate scientific object is not the traditional "materialist" object of a century ago. And it is actually made to act as a "spirit" to the concrete reality at the qualitied end.

What we call "dead" nature, or matter, is, according to this *abstract* doctrine, the work of the intellect. The intellect is responsible for all "deadness." But the external world is not really "dead" (it goes on to tell us), but alive — quite as alive as, if not rather more so than, the "mind." Behind the perceptual façade, or beneath the inanimate carapace, is an *organic* existence. Or perhaps the shell is ours. At all events, the real everyday world is nothing but a shell, or a kind of nothing.

The superior reality of this most abstract of the processes, or pictures of the reality, to which science enables us to reach, is what is here denied. The more abstract the less real, we would say, since however abstract, it is still an abstraction from what is dead. Into both the dead shell and the mechanical laws that obtain throughout "matter," and which are for us subjective appearances, we wish to put no more "reality" metaphysically, and as explanation of the world, than nature has provided it with. We experience no desire to bring it to life. So it is not as pure science (with all its great possible usefulness) that we are attacking these abstractions.

But science is metaphysical (today it has once more become fully metaphysical). "The more comprehensive a science becomes," Professor Alexander writes, "the closer it comes to philosophy, so that it may become difficult to say where the science leaves off and philosophy begins. . . . The highest generalizations in biology, in chemistry and physics, [illustrate this]."

Well, then, the "scientific object" becomes inevitably in due course "a metaphysical object." The point-instants of relativist philosophy — as interpreted by the philosophers Whitehead or Alexander — are as metaphysical as the "points métaphysiques" of Leibniz. Hence it is not *science* that I am criticizing, but metaphysics, if anything.

It was *abstraction*, Berkeley said — the admission of inferences and fictions of the mind upon an equality with perception — that caused men to believe in the reality of the external world. So the sign-world of verbal fiction established a competitive reality outside us: and the sign-world of mathematics, developing out of the abstraction of verbalism, can only reinforce that process. The berkeleyan doctrine, ideally, allowed no inference at all. You took your personal "external world" of handy and customary objects about with you on your back, as it were, or in your head, and when you needed it, spread it out or ran it up. But some inferential or sign-world is necessary; and indeed it is impossible in practice to say where "abstraction" begins and "concreteness" leaves off. Berkeley's extremism is, however, in keeping with his insistence upon the particular.

To the wonderfully fertile discussions of Berkeley I shall return in my concluding chapter, at the end of this book. Meantime there is an important matter in which we can make use of his teaching here. It is this. Berkeley was much concerned to destroy the myth of the superiority of the "abstract" over the immediate and individual. With us exactly the same preoccupation must occur, in the case of the advertisement of the mental at the expense of the concrete. That particular snobbery is a source of endless confusions, upon which such a mind as Bergson's, or Alexander's, is not slow to seize. It is exceedingly easy to confute, if the true values of "mental" and "concrete" as they emerge in the time-philosophy are attended to. This is what Berkeley (*Principles of Human Knowledge*) says on the subject as it concerned his doctrine, and the prejudices of his time:

I proceed to examine what can be alleged in defence of the doctrine of abstraction, and try if I can discover what it is that inclines the men of speculation to embrace an opinion so remote from common-sense. . . . [Locke] has given it very much countenance by seeming to think the having abstract general ideas is what puts the widest difference in point of understanding betwixt man and beast. "The having of general ideas," saith he, "is that that puts a perfect distinction between man and brutes, and is an excellency which the faculties of brutes do by no means attain unto. For it is evident we observe no footsteps in them of making use of general signs for universal ideas," [etc.] (*Essay on Human Understanding*, Book II, chap. xi, sects. 10, 11.)

Or, again, quoting Locke:

Abstract ideas are not so obvious or easy to children or the yet unexercised mind as particular ones. If they seem so to grown men, it is only because by constant and familiar use they are made so. For when we nicely reflect upon them, we shall find that general ideas are fictions and contrivances of the mind, that carry difficulty with them. . . . For example, does it not require some pains and skill to form the general idea of a triangle? [etc.] (Book IV, chap. vii, sect. 9.)

In short, Berkeley was busy attempting to dispose of that falsely founded snobbery where "the abstract" was concerned. It was a very paradoxical and difficult attempt: for any abstract notion does always seem to the general run of people as very much more important and clever than any form of concrete apprehension, so to reverse this opinion cannot be an easy task. Berkeley, of course, agrees that "all knowledge and demonstration are about universal notions"; but what he disputes is that these notions are "formed by abstraction." Universality, he says, consists *not* in "the absolute, positive nature or conception of being anything, but in the *relation* it bears to the particulars signified or represented by it."

Now, at first sight the particular snobbery set in motion by such a doctrine as that of Bergson, Alexander or Whitehead will seem a different, or in some respects an opposite, one to the snobbery Berkeley in the above passage is seen combating. The doctrine of Bergson, Alexander or Whitehead is labelled "organic": and its advertisement is that it is *life*, as contrasted with the mechanical "deadness" of materialist science. Unless you pay some attention to the ideas involved, therefore, you might mistake Berkeley's appeal to "common-sense," to the vivid and "individual," for a similar movement to that of the evolutionist philosophers.

The "organic" life-doctrine of the time-philosophy, advertising itself as the enemy of "materialism" or of matter, of all that is too "concrete," makes upon the surface, and with some speciousness, if not looked at too closely, a considerable sentimental appeal. It is an appeal *away from* "materialism or matter," in the direction of "life" and "mind." And it is not the easiest thing in the world to show the quite uninitiated what a false view of the position that appeal involves.

They are not, however, "idealistic," or anything of that sort. The appeal is skilfully handled and is often insisted upon. Yet there is no serious question at all that on the score of *life-value*, and as far as the advertisement of this particular warm and, with Bergson, ecstatic, appeal is concerned, the boot should be on the other leg. Whitehead is, I believe, an *honest* sentimentalist of the "radical" english-schoolmaster type. But Bergson, of course, is the perfect philosophic ruffian, of the darkest and most forbidding description: and he pulls every emotional lever on which he can lay his hands.

From a popular point of view, then, the main feature of the space-time doctrines (and with Bergson it was precisely the same thing) is that they offer, with the gestures of a saviour, *something* (that they call "organism," and that they assure us tallies with the great theory of Evolution—just to cheer us up!)—something *alive*, in place of "mechanism": "organism" in place of "matter." But the more you examine them (and the same applies to the doctrines of Bergson), the more you will feel that you are being fooled. For what the *benefit* to you, in this famous change from matter to mind, from "matter" to "organism," is going to be, it is very difficult to discover. For it is not *you* who become "organic"; *you* have been organic all along, no one has ever questioned that. It is your tables and chairs, in a pseudo-leibnizian animism, not you, that are to become "organic." As Professor Whitehead puts it, "the things experienced and the cognisant subject, enter into the common world on equal terms." But something *does* happen to you as well—the "you" that is the counterpart of what formerly has been for you a material object. You become no longer one, but many. What you pay for the pantheistic immanent oneness of "creative," "evolutionary" substance, into which you are invited to merge, is that you become a phalanstery of selves. The old objection to any pantheism, that it banishes individuality and is not good for the self, comes out more strongly than ever in the teaching of "space-time." So, as you proceed in your examination of these doctrines, it becomes more and more evident that, although it is by no means clear that you gain anything (except a great many fine phrases and exalted, mystical assurances of "cosmic" advantages), it is very clear what you *lose.* By this proposed transfer from the beautiful *objective*, *material* world of common-sense, over to the "organic" world of chronological mentalism, you lose not only the clearness of outline, the static beauty, of the things you commonly apprehend; you lose also the clearness of outline of your own individuality which apprehends them. You are told by Professor Whitehead that for the charm of the world of classical common-sense, the ordered and human world, you should substitute the *naïveté* of the romantic nature-poet. (The Child, that is, comes into this scheme of things, as is natural. It would be surprising if *naïveté* were not called in to assist, with its sentimental blandishments.) Apart from anything else, you would be genuinely "naïf," however, to fall in with these suggestions.

What is "eternal" for Professor Whitehead? The answer should be very significant; and indeed his answer reveals the very heart of all this type of thought. For him "eternality" is a quality of the temporal *real*. The abstraction, "colour," for instance, is, for him, eternal. Nothing that *it colours* is eternal, nor apparently suggests eternity to him. Just colour is *the eternal*; not its meaning or interpretation, but it, for this sensationalist philosopher.

There is yet a third fact to be placed [beside change and endurance, namely] — *eternality*, I will call it. The mountain endures. But when after ages it has been worn away, it has gone. If a replica arises, it is yet a new mountain. *A colour is eternal. It haunts time like a spirit. It comes and it goes. But where it comes it is the same colour. It neither survives nor does it live. It appears when it is wanted.* The mountain has to time and space a different relation from that which colour has.

So the equivalent to the "eternal forms" for Professor Whitehead are such things as "the colour green" or "dove-grey" or "crimson." That is certainly *abstract* enough! It disposes effectively of the notion of eternity as a thing in which we need be interested.

The "eternality" of Professor Whitehead is, however, also "externality" — the only objective, *material* thing at all. "The doctrine I am maintaining," he writes, in his *Science and the Modern World*, "is that the whole concept of materialism only applies to very abstract entities, the products of logical discernment." The only kind of thing that can be described as "matter," then, is such a thing as his "eternal" entity colour. A colour is eternal. "It haunts time like a spirit." Is it not strange that the only sort of "material" thing that Professor Whitehead will allow should remind him of a *spirit*? Yet it does; and that use of words is not without significance, nor a slip of the pen. Such "abstract entities" *are* the nearest approach to "spirit" in his system — such things as those eternal colours that come and go, always self-identical, never changing, haunting the mountain-side, or any other object, "like a spirit."

We know now what the only intelligible meaning of "matter" is for this doctrine. Let us next turn to "organism," since it is announced as a doctrine of "organism," as opposed to "materialism." How would you like to be the colour dove-grey, or the colour crimson? — (for it is to *you* that the appeal against "matter" is being made, in favour of "organism" or of abstraction). Not much, I suppose; it is scarcely a thing that, as an alternative to your personal life, you would trouble a great deal about. But an "organism" you are. That should be rather more interesting.

"The question is, can we define an organism without recurrence to the concept of matter . . . ?" That is the capital question, Professor Whitehead announces. And he decides, of course, that we can.

As an "organism" you do not become a thing-in-itself like those very abstract entities, or like the fundamental point-instant of space-time. You are not a self-existent entity: but provision is made for you, and you become, with some pride, a "thing-for-its-own-sake." I will now quote to show how the "thing-for-its-own-sake" comes about in Whitehead's system. What is it that makes value? he asks. ("Value," we have been told, is merely significance, a similar thing to what is commonly meant by "poetry.") What is it that results in a "real togetherness" in a pattern (which, consequently, excludes other entities for a certain time)? The importance or *"value"* of the new *pattern-thing* lies in its intrinsic essence. What is that?

Empirical observation shows that it is the property which we may call indifferently *retention, endurance* or *reiteration*. This property amounts to the recovery, on behalf of value amid the transitoriness of reality, of the self-identity which is also enjoyed by the primary eternal objects. The reiteration of a particular shape (or formation) occurs when the event as a whole repeats some shape which is also exhibited by each one of a succession of its parts. Thus, however you analyse the event according to the flux of its parts through time, there is the same *thing-for-its-own-sake* standing before you. Thus the event, in its own intrinsic reality, mirrors in itself, as derived from its own parts, aspects of the same patterned value, as it realizes it in its complete self.

To repeat certain mannerisms—which others recognize as "you," and without which they would be at a loss to distinguish you from another—that is to possess something in a very small way like the "eternality" of a colour, is it not? Your personality is like a colour or a smell; only, unlike things that have "eternality," you die. Just as the colour keeps on turning up when wanted, for ever and ever, so *you* keep on turning up, every morning, for a stated period. Then, one fine day, you do not turn up: and you never turn up again. For you are only a "thing-for-its-own-sake," not a "thing-in-itself." Still, "this property amounts to the recovery, on behalf of value" (you are "value") "amid the transitoriness of reality, of the self-identity which is also enjoyed by the primary eternal objects." So, in your perishable category, you do, for a spell, play at being the colour or the perfume.

You now see where the "organism" comes in. But you must not run away with the idea that "organism" is going to deliver you from *mechanism*—though it may enable you, for a brief period, to play at being "matter."

You may by this time have got rather confused as to what advantage precisely you are ultimately to derive from having discarded the concept "matter." For first you learnt that "matter" was like a spirit, whereas, of course, you knew that Professor Whitehead would never describe you as being "like a spirit." And then you found that, thanks to "organism," you became a sort of ephemeral understudy of "matter"—you "recovered," thanks to organism—which turned out to be a sort of "art-for-art's-sake" for the plain man, where his own sweet self was the "art"—some of the self-identity "enjoyed by the primary eternal objects" (the colours dove-grey or carmine, for instance). All this admittedly is puzzling and perhaps at first a little upsetting. But, high as our hopes still are, do not let us imagine that "mechanism"—what is so scorned and disliked by Bergson, Alexander, Whitehead, etc.—has been given the go-by.

"I would term the doctrine of these lectures [*Science and the Modern World*] the theory of *organic mechanism*." "That is not, Professor Whitehead, a very agreeable title," you might mutter at this point; "and further, sir, it is not exactly what I had been led to expect. Why should 'mechanism' come into it? *Organism*— as against mere 'matter': I should stand behind you, enthusiastically, if it were 'organism.' But why 'mechanism'?" And Professor Whitehead might reply, if he heard you, "Because, my little man, organism *is* mechanical: that is, after all, what it means!" That would of course be rather depressing.

However, by this time your emotionality will have evaporated. So let us look at this doctrine of Time reasonably, forgiving its supporters all the slight deception practised upon us. That there must be much more *mechanism* in the "organic" picture than there is in the "material" picture should have been obvious all along. For locomotion and movement, "organism" in the making, or *becoming*, not *become*, what is that but a machine? Indeed, since it is a function, not anything describable as a thing, it is a system or process and essentially *mechanistic*. And again, movement, or things apprehended in movement, are very much more abstract than are static things. The object of contemplation is less abstract, evidently, than the object of experience or the objective of action. To put this in another way, *time is more abstract than space*. But the process of *despatialization*, undertaken by Bergson and carried on by the philosophers we are considering, denies any "concreteness," except such as can be obtained from a time-pattern, like the structure of a piece of music. But it can only be apprehended as music can be apprehended, in *time* — not in space. It requires movement, as well as duration, to unfold itself. There is no one instant at which it can be apprehended in its totality; you have to take it in bit by bit, you have to *live* it, and its pattern will unfold as a melody unfolds itself.

Compare in this connection any two characteristic masterpieces from the arts respectively of music and of painting — a statue, say the Colleoni, and a piece of music, say a Beethoven quartet. You move round the statue, but it is always there in its entirety before you: whereas the piece of music moves through you, as it were. The difference in the two arts is evident at once, and the different faculties that come into play in the one and the other. When you are half-way through the piece of music, or it is half-way through you, if you did not *remember* what you had just heard you would be in the position of a clock ticking its minutes, all the other ticks except the present one no longer existing: so it would be with the notes. You have to live the music in some sense, in contrast to your response to the statue.

Supposing you could not see the statue *all at once*. Let us suppose that you were blind, and had to feel your way all over the statue, bearing in your mind all the details you had felt since you first touched it; there would be some slight analogy in that to what happens in listening to music. Certain rhythms and times unroll themselves in your brain, fixed for a brief period as the piece goes on acccumulating. These contrasts between the two arts have often been analysed, and I need not consider them further. I will merely resume the contrast as follows.

In the case of the music there is no concrete shape existing altogether, once and for all, or *spatially*. There is a shape, an organic completion, but it is a pure creation of *time*. It cannot spatialize itself. The representation goes on inside your mind, in making use of your memory. Its concreteness is not objective but subjective.

Without going further into this at the moment, all that it is necessary to say is that something resembling this pattern of the piece of music, existing ideally in the memory, but not susceptible of spatialization—having its being as a creature of Time—is the *time-object*, as it could be called, which is the sort of "object" that the time-philosophers contemplate. It is more "concrete" in a sense, since it has to be *lived*. *It has to be subject and object at once.* Its peculiarity is that it has to be *felt*—it is an *emotional object* as well as a *time-object*: there is an appreciable visceral and nerve disturbance accompanying the music, none or very little with the object that is an image. The statue, on the other hand, could be described as an *intellectual-object*.

Now if there is some advantage, as between one and the other of these objects, on the principle of the snobberies that, as we have seen, are generally invoked, it is difficult to see how the *musical object* can claim an advantage over the *visual object*. I am, in this particular case, a partisan witness. But I do not think that a quite unprejudiced onlooker would come to a different conclusion; unless he enjoyed so much having his bowels stimulated and his heart set throbbing by the accords of the musical object (but on the other hand, rather resented the calm of the sculptor's contemplative dream), that he cast his vote for the musical object, in which case naturally he would have been no longer unpartisan.

These illustrations should serve to direct the reader's understanding to the nature of the transformation that is proposed by time-philosophy in our conception of the object, and in our attitude to "the concrete." I do not say that these analogies should be pressed too hard, but the "musical" versus "plastic" is a useful *point d'appui* in arriving at an understanding of the theory. But however that may be, it is the transformation of a

space-reality into a time-reality that is involved—that is the trick
of the time-doctrine that it is important to grasp.

Dispersal and transformation of a space-phenomenon into a
time-phenomenon throughout everything—that is the trick of this
doctrine. Pattern, with its temporal multiplicity, and its *chronologic* depth, is to be substituted for the *thing*, with its one time,
and its *spatial* depth. A crowd of hurrying shapes, a temporal
collectivity, is to be put in the place of the single object of what
it hostilely indicates as the "spatializing" mind. The new dimension introduced is the variable mental dimension of time. So the
notion of the transformed "object" offered us by this doctrine is
plainly in the nature of a "futurist" picture, like a running dog
with a hundred legs and a dozen backs and heads. In place of
the characteristic static "form" of greek Philosophy, you have a
series, a group, or, as Professor Whitehead says, a *reiteration*.
In place of a "form" you have a "formation"—as it is characteristically called—a repetition of a particular shape; you have a
battalion of forms in place of one form. In your turn, "you"
become the series of your temporal repetitions; you are no longer
a centralized self, but a spun-out, strung-along series, a pattern-
of-a-self, depending like the musical composition upon time; an
object, too, always in the making, who *are* your states. So you
are a *history*: there must be no Present for you. You are an
historical object, since your mental or time-life has been as it were
objectified. The valuable advantages of being a "subject" will
perhaps scarcely be understood by the race of *historical objects*
that may be expected to ensue.

Since the one mind, in this issue, can be called a "spatializing"
mind, or a "space mind," there can be no objection to the other
sort of mind being called a *time-mind*. That is a better description of it than a *space-time mind* would be.

Reverting to the specific advertisement-value of the "organic"
theory, that advertisement should be regarded only as bluff. The
"mechanism" that, along with "matter," is to be combated, is
transferred into another category, merely—and for us a much
less comfortable one.

We find in the eighteenth century Paley's famous argument, that
mechanism presupposes a god who is the author of nature. But even
before Paley put the argument into its final form, Hume had written
the retort, that the god whom you will find will be the sort of god who
makes that mechanism. In other words, that mechanism can, at most,

presuppose a mechanic, and not merely *a* mechanic, but *its* mechanic. The only way of mitigating mechanism is by the discovery that it is not mechanism. (*Science and the Modern World.*)

The way to discover that it is not mechanism, however, is certainly not to pass over merely to a doctrine of "organic mechanism." All that the "organic mechanism" tells you is that *the machine is alive* — which is not such an agreeable belief, constituted as we are, as to believe that it is partially inert. It is preferable to believe that our tables and chairs are *matter*, than to believe them animated in some way, on the face of it. And, secondly, it informs you that *the machine (very slowly) transforms itself.* But that is obvious, and required no "organic" theorist to show it to us.

Everywhere the *snobbery of scale* is employed to drive home these doctrines. All recorded human history is *merely a ripple* on the immense ocean of being, etc., we are assured. And feeling very, very small indeed, after that, in the ensuing discouragement almost *any* "truth" can be put across. This browbeating by means of *scale*, the immensity of light-years, of geological epochs, of massed constellations and universes — that associated with ecstatic cosmic raptures — all the sickly flattery of the *élan vital* type of optimism — is how, on the emotional, propagandist side, the thing is done.

But Professor Whitehead commiserates with those figures of the Past oppressed by "materialism," and denied such help as his. Tennyson is dragged out and comforted publicly. Tennyson is evidently perplexed and appalled by the "materialist" picture of natural science. "It is the problem of mechanism which appals him."

"The stars," she whispers, "blindly run."

"This line," Whitehead goes on, "states starkly the whole philosophic problem implicit in the poem. Each molecule *blindly runs.*" Tennyson is forever consoled by being assured that, although it is true that the molecule *blindly runs* (as he put it), nevertheless it *runs according to a pattern.* (For instance: "the electron blindly runs either within or without the body; but it runs within the body in accordance with its character within the body; that is to say, in accordance with the original plan of the body, and this plan includes the mental state." The body and mind, in their turn, run blindly, too, within a still larger organism;

and so on. This may be true; but it is difficult to see how it is cheerful.) So the molecule is still a blind mouse, but it runs in the same way as a gigantic mouse which is its pattern. Happy little mouse! And (after hearing this) happy-ever-afterwards would, of course, Lord Tennyson be, if this good news could reach him. Or so Professor Whitehead thinks.

"In the present lecture," Professor Whitehead announces, "I propose . . . to consider how the concrete educated thought of men has viewed the opposition of mechanism and organism." But there is, as I have indicated, no opposition, in reality. The "organism" of Bergson, Whitehead or Alexander is perfectly *mechanical* — or at all events what " the thought of educated men" would term "mechanical." And it is far more "materialistic" (as the "thought of educated men" understands that word) than is the philosophy of Plato or Aristotle.

In handing the "secondary" qualities back to nature, Professor Whitehead is supposed to be cheering up nature and us at the same time. Shelley is called in as a witness.

Now the poet [Shelley], so sympathetic with science, so absorbed in its ideas, can simply make nothing of the doctrine of secondary qualities which is fundamental to its concepts. For Shelley nature retains its beauty and its colour. *Shelley's nature is in its essence a nature of organisms.*

The "science" of Shelley's day was a very different thing from the "science" of Professor Whitehead, for instance. And it cannot be enough insisted upon that a problem exists for everybody in this transformation of "science" of which they seem totally unaware. The "science" that today mixes the "secondary qualities" into the external world, is the same science that is mixing Time into it — "saturating" it with Time, as Alexander says. Everything which contributed to the isolation of "mind" as contrasted with "matter," or that tended to show "matter" to be a creation of "mind," has been put back where it *looks* as though it is. Mind has, in short, been moved into what was "matter" for the man-of-science of Shelley's day; and "matter" on its side has been removed into another dimension, and quite out of sight and out of reach; where, with Alexander, as "space-time" it becomes a sort of god. And the philosophy that presides at these various transformations has for its watchword something like *Down with matter!* and is consistently understood to be attacking the position of "materialism." It is highly important to understand the ins and outs of these significant arrangements.

What, in a few words, is contemplated by time-doctrine is this. Traditional "modern science" took all the heavily qualitied meaning out of nature — scraped off the colour, took away the smell, and otherwise denuded it. It treated it as (1) dead and (2) timeless. The main thing about this "dead" nature was that it is impossible to conceive it as *acting*, as possessed of any agent principle whatever. That is the guarantee, as it were, of its *unreality*; nothing so thoroughly as that secures the ascendancy of "the mind"; that "mind" that so entranced, as Whitehead says, the "century of genius," as he calls it, and which so disgusts and enrages the philosopher of the present time — a time which is scarcely likely to be described in the future as an age "of genius." Where Berkeley is proving that there is "no idea of spirit" — that there is no *image* of spirit or mind, that it is impossible to represent it objectively — he writes:

There can be no idea formed of a soul or spirit: for all ideas whatever, being passive and inert, . . . they cannot represent unto us, by way of image or likeness, that which acts. . . . Such is the nature of spirit, or that which acts, that it cannot be of itself perceived, but only by the effects which it produceth.

In this account, spirit *is* its *effects*. It is impossible to imagine or to form an image, of *a cause*. For Berkeley the causative principle was mind: for the time-philosophy it is some "very abstract entity" which is all that can truly be termed "matter."

I will quote another passage from Berkeley to make this point clearer, italicizing in some places:

All our ideas, sensations, or *the things which we perceive . . . are visibly inactive*; there is nothing of power or agency included in them. So that one idea or object of thought cannot produce, or make any alteration in, another. . . . A little attention will discover to us that *the very being of an idea implies passiveness and inertness . . .*

The "matter" of the typical man-of-science contemporary with Shelley was an *inert* and *passive* material. It was the laws of these "ideas" that he studied. It was perfectly plain that this material of his was not a real one in any absolute sense, but a convention. However, the researches of the man-of-science into the laws of "matter" had proverbially valuable results. He treated this "matter" of his as essentially a system of *effects*, and entirely left out of count all questions of a cause. Such a man-of-science, if rather a dry stick, was a respectable figure who did no direct harm to anybody, and was able, even, to do the richer members of the community — manufacturers, steamship owners, armament makers and so forth — a great deal of good. They formed a very high opinion of science and of "matter": and by means of their organs of publicity taught everybody else to value "science" highly, for the power it gave a ruling caste over its fellow-men (interpreted in the science-tract or the daily paper as "man's power over nature"). These activities continue as before. The theories of Einstein, for instance, have no immediate effect on the bank-balance of anybody. "Matter" and "mechanism" is still in full swing, for all the practical purposes of life. But theoretically science has become more ambitious. It has cut "matter" up into different categories; there is a theoretic "matter," there is the old "dead" scientific one, and several others: and in spite of all assurances to the contrary, it has introduced an *absolute* into the nature beneath its control (into its theoretic, not its practical, department).

Whitehead's or Alexander's "organic" nature is an absolute. Time and change are absolute; reality is, in its very essence, *historical*. The pattern that constitutes an organism — the new object — is the soul of the qualitied complex, and is the new "object." And what was "the spirit" for Berkeley (which could not "be of itself perceived") has turned from a subject into an object.

The most significant thing in the whole of the book from which I have been quoting, is the fact that Professor Whitehead, to illustrate his doctrine, goes to the poets of the *Romantic Reaction* — the title of his fifth chapter, and perhaps the best key to all this philosophy. *Just as we have seen Professor Alexander going to the sculpture of Rodin for support and illustration, so Professor Whitehead makes his way to the Romantic Reaction.* In the poets that came out of the nature-sentiment of Rousseau, and the politics of the French Revolution, Professor Whitehead, quite correctly, finds his analogies.

What, finally, the contemporary intelligence does not seem to have grasped is that the whole of this movement from Bergson to the philosophers who are interpreting Relativity, is *romantic*, with all that that word conveys in its most florid, unreal, inflated, self-deceiving connotation. As much as Montessori and her system are they in the tradition of Émile — children of Nature.

All their thought is weighted and drugged with an intense vehement unreality.

So these philosophers are busy disintegrating for us our public material paradise, and propose to give us in exchange the dark and feverish confusion of their "mental" truth, no longer confined to the units of the organic world, but released into everything. That this concrete and "material" world — which is all that is *common* to us, and which is therefore justly named the "world of common-sense," as opposed to the "mental" world — is a truly fantastic paradise, they are careful not to say. A person who believes in this concrete world is a "materialist" — a word conveying to the popular mind the very opposite of what here it describes.

The material world that the human intellect has created is still there, of course: but as it is a creation of our minds, it will no doubt be found that we can even physically disintegrate it. Already for the time-initiate it is getting a fluid, or flabby, texture and appearance. How would their ingenuity serve them, however, if these destroyers had to *create* the world of material beauty and order, as it appears to the senses we inherit from our marvellous ancestry? The thought alone of the genius that would be required to accomplish that should show us the true nature of the destructive enterprise in question. The world of classical "common-sense" — the world of the Greek, the world of the Schoolman — is the world of nature, too, and is a very ancient one. All the health and sanity that we have left belongs to that world, and its forms and impulses. It is such a tremendous power that nothing can ever break it down permanently. But today the issue, more dramatically than at any other possible point in history (owing to the situation created by the inventions of our science), is between that nature or some development of it on the one side, and upon the other those forces represented by the philosophy of Time. What is suggested here is that, in such a crisis, all the weight of our intelligence should be thrown into the scales representing our deepest instincts.

CHAPTER FOUR

PURE POETRY AND PURE MAGIC

WHAT I SHALL HAVE to say in this chapter would require very much more space than I can spare to demonstrate adequately, and to be certain that I had left no openings for grave misunderstandings. The complexity of the subject results in its bristling with traps. Shortly I propose to return to it; but with a little goodwill I hope that this mere outline will serve for the purpose of this essay.

If a definition were attempted of the position of literature among the arts, it would turn out to be in some sense a kind of half-way house. A piece of prose or poetry is not music; it does not, on the other hand, convey images with the definiteness of the plastic or graphic arts; it is less abstract than architecture, yet less defined; it is not so static as some, but more static than others.

That Professor Whitehead's war upon *clear ideas* is by no means new; that, as a result of Bergson's "anti-intellectualist" analysis, it had long been tabled in many different activities, and often has been heatedly discussed, I need not insist. Professor Whitehead, in his book (the epigraph of this essay could also be placed at the head of *Science and the Modern World*), has taken Science deliberately over into the neighbouring fields of the arts, and drawn from them his main inspiration, and illustrations. That is a gesture of considerable significance as his more intelligent critics (all favourable to him, of course, for such a writer as Professor Whitehead has no opposition at all) were not slow to notice. But the battle of the *clear idea* against the *cloudy idea* — or, if you like, the *static idea* against the *dynamic idea* — is a commonplace of continental criticism, especially since the overthrow of Bergson. (Before that Bergson had it all his own way, and for a considerable time no *clear idea* dare lift its head, or indeed, anything static at all.)

If anyone should wish to inform himself about the contemporary phases of that battle, they could not do better than read a book that has recently appeared called *La Poésie Pure* (published by Bernard Grasset, Paris, 1926). It is a series of discourses by two gentlemen, Henri Brémond and Robert Souza. I am not very conversant with the ins and outs of the literary world in Paris, but I imagine that M. Brémond, with his academic position, must represent the *quartier général* of critical mysticism. It is at all events from the extreme position of a mystical bergsonism that he speaks.

On the first page of M. Brémond's book, he immediately refers the reader to *Studies in the Genesis of Romantic Theory in the Eighteenth Century*, by J. G. Robertson; just in the same way, and of course on the same errand, as Professor Whitehead when he takes you to the poets of the *Romantic Revival*, or Alexander when he refers you to the sculpture of Rodin. Poetry is for him "this confused, massive experience, inaccessible to distinct consciousness." For all that is *distinct*, or *clear*, he has the same implacable aversion as has Professor Whitehead. This is how he contrasts Poetry and Prose—though he does not exclude Prose, finally, from mystic honours, nor deny it the title of "Poetry," provided it is vague enough.

Enveloping magic, as the mystics say, and which invites us to quietude, when our only duty is to abandon ourselves, but actively, to one greater and better than ourselves. Prose—a vivid and leaping phosphorescence which *draws us out of ourselves*. Poetry, *a summons from within*, a confused weight, said Wordsworth, a sacred heat, said Keats, a weight of immortality upon the heart; *an awful warmth about my heart, like a load of immortality. Amor, Pondus.*—That weight, where else does it wish to urge us except towards those august retreats, where we are expected, to which we are called, by a superhuman presence?

M. Brémond then recalls a saying of Walter Pater:

According to Walter Pater, "all art seeks to approximate to that of music." No, they all of them aspire, each one by means of its own appropriate magic—words, notes, colours, lines—all aspire to become a *prayer*.

Paul Valéry comes in for a good deal of very indulgent criticism, on the ground of his identification of music and poetry. Poetry is *not* music, M. Brémond says; it is a mystical communion with a supernatural entity. He agrees with M. Valéry that the less it *means* the better; but he does not agree with M. Valéry when the latter says the poet is simply a species of musician.

In the first of the above quotations Prose was described as "taking a person out of himself," as overcoming the self; Poetry as resulting in a *refoulement* upon the self, and in a self-aggrandisement. And Poetry is, at the same time as it leads to an enhancement of the self, an act of communion with God or nature or "space-time," or whatever your particular Absolute may be termed. So in this description of the difference between Prose and Poetry it is worth noting that the impulse towards the Not-self (which is supposed to rest with Prose) must really be taking you towards the *concrete*: it is seen as the pagan, non-mystical impulse. The *personal* emotion is always that of the mystic or religionist, the *non*-personal (or that in which you are taken out of yourself) also is what "time," or mental, expansion cannot provide. Or far enough down, everything is uniform; on the surface only are there modes and differences.

M. Brémond solicited correspondence from readers interested in the discussion he had started, and received, he tells us, a great quantity of letters in response. "I have been sent a quantity of beautiful quotations," he says, "*and naturally, first and foremost, from the text of Bergson.*" M. Brémond says that he will not essay what has already been so well done by M. Tancrède de Visan, who, in two remarkable books, "has shown us to what extent the philosophy of Bergson helps us to identify *pure poetry* — (*la poésie pure*) — that poetry which goes further than the word which expresses it." But he decides to quote a few passages from Bergson, passages used by de Visan, "avec la plus heureuse finesse." I will follow his example, and now in my turn reproduce these passages. The first is "of capital importance," M. Brémond tells us, for the theory of *pure poetry* championed by him.

The word which is sharply outlined, the brutal word, which is the receptacle of all that is *stable*, all that is *common, and consequently impersonal*, in human experience, crushes or at all events covers over the more delicate and fugitive impressions of our individual conscience. — (*Essai sur les données immédiates de la Conscience.* The italics are mine in this passage.)

His third quotation from Bergson is this:

[The object of art] is to send to sleep the active or rather the recalcitrant forces of our personality, and thereby to induce in us a condition of perfect docility, in which we realize the idea suggested to us, in which we sympathize with the sentiment expressed. In the methods employed by the artist you will discover, in an attenuated form, refined and in some way spiritualized, the methods by which in a general way the hypnotic trance is induced. (*Op. cit.*)

In the above passages two aspects of what we are considering are well brought out. The word that is clear and defined is, as described by Bergson, "brutal"; and whether you are a man or a word, to be called "brutal" is not the nicest thing that can happen to you; and it is quite certain that Bergson is aware of that, and that he uses it to prejudice us against the word he is attacking. But to be "brutal" (*i.e.* sharply defined) is also, it seems, to be "stable." And, further, to be "stable" is to belong to the physical world that we all share *in common* — that is to belong to our common world in which we all meet and communicate. And this world is the *impersonal world*. "All that is *stable*, all that is *common*, and *consequently impersonal*" are Bergson's words.

Next, the manner in which our minds are influenced against this "brutal," "impersonal" world by M. Bergson, is to suggest to us that we are inferior to it, and that it *crushes* us with its "brutality." We possess all sorts of beautiful "fugitive and delicate" sensibilities and sensations, peculiar to us — the material of our "personality," in short (our "individual conscience," here, it is). Finally, then, it is our *personality* that is being crushed by this "common," "brutal," world. It is our dear self, in short, to which this philosopher whispers that we do not get our due; that we are crushed, oppressed, brutalized, by this pact with other people, whereby a system of *things* — of words, of images, of emotions — long ago, it was agreed, should be held *in common*, and held as fact. Against this stable world we are stirred up to revolt.

But what a strange light the next passage I have quoted throws upon the first. It is *art* that relieves this oppression of the crushing weight of the "stable" world; breaks it up and uncovers the intense reality. That is M. Bergson's account of art, and it would also in effect be mine. But he goes on to explain that its function is to "send to sleep" the resistance of the active personality. Again I think he is quite right; but, if that is the case, what happens to the *personality* — and all its unique, precious, delicate, fugitive, incommunicable self-hood, that we were rescuing from the brutal stable world in the first passage? Surely the essence of a personality, or of an "individual consciousness," is that it should be *stable*. And how can it be stable if its resistances are overcome, and if it is "sent to sleep"? If it is reduced to "a condition of perfect docility," in which anything that is "suggested" to it it accommodates, in which it sympathizes ecstatically with its dear hypnotist

— that may or may not be very agreeable for it; but we certainly cannot claim, except with our tongue in our cheek, that, if we are the hypnotist, we are liberating it from oppression, or that we are enhancing its "individuality."

Yet throughout the world, since men first put in their appearance, there is no doubt at all that there have always been people who got the better of others less astute than themselves by offering to free them, and to enhance to a tremendous and unexampled extent their *personality*. The papers are always crowded with advertisements of individuals (whose photographs reveal them as men of the type of Napoleon, Rasputin, Mesmer or Mussolini) who promise to make hundred-per-cent business-magnates of you in three months, by letter or otherwise. The greek sophists guaranteed to teach a young man the art of statecraft in a fairly short time, and fit him for the highest offices of the state. There is no harm at all in any of those things, as a fool and his money are soon parted, also a fool and his freedom; and it would be a very foolish thing to waste a moment in attempting to keep money in a fool's pocket when it wants to fly out and jump into the pocket of some cleverer man with an empty pocket (even the feelings of a farthing, in such a case, must be considered), or to attempt to maintain in freedom a person who does not even understand what freedom means, nor ever will. Yet, in the world of ideas, and when we are attempting to hold the battered truth a little upright and to some extent in position, we are bound to point out the nature of these frauds.

These passages have, I think, enabled me to give you a sidelight on the particular system of intellectual fraud practised by Bergson. It throws a fresh light also upon the notions we have been scrutinizing elsewhere. And the reader who has followed me so far will not fail to have seen in all that I have quoted of this collection of opinions (it is M. Brémond's method to compose his case in that way, and it is an extremely illuminating one), a perfect confirmation of what I have said so far on the nature of these particular theories. Bergson has the place of honour (as he should have more explicitly with Whitehead and Alexander): an extreme doctrine of sensation is adumbrated, one avowedly "mystical," and to a fanatical degree hostile to all the works of "the intellect" — to what Whitehead would call the "spatializing" instincts of the natural man. The first and most famous protagonist of those attitudes in philosophy was Bergson, and in all that M. Brémond says there is nothing that has not already long ago been formulated by him.

The opposition that M. Brémond's campaign met with was very various, it appears; from the doctrinaire rationalism of his traditional opponent, M. Souday, to the timid objections, of which he gives an amusing sample, of a parish priest. He resumes his impressions of the non-professional objections as follows:

> It is always the same old scandal: people think that we are sacrificing the clear precisions of Reason to the cloudy lights of instinct, and that under the name of "poésie pure," we wish to glorify the pathetic, the vague, the obscure, the sub-rational, "the obscene chaos" where our human consciousness desperately battled prior to the *Fiat lux* of the Understanding.

This suggestion M. Brémond repudiates. *No!* he exclaims: *A thousand times No!* — But I do not think that anyone of much intelligence would believe him. I think it is evident that that is precisely what he and his associates are about. His is a *religious*, and not an *artistic*, intelligence. I am not suggesting, of course, that he is a rogue, but merely a religionist.

He *is* a kind of "illuminé" (as he says he is suspected of being); and his object *is* to convert the world to the doctrine of an ardent mysticism. And why not? But the loudest *No!* in the world will not, I am afraid, confute the soft impeachment. He is far more interested in *mysticism*, to say the least of it, than he is in *poetry* — "pure" or otherwise. And that seems to me what is the trouble with him, as with so many other propagandists; namely, that he is a religionist, masquerading as an artist or critic of art, or a philosopher. He is, in short, exploiting the artistic consciousness and the methods of the artist, just as Whitehead is doing; neither of them at all in the interests of art or of the artist. Brémond addresses his attention to art in the interests of religious mysticism; Whitehead in the interests of a scientific theory. But what is wanting in that scientific theory, as pure science, that it needs the support of *art*, all of a sudden? What is wanting in the world of the mystic of dogmatic religion we know. He is in very low water indeed. The artist might have anticipated *his* visit; but the polite attentions of the man-of-science are more surprising.

M. Brémond does not favour science; but he is far less preoccupied with science than you would expect. Perhaps he has met the man-of-science — in their respective calls upon the artist — so often now, that he has taken his measure; he has realized that science is no longer quite what it used to be, or at least that it is going out more, is less *farouche* and becoming civilized, and so is less to be feared. Science, when it has done its worst, he says confidently, will leave about "the poetic experience . . . a fringe of *the ineffable, un rien de je ne sais quoi . . .* a bridge between the infinite and us, between science and poetry." Whatever instruments of precision it may invent to record the pressures of the poetic afflatus, it will never be a match for *the ineffable*.

The word *ineffable* occurs on nearly every page of his book; nearly all his correspondents avail themselves of it. And indeed everywhere the language in which he expresses himself is of an unfortunately hyperbolic order, and should be more than sufficient to put anybody on their guard against views that require to shroud themselves in such verbal mists — unless of a very emotional nature indeed, and possessed of a great craving for ecstatic expansions. If of the latter order, Brémond will be your man, or one of them.

"Today," exclaims M. Brémond, "we not longer say: in a poem there are vivid pictures, sublime thoughts or emotions, there is this and there is that, and then, after that, there is *the ineffable*. We say: this is first of all and above all, *the ineffable* — intimately united, in addition, to this and to that."

Of course, it is to be hoped that *everybody* will not say, ever, when they wish to express themselves about a work of art, that "It is ineffable!" — and then some little time having elapsed, "It is a plate of apples," or it is "The rape of the Sabine women," or it is "About a work-girl in New York." It goes without saying, surely, that *everything* is "inexpressible," not only works of art — that, indeed M. Brémond's book, that the man who printed M. Brémond's book, that the postmen who carried and the sorters that sorted the correspondence that went to its making, that the academic robe of M. Brémond and the episcopal robe of the Archbishop of Aix, in whose company he met the Professor, bearer of the encyclical, which the quaint fellow placed to his lips like a trumpet; that the bocks consumed by M. Souday and the ink expended by M. Souza — that all these things are *inexpressible*. They are no more explicable in *clear* and *precise* terms than is the charm of Poussin or of Delacroix. All that he says, however, and he says a great deal, in spite of its unutterability, is a truism only, in particularly incontinent, florid and nebulous language.

One thing that it is interesting to note is M. Brémond's attitude
to the painter or sculptor. He is delighted with many of them,
in their rôle of "correspondent," and always for the same reason.
All you have to do, if you are a painter or sculptor, and wish
to please M. Brémond, is to describe your work in musical terminology. He will at once hail you as a brother, and announce you
to his public as an artist of the greatest value and discernment.
You need have no hesitation; *any* musical term will do; it *cannot* fail of its immediate effect; for M. Brémond's is a machine
that can be thoroughly relied upon.

Thus a painter writes to him from the country about "his art";
he is quoted at great length — for this painter uses the word
"cadences" to express the secret of his activities. "Cadences plas-
tiques" — what a fortunate phrase! But there is something engaging about M. Brémond, he is so easily pleased. "There is reason
to congratulate him [the painter] for not having explained to us
what he meant by his 'cadences.' It is quite enough for us that
this musical term is perfect for the mutual elucidation of time
and space. It is all the more expressive because it is not given
any precision, so that you can apply it to all the various values
of the composition." That is also a perfect brémondism. He con-
gratulates the painter upon not being clear. What he has said is
"all the more expressive because it is not given any precision."
That painter evidently knew the way to M. Brémond's mystical
heart; he brought nothing "clear" or "precise" with him, at any
rate; a great recommendation.

If M. Brémond shows a tendency to wish to improve on the
dictum of Walter Pater that "all art seeks to approximate to that
of music" — to take away from music what Pater bestowed on
it, and hand it to religion ("la prière"), nevertheless there is no
question, at least, which of the arts, religion apart, he prefers.

It is now that the danger of misunderstanding, and of appearing to go counter to my general argument (to which I referred
at the beginning of this chapter), will transpire — in what I next
have to say.

What M. Brémond is assailing is the extreme rationalist attitude
where artistic expression is concerned. His principal opponent
is M. Souday, with whose work I am unacquainted; but whom
I suppose to be, from what is said, an extreme supporter of the
sovereignty of Reason in artistic expression, though it is quite
possible that M. Brémond misrepresents his opponent's position.

In such a discussion, then, I should, if anything, be compelled to range myself on the side of M. Brémond, much as I should dislike to do anything of the sort. I think that all M. Brémond and M. Souza substantially say about the nature of artistic expression is true. I am in complete agreement with their position. What I am not in agreement with is their way of expressing themselves; I do not share what seem to be their motives for adopting it; I do not agree that religious mysticism ensues from it; I do not agree that plastic art can be reduced to terms of music; and a great deal of their interpretation, by the way, appears to me to be entirely and deliberately false. And yet if different people were professing these opinions, I should not have to put in these qualifications; they would, according to my view, be holding true opinions where the matter of the "spiritual" character of artistic creation is concerned.

To begin with, M. Brémond distinguishes between formal music and the "music" of words, I think very justly. The assertion of M. Valéry that a poet is simply a sort of *musician* appears untrue to me. M. Brémond contrasts two lines:

1. Nicole, apportez-moi mes pantoufles.
2. Mais où sont les neiges d'antan?

And from what he says elsewhere the implication in this contrast is that, as vowel music, one is much the same as the other. Indeed,

Dictes moy où, n'en quel pays,
Est Flora la belle Romaine?

is much the same, the rhythm aside, as

Dis! Gaston, où as-tu mis les plumes de ta grand-mère?

The upshot of this observation would be, I suppose, that as far as word-music goes, there is only time or rhythm; that it is of necessity all a matter of that in language. So in a sense it would be the ideal form for the musical sensibility of the specifically "time" order; if only the words would not insist on *meaning* something. It is that that drives such poets as Pound into pure music. After a time they can stand it no longer, and abandon language in disgust.

But those are, of course, not the conclusions drawn by M. Brémond. What he is anxious to demonstrate is something different.

"If all poetry is verbal music . . . all verbal music is not poetry," he says (and that has just been demonstrated above). "Fix, then," he goes on to say, "if you can, the exact, and exclusively musical, nuance, by virtue of which, of these two musics, one alone — and sometimes the least harmonious of the two, is *poetry*." Or again:

There is no poetry without a certain verbal music, but of such a special order that perhaps it would be better to call it by some other name; and as soon as that "music" strikes upon an ear, so constituted as to understand it, there is poetry. But we must add at once that anything so feeble — a handful of sonorous vibrations, a little air beaten upon — could not be the capital factor, still less the unique one, of an experience where the most intimate reaches of our soul are involved. Jingling rhymes, flux and reflux of alliterations, cadences by turns foreseen and dissonant — none of these pretty sounds reach the deep zone of the creative ferment where one is conscious of nothing, with the Pericles of Shakespeare, but the music of the spheres.

I will state very briefly my own belief as to the true character of artistic creation. The production of a work of art is, I believe, strictly the work of a visionary. Indeed, this seems so evident that it scarcely needs pointing out. Shakespeare, writing his *King Lear*, was evidently in some sort of a trance; for the production of such a work of art an entranced condition seems as essential as it was for Blake when he conversed with the Man who Built the Pyramids. To create *King Lear*, or to believe that you have held communion with some historic personage — those are much the same thing. The traditional romantic epithet for the poet — and as M. Brémond says, all creators are equally poets — namely, "dreamer" (which subsequently became a term of belittlement or contempt on the lips of the romanticist for positive knowledge or the science-snob), accurately describes all creative artists; though, of course, it need not apply, indeed could hardly do so, to the great number of practitioners of art who do not possess the essential qualifications of the artist.

If you say that creative art is a spell, a talisman, an incantation — that it is *magic*, in short, there, too, I believe you would be correctly describing it. That the artist uses and manipulates a supernatural power seems very likely.

The poet or philosopher in the non-religious greek states occupied, we are told, much the same position as the priest or witch-doctor or magician in a more religious or superstitious community. It was for that reason that a poet or philosopher was held responsible for his slightest or most casual utterance in the way that he was. He was recognized as the custodian of the spiritual consciousness of the race. The productions of art assumed somewhat the role of sacred books.

It is the appreciation of this *magical* quality in artistic expression — a recognition that the artist is tapping the supernatural sources and potentialities of our existence — that composes a good deal the attitude towards him and his creation that so often comes to light, and at some periods in a manner so unfavourable for his function. The artist is definitely, for the fanatical religionist, fabricating graven images, or tampering, in a secular manner, with sacred powers. The sort of material that Pirandello makes such a liberal use of in his plays, reduces itself to an expression of this consciousness: namely, the sort that realizes that Don Quixote or the Widow Wadman is as *real*, to put it no higher than that, as most people ostensibly alive and walking the earth today.

So the only dispute I am concerned to engage in with such critics as M. Brémond is such as is suggested by the question: All that being admitted as fact, where do you propose that that should lead us?

For me art is the civilized *substitute* for magic; as philosophy is what, on a higher or more complex plane, takes the place of religion. *By means of art*, I believe Professor Whitehead and M. Brémond wish to lead us down and back to the plane of magic, or of mystical, specifically religious, experience. And though the artist is certainly not devoid of religious emotion, it is exercised personally, as it were; and he is in temper the opposite of the religionist. The man-of-science is another sort of transformed magician. He, too, is opposite in temper to the religionist. The truly scientific mind — which Professor Whitehead, it is evident, does not possess, any more than he possesses, it is plain, the artistic — is as "detached," as we say, as is the artist-mind.

From this point of view the true man-of-science and the artist are much more in the same boat than is generally understood. The sort of time that would produce a great flowering of art would be apt to produce similar ferments in science. But the mixing of them up à la Whitehead can only have one motive: to retransform both of them into the primitive magician from which they both equally spring, or rather to retransform their chosen material into simple magic.

This, I am afraid, is a very imperfect statement, and requires, I am quite aware, considerable amplification. It is, however, all I can give for the moment. If I attempted a more detailed statement in this place, every further step would involve us in further elucidations, and I should risk extending this part of my argument at the expense of what I have to say elsewhere, and which at the moment is of more importance.

CHAPTER FIVE

ROMANTIC ART CALLED IN TO ASSIST IN THE DESTRUCTION OF "MATERIALISM"

EVOLUTIONISM, IN ONE FORM or another, is the prevailing creed of our time. It dominates our politics, our literature, and not least our philosophy. Nietzsche, Pragmatism, Bergson, are phases in its philosophic development, and their popularity far beyond the circles of professional philosophers shows its consonance with the spirit of the age.

So wrote Mr. Bertrand Russell in 1914 (*Our Knowledge of the External World*). He proceeds to analyse, in an unfavourable sense, evolutionism. He describes first the darwinian biologic revolution and the similar effects produced by the theories of Laplace.

The difference between man and the lower animals, which to our human conceit appears enormous, was shown [by darwinism] to be a gradual achievement. . . . The sun and planets had already been shown by Laplace to be very probably derived from a primitive more or less undifferentiated nebula. Thus the old fixed landmarks became wavering and indistinct, and all sharp outlines were blurred. Things and species lost their boundaries, and no one could say where they began or where they ended.

Bergson is, he recognizes, the most typical, as he is the most renowned and influential, "evolutionist," philosopher: and Bergson he will not have at any price.

M. Bergson's form of finalism [he says] depends upon his conception of life. Life, in his philosophy, is a continuous stream, in which all divisions are artificial and unreal. Separate things, beginnings and endings, are mere convenient fictions; there is only smooth, unbroken transition. The beliefs of today may count as true today, if they carry us along the stream; but tomorrow they will be false, and must be replaced by new beliefs to meet the new situation.

We shall have occasion, later on, to show how this account of bergsonian "truth" equally describes the doctrine of Alexander. However, here we find Mr. Russell describing Bergson as the perfect priest of the Zeitgeist — as of course that gentleman is, or was—and he finds that, as regards his general doctrine, "the motives and interests which inspire it are so exclusively practical, and the problems with which it deals are so special, that it can hardly be regarded as really touching any of the questions that to my mind constitute genuine philosophy."

Finally, although "it will . . . be admitted that the reconstruction (of physical conceptions of space and time and matter) must take more account of change and the universal flux than is done in the older mechanics," nevertheless Mr. Russell does not think that "the reconstruction required is on bergsonian lines, nor do I think that his rejection of logic can be anything but harmful." That there should be *no* "fixed landmarks"; that *all* should become "wavering and indistinct"; that *all* "sharp outlines" should be "blurred," all "things and species" lose their "boundaries," was not Mr. Russell's idea of what should happen, or in any case not on the lines of bergsonian time-philosophy—to all of which it is more than ever today easy to assent. But Mr. Russell has meantime abandoned that view of the matter (only, rather unreasonably, retaining his hostility to Bergson).

But at the time these papers were written Mr. Russell was already far over the lines of his own philosophic convictions, at the heels of theories that were (though it is evident from what he said, he was not aware of this) similar to the "evolutionist" theories which we here find him attacking.

I have been made aware of the importance of this problem by my friend and collaborator, Dr. Whitehead, to whom are due almost all the differences between the views advocated here and those suggested in *The Problems of Philosophy*. I owe to him the definition of points, the suggestion for the treatment of instants and "things," and the whole conception of the world of physics as a *construction*, [etc.]

So Dr. Whitehead woke him from his dogmatic slumber: but when first awoken he evidently did not for some time realize quite where he was. When he is describing bradleyan idealism he says, for instance: "The universe, it tells us, is an 'organic unity,' like an animal or a perfect work of art." This doctrine he flouts: but oddly enough, Dr. Whitehead—although apparently he was at the time not conscious of the fact—was telling him just the same thing. "By this it means," he goes on, "roughly speaking, that all the different parts fit together and co-operate, and are what they are because of their place in the whole . . . every part of the universe is a microcosm, a miniature reflection of the whole."

That certainly seems to describe Whitehead's doctrine of "organic mechanism." Take at random such a passage from *Science and the Modern World* as the following:

> The concrete enduring entities are *organisms*, so that the plan of the *whole* influences the very characters of the various subordinate organisms which enter into it. In the case of an animal, the mental states enter into the plan of the total organism and thus modify the plans of the successive subordinate organisms, until the ultimate smallest organisms, such as electrons, are reached, [etc.]

In what Whitehead calls "prehension," and in his particular variety of the doctrine of "perspectives," you get it still more clearly: in the passage I will now quote you have the underlying pantheism explicitly indicated as well. (He is discussing the fourth dialogue of Berkeley's *Alciphron*, in which the speakers are disputing about the respective reality of a castle as seen several miles away — the "little round object" that then is seen — and the castle when you are in it or at it.) Also a cloud and a planet come into the illustration.

> The things which are grasped into a realized unity, here and now, are not the castle, the cloud and the planet, simply in themselves: but they are the castle, the cloud and the planet, from the standpoint, in space and time, of the prehensive unification. In other words, it is the perspective of the castle over there from the standpoint of the unification here. It is, therefore, aspects of the castle, the cloud and the planet which are grasped into unity, here. You will remember that the idea of perspectives is quite familiar in philosophy. It was introduced by Leibniz, in the notion of his monads mirroring perspectives of the universe. I am using the same notion, only I am toning down his monads into the unified events in space or time. In some ways, there is a greater analogy with Spinoza's modes; that is why I use the terms "mode" and "modal." In the analogy with Spinoza, his one substance is for me the one underlying activity of realization, individualizing itself in an interlocked plurality of modes [p. 102].

If "Evolution is the prevailing creed of our time" is exact for 1914, it could certainly be said that "Time is the prevailing creed of our time" is still more closely true for 1927. And if Bergson stood, in philosophy, for "Evolutionism," he stood, and still stands, even more conspicuously for *Time*. Relativity Theory is of course also strictly a *time-theory* in the most general sense. Mr. J. W. Dunne, the well-known inventor, who is one of the most amusing of the time-romancers (following in the footsteps of Hinton, like Ouspensky and other highly picturesque fancy-thinkers), describes Relativity Theory in the following offhand manner: "Relativity is a *particular* theory grafted on the *general* theory of time-dimensional universes. Consequently, its survival or demise cannot affect the validity of that general theory." This certainly does not misrepresent it as regards its class, though it no doubt underrates its importance. Its interest for us here is, as was announced in my preface, confined to its *effects*, as observable in philosophical doctrine. As such it can be regarded certainly as a particular doctrine, of great mathematical prestige, belonging to the well-defined class of doctrines of time-dimensional universes. Its peculiar insistence upon personal time-systems is obviously of considerable moment in the metaphysical doctrines that it influences.

I will now turn to Whitehead again, with the object of answering more closely still the objection that my essay has already had to meet: namely, that the machinery of the physicist is one thing, and the predilection of the artist for concrete objects is another, and that in my criticism it is *only* that predilection that is at stake. As a matter of fact, Dr. Whitehead himself would be the last person, I suppose, to advance such an objection, since he has been at the greatest pains to *reinstate scientifically*, as it were, the art-object, as we call it, in place of the "scientific object." It is indeed his determination at all costs to effect this reunion that is so much objected to here, and it is that that has made me single his particular doctrine out for criticism.

I will arrange a few quotations from his recent book, *Science and the Modern World*, in such a way as to make what I mean quite clear, I hope. He is all for the poets and the artists, Dr. Whitehead: and in this first passage he is showing how right they were — "organic"-minded as of necessity such people must be — to reject the picture of the universe presented them by "materialist" science.

Nature is a dull affair, soundless, scentless, colourless; merely the hurrying of material, endlessly, meaninglessly. However you disguise it, this is the practical outcome of the characteristic scientific philosophy which closed the seventeenth century.

In the first place you must note its astounding efficiency as a system of concepts for the organization of scientific research. In this respect, it is fully worthy of the genius of the century which produced it. It has held its own as the guiding principle of scientific studies ever since.

It is still reigning. Every university in the world organizes itself in accordance with it. No alternative system of organizing the pursuit of scientific truth has been suggested. It is not merely reigning, but it is without a rival.

And yet — it is quite unbelievable. This conception of the universe is surely framed in terms of high abstractions, and the paradox only arises because we have mistaken our abstractions for concrete realities.

Indeed, that is the only case in which it could, or rather ever should, arise. But all this passage sounds to me strangely confused: for *who* has mistaken, or mistook, the very practical and useful abstractions of Science for "concrete reality" or for truth, who that any but such as our time-men would approve of or admire? The "materialists," at whom Dr. Whitehead's shafts are directed? But the naïf materialist is discredited long ago (and a far more insidious type of materialist has taken his place, as it is time we recognized, without wasting our energy in beating that dead donkey, the "materialist," pure, simple and unadorned). Nature, "the dull affair" of natural science, "soundless, scentless, colourless," *was never the business of the artist or the poet at all*; and if he romantically went over into it, and spoiled a good picture or a good poem, by his misguided enthusiasm, that was his own fault. Science was always purely the affair of the man-of-science — (poor devil! Dr. Whitehead would say, no doubt). His "astounding efficiency" is witnessed on all hands. What cause is there to wonder, therefore, that science has "held its own," and to marvel at the honoured place reserved for it in places of high instruction? The picture that it gives of the world is philosophically "meaningless," as Dr. Whitehead says, and is exceedingly "dull" and drab from one point of view. It is not "artistic." But surely, *as science*, and in its own province, "the better the uncouther." One cannot resist the belief that there is some extraordinary fallacy beneath all this discourse of his. And, if you consider what the author of *Science and the Modern World* is saying to you for a moment, the fallacy is not, I think, difficult to discover. It is *he*, Dr. Whitehead, who has *believed* in this "dull," "meaningless" picture, quite naïvely, no doubt. And now, with a gesture of enfranchisement and discovery, he announces that it is *"quite unbelievable."* But of *course it is unbelievable*. It always has been unbelievable. But, from certain aspects, and if kept in its own province, it can be extremely useful. So why not let its "dullness" and evident unreality alone, and allow it to go on doing its work?

But the mathematician today will have his *art*. The aesthetic factor that does play a considerable part undoubtedly in mathematics, as the theories the mathematician builds up become more and more faery-like and fantastic, asserts itself, and seeks to transform also the neighbouring more prosaic provinces of Science to its emotional nature. So much is comprehensible. But still the way it takes Dr. Whitehead appears particularly unreasonable. Einstein, for instance, is not a proselytizing *artist*: he even has rather the affectation, if anything, of being quite prosaic — the "simple physicist." That is one of the few things that, apart from his brilliant abilities, particularly recommend him.

Here is a second quotation from Whitehead. (He is still agreeing with the poet and the artist about Science: and he is using the poets of the Romantic Revival in England for his special purposes.)

Now the poet, so sympathetic with science, so absorbed in its ideas, can simply make nothing of secondary qualities which are fundamental to its concepts. For Shelley nature retains its beauty and its colour. Shelley's nature is in its essence a nature of organisms, functioning with the full content of our perceptual experience.

He next quotes some lines from the poem entitled "Mont Blanc," beginning "The everlasting universe of Things." Then he continues:

Shelley has written these lines with explicit reference to some form of idealism, kantian or berkeleyan or platonic. But however you construe him, he is here an emphatic witness to a prehensive unification as constituting the very being of nature. Berkeley, Wordsworth, Shelley are representative of the intuitive refusal seriously to accept the abstract materialism of science.

Indeed he truly is describing Berkeley there, in one sense: but Berkeley was not an "organic" theorist, and the objective nature of Berkeley was much more the nature of "common-sense" than is that of Whitehead. But what poet ever "seriously accepted the abstract materialism of science"? So all this arraying of the poets against the often very useful, and very brilliantly endowed, man-of-science, seems much ado about nothing. Also it is not calculated to benefit on the one side the poet, or on the other the man-of-science, very much. Very much the contrary, I am quite convinced.

The more you read Whitehead — especially in this phase of his writing — the more convinced you become that *he* is that "materialist" who "believed" in that "dull" world of scientific fact: that is why he is so excited at present. He finds the "Ode to the West Wind" a refreshing subject — it puts new life into him — after, say, "extensive abstraction." But even then Shelley as "an emphatic witness to a prehensive unification" is hardly the Shelley we all know!

He now (you will find this passage on page 126) tells us what he considers *philosophy* should be:

> I hold that philosophy is the critic of abstractions. Its function is the double one, first of harmonizing them by assigning to them their right relative status as abstractions, and secondly of completing them by direct comparison with more concrete intuitions of the universe, and thereby promoting the formation of more complete schemes of thought. It is in respect to this comparison that the testimony of great poets is of such importance. Their survival is evidence that they express deep intuitions of mankind penetrating into what is universal in concrete fact. Philosophy is not one among the sciences with its own little scheme of abstractions which it works away at perfecting and improving. It is the survey of sciences, with the special objects of their harmony, and of their completion. It brings to this task not only the evidence of the separate sciences, but also its own appeal to concrete experience. It confronts the sciences with concrete fact. The literature of the nineteenth century, especially the English poetic literature, is a witness to the discord between the aesthetic intuitions of mankind and the mechanism of science. . . . Both Shelley and Wordsworth emphatically bear witness that nature cannot be divorced from its aesthetic values; and that these values arise from the cumulation, in some sense, of the brooding presence of the whole on to its various parts.

Again, the same "emphatic witnesses"! And what they witness is that "nature" must be taken fully clothed in all its aesthetic values: it "cannot be divorced from" them. The answer to that is, of course, that it not only can be, but must be so divorced, for the purposes of science: and that that part is cut off by science for its especial purposes has to be left out — by the poet, for *his* business.

But in this last passage it is mainly the definition of philosophy that should occupy us. It is, we are told, the "critic of abstractions." Further, it is the *completer* of abstractions — their tailor, as it were. Its business is to dress them in the appropriate material of "concrete intuitions," and with the aesthetic stuff of the nature poet, or of the naturalistic artist. Its business is to mediate between the abstract — "dull" and "meaningless" — world of science, and the rich, qualitied and significant world of poetry and art. But this latter world is also that of "common-sense." So we see how Dr. Whitehead *states*, at least, the nature of his function.

I will recall the main objective of this chapter. We have seen that the external world can be looked at very variously, and that the same object, under the eye of science or under the microscope, and beneath the human eye, or, alternatively in the mind of the camera, or of the mathematician, or of "common-sense," will be a very different object. These "objects" for convenience could be arranged in a row. At one extremity would be the "scientific object," or the "physical object": at the other would be the "art object," or the object of "common-sense." And there are also a quantity of hybrids; and each distinct occupation, almost, has its especial "object." You could make a long museum gallery of them.

These objects are not all equally "real" or "true," it is our belief. But in consequence of that, such is the peculiar conclusion advanced here, there is nothing to be gained by mixing them all up together. That is, however, Dr. Whitehead's intention. If one is more *real* than the other, then let us mix the *less* real (which he seems to believe is the "scientific object" in the sense of the unreformed, naïf, "scientific object"), he says, with the more real. This will be more fair to the less real, among other things: and in the interests of what he calls "togetherness," this must be done.

The way this is brought about is by handing back the secondary (or as Alexander calls them, the "tertiary") qualities to nature: by robbing the mind of all the privileges bestowed upon it by the "century of genius," the seventeenth century — the great scientific century: and by creating a *mixed* nature, which exhibits none of the vigour or specific virtues of the purer duality from which it comes. We are told on all hands (by Whitehead, Alexander, Russell — and they were told by James) that the fundamental stuff of the world is neither "physical" nor "mental," but is a *neutral* stuff. That is information merely, as it is conveyed to us — of interest to the naturally inquisitive, that is all. We are not invited, exactly, to *return* to the more differentiated condition inferred for the benefit of our curiosity. We are told we *come from* it. But behold, as the discussion and exposition go on, we gradually become conscious of the fact that we *are* being invited — at least as far as our vision of the world is concerned — to *return to* it. We are asked, there is no doubt about it, to conceive of ourselves as neutral or neuter. It is definitely our segregations that are to be broken up, our barriers to be broken down. The paradigmatic "objects" that are held up to us, as our mirrors or as pictures of our reality, are of that mixed, fluid and neutral character; so that, if we survey them long enough, and accept them as an *ultimate* — as a metaphysical, as well as a scientific — truth, they will induce us, too, to liquefy and disintegrate, and to return to a more *primitive* condition. The word *primitive* is still the key to all these movements which in every case lead to some form of primitivism.

So of his romantic, pantheistic poets Whitehead says: "Thus we gain from the poets the doctrine that a philosophy of nature must concern itself at least with these five notions: change, value, eternal objects, endurance, interfusion." And the greatest of these is *interfusion*. But really these five notions are the same, except for the "eternal objects," which are too abstract to matter. Let us take them one by one. (1) *Change* is the melting of one thing into another — "interfusion," that is. (2) *Value* is emotion, again not at all a concrete thing; a factor of interfusion, that is. (3) *Eternal objects* are, as Dr. Whitehead describes them, "elusive." Or they "haunt the change which infects organisms." In other words, they are phantoms. (4) *Endurance* is the sort of stability that you get out of a thing that is always visualized as melting into another thing, or being brooded upon by a "creative," hen-like, evolutionist Whole, a Whole that according to Alexander is always brooding and brooding, but to no intelligible end. (5) The fifth is *Interfusion*, and there we have all the rest in one.

Dr. Whitehead's philosophy is the regular orthodox one of today — that of Change and Time. Under these circumstances it is not to be wondered at that it is *change* and *interfusion* that he stresses, as he says that Shelley does.

Shelley thinks of nature as changing, dissolving, transforming as it were at a fairy's touch. . . . In his poem "The Cloud" it is the transformation of water which excites his imagination. The subject of the poem is the endless, eternal, elusive change of things. . . . This is one aspect of nature, its elusive change: a change not merely to be expressed by locomotion, but a change of inward character. This is where Shelley places his emphasis.

And that is, of course, where Whitehead and all the school to which he belongs place their emphasis. It is a much more exasperated, mercurial form of the flux of Heraclitus.

This is one aspect of nature, says Whitehead. There is another, namely its opposite. Wordsworth, we are told, because he was born upon a hill, saw the other aspect of nature. He is the poet of *endurance.* And Spengler tells us that all Greeks, whether born on a hill or elsewhere, always had the misfortune to see that side of the medal — the enduring and concrete as opposed to the changing. And Alexander, in the passage I began this part of my essay with, also heaved a patronizing sigh over the limitation of the Hellene. Even Plato was *only a Greek;* just as, for the White overlord, Buddha was once *only a nigger,* in fact.

Both Whitehead and Shelley then, we are to assume, are looking at the same "nature." Shelley put all his emphasis (all the emphasis of an "emphatic witness") upon *change.* And surely no one will dispute that Dr. Whitehead, and the whole school to which he belongs, do the same? Whether the reason is that they were all born amongst a luxuriant tropical low-lying vegetation, I do not know. Perhaps the first of the school was: and all the rest — whether so favoured by birth or not — just followed suit.

My argument, then, is this. Upon his own showing, the picture of the world that Dr. Whitehead is offering us is an "artistic" one: it is one that is to include all the richness, intuitional concreteness, of nature: and presumably if such a slight cause as being born upon a (quite small) hill can influence a man to stress one aspect rather than another, so that he gives us an opposite world-picture to his friend in the fen, then surely mightier forces (such as are psychologically imposing themselves upon this time) can result even more effectively in his stressing or emphasizing one aspect rather than another of reality. This is, in fact, what Dr. Whitehead does, I think it is evident. And the object of his attention is the same object as that with which the artist or the poet deals. Hence I do not think it can be said that the artist is guilty of an impertinence in intervening at this point in the proceedings, and offering some criticism of that school which is so exultantly stressing one aspect of nature, and modifying everybody's view of the external world on a pattern of change and time — especially as no one else shows the least tendency to intervene.

With the following observations I will conclude this part of my argument. We hear usually in these sort of discussions of the "secondary qualities" of colour, scent and sound; and they are hustled about, first belonging here and then belonging there. But it is they that always stand for the immediate sensuous reality. I believe, however, that there is something else (equally, as I hold, a thing that should belong to the mind, be considered as "sub-jective") even more important than colour, scent or sound. It should always enter into the argument.

As a *realist*, in the most sensible acceptance of the word, and as of course we all are, whatever we are merely called, what is the strongest impression you receive from the external world, or nature? Certainly stability, I, as a realist, should say: decidedly not one of change. For change you have to look, to wait for, you have to detect it. And if colour, scent and sound must be given back to and draped upon the skeleton of Science, then, even more essentially, must immobility, the fastness and deadness of nature, be installed there too. This Dr. Whitehead is inclined to wish to leave out: he is all for colour, sound and locomotion. But *deadness* above all, for the fullest, most concrete "realism," is essential.

Surely it is the abstraction of the materialistic picture of science that puts the *movement* and the *fusion* into it? that "time," in short, that is the mind of Space, that stirs it up? It is certainly not our eyes that are responsible for it. Sound, it is true, sug-gests movement generally: but vision does not. And this *immobil-ity*, this *deadness*, this "concreteness," is, as I have said, exactly what Whitehead at all costs—in his new composite, half-scientific, half-aesthetic picture—wishes to leave out! Yet it is actually more important for the full, significant, "concrete" reality, let me again assert, even than are sounds, colours, or odours.

If there is one thing more than another that is essential to pro-vide a "sense of reality"—our sheer sensation that there is something *real* there before us—it is the deadness, the stolid thickness and deadness, of nature. No "eternal object," or buzz-ing in our ear, or whiff of perfumed air, can give that sensation of "the real," so surely as that. And it is because they know that this particular "concreteness" can be shown to be *unreal*, that these philosophers wish it away. What is most sensationally "real" (as ultimately it is, perhaps more than anything else, demonstrably unreal) is the *deadness* of nature, once more. And for any view of the world such as we are arguing for here to be successful, that *deadness* is essential. It is merely the enlightened materialism of Whitehead that makes him so eager to banish it, and to put a nervous tic into the limbs of the statue, or prove to us that all poets have been pantheists.

CHAPTER SIX

THE POPULAR COUNTERS, "ACTION" AND "LIFE"

FOR ALL PRACTICAL PURPOSES, "time" and "motion" are identical, as we find them applied in the philosophies under consideration. And all the so-called "dynamical" doctrines in the practical field lead to precisely the same conclusions as the central "Time" doctrine of the philosophers. The italian futurists — with their évangile of *action*, and its concomitants, speed, violence, impressionism and sensation in all things — incessant movement with the impermanence associated with that, as the ideal of a kind of suicidal faith — they were thorough adepts of the Time-philosophy: and Marinetti, their prophet, was a *pur-sang* bergsonian.

The fascists have the word *action* on their lips from morning till night. It is their magic word, recurring in all their speeches or incantations: violence is their god. Fascism is merely futurism in practice. Signor Marinetti has been fêted at Rome officially as the precursor of fascismo, indeed, so that connection has been publicly established. And Sorel — a disciple of Bergson — in his *Réflexions sur la violence*, sings the same bergsonian song; only in his case it is a sanguinary one, whereas Bergson is more "detached," and is not so specific as to what happens to you once you surrender yourself to the flux-god.

Bergson's philosophy was a *practical* one, as Mr. Russell long ago pointed out: and it may be interesting to quote what he says in support of that classification. In considering the nature and direction of Bergson's thought, he writes as follows:

Thus we shall have philosophies of feeling inspired by the love of happiness; theoretical philosophies, inspired by the love of knowledge; and practical philosophies, inspired by the love of action. . . . Practical philosophies . . . will be those which regard action as the supreme good, considering happiness an effect and knowledge a mere instrument of successful activity. Philosophies of this type would have been common among Western Europeans if philosophers had been average men; as it is, they have been rare until recent times, in fact their chief representatives are the pragmatists and M. Bergson. In the rise of this type of philosophy we may see, as M. Bergson himself does, the revolt

201

of the modern man of action against the authority of Greece, and more particularly of Plato; and we may connect it, as Dr. Schiller apparently would, with imperialism or the motor-car. (*The Philosophy of Bergson*, Bertrand Russell.)

Did this philosophy of *action* originate in the revolt of the man of action, the motorist, against the authority of the sages of antiquity and against all that immemorial life of restraint and love of wisdom with which the exclusively motoring and money-making habits could not come to terms? Was the shadow of that distant life like the presence of a "high-brow" at some smart or sporty philistine party? We are accustomed to think conventionally of these revolutions of feeling as belonging to the man-in-the-street, or to the "masses," and we forget that in reality it was the vulgar mercantile class (as the inventions of science made it richer and richer) which "revolted," their head completely turned by the sheer material power that had been lavished on them by the engineer and chemist. They did not want any critical, disillusioned, eye in their popular millionaire paradise. It was their vanity and insolence, "inferiority-complex" and "class-consciousness," that figuratively stoned Plato, and financed the revolt against the classical authority. But, until the coming of Bergson, they could not have found a philosophical intelligence sufficiently degraded to take their money and do, philosophically, their dirty work. The unique distinction of that personage is that he was the first servant of the great industrial caste-mind arriving on the golden crest of the wave of scientific progress. But perhaps that is unfair to Bergson, after all: the truth about him may be that he is in reality simply a very common but astute intelligence — naturally, and without other inducement, on the side of such a society, instinctively endorsing its ideals.

As to the motives underlying the thirst for action, Mr. Russell, from whom I again will quote, writes as follows:

To the schoolmen, who lived amid wars, massacres and pestilences, nothing appeared so delightful as safety and order. In their idealizing dreams, it was safety and order that they sought. . . . To us, to whom safety has become monotony, to whom the primeval savageries of nature are so remote as to become a mere pleasing condiment to our ordered routine, the world of dreams is very different from what it was amid the wars of Guelf and Ghibelline. Hence William James's protest against what he calls the "block universe" of the classical tradition; hence Nietzsche's worship of force; hence the verbal bloodthirstiness of many quiet literary men. The barbaric substratum of human nature, unsatisfied in action, finds an outlet in imagination. In philosophy, as elsewhere, this tendency is visible; and it is this, rather than formal argument, that has thrust aside the classical tradition for a philosophy which fancies itself more virile and more vital. (*Our Knowledge of the External World.*)

Mr. Russell, in a note, draws our attention to the fact that it was written before August 1914. It should be scarcely necessary to add how exceedingly out-of-date this picture of the man-of-peace amusing himself with the barbarisms of the savage past is today. It is very greatly to Mr. Russell's credit that he saw the true nature of those doctrines before the War came to enlighten us all. But even today, in their unfathomable conservatism, there are still masses of people who continue to think as though the War had never occurred, and still fall into these by now time-honoured traps, labelled for the unwary "action" and "life" — traps that are nevertheless choked with millions of corpses.

But the actual source of all this half-century of propaganda of *violence* or of *action*, is, of course, the darwinian doctrine of "the struggle for existence." From Darwin to Mussolini or Turati, is a road without a break. Bergson's "creative evolution" is as darwinian as was the "will to power" of Nietzsche. It is Darwin's law of animal survival by ruthless struggle, and the accompanying pictures of the organic shambles through which men reached world-mastery; broadcast throughout the civilized democratic world, it has brought in its wake all the emotional biology and psychology that has resulted in these values, for which fascismo is the latest political model.

The first people to whom it occurred to oppose *the living person* to the *image* or *representation* into which he or she projects himself or is projected, and to set these respectively living and dead things by the ears, were the futurists. To the beautiful young sitter they would whisper or rather shout: "You are more beautiful than that silly image in oil-paint of yourself, and you are *alive*; *it* is the rival of your *living* beauty. Rise up, hurl from its intellectual, snobbish throne, stamp upon, destroy, that *dead* pretence — your *rival* — into which so much of your vitality flows. People will praise *it* instead of *you!* What? Praise the dead paint above the living flesh? (And *such* flesh!)" And having added many other exciting and flattering things in the same strain, they would succeed in creating such a bad feeling and stirring up so much animosity between the sitter and the canvas, that it was as much as the discomfited artist could do to prevent the living beauty from setting her heel upon the neck of her painted counterpart (in the manner of the late Lord Leverhulme), or indeed from fetching him one in the eye for his part in the transaction.

None of the futurists were individually good artists. Severini has become a good if not very original painter since, but is no longer a futurist. Most of the others were killed in the War. They were a sort of painting, carving, propaganding ballet or circus, belonging to the milanese showman, Marinetti. One of the tasks he set them was to start making statues that could open and shut their eyes, and even move their limbs and trunks about, or wag their heads. The step from that to a living creature is a small one; and rivalry between the statue and the living puppet could be guaranteed to become rapidly acute.

An immense snobbery centering around the counter "life" had been built up to the bursting point when the War began; and at the end of four years of that, few people could have been found to exclaim any more about "life" for the moment. For it was then plain to the meanest intelligence for a month or two, that what that sort of "life" signified was death. All the sickly ecstasies of *élan vital* were drugs on the market. It was on the ecstatic "life" cry that Bergson was allowed formerly to provide the first (continental) wave of the High-Bohemia with an appropriate philosophy, showing it plainly that it was the roof and crown of things, and that the contemptible "intellect" was less than the dust beneath its chariot-wheels. Also, was it not the *fittest*, seeing that it was composed of such conspicuous *survivors*?

By an understanding of the value of such counters as "life," "dynamism," "progress," "time," the general tendency of all this movement can be grasped. Especially by finding out how these counters can readily coalesce can you arrive at a notion of the *one* head of thought that emerges, the characteristic Time-thought. So let us say that the "life" and "motion" ideas are seen to meet in the mechanical moving statue of the 1914 futurist.

CHAPTER SEVEN

"TIME" UPON THE SOCIAL PLANE
AND IN PHILOSOPHY

IN THIS CHAPTER I propose to go more carefully into the parallel manifestation of what I have called a *time-mind* in contemporary literature and social life on the one side, and the more abstract plane of philosophy and all the field of theoretic thought on the other. In both, the hypostasization and glorification of the concept *Time* is the central fact. As to the existence of the *time-mind* on the social and literary plane, my first book was designed to answer that question. Does it also exist upon the philosophical plane? Is it the same concept, only on another plane? Is there a close connection between the one and the other? Or is there no connection at all between the concept *Time* of speculative thought, with its doctrinal ascendancy, and the popular and literary pre-occupation with Time, that of what I have called the *time-mind*? Finally, if there is some close association of thought and feeling between the one and the other, of what nature is it exactly, and how does it come about? These are the questions we now have to ask ourselves.

Reverting to the objections that were answered in the chapter headed "Spatialization and Concreteness," I had perhaps better specify them a little more fully. The criticism to which I refer has taken somewhat the following form. My critic, if he wished to be amiable, would say: "I agree that there is a *time-mind*, as you call it. I think you have proved in your 'Revolutionary Simpleton' that such a thing as a 'time-mind' may be said to exist. With your concrete analysis I am in agreement. But the existence of this 'time-mind' has nothing whatever to do with Einstein, Bergson, or with Whitehead or any of the philosophers you mention, who depend on Relativity. Your association of Einstein with Miss Stein, of Swann and Stein, of Bergson and Bloom, of Miss Loos, Charlie Chaplin and Whitehead, is still to me meaningless. There is no connection that I can see. Such a connection, I protest, is not proved by you, nor can it be proved."

Another sort of criticism, which we can neglect, but may just refer to in passing, is to the effect that a physical giant, hiding his head amongst a crowd of stars, an Einstein or a de Sitter, cannot be compared, or forced into the same frame, without absurdity, with a jazz poetess or a circus or cinema clown. That is a snobbery of a similar sort to such as would lead the person possessed of it to resent your associating such a monster as, say, a stellar universe with a primrose or a tadpole. All I can say to that is that my values, though exacting enough, are of a different order from that of such quantitative pomp.

So let us now turn to the first of these two criticisms, and try once more (and this time I hope in such a convincing manner as will leave no further room for honest criticism on that count at least) to make clear the connection of the time-cult as manifested upon the social plane with that manifested upon the theoretic. I reached the particular conclusions set forth in this book inductively. I became aware that a great orthodoxy of thought of some sort was in process of consummating itself. Having satisfied myself of that and analysed its nature on the spot, and upon the living model, I thought I would see whether a similar orthodoxy was to be found in the theoretic field. Should I find that that were so, I said to myself, it would be fair to assume that the one must have something to do, at the least, with the other. The result of my investigation was that I found the same unanimity rampant throughout the contemporary theoretical field. Point for point what I had observed on the literary, social and artistic plane was reproduced upon the philosophic and theoretic: and with a startling identity, the main notion or colour at the bottom of the theoretical system (however misleading the tags and descriptions of the various schools might be) was precisely the same thing as what was to be observed throughout the social and literary life of the day.

It resolved itself in both instances into *a cult of Time*. There seemed no doubt, after a little examination of the facts, that the more august of these two regions had influenced the lower and more popular one, and that the great principle of its cult, namely Time or History, had reproduced itself with a god-like fecundity, taking a multitude of original, hybrid, and often very grotesque forms upon the mundane plane of popularization and fashion.

I will begin my further evidence upon this initial point with Professor Alexander: in the following passage it will be seen that he, at least, would hardly have been able to make the sort of objections to my earlier statement that I have outlined above: for he brackets Bergson (and his famous principle of time or *durée*, for him "the animating principle of the universe") with the "mathematical physicists," the most celebrated of whom is Einstein; and associates his own philosophy, that of *Space Time and Deity*, with the Time-attitude implicit in both.

In a famous passage Kant, speaking of our need of immortality in order to approximate to perfect virtue in an infinite progress, says, "The infinite being for whom the condition of time does not exist sees what for us is an endless series, as a whole . . . and the holiness which his command inexorably requires is present at once in a single intellectual perception on his part of the existence of rational beings." . . . A person might well be content to be an idealist in philosophy in order to have the right of saying these noble things. But all these questions arise not before but after the empirical inquiry into the nature of Space and Time, and this inquiry should answer them directly or indirectly in its course or in its outcome. *At the present moment the special question of the exact relation of Time to Space has been forced into the front, because Time has recently come into its full rights, in science through the mathematical physicists, in philosophy also through Prof. Bergson, who finds in Time conceived as duree . . . the animating principle of the universe.* . . . One welcome consequence of [Bergson's] work is that it imposes on philosophy the duty of considering, like the mathematicians in their way, what exactly Space and Time are in their relation to one another. (*Space Time and Deity*, vol. i, p. 36.)

And a few pages further on Professor Alexander says again:

The most important requirement for this analysis is *to realize vividly the nature of Time.* . . . We are, as it were, *to think ourselves into Time. I call this taking Time seriously.* Our guides of the seventeenth century desert us here. Besides the infinite, two things entranced their intellects. One was Space or extension; the other was Mind. But, entranced by mind or thought, they neglected Time. *Perhaps it is Mr. Bergson in our day who has been the first philosopher to take Time seriously.* (*Space Time and Deity*, vol. i, p. 44.)

There is the following footnote to the first of these two passages:

Even Mr. Russell writes . . . "The contention that time is unreal and that the world of sense is illusory must, I think, be regarded as based on fallacious reasoning. Nevertheless there is some sense . . . in which time is an unimportant and superficial characteristic of reality . . . a certain emancipation from slavery to time is essential to philosophical thought. The importance of time is rather practical than theoretical, rather in relation to our desires than in relation to truth. . . . Both in thought and in feeling, to realize the unimportance of time is the gate of wisdom."

I should say that the importance of any particular time is rather practical than theoretical, and to realize the importance of Time as such
is the gate of wisdom. (*Space Time and Deity*, vol. i, p. 36.)

So Professor Alexander, as you will see, will not have Mr.
Russell's hedging on the subject of such a thing as *Time*. No, with
such a thing as that there must be no trifling or short measures:
you *must* take Time seriously! None of your intellectualist airs
where the great god Time is concerned! The "unimportance of
Time," indeed! "The importance of Time is rather in relation to
our *desires* than in relation to truth." Our "desires" and "truth,"
forsooth! — as though our *desires* were not *truth*, and truth just
our desires! "Practical" and "theoretical"! As though the "practical" were not of more importance than the theoretical, instead
of *vice versa*, as poor little Mr. Russell arrogantly, sentimental-
ly but hopelessly asserts! Some such response as this was evidently
that of the offended mind of Professor Alexander.

To take Time seriously — that has never been done by
philosophers, and that is what we now must do. In the two
passages I have quoted above, Professor Alexander associates
the mathematical physicists and Bergson as the two main sources
of this new attitude — it is to them jointly that we owe this striking advance. The seventeenth-century philosophers were (1)
"Spatializers," entranced with Space or extension; and (2) they
had the cult of the Mind, were "entranced with Mind." So they
are of no use to us, as little use as Plato, where this great innovation is concerned. We must be *entranced with Time*, instead
of being "entranced with Space," or "entranced with Mind." And
if we would be so entranced, it is no use looking for support
anywhere earlier than Bergson. *Bergson was probably the first
man in the world, calling himself a philosopher, to "take Time
seriously."* What Mr. Russell would call "practical" men, what
others call Plain-men, or sometimes Men-in-the-street, have
always taken time seriously. They have even named it the
"enemy," and they have a proverb to the effect that "Time is
money." But Professor Bergson was the first "theoretic" man (as
Mr. Russell would innocently call him) to "take Time seriously."
That is in substance what Professor Alexander says to us above.
I take it that that is unambiguous enough to satisfy the requirements of any criticism on this point, at least as far as the
testimony of Professor Alexander is concerned. But I will finally
quote another considerable authority as to the place that should

be assigned to Bergson, and his responsibility for most contemporary philosophic thought having the concept "Time" at the heart of it. Dr. Sheen is the authority to whom I refer, and this is what he says:

Whatever philosophical criticism is given today is in greater part a repetition of that made by the great French Academician, Henri Bergson. It is under his leadership that the intellectualist position has met its severest attacks, and it is round his arguments that all modern anti-intellectualists rally. Not only to his anti-intellectualism, but also to his positive doctrine, English philosophy is profoundly indebted. The greater portion of English and American philosophy which has appeared in recent years is Bergsonian in inspiration. (*God and Intelligence*, Longmans, Green & Co., 1925.)

To Whitehead, to the neo-realists, to Croce and Gentile, and to Spengler, I will revert in a moment. But first I will quote some remarks of Bosanquet's, from his *Meeting of Extremes in Contemporary Philosophy* (Macmillan, 1921). I find it very difficult to understand, in following Bosanquet's excellent account of the contemporary metaphysical situation in this last book of his, which I have only recently come across, why, seeing the situation with such clearness, he should have been so accommodating. It is that vice of mildness, or that readiness to be flattered and intellectually cajoled, on the part of such people as Bosanquet, that has made the unification in question possible. For Bosanquet saw very clearly with one eye a part, at all events, of the time-manoeuvre; the other eye he kept, not very tightly, closed. But apparently in that way he gradually grew cyclopian, and mutilated his thought with a false Unity. With his trained mind he could scarcely help immediately putting his finger on the spot of vital importance, guided to it by his technical equipment. He saw clearly that what really was significant in most contemporary philosophy was (*a*) the strange unanimity on great issues between these various schools, labelled in such opposite fashion, yet really agreeing so much; and that (*b*) the critical point of their agreement, the capital issue — and in that they are without any exception unanimous — is as to "Time." For them all, the fundamental character of the real is *temporal*.

Time is the supreme reality.

Time as a whole and in its parts bears to Space as a whole and its corresponding parts a relation analogous to the relation of mind to its equivalent bodily or nervous basis; or to put the matter shortly, Time is the mind of Space and Space the body of Time. (Alexander, *Space Time and Deity*, Book III, chap. ii.)

Bosanquet had been too long associated with Bradley not to have inherited some of his weaknesses. But whatever was the conclusion he came to about what he saw, he certainly did see these two things very clearly, and expressed himself with admirable lucidity: the two things being, once more, the very odd fact, as it seemed to him, of a sudden orthodoxy, where he had always been accustomed to the disputes of the metaphysical party-system (of "realist" and "idealist," rationalist and empiricist): and secondly, the position of Time at the bottom of this new brotherhood, in a position of dictatorship with regard to all other concepts or systems whatever. The details of his analysis can be read in independence of his conclusions. What is unsatisfactory and vacillating in Bradley is what, in Bosanquet, inclined him to this agreement with a system which he nevertheless saw clearly was embarked on a mass-organization of all the principles that the "Absolutist" had always recognized as the opposite of his own thought. The "Absolutism" that he represented had received into its bosom too much doubtful matter, however, and had been too weakened by constant attack, to behave differently in its last great representative, Bosanquet.

In the next chapter I shall be dealing with the phenomenon of Unanimity, as I am here with the Time issue. On both Bosanquet has very valuable things to say. This is how he opens the first chapter of his book:

I will not begin my discussion with *that most striking antithesis and identity* to which I referred in my Preface — *namely, the main relation between the neo-realists, and, as I will venture to call them, the neo-idealists, consisting in their doctrines of time and progress as ultimate reality.* For this remarkable agreement involves one entire philosophical position of today. . . . [The italics are mine.]

That is how Bosanquet opens his book; and, as you see, this celebrated metaphysician goes straight for the fundamental peculiarity of the situation (as I have described him as doing), namely, the *identity* of the standpoint (beneath the superficial variety of approach) of all that is influential, and all that has been influential for a very long time now, in the philosophic thought of the West; and at the same time he proceeds immediately to the fact that that identity is above all seen in the conferring upon

Time of an absolute and unique reality — in "taking Time seriously," as Alexander would say. What I next shall quote, from a
later chapter of his book, will fully confirm the clairvoyance of
this opening. It also introduces the other element, the political
element, which apparently he thought accounted for this strange
phenomenon, and which subsequently must be one of our main
subjects of debate.

I said in the Preface that when we began to deal with ultimate problems it would be necessary to insist on the most startling of all coincidences between extremes in the modern philosophical world. . . . But
now we have to consider the influence of the characteristically modern
attitude, dating, I presume, at least from what Carlyle would call the
Progress of the Species theories of the French revolutionary period,
which is asserting itself with decided superficial resemblance in neo-
realism and neo-idealism alike.

The three naturally connected characteristics of this position are the
acceptance of time and change as ultimate characteristics *of* (not
"within") the universe as such and as a whole; faith in the progress and,
in some sense, the perfectibility, of the human species . . . and the identification of morality and religion with the faith in this law. . . .

The school of neo-idealists in question, of whom Croce and Gentile
may be taken as typical, have, in the first place, thoroughly admitted
time and change into the core and basis of reality. Reality *is* "divenire,"
"becoming"; the idea of evolution in time is taken by them, in conscious
harmony with the trend of thought throughout the philosophical and
scientific world, as the very spirit of their philosophy. They have not
yet, so far as I know, dealt theoretically with the modern problem of
space-time; but I do not think that this need affect their position, and
if it did, according to current ideas, it would be taken to confirm it. . . .

Arguments could be alleged in their case, as in that of Professor
Alexander, to prove that so much of unity and wholeness is admitted
. . . that a change *of* reality, as distinct from changes within reality,
ought not to be taken as what they contemplate. But there is no question that in their minds this is what they intend to affirm — viz., that
in its very basis and meaning reality is a history or an unending dialectical progress.

That "most startling of all coincidences" is, of course, the identity of attitude on the subject of Time. Then he gives the practical bearings of this attitude towards that fundamental concept,
and its close alliance, as it is envisaged today, with the old revolutionary formula of *Progress* — the "Progress of the Species theories
of the French revolutionary period." And he then shows Gentile
and Alexander alike, and the Six — the six american neo-realists,

Holt, Marvin, Montague, R. B. Perry, Pitkin, and Spaulding — (with Whitehead and others) at his heels, admitting "time and change into the core and basis" of their Reality. Finally, he hints that no doubt the supporters of Professor Alexander, as of the italian philosophers associated with him in Time-worship, would find arguments to show that no fundamental change of reality itself was contemplated by them, but only changes *within* it. But he doubts the validity of such arguments, even if he accepts their sincerity. For them all, without exception, "in its very basis and meaning *reality is a history.*" It is a pure dialectical progression, presided over by a time-keeping, chronologically-real, super-historic, Mind, like some immense stunt-figure symbolizing Fashion, ecstatically assuring its customers that although fashions are periodic, as they must and indeed ought to be, nevertheless, by some mysterious rule, each one is *better* than the last, and should (so the advertisement would run) be paid *more* for than the last, in money or in blood.

To Bosanquet's identification of the attitude of these idealo-realist philosophers to the concept Time, with the "Progress of the Species" notions of the french revolutionary period, or all "Progress," in fact, and to the interesting means he takes to trace this deep liaison, I shall return presently. Whether we agree with him or not (and on the political ground I do not entirely), to have the hidden cable — as he sees it — connecting philosophic speculation with politics exposed by a master hand, is a valuable and suggestive experience. At least, I think, we shall have to allow that Bosanquet was not so far wrong even in this respect, where he directly describes the whole of this movement (and it must be remembered that it is universal, and is shared by almost every philosopher alive today) as "democratic" in its essence: that is to say, definitely *"political"* in its impulse, and not speculative at all. *"It is the assertion,"* he says, *"of the immediate and the practical, of the democratic element, it might be said, in thought,* just as is the affirmation of external being, and of all the forms of instinct and emotion which bring home to us ontological and cosmological truth in a simple and coercive manner" (*Meeting of Extremes*, etc., page 125). After this admirable statement he falls into compromise: but he ends his chapter with these words:

"The distinction at stake is that between time in the Absolute and the Absolute in time."

And on that plane and capital issue he might really have argued, with more effect, with rather less seduction: for what he was called upon to meet will scarcely be won by seduction. But let us assemble, without yet passing over into the very complex region of half-political, half-speculative argument and counter argument (where we shall be called upon to decide how far Bosanquet was right in identifying these attitudes in philosophy with specific political revolutionary idealism, how far the philosophical concept "Time" in its theoretic aloofness is in reality the old political "Progress" transformed for the occasion), still more evidence of the concrete existence, throughout all the field of thought and life, of the time-obsession, or the cult of history, of the "reality-as-history."

But "reality-as-history" is a pure Spenglerism—the *world-as-history* is one of his favourite phrases. And to Spengler I will now for a moment turn, forestalling my subsequent analysis. Spengler is perhaps the most undiluted and intensest specimen of the theorizing time-mind that has so far been produced. Spengler is expounding the "world-as-history"; in this passage we surprise him at his characteristic work. He is contrasting the historic mind with the "ahistoric," or "classical." In his pity for the poor Greek you will see the same sort of thing in operation as in the case of Professor Alexander (where the latter was comparing our "dynamical" advantages with the "static" shortcomings of the contemporaries of Plato or of Socrates).

It makes a great difference whether anyone lives under the constant impression that his life is an element in a far wider life-course, that goes on for hundreds and thousands of years, or conceives of himself as something rounded off and self-contained. For the latter type of consciousness there is certainly no world-history, no *world-as-history*. But how if the self-consciousness of a whole nation, how if a whole Culture rests on this ahistoric spirit? . . . Consider the Classical Culture. In the world-consciousness of the Hellenes all experience, not merely the personal, but the common past, was immediately transmuted into a timeless, immobile, mythically-fashioned background, for the particular momentary present. . . . Such a spiritual condition it is practically impossible for us men of the West, with [so strong] a sense of time-distances . . . to reproduce in ourselves. . . .

What diaries and autobiographies yield in respect of an individual, that historical research in the widest and most inclusive sense—that is, every kind of psychological comparison and analysis of alien peoples, times and customs—yields as to the soul of a Culture as a whole. But the Classical Culture possessed no *memory*, no organ of history in this special sense. The memory of the Classical man . . . is something different, since past and future, as arraying perspectives in the working consciousness, are absent, and the "pure Present," which so often roused Goethe's admiration in every product of the Classical life . . . fills that life with an intensity that to us is perfectly unknown.

This pure Present . . . in itself predicates the *negation of time* (of direction). For Herodotus and Sophocles, as for Themistocles or a Roman Consul, the past is subtilized instantly into an impression that is timeless and changeless, *polar and not periodic* in structure . . . whereas for our world-sense and our inner eye the past is a definitely periodic and purposeful organism of centuries or millennia. . . . *Inevitably* . . . the Greek man himself was not a series but a term. . . .

As regards Classical history-writing, take Thucydides. The mastery of this man lies in his truly Classical power of making alive and self-explanatory the events of the *present*, and also in his possession of the magnificently *practical outlook* of the born statesman. . . . But what is absolutely hidden from Thucydides is perspective . . .

Turning from Greece to India, Spengler tells us:

> In the Indian Culture we have the perfectly ahistoric soul. Its decisive expression is the Brahman Nirvana. . . . Of the visible course of their Culture . . . we know even less than we do of Classical history, *rich though it must have been in great events between the twelfth and eighth centuries.*

Alas, the poor Indian! and his untutored ahistoric mind! Spengler treats the poor Indian, or Greek, that he visits in the course of his time-travel, with the same lofty pity and disdain that the conquering White showed for the "poor Indian" of the english verse. Is it not at least strange that we today (as represented by Spengler and Alexander) are behaving to the Greek and Indian (*whose period we have historically overrun, as our ancestors overran the New World and the Orient*) just in the same way as the colonizing European did to the populations upon whom he fell? Is it just that same blind conceit (but nourished upon a sort of *time-jingoism* rather than upon the conditional sense of the superiority of the country of his origin possessed by the marauding White) that speaks in Alexander and Spengler? Or is it something else? That of course our subsequent investigation should bring to light. But in the name of common-sense, of the most immediate reality of the direct observation available to all of us, what today in Europe or America is there to give our representatives this insolent confidence in the superiority of our time? Have we at last become truly mad? For not since the Dark Ages has there been a time about which the time-jingo has as little right to boast as

the present. And it is difficult to see how any man could believe
in these irrational and pompous vaunts. So perhaps we should
look elsewhere, and not attribute these attitudes to confidence
or overweening belief. Let me recall, to place beside Spengler,
Professor Alexander's words, so similar in tone and significance.

It is in fact the cardinal defect of universals as conceived by Plato
and the Pythagoreans that they were changeless and immovable and
eternal. For not even the mind of Plato could be free from the habits
of his age, one of whose tendencies was to seek the highest ideals of
perfection in gravity of action and statuesque repose rather than in
restless motion.

Either the person responsible for those words is something like
a fool, or there must be some other explanation: for he cannot
believe in their good sense. And as he does not appear to be a
fool, then probably the reason for his expressing himself in a manner that he knows to be neither sensible nor true must be sought
elsewhere, in some region of pragmatical adjustment.

But Spengler is really a foolish, an exceedingly foolish, writer:
so let us stop and interpret this oracle, beginning at the end of
our quotation and working backwards. Indian history between
the twelfth and eighth centuries "must have been rich in great
events," he exclaims, full of time-hunger and despite at the thought
of lost historical opportunities. But these "great events," and the
certain people of importance who were undoubtedly engaged in
them, were so many pearls before swine as far as the poor Indian was concerned. Spengler shows no sign of its having occurred to him that these "great (historical) events" may not have
appeared of such vast importance to the contemporary indian
intelligence as they would be to Spengler. We often see lengthy
discussions in the papers as to whether Churchill or Briand is
the "greater" man of the two: or which of the recent american
presidents is as "great" as Pericles, Pitt, Dante or Galileo.
Spengler's responses to life are of course of the same order as
are those of the writers of such articles. The thought of all the
thousands of "great princes," gigantic harems, large meaty political
massacres, wars, rapes, manifestoes, criminal trials, gladiatorial
contests and so forth, that have been lost forever by the
"ahistorical" disposition of the benighted Indian, overwhelms
Spengler with astonishment, regret and disgust. It is just as though
he had learnt, suddenly, that all the records of the battles, raids,
destruction of ships, statistics of dead, prisoners, wounded,

maimed, gassed or lost, during the Greatest War of All Time (the one that ended nine years ago) were being neglected and lost, and that probably in another ten years it was announced not a line would be left to remind the historically-minded of the future (men like Spengler) of all these "great events." So, very much as the Greeks amaze and irritate him, the Indians do so even more.

His admissions, even, are not undiverting, for they are admissions that would weigh a little upon anybody except Spengler. Thucydides, for instance, was "a master" — *because* of his classical concentration upon the Present. He possessed a "Classical power" of making that Present of his "alive," in a way that we could not do: for *we* do not believe in the Present. Again, Goethe is one of Spengler's great heroes: yet Goethe was lost in admiration, he says quite simply, of the "pure Present" of the Hellene (when he compared it with his own romantic, time-obsessed, "Faustian" dream), manifesting itself, so Goethe thought, in every product of the Classical life. It is at least strange that the creator of "Faust" (and so indirectly of the notion of the "faustian") should have been so short-sighted and so easily amused.

But that, of course, is not quite Spengler's attitude either. He is *so* historical that he is impartial, he would tell us. Really Spengler's "fatalism" is the most marked thing about him, next to his congenital stupidity: because things are *so*, and not otherwise (as though they had occurred — in the "fatal," "incidental" course of things — and other human beings had had no hand in the transaction), they must, without any criticism or mitigation, remain as they *are* until they change of their own accord. It is true that an "ahistorical" people may change things if they don't find they agree with them: but not so an "historical" people. An historical people is very superior, superior to mere self, and far too respectful towards "destiny" to dream of changing *the Changing*. The chronological, the critical, mind, never attempts to alter anything: its rôle is passive, essentially. What *is* is sacred to it, in fact. The mere fact that it *is* just what it is, shows its superiority to us (who, however, are also just as we are). It is not our place — what next! — *to make History*: it is History that makes us. A truly chronologically or time-minded person knows better than to alter or criticize anything. This is called by Spengler "the historical capacity." (Cf. "From our standpoint of today, the gently-sloping route of decline is clearly visible. . . . This, too, the power of looking ahead to inevitable Destiny, is part of the

historical capacity that is the peculiar endowment of the Faustian." — *Decline of the West.*) So our Spengler is a description of
eternally time-trotting dilettante, who trots about his own time
along with the rest: and all he sees is a part of *history*; and he
would no more think of touching it than he would touch the objects displayed in a museum. Time could not be more static, even
as it appears in Weyl's physical system, than it and all its objects
are for Spengler, and this in spite of the dithyrambic orgasm that
occurs with him whenever he mentions "Time." He thinks, for
instance, that he notices "The West" rapidly "declining" — and in
any case it is about time it did; to satisfy the periodic principle,
and to satisfy chronology, it is about *time* the West "declined"!
So he writes *The Decline of the West.* The last thing that it would
ever occur to Spengler to do, even if he were able, would be to
interfere with this process, to challenge *this historically fated*
"Decline," for which he entertains the profoundest fatalistic
respect. This fatalism should be particularly noted, for it
characterizes most Time-thought. It results in an effect as though
its theorists were crawling about a reversible time-region which
was fixed, closed-in, and as though life consisted entirely in a
repetitive, periodic oscillation. And this applies to the same extent whether their "time" inclines to the physical side, as an ex-
tra dimension, or whether in the tracks of Bergson they treat "time"
as a thing of a quite different character to space. With this you
arrive at what is certainly the greatest paradox in the mass of
time-doctrine taken as a whole: namely that, advertising itself
as "creative," "evolutionary" and "progressive," it is yet the deadest
system, productive of least freedom, that you could imagine.

    If you consider a moment what the Spengler-ideal of the
"historical" mind implies, you will see how this indeed must ensue. It is equally evident that the mind of the "pure Present" must
be productive of the reverse. It fills Classical life, Spengler himself
tells us, blandly, "with an intensity that to us is perfectly
unknown." The pretentious omniscience of the "historical" intelligence makes of it an eternal dilettante, or tourist. It does
not live in, it is *en touriste* that it tastes this time-district, or
time-climate, and that. This mental world becomes for it an
interminable time-preserve, laid out for critical, disembodied
journeyings.

    Again, the mental world of *memory*, the image world, is not
in the nature of things as "intense" — if it is intensity that you

want—as the spatial world of the "pure Present" of the classical heyday. The *image* is not as strong a thing as the direct, spatial *sensation*. And the time-world is a world of images: that is one of the main things to remember about it, and to that presently I shall return.

How it is that many contemporary thinkers arrive at a kind of fixed world it is easy to grasp imaginatively by means of these analogies. The world of the "pure Present" of the Classical Ages is obviously the world that is born and dies every moment. (It is not the time-world, as Alexander asserts, but the space-world that does that.) The world of Space—as opposed to the mental world of memory—is the world of a "pure Present." For the past of that space-world is dead and gone; all its elements are regrouped: it is only in memory and the mental life of organisms that it survives. For the world of Space, used in this sense, yesterday no longer exists. But for the mental world of Time, the psychologic world, yesterday is still there, often exceedingly vivid though of a different quality to the Present.

Where the importance shifts over to the time-world, or mental world, it is natural that our conception of things should grow more static in one sense; for the time-world does not grow, decay, and die, as does the world of physical objects. It is always there: no bergsonian would be able to banish it—his efforts to do so and pull up all his Past into his Present would only result in his living in it more than anybody else in the end. In his private time-sense a man can move up and down, backwards and forwards, at will, in his gallery of memory-images. And it is natural at a period where this world of the "inner eye" is stressed, that men, whether physicists or philosophers, should begin constructing systems which are, as it were, dead worlds, laid out endlessly in what we know as Time. In their midst they imagine themselves moving about like sleepwalkers, placing themselves over against quite arbitrary perspectives, but perspectives of a sort of crystallized Time, instead of receding space-vistas. This time-world that they will imaginatively construct will naturally be difficult for the space-sense to imagine: but in effect it will consist of a time-sense *all there at once*, just as a space-sense is; yesterday, for example, will be five hundred yards away and in perspective, and last year will be a group of features in the middle distance. It is *we* who will be moving about in this time-scene. We, in short, shall be Time. (Cf. Spengler: "We create [Time] as an idea or notion and do not begin till much later to suspect that *we ourselves are Time*, inasmuch as we live.")

The difficulty comes in when this type of conception takes to itself the name "creative" or "organic," or has "Progress" conspicuously painted on its banner. For nothing could so ill describe it. Certainly it must be the instinctive "spatialized" world of the "pure Present" of Antiquity that is "creative," if anything deserves that name.

If we look at this problem with the eyes of the pure theoretic vision, which will probably at some point merge in some emotion that may be termed religious (of the sort that is not morals, it is understood, nor indeed practical at all), it is clear that what will satisfy us best will be the world of the "pure Present," the pagan system of Greek Antiquity, rather than the time-world. For that which is dead should be well dead—*bien mort*; and an account of things in which the only reality of this order is the *present* reality, consorts better with the instincts of the pure theoretic or highest religious vision, that is certain. This will have at first sight the appearance of a paradox. But when you consider the matter a little you will see that to wish to cling to this dead stuff or slough of the Past, and to treasure it, or (still more) to mould it into an ultimate system of truth, to make a finality of it, and invoke the conception of a finite universe to enhance and consummate, theoretically, this time-reality, and secure that there should be no escape, must seem to such a speculative sense strange and meaningless indeed. There is such and such a thing, or person, one moment, then it ceases to be: that is the "spatializing" truth. And in the end it certainly is a far less "materialistic" one. For that all that suffocating plethora of rubbish that collects within the infinitely extended field of memory can be very real indeed, is clearly shown by the various time-books we considered in the earlier part of this essay.

Next, I will quote Bergson's english disciple, Dr. Wildon Carr. He gives exactly the same account of the matter as Bosanquet, only he notes the same things naturally in a mood of exultation. The school to which he belongs has become an orthodoxy, he assures us.

There is every indication that a new concept of the fundamental nature of reality is emerging. . . . *The change, moreover, is distinctly in one definite direction.* ("Time" and "History.")

"Time" and "History," the title of the tract from which I am quoting, speaks for itself. It is a comparison of the philosophy of Croce (standing for "History") with the philosophy of Bergson (standing for "Time"). And Bergson's english disciple finds Bergson's *durée* and Croce's "historia" just as identical as does Bosanquet, although, of course, he is not quite so surprised.

The comparison I wish to make and the fundamental agreement I wish to indicate between the philosophy of Bergson and that of Croce does not consist in any material or formal identity . . . but in the fact that each has focussed the attention on the dynamic aspect of reality. . . .

He will go, he says, for his illustration of the "fundamental agreement" to:

First, the theory of Bergson that time is a material and not merely a formal element of the world . . . the "stuff" of things. Second, the theory of Croce that history is identical with philosophy, that there are no external events . . . that the historian, like the philosopher, is engaged in interpreting a present activity, and that history is therefore contemporaneous.

The reader will see that Dr. Carr's account bears out, with the authority of an official disciple, what I have quoted of Bosanquet. Or let us take this other passage of Dr. Carr's from the same pamphlet:

It will be seen that the two philosophers whose writings I have had mainly in mind [Bergson and Croce] reach, by entirely different routes and from entirely different standpoints, practically one identical concept. I do not think this is a mere coincidence. It marks a tendency to emphasize the dynamic aspect of reality as more original and more explanatory than the static aspect, and also to recognize that the static is derived.

The following very instructive passage will make still more precise our notion of what this philosophy means by "history" and "time." (It is from a lecture delivered during the War, apparently.)

The concept of history as present reality is the leading motive in Croce's philosophy. We may make the concept clear to ourselves by reflecting on the great world events in the midst of which we are living and in which we are taking part. We know that this world war will furnish to future generations the subject of historical research. Yet we distinguish. We suppose that we are making history, but that the history we are making is not history for us; it will be history only to those for whom it is past accomplished fact. To the philosopher this is not the pure historical concept. History is what we now are and what we are now doing, it is not a character our actions will assume only when they have receded into the past. The basis and the substance of this concept is that our present actions lose their meaning the moment we regard them as new existence *externally* related to another and past existence. To carry our past in our present action, we do not leave it outside and behind us. Not only is there no break between the present and the past, but both the form and the matter of present reality, what we now are and are now doing as individuals, or as nations, is in its essence *history*.

This is a description of one of the most fundamental concepts of the whole of this school, and it is equally shared by Croce and Bergson, and by all such philosophers as Alexander, who have followed them. I will proceed to interpret it, and make it even "clearer" than Dr. Wildon Carr has done. *History is the present reality* for Croce. That is the familiar Bergson doctrine of the Present being all-at-once, in one concentrated *now*, all the Past, as well as the present moment. Actually, there *is* no Past at all, in this view, strictly speaking: for the Present continually modifies it, so that the "Past" of yesterday is not the Past of today, for even with your dreams during the night you were altering it.

The extreme form of this doctrine is that recently advanced by a relativist; he holds apparently that we are able to change physically or even cancel the Past; so that it might no longer be true to say, for instance, that Napoleon had crossed the Alps, for we are able to abolish that event; to prevent him from crossing the Alps, in fact, as though there with a modern army to stop him. All the Thermopylaes and Waterloos could easily be reversed by our god-like relativist powers — if we had those powers, that is.

History is not something we have [Carr says], it is something we are. . . . Present reality is not in external union with past reality, the present holds the past in itself, it is one with the past and it is big with the future. *Not only does every new present action modify the past,* it reveals the meaning of the past, and even in that external sense the past is not dead fact to be learnt about, but living development changing continually. (*"Time" and "History."*)

Let us turn the bull's-eye of the pragmatists upon this account of things. Is it not evident that sharing your life with your descendants in this manner, and your ancestors' being dependent on

you for their very souls, is a purely "materialistic" doctrine—
not at all "idealist," as Carr calls it, but is indeed one of the subtlest
blows it would be possible to deliver at the notion of individuality,
and of individual freedom. Let us visualize in the concrete what
this teaching would involve; then we shall become immune from
its lyrical glamour, I think. (Professor Hoernlé says, in his *Studies
in Contemporary Metaphysics*: "Poetical metaphors seem almost
unavoidable in the attempt to render Bergson's theory." Poetry
is necessary, that is true, with Bergson. It is a pity Bergson was
not able to "say it with flowers"; but of course he does as often
as he can, and any attempt at interpretation, even in the driest
hands, has always had to *blossom*.) On what part of the picture
are the flowers heaped and the scent squirted, here?

You are supposed to burst into rapturous song at the mere
thought that you are *co-operating* in one "great" (very great) communal work (of art), with a toiling, joyous crowd of forbears
and descendants. (You know that in cold fact you have nothing
much yourself to be joyous about; you are aware that the generations behind you, could you visit them, would scarcely be found
so romantically situated as in this Santa Claus dream for good
little "proletarians." But no matter. Do not let us spoil the picture.) It is *tremendously exciting* to think that we are actually
making history with our own hands—and—just think of it!
"History" is *all there is!* So *we* are all there is, too! We are
creating—anything there is to create. Again, history does not *stay
put*. It jumps up and helps us. We find, with a gasp of delight,
that *it* is *us* all the time. We look round, and there is Julius Caesar,
with a cheery smile, in blue overalls and sandals, come to give
us a hand! It is all so glorious and splendid, when you come to
think of it, that it makes one happy to be alive, and at the same
time quite ready to die. Hard work—why, *no* work is too hard,
if you only reflect what it's all for, just as no death is too unpleasant! That's the spirit!

That is the sunday school magazine side of the "historical" doctrine of Croce and Bergson. The other side of it, the practical
side that would claim our attention immediately in real life, is
this. This immanent, "historical" doctrine, like any other form
of pantheism, has as its capital drawback that it leaves very little room indeed for the individual, the person—that is if you
regard that as a drawback. Human life, beneath the reign of
"evolutionist" politics, would be a colourless affair for anything

more complex than an ant. Your *individual* life, however miserable an affair, is the thing you make, or that you have the sensation of making. That is your bird in the hand. That you build for your personal use; all the pleasure is in the personal. Once you are no longer there, you would prefer it should vanish. But some patronizing high-bohemian family, with a far larger and quicker motor-car than any you could possess, infinitely more highly "evolved" and sanitary and clever than yourself, come to live in it, constantly changing and *improving* it. You remain there as a servant or gardener. Later you fall lower than that, but you are always there. That is one sort of picture. Or consider what such a person as Michelangelo would be apt to reflect if he learnt that each fresh half-century would see the frescoes he was labouring at improved and "evolved." As an artist he would know, of course, that such things were not susceptible of such barbarous "improvement": that they were not in the same category as types of rapidly "evolving" engines: that they were there for good or ill, once and for all, and that a race of people, mad and pretentious enough to adopt the feature of "progressiveness" indicated, could merely ruin them. This is, of course, a thing that has often happened to works of art, as gothic churches notably testify.

The reader perhaps could have supplied better illustrations himself, or ones more persuasive for him personally: but my argument I think is now evulgated sufficiently. The Past as *myth* — as history, that is, in the classical sense — a Past in which events and people stand in an imaginative perspective, a *dead* people we do not interfere with, but whose integrity we respect — that is a Past that any person who has a care for the principle of individual life will prefer to "history-as-evolution" or "history-as-communism." As to the extremest form this sort of "historical" or "time" doctrine has taken, we can say that to desecrate a grave is a mild offence compared to the possibilities involved in the theory to which I have already alluded, that men may one day be able to poke into the Past, as it were resuscitate it, and dragoon the dead — in the way that Spengler would the ancient races of the East, if he could, making Buddha swallow his words, and Confucius learn to play the ukulele; rather, of course, much more than that — decree that such people should cease to darken existence at all, and abolish them.

So "new existence *externally* related to another and past existence," so disliked by Dr. Carr and his master Bergson, is what we prefer. That is the condition of the "classical Present" referred to by Spengler — though Spengler always talks as though it were confined to Greece, whereas it has been most men's Present excepting ours. We have indeed *lost our Present*: in a bergsonian attempt to crush all the Past into it, and too much of the Future at a time, as well. It may be thought that my extreme antipathy for this "community-history," or chronological merging, is because I know that the intellectual principle would suffer first in the "progressive" readjustment, as indeed we already can perceive it suffering today. Mr. Bertrand Russell, in his excellent pamphlet, *The Philosophy of Bergson*, describes the situation of the intellect in the bergsonian dispensation as follows:

Among animals, at a later stage of evolution, a new bifurcation appeared: *instinct* and *intellect* became more or less separated. They are never wholly without each other, but in the main intellect is the misfortune of man, while instinct is seen at its best in ants, bees and Bergson. . . . Much of [Bergson's philosophy] is a kind of Sandford and Merton, with instinct as the good boy and intellect as the bad boy.

And we know what would happen to the "bad boys" of the Past if Bergson had his way, especially the hellenic monsters, headed by Plato. But it is not only on account of the intellect that I adopt this attitude. I am just as concerned for "instinct," which I do not regard as being quite at its best in ants, bees and Bergson.

Some ambiguity is apt to cling to a first statement of anything. What this problem hinges on is the very question of *reality*, nothing less, and what you are going to mean by it. The time-mind makes Time "a material element of the world," and the ultimate and supreme reality. The absent, the past — *all* time is actual. Professor Alexander's god is Time: for of his god, Space-time, *Time is the mind*: and one is never left in any doubt as to which of these two, Space and Time, in their new union, is in the ascendant. So what occurs in this philosophy is that Time is made *more* real than was the "pure Present" of the antique world (as described disparagingly by Spengler, or extolled by his hero Goethe). For the "idealist," or platonic side of that antiquity, the "pure Present," though far more real than any Past, was not entirely real. There was something else, that was neither "pure Present" nor Past nor Future, that was infinitely more so. This hypostasized "something" was the Reality — for one thinker it took one form, for another another. But for the time-school in the bosom of which, as though in Abraham's, we dwell for the moment, the Reality is *not* the Present, but it is the stuff of which the Present is an arbitrary perspective: and it is always, ultimately, *Time*. So, as Bosanquet puts it, "the distinction at stake is that between time in the Absolute and the Absolute in time": that is the capital issue upon which you have to come to some decision.

If I fail in this attempt to make the Time problem plain, it will be the result entirely of my own incompetence and lack of the most elementary powers of persuasion, that is quite certain: for my case is an overwhelmingly good one, the material inexhaustible, and really all that is necessary is, by some device, to prop people's eyes open for half a minute, and my point would be perfectly clear to them: for the landscape I am describing lies all round them: or rather, the main feature of it, to which I am drawing attention, it is impossible to escape from: it is as ubiquitous as Fujiyama in a japanese print. But I obviously cannot fail in this attempt: still the relevant material has to be carted up and dropped down on to this paper, so that we may examine it without preliminary confusion: and it is my object to make this task as light as possible for the reader. About the time I was describing above the *stuff*, the colossal mountain of sheer material, that the time-view involves — stuffing up and constipating the "pure Present," impeding clear-cut living and sane, resolute, "classical" action, like a rising morass of mud — I was reading again Miss Jane Harrison's book, *Ancient Art and Ritual* (which I used extensively in my *Dithyrambic Spectator*), and there I found the following account of her idea of what I have called a "timebook."

Science has given us back [she says] something strangely like a World-Soul, and art is beginning to feel she must utter our emotion towards it. . . . The art of Mr. Arnold Bennett gets it bigness, its collectivity, in part — *from extension over time*. Far from seeking after beauty, he almost goes out to embrace ugliness. *He does not spare us even dullness, that we may get a sense of the long, waste spaces of life, their dreary reality*.

Miss Harrison's mind, as you will observe, is a perfect *timemind*. Her concluding chapters swarm — for the time-hunter — with such stuff as the above. If you are a time-critic, turn the pages over, and the fruit will drop into your hand, or the game offer itself in a mad profusion to your eye. That anybody who erects

Time into a reality should have to deal with "long waste spaces," interminable spaces, full of an infinitude of material—the material of memory, but none the less filling for that—that "dreary dullness" should be essential when the creative artist of the time-sort enters these "waste spaces," is inevitable. But Miss Harrison tells us that in Mr. Bennett you get "bigness, collectivity."

We are keenly interested [she writes] in the loves of hero and heroine, but all the time something much *bigger* is going on, generation after generation rolls by in ceaseless panorama; it is the life not of Edwin and Hilda, it is the life of the Five Towns. After a vision so big, to come back to the ordinary individualistic love-story is like looking through the wrong end of a telescope.

Miss Jane Harrison is an extremely well-known writer, and representative, no doubt, of a very large class of scholarly people; and here she expresses perfectly the time-idea, associated, of course, with the communistic or collectivist—which, as she accurately observes, "Science has given us."

The "bigness" to which she refers is plainly quantitative: she is being lyrical about a hundred billion Hildas and Edwins. "Generation after generation rolls by." The *bigger* the generations, and the *more* of them that roll by, the more Miss Harrison is impressed, the more she exclaims and points, and opens wide her eyes, and desires to impress us, or takes it for granted we shall be impressed. "It is the life of the Five Towns" we are beholding—nothing so "paltry," really, as the poor, *little*, merely individual, existence of Hilda and Edwin. "After a vision so *big*, to come back to the ordinary individualistic love-story is like looking through the wrong end of a telescope."

The individual, in short, is dwarfed by these perspectives: we return condescendingly (after the impressive privilege of looking at "the Five Towns" in person, as it were—telescopically) to the two little specks, mere *individuals* belonging to this colossal aggregate.

The assumption in this passage of Miss Harrison's of a "collectivist" emotionality in the reader, of an ecstatic stupefaction at the picture of the colossal, of a ready contempt for a mere "individual" (like himself or herself), is very curious. It would seem intensely stupid if it were not the sort of assumption that could be matched in so many places or persons that it would be presumptuous, in face of this unanimity, to think of it as stupid.

We say, perhaps to ourselves, patiently, "Why should the

bigness be so important, or has *importance* of that sort so much meaning? Has it so much meaning, above all, for us — for it is *we* for whom "art is beginning to feel she must utter *our* emotion." What is the "Five Towns," *big* as that pentamerous mammoth is, without us? We are not *mere* individuals: on the contrary, it is the Five Towns that is a mere immense "dreary reality," a huge Nothing, without us. It was that sort of abstraction that Berkeley could simply not find, when he looked for it, in his mind. And it does not, nor could it, exist, in spite of the time-mind, without our "pure Present." This immense smoky dragon made out of generations and generations of billions of Five Towns rolled into one great time-mass, and seen with the chronological eye *all-together*, as *one* huge thing, of which any Edwin and Hilda are a tiny cell, is not a reality; and, apart from that, it is a particularly *useless* invention.

The memory of the Classical man is . . . different [from ours] since . . . perspectives in the working consciousness are absent, and the "pure Present," which so often roused Goethe's admiration in every product of the Classical life . . . fills that life with an intensity that to us is perfectly unknown.

At all events it is unknown to the Hildas and Edwins, with Bennett at their head, and ignored also most probably by Miss Harrison, the devotee of the "long waste spaces . . . of dreary reality" that she assures us are provided for the devout time-sense by Mr. Arnold Bennett. (I do not know whether her account of this book of Mr. Bennett's is accurate or not, as it is one I do not happen to have read.)

At this point I shall venture to digress for a moment, as perhaps a few further remarks on the subject of that quantitative piling up of material and its advertisement (that vaunted "bigness" or "collectivity," as Miss Harrison calls it) are needed, to further advance my meaning. Perhaps it will seem a great way off to step from the "dreary reality" of the Five Towns to Bradley's Absolute: but by doing so, if you do not object to that precipitate anomalous translation, I think the problem of scale and of quantity, on which we have just touched, will be advanced, and a further light be thrown on that common advertisement of "bigness" and "collectivity."

When Bradley is discussing one of the objections to his Absolute ("drawn from a common mistake"), he writes:

Quantity is often introduced into the idea of perfection. For the perfect seems to be that beyond which we cannot go, and this tends naturally to take the form of an infinite number. But. . . [I] will pass on to the objection which may be urged against our view of the perfect. If the perfect is the concordant, then no growth of its area or increase of its pleasantness could make it more complete. We thus, apparently, might have the smallest being as perfect as the largest; and this seems paradoxical. But the paradox really, I should say, exists only through misunderstanding. For we are accustomed to beings whose nature is always and essentially defective. And so we suppose in our smaller perfect a condition of want, or at least of defect; and this condition is diminished by alteration in quantity. But, where a being is really perfect, our supposition would be absurd.

In "smallness," Bradley says, we see "a condition of want." And as our notion of a more-perfect-thing is always additive — since our units of experience are invariably poor and defective — so "bigness" in our minds comes to have some connection with the notion of perfection. How this applies to the passage from Miss Harrison's book we have been discussing is as follows. We commonly suppose that if we multiply Hilda and Edwin a million-fold, we get something more perfect, and more to be admired. We do in reality get something "big" — a large "collectivity." As the "generation after generation rolls by," we do think that we are really arriving somewhere, or at least Miss Harrison assumes that this is how we do, or should, feel. But it is really not to be wondered at, if you come to consider it, that this *quantitative perfection* should (after our first awe-struck genuflections at the *scale*, the "bigness," the "collectivity") a little pall on us. This "dreary reality" reached across the big "waste spaces of life" is, however much we are worked up by able propaganda, such as the eloquence of Miss Harrison, not very inspiring. No *quantitative perfection* can be: and of such stuff is the "Five Towns" (as interpreted by Miss Harrison) made. The "Billion Towns" would be the same. Hilda and Edwin, whatever they may be, are more important than the "Five Towns" — the abstract collectivity of all the Hildas and Edwins. And some modification in their favour, and away from the Absolute, is to my mind required, where Bradley's values are concerned: for Bradley's Absolute is a little too much of a ponderous abstraction, a "Five Towns," Itself, it must be said.

I could, of course, accumulate here many illustrations of the type of the short passage from *Art and Ritual*, for such confirmatory material abounds, and everybody can apply the principle, suiting themselves as to their illustrations. The remainder of the essay will progressively provide further confirmation as to the supremacy of the notion of Time in contemporary philosophic thought, and attempt to make clear the nature and meaning of that ascendancy.

CHAPTER EIGHT

THE FUSION OF IDEALISM AND REALISM

IN THIS CHAPTER I am going to discuss the nature and extent of the *unanimity* which I have said I believe to be one of the most peculiar things about the present time, or as Bosanquet describes it, "the meeting of extremes." Many people will be found, probably, to deny absolutely that any such orthodoxy exists. There is no "meeting of extremes," they will say. There are still fierce fanatical "idealists" contending with strong, silent "realists," and all is just as it has always been. Others will say, "If that ancient strife is ended, so much the better; it is about time." Others might argue, "There has always been a *meeting of extremes.* There is nothing new in that." This chapter is devoted to answering those arguments and objections, and to defining the nature of the fusion alleged.

What are these "extremes" that "meet"? The most general terms by which they respectively would be indicated are "idealism" and "realism." So let us start by considering for a moment what meaning can be attached to those terms. And let us take the bergsonian convert to thomistic thought, Jacques Maritain, as our guide, for he holds very strong, bergsonianly strong, views upon what is apt to be grouped beneath the term "idealism."

Idealism [he writes] strikes at the very life of the intelligence, it misunderstands radically the intelligence even while it affects to exalt it. At the same time, and for that very reason, one discovers it at the root of all the ills from which today the mind is suffering. (*Réflexions sur l'Intelligence*, chap. ii.)

If idealism is all that, and more, it is an important disease at least, and is worth paying some slight attention to. But what is "idealism" for M. Maritain? Idealism is the enemy of "the real" for him, we must suppose (for whether you are an "idealist" or a "realist," what *you* are is always "the real"). So, of what "real" — or "ideal" — is "idealism" the enemy?

For Maritain "idealism" has its roots in Descartes. This is his account of its origin.

Did not Descartes pretend to replace the syllogism by intuition —
by an intuition, certainly, multiple and discontinuous, like a succession of angelical *coups d'oeil*? Does not he wish our ideas to be innate,
resolved into the very truth of divine ideas, like the truth of pure spirits?
That we know nothing except in first knowing ourselves, as happens
with the angels? Does not he believe our reason to be so naturally excellent that common sense is sufficient (along with method) to enable
us to penetrate into the secrets of the most curious sciences, and that
there is no more occasion for an intrinsic process of perfectioning or
for a *habitus* for the human understanding, than for the angelic intelligence in the system of nature? But there we have, in the cartesian
revolution so interpreted, the first seed, certainly very general and
undefined, but very real . . . of modern idealism: having for its result
that our ideas become ideas of angels, directly and immediately contingent upon the First Cause and Creative Truth.

First of all, if Descartes was under this (very favourable) impression with regard to the angelic status of our ideas, it was no
doubt largely because he himself was an "angelical doctor." For
was not the "Angelical Doctor" himself a kind of angel? Was not
the "Seraphical Doctor" the only true seraph? But those two fundamental and realistic considerations will not, it is true, in this
case help us. Maritain means, of course, that Descartes, with his
subjective truth, pushed up the human mind too near to God,
and crowded out the magian angels of St. Thomas. Such people
as Descartes, with their *genius* (which is such a complication in
dogmatic systems, which of course in the nature of things can
make no allowance for such *sports*) always have this tendency
to telescope the hierarchy. Any intelligent thomist would admit
the difficulty; a purely disciplinary difficulty. The philosophical
superman, the mind that so outstrips the average that it dislocates
any orderly conservative system, must be repudiated and denied
both by the dogmatic authoritarian and by the communist; when,
that is, the unusual person shows a tendency to behave as though
he were already in Paradise. Descartes was such a freak, and in
his natural life behaved as though truth were of this world and
permitted to men.

But it is not the evulgating of this truth, on which point
we should be in agreement with the thomist to some extent, but
the truth itself, which is to be considered. Is the "subjectivity"
initiated by Descartes, is the "idealism" of Leibniz, Spinoza,
Berkeley or Kant, responsible for all the ills of the modern world?
That question cannot be answered, simply because "idealism,"

"subjectivity," are terms that are worlds in themselves, and contain everything from positivism to solipsism, it could almost be said: just as "christianity" covers the extremest mysticism and the utmost materiality. It depends on the "idealism" in question, upon the time that that acts upon, and so forth. But I shall shortly be giving such answer as can be given to any inquiry of that nature.

As far as Maritain personally is concerned, once a bergsonian always a bergsonian. It would be naïf to place too much reliance upon his "conversion." He seems to me to be saturated with the lyrical and shoddy impulses of his master, some of his tracts are so effusive that it is impossible to read them without feeling seasick: and he seems to me to retain all his old master's hatred of the "intellect," so that it often seems as though he might perhaps without too conscious a guile have disguised himself as a thomist in order the better to attack it.

When Maritain attacks the "ideality" of Relativity Theory, and describes the Relativists as "ces petits-neveux de Kant"; or when he attacks Descartes as the ancestor of Kant; or when he attacks Kant as this "docteur brutal," and so forth, he is describing systems and people who are respectively so extremely dissimilar in their "subjectivity," that it is impossible to answer him on behalf of "subjectivity"; and the individuals involved could not answer him in that general way either, they would disagree with each other too much. The "subjective" private systems of *real* Time of Relativity is an exceedingly different thing from Descartes or from Berkeley, both of whom started from a God as much as did St. Thomas. These few remarks will enable the reader, I hope, to find his way into what is really the maze of these classifications, with which, however, we are bound now to deal.

The doctrine of "Time" was identified, in Book One, with the doctrine of the Flux. With regard to that statement, it is perhaps necessary to draw attention to the following obvious qualification —for not only is "time" not nothing but the Flux, but a belief in or recognition of the Flux, or the "Becoming," by no means involves a doctrine of temporal supremacy. So, to start with, it is probably as well to point out that no Western philosopher who has ever lived has denied that there is a constant empirical flux and change in time, at least in appearance. Plato, in this respect, gives exactly the same account of things as Heraclitus. It is not there that the capital antithesis in traditional philosophy is to be sought. The radical difference between one kind of doctrine and another has consisted in whether it was held that there was anything *besides*, behind, or over and above the Flux, or whether, on the other hand, there was nothing but that. Such, roughly, is the basis for the popular contrast.

Heraclitus was the first celebrated Western protagonist of the Flux and nothing but the Flux. In this he was in the ionian naturalist tradition. For him it was insupportably real: he was known to the Ancient World as "the weeping philosopher," because, in believing that there was nothing but dissolution and vanishing away, so that the river into which you step is never twice the same river, but always a different one, and you yourself of yesterday are as far away today, and as much scattered and changed, as are the waters of yesterday's river, he was rendered very gloomy, or people took it for granted that such must be the case, in consequence. "Où sont les neiges d'antan?" could be taken as typifying, in inconsolable reiteration, the burden of his thought. He could scarcely be said, from that point of view, to be a man of a "pure Present," although standing conspicuously for the Classical Age. So that, in passing, is a good illustration of how we must beware of "Classical," "Modern," "Faustian" generalizations, side by side with "Realist," "Idealist" ones. On the other hand, Bergson, professing much the same belief as Heraclitus, has always exhibited a highly advantageous and popular optimism at the same sight. But of course it is not really the *same* Flux at which Bergson has beamed, and at which the primitive Ionian disconsolately gazed. That is another difference that we have to be careful not to forget, apart from the great discrepancies in personal character.

To represent the other great division in philosophy, the opposite to that that insists upon the ultimate reality of the Becoming, Plato is the figure usually chosen. The world of Time or Becoming was for him the "moving image of Eternity," a kind of false Eternity; or, in another myth of his, shadows upon the wall of a dark cave, cast from real but unperceived originals. He believed that there was something indestructible and constant behind the phenomenal flux. But one or more "faulty souls" betrayed their presence by many inharmonious happenings in our universe. So he exonerated the divine principle. The discordant facts are accounted for by most people today not, of course, by reference to occult "powers" of that sort, but as part of the natural and fatal process of relentless struggle which characterizes organic and physical life, and this irrespective of whether the person in question inclines to the "platonic" side or to that of an ionian naturalism.

As to the time and place of appearance of these opposed standpoints, no race or period has, of course, conformed to either entirely. Western Europe has been more inclined (in contradiction to its "idealist" religion) to the naturalist or mechanical; being less "strong in mystery" and more disposed to the practical roman model. Yet the european religion grew up in response to the picture of a finite God, one well within the universe: and so even theologically there was not such an irreconcilable contradiction. Greek thought, for its part, was inclined to mix politics into its philosophic speculations; early indian thought, we can assert more perhaps than of any other, was purely speculative. And politics and dogmatic coercive religion, these kindred activities, are the influences that are most able to distort and cancel the pure speculative impulse.

In the history of indian thought both these principles exist. For the buddhist religion the older and profounder upaniṣadic thought is transformed in two important respects. First, the reality of the self is denied: and, secondly, in order to obtain more leverage for proselytizing purposes, the conception of the unreality of the empirical manifold is sensibly reduced. The practical reason for this is manifest. The buddhist religion is founded upon the advertisement (in the interests of professional salvation) of the fearful misery of human life. But if the misery were shown not to be *real*, then obviously there would be less need for the intervention of the salvationist. The world, in spite of its flux, has to be, for the buddhist, as unquestionably real as it was for Heraclitus. And a similar phenomenon, a deliberate blackening of the natural colours of the picture, a policy of sabotage, may often be observed where politics are concerned in all times and places.

So the political mind of Greece and the materialistic, pragmatical mind of the modern West, equally with that of the religionist of India (as opposed to the indian philosopher or to occasional philosophers making their appearance in any period or place), has tended to make the flux real: it has not wanted to throw doubt upon the empirical "reality"; that which clearly makes the Flux, or the Becoming, a matter of overwhelming importance to the world at large. It is curious also to note that the conception of the "self" is apt to suffer more with a dogmatic religion, or with political thought, than with pure philosophy.

By far the greater number of the famous greek philosophers were ionian or italic. Plato and Socrates are almost alone, among those of the first order, in being athenian by birth. In both the Academy and the Lyceum the Ionian predominated. Applying these few generalizations to *"le miracle grec,"* it is safe to describe that miracle as a *scientific* miracle. It was science, more than art, that made a "miracle" of the few centuries of greek activity. The "greek miracle" was the first example in history of *scientific magic* (with which we are so familiar today).

The fluid, naturalistic, greek sculpture was the outcome of greek science. It was as a consequence of contemporary medical prowess, of the ionian surgery and anatomical knowledge, that the marble athletes and gods of the Hellenes were so very like living models. And there are many people today (among them the present writer) who consider this art less good as art because of its scientific naturalism. Yet it is, of course, impossible to dissociate greek philosophical thought, in the aggregate, from the plastic art which accompanied it or the art from the philosophy; and both the art and the philosophy came out of the science of Ionia. (Whether that, in its turn, as Elliot Smith and his school would have it, came from the egyptian embalmers, and their intimate professional familiarity with the human corpse, is an interesting speculation, but does not affect what we are advancing here; for the greek civilization was independent in character, whatever its origins may have been.) And, finally, both art and science in Europe, and indeed the whole basis of thought, have been the result of the "greek miracle." Our attitude to that miracle at the present juncture is of capital importance, it is clear: and if we were capable of producing a "Western Man" (which would, of course, be another "miracle," at least equal to the greek), it would be necessary to decide how much and how little was to be retained of the greek heritage.

Probably, and that is the line of argument I shall pursue with regard to this problem, science and art should be kept rigidly apart, in our present situation, and with our greatly enhanced resources. (The fusing and unity against which I am arguing is natural only to a more primitive condition: and it is in fact as a result of our false "primitivism" that such a process has occurred.) When science passes over into art, as happened in Greece, it produces indifferent art, or at the best an art that is too "scientifically" close to nature. The modern man, our perfect "Western Man," would have to be about six different people, perhaps; taking his science, and the scientific spirit, still from Greece, its home, but taking his art from somewhere else — only to consider these two factors.

Then we have found (in Book One) Professor Alexander congratulating us upon not having as our contemporary ideal one of "statuesque repose," like the Greeks. In that connection it is well to remember that if greek statues awaken Professor Alexander's compassion because of their quietude, then his pity must deepen as he turns his eyes Eastward, or down towards Africa. In front of a Pharaoh or a Buddha, what would Professor Alexander feel? He would certainly experience a very deep pity indeed at the thought of all those poor misled and ignorant generations, at the mere thought of all that those ancient arts had lost by being so very "undynamical." If they could only have seen Rodin's fluxions in soapy white stone! *That* would have opened their eyes for them! No doubt they would on the spot have abandoned their ignorant static dream.

The historical attitude in philosophy was assailed by William James with considerable point: he said that the modern philosopher was too apt to state his position in historical terms, in terms of its distance or nearness to Kant, of its affinity with Giordano Bruno, or Jacob Boehme, or of its indian descent. He said that philosophy would be freer today if it could forget its past, and detach itself from the complex mass of thought it carries with it. We would subscribe here very much to that attitude. But that, too, is an ideal of method (rather like the advice of Descartes to his followers never to open a book). If we had never acquainted ourselves with the art of all periods and countries, as we have done today, we should, after all, probably still be copyists of the greek; or, without the historical-minded Renaissance, not even that. But the protest of James can be quoted with advantage.

Russell's rule for the classification of philosophies is by method or by results. "Empirical," "a priori" is classification by methods, "realist," "idealist" is classification by results. But such classifications are very relative indeed. Plato, for instance, was in a very important sense a "realist." Neither Plato nor the pythagorean doctrines were so "ideal" as the word "idea" popularly suggests. Parmenides and the Eleatics answer to the popular meaning best in greek philosophy. After wandering for a while, however, in the interpenetrating groves of the Academy and Lyceum, and tracing the contributions, in both, of Elia and Miletus, you will find that there remains, nevertheless, the great main demarcation you started with. There in Athens it is a reality: and the first simplified view to some extent returns. But in contemporary Western secular thought, the thought of this decade, there is no such demarcation, whatever antagonistic names you like to bestow upon the supposedly differing schools. When it comes to the point, where the main and central problems are concerned, they all agree.

The gap has closed up. Today we are all one. The question is whether we should rejoice or not at this reconciliation; and probably our answer will depend upon which side of the ancient conflict we think that the opposition has been resolved, and then whether our interests lie on that side or the other.

When Kant was woken from his "dogmatic slumber" he proceeded to invent what he called "criticism," and since the main characteristic of that slumber was that it was "dogmatic," his "criticism" was in the nature of things an *undogmatical* gesture. He became the greatest of all "mediators" of the modern age. Ever since Kant people have gone on being "critical," and consequently gone on "mediating." It is at the present stage of the proceedings highly questionable if this particular "critical" gesture of Kant's was such a blessing as it has been represented, or even, in the upshot, so undogmatical: for an orthodoxy of a critical order, founded in the "meeting of extremes," has now become a dogma. Perhaps it would, after all, have been better if Kant had never woken from his "dogmatic slumber," nor patented "criticism" at all — teaching others the trick of "mediation." In our day such a title as "critical realists," for instance, merely indicates a band of militant "mediators," with a strong "realistic" bias, in the way that Kant had a strong "idealist" bias.

As to the nature of Kant's meditation, it may be instructive to quote from Edward Caird's excellent account of this phenomenon. I will quote rather fully, for it will serve to throw considerable light upon the question that, to the best of my ability and in my unpractised way, I have been attempting to expound a little:

It has been noticed [he writes] that Kant, from the beginning to the end of his career, shows a tendency to seek for some middle term or higher reconciling principle between opposite schools of thought. . . . To mediate between Leibniz and Newton was the aim of his first philosophical essays; to mediate between the English Empiricism and the German Rationalism may be said to be one of the main objects of the Critical Philosophy. The idea of *criticism* itself . . . springs out of the opposition of different dogmatisms, and of dogmatism to scepticism, and it is essentially an attempt to reconcile them. Note, however, that Kant always demands a real mediation of the opposite dogmatisms by "going back to the point from which the divergence began": . . . he had no toleration for a mere "splitting the difference." . . . "Moderation," he declares, "which tries to hit the mean between extremes and thinks it can find the philosopher's stone in subjective probability . . . is no philosophy at all."

To try *to hit the mean between extremes*, we see Kant saying here, is no philosophy at all. Yet he was "mediating" the whole of his life, and his famous "Criticism" is what we inherit from him as the supreme trick of this mediation. But there is really no more difficult question in speculative thought than this that we are occupied with. There is the "dogmatic slumber" or equally the dogmatic wakefulness on one side, and on the other "the meeting of extremes." All that it is intended to do here, in relation to this baffling question, is to make the reader aware of it, awake his interest in it, and draw his attention to a few of its main implications.

The question of this possibility, likelihood or desirability of a unification of thought has occupied many people for some time. Perhaps that is why they have never noticed that what they were deciding upon had already happened. It may be interesting to quote the following passage from Mr. Morris Cohen's introduction to the essays of C. S. Peirce (Harcourt, Brace and Company). It shows admirably how this question is most generally regarded today.

Not only the pragmatism and radical empiricism of James, but the idealism of Royce and the more recent movement of neo-realism are largely indebted to Peirce. *It may seem strange that the same thinker should be claimed as foster-father of both recent idealism and realism*, and some may take it as another sign of his lack of consistency. But this seeming strangeness is really due to the looseness with which the antithesis between realism and idealism has generally been put. If by idealism we denote the nominalistic doctrine of Berkeley, then Peirce is clearly not an idealist, and his work in logic as a study of types of order (in which Royce followed him) is fundamental for a logical realism. But if idealism means the old Platonic doctrine that "ideas," genera, forms, are not merely mental but the real condition of existence, we need not wonder that Peirce was both idealist and realist.

"Realist" and "idealist" are still the two terms most generally used to express the supposed contemporary phase of the great traditional antithesis. This duality was "Nominalism" and "Realism" for Roscellinus and Anselm, for William James "Rationalism" and "Empiricism": but whatever the terms employed, in accordance with the shifting of the interest in the doctrinal battle from one spot to another, substantially the same types of thought are opposed, or have been up to the present period.

Mr. Cohen's reference to Plato is particularly interesting. Plato today is coming to occupy the position of a symbolical meeting-ground and rallying-place for the united idealo-realist philosophy. For was he not, it is said, a "realist," in the sense that he believed his "forms" to be ultimately real? And yet he is notoriously a figure representing "the ideal." So he is ideally fitted, it seems to have been felt, to serve as *ancêtre* for the "real" of this day. But this being so, and since "idealist" is today a meaningless and, by association, semi-idiotic word, it is to be hoped that the fact that Plato has been taken possession of by the idealo-realist orthodoxy (or the neo-realist-platonism, or whatever you care to call it), or may soon be so accommodated, he will — if the principle for which he once traditionally stood revives — be unable to dispense with the tag issuing from his "ideas" or forms. So, that Peirce was "both idealist and realist" we should make no difficulty in accepting: nor, with the growing evidence of the "convergence" and intellectual fusion now before us, should it be difficult to see how this fusion should have had such a figure as Peirce for its father.

I will now turn to the evidence on this matter afforded by Bosanquet's very acute analysis. Everyone must agree with Bosanquet, of course, in his weariness with the war of "Idealist" and "Realist": and everyone will be ready to concede that any philosophy whatever must attempt "to do justice to the standpoint of *the whole*" (Alexander's formula — quoted by Bosanquet). Yet, once more, it is regrettable that Bosanquet should have been afraid of taking a more clearly defined position.

It is certain [Bosanquet writes] that each of them ("Realist" and "Idealist") if he follows his primary clue freely, with an open mind, and his eye upon the object, may, or rather must, be led to investigations and appreciations which will carry him to seek completeness in regions within his opponent's spiritual home. It is . . . at least one party of the most realistically minded who care most intensely for transcendent theism or polytheism, and for the persistent finite individual subject—for spirit and spiritualism, in short: . . . it is at least a faction of the idealistically minded who refuse to see in mind and nature either the factors of an ultimate antithesis, or provinces of data either of which is simply reducible to the other. Each of them . . . finds room for the complementary elements; and the freer, more subtle, and more penetrating their respective explorations, the more they show indications of supporting one another. The substitution of these fine and dissolvent analyses, of this sapping and mining under fortifications of an obsolete type for a new warfare of crude antagonism . . . is perhaps on the whole a new thing in the history of philosophy (though indeed it began with Plato) and is a feature of remarkable promise in the philosophy of today.

So Bosanquet describes accurately enough this fusion, and gives it his benediction. Above you see this philosopher, the War (the real, so-called "Great War") still fresh in his memory, comparing what he saw in philosophy with what he had heard about in War. What an unfortunate comparison! For as War, or as anything at all, who today believes that the scientific positional Warfare of "sapping," of "subtle interpenetrations," etc., is an improvement on the more primitive combats, when individual intelligence, valour and endurance played a more conspicuous part in the result? But the parallel is not inexact. And he finds it "a feature of remarkable promise." He wants to be nice and friendly and see the best in everything, and to be cheerful and not "narrow-minded"—to be "open-minded," as he says.

Yet how clearly Bosanquet saw the nature of the confusion can be judged from the following passage:

What first attracted my attention to this point of view (namely that of the "convergence of investigations" in contemporary philosophy) was the really startling difference and agreement between the Italian neo-idealists who follow Croce and Gentile, and the English and American neo-realists, who are represented, say, by Professor Alexander and the Six. On the one side thought, self-creative and all-producing, the ultimate principle and even the ultimate type and form of reality; on the other, a self-existent universe, actual in space and time, in which mind—that is, distinct individual minds—holds a place on equal terms with the other finite things. *And yet in both alike . . . we have the actual and ultimate reality of Time, progress to infinity, as the fundamental character of the real,* and with these inevitably (what I suspect to be a deep-lying motive in both) the specifically ethical and non-religious attitude, for which, to quote the old humanistic watchword and paradox, "the end is progress."

The true mechanism of the time-thought, and possibly much of the secret of its origin, seems to lie directly in the outcome of the technical philosophic situation. The substitution of the mental for the physical (only a "mental" that is almost more "physical" than matter) — it is in that transaction that we should look for its secret. When you get well into the centre of the consciousness of any time (and we have just illustrated this by the greek consciousness), there is certainly a unity there, for, if for no other reason, it is after all a time. But it is also, in the case of ancient thought, very definitely also a place. Now what I am advancing is that, first of all, our time is very fully *a time*, but very little of *a place*. We have come to live mentally and historically so much more than did the Hellene, for instance, or an ancient Indian, that we are justified in referring to what we have as *a time, tout court*, with the minimum of *place*. And the "new thing in philosophy," namely, the unanimity of our philosophers and teachers, is largely due to that, no doubt. The psychological reason for what he noticed accurately enough, Bosanquet, for instance, failed to grasp. Hence, I think, his unique stress upon the political nature of the impulse. As a matter of fact the inclusiveness, and sort of bastard universalism, naturally arrived at by this mercurial spreading-out in time, and this overriding of place, might by itself produce such a result as we find. Having absorbed all the otherness, or such great tracts of it, a Oneness would naturally result. And having grown accustomed to go backward and forward, at all speeds, in all places and times, a certain attitude must also be induced towards displacement itself, and with it would come naturally a contempt for spaces, as well as an instinctive substitution of Time for any other values, quite apart from the especial political utility of that idea at the moment. But many factors have, I believe, contributed to the total result, to the unification, this "new thing in philosophy," which characterizes the present age, which is less "a time" than any other, in one sense, and so much more acutely so in another sense. These various factors I shall subsequently be reviewing, though I by no means wish to exclude the political. It is a very important motive indeed, the most important almost certainly where the second-rate is concerned. All I wish to point out is that it is not the only one; that there is something beside the second-rate in any time, though not enough, under unfavourable conditions, to electrify it.

So we must in this investigation remember (that has been the object of this long preliminary argument) that, though a "new thing in philosophy," nevertheless some and indeed a great deal of merging and interpenetration is to be found everywhere in the world of thought of any time whatever. Professor Alexander writes: *"No sane philosophy, Plato's or any other's, has been definitely this or that."* And that we must constantly bear in mind in handling what we have now set out to analyse. But the *definiteness* that I am seeking here is not a definiteness of the kind implied in the above remark.

In these difficult new adjustments that I am here proposing to you, our *definition* must be sought in the rigidity of the princi-ple at the base of all our arguments; a rigour as though there, at the base of the necessary dialectical instability, there were planted a God. The idealo-realists, or to name a few, Alexander, Whitehead, Cassirer, Gentile, are just as adamant as that: *their* principle is just as rigid, indeed more so. For there is no princi-ple more pervasive, ubiquitous, exacting, and hence absolutist and rigid, than is *Time.*

Otherwise, and apart from this stubborn *definiteness* under-neath, we can all meet and exchange ideas upon the best of terms: you could almost say, indeed, that it matters hardly at all what we *say* or what arguments we use, at least that is the case with the Time-school, for it all returns to the same absolute centre, and that centre, or base, is of so barren a nature that more and more what is said as its justification is in the nature of a raree-show, and pure entertainment. This is especially the case with Alexander, and all his traditional apparatus of categories and metaphysical fustian.

As is perhaps natural, it is with the most important, truly in-novating, of the group, William James, that most agreement is possible — and this is saying a good deal, for with all there is so much on the surface with which it is easy to agree. As to James, with a great deal that he says, and with the spirit of a great deal of his writings, I am much in sympathy. Underneath, one knows what is there: but philosophically, he is the best of company.

PART II

"It is only by such external functions as the millions have in common, their uniform and simultaneous movements, that the many can be united into a higher unity: marching, keeping in step, shouting 'hurrah' in unison, festal singing in chorus, united attacks on the enemy, these are the manifestations of life which are to give birth to the new and superior type of humanity. Everything that divides the many from the one, that fosters the illusion of the individual importance of man, especially the 'soul,' hinders this higher evolution, and must consequently be destroyed."

The Mind and Face of Bolshevism,
René Fülöp-Miller

CHAPTER ONE

HISTORY AS THE SPECIFIC ART OF THE TIME SCHOOL

IN THIS AND THE NEXT FEW chapters I shall be mainly concerned with the problem of which so far I have postponed examination, but to which several times I have had occasion to refer: namely, how far the philosophic thought of a period is influenced by the current political or religious atmosphere, this with especial regard to the present time.

At the start I will give my view of the matter briefly, and then proceed to elaborate it a little. Millennial politics, it seems evident enough, have a very pervasive influence on philosophic thought today. The latter places its purely theoretic concepts, I believe (such as "Time," notably), in a light that will be found attractive to the majority of contemporary political sensibilities. . . . "There are progressists . . . who seem to understand this whole relation, and yet to be coerced by the spirit of the age into an ethical approximation-theory after the manner of Kant," says Bosanquet, lamenting what he appears to regard as the rather wild ways taken by Alexander. Certainly the "coercion," it must be admitted, is there. Many people *understand* perfectly well, as Bosanquet put it, but still they take the line most likely to ensure them efficient support. Next, as to the mathematician or the chemist, there is a very good chance, on the other hand, surely, that he is led wherever he goes in his theoretic evolution, simply in response to the technical problems that confront him. That does not apply, of course, to such a doubtful science as psychology; and history, proto-history or sociology are apt to be almost purely political activities.

But most of the things that in due course take a more and more political colour, were not originally political, but speculative. The opportunist mind seizes on this or that theory and adapts it to its needs; and politics and philosophy in Europe are tradition-ally a little too close together. But further than this, you may be right in saying, I believe, that many philosophical doctrines that *look* political are in reality the result of some purely technical, theoretic peculiarity.

I believe that it requires a really very foul or else very fanatical person to live with ideas, and consistently to betray them: and secondly, the ideas themselves are apt to be refractory, and to have some say in the matter. The material of theoretic thought, at least, is not "personal," if its manipulator is. That preliminary statement will serve to indicate my standpoint.

There is no person more persuaded of the political, or historical, nature of *everything* than is Spengler: and that is, of course, the "Time"-nature. That is his main source of argument: all his very long book is written to show, scientifically, how everything is a factor or creature of Time, and as entirely contingent upon the time-atmosphere or time-climate as is a fish or bird upon the presence and structure of its native medium. I will begin my criticism of this materialist ultra-political — pan-political — doctrine with the *Decline of the West.*

If music is the art most appropriate to the world-view of the time-philosopher, then history is certainly the form in literature that must be above all others congenial to him. For the "time" view *is* the historical view *par excellence.* And the great prevalence of archaeological and scholarly subject-matter in contemporary art is, aside from the effect of the rapid elaboration of the technique of research, the result of the hypnotism of the time-cult.

Spengler is the most characteristic bloom that has so far made its appearance out of this entire school. The mere title of his book is an invitation to extinction for the White European, or Western Man. It says to the West: "I am an *historian;* I have all the secrets of *Time;* and I am able to tell you with a wealth of detail that will take your breath away (if you have any left after your War) that you White Peoples are about to be extinguished. It's all up with you; and I can prove to you on the testimony of my data of research, and according to my new science of history, which is built on the great time-system in the mode, that that must be so." This thesis is in itself, and apart from anything else, such an immensely popular one, that the book was assured an immediate and overwhelming success everywhere, from Moscow to Johannesburg.

The hypnotism of the crater-mouth of "catastrophe" — not marxian "catastrophe" this time, but a fatalist, "scientific," "detached," "*historical,*" catastrophic picture — should surely draw the awestruck sheep of as many mass-democracies as the book could rapidly be translated for, and in imagination at all events they would be engulfed.

Where history is concerned no one is able to contend that the historian is not a politician. The *Decline and Fall* of Gibbon, or the *French Revolution* of Carlyle, are political and moralistic romances. History is an account of the Past, seen through a temperament of a certain complexion, and intended to influence its generation in this sense or in that.

But to the popular mind "a history" is always a true account of something as it *really* happened; and the historian is an impassible and incorruptible recorder of *the truth*, and nothing but the truth. It certainly never occurred to ninety-nine per cent of the readers of the *French Revolution* to question the veracity or the disinterestedness of "the historian," at the time at all events. That book became — the French Revolution. Tacitus, the greatest of Western historians, was similarly a violent partisan and militant political moralist. But his books were put forward as veracious descriptions of fact.

If, however, in place of a highly-coloured narrative of particular events, you get such a book as Spengler's, surveying the whole of "history" *sub specie aeternitatis*, and promulgating a set of flamboyant, easily-grasped, picturesque rules for its understanding, then you have the same order of stratagem; but it applies to the whole of mankind, past, present and future. So the concentrated humbugs of three great superstitions — that of *historical* fact, that of *scientific* fact, and that of *philosophic* truth — humbugs, that is, if they are received with too helpless a credulity — come into play.

I am not here superciliously underrating the intelligence of the majority of readers. Most non-professional readers of such a semi-popular book as Spengler's (which proved actually the greatest highbrow best-seller of the last ten or twenty years) have very little leisure for reading. They never read such a book as Spengler's unless it is thrust under their nose. Most of the things it treats of, even commonplaces of philosophy or criticism, appear to them as marvellous and arresting discoveries — for it is the first time that they have made acquaintance with them. If educated people, as students they were far too busy enjoying themselves or cramming for an exam to attend to such austerities or luxuries of the intellect. So they are totally unprepared for such a reading, and certainly unqualified to arrive at an informed opinion. This is not a question of intelligence or of aptitude so much as one of training.

How much ethnology, biology, archaeology, sociology and so forth today is really *history*, is not sufficiently realized. Darwin was, after all, a history of our species. Much of psycho-analysis is history of the Past of our species. And all those various forms of history have this in common: they all affect to give a correct account of the Past. The Past is the preserve of the historian; and, as I began by saying, the science or art which is *par excellence* that of the time-philosophy, is *history*. In most cases, further, the historian is a politican; attempting, by the colour he gives to his version of the Past (as Tacitus in his *Germania*), to influence his contemporaries to imitate that particular version of the Past.

If this is so with the historian dealing with historical times or a fairly recent epoch, is it likely that this is not also the case with the ethnologist and every other form of veiled historian? Often that assuredly is the case — as with Professor Perry, for instance, or with Perry's disciple, Mr. H. J. Massingham, with his *Downland Man*. There, of course, a benevolent picture is zealously imposed — one of the few cases in which that view of the matter is taken, though it is at least as likely to be true as the other. Indeed, Spencer and Gillen and the australian investigators — certainly unpartisan observers, rather perplexed at what they found — seem to point that way rather than to the Primitive Past saturated with blood and incest so generally favoured.

What reason have we to suppose that this more or less political intention is not always present? It seems at least likely that the sociologist-ethnologist (like Mathilde and Mathias Vaerting) who is also a militant feminist will invariably arrange his *soi-disant* scientific account of primitive matriarchates, for instance, to suit his political beliefs. And where the evidence, in spite of all the ardour of research, is extremely meagre, and it is consequently very easy to manipulate the material, we should be still more on our guard with the proto-historian than with the historian.

With the history of a person written by himself, or any form of autobiography or self-portrait, the same impulses are at work. They are often propagandist — propaganda for all that the "time"-hero depicted has favoured. In Proust, for instance — one of the ideal examples of a projection on the grand scale, in narrative form, of the philosophy of "time" — we have in a sense a new type of historical practitioner. Proust embalmed himself alive. He died as a sensational creature in order that he should live as an historian of his dead sensational self, which expired about the time that lyrical poets are supposed to snuff out. Or rather he did in a sense really die; when those complicated and peculiar meeds of admiration exacted by his slight, ailing, feminine body, with deep expansions of bottomless vanity, were in the nature of things no longer forthcoming, and life's (for him) paradoxical receptive trance was terminated, he bleakly awoke; in his wakeful industrious nights he began stealthily revisiting the glimpses of the sun of the past time-scene. That was his way of making himself into an historical personage, by embalming himself in a mechanical medium of "time."

And here we should establish another accompaniment of the historical function. The historian himself is virtually inexistent, as he must be invisible. He comes to life in his historic Past; and the implication in most of the more vigorous historical intelligences is that the Future must resemble the Past; some degree of mechanical repetition, of recurrence, of periodicity, is involved and insisted upon. The historical writer, in every case, is distracting people from a living Present (which becomes dead as the mind withdraws) into a Past into which they have gone to live. It is a hypnotism that is exercised by the time-vista, or by those time-forms or exemplars that are relied upon for the mesmeric effect. The intelligence to which this method is natural is the opposite of the creative, clearly.

The metaphor employed above, to describe the procedure of Proust, suggests a further illustration that may assist in clarifying the subject. The ancient Egyptians who embalmed their dead were constantly in the presence of the Past of their race. Imagine some english country-squire, who possessed, instead of a set of family portraits, a cellar-full of the carefully embalmed remains of his ancestors, to which he could stroll down, when he felt inclined, and spend a half-hour examining. That would be more impressive than dingy oil-paintings.

But how much more impressive would it not be if with the assistance of a gramophone and domestic cinematograph, or a vocal film, men were, in the future, able to call up at will any people they pleased with the same ease that now a dead film-star, Valentino, for instance, may be publicly resuscitated.

A quite credible domestic scene of the future is this. Mr. Citizen and his wife are at the fireside; they release a spring and their selves of long ago fly onto a screen supplied in the Wells-like, or Low-like, Future to all suburban villas. It is a phono-film; it fills the room at once with the cheery laughter of any epoch required. "Let's have that picnic at Hampton Court in such and such a year!" Mrs. Citizen may have exclaimed. "Yes, do let's!" hubby has responded. And they live again the sandwiches, the tea in the thermos, the ginger beer and mosquitoes, of a dozen years before.

People with such facilities as that for promenades in the Past — their personal Pasts in this case — would have a very different view of their Present from us: it would be Miss Stein's "continuous Present" in fact. And all the Past would be similarly potted, it is to be assumed; celebrated heroes like Lord Kitchener would be as present to those happy people as were their own contemporary Great.

Art — whether in pictures, music, the screen, or in science or fiction — is already beginning to supply us with something of that sort. The mechanical photographic reality of a perpetuation of the Past is not here yet; art leads the way, the photograph will follow. And people have, already, somewhat that sense of things laid out side by side, of the unreality of time, and yet of its paramount importance, that the conditions indicated above would breed.

Confining ourselves to what has already been done towards this reversal, the tendency, even upon the most popular plane, is evidently to substitute *time* for *space* in human psychology. The geographical novelties of the earth (as they presented themselves to the contemporaries of Magellan or Marco Polo) are now exhausted. In our mind's eye we see all around the physical world, and into every corner of it. Our voyages of discovery now have become time-voyages, as it were, in consequence of the sudden physical shrinkage.

Yet, evidently, explorations, journeys, tours, expeditions in *time* are as "romantic" occupations as were similar journeys in space. As there was the globe-trotter, so there will be the "time"-tripper. Men have taken up with time, where space ended, but they have not changed their habits. But certainly this change-over, or revolution, if they go through with it, will give them a new psychological outfit — suitable for mind-travel — imposed by the different character of their new functions — opposite in a sense as they will be, when fully realized.

For what is the basis of these new journeys or travels in time? Where do they occur? They occur, of course, *inside the head* — that is where the time-tracts lie — the regions of memory and imagination, as opposed to "matter." It is in short a mental and psychologic world. Or it is memory associated with the Present in the bergsonian combination (as that works out in practice rather than as theory), or that of Miss Stein's "continuous Present." So it is that we get such phrases in Whitehead as "mental climate." The phrase is exact for the Nature or topography into which that philosopher and his friends would invite us to pass.

CHAPTER TWO

THE "CHRONOLOGICAL" PHILOSOPHY
OF SPENGLER

1. IN ORDER TO DEMONSTRATE effectively the true character of Spengler's book will require almost as much space as I have devoted to *Ulysses*. And certainly as a book it deserves it far less. When I open it now I am at once impressed, once more, by the way in which it is able to reveal, as no other time-book could, the fat and flabby heart of this philosophy. It so teems and swarms with everything that I have been attacking, it is so picturesquely "provocative," and it so expansively offers itself in redundant self-exposure, that the very *embarras du choix* overcomes me for the moment. Surely the god that is the enemy of the Time-god, put it into Spengler's foolish head to write all this, so that the doctrines of "Time" should be overthrown, and their essential weakness be at once manifested! If that is so, I offer up a short prayer of thankfulness, at this juncture, to the unknown god, our mighty friend.

First I will choose such passages as relate directly to the problem of *time*.

"*We ourselves are Time*," Spengler writes and italicizes; and he could say no more if he were Bergson. Time is the personal and organic; "*Time is a counter-conception to Space*." "Between Becoming [and, hence, Time] and any part whatsoever of mathematics, there is not the slightest contact." Or here is a statement, of many, that should answer all our requirements:

Mathematics as a whole—in common language, arithmetic and geometry—answers the *How?* and the *What?*—that is, the problem of the Natural order of things. In opposition to this problem stands that of the *When?* of things, the specifically historical problem of destiny . . . all these things are comprised in the word *Chronology* . . .

What to the time-philosopher, such as Spengler, is significant about a person or a thing, is *when* it or he is, not *what* or *how* he or it may be. The chronological truth is the only truth. But it is a very "mystical" and unseizable one, we are assured, in case that should seem too simple.

"Understanding loses its way when language has emancipated it from sensation," he tells us. (To be "emancipated from sensation" is the most detestable thing that can befall a time-man.) For Spengler, as for all time-philosophers, intelligible language is the arch-enemy. For what he has to communicate is strictly and portentously unintelligible—a mysterious *something* that defies definition, and is the foe of all *words*. "All systematic philosophies use mere names . . . for getting rid of the Incomprehensible . . . We *name* . . . something the 'Absolute.' . . . What is *named*, comprehended . . . is *ipso facto* overpowered . . ." *Systematic* philosophies Spengler dislikes; they are means of "getting rid of the Incomprehensible," and of Spengler along with it—far too effective means to please Spengler. He objects to *naming* for the same reason. Jahweh put his name upon, or *named*, the people of Israel; and as a consequence they became *his*, it will be recalled. The power of the *word*, or the name, is very naturally redoubted.

But a *word* is one thing, an intelligible name or word; and a big, misty, rolling *sound* is quite another. So Spengler has two ways of talking about words, or language. The one is the abusive manner employed when a word has a *meaning*; the other is the fulsome manner employed when the word has *no meaning*—or is "incomprehensible"; or when it can be made incomprehensible, or when it lends itself to incomprehensibility. When it is what could be called a *sensation-word* it is splendid; when it is an *intellect-word* it is detestable, and to be fiercely scorned.

What is not experienced and felt, what is merely *thought*, necessarily takes a spatial form, and this explains why no systematic philosopher has been able to make anything out of the mystery-clouded, far-echoing sound-symbols "Past" and "Future."

When the word can become a "mystery-clouded, far-echoing sound-symbol," all is well, says Spengler. It means nothing, or anything. It becomes material for music, and is no longer a part of human language at all. Then it is quite all right. The light that all this can throw, incidentally, upon the purely literary problems we have been discussing, will be at once obvious. All the problems of *language* and *music*, respectively, that preoccupy Pound, or Stein and Joyce, are implicit in Spengler.

In the beginning there was the time in the composition that naturally was in the composition but time in the composition comes now and this is what is now troubling every one the time in the composition

. . . the time-sense that is at present the most troubling is the thing that makes the present the most troubling.

So delightfully and archly stammers Gertrude Stein. Spengler says the same thing in his way.

What is thought takes the *spatial* form; what is felt takes the *time* form. "What is not experienced and felt, what is merely *thought*, necessarily takes a spatial form." And the "experienced and felt" of Spengler is absolutely and in the smallest detail identical with the sensationalism of Bergson. But the "time" — that is where space is not — which is, as we have seen Spengler describing it, a *counter-conception* to space — the "time" that is the mental and the personal, the psychologic, is the "time" that so troubles Miss Stein that she constantly stammers in an eternal false-naïveté. And what effect "time" has on the attitude of a philosopher to *words*, or to language, we have just seen in Spengler's case. And we know what effect "time" has upon Miss Stein according to her own account in *Composition as Explanation*. Already I think we can be said to know more about what Miss Stein means by "time" through having gone to the "mystery-clouded" Spengler for information. For though certainly triple-clouded in a mystical "incomprehensibility" from one point of view, he is in another way extremely lucid; and he has the advantage (or disadvantage for the "mystery-clouded") that he does not stammer.

The "time" of Spengler is sensation, that we now have learnt. And *sensation* is what is *us* (for "We ourselves are Time"); whereas what we *think* is not us, or is the Not-self; what is not personal to us. And what is merely "thought" or the material of the intellect — that part of us which reflects what is not immediately us — is cold and unreal compared with what is us. It is a *dead portion* of us, as it were. It is not susceptible of *sensation*, else it would be us; for anything that is sensation is us.

It is a consequence of this form of reasoning that (whatever the superficial doctrine may be) a time-book must always be obsessed with the personality of the author. In *Ulysses* we find on the surface the naturalist tradition of a scientific "impersonality." But the "time," the "mental" — the telling-from-the-inside method — makes it gravitate everywhere on to the ego of the author, to the confusion of the naturalist machinery pulled out and set going for nothing. And the writing of Miss Stein is, of course, as undisguisedly personal as it is lyrical.

Yet the Not-self, and especially the physical, is almost the patent and property of the Western genius. The "natural magic" of Western poetry owes its peculiar and penetrating quality to the intense relations of the Western mind to this *alien* physical world of "nature." It is in the detaching of himself from the personal that the Western Man's greatest claim to distinction lies, from the Greeks and early Celts to the present day. It is in non-personal modes of feeling—that is in *thought*, or in feeling that is so dissociated from the hot, immediate egoism of sensational life that it becomes automatically intellectual—that the non-religious Western Man has always expressed himself, at his profoundest, at his purest. That is, of course, the heritage that is being repudiated in the present "time"-modes. We are busy in everything, in the West, substituting the personal for the impersonal, the private for the public.

Again, the hatred of *exteriorization* is well brought out in these words of Spengler's:

All that has been said about time in scientific philosophy, psychology and physics — the supposed answer to a question that had better never have been asked, namely, what *is* time? — touches, not at any point the secret itself, but only a spatially-formed, *representative* phantom.

You *ought never to ask*, even, what time is, for it is ineffable, you see. It is a "secret"—the Holy of Holies of the "time"-cult. But at least whatever else in your ignorance you do, you must not identify it with anything exterior or merely *spatial*. That is the supreme offence. And you must remember, too, that you are in the presence of an extremely fanatical cult. When you approach the "mystery-clouded, far-echoing" sound-symbol, *Time*, you must bare your head and avert your eyes. A "spatially-formed, *representative*" "thing," is in the nature of a graven image. With Space, and its spatially-formed, representative objects, you enter into the regions of idolatry!

This is how Spengler begins his reflections on the subject of Time:

The way to the problem of Time, then, begins in the primitive wistfulness. . . . The *word* Time is a sort of charm to summon up that intensely personal something designated earlier as the "proper," which with an inner certainty we oppose to [what is] alien. . . . "The Proper," "Destiny" and "Time" are interchangeable words.

The problem of Time, like that of Destiny, has been completely mis-understood by all thinkers who have confined themselves to the system-atic of the Become. . . . But what *is* time as a length, time without direction? Everything living, we can only repeat, has "life," direction, impulse, will, a movement-quality . . . that is most intimately allied to yearning and has not the smallest element in common with the "mo-tion" . . . of the physicists. The living is indivisible and irreversible, once and uniquely occurring. . . . For all such qualities belong to the essence of Destiny, and "Time" — that which we actually feel at the sound of the word, which is clearer in music than in language, and in poetry than in prose — has the organic essence, while Space has not. . . . Space is a *conception*, but time is a *word* to indicate something inconceivable, a sound-symbol; and to use it as a notion, scientifically, is utterly to misconceive its nature. Even the word "direction" — which unfortunately cannot be replaced by another — is liable to mislead owing to its visual content. The *vector-notion* in physics is a case in point.

That such flimsy stuff as this should have to be considered at all as a contribution to philosophy, much less seriously answered, is the fault of the intellectual standards of our time. As politics it has, alas, a paradoxical usefulness, for it foretells the almost immediate doom of our race. And it has been, perhaps for that reason, everywhere solemnly discussed. For intellectual, not for political reasons, we have to follow suit.

This "Time" that is wistful and "yearning," is "a charm," then. *"Forlorn! the very word is like a bell,"* etc. Time! the very word for Spengler is a charm; but not, as with Keats, to drag a reluc-tant creature back to himself; quite the contrary. It summons up "the intensely personal" to the delight of the ravished listener. It whispers "self"! "Time" is the magic "Sesame" that opens the cave of all that is most intensely *personal*, and "proper" to the self alone. It excludes the alien, or the Not-self. That is the word for me! exclaims Spengler, more or less. And Time, Destiny and Self are commutative terms, he then goes on to say.

The "movement-quality" of Time, or the mind, is not the same as physical "motion." Oh! that one should have to use the base physical counter "direction" to express this ineffable movement of movements, and so allow it to be classed by the less sensitive reader with vector-notions! All these words are disgusting travesties — except when they are "a *word* (it has to be italicized to distinguish it from ordinary words, and capitals cannot be employed, for that is the prerogative of the Logos) — a *word* to indicate something inconceivable, a sound-symbol."

Why cannot Spengler "say it with flowers" (as we have

suggested would be Bergson's natural outlet), or say it in music —
in something more beautiful and seductive than mere words (not
italicized) — anything rather than that! But such is the cross that
the philosopher has to bear. He cannot be a philosopher or an
historian in anything but words. So it is that "Time — that which
we actually feel at the sound of the word, which is clearer in music
than in language" — the great god "Time" has to be adored in this
inadequate manner; and Spengler has to keep up a running
apology for his language to his resounding, inexpressible, sound-
symbol of a deity.

The above passage is too palpably confused even for Bergson
to have written; but otherwise it is, again, the purest bergsonism.
This "life," "will," "movement-quality" is surely that once celebrated
counter *l'élan vital*? The "wistfulness" and the "yearning" are reminiscent of the first great time-philosopher; and, like Whitehead,
Spengler is a follower of the "organic theory of nature."

It is as an historian, however, that Spengler has been privileged
to give away "time" most completely. The next passage I will quote
shows him again at work, incidentally, in his war upon language:

Every higher language possesses a number of words such as luck,
doom, conjuncture, vocation, about which there is, as it were, a veil.
No hypothesis, no science, can ever get into touch with that which we
feel when we let ourselves sink into the meaning and sound of these
words. They are symbols, not notions. In them is the centre of gravity
of that world-picture that I have called the World-as-History as opposed to the World-as-Nature. The Destiny-idea demands life-
experience . . . *depth* and not intellect. There is an *organic logic*, an
instinctive, dream-sure logic . . . a logic of direction as against a logic
of extension — and no systematist, no Aristotle or Kant, has known how
to deal with it.

We are amongst the "mystery-clouded, far-echoing" type of
word once more; amongst words "with veils about them" — words
that are not words. "When we let ourselves sink into the meaning and sound of these words" — as Bergson, in identical language,
would recommend us to do — then we get in touch with the Incomprehensible. In their veiled and mystery-clouded depths, the
"deep," not the intellectual, man will intuit the *World-as-History*.

The *World-as-History* is simply the world of human emotions,
the psychological world, of course; and it could be called the
World-as-Time just as well. This misty object is the cornerstone
of Spengler's edifice.

2. Spengler's book on the theoretic side is simply the elaboration (on a basis of bergsonian, or italian idealist philosophy) of the widely-held belief that everything whatever—as much a scientific theory as the hat you wear—is a phenomenon of fashion, a Time-phenomenon—a "history," and not a "truth," whatever its pretensions to be the latter. Spengler is very exactly the philosopher of Zeitgeist. The rest of our analysis of Spengler will be an examination of his theory from that point of view. If you open Spengler's book at almost any page you will meet some elaboration of this belief. Let us take, for instance, his account of the principle of causal necessity in Western physics, compared with those of the Greek and Arabian.

We see then [he says] that the causality-principle, in the form in which it is self-evidently necessary for us—the agreed basis of truth for our mathematics, physics and philosophy—is a Western and, more strictly speaking, a Baroque phenomenon. It cannot be proved, for every proof set forth in a Western mind presupposes itself. . . . Beyond question, the notion of laws of Nature and the conception of physics as "Scientia experimentalis," which has held ever since Roger Bacon, contains *a priori* this specific kind of necessity. The Classical mode of regarding Nature—the alter ego of the Classical mode of being—on the contrary, does *not* contain it, and yet it does not appear that the scientific position is weakened in logic thereby. If we work carefully through the utterances of Democritus, Anaxagoras and Aristotle . . . we look with astonishment into a world-image totally unlike our own. This world-image is self-sufficing and therefore, for this definite sort of mankind, unconditionally true. And causality in our sense plays no part therein. The alchemist or philosopher of the Arabian Culture, too, assumes a necessity within his world-cavern that is utterly and completely different from the necessity of dynamics. There is no causal nexus of law-form but only *one* cause, God, immediately underlying *every* effect. . . . If a rule seems to emerge, it is because it pleases God so. This was the attitude also of Carneades, Plotinus and the Neo-Pythagoreans.

But the "Faustian," "Western," "Classical" periods are divided into many sub-classes for Spengler, and each has its own physics, philosophy and art, its particular time-blend.

Professor Whitehead (*Science and the Modern World*, page 25) refers to "the particular conceptions of cosmology with which the European intellect has clothed itself in the last three centuries." And he proceeds:

General climates of opinion persist for periods of about two to three generations, that is to say, for periods of sixty to a hundred years. There are also shorter waves of thought, which play on the surface of the tidal movement.

These "climates of opinion" of Whitehead are as peculiar and exacting a medium as are the time-atmospheres of Spengler, and presuppose organs and morphological variations to match. Whitehead's account of Western science is much the same as Spengler's. "The inexpugnable belief that every detailed occurrence can be correlated with its antecedents in a perfectly definite manner, exemplifying general principles," that was for Whitehead the necessary, naïf basis of the Western scientific impulse.

I am not arguing [he says] that the European trust in the scrutability of nature was logically justified even by its own theology. My only point is to understand how it arose. My explanation is that the faith in the possibility of science . . . is an unconscious derivative from mediaeval theology.

Again:

When we compare this tone of thought in Europe with the attitude of other civilizations when left to themselves, there seems but one source for its origin. It must come from the mediaeval insistence on the rationality of God, conceived as with the personal energy of Jehovah and with the rationality of a greek philosopher.

Or yet again:

Faith in reason is the trust that the ultimate natures of things lie together in a harmony which excludes mere arbitrariness. It is the faith that at the base of things we shall not find mere arbitrary mystery. The faith in the order of nature which has made possible the growth of science is a particular example of a deeper faith [page 27, op. cit.].

Here is what Spengler says on the same subject:

The appeal to "experience" . . . [is] characteristically Western. . . . But no one has noticed that a whole world-view is implicit in such a concept of "experience" with its aggressive dynamic connotation, and that there is not and cannot be "experience" in this pregnant sense for men of other Cultures. . . . We have never yet given adequate thought to the singularity of this, the pure Faustian, conception of experience. The contrast between it and faith is obvious — and superficial . . . sensuous-intellectual experience is in point of structure completely congruent with that heart-experience . . . , that illumination which deep religious natures of the West (Pascal, for instance, whom one and the same necessity made mathematician and jansenist) . . . [etc.]

It will be seen that Whitehead and Spengler say exactly the same thing: they both identify religious faith with the scientific passion. *What makes Pascal a jansenist also makes him a mathematician.* Science and religion, and science and art, are, for both Whitehead and Spengler, one activity, as it were, and both, in their respective books, are busy drawing parallels between, or fusing together in their interpretations, painters, poets and musicians or "deeply religious natures" on the one hand, and men of science on the other.

But, you may say at this point, if this is true of the past, then it is also true of the present. And that I would not deny. What made Pascal a jansenist *and* a mathematician has made also no doubt Einstein a mathematician and something or other (not a jansenist). Indeed, as to Einstein, Spengler does not mince words: he has him firmly fixed into a little box upon the giddy declivity arranged upon his "faustian" switchback, hurrying to perdition. This is his contribution to the subject of Relativity:

> . . . the ruthlessly cynical hypothesis of the Relativity theory strikes at the very heart of dynamics. Supported by the experiments of A. A. Michelson . . . and prepared mathematically by Lorentz and Minkowski, its specific tendency is to *destroy the notion of absolute time.* Astronomical discoveries (and here present-day scientists are seriously deceiving themselves) can neither establish nor refute it. "Correct" and "incorrect" are not the criteria whereby such assumptions are to be tested; the question is whether, in the chaos of involved and artificial ideas that has been produced by the innumerable hypotheses of Radioactivity and Thermo-dynamics, it can hold its own as a *useable* hypothesis or not. But however this may be, *it has abolished the constancy of those physical quantities into the definition of which time has entered,* and unlike the antique statics, the Western dynamics knows *only* such quantities. Absolute measures of length and rigid bodies are no more. . . . If we observe how rapidly card-houses of hypothesis are run up nowadays, every contradiction being immediately covered up by a new hurried hypothesis; if we reflect on how little heed is paid to the fact that these images contradict one another and the "classical" Baroque mechanics alike, we cannot but realize that the *great style of ideation is at an end,* and that, as in architecture and the arts of form, a sort of craft-art of hypothesis-building has taken its place. Only our extreme maestria in experimental technique — true child of its century — hides the collapse of the symbolism.

To understand ultimately why Spengler is so fierce about this theory that *destroys the notion of absolute time,* it is necessary to discover more exactly than we have done so far what he means by "time"; and that, in its place, we shall do. Meanwhile I will quote a further four short passages relative to the Theory of Quanta and the atomic theories, full of similar denunciation. All these passages reveal the same idea, namely, *the close association of scientific theory with the ethical or political attitude of the Zeitgeist contemporaneous with them.*

> *There is a Stoicism and there is a Socialism of the atom* [Spengler asserts]: the words describing the static-plastic and the dynamic-contrapuntal ideas of it respectively. The relation of these ideas to the images of the corresponding ethics is such that every law and every definition takes these into account. On the one hand, Democritus's multitude of confused atoms, put there, patient, knocked about by the blind chance that he as well as Sophocles called ἀνάγκη, hunted like Oedipus. On the other hand, systems of abstract force-points working in unison; aggressive, energetically dominating space (as "field"), overcoming resistances like Macbeth. . . . Democritus merely regards shock and countershock as a form of change of place. Aristotle explains individual movements as accidental. Empedocles speaks of love and hate, Anaxagoras of meetings and partings. All these are elements also of classical tragedy; the figures on the Attic stage are related to one another just so. *Further, and logically, they are the elements of Classical politics.* [These last italics are mine.]

So for Spengler, *logically*, and as a matter of course, the conceptions obtaining in the art of the theatre are identical with the political conceptions of the same period, and the "discoveries" of science (whether the atom is envisaged as an aggressive "force-point," full of purpose, or is a little ball knocked blindly hither and thither by fate) are also reflections of the political and social ideas of the time. All the most abstract science as much as anything else, in politics, is Zeitgeist. The claim of the man-of-science to an absolutist status, to being a "discoverer," independent of the march of political and social events, is humbug, or at least self-delusion. It is interesting in the above passage to compare the analogies taken from the tragic stage of Greece with the account I have quoted above of the same things by Whitehead. It will be noticed how close their statements lie together. I will give three more passages to further illustrate this point of view:

> It is tension that is missing in the science of Democritus. . . . And, correspondingly, the element of Will is absent from the Classical soul-image. Between classical men, or states, or views of the world, there was, for all the quarrelings and envy and hatred—no inner tension, no deep and urging need of distance, solitude, ascendancy; *and consequently there was none between the atoms of the Cosmos either.*

(I have italicized this last sentence, which sums up very well what is the constant attitude of Spengler.)

Every atomic theory, therefore, is a myth and not an experience. In it the Culture, through the contemplative-creative power of its great physicists, reveals its inmost essence and very self.

Lastly, I will choose the following passage:

Goethe once remarked (to Riemer): ". . . *The great views of Life were brought into shapes, into Gods* [in the earlier centuries]: *today they are brought into notions.* Then the productive force was greater; now the destructive force or art of separation." The strong religiousness of Newton's mechanics and the almost complete atheism of the formulations of modern dynamics, are of like colour, positive and negative of the same primary feeling. *A physical system, of necessity, has all the characters of the soul to whose world-form it belongs.* The Deism of the Baroque belongs with its dynamics and its analytical geometry; its three basic principles, God, Freedom and Immortality, are, in the language of mechanics, the principles of inertia . . . , least action . . . , and the conservation of energy . . .

There you have excellent examples of the extreme view in the question we are discussing in this chapter. It is as extreme a statement, indeed, as you could have of the position that politics, art and science are one, and work in with each other. But I do not believe the general view of educated men (not what they would say, polemically, if taxed with it — for "the disinterestedness of science" is also, of course, a great dogma with them — but what they for the most part think) would be so very far behind this extremist view of Spengler's. On this view Relativity, the space-time notions in philosophy, "emergent" or evolutionary theories, all would be expressions of the time-spirit, and would have no more general or absolute value than that. They would be a deliberate and arbitrary structure of hypothesis and myth, approximating as closely as possible to some atomist aspect of experimental truth, this specious approximation reached, in the case of the contemporary physical theories, by a tour-de-force of mathematical *craftsmanship.* This "maestria," Spengler says, could, with its brilliant and dexterous fancy, cover up and disguise from us all the contradictions existing underneath. So we would be living, with sublime naïveté, according to this point of view, in *one* particular little house of cards: the contemporaries of Newton would be squatting peaceably in *theirs,* the good Newton, full of the most pious but one-sided intentions, busily running it up and perfecting it with a marvellous exactitude and with a fine eye for the great architectural effect. Einstein, a more finicky, fastidious and at the same time bizarre architect, produces an unsimple, intricate, amorphous thing, like a mathematical Boro-Budur.

What we have to ask ourselves is whether this extremist account of Spengler's is true, or only partly so, or whether it is without any basis at all, in fact. If we are spenglerites, we could scarcely ask ourselves these questions, of course; for, to be consistent, it would have to be admitted that our answer would inevitably be influenced by the fact that we are in the middle of the time-illusion, and could scarcely be detached from the apocalyptic medium emanated by the "faustian" soul in its immense and tragic decline — though how Spengler our master does it and is to some extent exempt, would remain a mystery.

The fundamental attitude of Spengler I entirely reject, as I have already indicated — this quite apart from any question of the hideous and inflated form in which he presents his mechanical vision of things, or his light-hearted inconsistency. Yet no one can deny that the attitude to the liaison between the various activities of any time outlined above in the passage I have quoted responds to some sort of truth. At present I will only make one specific criticism of this doctrine. Where he is discussing the various european conceptions of force — the *nisus, potentia, impetus*, etc. — he makes the following statement:

We can indeed quite well differentiate between Catholic, Protestant and Atheistic notions of force. But Spinoza, a Jew, and therefore, spiritually, a member of the Magian Culture, could not absorb the Faustian [Western] force-concept at all, and it has no place in his system. And it is an astounding proof of the secret power of root-ideas that Heinrich Hertz, the only Jew amongst the great Physicists of the recent past, was also the only one of them who tried to resolve the dilemma of mechanics by eliminating the idea of force.

First of all, this statement obviously contradicts his own Zeitgeist doctrine. For, apparently, there are people in Europe who are mysteriously *outside* the great Western dynamical ("faustian") illusion, namely the Jews: and they have been at all times fairly influential. But if his time-doctrine or period-doctrine is to be based upon *race* (and the passage I have just quoted shows it to be so based), then it at least would be very difficult to imagine the "faustian" uniformity he supposes obtaining among such a heterogeneous population as that constituting Europe or "the West" — so that, whether it be a Finn or a Sicilian, a Roumanian, a Hebridean or a peasant from the Rhone, the moment he begins thinking he begins thinking *dynamically*, in terms of *force* and *power*: for what applied to the Jew must also apply to the differing race oppositions among Europeans.

Then if you say that Hertz, because he was a Jew, was baffled by the Western conception of "force," and proceeded, since he found he could not make any sense of it, to banish it altogether from physics, you would also have to say the converse should happen, and that Einstein, who is also a Jew, should meet with a similar opposition in the "faustian" soul, where his physical conceptions are concerned: you would expect to find that the Western "faustian" Culture, finding *his* non-dynamical doctrines difficult to assimilate, rejected them. Mr. Bertrand Russell, for instance, gives this picture of the einstein universe:

If people were to learn to conceive the world in the new way, without the old notion of "force," it would alter not only their physical imagination, but probably also their morals and politics. . . . In Einstein's world there is more individualism and less government than in Newton's. There is also far less hustle: we have seen that laziness is the fundamental law of Einstein's universe. The word "dynamic" has come to mean, in newspaper language, "energetic and forceful"; but if it meant "illustrating the principles of dynamics," it ought to be applied to the people in hot climates who sit under banana trees waiting for the fruit to drop into their mouths.

There Mr. Russell is discussing the same phenomenon as Spengler is discussing, where he disparages the effort of Hertz to get rid of force in Western physics. But Mr. Russell (unlike Spengler) is enchanted with what has happened: and Mr. Russell is a true and typical Western man. But perhaps, as regards his "faustian" theory, Spengler is the exception that proves the rule.

Actually, if the Jew could, by physics or any other means, cure us of what certainly is a characteristic of much european life, a belief in and worship of the most brutal and stupid sort of "force," he would deserve our deepest thanks. But that is another question.

The *race* basis is, at all events, a hopeless one on which practically to found anything of this sort at all. Your Faustian Culture would swarm with exceptions — not one solitary Hertz, as cited by Spengler, but a multitude of people, not Jews necessarily, but

simply *not "faustian"* (whatever that may be), would not conform to the unanimous picture. Far more would fail to conform
than would be found to conform in any such arrangement. And
indeed that is precisely what, in practice, happens. All the types
and genera that Spengler describes have occurred in every
period—the "faustian" age is full of "classical" men (his great hero
Goethe, even, to some extent is one of them), and Greece was
packed with ill-disciplined "faustians."

In spite of this entire rejection of a theory that I consider, in
whatever form it be stated, a foolish one, I am very far from
asserting that religion, politics or social thought cannot or does
not influence speculative thought, and indeed colour and distort
it, often, altogether. But it does it very differently, I believe, from
the manner of Spengler's description; in a sense even more radically, perhaps, but nothing like so neatly nor on an ordered plan,
nor in disciplined, pre-ordained cycles, revolving with the exactitude of a battalion of prussian infantry at manoeuvres.

This second section of my analysis of the time-consciousness
of Spengler will be for his most direct contribution to what we
have subsequently to debate apart from Spengler's theories:
namely, what rôle the political movements of the present time
play in the parallel philosophical or physical systems.

3. Now I will turn to the shape the doctrine of *organism* takes
in Spengler.

First, the emphasis on the *periodic* goes hand in hand always
with a doctrine of *organism*. The universe becomes an animal,
whose organic periodicity we study. In philosophic theory
"periodic" implies "organic"; and when Whitehead says that he
is advancing (as Bergson did) "the organic view," that involves
the stressing of a regular time-pulsation of things, and a periodic
re-enacting and repetitive pattern, in everything, as we have seen.
The "world-as-history" could equally well be expressed as the
"world-as-cycles." It involves insistence upon the pervasive existence of a fatal, mechanical periodicity, in the working of the
empirical Flux: in short, the reference is directly to the organic
mechanism of your body, with systole and diastole, periodic
changes, and its budding, flowering and decaying. The "mind"
has ceased to exist. The universe is an animal resembling your
body, with a mind composed of *time*. You are invited to listen

for the creaking and churning of the world as it whirls round upon its axis, the beat and thunder of its movement, for the repetitive music of the spheres, for the *breathing*, the "heart beats" of the sun (which instruments, it is thought, very soon may be invented to register), and for the "chug-chug" of your own blood, the rhythmical vibration of your own circulative machinery, as you forge ahead, like a gently-heated, purring steamer, upon the breast of the river Flux.

That picture, to begin with, is not the picture of the normal consciousness. Pushed down, or sunk down, on to a purely automatic motor-plane, all the functions upon which our conscious life depends are totally forgotten. Except when violently exerting ourselves, or when acted upon by the rush of what Spengler calls the "megalopolis," our consciousness is quite static and still, as serene and unmoving as our position upon the earth in the midst of Space appears to be. This essential quietude of our consciousness, if it did not exist, would be a thing that a thousand people would be recommending us to acquire. If Time is "a moving image of eternity," our consciousness is a non-moving image of it, or else it is the thing itself. Nature, and we in nature, are balanced so perfectly, and move so quietly hither and thither, in such a dream-like suspension, in our most normal life, that it would require an equal effort to reverse this illusion of eternity, and convert it into the heavy, unquiet, shattering pulsation of Time, to what it must have needed, according to our standards, to create it. So the theoretic view in question is a very different one from the teaching of experience.

The "historic" picture is in reality a description of the Unconscious, as exactly as is the teaching of von Hartmann or of Freud. When it is brought to life by time-consciousness, it exists only as an *immense image*. So there is in the life of the time-conscious individual a crushing preponderance of image-material. What next we have to ask ourselves is if this inflated image-world is real in its own right, or if not, on what terms it is endowed by us with reality. There is also the practical question of its influence upon our "actual" existence.

The rise and fall of Empires — one of the obvious illustrations and starting-points of "organic" historical myth — is only true of a very small stretch of historic time. It is not fundamental; not a fact of the same order as the growth and decay of individual man. With "Cultures" it is the same thing. If the European has not broken the vicious circle and the world entered on a period of pacification, it is not from lack of opportunity. The Great War and the wars that are now threatened are the result of the historic mind. It is the time-mind at work: indeed, it is peculiarly useful to the promoters of wars, hence its popularity. It says, "It's time for another war." The fact that world conditions have been completely changed by the "scientific age" means nothing to it. Shut into its dogmatic history-picture, it clamours for repetition. It does not see, nor wish to see, very new facts. It wishes only to see history and the habit-picture. Life is quite exactly for it a drama (as we have seen Spengler and Whitehead describing it). Or it is a melodrama — a musical drama. For the historic-mind is that of the sensationalist gallery or pit of tradition. It expects images of "power" and of exaggerated "passion," then a great deal of red blood and good blue entrails. Then the curtain: a pause: then the same thing over again.

The clockwork rising and falling of empires, with the regular oscillations of great wars, plots and massacres, seems, according to all unprejudiced information, to refer to a certain limited period of history only. It had a relatively recent beginning, very special, not universal or necessary, causes, and it is to be assumed that it is amenable to an end. This seemed, but recently, within sight. But even if that were not so, still not to struggle to alter such things, however profound the rut in which they run, would display very little spirit or perseverance, "evolutionary" or other. Had men never sought to alter things no historical, cyclic changes could ever have been got going, to start with: for you cannot have a period or a "culture," even, without un peu de bonne volonté.

"Arts [are] organisms of [a] Culture, organisms which are born, ripen, age and for ever die," writes Spengler. The rationale of this emphatic for ever of Spengler's is of course that for him the "organism" that we call an art (such as "Impressionist art," "Geometric art," or "Renaissance art") is conceived in its full, coloured, breathing materiality, it is bergsonianly "alive," and so it not only dies for ever, but everything about it dies for ever. There is nothing "universal" left in it except entities of an extremely low and feeble order. It is, in short, the super-sensuously real — the daily "copy," the topical, what has "news-value" — that dies so absolutely. The "arts" that "are organisms" within a great Culture, or historical body, can be visualized on the same principle as the electron of Whitehead's illustration, "blindly running," but deriving importance from the fact that it is an integral part of a whole greater than (though possibly as blind as) itself, and not a mere lonely, alien atom. That is why those arts, with the culture-body, behave so "organically," why it is necessary to italicize *for ever* when we come to mention their lamented decease.

Returning to the imperial organisms that are the patterns for Spengler's apocalyptic zoo, we have many excellent reasons to inquire whether societies *must* see-saw up and down, with Apocalypses, "Declines," or "*never-more*," wistful, and dramatic Culture-periods, for the benefit of sentimental historians of the type of Spengler?

The extremely "ahistoric" Chinese are more troublesome than the Greeks for the chronological philosopher. The ancient Egyptians are as bad. The Indians are even worse, perhaps the worst of all. But then when you come to think of it, there is no civilization of any magnitude or importance that was not "ahistoric" — all except the "Faustian West."

Here is Whitehead on the Chinese problem:

. . . the more we know of Chinese art, of Chinese literature, and of the Chinese philosophy of life, the more we admire the heights to which that civilization attained. For thousands of years there have been in China acute and learned men patiently devoting their lives to study. Having regard to the span of time, and to the population concerned, China forms the largest volume of civilization which the world has seen. There is no reason to doubt the intrinsic capacity of individual Chinamen for the pursuit of science. And yet Chinese science is practically negligible. There is no reason to believe that China if left to itself would have ever produced any progress in science. The same may be said of India. Furthermore, if the Persians had enslaved the Greeks, there is no definite ground for belief that science would have flourished in Europe.

The Greeks are alone responsible for modern science, it seems, and so for Progress; and (although so "ahistoric" themselves) for the historical, chronological mind. But there seems no reason at all why the present great ferment should not eventually return to the chinese, indian, egyptian, persian, etc., etc. condition. We are perhaps in the last phases of greek "progress" — phases that are extremely ungreek, however. Progress may even itself bring Progress to an end. Indeed, already the bottom appears to be entirely knocked out of Spengler's "historical," periodic picture, by such things as wireless, air-travel and so forth — actually by Progress itself. How *can*, in fact, the old competitive "rising" and "declining," clashing of crowds of rival states, continue at all, unless science is abolished, or else unless that state of historical rivalry is artificially maintained? It is because Spengler is so very romantic that he is so objectionable: and anyone who cares to argue it out for himself will soon see that the "historical" view is the opposite of anything that could be called "realistic," in anything but a false and indecent sense.

His "organic" antithetic Cultures are the result of the hypnotism of the Rise-Decline-and-Fall of empires and aggressive military states, it is plain. That Spengler imparts a pan-german pugnacity, of all foolish things, into his Culture-partisanship (it is the Musical, the Nordic, the Faustian Culture that is the "profoundest," etc., etc.) proves it, if that were needed. Nietzschean power-metaphysics have long obsessed european ideology and speculation. Spengler's violent power-doctrine applied to History is still Nietzsche, as Alexander and Whitehead are still Bergson.

The mark of the darwinian matrix from which this thought comes is very plain in the following passage, where he is showing "static" Classic Man to be lacking naturally in "tension."

> It is *tension* that is missing in the science of Democritus. . . . Between Classical men, or states, or views of the world, there was — for all the quarrelling and envy and hatred — no inner *tension*, no deep . . . need of . . . ascendancy. The principle of *tension* . . . has become for Western physics fundamental. Its content follows from the notion of . . . the *Will-to-Power-in-Nature.* . . . For the Classical thought it [would have been] impossible.

Inner tension between men, between states, between the points of view embodied in them, or even between atoms, or indeed between *everything* existing in the Western World, hypothetically or otherwise, in theory or in life — that is the stirring burden of his historical vision. All this tension — especially "inner tension" — comes straight out of the *Will-to-Power-in-Nature.*

Finally, his theory of art is highly "organic" in all its details. What he constantly contrasts are the Classical point of view and the Faustian, as he calls it, or "gothic-european." Whenever a Classical "thing" *comes to life*, then it immediately becomes "Musical." When the greek statue, for instance, came to life in Byzantium or Alexandria by receiving soulful eyes that *"entered into"* the onlooker — then it is Faustian and non-Classical. The

Faustian building, for instance, is *alive*. "The Faustian building has a *visage* and not merely a *façade*": and with this visage, this head, is associated "an articulated trunk, that . . . erects itself to the heavens like the spires of Rheims." These buildings, whether of Speyer, Rouen or Rheims, are alive: they have a face, instead of façade: they are also "a cathedral of voices" — they *sing* (as well as rumbling with organs). They are apocalyptic "musical" animals, where the Classical temple was a songless embodied ethos, the blind, nude, static body of a man.

So much for the "organic" nature of his picture of the world. I will now turn to his art-doctrine.

4. Spengler is very preoccupied with the greek idea of Tragedy. He cannot drag his mind away from the picture of all the athenian population squatting in its theatres and "purging" itself. It seems to him, no doubt, such a waste of good "historical" material. He feels cheated of *real* live "events," by the athenian poets. The stoic philosophers even went further still, and transplanted this quietism and staticness into everyday life!

> The seated Buddha-statue . . . and Zeno's Ataraxia are not altogether alien to one another. The ethical ideal of classical man was that which is led up to in his tragedy, and revealed in its Katharsis. This in its last depths means the purgation of the Apollinian soul from its burden of what is *not* Apollinian. . . . That which the drama [the attic-drama] effected in a solemn hour, the Stoa wished to spread over the whole field of life; viz., statuesque steadiness and will-less ethos. Now, is not this conception of κάθαρσις closely akin to the Buddhist ideal of Nirvana? . . . And does not this kinship bring ideal Classical man and ideal Indian man very close to one another, *and separate them both from that man whose ethic is manifested in the Shakespearean tragedy of dynamic evolution and catastrophe?*

We could add, separate from *all* apocalyptic men whatever — all those labouring ecstatically under aching burdens of "fate" or "destiny," that require "dynamical" and "evolutionary" purgations — all those temperamentally in love with "tragedy," and bitterly resenting the model picture presented to us by Aristotle of its being gently purged out.

All art, except modern german music, becomes, in Spengler's account, a sort of buddhism. If allowed to have its own way, even a god of Peace might be evolved. Anything really might happen! Something like a chinese or an indian civilization might ensue.

So what Spengler says, in effect, is this. The poor, ignorant, unenlightened Greeks went into a theatre and worked off their tragic deposits of thought and feeling in watching a *make-believe* agony and death. They were so *superficial, the Hellenes, and had so little care for reality* (these confirmed "idealists"), that they were satisfied with that mere *picture* of tragedy, that second-hand reality. *We*, "faustian," modern, Western Europeans (and especially Nordics), have a better way of purging ourselves. *Our* catharsis is not of that roundabout, feeble, static sort. *We* engage in gigantic exterminatory wars to purge *our* feelings. We exact *real* blood and tears. We want, in short, *reality*: whereas the poor Greek only wanted a show, a picture, a representation in a theatre.

All the problems presented by the arts, and the meaning of their relation to our life, and so, as I see it, all the problems of our life at all, today, lie in this reasoning. On whether you see through, or whether you accept, this romantic, self-styled "realist" version of things, will rest a great deal your general position.

The Romans, never strong in art or speculative thought, at the best of times, gradually sank during the Empire to a condition in which art became more and more "naturalist" and *real*. They arrived at the veritable pitched battle in the gladiatorial games, in which quantities of men fell upon and killed each other for money; and, as Seneca describes, they crucified and killed real men upon their stages. It was those ultimate forms of "realism" in the later Western Empire that ushered in the Dark Ages. Today, our wars and revolutions, and all the feverish emotionality associated with these, appear to be doing the same with us. I am merely stating the case for *art*, as against what is vilely misnamed "reality."

5. Just as Whitehead (in his *Science and the Modern World*) wishes to identify art and science — to suggest that they are at bottom an identical activity (Whitehead being quite prepared to say, I should imagine, that art was equally "scientific," and in many ways more exact), so does Spengler. This is Whitehead on the subject of Leonardo da Vinci, for instance:

Perhaps the man who most completely anticipated both Bacon and the whole modern point of view was the artist Leonardo da Vinci, who lived almost a whole century before Bacon. Leonardo also illustrated the theory which I was advancing in my last lecture, that *the rise of naturalistic art was an important ingredient in the formation of our scientific mentality.* Indeed, Leonardo was more completely a man of science than was Bacon. The practice of naturalistic art is more akin to the practice of physics, chemistry and biology than is the practice of law. . . . Da Vinci and Bacon stand together as illustrating the . . . legal mentality and the patient observational habits of the naturalistic artists.

It is interesting to note, in connection with this passage, that Duhem believes that we have in Cardan (*De Subtilitate*) the thought of Leonardo, since Leonardo's unpublished MSS. were in the hands of Cardan, and he is proved not to have been over-scrupulous. Descartes, the father of the modern age, was very indebted to Cardan; and so, if Duhem's supposition is correct, you have in Leonardo, more than in any other single person, the source and origin of the modern scientific outlook. At all events, there is no intention here of disputing the importance attributed to Leonardo by Whitehead and Spengler.

Whitehead's account of Leonardo is the exact opposite to that of Spengler; for no consistency must be expected in "Time" enthusiasms. Both believe Leonardo to be almost the most important figure of the last five hundred years, but for opposite reasons. Whitehead sees him as a very scientifically-minded *observer*, patiently dissecting corpses and immersed in the technical, physical problems of "naturalistic art." Spengler would regard this view of his hero as repulsive and untrue. For him Leonardo was, on the contrary, the person who took the art of painting out of that Renaissance naturalism into the region of "faustian" infinite Space and "Music."

Oil-painting, on the other hand, sees and handles with ever-growing sureness extension as a whole, and treats all objects as representatives thereof. The Faustian world-feeling created the new technique that it wanted. It rejected . . . drawing . . . It transformed the linear perspective . . . into a purely aerial perspective. . . . Some ventured [on the Faustian road], some guessed, some fell by the way, some shied. *It was, as always, the struggle between the hand and soul, between eye and instrument, between the form willed by the artist and the form willed by time — the struggle between Plastic and Music.*

The "hand" is of course here the symbol of "the Classical"; the line (or "drawing," in whose repudiation by his faustian spirit you see, above, Spengler exulting) is the Classical; whereas the aerial perspective, chiaroscuro, is the *musical* invention of the germanic North. It is also worth noting the identification of "time" with "music," and Music contrasted with Plastic—that "timeless" thing, as he elsewhere describes it. The cult of time or feeling for time, he also, elsewhere, identifies with "the feminine." (These associations of terms are interesting as revealing the true nature of his thought.)

In the light of this [account of the melting of the Renaissance into the Gothic or "Faustian"] we can at last understand that gigantic effort of Leonardo . . . the Adoration of the Magi. . . . Nothing like it was even imagined till Rembrandt. Transcending all optical measures, everything then called drawing, outline, composition and grouping, he pushes fearlessly on to challenge eternal space; everything bodily floats like the planets in the Copernican system and the tones of a Bach organ-fugue in the dimness of old churches.

Further on you read:

In Fra Bartolommeo the material bounding-line is still entirely dominant. It is all foreground, and the whole sense of the work is exhaustively rendered by the definition of bodies. But in Raphael line has become silent, expectant, veiled, waiting in an extremity of tension for dissolution into the infinite, into space and music.

Now "the dimness of old churches," bodies "floating" in infinite space, or a technique where things are "veiled," shuddering and expectant, prior to their thrilling plunge into dissolution, "the infinite," and into Music, is not what Whitehead was thinking about when he mentioned Leonardo. Of course he had in mind quite the opposite of such happenings as those. But I believe that Spengler understands himself, and the time-material he is handling, better than does Whitehead. When Professor Whitehead identifies his scientific and mathematical theories with Romantic Art, he does so with a sense of paradox: he has the air of thinking that by bringing together such things as electro-dynamics and "Hail to thee, blithe spirit," or Wordsworth, he is treading with some daring a novel—if not a naughty, a peculiar—path. A little less english stiffness, and we should find him splashing about in a faustian bath of Music and Infinity with Spengler.

6. In this section I will set out fully the meaning of the antithetic "Classical" and "Faustian" (or "Gothic"), or the "Plastic" and "Musical," of Spengler's vocabulary.

Classical Man and the "Classical" Culture is for Spengler hellenic civilization. This, with its definiteness, its immediacy, he is against. He is for the "Faustian" Culture (which resolves itself into modern Western Romanticism). That is "far-away" (or "infinite," "yearning," etc.): that *hates the line*, that loves the "perspective," in which "things" only exist in their relation to a misty, "far-echoing" Whole, not for themselves: it is those attributes that he likes and teaches.

Let him describe to you the advantages of the "Faustian" over the "Classical."

Consider, now, Western painting as it was after Leonardo, fully conscious of its mission. How does it deal with infinite space as something *singular* which comprehends both picture and spectator as mere centres of gravity of a spatial dynamic? . . . The [Faustian] picture no longer stands for itself, nor looks out at the spectator, but *takes him into its sphere.* . . . Foreground and background lose all tendency to materiality and propinquity. . . . Far horizons deepen the field to infinity, and the colour-treatment . . . expands the field so that the spectator is *in* it. It is not he, now, who chooses the standpoint from which the picture is most effective, on the contrary, the picture dictates position and distance to him. . . . The Greek spectator stands *before* the fresco of Polygnotus. We *sink into* a picture: that is, we are pulled into it by the power of the space-treatment.

In the *Dithyrambic Spectator* I have dealt with this particular phenomenon of merging recommended — dithyrambically — by Spengler. I will now place beside the above quotation from the *Decline of the West* a passage from the excellent *Belphégor*, by Julien Benda, in which exactly the same process is described, but in Benda's case described with as much disgust as in the case of Spengler it is pointed to with gusto. *Belphégor* is a critical study of the "democratic" post-war society in France: all the mass-democratic vices and weaknesses are exposed in a masterly fashion. When, however, he uses the word "democratic" he wishes us to understand exactly what he means, he tells us, and this is how he defines it:

We speak of the bad taste of our "democratic" society. We mean by that a society whose tastes have become those of the people or at least such as we usually expect of the people (namely, indifference to intellectual values, religion of emotion). We intend by that neither to curse nor to flatter any particular political régime. We would willingly say with a woman of the eighteenth century: "I will call 'people' all those who think commonly and basely: the court is full of them."

After the alternations of romantic power-snobbery, and astute provision of gaudy and gigantic morsels destined for the most plebeian of palates, found in Spengler, this good sense of Benda's is refreshing, is it not? This is the passage from Benda that can usefully be read in conjunction with the above passage from the *Decline of the West.*

Art (in contemporary doctrine) [he writes] must *identify itself* with this principle: it must not *observe* it, or describe it, which implies *remain distinct from it*, it must *unite itself to it*, more precisely, *fuse, confound itself with it.* . . . When our teachers announce that art "should cease to walk around things, but should take up its position *inside* them," that by no means signifies, according to them, that art should *look into* the inside of things, but, quite the contrary, that it should *die to every kind of* (*mere objective*) *vision* (in so far as to *look at* a thing is always to remain exterior to it) and *merge itself in* (*se confondre*) the life of things. Constantly we hear our prophets declaring that the artist should "marry the eternal rhythm of things," "become the life of things," "*live* things."

As you see, this passage describes spenglerism with great accuracy, only it refers not to Spengler but to a flourishing mode in France a year or two before Spengler made his appearance.

I will quote a few remarks of Spengler's to define further the meaning he attaches to the word "classical," arranging my quotations in subsections:

(1) The "Nature" of Classical man found its highest artistic emblem in the nude statue, and out of it logically there grew a *static of bodies, a physics of the near.* (. . . Faustian man's Nature-idea was a *dynamic of unlimited space, a physics of the distant.*) To the Classical belong the conceptions of *matter and form*: to the Arabian . . . the idea of *substances* . . . to the Faustian the idea of *force and mass.* Apollinian theory is a quiet meditation, Magian a silent knowledge of Alchemy . . . (even here the religious source of mechanics is to be discerned): the Faustian is from the very outset a *working hypothesis.*

(2) An Attic statue is a completely Euclidean body, timeless and relationless, wholly self-contained. It neither speaks nor looks. *It is quite unconscious of the spectator.* Unlike the plastic forms of every other Culture, it stands wholly for itself and fits into no architectural order; it is an individual amongst individuals, a body amongst bodies. And the living individuals . . . perceive it *as a neighbour*, and do not feel it as an invasive influence . . .

(3) The Greeks inquired as little into the interior of their own organization as they sought for the sources of the Nile: those were

problems that might have jeopardized the Euclidean constitution of their being. . . . Classical man took good care not to take the cover, the material wrapping, off anything cosmic. . . .

(4) All Classical building begins from the outside, all Western from the inside.

(5) The history of the Classical shaping art is one untiring effort to accomplish one single ideal, viz. the conquest of the freestanding human body as the vessel of the *pure real present*. The temple of the naked body was to it what the cathedral of voices was to the Faustian . . .

(6) For Classical man . . . the gods were, like a statue or a polis, Euclidean bodies having locality.

(7) The bases of the Apollinian and the Faustian Nature-images respectively are in all contexts the two opposite symbols of *individual thing* and *unitary space*.

In the above passages, chosen at random, you obtain a quite definite picture of what Spengler considers the attributes of the "Classical," and what he means by Classical man. He goes indifferently to art and physics for his description. The "Classical man" is, however, the Greek man: and the attic statue is the central symbol, for Spengler, of all that is "Classical."

The attic statue "neither speaks nor looks." The sculptor makes its eyes *blind*. It is a *thing*, really, an object among other objects. It is, in short, "the individual thing," without a "soul." The Greek regarded himself as surrounded by static and soulless "things"; whereas we, and our "Faustian" brothers, regard ourselves as surrounded by "forces," and as dynamically involved in a World-Soul.

In contrast to the "Classical," the byzantine artist supplied his human figures with enormous eyes: "the beholder's sphere is invaded by an action-at-a-distance," emanating from the picture, by means of these fixed and hypnotic, almost living, *eyes*. Art has come to life. The repose of *things*, of a dead and soulless universe, such as you get in attic art, has come to an end forever. These are the Dark Ages, and then the Gothic North begins its great Culture, of which its vast and profuse cathedrals (from which the hated "classical" line is conspicuously absent) are the culmination. After a slight rebuff (namely the Italian Renaissance) the Gothic soars on till it builds up German Music as a fitting sequel to its cathedrals — (which, as Spengler truly remarks, are only half-plastic art or less than that; they are really *music*). In

Beethoven and Wagner this disembodied, soaring, mystical afflatus makes its most expressive finale of achievement. That is the "Faustian" Infinite in full blast.

So "Music," in the spenglerian account of things, which agrees with a widely held view (cf. M. Brémond, chap. iii, etc.), is the supreme expression of Western Culture: with Chamber-music "the Faustian music becomes dominant among the Faustian arts. It banishes the plastic of the statue and tolerates only the minor art . . . of porcelain."

Spengler sets "Plastic" and "Music" at each other's throats, in an eliminating contest. It is world-power or downfall for Gothic Music as interpreted by this warlike professor; and the arts become weapons in his hands, which he wields with a picturesque barbaric clumsiness, brandishing them hither and thither. There is no room upon the same earth for two such *opposite* things as Plastic and Music. He insists characteristically on a *unity* in everything. So Music eats up the Plastic, dissolves it, and it streams out to "infinity." There is then *only* Music throughout the triumphantly Gothic World.

Spengler's "Faustian," "Musical," and "Gothic" has its culmination in Wagner, that, for an artist, is the thing of crowning significance.

A whole world of soul could crowd into these three bars [of Wagner]. Colours of starry midnight, of sweeping clouds, of autumn, of the day dawning in fear and sorrow . . . world-fear, impending doom . . . all these impressions which no composer before him had thought it possible to catch, he could paint. . . . Here the contrast of Western music with greek plastic has reached its maximum.

Indeed, I think it did. But is Spengler's whole book a subtle argument *for* the Classical, after all?

7. By "Music" Spengler means something peculiar to his own artificial system: and by "Plastic" he means something unusual too.

Most of his chapter — the most instructive in his book — called (in the english translation) "The Arts of Form," is taken up with contrasting "Plastic" and "Music." What he means by "Music" is evidently a late Beethoven quartet rather than a Bach fugue: for I suppose (I am ignorant) that a Bach fugue would offer too many analogies to the "Classical," would be too *structural*," to satisfy the "faustian," romantic, "musical," ideal. *It is not really with the*

*art of music, that is, or with the art of painting, that he is deal-
ing, when he is contrasting Plastic and Music, but with a certain
kind of nature that has expressed itself in one art or the other.*

My standpoint here is that when he says "Music" he does not
mean what Bach, for instance, would mean by music, but merely the german "soul" expressing itself in that medium. And I suggest that other "souls" have expressed themselves just as beautifully
in music, but "Classically," as he would call it. In spite of the
fact that he uses Bach and counterpoint often as a typical "Faustian," I should imagine that many musicians would be found to
disagree with him, once they understood exactly what he meant
by his term. Similarly for him "Plastic" means greek or plastic
art: any plastic art in Europe that is not greek or greek-influenced,
he calls "music." And by "music" he means, as I have said, not
what other people mean by "music," but the expression of a certain type of romantic mind, for which Germany has been mainly responsible.

Just as he sees underneath all physical theory the "soul" or "will,"
of some *particular Culture* (so that "there is *no absolute science
of physics*, but only *individual* sciences that come and go, within
the individual Cultures"), so underneath any phase of plastic art
he sees no universal and peculiar problem of form. No art has
a philosophy of its own for him: indeed all arts, the moment they
really begin to understand themselves, show a tendency to melt
away into "music" — into something intangible, abstract, non-
plastic — "infinite." The saying of the great nineteenth-century
romantic and aesthete, Walter Pater, can again be usefully recalled: "All art seeks to approximate to that of *music*."

As regards Painting or Sculpture, "the technical form-language
is no more than the *mask* of the real work." Style is not a product of material, of technique, but of "a mysterious *must*, a
Destiny." Oh, those mysterious *musts* of Spengler's! one had supposed that no more such eternal teutonisms were to be found.
At all events, in spite of the emotional pretensions of the terms
in which he sees fit to express himself, there is something definite
enough here. He objects to the arts of architecture, music and
painting being "determined by perfectly superficial criteria of
medium and technique," endowed with eternal validity and immutable principles of formal expression. The "Science of art" has
always attached importance "to a timeless delimitation of the individual art spheres": and it is the ahistorical character of this

"science" (invented by "Faustians," like so many other "timeless" things, oddly enough) that annoys Spengler, rather than its claiming for the plastic arts independence of "Music," or rather ignoring the imperialistic rôle of Music altogether. "If an art has boundaries at all . . . they are *historical*, and not technical or physiological boundaries. An art is an *organism, etc.*" To be an "organism," to be "historical," to be saturated with and fully possessed of *Time*, it is essential that it should be physiologically castrated and absolutely despecialized. Otherwise we should get just *artists* — whether chinese, tuscan, arabian or mayan; and that would not at all suit Spengler's book. For him a tuscan Quattrocento painter is not an *artist*, but a "Classical" man in disguise, struggling to reincarnate himself in an italian "Goth," engaged in the vain attempt to vanquish by means of his old weapon, plastic form, the surging, "infinite," "gothic" Music of the "faustian" man; who, of course, without any difficulty discomfits him, and re-establishes the "gothic" (in the form, this time, of german music) more firmly than ever before. Today it *declines*: for even "Goths," apparently, must die. And "every individual art . . . is *once existent*, and departs with its soul and its symbolism never to return."

8. For Spengler's militant picture, in which it is his idea to set by the ears something he calls "gothic" or "faustian" on the one hand, and "classical" (that is to say, greek) on the other, there is one very troublesome event. That is the Italian Renaissance.

For the culture of Europe the Renaissance stands as a great and unparalleled cultural awakening. Just as the Englishman regards the Elizabethan Age as a short but select period, when England produced its greatest intellect, and many scarcely less important ones, at the most heroical moment of its history; so Europe in general is accustomed to look back on the Renaissance as its culminating intellectual effort, when genius reached its greatest pitch, in unexampled abundance.

But for Spengler's World-as-History and his glorification of the "gothic" soul, the Renaissance is a most disagreeable retrospective contretemps. Renaissance Man was almost Classical Man over again. And what is the value of his "gothic" panegyric if upon the only occasion on which Europe reached the greatest levels of art and really put forth all its genius — or if that estimate of the Italian Renaissance is accepted — it simply became *Classical* again, as though there were nothing better to do than that, and as though its true soul were in reality a Classical soul! That would be very awkward. So the prestige of the Renaissance has to be destroyed.

First, he sets himself to suggest that any artist whom he finds it is quite impossible to belittle without being even more absurd than he wishes to be — such as Leonardo or Michelangelo — was in reality a "Gothic." Michelangelo was, with St. Peter's, *primitive Baroque*, not Renaissance. Leonardo was Baroque too: he, as we have seen, is not only the founder of modern, anti-classical, science; he is also for Spengler the forerunner of German Music, the enemy of the Classical "concrete," the first great artist to envelop his pictures in a romantic "infinity" of pure "faustian" Space.

But no Renaissance artist was really "classical": they were all members of a very obstinate, irrelevant, "anti-gothic," movement, that flared up and then quickly died down, all the greatest ending their days as musical baroque primitives.

It was the "musical" Baroque that, for Spengler, gave the *coup de grâce* to the Renaissance. Jesuit art, as seen in the venetian churches, brought "music" into its own again: and with the "real" or "alive" quality of its ornamentation, that everywhere broke up the "classical" and static; with its architectural surfaces and vistas that were *alive* instead of classically objective and *dead*, it was the aerial bridge back into the region of Music and the abstract. Here is his description of Rococo, which, in its function of a dissolvent of the Plastic, is analogous to Baroque.

> With the eighteenth century . . . architecture died at last, submerged and choked in the music of Rococo. On that last wonderful fragile growth of the Western architecture, criticism has blown mercilessly, failing to realize that its origin is in the spirit of the fugue, and that its non-proportion and non-form, its evanescence and instability and sparkle, its destruction of surface and visual order, *are nothing else than a victory of tones and melodies over lines and walls*, the triumph of pure space over material, of absolute becoming over the become. They are no longer buildings, these abbeys and castles and churches with their flowing façades and porches and "gingerbread" Courts, and their splendid staircases, galleries, salons and cabinets; they are sonatas, minuets, madrigals in stone, chamber-music in stucco, marble, ivory and fine woods, cantilene of volutes and cartouches, cadences of fliers and copings. The Dresden Zwinger is the most completely musical piece in all the world's architecture. . . .

Again, the Renaissance was not the expression of *the time*, nor was it the expression of the people among whom it occurred. Here is his full statement:

We have only to think of the bursting passion with which the gothic world-feeling discharged itself upon the whole Western landscape and we shall see at once what sort of movement it was that the handful of select spirits — scholars, artists, and humanists — initiated about 1420. [It was purely Florentine, and even within Florence the ideal of one class of society.] In the [gothic] the issue was one of life and death for new-born soul, in the second it was a point of — taste. The gothic gripped life in its entirety, penetrated its most hidden corners. It created new men and a new world. . . . But the Renaissance, when it had mastered some arts of word and picture, had shot its bolt. It altered the ways of thought and the life-feeling of West Europe not one whit. It could penetrate as far as costume and gesture, but the roots of life it could not touch — even in Italy the world-outlook of the Baroque is essentially a continuation of the gothic . . . the Renaissance never touched the people, even in Florence itself. The man for whom they had ears was Savonarola . . . all the time the deep undercurrents are steadily flowing on towards the gothic-musical Baroque. The Renaissance [is] an antigothic movement and a reaction against the spirit of polyphonic music. . . . [The Renaissance is in the nature of] a stand that the soul attempted to make against the Destiny that at last it comprehends. The inwardly recalcitrant forces . . . are striving to deflect the sense of the Culture . . . it stands anxious in presence of the call to accomplish its historical fate. . . . This anxiety fastened itself in Greece to the Dionysus-cult with its musical, dematerializing, body-squandering orgasm, and in the Renaissance to the tradition of the Antique. . . .

Culture conceived as "fate" or "destiny," as you see, is far from an agreeable thing: it is a thing against which the "soul" reacts with considerable violence, as the Renaissance as seen by Spengler surely proves. But why should the soul of the West be so "anxious," and so unwilling to fulfil its "destiny" — since this "destiny," after all, was presumably just *it*? The answer seems to be that that Destiny was "a musical, dematerializing, body-squandering orgasm": that it did not *want* to have its body "squandered" in an "orgasm," any more than a people (though it may be their "destiny") want to become "cannon-fodder," and engage in a murderous "orgasm." That seems reasonable enough: but it suggests unmistakably another thing: namely, that the soul of the West was *not* so purely "gothic" and musical as all that: that it certainly was not *all* gothic and musical: that it differed from district to district and man to man, as anybody would expect, who had not a *Destiny-theory* of history, or who had not history on the brain or an "historical complex." In short, it would seem to point to our conclusion rather than to Spengler's.

9. Finally let me quote this: "What Darwin originated is only the 'Manchester School' system, and it is this *latent political element in it that accounts for its popularity.*" (The italics are in the original.) What is it accounts for Spengler's popularity? I hope not any *latent* political element which may have escaped me! In any case, in this last section we will turn to the politics implied in all this profuse bric-à-brac.

Spengler is a host in himself: he dispenses us from picking amongst a hundred less open and slightly more circumspect minds: for he goes out of his way to give us all the material we want in just the way that we want it. He not only makes life easier for the critic of "time," but he should make it a lighter affair for the more delicate reader. But if the rather lazy and easily fooled general reader suddenly opened Spengler's book and began plunging about in its immense and portentous material, he might, it is true, be baffled. He would be very much impressed, perhaps, by all this mass of "learning" and of intellectual apparatus; but it would confuse and exhaust him so much that (at the end of it all, or when he finally gave up, dead-beat) he would not know *what* Spengler had told him quite, or whither it had all led. He would only feel that he had been globe-trotted more intensively than ever before — had heard more paradoxes about more "sights," and had really learnt the latest opinion about the thousand and one wonders of the world. A notion that Spengler was not very favourable to socialism might remain with him; but all that side of the trip would be misty. If a socialist, he would enjoy the haughty abuse of the masses, of course: just as, if an Englishman or American, he would relish the contempt shown for those peoples. In the main, all would be covered over for him (when looking back upon his experience) by oceans of words, a large proportion of them as it were uniformed, many decorated and embossed with immense and overpowering symbols.

It will now be my task to put a little order into that department of spenglerism that would come under the head of *politics.*

Spengler affects to be an "anti-popular" writer. On exactly the same principle as Nietzsche — though of course without the latter's initiatory genius or his thoroughness — he affects to be a writer by no means "for the crowd."

In this Spengler is only humbugging, of course: he is in reality a popular writer: not because of any clarity to be found in his exposition, but in its "direction," to use his favourite word. It is an intoxicant for herd-consumption.

But his reiterated complaint about "Classical Man" is that he is "popular."

The Classical Culture is the most popular and the Faustian the least popular.

He adds this definition:

A creation is "popular" that gives itself with all its secrets to the first comer at the first glance, that incorporates its meaning in its exterior and surface . . . generally, *that which is immediately and frankly evident to the senses* . . .

This, too, when it is not mere bluff, is just excitement, and various contradictory emotional habits asserting themselves.

Spengler identifies the "classical" with the "popular." He makes a great pretence of providing a very distinguished, not to say aristocratical, version of the things of which he treats. The preoccupation of the Greeks with the sensuous life of immediate objects revealed a rather low taste — at best it was merely "popular." The German Valhalla, the misty musical dynamics of Wagner or Beethoven, the mystical "yearnings" for infinity of the Northern ("Faustian") man — that is a very distinguished thing, on the contrary. "Music" is, put crudely, gentlemanly; "Plastic" is not. Emotion is an exceptional and very noble thing, the intellect is a "popular" one. This is the opposite to the view taken by Benda, or even, for that matter, by Nietzsche, or indeed by almost anybody. The general view of the Intellect is that it, above all things, is the aristocratical attribute; so much is this the case that in the present egalitarian and popular age it, and all its "highbrow airs," are exceedingly disliked.

I suggest that this view is merely adopted by Spengler to enlist the sympathies of what he knows quite well to be a large, popular, and for the most part extremely vulgar, audience. He understands his public in very much the same way that a socialist orator does his: in modern socialism "vulgar" means all that is not proletarian, noble means all that is socially insignificant: both terms, in their paraphrases, are essential to the orator. Of course, if we know

how very vulgar most that is not proletarian in fact is, this will
not strike us as any particular paradox: but the fact remains that
the speaker is indulging in sleight-of-hand. The same applies to
Oswald Spengler.

In the passage quoted in the last section Spengler describes the
Renaissance as an aristocratic event, an affair of a "handful of
select spirits," which did not touch "the root of life": it "never
touched the people": Gothic did do that: indeed it "gripped" them,
and "penetrated" them in a truly "musical" and mystical fashion.
It was *dionysiac* — so, with that misbegotten word (in its modern
use in popular propaganda), we get back to Nietzsche once more.

I do not know if it will appear to every reader worthwhile
detecting and exposing the almost insane inconsistencies of such
a writer as Spengler: but I think that it is so because this kind
of sham does take in a great many people, and it does have a
far-reaching and extremely poisonous effect. The swallowing of
such inconsistencies means that *people are being taught not to
reason, to cease to think.* So it has appeared to me worthwhile
to expose it at some length.

Let us place beside the passage above a passage from another
chapter of his book. You will see him using the same argument
for as he above was using *against.*

Every high creator in Western history in reality aimed, from first to
last, at something which only a few could comprehend. Michelangelo
made the remark that his style was ordained for the correction of fools
. . . the same applies to every [Western] painter, statesman, philosopher.
. . . What does it mean that no German philosopher worth mentioning
can be understood by the man-in-the-street, and that the combination
of simplicity with majesty that is Homer's is simply not to be found
in any Western language? . . . We find everywhere in the Western what
we find nowhere in the Classical — the exclusive form. Whole periods —
for instance Provençal Culture and Rococo — are in the highest degree
select and uninviting, their ideas and forms having no existence except
for a small class of higher men. . . . For us, popular and shallow are
synonymous — in art as in science — but for classical man it was not so.

He cites the Renaissance, too, as he no doubt remembers mistily
that he used this argument in an opposite sense elsewhere, and
thinks the reader might notice it. But he says that that only shows
that the Renaissance was thoroughly Western.

But where is the "Gothic" and "Musical," now, that "gripped"
the "people": and where is the sting in his former argument, to
the effect that the "anti-gothic" Renaissance touched only the

surface of the life of the people, and left its great heart untouched, which was all for Gothic, for "Music," for Savonarola, for the Apocalypse? Here we are shown the flower of the "Gothic" élite likewise so many miles above the heads of the "man-in-the-street" (the romantic "people" has become the prosaic "man-in-the-street" for the occasion) that he does not so much as touch him with a barge-pole, much less "grip" his vitals and penetrate him through and through. And surely if Classical man is *popular* in his art, that should appeal to "the people," in contrast to the faustian autocrat who is not? And is it not strange to argue against the "classical" Renaissance man that he failed owing to the fact that he was not "popular" enough?

Is it bad or is it good to be "popular," Mr. Spengler, which do you mean? for you must mean something. Or, more difficult still for you to answer, is it "faustian" and gothic to be "popular," or on the contrary, is that *not* gothic or "faustian"? Is it both and neither and absolutely anything, though: and shall we just shut up the book and admit that in such a wild world there is no time to go into such details, and that what the tongue says at 3 P.M. is not necessarily what the tongue says at 4:30 P.M., and that in any case it will be all the same a hundred years hence? Have I got the drift, and is that the idea? That is the only guess, at all, that I can make.

Wagner's Nibelung poetry . . . expresses his social revolutionary ideas . . . his Siegfried is still a symbol of the Fourth Estate, his Brunhilde still the "free woman." The sexual selection of which the *Origin of Species* enunciated the theory in 1859, was finding its musical expression at the very same time in the third act of *Siegfried*, and in *Tristan*.

To Goethe evolution meant inward fulfilment, to Darwin it meant "Progress."

Nietzsche . . . as a derivative of Darwinism, presupposes Socialism . . . this "dionysiac" idea (of breeding a class of supermen) involves a *common action* . . . is democratic.

As Wagner is the culmination of the Faustian, and as Nietzsche, though so much disliking Wagner, was the first high-priest of self-conscious "faustianism," we must assume that "socialism" is an excellent thing.

Yet —

The great mass of Socialists would cease to be Socialists if they could understand the Socialism of the nine or ten men who today grasp it with the full historical consequences it involves.

That Wagner is the supreme example of Music (of Faustian, and as he calls it Western, art) as understood by Spengler, seems exact enough. He embodies, too, the emotionality of egalitarian Social Revolution (or have my eyes deceived me?): further, he expresses the Western "power-complex" (in all the colossal apotheosis of a romantic musical drama) as nothing else has. (It appears to be abominable music, most musicians today seem agreed about that.) That Nietzsche thundering and screaming is purely "darwinian": that Darwin means "Progress of the Species" (what Carlyle thundered about): that seems quite true. That socialism as taught and understood by many people deserves all the disobliging things that Spengler can say about it, is undeniable. But why should Spengler wish us to believe that these things all fit in with each other in such a way that he can say, as a result of assembling them, that he has shown this "Progress of the Species" set to *"Infinity"-Music* at Bayreuth, and all this colossal confusion of the "faustian" soul, to be *better* than the Classical? Yet everywhere he is affecting to scorn and pity the Classical, and to persuade and hypnotize us into believing that the Faustian or Western is a far finer thing.

CONCLUSION OF ANALYSIS OF SPENGLER

ONLY A FEW GENERAL observations remain to be made: for as I went along I gave my view of what I was quoting or exhibiting.

First, if it is the "faustian" culture-atmosphere that induces Spengler to be so "chronological," then the *Decline of the West* is merely a manifestation of an untranslatable Culture, with no validity beyond this period. Indeed, if Western man were to accept Spengler as his spokesman, to other Cultures the "faustian" would be a sort of outcast. For they are, up to date, all "ahistoric." Only "faustians" are "historic." So they would say between themselves that "faustianism" was false.

Next, when Spengler is attacking "Classical Man" he always means the Hellene. But anything he says about the Hellene (in contrast to us — the "dynamic" to the "static") would apply equally to the Chinese, the Indian, the ancient Egyptian — only they are all *more* static, as has elsewhere been pointed out, than the Hellene. So, my "Classical" is not the Hellenic Age, as it is Spengler's: and my Western is not his "Western." For me the contrast is no longer Modern Europe and Classical Greece. We can very well be the healthy opposite of "romantic" (and all that entails) without being greek. On the other hand, if Time-travel were able to offer us the alternative of residence in New York or residence in Periclean Athens, I should choose the latter.

It is a matter of fairly common agreement today that Asia has produced plastic art of a far higher order than Europe, in many ways more complex, mature, sensitive and beautiful. I don't think the Europeans generally realize how little original plastic art has come from Europe. If you could get rid of the Renaissance (as Spengler does) it would be very noticeable. If there is one thing that eastern art is characterized by more than another it is "line." With greek art the "line" suffers from the intrusion of the dogmatism of ionian science — of "nature," in short. It is legitimate to regard greek sculpture as part of platonic doctrine, as philosophy rather than as art. That is, at all events, how I have always regarded it, and valued it, and in that sense discuss it here.

What, on the other hand, is your Western Man, when he is not musical? *When he is not musical*, Spengler might reply, *he is not a Western man!* Western Man, according to me, made the Renaissance, and he was not "musical" but "plastic." He is still here: and he is "plastic" *now*. It is merely the German man, the least plastically gifted of any race in the world, who made German Music (but not *music*). Musical, and unmusical, men abound in the East as in the West. The substitution of *art*, or of technique, for *period*, is essentially vicious. Greek science has been very bad for the non-musical and musical East: but it may, on the other hand, be favourable to the "musical" East.

To say that I disagree with Spengler would be absurd. You cannot agree or disagree with such people as that: you can merely point out a few of the probable reasons for the most eccentric of their spasms, and if you have patience—as I have—classify them. That, I think, I have done enough.

What I now propose to do is to give an outline, in some detail, of what I believe to be the true account of the historic progression by which we have arrived at the present impasse, for also I do not deny—who can?—that there is a fearful state of chaos throughout the world. I indeed observe it with far more anguish than does Spengler, perhaps because of the "dynamical" residue in my "faustian" soul, and because I am not so happily constituted as he is, and am unable to detach myself from this "decline," and regard it as a spectacle arranged for all of us by the historically-minded god of Time, as though for an attic audience. But that is really not because I am lacking in "stoical" qualities, but because his fatalistic, mechanical account of the matter does not seem to me to be true. I, unfortunately, *live* in this Present; I have not the time-mind. I am what Spengler would call a "Classical" intellect. That is why I do not understand.

CHAPTER THREE

THE SUBJECT CONCEIVED AS KING OF THE PSYCHOLOGICAL WORLD

1. IN THE ENSUING HISTORICAL account of a certain aspect of that movement that has resulted, at last, in those typical doctrines merged in the central conception of space-time, to some readers, as I proceed, it may look as though I were merely providing confirmation of the "historical" account of Spengler. For I shall everywhere trace the curiously exact parallel between the march of political and social thought with the evolution of concepts in the philosophic field. This parallel I regard, however, as an established fact, fairly obvious and at present fairly widely recognized: it is the interpretation only that you give to it that seems to matter, or that seems to differentiate the view of one person from another. Afterwards, which of these two activities, the theoretic or practical, affects the other, or how much and according to what laws, we shall have finally to decide. I must leave it to the conclusion of my evidence to enlighten you as to my final solution of this problem. This short historical survey will resolve itself into a history of the ego since the revolutionary period of the eighteenth century of the european Enlightenment. That, it seemed to me, would be the most satisfactory way to get at what I wanted: for by confining ourselves in the main to the fate of this particular concept — and its part-ner, "consciousness," the last of the two to go, under the battery of William James — we shall be able to concentrate our historical argument, and at the same time, in tracing the all-important career of this arch-concept, to include all that is germane to what we wish to prove. First I shall define from our standpoint the position of Science in the modern world, and then turn to my account of the vicissitudes and final extinction of "the Subject."

In the first part of this book a passage from Professor Whitehead was quoted, in which he described Aristotle as the last *free* great european philosopher. With that statement we agreed: and at the time some brief description was given of what interpretation we should attach to such a statement. To that we will now add the following observations.

There is no great european philosopher of the modern age more worthy of admiration than Leibniz, both on account of his extraordinary gifts, and the humane gentleness of his nature. Yet he fell a victim to his dogmatic theology: compared with the freedom of hellenic thought both from theological and political exactions (though less the latter than the former), he was as unfortunately burdened from the start as were the Schoolmen. The advantage of Averroes over his christian contemporaries, or in a different way of Maïmonides and his pupil Spinoza, would have been enjoyed fully as much by a contemporary of Leibniz with regard to him. We are anxious to suggest the possibility that he would have been a truer servant of God if he had turned his back on God for practical purposes, and almost forgotten Him.

The leibnizian monad is a marvellous, though imperfectly conceived — confused, as he would have said — intuition of genius. But it was also, on its confused side, nothing but the little aspiring Everyman of the Enlightenment. The too literally theologic bias of his thought, and his gentle but misguided heart, his enthusiasm for an impossible "freedom," degraded the monad into a political construct, highly finished, though ill-built because of these — in themselves — noble distractions. Accommodated with a private, independent, psychic cubicle, and placed in a heaven lighted and furnished in the style of Swedenborg, it satisfied the "enlightened" of that day, but was very easy to storm when the critical period set in. Had he, with all his genius, built his system of a purer stuff, it might have served us today, instead of serving our enemies: and it might also have better served his God.

Bergson and Nietzsche have been (without the genius of Leibniz) popular purveyors to the enlightened Everyman of their day. Bergson supplied him with a certificate of "creativeness" and of "uniqueness": Nietzsche with a certificate of "blue blood." What it is really essential to press upon the attention of the reader is this: that the least distraction on the part of a great intelligence from his task of supplying pure thought, is fatal; its result is the same as in the case of a plastic or other artist when he allows himself a similar distraction. So if, then, political and theological distractions must exist, for truth's sake, the less the better: and far too much, I believe it can be shown, of the doctrine in which today we find ourselves standing, is sandy, in that sense.

Again, the belief that the mediaeval age of the Schoolmen, of Abélard, of Saint Bonaventure or Saint Thomas Aquinas, was one age, and that then came the age typified by Descartes, which was another, is a delusion (of the spenglerian order) which is responsible for a great many mistakes. It is better to regard the *Sic et non* of Abélard as a revolutionary document, than to regard his age as an age of pure faith, and that which succeeded it as an age of pure reason. The truth is that both, in different degrees, according to character and opportunity, were *mixed* ages, of revolutionary speculation associated with dogmatic faith.

2. Our next proposition will relate to Science and its contemporary status. First, Science gives as much power, and power of the same nature, as was formerly given by magic. Science is in one sense a new animistic religion, operating definitely as *magic* for the Black Boy or Redskin when he was first invaded by the White. White ascendancy in that way has truly been *White Magic*. But the White did not know that he owed his success to White Magic; he had a very different, and much less real, conception of its significance. Nor did he regard his magic as in any way "magical." He thought of it very prosaically, and a little contemptuously. He supposed his marvellous success to be due to his own unusual qualities, and his possession of the only true faith.

His magic was, however, so powerful that, in spite of his shortsightedness and self-delusion, and all he could do to discredit it and cheapen it, it has taken some time for the other world (not possessed of such formidable "medicine," to start with) to recover itself.

Science again differs from all former types of magic. It is an inexhaustible, and a public, magic. Everyman is behind the scenes, everybody is in its secrets. All the tricks are done with sleeves rolled right up to the shoulder. The audience participates fully: everyone, from the smallest errand-boy, assists at the performance. Wireless has the same magical appeal for the modern industrial savage, it is true, as the rifle had for the Redskin confronted by the early colonist. But he is in a sense the magician himself. He does not invent the spells, but he uses them and handles the ritualistic implements.

Next we will turn to the inventor, the true magician. But he, also, is different from the old or primitive magician. "Science gives as much power as was formerly given by magic," we started by saying. But it does not give it to the true magician, to the maker of the spells and the engineer of the machinery. Nor, still less, does it give it to the Everyman who handles the machinery and magical properties. There is a third character in the plot: and he alone is invested in all the marvellous power of Science.

Still the *de facto* magician, the possessor not the maker, requires the close cooperation of the inventor. And they work together, to some extent in league as regards the mass, their ostensible third partner.

The magician or religionist operates, at all times, on behalf of an unseen god who in a curious manner is of the same opinion on most matters as himself. Fact and "truth" are what the man-of-science works with: but that also has a way of accommodating itself to his interests and those of his partner (not the sleeping one). But what he operates with is more persuasive, for fact is more democratic and above-board than is faith or dogma. So Science has to its credit this patent: namely, the *popularization of magic*. It is a democratic God letting his creatures into the secrets of their creation. "Then I mixed a little pigment, *so*, and *so*, and that was the twenty-carat gold of your hair: a little paste, evenly applied, and that was the enamel of your teeth, so much prized and regarded as conferring value, the value 'beautiful,' upon its proud possessor."

I think for the foolishness of the European where the uses to which he has put his magic is concerned, we must go to the marcionite heresy. The student of the early christian age will recall that the great heretic Marcion found it impossible to reconcile the god of Justice with the god of Mercy: his gentle master, Christ, he found represented such an opposite doctrine to that of the supreme member of the Trinity, that he was compelled to repudiate the latter, or at least to distinguish radically between them, a very difficult and ticklish operation, but, for him, essential.

The sacred books inherited by the christian European were in two contradictory parts. One was a very "realistic" account of things indeed—as barbarous and "pessimistic" as darwinian theory—namely, the Old Testament. The other part was the exact opposite: it was an extremely "idealistic" book of humane injunctions, full of counsels of perfection—namely, the New Testament: the existence of this mad contradiction at the heart of his intellectual life has probably been the undoing of the European. The habits induced by the pious necessity of assimilating two such opposed things, the irrational gymnastic of this peculiar feat, installed a squint, as it were, in his central vision of his universe.

The actual *behaviour* of the European was for the most part thoroughly "Old Testament." Wherever he went, and that was everywhere, people were exterminated and enslaved by him in true Babylonian style: his behaviour was that of a very practical man-of-the-world indeed, of a child of empire worthy of Assur or of Babylon. But then, to the stupefaction of the survivors, or of his abject "native" subjects, he began wiping away a tear from the corner of his eye (in the manner of Wellington after Waterloo when he shut himself up alone for some hours to weep), exhorting the creature beneath his heel to gentleness and brotherly love. It was the New Testament asserting itself — the slaughter over and the berserker rage past. But he really carried this contradictory vice of mercy too far: what must have seemed merely ridiculous and disgusting to his victim, developed into a weakness: he not only had a good cry over what he had done, but he persevered beyond the limits of safety, where his colonial rule was concerned, with this non-sense of his double-sided theology. And his success was so overwhelming (owing to his superior science) that he never was forced into a salutary self-criticism, until, at last, from a practical standpoint, it was too late.

Had his doctrine from the start been that of the Old Testament, he could not have been less humane, and would probably in fact have been more reasonable and his conquest would have been more orderly and productive of a useful power. Had it been that of the Gospels only, he would never have been a conqueror. It was this unhappy blending of disparate things that was his curse.

But in many cases the White European has been the curse of the conquered races as well. He had a very debilitating effect in many parts of the world. When what was the "savage" for our christian grandfathers opened the sacred-book of his White conqueror, he found the first part devoted to a long account of implacable warlike activities undertaken on all hands, and prosecuted with a studied ferocity, in which the various contending heroes were assisted by a pantheon of bloodthirsty gods. This made his hair stand on end and his teeth chatter. That was "the Old." The second part — called "the New" — made him cry, it was so soft and gentle. He grovelled in terror before the superior bar-barity of the first, or "Old": and always cried when he read the second. These two sensations, so far apart, and yet so closely associated in the teaching of his new masters, ruined him, as even-tually it appears to be ruining them. He became incapable of coping with any of the eventualities of life: he too became the victim of a contradictory ferment: he lost his zest in his old self because of this humane and other-worldly criticism, and yet his Old Testament self would not allow him to integrate properly the "New."

But then Science slowly began asserting itself, in contradic-tion to the dogma of religion. Darwin appeared on the White horizon, and the White conqueror began regarding himself as a kind of monkey, no longer so very little beneath the angels, but wholly of the animal creation. Darwin was like another, and worse, Old Testament. The "New" lost ground daily. But still it interfered.

Into European Science the same anomalies have entered, however. For it has been the same confused and contradictory mind of christian civilization that has evolved and interpreted it. White Science, like White Religion, has its New Testament, as it were, as well as its Old. And it has introduced the bibles of its new religion, Science, to the "native." Its new sacred-books take the form, of course, of "Popular Science Series." All these books are infected with christian ideology. If possible, the new sort of sacred-book is more contradictory than the old. But the European is supplying the defeated races with his manuals of magic. They will no doubt be made a different use of from his bibles.

The new sacred-books of Science, then, are also in two con-tradictory parts. Horrors that make the industrial and other savages' flesh creep (for White civilization now knows that it has "savages" and natives of its own, and treats them accordingly) are found in *one*, of more ruthless struggles for existence than even he has ever known. But they are also full, in the *other* sec-tion, of melting pictures of "progress," the gift of the good God, Science. In this they give away no weight to christianity. One part roughly goes by the name of science: the other of socialism. In the latter, in the socialist portion, Everyman — Black, White, and Yellow — becomes a leisured gentleman; with the aid of machinery (the good God Science) he only needs to work two hours a day. All the rest of the time he sits in a velvet jacket and paints a field of buttercups, one eye on a copy of the "Idylls of the King," while his mate feeds his ear with Puccini and Offenbach.

The same process repeats itself in this traffic of ideas as in the old one of moral and immoral injunctions. The propaganda of ideas — that spread by the Science-bibles — is especially destructive where the modern industrial "savage" is concerned. The humbug and illogic robs him of his will, and even tends to impair his reason; in this resembling the effect of the christian bible on the primitive races. And if in christianity the elements become extraordinarily mixed, resulting in the most surprising hybrids of angel and devil, the religion of Science — Science as a religion, not pure science, it is understood — can show even stranger confusions. That is the position that we have reached today.

These remarks on the subject of the religion of Science can be concluded by once more recalling the immense and unprecedented power of this White Magic, so dangerously broadcast, and now shared in by all races — dangerous, at least, from the practical standpoint of its originators. It represents *power* and nothing else, denuded of its altruistic equipment of humbug. If a primitive race had carefully taught its neighbours its warlike arts and the secrets of its success in aggression, it would have known what to expect. But the stupendous power of these inventions is the thing to recall. That alone, in conjunction with the democratic, altruistic, christian idea, is what must with great rapidity transform all the balance of power in our world. A gigantic plague of numberless mechanical toys meanwhile everywhere has resulted in a weakening of the system attacked, turning the White populations into not an irresistible race of supermen, but a horde of particularly helpless children.

3. Modern Mass-Democracy and Modern Science took their rise together principally in the free city-republics of Italy. Science began as hard and visible truth: but now that which began as a hard and visible truth has become a fluid and infinitely malleable one. It flows out everywhere. There is the tacit assumption that truth *can* be reached, other than symbolically and indirectly: with the habit of the fluidity comes just as firmly the belief that it cannot.

Perhaps the search for *power* may be for us yet the new philosopher's stone — not power, need I say, however, in the spenglerian sense, or such as is expressed by romantic german music: nor, of course, literally would it be the dynamical concept first undermined by Hume. Certainly all "creative" or "emergent" life doctrines we must regard as semi-magical prescriptions for the *power* we have lost, like a sort of stimulant for the impotent. These doctrines all start by accepting, and taking a step further, the machinery used for the elimination of power. Having done this, they hand it back, in a gush of hideous optimism, as a "they-lived-happily-ever-after" anti-climax on the pattern of Kant, in his reinstatement of God. Some start with the indescribable creative gushing of the life-force, and then proceed to destruction. But optimism is the order of the day, used to disguise the increasing depredations made upon what is necessary for human life by popularized scientific thought. It is, *de rigueur*, on the same principle as were the masses of powder and scent for the stinking, unwashed mistresses of Louis the Fourteenth.

All the modes of feeling and of thought that hang upon the suppression of this notion are worth giving some attention to. That for a moment I will do.

First I will take the disbelief in will, the dogma of mechanical accidence (the "incidental" of Spengler): how it is affected that things drop from the sky, as the victorian doctor was supposed to bring a new baby to mamma in his bag, or as Santa Claus put the gifts in the stockings. In periods when fashion has imposed a particularly short skirt, for instance, often some self-conscious woman will be seen behaving strangely, as though it were not she who had bought and put on what she is wearing. In the adjustment of the curtailed sheath to her legs, in her expression as she arranges it, or simply as she parades it in the street, there is an implied detachment. Her manner or expression suggests that it is a part of her person which has grown there, as fatally fixed as the feet on the end of her legs. That is a familiar illustration of the instinctive, rather than indoctrinated, denial of volition. The *occurrence* of things, independent of the personal will, is implied in the relation of the self-conscious woman to her dress, whose "extremism" has enveloped her, or left her uncovered, in a semi-elemental manner. This, though no doubt found in all periods, is especially characteristic of ours. For such instinctive, volitionless detachment has become a cult that is publicly taught. It is the child-cult, for now is the child-period, in which all initiative has been removed from people, and they have been reduced literally to a childlike condition of tutelage and dependence by urban mass-life and by the prevalence of machinery. Daily the instances of this way of thinking or feeling multiply. Responsibility or personal will is, it seems, gladly repudiated; fresh theories are constantly put forward to encourage this attitude, or such as will encourage it. *Discouragement of all exercise of will, or belief in individual power*, that is a prevalent contemporary attitude, for better or for worse. Why will is discountenanced or discouraged is not hard to understand. There is not space in a crowded and closely-organized world for initiative, or for the play of those instincts that arise as a result of this energetic self-feeling of the natural, autonomous man. The sense of *power*, the instinct for freedom, which we all have, would cost too much to satisfy. We must be given, therefore, a dummy, sham independence in its place; that is, of course, what democracy has come to mean.

4. If you ascend, for a century, the evolutionary road or track, at any point you like to take you will meet with criticism of the direction thought was taking. Criticism of opposition cannot *always* be wrong, unless you accept the "historic" or "Time"-view, when, of course, there is no value of that sort. In the history of the personality, for instance, here is a remark of Lotze's, from Book II, Chap. viii of his *Metaphysic*, at which we can pause for a moment:

It cannot however be ignored [he writes] that many of our contemporaries are animated by a profound hatred of everything that goes by the name of Spirit; and that, if a principle were submitted to them which seemed to bear traces of this, even though it were not opposed to any postulate of science, they would, none the less, turn away from it in indignation to enjoy their feast of ashes, and delighted to feel that they were products of a thoroughly blind and irrational necessity.

Lotze is, in these words, opposing himself to the most powerful tendency that he felt in those around him — a tendency that, on the single-gauge evolutionary track, has arrived at the behaviourism of Watson — unless, perhaps, my presence here contradicts that. *Must* those of us today who demur when we come to examine some of the ordinances and tendencies of this Best of All Possible Times of so much philosophic advertisement, be necessarily wrong? It seems very unlikely.

5. We will now track the Ego, briefly, from where we find it fully substantival at the time of the opening of the great period of democratic stir and ferment in Europe, down to the time of its death in "action," of recent date. (This refers, of course, not to "action" in the military sense, but to the final overwhelming of this static "substance" in the "motor" explanations of contemporary psychological research.) When we see Flourens "cutting away the soul from his fowl bit by bit," in his operation upon the chicken, we shall neither applaud nor rebuke his success as he drives the higher mental faculties into the cerebrum, where they will have a precarious home for a moment. But we shall state, with fairness, as we go along, all the advantages for man in having a specifically intellectual centre of control, and principle of authority.

   Persona for the Roman, meant a *free* person only; a slave was not a *person*, but a *res* or *thing*. We shall not deny that human freedom is also, in our opinion, bound up with this *personality* which is so rapidly being given away to sensational interpretations of life. But as to the value of human freedom as enjoyed at any time by the general run of men, we shall express no opinion, or one partly unfavourable to its too crude, undisciplined continuance. Our freedom is another one to that. Or rather, all that will be necessary to notice will be something to this effect: that the life of the large-sized mammal is "individualistic" and free, but also is lived under conditions of relative solitariness; whereas the swarming of insect life is lived more in accordance with a rigid communistic plan—it is the community that lives, not the individual. But the *community* in this second case is no doubt as "individualistic" and "free" as the individual of a larger and scarcer species, taking up more room, living longer and breeding immeasurably less. And so there is not much in it. The handing over of your life to the community is like resigning yourself to living in *bits*. Imagine your body an ant-hill: suppose that it is a mass of a million subordinate cells, each cell a small animal. That it more or less is, of course, so it is not difficult to imagine. We live a conscious and magnificent life of the "mind" at the expense of this community. This, in a passage I shall shortly quote, is how Lotze (in his *Microcosmos*) pictures it. But in sympathy with the political movements today, the tendency of scientific (in which is included philosophic) thought is *to hand back to* this vast community of cells this stolen, aristocratical monopoly of personality which we call the "mind." "Consciousness," it is said, is (contrary to what an egotistic mental aristocratism tells us) not at all necessary. We should get on just as well without it. On every hand some sort of *unconscious* life is recommended and heavily advertised, in place of the *conscious* life of will and intellect which humanly has been such a failure, and is such a poor thing compared to the life of "instinct." But what would Rousseau have thought of Professor Watson or of Mr. Yerkes' american army-tests, and our militarized, "dry," over-controlled, industrial colonies? The bird-on-the-bough of Rousseau's fancy has slowly been transformed into the rat: still technically out of doors, but of all nature's children the most mechanical. Yet Froebel and Maria Montessori (whose curriculum for the modern child is Rousseau's ideal of "freedom," as expressed in Émile) would be regarded as part of the same movement of human training with Yerkes and Dewey: and actually, as exponents of the practical application of the discoveries of natural science, have many points of resemblance. But as these systems become more systematized, and brought into a rigid conformity with the effective practical life of the child — that is, of the future worker — they will obviously end up at the other pole from Émile. And it was Émile and his "freedom" that all egalitarian ferment was supposed to be about.

6. The subject, or ego, is a sort of primitive king of the psychological world. He is an "intellectualist" monster; and apart from his "reality" or the reverse, he could never have hoped to survive in a democratic environment. Actually he excites very special displeasure, and has done so from the start. Science has been in one sense a *revolutionary tribunal*: and the scientific method is the most admirable guillotine. Like all violent dictators, there has been some crudity in its fiats and sentences. It is, of course, to the masses of the smaller servants of science, and to a more influential type of person to whom science is apt to give power, that the passion of levelling, the crowd-passion, is principally to be traced. However this may be, the INDIVIDUAL has

been from the first proscribed. And the Conscious at once became suspect to the fanatical revolutionary mind.

Whatever science might, or has in some men's hands, become, or fundamentally is, it is undoubtedly recognized today as the expression of the aggregate or crowd. It is a kind of *practical art*. It is, as it were, the art of the crowd-craftsman. We have seen Miss Jane Harrison saying, "Science has given us back something strangely like a World-Soul." Why *strangely* like? we might ask. However, it is in this capacity that it becomes the natural ally of the Unconscious. That there is some passion, and more interest than we associate with a scientific inquiry, in the attitude of many men-of-science and psychologists to the "thinking subject," is borne in upon us in a hundred ways. The most sincere and gifted early propagandist for the scientific, methodological standpoint in life — Lange (who was also an ardent revolutionary politician) — expressed this with exemplary plainness:

Never was the gulf between the thought of this privileged society and the masses greater than now, and never had this privileged society so completely made its egotistic and separate terms of peace with the unreason of things. Only the times before the fall of ancient civilization offer a similar phenomenon; but they had nothing of that democracy of Materialism which today, half-unconsciously, revolts against this aristocratical philosophy.

Lange, the great historian of Materialism, was himself — as it happened — interested to advertise the identity of Materialism with Democracy. Also there is nothing half-conscious or half-unconscious about him. But were this not so, the connection between this political mood, and this particular philosophic aspect of the scientific creed, is very plain. In any case, a long time ago a battle was engaged between the *Unconscious* and the *Conscious*: and we have been witnessing the ultimate triumph of the *Unconscious* of recent years. The *Individual* and that part of him that is *not* individual, also joined issue: for the civil war was taken up, in the interior economy of the personality, sympathetically, at once. Inside us also the crowds were pitted against the Individual, the Unconscious against the Conscious, the "emotional" against the "intellectual," the Many against the One. So it is that *the Subject* is not gently reasoned out of, but violently hounded from, every cell of the organism: until at last (arguing that "independent," individual life is not worthwhile, nor the game worth the candle) he plunges into the *Unconscious*, where Dr. Freud, like a sort of mephistophelian Dr. Caligari, is waiting for him. "Consciousness" is perhaps the best hated "substance" of all: but there is a technical specialist reason for that. Consciousness is the most troublesome common-sense *fact* of any for scientific analysis. The hardiest investigators approach it with trepidation, and apologize beforehand for the poor show they are likely to put up in grappling with it.

Politically, of course (and envisaging science as the supreme functioning of the consciousness of the crowd), "consciousness" is equally objectionable. For so long as that, in any sense, and in whatever disguise, holds out, it is very difficult to get the *individual* firmly by the scruff of the neck, and seat of the trousers, and fling him into the "Unconscious." How the "Unconscious" comes to be the great democratic stronghold that it is, may require, in passing, a little further explanation.

The "Unconscious" is really what Plato meant by the "mob of the senses," or rather it is where they are to be found, the mother region of "sensational" life. It is in "our Unconscious" that we live in a state of common humanity. There are no *individuals* in the Unconscious; because a man is only an individual when he is *conscious.*

He [Leibniz] declares unconscious ideas to be the bond "which unites every being with all the rest of the universe," and explains by their means the pre-established harmony of the monads, in that the monad as microcosm unconsciously represents the macrocosm and its position therein.

That is a passage in E. von Hartmann's *Philosophy of the Unconscious* (shortly to be republished by Harcourt, Brace & Company). Von Hartmann, in quoting this brilliant observation of Leibniz (one of those fertile notions of which his scattered writings are so full), puts before us at once the key of all these questions.

The "Unconscious" itself, become such a mountainous phenomenon in recent mystical psychology, was invented by Leibniz, in any case, in the course of his lifelong struggle with Locke. With his egalitarian predilections, he located in *the Unconscious* the pantheistic egalitarian heaven for his monads to pass into when they wished; just as, with his monad, he invented the smallest possible form of god.

Kant identified the Unconscious as the seat of sexual love (*Anthropologie*). And placing that alongside Leibniz's identification of it with the common soul of humanity, we have at once the basis of a definition of it, which can be applied in consideration of any of its uses. "That only a few spots on the great chart of our minds are illuminated may well fill us with amazement in contemplating this nature of ours," Kant writes; and we are all agreed how ideal and shifting this spot is, and how in its penumbras and depths it is fused with the Unconscious of our kind. The rage for what is "real," as opposed to "artificial," tells against this spot. But it is not sure that this is not the best challenge of man to science. At least of this we can be certain where Consciousness is concerned, and in its favour; that in order to fit in with the only explanation of it that science is able to provide — the mechanistic, behaviouristic explanation — the actual standard of human consciousness and human ambition will have to be indefinitely lowered and debased. For it is only by approximating themselves *en masse* with the performing dogs and social hymenoptera of the laboratory of positive science, that men will not confuse and discomfort the scientific investigator. Only in that way can they satisfy the requirements imposed on life by the necessarily limited powers of mechanical explanation possessed by the scientific method.

Before leaving this subject, I will use a passage from Freitag, quoted by von Hartmann, in which the conclusions to which we wish to lead are implied:

All great creations of popular force — ancestral religion, custom, law, polity — are to us no longer the outcome of individual effort; they are organic products of a higher life, which in every age only attains emancipation through the medium of the individual and in all ages gathers up into itself the spiritual wealth of individuals into a mighty whole. . . . Thus one may speak, without intending anything mystical, of a *national soul*. . . . But *no longer conscious*, not so purposive and rational, as the volition of the individual man, is this life of the people. *All that is free and rational in history is the achievement of individuals;* the national energy works untiringly with the dark compulsion of a *primitive power,* and its spiritual productivity sometimes corresponds in a surprising manner to the formative processes of the silently creative forces of nature, which urge stem, leaves, and blossom out of the seed-grain of the plant.

7. Our tracking of the ego must be brief: all we can do under the circumstances is to flash our light on to a few aspects of its changing history since, let us say, Descartes. Leibniz is much

more the "father" of very recent doctrine than is Descartes. Leibniz with his "monad" created a particular psychic genus of his own. There is no occasion to describe his monad: but before passing on it may be useful to quote a passage which will have some bearing upon what we shall have subsequently to say.

When I am asked [he says] if there are substantial forms, I reply in making a distinction. For if this term is taken as Descartes takes it when he maintains against Regius that the rational soul is the substantial form of man, I will answer, Yes. But I answer, No, if the term is taken as those take it who imagine there is a substantial form of a piece of stone, or of any other non-organic body; for the principles of life belong only to organic bodies. It is true (according to my system) that there is no portion of matter in which there are not numberless and animated bodies; under which I include not only animals and plants, but perhaps also other kinds which are entirely unknown to us. But for all this, it must not be said that each portion of matter is animated, just as we do not say that a pond full of fishes is an animated body, although a fish is. (*Considerations on the Principles of Life*, etc., 1705.)

This last quotation is interesting, as it embodies the attitude of Leibniz to the question of the unanimated background on which even the feeblest entelechy would show up and count. He here, it will be seen, contradicts the average space-timer of post-Relativity philosophy, for whom *the pond* too is virtually organic.

Descartes called animals *machines*: they had not the rational spark. But men use their rational spark so unequally, and are so much machines too, that, on the face of it, that generalization is a very superficial one — one that you would expect in "the antechamber of Truth" (as Leibniz called cartesian philosophy), but not in Truth's presence. Many animals, indeed most, are more dignified, much freer, and more reasonable than men, in the conduct of their lives: and the "language habit," as the behaviourist calls it, is a servitude for those who are unable to use it, but have to be content to be used by it. It is not a thing to boast about that you *talk*, and that the elephant does not. It depends on what you say.

Again, there is the problem of "Socrates awake" and "Socrates asleep," and the manner in which, in this sort of extinction, his super-monadhood shrinks to a dim animal entelechy. But the difficulty does not end there: for the *waking* Socrates, even, is not uniformly socratic. At certain times he is more awake than at others. The divine spark or "soul" or principle of reason is (to employ a metaphor that is exact enough) comparable to the penis:

in repose it may shrink to entelechial proportions; and in its erected state may transform itself into something belonging, pro-portionately, to another category. An interesting study could be made in collecting psychical statistics as to the range of the mental variability — disparity of intellectual power or of personal character between the lowest ebb and the highest flood — in the case of specimen-men. It would be found that some natures were of an eminently *transfigurable* type, very plastic and sinking to annihilation almost when in repose (to again use the physical parallel, reminiscent of the young venetian noble in Boccaccio whose deceptive virility caused the bathkeeper so much amuse-ment, to his cost): whereas others maintained a fair level of stable erectness. As an example of a parallel phenomenon, physical courage could be cited.

This great variability of *life* or *"genius"* in the same person gives at once a sensation of unreality where psychic identity, and in-deed individuality altogether, is concerned. "Mind" is an artificial, pumped-up affair — just as the "male" is a highly unstable and *ar-tificial* mode of life. All we can say is that certain entelechies (to use the phraseology of Leibniz) are adapted to sustain these sporadic feats of superlative activity, and others are not. From this catalogue of difficulties it will be seen how very embarrass-ing it becomes to settle the frontiers for the "soul" or "subject": and how it is not only a case of a competition between a man and a brick, or Shakespeare and a toad, but between more near-ly related aspirants.

8. Lotze's criticism of the walled-in-monad, from which I will now quote the principal passage, occurs in his *Metaphysic*.

In laying down the principle that "the monads are without windows," Leibnitz starts from the supposition of a relation of complete mutual exclusion between the simple essences on which he builds his universe. The expression is one that I cannot admire, because I can find no reason for it, while it summarily excludes a possibility as to which at any rate a question still remains to be asked. That Monads, the powers of which the world consists, are not empty spaces which become penetrated by ready-made states through openings that are left in them, was a truth that did not need explanation; but this proved nothing against the possibility of a less palpable commerce between them, to which the same "reciprocal action" might have been fitly applied. It would not therefore have caused me any surprise if Leibnitz had employed the same figure in an exactly opposite way and had taught that the Monads had windows through which their inner states were communicated to each other. There would not have been less reason, perhaps there would have been more, for this assertion, than for that which he preferred.

In place, however, of this interchange of states that Lotze would have preferred, Leibniz locked up his monads in narrow cells, condemning them to solitary confinement to perpetuity; only, in place of the intercourse of their kind, allowing them the supreme blessing of intercourse with the high-god. And I think that whatever objections are brought against this obstinate scheme of his, there is something in its favour: namely, that it provided a basis for (or, rather, ensured) a clearly-cut, individually-defined universe. As a dogma, or a myth, it is at the other extreme to the impressionistic disorder of contemporary psychology or the cheerless mechanism of the Tester.

In examining the credentials of these *"points métaphysiques"* proposed to us, as our portraits, we feel that their rather shallow claim to eternal self hood is in conflict with their claim to contain something of the Absolute.

The finite individual of Spinoza was, like the lutheran ego of the Reformation, passive. Or if he was active, it would only be in a possible frenzy of mutilation in the attempt to reach God; in cutting everything away, and ridding himself of all that would interfere with his translation towards divine perfection. The finite individual or monad of Leibniz was *active*. He was a little world all to himself, saturated with "force" or enthusiasm. Voltaire's caricature of Leibniz (although as it came from Voltaire it would necessarily be pointed to the objects of a mechanical persiflage) had some relation to the real Leibniz. *"Enthusiasm* signifies that *there is divinity in us*: est deus in nobis" (*Nouveaux Essais*). There was too much "divinity" at all times in Leibniz, and his "enthusiasm" was his weakness. For his sort of "enthusiasm" was "illumination."

9. We will next get in touch with the notion of *the individual* in the post-revolution epoch in nineteenth-century Europe. I propose to get at it first by way of the question of the Freedom of the Will, with whose destiny its own is bound up. And I will take Schopenhauer's great book upon the subject of the Will, published in 1818, to illustrate this progress — though it is true

he is a theorist with a most personal metaphoric scheme. To his exposition I will add that of his disciple Eduard von Hartmann, both by training and disposition much more positivist even than his master.

Arthur Schopenhauer, is, I believe, the philosopher who has given the fullest and most intense interpretation of what must be the unchanging philosophy of exact science. He gave it in the language of early nineteenth-century scientific mythology, but it is none the less authentic, and is easily brought up-to-date. There is one philosophy for the surface skin (for everyday "life"), and another philosophy for the intestines. Schopenhauer's, and that of his disciple Eduard von Hartmann, is of the latter type. The dark volitional Unconscious on which their system is built, with *music* as its highest accompaniment, unsealed forever the lips of the science-sphinx. What philosophically results from science, not merely used as a technique, but allowed to sway us as a philosophy, is laid bare in the "pessimism" of the schopenhauerian system.

The *individual*, for Schopenhauer, was a thing confined entirely to perceptual life. Schopenhauer insisted that under all circumstances the individual should be kept in the most unequivocal subordination to his conception of the Will. *Up to a point* he would protect the "self" from molestation, against predatory idealists, for instance, disposed to ravish it into a Unity. But his demonic Will was absolute: with the prerogatives of that he would have no tampering.

Whilst I defend and uphold the uniqueness of the Individual and its right within the real world as against abstract Idealism and Monism, as energetically as Herbart, I just as decidedly dispute the claim of the individual to a transcendent-metaphysical validity, extending beyond the world of objective appearance, as unfounded, unwarranted and presumptuous; and deem even that Pluralism which *flatly denies* all transcendent-metaphysic behind the real world, to be *more endurable* and *philosophical*, than that which inflates the individual to an eternal transcendent essentiality or substance: for the former merely foregoes all metaphysic in favour of physics: but the latter has a false metaphysic, and that is far worse.

The world for Schopenhauer consists of two things—of Will and of its objectivation (or representation or idea). All *object* or idea is *phenomenal* existence; only the Will is "Ding an sich." "As such it is throughout not idea, but *toto genere* different from

it. It is that of which all idea, all object, is the phenomenal appearance, the visibility, the objectivation."

The *Will* is unconditioned: it is "free from all multiplicity. It
is itself one," etc. The Will is outside the *principium individuatio-
nis, i.e.* the possibility of multiplicity, altogether. Schopenhauer's
Will is really the "life force" or "élan vital," the hypostasized
"duration" of Bergson, the Time-god of Spengler, Alexander,
Whitehead, etc. By means of it, which is *Ding an sich*, we
share the "inner life" of other individuals, are indeed identical with them, though outwardly we are cut up into Thises and
Thats.

This pantheistic unity makes Schopenhauer a less reliable champion of the *individual*, it may be noted, than he has pretended
to be above. Life was at the most a roundabout, meandering
renunciation of the *self*—the climax could not be long delayed.
In an essay called *An apparent design in the fate of the Individual*,
he puts this point of view very clearly:

Although the Will to Individualism is illustrated by every action and
happening throughout the world, as the objectivation or appearance
of its impulse, none the less every human being is that Will for Individualism in a wholly personal and specialized way . . . since now
from my Philosophy—which, as opposed to professional or burlesque
philosophy, is serious—we have learnt *renunciation of the Will to Individualism* to be the final goal of a temporal existence, it must be accepted that everyone, step by step, is being conducted thither on his
own specially appointed line—that is to say, often very circuitously.
In the life that ends tragically it seems as if the Will were, in a sense,
forced to renounce life, and that its re-birth were obtainable, so to speak,
by the caesarian section.

As the will-to-individuality, or self-will, is the powerfullest will
we have any experience of, and surely is (if anything is that) the
most characteristic expression of the "life force," Schopenhauer's
will to death, or *will to merge* (which this "will" of his should
be recognized clearly as being) is a confusing term. And what
a good preparation for the modern industrial world this pseudo-
asiatic *renunciation of the will to self* was, needs no underlin-
ing. It is the *will-to-willessness* exacted as the first step in all
mystical "merging."

A sort of *roman genius* or psyche is provided for each individual by Schopenhauer—a little private Will, which is yet
identified with, and possesses some of the resources of, the great

pan-Will. He illustrates this in the essay I quoted from just now in the following way. He says that the great Unconscious to which we are attached is naturally able to warn our *private* Unconscious of danger, or of anything that it might be useful for it to know. His analogy is to the contretemps of our dreams. He reminds you how, in certain dreams representing your pursuit of some appetizing phantom (he takes it for granted that your sex is the same as his own), some obstacle is incessantly obtruding between yourself and the object of your desires. You are just about to couple with your dream-mate, when you are snatched away or interrupted. In other cases all goes smoothly, on the other hand; you effect your purpose, your desire is consummated. The former of these two occasions — that in which you are prevented from reaching a crisis — is an example, he suggests, of the vigilant intervention of the Unconscious Will on your behalf. It is your sleepless "double" (who knows that the event you contemplate is an organic extravagance which at the moment would be inopportune) interfering with your design.

Physiology explains the body, he says, in the same way that motives explain actions. "The whole body . . . must be simply my Will become visible, must be my will itself." *My will* is, of course, my private portion of the general fund of aimless power. Sometimes when he speaks of his will it sounds like a blind animal bundling about inside him. ". . . every impression made on my body also affects my will at once and immediately." ("Pain" is thus what my will dislikes, "pleasure" what gives it satisfaction.) Violent movements of the will (emotions or passions) convulse the body and disturb its functioning.

The parts of the body must . . . completely correspond to the principal desires through which the will manifests itself; they must be the visible expressions of these desires. Teeth, throat and bowels are objectified hunger, the organs of generation are objectified sexual desire; the grasping hand, the hurrying feet, correspond to the more indirect desires of the will which they express.

The Unconsciousness of the Will (or schopenhauerian *élan vital*) is insisted upon. "To the Unconscious we can ascribe no memory." The *unconscious* needs no experiences (which is the same thing as memory). The *unconscious* thinks everything that it needs for a special case implicitly in an instant. It is the *present*, it is the agent, and we alone "look before and after," compose our reveries, and tot up the accounts. ("Si l'homme *pouvait!* Si la volonté

savait!" we could parody the proverb.) The Will, or the unconscious life force, needs no documentation, no memory, or
any of the intellectual machinery that we carry about. It acts,
unerringly and at once. It is instinct, personified as *the Will,* it
is bergsonian "instinct" and "intuition." It is also the first great
"Unconscious," dated 1818.

Up till now, Schopenhauer said, we have regarded consciousness, motive, or idea as essential to the full animal dignity.
For *animal* dignity, it is true, that may be requisite. But Will,
or the Unconscious, expresses itself not only in animals, but in
stones, tables and chairs, anything which exists in short, and
which can be affected by mechanical laws. He quotes Bacon and
Kepler, and warns us not to regard their statements as as wild
as they might at first sight appear. Bacon considered that all
mechanical and physical movement of bodies has always been
preceded by perception in these bodies. In Dr. Whitehead's
Science and the Modern World, the same quotation of Bacon
is conspicuously used to uphold its doctrines, just as it was
by Schopenhauer more than a century ago. You could not
have a better example of the continuity of thought of this type
than the coincidence of this quotation, the same use for the same
end, of this passage from Bacon: 1818 and 1926 are one in
principle.

Kepler (*De Planeta Martis*) says that planets must have
knowledge "in order to keep their elliptical course so correctly,
and to regulate the velocity of their motion so that the triangle
of their course always remains proportional to the time in which
they pass through its base." He does not say that stones and chairs
and tables *think;* but his attitude to the matter is rather what
any behaviourist's, or that of any member of the most influential
school of post-Relativity thought, would be.

If there is one thing that may be said, in the popular estimation, to
characterize mind, that one thing is "consciousness." We say that we
are "conscious" of what we see and hear, of what we remember, and
of our own thoughts and feelings. Most of us believe that chairs and
tables are not "conscious." We think that when we sit in a chair we
are aware of sitting in it, but it is not aware of being sat in. It cannot
for a moment be doubted that we are right in believing that there is
some difference between us and the chair in this respect. . . . But as
soon as we try to say what exactly the difference is, we become involved in perplexities.

That is from Mr. Russell's *Analysis of Mind* (1924). As it is in order to establish these parallels that we are going through these older systems of the early and middle nineteenth century — of the time, that is, that saw the birth of darwinism, and the triumph of the modern "scientific" outlook — dating, in its popular form, from Condorcet — we will frequently interpolate, for comparison, in this way, passages from contemporary work that bring out the identity we are tracking.

All the characteristic semi-animistic, mystical-unconscious, present-day perplexities are emphasized in Schopenhauer. His Unconscious or Will informs stones as well as men, and his Will, before animals arrived, can have been little more than an inert mass, as conscious as, or no more conscious than, a planet or an armchair, just like the "Space-time" of Alexander, in short; an infinity, but "a very low type of infinity," as Bosanquet remarks. It is difficult for us to realize how life could be lived without "consciousness." Consciousness is, he tells us, a confession of weakness, a need to hoard up experiences and compare them, in order to know how to act by analogy. It should be regarded as the result of an inferior knowledge, and not a finer or better-documented one. "Only those changes which have no other ground than a motive, *i.e.* an idea, have hitherto been regarded as manifestations of Will. Therefore in nature a will has only been attributed to man, or at the most to animals; for knowledge, [or] the idea, is, of course . . . the true and exclusive characteristic of animal life." But that the Will is also active when no knowledge guides it, we see at once in the instinct and the mechanical skill of animals. That they have ideas and knowledge is here not to the point, for the end towards which they strive, as definitely as if it were a known motive, is not guided by the idea, and shows us first and most distinctly how the will may be active entirely without knowledge. The bird of a year old has no knowledge of the eggs for which it builds a nest; the young spider has no idea of the prey for which it spins a web, etc. *Idea as motive is not a necessary and essential condition of* the activity of the Will, etc.

The result of Schopenhauer's doctrine of the Will is to create at first some uncertainty as to how the situation depicted should be regarded. An imperfect, animal-like god, *tries and tries* — for *something*, for no assignable reason: and he comes out into self-consciousness in men — a thing he has not done here, it is to be assumed, prior to the existence of men on this planet. Yet our "consciousness" (which is his self-consciousness) is a less perfect thing than his less conscious instinct. But a bee has this marvellous instinct to the full; and yet we regard ourselves as an improvement on the bee, or on other social hymenoptera. In that we are evidently wrong. For, judged by the standard of this god, the bee is more god-like.

Is our "consciousness," we could ask ourselves, a little bit of the Will gone dead, as it were, or gone to rot? *Is our "consciousness" the deadest, and not the livest, part of the universe?* (We know already the bergsonian or behaviourist answer to that question.) Our position in the animal scale makes it difficult to accept that estimate of our special peculiarity; and yet the more we consider this Will-god, the more reason we find for diffidence. In that he is like natural science. But Schopenhauer's pantheism (although he did not wish that term used of his philosophy, as he felt he was not able to produce a purposive god, so should not be called a pantheist) is the pantheism of science. And it appears to us to be the first philosophy that natural science, of the modern age, can lay claim to, or that would fit its subjective and one-sided mood.

Every occupation has its philosophy — we have taken that fact, in a way, as our starting-point — a sort of personal and functional philosophy adapted to it. With the doctor, lawyer, engineer or schoolmaster, this equally is the case. It sees the world through the modes of its specialist experience. A doctor, a soldier, a prostitute, a dentist, an undertaker or a pearl-fisher would not, unless a very extraordinary individual, be able to keep their shop out of their general philosophic speculation. In order to be humane and universally utilizable, philosophy must be abstracted from these special modes and private visions. *There must be an abstract man, as it were, if there is to be a philosopher*: the sort of man that Plato was thinking of when he wrote the remark in the *Theaetetus*, used as an epigraph on page 127 of this book. So exact research into physical phenomena must provide us, when it speaks and reasons, with too "shoppy" and one-sided a theory of things. But an *abstract* man in any sense Schopenhauer was not. He was a dark, romantic, concrete intelligence, working through the temper of the discoveries of natural science, and speculating closely along the lines of these specialist habits of mind. His god (or Will, as he prefers to call it) is a vast, undirected, purposeless impulse: not, like us, conscious: but blind, powerful, restless and unconscious. It is indeed the opposite of our *purpose* (which is identified with consciousness): for it is purposeless (which is identified with unconsciousness).

The Will that "objectifies" itself in this way is a will *to what?* To nothing, Schopenhauer replies. This is, of course, his celebrated "pessimism": the picture of a Will that just goes on for some reason "objectifying" itself, resulting in the endless rigmarole in which we participate, and of which (*qua* Will) we are the witnesses. It produces Charlie Chaplin, the League of Nations, wireless, feminism, Rockefeller; it causes, daily, millions of women to drift in front of, and swarm inside, gigantic clothes-shops in every great capital, buying silk underclothing, cloche-hats, perfumes, vanishing cream, vanity-bags and furs; it causes the Prince of Wales to become one day a Druid, and the next a Boy-Scout; it enables Dempsey to hit Firpo on the nose, or Gene Tunney to strike Dempsey in the eye, and the sun to be eclipsed; for one thing to "build bonnie babies," and another universally to sustain "schoolgirl complexions." It is a quite aimless, and, from our limited point of view, nonsensical, Will. Identified as it is with the creatures of its mania for objectivation, if it were a Will worth its salt, would it not, sharing as it does their struggles, contrive less ridiculous and more pleasant modes of life for them?

As a *Will*, and as it manifests itself in us, it certainly seems to be a Will to something pleasant; and in the case of some people to something quite sublime. (Where does it get its notions of sublimity from?) But yet it is the feeblest of Wills with which any unhappy universe was ever afflicted. For it cannot get anything that it wants. All that it can do is to tear itself to pieces. If it replied to us — we having expressed ourselves in its hearing more or less as above — "No, it is you (because of the contingent and ineffective sort of 'objectivation' that you represent) who are responsible for all the sloth and misery"; we could reply: "But we are *you*; 'objectified,' it is true, but identical with you! It is only a bad workman that complains of his tools. If you find the material conditions of this existence beyond your powers, do not stupidly blame our little will-filled bodies. It is the poor quality of the volition we are supplied with that is the trouble. 'Those that level at my abuses reckon up their own!' When you gird at us, the boot should be on the other leg." The schopenhauerian

Will would find this speech unanswerable, at least as far as our poor human logic will take us.

Under these circumstances Schopenhauer decided that, as there was nothing to be hoped from it but its eternal mechanical buffooneries, the best line to take was to remove yourself as far as possible from enforced participation in its quite imbecile impulsiveness and fuss, and to employ to that end the traditional strategy of the hindu sage. All this did not prevent Schopenhauer from writing a good deal of carefully-thought-out criticism of life, and so of Will (pushed to this no doubt by the Will), from throwing a woman downstairs, entertaining close and satisfactory relations with other women wherever he found himself, and of being so noisy in the expression of his despair that he was known as Jupiter Tonans to his friends and disciples. All this he quite well understood; "he was afraid" (he would say) "that his energetic disposition did not suit him for Nirvana." So the "strange fact that everyone believes himself *a priori* to be perfectly free, even in his individual actions," is because the great universal Will is *inside* him, and as a part of that he is liable to this sensation. But he has reckoned without his stomach, legs, organs of generation, heart and liver. They pin him down to one unchangeable personality, from the cradle to the grave.

We have now completed a brief survey of one of the principal dogmas of a famous philosophic myth, of great value as assigning a philosophic meaning to science. We possess no better metaphysical or symbolical rendering of the science of the modern world, given, in this case, a "pessimistic," hindu conclusion of nirvana and renunciation. Whereas Kant leaves room for a god, Schopenhauer (as his most enthusiastic disciple, Frauenstaedt, was reproved by him for revealing) is unavoidably atheistic. He also holds firmly to the *purposelessness* of everything. And science (which as a sort of Unconsciousness, is blind and dumb, of course, and without "personality") must, if it could speak, and were prepared to explain itself, give a similar account of a non-human, purposeless, mechanical force. Heavily disguised with an optimistic réclame, the Time-god of Bergson, or that of the more recent space-timer, is the same god as Schopenhauer's, still the god of positive science. The name changes, only, from a hypostasized Will to an hypostasized Time; it is introduced now with ecstatic rejoicings and new decorations, such as terms like *things-for-their-own-sake*, etc.: now with an unfathomable gloom. Schopenhauer was completely sincere, hence his "pessimism": Bergson was not sincere, hence his optimism. The version of Schopenhauer is therefore a better guide to the true nature of this deity.

10. Eduard von Hartmann carries on with few alterations the system of Schopenhauer. What is new is that he uses "Unconscious" where his master would use "Will": just as Bergson substitutes "Time" for "Unconscious," as do the philosophers of Space-time following Relativity. The principal work of von Hartmann is called *Philosophy of the Unconscious.* Leibniz is claimed as the father of his particular "Unconscious," just as Leibniz today is pointed to by Spengler and many of the Time-philosophers as being, among their european forerunners, probably the one nearest to their thought and method. "I cheerfully confess that it was the study of Leibniz which first incited me to the present investigation," von Hartmann writes, and he then proceeds to trace the road by which Leibniz reached "the Unconscious." Leibniz was led to his discovery by the endeavour to save innate ideas and the ceaseless activity of the perceptive faculty (which he was especially interested to preserve). For when Locke had proved that the soul cannot consciously think if the *man* is not conscious thereof, and yet *should* be always thinking, there remained nothing for it but to assume an *unconscious thinking.* Leibniz therefore distinguishes perception, ideation, and apperception, conscious ideation or simply consciousness (*Monadologie*, sec. 14), and says: "It does not follow because one is not conscious of thought, that for that reason it ceases."

What Leibniz contributes to the positive establishment of his new conception is unfortunately scanty, von Hartmann says, but for "instantly perceiving with the eye of genius the range of his discovery, for penetrating into the dark inner laboratory of human feelings, passions, and actions, and for recognizing habit and much else as effects of an important principle only too briefly expounded," he deserves the greatest credit. Leibniz declares unconscious ideas to be the bond "which unites every being with all the rest of the universe," and explains by this means the pre-established harmony of the monads, in that every monad as microcosm unconsciously represents the macrocosm, and its position therein.

So the historic sequence was (1) the cartesian statement that *"the soul, as a thinking being, must think incessantly."* (2) Locke, who then appeared, with such statements as this: that "To ask at what time a man has any ideas is to ask when he begins to perceive: *having ideas,* and perception being the same thing." There would be as much sense in saying that "a man is always hungry, but that he does not always feel it. Whereas hunger consists in that very sensation, as thinking consists in being conscious that one thinks." It will be clear from this that Locke was willing enough to take things as he found them, and the Individual where he found him — that is, just wherever he declared himself, by starting thinking and "having ideas." For the rest of the time he felt that the Individual could look after himself — he always turned up again, in any case. And Locke was not at all concerned to maintain the visible continuity of that entity. (3) Then came the decisive contribution of Leibniz to the theory of the Unconscious. For Leibniz these blanks (which he was forced to admit) had to be filled up. It also seemed unreasonable to suppose that the Individual, when asleep, ceased to be an Individual, and was reborn when he awoke. So he was led to the idea of the Unconscious.

Hume (whose principal concern was Causality), by allowing Causality an *instinctive* basis, opens the road to the Unconscious. Hume does not dispute the fact of Causality, he only opposes the empiricists (Locke) with respect to its abstraction from experience, the *a-priorists* (cartesians) with respect to its apodictic certainty. But in his concession to the *a-priorists* he affords a support for the assertion that our thinking and inferring according to causal relations is a manifestation *unconsciously to ourselves* of an *instinctive* power far removed from discursive thinking, which like the instinct of animals is a gift of nature. . . . Von Hartmann, with his Unconscious, supplements the schopenhauerian metaphysics of the Will. The Unconscious with him has the same "unerring prescience" and happy knack that the Will has with Schopenhauer. That is natural, since they are the same thing. The "intuition" of women is dragged in to illustrate and confirm this, and The Feminine is identified with The Unconscious.

The union of the Individual with the Absolute is effected by way of a marriage of mysticism and science. The conscious self-activity could not compass it: the notion of the *Unconscious,* however, makes it at once intelligible. It is the cognition of the

Unconscious which makes this possible and evident, by bringing into scientific clearness the hitherto only mystically postulated identity of the Individual with the Absolute, yet without effacing their difference, which is a not less one than that of metaphysical essence and phenomenal existence.

For the exercise of the Will (or of the Unconscious) *no brain at all* is required, von Hartmann points out. Ganglionic impulsion is just as good. For the Unconscious (or on the plane of the Will) the body is an egalitarian and self-sufficient commonwealth. Since in invertebrates the oesophagal ganglia take the place of the brain, we must assume that these suffice also for the act of will. In decapitated frogs the cerebellum and spinal cord supply the place of the cerebrum.

But we cannot confine the will of invertebrate animals to the oesophagal ganglia; for when the *anterior part* of one bisected insect continues the act of devouring, the *posterior part* of another the act of propagation; when praying crickets with their heads cut off even seek their female for days, find them and copulate, just as if they were unscathed; it is tolerably clear that the will to devour has been an act of the oesophagal ring, but the will to propagate . . . an act of the ganglia of the trunk. The like independence of the will in different ganglia of one and the same animal is observed, as when two halves of a divided earwig, or of an australian ant, turn against one another, and under the unmistakable influence of the passion of anger . . . contend furiously with their antennae till exhaustion or death ensues.

Or again:

Let anyone take a glass of water containing a polyp and place it in such a position that a part of the water is illuminated by the sun: the polyp will instantly propel itself out of the dark towards the illuminated part of the water. If now a living infusorian be placed therein and it approaches . . . the polyp, the latter perceives it — God only knows how — and produces a whirlpool with its arms, in order to draw it within its grasp. On the other hand, should a dead infusorian, a small vegetable organism, or a particle of dust, approach quite as close, it does not trouble itself at all about it. . . .

When we see acts of will in animals destitute of nerves [an infusorian, for instance] we can certainly not hesitate to recognize the same in ganglia. This result is also suggested by comparative anatomy . . . physiologists assume as many independent centres in the spinal cord as there are pairs of spinal nerves issuing therefrom. Among the vertebrata there are fishes, whose brain and spinal cord consist of a number of ganglia, which lie in a row behind one another. The composition of a central organ from several ganglia is positively confirmed by the metamorphosis of insects, where certain ganglia, which are separate in the larval state, appear consolidated at a more advanced stage of development. These facts may suffice to prove the essential resemblance of brain and ganglia, brain will and ganglia will.

This swarm of "substances" called "wills" would be objected to as much as a "soul" by the dogmatic positivist: but it gives a picture of the Schopenhauer–von-Hartmann world-picture. We also see in this philosopher, in the use he makes of the biologic science of his time, combined with his mystical tendencies, the basis of bergsonism or "creative evolution," the last and final stage of this particular philosophic progress or process. Von Hartmann's transformed schopenhauerian Will (become the Unconscious, but still *will*) is a first cousin to bergsonian "intuition" and "élan vital," but better turned out and more consistent as doctrine.

Having got the brain down into the ganglia, and made of the body a commonwealth of Unconscious "Wills," we have taken the personality a step further on the road to destruction. The personality of the animal, in this way decentralized, and characterized essentially by *will*, not "thought," can be decomposed before our eyes. The stomach can be used to make war on the head, the left hand on the right. The *praying cricket* deprived of its head, the organ of generation takes command, and off it (this organ) marches (quite like Gogol's Nose) in search of a female; and when he (or what remains of him) finds the female, he addresses himself to the act of generation as though nothing had happened. An earwig, or an ant, similarly, cut in half, engages in mortal combat with itself. The proceedings of these insects is a blow to the human personality as well as to their own, employed in this connection. We since have reproduced progressively in our own proper persons the phases of their mortal division. Every organism or *Unity* whatever, political, social or physiological, has fallen apart in hostile conflict. Will and intellect are two things, Schopenhauer was found to have shown in contrast to all other philosophers. The "intellect" of von Hartmann is the same as "the conscious." And any animal (man included) can get on better without it. The whole organism is a commonwealth of "wills." "The brain is the will to know, the feet the will to go, the stomach the will to digest — it is only on the basis of their active self-expression that the thought-life arises." When again von Hartmann says that christian providence is confirmed by the "fitness" of the proceedings of the motiveless, blind, and not even free, schopenhauerian Will, it is apparent that he is becoming either foolish or no longer sincere. For as to the "absolute wisdom" of the proceedings of this blind, mechanical Will, what sort of wisdom can possibly be intended by that? he could well be asked. The "absolute fitness" of what happens is merely that *nothing else could possibly happen*: so *in consequence it is "fit" and proper that it should happen.* This form of argument is not likely to be found very satisfactory in the end.

But as to the *wisdom* of the unconscious Will, we are naturally disposed to deprecate so much human modesty; and ask in any case *why our human word,* "wisdom," should be used about it. The "Never-Erring Unconscious," so respectfully treated, whose "unerringness" and "fitness" and "wisdom" we are asked so much to admire, we get tired of before long. For we feel that the flattery is misplaced: our intelligence rebels against this blind god. And (since, according to von Hartmann himself, it will all end the same way in any event) we pit our *human* wisdom against this "unerring" mess; and determine (for our short life, and according to our feeble means) to "live our life" with the starkest impiety where this "substance" is concerned, and to have as little to do with it as possible. At least this is a very likely reaction from this "Unconscious" version of the schopenhauerian pessimism. Despair is a stimulant, and as a doctrine of despair we are inclined to welcome the creed of Schopenhauer. But if we are asked to convert our despair into an official religion, to venerate our discomfort, and kiss the toe of our blind executioner, we should then no doubt rebel. But that was exactly what Schopenhauer asked us to do; resignation being his solution, brightened somewhat by string-quartets.

11. Why it has been necessary to supply this historical outline is, first of all, because it is not generally realized by those very many educated people who yet have given little time to the study of philosophy, by what process of thought the contemporary European arrived at the highly complex, "emergent," empirical doctrine most generally accepted today. On examination, however, it can be said without exaggeration that as far as the mystic-positivist-cerebralist is concerned (it is only by such a *group* of words, or word-group, that we can designate this heavily-mixed, over-complex group-intelligence) the nineteenth

century possessed, but for a few changes of names, and a prodigious fresh deposit of scientific material, systems in all respects
representative of the mind of the most modern science, which
has been fairly constant for a considerable time.

So a rough history of the vicissitudes of the notion of the ego
during the last century, or at least some indication of how it
reached its present status, seemed necessary. Of course to do this
fully would be a long and exacting task: here we can only illuminate certain characteristics on the road. Whether you go out
with your little bow and arrow to kill "that absolute bird," as
James called the God of Idealism, or the other bird, that *ka* or
sparrow-hawk, which perches beside the egyptian dead, you will
find today that you will have to travel very far indeed to find
any trace of them. This absence of game of any sort, small or
large, is a circumstance that should not be without its effect. The
sport of destruction is almost at an end: that is, speculatively,
almost a novel situation. And the sport or *fun* factor is one of
great importance in philosophy.

Looking back towards the days of the active career of William
James, for instance, though he, no doubt, thought at the time
that game was "getting scarce," and wasn't what it used to be,
yet, to us, his landscape seems positively to swarm with
"substances." The final finishing off of "our consciousness" was
left to Professor Watson, and that was about all that was left
for him, poor man, and that James had already almost disposed
of. You are sorry for Professor Watson: he has to say the same
things over and over again: for the whole of what he effectively
has to say can be put into two lines. It is the last, monotonous,
dogged negation of scientific or critical philosophy, before the
last tattered shred of the last exploded entity. So, recalling what
was said at the start of this historical outline, Watson could have
existed in no time or place except modern industrial America:
that must absolutely be admitted, and that whether Aristotle was
"to some extent a behaviourist" or not. That is what he *means*
as much as a newspaper article means that what it hands out as
fact is what it is suitable that the "public" should know, and (by
herd-suggestion, and natural gullibility where printed matter is
concerned) be made to *accept*. But to that statement we must
attach a further one: namely, that all philosophers, even some
modern ones, have not been so pat a product of their country
and time as is Professor Watson. But we will now examine in

passing this figure, one that is surely the most locally, and temporally, coloured of any which it would, anywhere, be possible to find. I refer to the american Tester.

12. A "Tester" is a very peculiar product in some ways. He is, as it were, *nothing* but the outcome of a certain society and a certain time; for no society in its senses would have any use for such a thing as a "Tester." He is an ideal illustration for Spengler's *world-as-history* theory. Most reasonably sane societies wish if anything to have their habits broken up, not stereotyped. Like the phrenologist, or character-reader in the tent at the fair, the "Tester" "tells your character," only he has a pretentious "laboratory" to do it in. Beyond that he does nothing except testing your "intelligence," and writing books for the educationalist department of health, for the employer of labour, and, generally speaking, anyone who may be interested to learn how to train human beings, and transform them into tractable machines. As a behaviourist, the "Tester" takes on some importance: he intervenes in psychological disputes, puts to rout the Introspectionist, and affirms loudly that those who still attach themselves to the traditional *psyche* are wasting their time; and that *his* plan is the only fruitful one — namely, that of "peripheral" observer, and recorder of the inevitable reflex; that the "mind" is action: the human being a machine into which you drop a penny in the form of a stimulus — and sooner or later the figure works. And the *sooner* the *better*! Let there be a clear understanding about that at once. Quickness is his motto — *time is money*: the Tester's master is a money-man. When the figure works slowly, you call it "thought." When it works quickly, you call it "reflex." But they are the same thing. There is no "mind": men are "reaction masses." The whole bag-of-tricks is contained in physiology. "Tester" is the only word you can use because he is not a physiologist: he is not a psychologist (since there is nothing to psychologize, he cannot be that): he is not a biologist: he is not a philosopher (since there is nothing to philosophize about): he is not a psychiatrist or any sort of healer, as he does not pretend to heal. He therefore is called a "Tester," simply: he registers your tics and tells (by means of little tests) your rate and quality of response to stimulus, that is your character; and that is the end of it. All is perfectly simple; and he is a plain, straightforward man. And you can take

it or leave it. . . . Binet was the first "Tester." Professor Watson is, however, the one who has most to say for himself — whose "testing" has a philosophy attached to it. It only consists of a few words repeated in various ways, like an opinionated but quite straightforward parrot: for if you deny the existence of everything except knee-jumps there is not much to say about life. It is a very austere position indeed, and you can become a man of few words. Professor Watson is, of course, a man of many words. But they are *all the same*, or almost so. Mr. R. M. Yerkes (the american translator of Wundt) is, however, the first one I will take.

Mr. Yerkes is even simpler than Professor Watson, and is the purest form of "Tester." During the War he organized, or was one of the principal organizers of, the American Army Intelligence Tests. And it is from his book, written in partnership with Mr. Yoakum, that I shall principally quote. He, of course, points out that army-tests did not give full scope to the Testers. But his characteristic work can be seen there with greater clearness, probably, because a little simplified for application to the illiterate imbeciles of which, if you were to judge from Mr. Yerkes' Test, you would suppose that army to have been composed. Anyone who had the advantage of meeting some of its members at the time (and who is therefore in a position to know how irksome and unnecessary these Tests must have been) will be in no doubt as to their inappropriateness. "Our war department," this individual writes in his *Mental Tests in the American Army*, composed in company with C. S. Yoakum, "nerved to exceptional risks by the stern necessity for early victory, saw and immediately seized its opportunity to develop various new lines of personnel work. Among these is numbered the psychological service. *Great will be our good fortune if the lesson in human engineering which the War has taught us is carried over, directly and effectively, into our civil institutions and activities.*"

The magnitude of this "good fortune" for all of us is, of course, the question on which it is difficult to feel so confident as Mr. Yerkes. Messrs. Yerkes and Yoakum are, however, thoroughly satisfied on this point, as on any other that engages their immediate interest. (Also, if I had a name like Yerkes I should avoid associating myself too closely with a man called Yoakum. The feeling of almost insane uniformity produced by this must be highly displeasing to anyone except a habit-adept.)

Whether, then, the War once done, and its feats of "human

engineering" — its mechanizing of millions of mankind — it is advisable that its spirit and methods should be perpetuated, is a subject on which many different opinions must be held. The "captains of industry" (and no doubt also the general staff) are of one mind: the military organization of the vast masses of people militarized during the War must be carried over into "civil life." We are naturally not of that opinion. The napoleonic wars were pointed to by the french syndicalists of the Sorel–Péguy type with admiration, as excuses for the organizing and industrializing of France: and Sorel and Péguy were men of irreproachable honour, especially Péguy. Little as theoretically your enslavement matters to me, or mine to you, it is uncertain still whether universal enslavement would benefit either mankind, you or me. That is the point in dispute, in any case.

As to the nature of the Yerkes–Yoakum Intelligence Tests, in a society where the modicum of success within the non-competitive democratic cadre allowed a salaried servant depended on Intelligence Tests, there is one thing that is clear. Every person of exceptional ability would straightway sink to the rank of a nonentity, and be branded as an imbecile. Indeed, *the rôle of imbecile* would offer the only possibility of *life* for such a person. The habit of imbecility, like the habit of femininity, or shamanistic transformation, is a habit that will probably in the near future be acquired by all sensible persons as soon as they are out of the cradle.

"The purposes of psychological testing," the official medical inspector of the Army wrote, "are (*a*) to aid in segregating the mentally incompetent, (*b*) to classify men according to their mental capacity, (*c*) to assist in selecting competent men for responsible positions." For the most part, these are tests of memory at short range, or of presence of mind. *Presence of mind* is the principal thing invoked indeed: and that is not alone a military virtue. Another thing provided for the Tests was a "Foxy Grandpa" picture. This is a set of six designs. "*These pictures tell a funny story if they are placed in the right order.*" They are jumbled, three minutes is given for placing them in their correct sequence. Readjustments of this sort are important items of the Tests. Then there are the MAZES. With them the "Tester" gets on to one of his favourite hobbies, and you, at the end of your pencil, become for him the Dancing Mouse. The mazes used are similar to those employed in the mouse-tests of habit-formation with Mr. Yerkes' labyrinth. Transferring our attention at this point from soldiers to animal research, we will have a look at another side of Mr. Yerkes' activity.

In the case of the Dancing Mouse he found that, in order to obtain accurate measurements of the rapidity of learning or of the permanence of the effects of training, a labyrinth was a useful device. In his *Dancing Mouse*, Mr. Yerkes says:

The four labyrinths which have been used in the investigation may be designated as A, B, C, and D. They differ from one another in the character of their errors, as well as in the number of wrong choices of a path which the animal might make on its way from entrance to exit. . . . At the outset of this part of my investigation, it was my purpose to compare directly the capacity for habit-formation in the dancer with that of the common mouse. This proved impracticable because the same labyrinth is not suited to the motor tendencies of both kinds of species.

A record was kept of the time occupied, and the number of errors made, by the mouse, from the moment he entered the maze to the time he left it. There is no necessity to pursue Mr. Yerkes into the heart of these experiments. In passing it is interesting to note, however, that "in the most intricate labyrinth, labyrinth A, the mouse gave a poor performance."

There was no motive for escape sufficiently strong to establish a habit of following the direct path: often, especially after a few experiences in the maze, a dancer would wander back and forth in the alleys and central courts, dancing much of the time and apparently exploring its surroundings instead of persistently trying to escape. This behaviour, and the time and error results of the accompanying table, lead me to conclude that the labyrinth method, as it has been employed in the study of the intelligence of several other mammals, is not a satisfactory test of the ability of the dancer to profit by experience. That the fault is not in the labyrinth itself is proved by the results which I obtained with other mice.

In examining the objections to labyrinth A, Mr. Yerkes says: "Its passages are so large that the mouse is constantly tempted to dance. . . . [A new maze was constructed] with the wires of an interrupted electric circuit installed on its floors to punish the dancer for its mistakes. The formation of the labyrinth B habit was more satisfactory. It enables the experimenter to test the dancer's ability to learn to follow a simple path: but it is not an ideal means of measuring the rapidity of habit formation." The "study of intelligence of several other mammals" includes man, of course: but if that terrible human aristocrat, man, shows a tendency to rebel at those classifications—even to break up the mazes! —he gets short shrift from the tongues of Messrs. Yerkes, Yoakum and Watson. A great deal of chaff is administered, on the score of his high opinion of himself, his being too good to associate with poor mice and dogs, a great many disobliging references made to his dancing prowess and other questionable accomplishments.

13. Professor Watson represents the most powerful movement of extreme positivism in american psychology today. And this movement is deeply influencing english work in the same field and in philosophy: Mr. Bertrand Russell being its most distinguished adherent, withholding his assent only on one capital point, that of the "image." The "image" is a thing of capital importance elsewhere, so as to the "image" Mr. Russell begs to be excused. *Comparative Psychology* or "Behaviourism" (as opposed to Traditional Psychology or Introspective Psychology) substitutes the body for the "mind." There is not, for it, so much as a pin's point of the "psychic" left anywhere in the field of observation. Everything about a human being is directly and peripherally observable: and all the facts about the human machine can be stated "in terms of stimulus and response," or of "habit-formation." Therefore in the history of the Subject, we reach, with Professor Watson, the last ditch. Beyond him (or already with him), for the Subject, there is nothing.

The human personality is a "reaction-mass": it is a very complex edifice of reflexes. An observer, at its periphery, noting the stimulus going into this "mass," can confidently await (if he has the time and is allowed the opportunity) the response. Somewhere in the circuit—in no "mysterious within," but at a quite unimportant point in the material circuit traversed—a thing may or may not occur which we call "thinking" or "consciousness." The only importance that could possibly be attached to this little oddity of what is, of course, a very intricate mechanism, is that it may hold up the transit of the stimulus-response movement indefinitely, and so can be a matter of great inconvenience to the peripheral watcher: a fact that does not endear it to him.

In setting out to give even the briefest account of behaviourist theory, the first thing you become aware of is the slenderness of its material, and in the sense that it reduces itself to a simple negation, and to an account of a series of not very satisfactory experiments on dogs, chickens and rats, and a few on men. The ones on men seem to have been universally admitted to have been very disappointing. Those on rats and birds, by putting these animals in mazes, have shown that the rat mechanizes itself — becomes a pure automaton — much more quickly and naturally than the bird. Pavlov's apparatus is able to draw a good deal of saliva from the salivary glands of a large dog; but it is unfortunately not very successful with smaller animals, such as rats, because (1) these smaller animals have not much saliva at the best of times; and (2) having a cup and funnel hung at their salivary glands makes them fidgety, and sometimes no saliva comes at all. But even with the dog, the responses tend to become slacker, and the saliva flows less and less freely; until eventually the animal dispenses with saliva altogether.

As to experiments on animals and men undertaken with the object of obtaining proof for the theory of "substitution," they have met with nothing but hardships. The "Substitution" theory is roughly this: that when we admire what we call the "beauty" of a peach, not only does our "mouth water," but our organism (in other words, our resourceful and ingenious "reaction-mass") *calls up* the sex-circuit, and brings into action the full, or part of the, affective resources of the apparatus controlling our reproductive functions. With the aid of this mighty ally, we are able to become quite sentimental about the velvety bloom on the cheek of the peach. It reminds us of the bloom on the cheek of more human peaches — peaches on two legs. (At the word "legs," in conjunction with "peaches," the salivary glands come into play again.) So we are able to *humanize* the down of the peach: and so we arrive at what we call *abstract* beauty. Similarly when our eyes fall upon Cynthia, Mabel or Joan, and the headquarters of the general staff of the "reaction-mass" is momentarily in what Donne calls the "centric part," then the salivary glands will come in handy as well, and suggest — while what Professor Watson calls the "expansive or seeking movements" are in progress — that Cynthia or Joan be chewed and devoured, as well as "loved."

But when you have run through the list of these failures with animals of various sorts to establish anything that was not known before the behaviourists began, there is not much left except a *theory*. And that theory is very easily stated. And, indeed, it is stated over and over again by Professor Watson in his books: you are expecting something else, perhaps, to follow it, but nothing comes. All he has to say is what I have already told you, namely, that the human body is a machine: that it has no "mind": that it possesses two things — (1) instinct, that is inherited muscular habit, and (2) habits (speech and others), that it acquires: and that it can be trained better by a behaviourist than by an ordinary pedagogue with a birch: and that the working of what is called the "mind" can be observed from outside by watching what it *does*. Add to this a series of vague and not very useful experiments, precisely like the experiments any biologist is likely to make while observing the ways, habits or "behaviour" of any particular animal, and you have the whole of behaviourism.

Under these circumstances, why the pretentious apparatus and nomenclature, widespread movement, and rumours of a scientific event? The reason again is a simple one. Men naturally gather and exclaim to watch the final extinction of such a redoubtable human myth as "the mind." And it is in what Professor Watson calls his laboratory that this is taking place. But there are less substantial reasons for that. The first is that psychology had reached a point where, converging for a long time, it had almost met physiology. For fifty years it might at any moment have come face to face with that sister science at any neural cross-road or nerve-ending. And at last, *Ça y est*: it has happened. Henceforth they are one.

So it is rather psychologists, than mere men, who have gathered to watch the administration of the *coup de grâce* to the ego. For with it their occupation will be gone, or they will have to turn behaviourist. They have enough sense probably to see, after a look round at the dejected rats, who have not satisfied experimental requirements, at the performing dogs with their tails between their legs, who have ceased to "respond," gathered in the behaviourist laboratory, that there is no great future for anybody *there*. Once the "mind" is finished for good and all, the excitement will die down, and the behaviourist (*qua* behaviourist) will also have little to occupy himself with. For behaviourism is rather a *biological façade* than anything else. The behaviourist is the *bravo* sent by positivist science over to psychology to make an end of consciousness once and for all. For this purpose biological research has lent him a lot of old "mazes" and odds and ends of laboratory furniture that it did not require, and which the behaviourist himself admits that he does not know what to do with. So Professor Watson's mock-modest, his monotonously repeated, expressions of disappointment, apologies for poor results, is a bluff. For there is nothing to apologize about! The behaviourist is a specimen of a very queer product of our time — a dogmatic destructive philosopher and dogmatic educationalist, disguised as a man-of-science to further his theory. Each one carries with him and insinuates, either the philosophy of his particular sort of research, or else associates to his particular philosophic temperament the science suitable to his philosophy. Professor Watson is a fanatical product of modern american civilization, an impassioned mechanistic theorist, and a believer in the possibility and desirability of mechanizing men much further and more thoroughly than has been done even at present. At the bottom of his false-science ("behaviourism") is a crude and mechanical educational theory.

But every convinced educationalist is a utopian of some sort. He wants to *educate* people in order to make the world *thus* or *thus*. Professor Watson's Utopia is best represented by the life of the american industrial colonies. This as a practical scheme for getting rid of masses of people, by concentrating them in big centres, like millions of specialized insects, and leaving them to go on turning their silly wheel eternally, is a good one.

As I have said, the doctrine of Professor Watson contains only one idea. Then why so much display about such a simple matter? But that is just one of the things that must inevitably happen when a research-road (as when an art-road) comes to its inevitable conclusion. Only a final kick or touch was required to precipitate the "mind" into the abyss. Once that has been done there is nothing but the body left to play with: and for a very long time men-of-science have busied themselves with that; and it should not be a cause of surprise that Professor Watson is somewhat at a loss once this last kick or touch has been administered, or that he should go on talking rather monotonously about this little event.

I will now quote from the text of behaviourism, and so show more concretely what we are talking about:

We see in passing through a forest, a youth trained to hunt, firing upward into a tree, and we note that the dog he has with him has "treed." An observer responds to this picture by telling his companion that the boy is hunting *squirrels*. But if he sees the boy firing in another way, say horizontally, and sees a dog in the act of pointing, he will state that the lad is hunting *quail*. If a boy fires towards the ground, and has a hound with him, he is shooting *rabbits*. Finally, if he is seen in the hunting-fields on horseback, with no gun, but accompanied by a pack of hounds in full cry, our observer remarks that the boy is hunting a *fox*. Watching his actions, and taking note of all attendant circumstances, enables anyone to tell, with some degree of probability, what the immediate situation is leading to the boy's actions.

There you have a characteristic glimpse of the behaviourist engaged in what he calls "field-work." He is (at the moment you discover him) engaged in observing "the repertoire of acts" of the boy in question. "The more constantly we are thrown with an individual the more accurately we can map out his programme for the day." Some people's "repertoires" are more eccentric than others. But as a rule these things are readily predictable. "An equally important result coming from psychological study, is our *formulation of laws and principles* whereby men's actions can be controlled by organized society." It is only a step from observing a man engaged in a very clear-cut " 'stimulus'-response" (rigidly-habitual, readily-observed) type of action, and to persuade him to continue doing that harmless simple thing till the machine stops. For "the control of organized society" is always at the bottom of his mind. Professor Watson, of course, gives no hint of what sort of society he thinks would be a good one. A society in which people were trained not to interfere with their neighbours is, whatever else, not the one he has in mind. Organized interference, of unprecedented closeness and severity, is what would await, it would be safe to say, the unfortunate men and women whose "behaviour" will eventually be manufactured by this type of man.

Professor Watson is himself a very "clear-cut" and perfect type of american *agent-heroism*, or of the typical american gospel of *action*. He is the most perfect logical product of that process by which in the american world (initiated by the practical "matter-of-fact" anglo-saxon puritan stock) the human civilized notions that, up till the beginning of the nineteenth century, Europe retained, its graeco-roman heritage, have been transformed into an unwieldy and breathless mechanism, from which, quite apart from any "theories," behaviourist or other, on the subject, "mind" is gradually crushed out.

There are for Watson two main points of behaviour, and two only. And in these two physiologically controllable forms the whole of the human personality is contained. There is no metaphysical or non-metaphysical element of personality. These two forms of behaviour are the big and the little; or, as he puts it, those affecting the large musculature of the animal, and those affecting the small. The former, the big, he calls *explicit* behaviour. The lesser, the small, he calls *implicit* behaviour. Stowed away in this second category, hidden in the almost imperceptible movements of the language machinery, are all the mysteries and metaphysics of life. "The larynx and tongue, we believe, are the loci of most of the phenomena (*i.e.* of implicit behaviour)." For the observation of this there exists no method at present. A man hits you on the head. Either (1) you respond by striking him back: in which you are giving an example of *explicit* behaviour, or (2) you go away and think it over, and perhaps ten years after you approach him again and return the blow. His blow is a *stimulus*, whose response (your blow) will then be ten years overdue. Where explicit behaviour is delayed (*i.e.* where deliberation ensues), the intervening time between stimulus and response is given over to implicit behaviour (to "thought processes"). That is, in the example shown by me, you would have been engaged for ten years in implicit behaviour: or, in other words, you would have been "thinking." Thereby you would have been causing the behaviourist a great deal of trouble.

Word-habits make up the bulk of the *implicit* forms of behaviour. "Now it is admitted by all of us that words spoken or faintly articulated belong in reality in the realm of behaviour, as do movements of the arms and legs. If implicit behaviour can be shown to consist of nothing but word-movements (or expressive movements of the word-type), the behaviour of the human being as a whole is as open to objective control as the behaviour of the lowest organism." Of all the enemies of behaviour (and the behaviourist is not slow to see it), Words and Speech (next to consciousness) are the greatest. It is in the forest or undergrowth of words that the behaviourist tiger of clear-cut stimulus-response, or his "futurist" maker, can become entangled. "As language habits become more and more complex, behaviour takes on refinement: short-cuts are formed, and finally words come to be, on occasion, substituted for acts. That is, a stimulus which, in early stages, would produce an act (and which will always do so under appropriate conditions) now produces merely a spoken word or a mere movement of the larynx (or of some other expressive organ)." In the mere spoken word (which might have been a fine blow in the solar plexus, or a grant sprint for a 'bus, had the principles of behaviourism been observed) so many good *actions* are, alas! lost to this world for ever. When you think of all the good actions that have been lost in this way, it makes you feel mad!

We live largely, then, in an indirect world of *symbols*. "Thought" having been substituted for action, the word for the deed, we live in an unreal word-world, a sort of voluminous maze or stronghold built against behaviour, out of which we only occasionally issue into action when the cruder necessities of life compel us to. Some of us live in this world more than others, of course. Some actually like it. And (a democratic note) *what* sort of person, do you suppose, enjoys living in this word-world? Words are symbols of ideas, as the old psychology would put it — some people "have ideas" — are "theorists," "highbrows," and so forth; and SOME (like You and Me) are just plain people who *prefer deeds to words*. That's US — that's our way! What's the use of a word-world to us, anyway? We're not brilliant conversationalists, or anything of that sort! Speech is of silver, silence is of gold. And this is the age of *iron*, the age of *motion*. We may not have much to *say* for ourselves: but we can hit a ball or turn a screw with the best. To hell with mere Words! Up behaviour! — Once upon a time our world was nothing but *action*: it was entirely a stimulus-and-response world of "unconscious" behaviour. The behaviourist as observer of *action* is frequently baffled in the maze, and even indefinitely held up. This must unfortunately be *admitted*.

So insensibly the behaviourist (on account of the inadequacy of his method where the word-world is concerned) is driven into an utopian attitude. Like all other animals, the behaviourist-animal dreams of a *perfect* world (for behaviourists) where everything would occur "in terms of stimulus-and-response" (immediate, evident, unequivocal, objectively-ascertainable response) and "in terms of habit-formation." And insensibly he is driven into a frenzied dogma of *action*, and into a more or less disguised attitude of impatience with human beings who "delay" or hold-up their natural responses an undue length of time, or who convert them into words.

Words are the arch-enemies of behaviourists (comparative psychologist, physiologist, vitalist, or actionist) of any sort. You meet this as a refrain throughout philosophy today. (We have seen it characteristically in full flower in Spengler.) *Hostility to the word* goes hand in hand with propaganda for the intuitional, mystical chaos. It is here that we touch the point at which Watson and the time-mystic connect.

14. The philosophy proper to physical science, especially with regard to its effect on the conception of the human personality — that has been up till now the subject of our scrutiny. We have attempted rapidly to show how science possessed already in 1818 a philosopher faithful to its teaching — Schopenhauer, who, allowing for the piling up of further technique and experiment, responded as exactly as could be wished to what science still is. But the science-philosophy of the nineteenth century differs in one very important point from its more recent correlates. It tells the same story and is based on an identical base, of course: but its *conclusions* are quite different.

Schopenhauer is a notorious *pessimist*: Bergson is a notorious *optimist*. Bergson's own private responses are probably far more disillusioned, drearier and less animated than were those of Schopenhauer. But that optimism is not peculiar to Bergson, or the result only of lack of integrity. Many transparently honest persons conform to this changed tone. They are as cheerful as schoolboys about it all, as hearty and smiling as a suburban scoutmaster in the midst of his "cubs" or "wolves."

Specifically, nineteenth-century thought was very different from that. It had the same material to work with, but it used it differently and it caused it to come to very different conclusions. The notorious "pessimism" of the great nineteenth-century school of Russian Fiction comes to mind: but with their national reputation for "morbidness" or "pessimism" they are perhaps not the best examples to prove our contention. Let us rather take the French, notoriously high-spirited and full of common-sense: and, choosing such figures as would be expected to interpret most completely and intensely the thought around them, you will find that the French do not yield at all in "pessimism" even to the nineteenth-century Russian. I suppose there is no greater intellectual figure in the France of the last century than Gustave Flaubert — let us take him. And in Gustave Flaubert you have the darkest "pessimist" that you could easily find. It was he who said that as a boy he had a distinct premonition of what life really signified: for that as he was passing before a house a smell arose from the window of a scullery, and the odour of stale greens attacked him: instinctively and at once he realized that that was really what life was like — and of course he rapidly found out that he had not been mistaken. His *Bouvard et Pécuchet* is the absolute fulfilment of this promise. His brilliant disciple, Maupassant, had the same tale to tell, but was unfortunately not able to work off his knowledge, or foreknowledge, as was Flaubert, in acute nervous seizures. Among his memorable statements relating to his own attitude towards the life he so bitterly represented in his stories (which are far more despairing, in truth, than anything written by a Russian of his day), is that in which he says: "If I could groan as (dogs) do, I would go out into some vast plain or into the depths of a forest, and I would howl as they do for hours together in the dark. It seems to me that that might ease me." These splendid artists, of course, were of a different calibre from the more recent *co-optimists*. But they nevertheless represent a deep difference, not in the apprehension of the facts, but in the conclusions drawn from them, between, roughly, the european intelligence of the mid-nineteenth century, and that of the twentieth century up to date.

15. If we take now, to illustrate this view, what is obviously a negligible and ridiculous figure, you cannot accuse me of picking my examples to suit my case, for the person I next will use is taken seriously by quantities of people, occupies responsible positions in the scientific world of America, and is extremely typical — not at all, unfortunately, an exceptional or extreme case: there are thousands who think and express themselves almost exactly like him. We choose him because he is one of the best-known american champions of the gland-theory — the theory that sees in the glands of internal secretion the key to life's mysteries. He has the further advantage of having stated fully and picturesquely in a long book the relation of his theories to the human personality, which has also been our major concern. His name

is Dr. Louis Berman, and his book is *The Glands and Human Personality*.

His book is so naïvely, unguardedly, self-expressive, that it can provide the distrust and critical doubt, which is at last showing itself in some quarters where such theory is concerned, with a good deal more substance than could be relied on in the case of most men-of-science, who are almost unnaturally wary of giving themselves, or their occupation, away. The sphinx-like silence at most times of the scientific man results in his sporadic utterances on the subject of his craft having a peculiar impressiveness. When the specialist in Bright's disease speaks, it is as though you heard the kidneys speaking. When the astronomer speaks, it is not so much the music of the spheres, as a still, small and infinitely distant voice reaching us. Science can be regarded from that standpoint as the means of communication that matter has found to explain itself, full of coldness and lassitude, pessimistically, to man.

Dr. Berman, then, speaks principally for the glands of internal secretion; it is they that speak in a hot and oily language to us through his lips. But he is not at all backward where speech is concerned; and is indeed one of the most loquacious people you could ever meet with, in or out of natural science. He is quite ready to speak for the entire organism: to improvise as the poet not only of the glands, but of any other portion of the body. His most eloquent flights are, of course, called forth by the reproductive apparatus. But in every department of his subject, or in the neighbourhood of his subject, he exhibits a genial warmth which enables one to appreciate the reticence and chilliness of some of his colleagues. Many exponents of psycho-analysis approach him in this respect; but he is excelled by none where physiological poetry is concerned, or rather rhapsody. He even provides us with passages on the religion of science; so well equipped is he for our purposes. These are worth reproducing.

"*The religion of science.* Science also as a religion, as a faith to bind men together, as a substitute for the moribund old mythologies and theologies which kept them sundered, is commencing to be talked of in a more serious tone. . . . Presently the foundations and institutes, which coexist with the cathedrals and churchs, just as once the new christian chapels and congregations stood side by side with pagan temples and heathen shrines, may oust their rivals, and assume the monopoly of ritual." There is no difficulty in imagining what such ritual, formulated by Dr. Berman, would be like. I will describe what I am sure it must look like inside the head of Dr. Berman. On an operating table, which would be the high-altar, a pregnant woman (*genre* Rozanov) would be placed: the crisis would be precipitated, and, with weeping and gnashing of teeth, the congregation, overcome with a primitive sense of the importance of the occasion, would participate in the obstetric solemnities. A semi-chaldean staff of Hollywood priestesses would perform a dance of ecstatic abandon; and the function would probably conclude with a tableau in which human fertilization figured; for which purpose a buck nigger would be employed, and be coupled with one of the priestesses, the organ booming the Venusberg, jazzed by the organist. "If at all," he says, magnanimously prefiguring this glorious future in a sense satisfactory to all concerned, "the resolution of the conflict will come by a pooling of actual powers and interests, in which the religion of science will play the great part of the Liberator of mankind from the whole system of torments that have made the way of all flesh a path of rocks along which a manacled prisoner crawls to his doom." Freud, from the point of view of the intelligence, is written all over his book. Its pages swarm and fester with florid contradictions of huge emotional bulk. He says, for example, to contrast his lyricism about science: "Darwin changed Fate from a static sphinx into a chameleon flux. Just as certainly as man has arisen from something whose bones alone remain as reminders of his existence, we are persuaded man himself is to be the ancestor of another creature, differing as much from him as he from the chimpanzee, and who, if he will not supplant and wipe him out, will probably segregate him and allow him to play out his existence in cage cities." What becomes of the cloud-capped towers and gorgeous palaces and temples of science he was speaking of above? How about "Science," the Liberator of mankind, and the "manacled prisoner" of the old, bad days? What, "cage-cities"? Oh, Bolivar Berman!

The real Dr. Berman — not the humanitarian enthusiast — of course knows that the future is what indeed every pointer of our time shows us: a mechanical humanity, caged in huge cities, allowed once a week to prostrate themselves in the mechanical temples reared to a god that, in their ignorance, they have chosen. "The chemistry of the soul!" this enthusiast exclaims. . . . "The exact formula is as yet far beyond our reach. . . . But . . ." And

he goes on, with his invariable exclamatory unction, to show us
how the glands of internal secretion — the thyroid, pituitary,
adrenal, thymus, pineal and sex glands — are the *soul-stuff*. He
quotes Llewellys F. Barker:

More and more we are forced to realize that the general form and
external appearance of the human body depends, to a large extent, upon
the functioning, during the early developmental period, of the endocrine
glands. Our stature, the kinds of faces we have, the length of our arms
and legs, the shape of the pelvis, the colour and consistency of the in-
tegument, the quantity and regional location of our subcutaneous fat,
the amount and distribution of hair on our bodies, the tenacity of our
muscles, the sound of the voice and the size of the larynx, the emotions to which our exterior gives expression — all are to a certain extent
conditioned by the productivity of our glands of internal secretion.

Brown-Séquard (the first man to advertise the "hormones") at
seventy years old began experimenting with the testes of monkeys.
He went right to the heart of the matter with a primitive simplicity; concluding that the same reproductive juices that could form
new beings could also, injected under the skin, revive old ones.
He did not succeed; but he directed people's attention to these
particular problems of rejuvenation. Dr. Berman's mind resorts
frequently to the specifically sexual sources from which Brown-
Séquard proposes to derive the wine of life. Although he has
nothing new to say on the subject, he leaves it in no doubt as
to which part of the body (were he himself of an inventive turn)
he would direct his attention.

The supposed functions of the glands of internal secretion are
briefly as follows. The pituitary is supposed to control physical
growth; an excess of this resulting in unusual physical dimensions. (When you see a woman, for example, of six foot, with
a pin-head at the top, that would be, according to this theorist,
an unfortunate result of an overdose of this gland.) The *thymus*
is supposed to be the childish gland — that preserving the juvenile
qualities of "heart" and body (so the numerous instances of prolonged childishness or Peterpanism in people of mature years
would, on this system, be the result of the unusual power of their
thymus apparatus). The sex glands (not themselves hormones)
naturally control the sex areas and functions, subject to a great
deal of interference on the part of the other glands, and represent sex-interests in the gland-parliament. "All the glands, in fact,
work in unison, with a distribution of the balance of power that

diplomatists might envy." But the "harmony of the Hormones," as Berman likes to call it, is not of the nature of a phalanstery of sucking-doves. "The Kinetic Chain is about as good a case as there is of the glands of internal secretion co-operating. The Check and Drive systems, with the adrenals and thyroid oposed, are one of the best instances of their antagonisms." Next we come to the combination of the internal secretions and the vegetative system, ". . . modern thought does not regard the brain as the organ of mind at all, but as one unit of a complex synthesis, of which the mind is the product, and the vegetative apparatus is the major component. That involves the blasting of the last current superstition of the traditional psychology, the dogma that the brain is the exclusive seat of mind." The "mind" and "soul" he has a great deal of information about. The vegetative apparatus is the "oldest part of the Mind." "There is indeed room for rhetoric, even poetry here," he tells us. This is of course bluff, for he finds an outlet for these two natural expressions of his nature *everywhere*. But at certain chosen points in his argument — when he comes to speak of the ovaries, for instance, or the digestive system, he will pause and emphasize the possibilities for a poet or a rhetorician more especially. His endocrines might be said to be virtually bathed in both poetry and rhetoric.

". . . We think and feel," he goes on, "primarily with the vegetative apparatus, with our muscles, and particularly with our internal secretions. Wherever there is thought and feeling, there is movement, commotion, precedent, and concomitant, among these. They are the oldest seats of feeling, thought and will, and continue to function as such." ". . . There is the fascinating story of the origin of vertebrates from invertebrates of the sea scorpion and spider type." Then there is a whole group of data which demonstrate that the primitive wishes which make up the content of a baby consciousness are determined, settled by states of relaxation or tension in different segments or areas of the vegetative apparatus. According to this, the brain enters only as one of the characters into the play of consciousness. It is just the organ of awareness within the disturbed vegetative apparatus. Consequently the brain emerges, not as the master tissue, but as merely the servant of the vegetative apparatus. In all these statements it is the *primitive* that is stressed. There is more "room for rhetoric and even poetry," he never fails to make clear, where some organ is concerned which, when for the moment it has the spotlight, makes us into some very much earlier, less evolved, being. The caveman is a mere child compared to some of our organs. These are the ones for the poet — or rhetorician — to tune up for: the viscera should certainly, if they are poets worth their salt, cause them to burst with uncontrollable song: but *not* "the *face*" — that physiological parvenu — not the face that launched a thousand ships, or any other — to hell with Helen! But to hell, above all, with words, which, damn it all, have no *guts!* Such is Berman — gland-man, colleague of the Tester.

16. James is the hero of the final rout of the Subject, and to him we will now finally turn. All the motivation for that fanatical war upon the Subject, mind or psyche, and its associated entities, transpires in the course of a reading of him. James is, in his attitude to causation, opposed to Hume. He wants things *real*: and yet he wants them in one sense as Hume describes them. "Events rattle against each other as drily as dice in a box in Hume's philosophy," James, with great relish, exclaims. Yet in spite of this initial advantage of a "pluralistic" material, Hume sternly sets his face against novelty. Now as to the "dry rattle in the box," James can certainly be said to have achieved that — but with the material of the human personality — to admiration. In his account of it the different *selves* rattle against each other like dice in a coffin: for no dice-box would hold all the selves that James provided for any man, once he has done cutting them up: and for all his claim, or that of his friends, to bring the full pulsing of the intensest "life" to us, nothing could be more dead than this psychological assemblage of particles.

No psychology, James reassures us to start with, can question the existence of personal selves. *"The worst a psychology can do is so to interpret the nature of these selves as to rob them of their worth."* These words of James describe what is achieved by his psychology, of course. The worthlessness of your personality, once James has finished with it, has no bearing upon the truth of his analysis. But its truth rests on a method not dissimilar to that of Hume, and which could be objected to on the same grounds.

In behaviourism — the subject of our last scrutiny, and which is so implicated with James that to talk of one is to include the other — it reaches results at least as "preposterous" as those of

Hume. In dealing with the question of the *sense of personal identity*, James says that our belief that the *Me* of yesterday is the same as the *Me* of today is "a mere subjective phenomenon." It belongs to the great class of judgments of sameness. (The law of Identity, misinterpreted, is the arch-enemy of James, as it is of Gentile and most contemporary philosophers.) So whether I say "I am the same person I was yesterday," or "This pen is the same pen that it was yesterday," is the same thing. And the *Me* of James is dismissed by the same arguments as those employed by Hume for material objects. These different *Me's* — like those chairs and tables — have, it is true, a resemblance to each other: and there is a temporal continuity. But there the sameness ends. There is a separate *Me* on Monday, a separate *Me* on Tuesday, Wednesday, and so on. Reflection does not warrant the belief in any *unity*, metaphysical or otherwise.

For James — and that has hardened into an absolute and often fanatically-held dogma for those who have followed him — no thoughts are owned, there is no "mine" or "yours" in reality; "it thinks here" is as good sense as "it rains here," the thought merely getting a certain colour from where it occurs, or through what, like a wind or a stream, it passes. We are the spot where a bundle of things is tied: we are the intersection of a multitude of paths. We benefit, naturally, by our position — heaven be praised, we can get something out of it — just as a village benefits by being at a junction of waterways, or near a ford, and, with a little luck, grows into a prosperous town. But some of us *abuse* this position. It is then that Professor Watson and all good behaviourists lose their tempers. They say it is indefensible to *hold up*, or *delay* our responses for so long as sometimes we undoubtedly do, if not *prime-sautier*, entirely, by disposition. The behaviourist, we forget, may be there waiting to register them. A "stream of consciousness" is passing through us — in and out again. But it is a *public* stream. This some of us do not properly understand. We treat it as though it were a *private* stream. We take advantage of our strategical position (namely, inside our heads) to hold up, sometimes indefinitely, in the cerebral cortex — to confiscate sometimes *for ever* (in which case they are *for ever* lost to the dialectic of "history") — things which are meant to *pass through*: and which, in any well-regulated organism, should issue immediately, or with as brief delay as possible, in *action*. Consciousness is given us to use. If a fine tree passes into our consciousness we should not hold it up inside, idly contemplating it. We should at once do something about it; perhaps praise the Lord that such a fine tree has passed into our consciousness; then go over and pick a chestnut from it, climb it, cut it down, sit under it and read the *Chicago Daily Vigil*, suitably shaded, or in some other way exhibit our perception of it, and our appreciation of its many uses, by a suitable instantaneous "response," so that we can be labelled by the behaviourist observer as though we were mannikins in a Mutt and Jeff set, from whose mouth could be made to issue, "Ah ha! a fine tree! that is where I will sit and read the paper!" or, "Ah ha! What a fine tree! I will get an axe and cut it down!" To satisfy the behaviourist, we should be amenable to that simplified treatment. Our brains, in particular our hemispheres, are storehouses of past experiences: it is in the storehouse that we are apt to dream away our day, fancifully fitting together mnemonic lumber.

The conversion by James of the *Me* of common-sense into a meeting-place of abstract *actions* or *objects*, mysteriously turning into causes once they are inside, is a similar operation to that of Hume, performed with the causal nexus — which for James (when it is Hume, not himself, that does it) is too "intellectualist" a proceeding. Ah! he exclaims (where pharasaically he surveys the distinctive work of Hume), so is fact maltreated by the translation of the conceptualist, who "pulverizes perception and triumphs over life!" But his *Me's*, or his *I*, are overwhelming facts too, which he maltreats. And for his followers today this long-bludgeoned and assiduously-bled fact has become without further ceremony "it." Where people resist the conclusions of the behaviourist, they still sometimes get on with James. Yet all of behaviourism is in James, or it carries his views to their ultimate conclusion.

One of the aspects of this question that should interest us most is that, in this jamesian dispensation, the one *Me* or *Subject* of tradition becomes a *class of Me's* or a crowd of Me's. "Nothing," it is said, "necessitates the use of nominal entities of this sort. *Classes* or *series* can perform these functions as well as they." The distinction between sensation and sense-datum vanishes. You are forced to a fusion of the world of objects with the fact of apprehension, so that when you see a tree you *are* the tree — or, since there is no "you," *the seeing of* the tree *is* the tree. If there is no *you* this must be so: there is only the tree — which, however, is not a tree properly speaking. There *are* trees, kettles, chairs, dogs, men, billiard-balls (of sorts). But it is undemocratic to suggest that the man sitting on the chair thinks, but not the chair: or that the billiard-player hitting the ball thinks, and not the ball, too, as it is hit. At least if it does not think "He struck me: the great ugly blackguard," it *perceives* that it is struck: and Bacon is brought from the dawn of modern Science, to say to us: "It is certain that all bodies whatsoever, though they have no sense, yet they have perception." So that the tendency is to admit thought into everything, on the leibnizean pattern of the entelechy, or more confused inferior percipient, only with a difference. Animism is reinstated. If *you* are not, but the tree you see *is*, if only physical objects *are* (though for "object" you must understand some dynamical group of stated duration, not the "object" of general perception), then they must be admitted into the psychic league of minds. The "psyche" disappears; but everything becomes psychic.

The psychic fact cannot be disposed of, "thought" and "meaning" has to be there; and in this way the spoils of the "transcendental ego" are distributed throughout the "inanimate" world. Every stick and billiard-ball gets its bit of "psyche," confiscated in this upheaval. It is "matter," always, that gains by these transactions, though it gains by way of the maxim that there is no matter. It gains in one sense, that is, but it at the same time ceases to be "matter." It loses its alien and concrete integrity, so useful, and indeed necessary, to mind. If this is visualized as a war between "matter" and "mind" — and this is the aspect it has been given in much philosophy — you will see that indeed by appearing to *deny itself*, it escapes the stigma of "materialism," and at the same time diminishes mind by overrunning it, invading it with its mechanism. On the other hand, it confers a material quality upon Time and floats it as a sort of bastard "mind."

You may at this point offer an objection on somewhat the following lines. You may say: But what you have described appears to be a double and contradictory movement. For it results at one point in a fusion of kinds, and at another in a differentiation into a multiplicity of individuals: when the *one* self, for instance, becomes *many selves*. Why you should care one way or the other whether you are one self always or "successive thinkers," *one* Smith or on the other hand *a colony* of little Smiths, one behind the other, I find it hard to understand. To be *a new self* every morning is surely not a hardship. I always want for my part to change about, and can't. I am *too* fixed and unified.

Those are the sorts of objections to this phase of my argument that, I suppose, might be advanced by some readers. My answer to such objections would be as follows.

I, of course, admit that the principle I advocate is not for everybody. Many must seek and find in a mercurial surface change their principle of life and endurance: action and not contemplation is most people's affair: "Personality" is merely a burden and hardship to many. Still, to meet your objections in their order (and to include in our outlook types of mind of a more energetic stamp): First, if you wish to reduce two large objects to one triturated mass, what you begin by doing probably is to break up each object into a heap of smaller particulars. You may remark as you are doing this to the little particulars as they appear: "You will be very much more *important* now as *individuals* than as part of that big lump. I am giving you your *liberty*: I am restoring to you an identity that was lost in your adherence to that large unit." If they are wise little particulars, they will distrust your disinterested activities, and say to themselves: Once become small imitations of the big object, we shall probably be still further disintegrated. Beyond the flux and tripsis, new distinct objects will emerge: but then on the other hand, what is that distant future to *us*: why must we live only for some problematic grandchildren? Transition and change spell nothing but misery for the mass of small particulars. And the new grouping, for all its advertisement of newness, is much the same, for us, as the old. We always lose, whoever wins. That is how the really astute mass-midget would soliloquize.

As to the other part of your objection: opposition to the ideologic disintegration of the notion of *the one personality* is an extremely well-founded one. For it looks to the inevitable result of that separation in everyday life — the conviction of its theoretic untruth aside, that is. In a man's way of regarding himself, it is socially of capital importance that he should regard himself as *one person*. Is it not? That is surely beyond any possible question. It is only in that way that you can hope to ground in him a responsibility towards all "his" acts. Constantly encouraged to regard himself as a mass of Hydes and Jekylls — and he is only too willing to fall in with that relaxed, amusing, sensational view — he throws all his useful obligations to the winds (useful to each and all of us, for it is upon the "behaviourism" inbred in our neighbour, of moral and unselfish precept, that our personal comfort and peace depend). If yesterday's self is not today's, then also the obligations contracted yesterday are no concern of today's self, and so on. There was a comic heraclitean, I think it was, on the attic stage, who refused to pay the rent for a house he had taken, on the ground that he was no longer the same man who had rented it. That is the most utilitarian view of the matter. Then another, in some respects more fundamental, thing, results. If the comedian got for himself a philosophy, it would, on one side, work out very much like the theories of the analytical psychologists (since a philosophy is always a thing that helps a man to live and to enhance his powers). The comedian, in the picture of these many distinct, intermittent *selves*, would find his professional paradise. For all comedians are necessarily volatile, love change for change's sake, prefer parasitically other personalities and other lives to their own — such is their faculty and function: they would desire never twice to be the same thing: to have at their disposal an infinite number of masks. So it is *an ideal comedian's philosophy*, we shall find, the one composed by this type of psychology.

But the transition society of today, no doubt inevitably, is essentially an actor's world. The successful personality of the moment is generally an actor-mind (Mussolini): with all the instincts bred behind the footlights, the apotheosis of the life-of-the-moment, of exteriority, display and make-up; and of an extreme instability, fundamental breaks and intermittences, the natural result of the violent changes of, and the return of great chaotic violences into, our time. In the arts themselves this tendency issues in the form of prodigious virtuosity. The work of one person will consist of the schematic juxtaposition of a series of disconnected stylizations; and therefore, since the "style is the man," of a crowd of men, not one man at all. So the co-existence is achieved of many persons and times in one. This often-remarked-on "timelessness" is "timeless" in a very particular sense, and is actually a result of the Time-philosophy, of an insistence upon "Time," in fact, as already remarked in an earlier part of this essay.

So the *one* personality, as found in the Renaissance, for example, hardly exists with us. Each man is *every man*, an abstraction, not a *concrete person*. And we wear the coat of one neighbour one day, and of another the next. The stable personality is indeed suspect, as *all* personality is suspect — for "personality," as we use that term, is nothing but stability, and stability of any sort at all is hated and is suspect, necessarily, in a period of revolutionary change so absolute as the present — even stability in revolutionary principles.

This part of my argument — connected with the radical revaluation of the psychic — will contribute especially to the throwing into relief of the particular interlocking today of practical and theoretic interests. The fashionable doctrines in psychology may without spenglerian phantasy be regarded as very much one with the social tendencies of the times. Is it too rash to assume that, with another kind of social structure, less deliberately fluid and destructive, more favourable to stability and to personal, secure and constructive achievements, we should have other psychological doctrines, as indeed all the Past seems to show us? Or will the scientific "truth" of today be an eternal obstacle to such a reversal? Such does not appear to us to be the case. Because often it can be proved that thought is an *historical* phenomenon, in the Spengler sense, it does not follow that has always been, or need in the future be, the case. It is to see that it should become less so, to circumscribe the power of *history* and fatalism (or "Destiny," as Spengler calls it), that we should exert ourselves, surely.

With that I bring to a close my short account of the extinction of the "thinking subject," "mind," "psyche," or by whatever name it has gone. I have shown it first cast down from its position of pre-eminence, and then hunted from spot to spot until finally made an end of by the Tester. And I have shown how (as it happened, or else because of some intimate connection between the two events) this sad history ran parallel to the libertarian process of the suppression of all visible authority, and the rooting-out of our Western society of all its emblems. What it *looks like* is that man, as he has been engaged in an internecine war with other men on the grounds of the inequality found among us, has fanatically, at the same time, been engaged in tearing off and out of himself everything that reminded him of the hated symbols, "power," "authority," "superiority," "divinity," etc. Turning his bloodshot eyes inward, as it were, one fine day, there he beheld, with a start of horror and rage, his own proper mind sitting in state, and lording it over the rest of his animal being — spurning his stomach, planting its heel upon his sex, taking the hard-work of the pumping heart as a matter of course. Also he saw it as a *mind-with-a-past*: and he noticed, with a grin of diabolical malice, that the mind was in the habit of conveniently forgetting this *humble* (animal) and *criminal* past, and of behaving as though such a thing had never existed. It did not take him long to take it down a peg or two in that respect! The "mind" — that greek divinity or egyptian spirit, that celtic paladin, that symbol of everything that was, for those hated feudal times, "pure" and "noble," save the mark! — was soon squatting with a cross and snarling monkey, and scratching itself. That is the sort of picture that the facts certainly suggest, and it is the one I have stuck closely to in my exposition, for clearness' sake. But it is only half true, I believe, and what has happened is a sort of coincidence.

PART III

"By space the universe encompasses and swallows me as an atom; by thought I encompass it."

Pascal

"But the chief advantage arising from it is, that we are freed from that dangerous dilemma, to which several who have employed their thoughts on this subject imagine themselves reduced, to wit, of thinking either that real space is God, or else that there is something beside God which is eternal, uncreated, infinite, indivisible, immutable."

Principles of Human Knowledge, *Berkeley*

"To be plain, we suspect the mathematicians are, as well as other men, concerned in the errors (1) arising from the doctrine of abstract general ideas, and (2) the existence of objects without the mind."

Principles of Human Knowledge, *Berkeley*

CHAPTER ONE

SCIENCE AND SCEPTICISM

[NATURE] IS THE ASPECT most opposed to self-dependence and unity. It is the world of those particulars which stand furthest from possessing individuality, and we may call it the region of externality and chance. Compulsion from the outside, and a movement not their own, is the law of its elements; and its events seem devoid of an internal meaning. (Bradley: *Appearance and Reality*.)

It is the laws of this zone of chance and externality, as it were artificially segregated by us, and set over against our purposeful, if limited and obscure, existence, with which Science occupies itself. Today the chastened man-of-science is extremely conscious of the criticism of sceptical philosophy; even the means he takes to repudiate it show that. Meantime he sees to it that he gets more and more *mind* into his abstraction, or at least — which is much the same thing — more Time, more movement. He arranges his physical world to look as unsubstantial and immaterial as possible. In this he notably succeeds.

Come upon unexpectedly, his nature would look more "idealist" than the ideal. (For the ideal "thing," even when most unearthly in character, looks overwhelmingly solid compared to the realest and least "ideal" affair in fairly rapid translation.) Though there is no agreement at all as to terms — for Russell thinks, for instance, that Relativity must result in some kind of "berkeleyan idealism," and Eddington bears him out, whereas Alexander, and less so Whitehead, would not endorse that view — all the same, in practice the world-picture ensuing in contemporary theory *looks* more like "idealism" than the reverse, and that is one reason why it is very necessary to scrutinize it with unusual attention.

This interchange of influence — the sort that we can imagine might have occurred, under other circumstances, between Berkeley and Newton, let us say (had it been Berkeley rather than More who had been the nearest metaphysical influence), between metaphysics and psychology on the one side, and physics on the other — is slowly producing a certain uniformity. A *third* "nature," as it were, common to both, is being invented.

347

That such a "nature" is, from the point of view of the metaphysics concerned, strictly impossible, is true. From a sort of materialistic solipsism, Science is saved by the fact that it is universally recognized as a somewhat scandalous extremism, fatal to all concerned, so the route is barred in that direction. Philosophy is glad, no doubt, to be held back by physical science from this too mortal conclusion. No one but the disreputable Agrippa has even entirely embraced it. So a "phenomenalist" compromise is arrived at. With Einstein a physical residue is arranged for — the most satisfactory compromise so far achieved, we are told: for the residue, the ascertainable physical residue, is the smallest yet agreed upon.

This third, go-between, "nature" is naturally, however, riddled with inconsistencies. But there is goodwill, indeed, the instinct of self-preservation, on both sides. And so, the reformed but still at heart materialist Science, Nelson-like, with a blind eye to its microscope half the time; and Philosophy, on its side, with an eye perpetually winking at the assumptions that rash Science will, and indeed must, indulge in (however "phenomenalistic" in principle); a sort of hybrid "nature," half physical, half mental, does grow up, and does take shape. It is this nature against which, in one or two of its most crystallized aspects, we here bring a first brief criticism.

Remembering Kant's remark that "natural science is nothing but a pure or applied doctrine of motion," to be "empirical" any doctrine must be *a science of motion,* essentially. In place of objects, which are alien to its methods (for "classes" are, in the nature of things, its "objects"), Science has to possess impersonal units of some sort. It consequently assembles the movements it is studying into "events" or serial "groups" — but always groups and aggregates: and so, as regards the "nature" it shows us, it arrives at a sort of shimmying, contourless metis. Some groups are unconscionably *slow* in their movements (they are indeed about as bad as a reflective man — "holding up his responses" — appears to a behaviourist): for instance, a mountain remains very much longer in the same place and of the same shape than does the ocean-wave. So the mountain has a certain spurious status as an object, and is disliked by time-science accordingly. Men deliberately make such objects, too, some very complex, like St. Paul's Cathedral; or some simple, like an egyptian pyramid. But natural science, observing them, knows that they are only humbugging, in a sense. They are, in their degree, as liquid as the wave or as gaseous as a puff of smoke. That is what was meant by the "cloud capp'd towers," etc., of *The Tempest* — a reaction, as well, against "common-sense." But it is still proper to note that the latter remark about the impermanence of what men regard as permanent, is put into the mouth of a *magician*; and that all magicians dislike permanence, and are naturally sympathetic towards the flux. For operations involving *disappearances* are their *métier*. Nearly all their tricks are *vanishing tricks*. So the interests of the man-of-science and of the magician are identical where impermanence and change are concerned: and both their interests are only accidentally identical with those of mankind.

Now in an earlier chapter we have seen Professor Whitehead repudiating the "dull," "meaningless" abstractions of science, in favour of a highly-qualitied world of poetry and romance, brimful of secondary (or "tertiary") qualities, of colours, scents and sounds. That is the *real* world, he says. The abstract, *materialistic* world of traditional science he pretended to scrap altogether. He displayed his intention of throwing in his lot with the artist and the poet. And against him I found myself in the curious position of defending the mechanical world of the popular conception of science.

The semi-"idealist" world that just now I was describing science as having arrived at — a world of very abstractly conceived groups and classes, *painted* to look alive and "individual," but essentially depersonalized and robbed of will, kept jigging and moving, and never left to its own resources, or allowed to *reflect*, for a moment — is the world of Professor Whitehead's teaching. It is, I believe, a complete sham. *Every* criticism that Professor Whitehead levels at the "abstract," "meaningless," "dull" world produced by sixteenth-century mechanical science can, on the grounds of "materialism," be levelled at it. It is, very strictly and technically speaking, a *sham* world of images and appearances, where secondary qualities are brought in to *paint* it — to give it colour — and where sounds and perfumes are introduced, as it were, by mechanical means. It is an attempt at producing life. But it remains unreal, for the reason that it obstinately, and in conformity with its method, leaves out the only thing that gives the "real" world of our experience *life*. That thing it cannot manipulate and cannot explain; and although it affects to explain nothing, it in reality pretends to explain everything, and at least is generally maddened by what it finds recalcitrant to its methods.

To make things *endure* (to make something *solid*, relatively indestructible, like a pyramid) is of course, as well, a sort of magic, and a more difficult one, than to make things *vanish*, change and disintegrate (though that is very remarkable too). Of these opposite functions of magic we daily perform one, in our sense-perception activity, better than magic could. This function we justly call "creativeness": and, we have just said, it is a much more difficult type than that of destruction. (That it is not we, individually, who thus create, is true; but what we do is none the less marvellous for that.)

When Kant is showing that the substantival principle can be educed from time, but that space is not only indispensable, but capital, for its generation, he says, "In order to supply something *permanent in perception*, which corresponds to the conception of substance, we need a perception (of matter) in space; for space alone is determined as permanent, while time and all that is in inner sense is in constant flux." The objects of our perception, with their mystifying independence and air of self-sufficiency (around which strange and arresting characteristics have gathered all the problems of cause and effect, ground and consequent), are far more uncanny than the unity we experience in our subjective experience. These strange *things*, that stand out against a background of mystery, with their air of being *eternal*, and which really appear to be "caused" by nothing that we can hold and fix, and from which we can see them being actually produced, arc far stranger than we are, or more brutally and startlingly strange. If architecture is "frozen music" — as it has been rather disgustingly called — what are we to say of these trees and hills and houses? They, at all events, seem far nobler and severer than our minds, or our "inner sense," which, in the words of the foregoing quotation, is always in "a constant flux." But these "objects" are the finished product of our perceptive faculty, they are the result, as we are accustomed to explain it, of the organizing activity of our minds. When we say we *see* them, in reality what we perceive is not the direct datum of sensation, but an elaborate and sophisticated entity, or "object." We do even in that sense "create" them more than "see" them.

CHAPTER TWO

BELIEF AND REALITY

FOR THE UNDERSTANDING of "reality," and to get at the meaning of
the problem suggested by the term "reality," there is no term so
important as "belief." *Reality* is in fact simply *belief*. What you
"believe in" is a thing's "reality": that is the realistic, not of course
the logical, account of it. That which a thing *ceases* to be for you,
when you cease to believe in it, is "real." And the sensation that we
define as "reality" is the thing whose nearest specification is described in the word "belief." To *believe* in a thing's *existence* is
to experience its *reality*. Reality, then, is simply a way of describing our capacity for belief, and the things in which we believe.

David Hume insisted that not even the most sceptical
philosophy is ever likely to "undermine the reasonings of common life; nor need we fear that it will *destroy all action, as well
as speculation.*" Nature will always maintain her rights and prevail
in the end over any abstract reasoning whatever. Nietzsche
remarks somewhere that we experiment with ourselves in a way
that would revolt us, and that we should not allow, if it were
animals that were to be the victims: and when he is engaged in
one of his daily sallies against asceticism, he admits that there
must be "a necessity of the first order which makes this species
[the ascetic species], *hostile* as it is to life, always grow again,
and always thrive. *Life* itself," he says, "must certainly *have an
interest* in the continuance of such a type of self-contradiction."
This passage may be usefully compared with the remark of
Bergson, to the effect that life evidently seeks to establish isolated
and closed systems — exactly what Bergson's philosophy, stridently
claiming "life" as its patron, seeks, in its turn, to break up.

But the same thing may be said to apply to the propagation
of any destructive truth to some extent, and both Hume and
Nietzsche may be in some sense right. Thorough destruction, cast
wholesale amongst people, withering every belief, may give a
tragic zest to existence: and certainly the agents of the most
destructive truths are often themselves the most contented and
high-spirited of men. This is really Nietzsche's subject: I will take

351

what he says again in the same connection, as it refers directly to one of the psychological problems of "idealism." The problem of the real and the apparent world, eagerly debated in his time, is occupying his attention. The fanatical advocates for "appearances," he points out, are not all people consumed with the "will to Truth" at all costs, nor yet are they people predisposed to a nihilistic despair. On the contrary, many, the "stronger and livelier" ones, are still consumed with an appetite for life. How does that come about, he asks?

"In that they side against *appearance*," he says, "and speak superciliously of perspective"; in that they rank the credibility of their own bodies about as low as the credibility of the ocular evidence that "the earth stands still," and thus, apparently, allowing reality to escape (for what does one at present believe in more firmly than in one's own body?) — who knows if they are not really trying to win back something which was formerly an even *securer* possession, something of the old domain of the faith of former times, perhaps the "immortal soul," perhaps "the old God"; in short, ideas by which they could live better, that is to say more vigorously and more joyously, than by "modern ideas"?

With his fine nose for the dramatic-intellectual situation, Nietzsche saw the paradox implicit in the destructive beliefs of those healthy, happy men of his time, announcing their own unreality and nothingness, and gave the above characteristic explanation of it. I dare say he would say that, taking in many ways a different road, we were, here, upon a similar quest. We are far from agreeing with Hume or with Nietzsche that destructive thought can be indefinitely absorbed by the plain-man without a destructive effect: nor do we agree that the salt of destruction, and the zest of life induced by it, is a good thing of which you cannot have enough. (Perhaps that may be because in this time we have had so much more of it than even Hume or Nietzsche can have experienced.) Nietzsche had very little in his composition of the health, balance, measure, and fine sense of the antique world (of Spengler's "Classical" and Goethe's before him) towards which he turned so often: he had much more of the frantic, intolerant fanaticism of a genevan reformer or an Old Testament prophet. This is even illustrated in his picture of the self-destructive road taken by the idealistic philosophers of his time in order to reach, *perhaps*, he intimated, *after all*, the antique heaven of health and security. It is actually the road he took, and induced many others to adopt, with the results we today in Europe are able at length to estimate. However, Hume, whose remarks we began with, insisted that there was a principle that would overcome all abstract reasoning whatever. And that for him is Custom or Habit.

For Hume, habit is the only *law* to a notion of which we can attain. An arbitrary and casual, but habitual, conjunction of a whole system of things, having between themselves no necessary connection (which is evident to us, at least), is our *causation*. But before returning finally, as far as our argument is concerned, to causation (in order to consider *belief*), I will interpose a few remarks, as I wish to step aside for a moment and consider "will" before I come to that.

If you were asked to provide some definition of what you meant by "will," how would you go about it? It might be that you could provide me with a kind of reasoning that would be useful to my argument. For instance, you might argue somewhat as follows: "Will," you might say, "is habit — that which, as Hume quite truly says, trips up the philosopher and his innovating mind. What we term a 'voluntary' movement would be impossible without memory, the seat of repetition and habit. We should form no habits if we could not *remember*. Will is the sensation we get when we are picking about in our memory and deciding which of a variety of specimen-actions we shall pull out and use. It is always a repetition of some movement, originally performed involuntarily."

"Then consciousness is habit, or rather could not exist outside a habit-system?" I should ask you. And you perhaps would reply to that: "That is so. It is the movement we describe as 'thought'; it is thought surveying its historical picture-gallery of images of past movements of a similar type *en connoisseur*, and ultimately choosing what it regards as the most appropriate for response to the stimulus of the moment."

Let us pursue this imaginary dialogue for a moment. I then ask you:

I. "In the necropolis of images or mummies of its dead selves is there a live self that moves? What is it?"

YOU. "There is something that *moves*."

I. "Can you give me the likeliest account of what it is that moves, conform with your other definitions?"

YOU. "Why, what we all observe to move every day of our

life — ourself and the various habit-patterns by which we are surrounded. That which moves (us) sticks extremely closely to the
main-habit-pattern, but it embroiders it with small variations,
suggested by the occasion, of a 'voluntary' sort, and is deceiving
us into attending to the superficial, 'living' elaboration, rather
than to the dead skeletal habit-structure. In its week-end golf,
its verbal interplay with its mate, etc., it is a similar automaton.
Any human organism is essentially a repeating-machine, a habit-
machine, a parrot of itself. It is an affair of easily-checked immanent causality and motor-responses. The 'self' that moves in
the picture-gallery is a *movement.* Or better still, it is our way
of describing the *time* at any particular moment in the picture-
gallery. 4:30 or 10 A.M. would be (given the picture-gallery, and
given a periodic fluxion of a point around it) a description of
the 'self' of a more accurate kind than James Jones, or some other
irrelevant label."

I. "Mr. 4:30 or Mr. Eleven o'clock is a truer name than Smith?"
You. "Certainly."

I. "The harmonious and established habits, our 'laws' of
science — the 'skeleton' that Poincaré calls 'beauty'; rather than
the qualitative filling-in, the accidental padding, of 'living' process and event: the uniformity steadily settling down and
straightening out — the dead ossature — *that* is the region of the
human will, of our 'voluntary' life, in which it apparently has
been conceived, and from which it operates: the sensation of personality, or that of a central 'self,' or of the psyche or genius,
or that of any complex idea of a 'high-god,' or that of only an
unimportant domestic 'numen'; all these entities, whether fictional
or not, are creatures of the habit-world, which system we interpret as causative? As regards our 'voluntary' life this indeed must
be so: since it is only among dead times, immovable and stable
things, that we exercise any *will* at all, in the free and uncondi-
tional sense. When most bergsonianly *living* — that is acting —
we are least *ourselves.* We are then just bemused *instruments,*
rapt in the ecstasy of 'action.' The moment we apply our will
to fact, it becomes something different. And our *will* is the expression, the definition of our 'self.' "
You. "Yes."

You perceive that for the occasion I have made you into a time-
adept, and you have been made, reluctantly, I hope, to provide
the sort of argument that would be anticipated from the mouth

of such a figure. I will now turn to Hume, and let him speak in place of the hypothetic You.

"If I ask you why you believe any particular matter of fact, which you relate," Hume writes, "[your] reason will be *some other fact, connected with it.*" Again, "all belief of matter of fact or real existence is derived merely from some object, and a customary conjunction between that and some other object." *Belief* in matter of fact, or in real existence, is derived from *customary conjunction*, and, it follows, from some *persistence*, and repetition. A thing only occurring *once* in a universe of things only, each of them, occurring *once*, and we should never have the notion of reality at all. A purely sensational existence would not be capable of supplying this notion, "reality," at all.

So we see that "reality" as a notion, and in its generally accepted sense, is not what it usually represents itself to be. We need *time to think*, in short, and the leisure which habit supplies us with, to arrive at the notion of the "real"; we require the sort of loose, disconnected "self" of our non-sensational, abstract life to get this sensation with. The purely sensational creature (like the newly-born baby) would not discriminate between itself and the exterior world. It would *be* what happened to it. It would *be* everything with which its senses presented it. There would be no question of a "self." There would only be a not-self of pure sensation—which is, of course, the evangelical christian and communistic "self," as it is also the self of "action" and "function": the time-self. As regards a man's transactions with his store of private images, or "ideas," he can be said to be supremely "free": "Nothing is more free than the imagination of man," as Hume states it. And with this mental, private and imaginative condition Hume associates the word "will." This world of *fiction* is his world of *will*. Now, the difference between *fiction* and *belief* "lies in some sentiment or feeling." This we can call the belief-feeling. So we reach Hume's definition of *belief*.

Belief is nothing but a more vivid, lively, forcible, firm, steady conception of an object than what the imagination alone is ever able to attain.

Or:

Belief is something felt by the mind, which distinguishes the ideas of the judgment from the fictions of the imagination.

Again:

This manner of conception [of an object, the conception accompanied by *belief*,] arises from a customary conjunction of the object with something present to the memory or senses [that is the system of habit].

The main material for the phenomenon of *belief* is drawn from the experiences of causation: the notion of cause and effect is necessary for any human belief. And cause and effect is simply an arbitrary and unnecessary repetition, the machinery of our "system of habit," according to Hume, a "habit of space-time" according to the space-timeists.

So "reality" is a sensation arising from and depending on the phenomenon of endurance, and so familiarity. Unless we are familiar with it, unless we have the habit of it, nothing can seem "real" to us. Such a notion would otherwise, in fact, never enter our head at all. As it is, a thing occurring only for a moment, like a flash of lightning, however often repeated, always has a certain "unreality" about it. And instantaneous things like that which occur once could never enter the category of "reality."

Belief, then, for Hume, is *belief in cause and effect*, his definition conveniently reduces itself to that. And belief is an extremely important conception to familiarize yourself with. In our day, for Mr. Russell, "on the view we take of *belief* our philosophical outlook largely depends." But the problems of "reality" and of "belief" are so intimately connected that they are one. And you could equally well say — and that would be an even profounder test — that "on the view we take of *reality* our philosophical outlook largely depends." Reality is today, indeed, a better term to take than "belief," for these crucial purposes. So let us attempt a realistic definition of reality in the same way that Hume attempted one of belief. But for that, again, we must travel some distance first and assemble a little material, with which the general educated reader may not be familiar.

The humian analysis of "sensation" and "image" (or, for Hume, "impression" and "idea") used principally the test of *distinctness*, as did Leibniz, Descartes, and others of that time in their early psychologies: and we have seen Hume using "vivid, lively, firm and forcible" as adjectives to distinguish our apprehension of a "real" object from our apprehension of a fictitious one, reposing only on our free imagination. It was the *vagueness* or the *distinctness*, feebleness or force, poorness or richness, of the "impression" that gave it "reality" or the reverse. It is the *abstracting* tendencies of the philosopher today that causes him to attack this "distinctness," or those "clear ideas" of the great seventeenth-century realists.

So to induce "belief" and earn the title of "existence" or "reality," a thing must, first of all, not be dim or vacillating. Men early learned to be on their guard against the crowd of imitation-sensations, images or ideas, that they knew their heads to be full of, but which responded to no exterior, causal arrangements of the not-self. So to be "real," again, would mean *to be beyond the influence and reach of the individual's active and naturally imitative, but unreliable, mind.*

When men first began establishing this necessary distinction, *the dream* would be the arch-deceiver, with its sham-sensation building up an imitation-reality, which was the most likely to trip him. But today, through the propaganda of psycho-analysis, *dream* and *hallucination* are the most customary ingredients of our speculation, and thence to a large extent of our thoughts. The *mirror-image*, in post-Relativity philosophy, of Whitehead or of Russell, is the most common object of reference, and perpetually the phenomena of our everyday life are referred to that as to some sort of prototype of sensational existence. In theory, "reality" has recently not only shifted considerably from its traditional realistic seat, but also it has moved very much nearer to the subjective, or "private," end of the scale. The barriers set up by "belief" have been broken down. And that is to say that the barriers between the "real" and the "unreal," between the not-self and the self, have been everywhere impaired.

There is no need to stress the debt to the system of Berkeley in these teachings of Hume. Our absolute dependence upon sensation was for Hume a weakness, for Berkeley a necessity of the ultimate fact of our status of relative and "unreal" creatures. If our conceit, or even our incredulity, revolted, Berkeley might have inquired (by means of an illustration), "What do you suppose it would feel like to be a character of fiction — a Sancho Panza or a Don Quixote?" "Much what it does to be what we are at present," we could only, sensibly, reply. And God the artist is a more significant image than God the mechanic.

For Hume the world of imagination or of images was what the *abstract* world was for Berkeley: it was not real. The insistence upon the world of sensation was the insistence of Berkeley. The necessary "inertness" of the external world of things of Berkeley is what makes things "rattle against each other drily" in Hume's philosophy, for James. And the "reality contingent upon habit," for Hume, was perception rather than sensation, though sensation was its ultimate material. Neither believed in the reality of *the abstract*, or the image-world, that is the main thing.

In all movements we have under consideration the thing to be stressed more than anything else is the disposition to bestow "reality" upon *the image*, rather than upon *the thing*. The reality has definitely installed itself *inside* the contemporary mind, that is to say, as it did with the Stoic and other post-socratics of the greek political decadence. The external world is no longer our affair, as indeed it ceases to be ours in any civic or political sense. At first sight it is easy for the former, at least, of these tendencies to pass itself off as suggestive of an enhanced appetite for *life*. To plunge into sensation, in the bergsonian manner, is surely a movement in the direction of "life"? But yet, if you follow it out — if you observe a little closely the attitudes, vital equipment, and then what soon becomes of all these ecstatic, vociferating divers; or if you ever consider the sort of person that such a cult must cater for, you will form an opposite opinion. So the frenzied propaganda for sensation — for moments, that is, without the "reality" of custom and endurance — in the general way, and of which we see too clear reflections, we think, to be mistaken, in philosophy: this propaganda that is such a strident accompaniment of the most recent industrial and urban life, is rather the experience of an aged organism than of a vigorous and fresh one. For what need has a vigorous one to be told to plunge, to immerse itself? It is immersed naturally, and without instruction, and certainly not as a cult or a philosophy. This is new with us in the West: Whitman was, I suppose, its earliest professor — *Specimen Days* one of the first characteristic utterances of what since has taken on a universal complexion. It is in its wide extension a relatively sudden occurrence, resembling an overwhelming infection. All that doctrinaire barbarity of the sorelian and nietzschean spirit, leading to the "blood-baths" of immense wars and revolutions, are like gigantic and ghastly prescriptions for the rejuvenation of some aged thing which had suddenly thrust itself among us. The insistence on sensation-at-all-costs, then, like the incessant emphasis upon "virility," or "sex," or "stimulation," suggests an unaccountable consciousness rather of an absence than of an abundance of life. So much discussed, the subject of so many inflammatory doctrines and ingenious dissertations, claiming for its realization such insane sacrifices, such insane expense of healthy life, it rather is a sadist corrupted, sickly, leviathan than a triumphant organism, this thing that usurps the name of "life" today; and it displays such an appetite for "reality" that it is natural to suspect it of having been too long unacquainted with it; or else, as an alternative, to have suddenly lost it. So in conclusion, and as regards that feature of our argument, the tendency to bestow "reality" upon images can be interpreted with even less difficulty as a confession of the stage of unreality and sensational dimness or "vagueness" that has been reached. It is not the primitive vigour and pictorial sharpness of the image-capacity of the true savage, of the true child, or of the artist, that would accommodate itself to the atmosphere now prevalent in the world of thought.

As to causality, Time, or motion, has to some extent solved the problem for such people as Alexander: but of course it has not in any way been reinstated. It is a thoroughly discredited principle, but it has its tempting uses, and has recovered a little, here and there, from its neglect. It is not the same *cause*, either, that has been partially rescued; nor has it returned to its traditional seat. The melting of the causal ties of habit into the events or things held apart by the schematization of conceptual thought, so that they *flowed into each other*, reached its climax in Bergson. (The well-known figurative habit in which he described the "past penetrating the present," "the present eating into the future," etc., is that to which we refer.) And today Alexander follows the same course. *Motion* is the secret of *connection*, for him, as we have said, a secret that Hume was unable to discover. Motion, in its turn, is more or less commutative in Alexander's space-time system with Time. So it is really Time that steps into the shoes of Cause: and in consequence Alexander is disposed to put in a good word for the causality principle. It is the *connective motion* only that gives rise to power, or *is* power, rather: not any existent thing, or person, that is causally possessed of power. Causation is a pervasive force, the *force of change*, percurrent or overriding our accidental sequences. However, "since the idea of a power in the cause to produce its effect suggests that the relation is presided over by something akin to 'spirit,' some entity behind the relation which brings it into existence, we are perhaps well rid of the conception . . ." A "spirit," an "entity behind the relation," is what the notion of *power* brings in, there is no escaping from it; you cannot really keep it out, if you have "power" at all, instead of an inert dance or crawl of wandering groups. So, useful as "power" is, and inclined for various reasons as these philosophers are to admit it, along with causation — for where Hume left causation, high and dry, does not at all suit their book, or tally with their fluid mechanism — nevertheless they exclude it on account of what they know it is so difficult not to annex to it, the hated "entity" — something that would dispute "reality" with Time.

Causation is let in, provided it does not have any "power," and provided it is clearly understood that it is "time" or "motion." The traditional *cause* was as bursting with life and purpose as a little Napoleon. But the later *cause*, the *cause-without-"power,"* is very sluggish. It demands some *"inducement* to stir it into activity" (cf. *Space Time and Deity*). It does not at the best of times become its "effect" with any *entrain*. It can be most accurately described as *falling into its effect*, or bursting into it gradually and blindly, with the weight of the oncoming change-stream behind it. It flops with a stagnant release, when sufficiently pushed, into the neighbouring compartment, the next in temporal succession. "Its real activity consists in passing over into its effect," says Professor Alexander. If there were no "time" there, you gather, to hustle it continually, it would certainly never move at all, and if there were no "effect" it would never appear at all. That, then, is what has become of the once so vivacious "cause" — of any "effect" whatever. It has become a sort of Time-and-motion entity, of a minor sort, whose indolent habits are becoming proverbial, and which habits men now share with things. And every day the "cause" requires greater "inducement" to move — more "stimulation" and "provocation"; until eventually it will become as spoilt — and as helpless and sluggish — as the most british of workmen.

CHAPTER THREE

GOD AS REALITY

IN DEVOTING AN INSIGNIFICANT space to this great principle, I am only following the plan with which I set out: namely, to confine myself to what was necessary for the criticism of the time-doctrine, although my argument must certainly reveal its directing impulse, and so to some extent pass beyond criticism. But among the time-philosophers a very considerable theological literature has sprung up — William James, in that matter, as usual, supplying the starting-point of most contemporary speculation in his *Varieties of Religious Experience.* But there is another reason why in this place and for the purposes of this book, it is less necessary to devote time to this subject than to the attack upon the Ego or "thinking subject" or the "object": and that is because there is no attack made upon God in the contemporary time-philosophy we are analysing. Rather is it the contrary. Most contemporary philosophers adhere to the results of the kantian criticism, and provide a handsome place in their time-system for Deity of some kind. Both Alexander and Whitehead place God at the end of the "emergent" road. The reasons they have to offer for this accommodation are often very unsatisfactory: but having discoursed empirically upon "Space and Time," they still add "Deity," with a more or less kantian, pragmatical, gesture, at the end. And they are able to do this all the more heartily because the "deity" thus introduced is a very different one from the entity with which Kant had to deal, and which he found it necessary, for pragmatical reasons, to accommodate with a rationale or "reason" of its own.

Constantly in our criticism we march with the "thomist"; and this is perhaps the best point to make clear where our positions differ, as where they merge or overlap. The catholic criticism of "modernity" is as irretrievably "historical" as the doctrine of Spengler. It is really a "time"-doctrine too, as in the nature of things, perhaps, it must be, but the converse of that of the "evolutionist." It attaches a disproportionate importance to *one* time, as its opponents do to *all* time. In opposition to the "modernity"

they attack (and everything is "modern," and therefore to be attacked, which is not thomist or aristotelian, for the typical contemporary catholic theorist) is, in their system, "antiquity," which
is equivalent to the "Classical" of Spengler, and is just as
inalterable, unique and fixed. Those are two of the extremes of
contemporary controversy: indeed, when we said there was *no*
"opposition" today, that would, in this sense, be inexact: for there
is, of course, always the catholic opposition. It is because that
is a purely theological or political "opposition" that we considered
it could be neglected, in the sense that we were using that word.
There is *no* theoretic "opposition": there is only the theologic "opposition": which is discredited, popularly, and we think not
without considerable reason, in advance.

I will take the very interesting book of Dr. Sheen (who is an
american priest, and professor of philosophy at Louvain) for the
purposes of this brief survey. He outlines the thomist case with
the greatest lucidity, and in such a matter it is important not to
have to deal with such a "personal" account as that of Maritain
(the renegade bergsonian, and still far too tainted with the manners of thought of his original master, as I suggested in a previous
chapter) would be able to provide. Dr. Sheen's statement of the
position of the contemporary catholic theorist is very exact, and
can be recommended to the student. (It is to be found in *God
and Intelligence in Modern Philosophy*. Longmans, Green & Co.,
1925.)

The first and great objection that I have to the neo-scholastic
attitude is precisely its incurably *historical* view of things. It is
incurably "conservative": it is forever the "old" against the "new";
it is "anti-modern" in a, to me, stupid, "historical" manner. It says
many shrewd and damaging things about "modernism": but
because all that is contemporary (except thomism) is vowed —
such is its unanimity and herd-discipline — to silence about
anything that is not very delightful or intelligent about "modernity," that is no reason why the epoch and the ideas that produced
scholasticism, to which catholicism points, should be wholly
beautiful and true. It is surely not a bad thing to remember that
that system was unified, too, into a tyrannic orthodoxy, with
every theological sanction; and that it was impossible then, as
it is now, to think except in one way, and according to an intolerant unique and jealous standard. There was no arguing with St.
Thomas about the angelic nature (from which he derived his

soubriquet) any more than it is exactly easy to argue with Alexander, and his colleagues, about "Time." Indeed, a frantic, hallucinated, "soul"-drugged individual such as Maritain or Cocteau, in France, or such a ferocious and foaming romantic as the dogmatic Toby-jug, Chesterton, in England, are not easy to reason with; were their orthodoxy rampant, they would be worse than the disciples of "Time." So in that particular battle I am neither for "Time" nor for its enemies: but of the two the line of argument adopted here has more in common with St. Thomas than with "Time."

The "God" with which Dr. Sheen has dealt in the critical part of his essay is not so much the God "Time," as the God that is the subject of the mystical experiences of James and others, who have turned, as a relaxation, from their massacre of smaller entities, to genuflect in the direction of this greatest hypostasized feeling, or belief, of all.

This God of the philosophy of change and time, "though coming from the past, differs from all that has appeared in the past. It is, as it were, one of the novelties of evolution." It brings man into greater prominence. It exalts him even to the extent of giving him a "vote in the cosmic councils of the world." It is, in a word, the "transfer of the seat of authority from God to man." This is "God in evolution. God *is* not. He *becomes.*" Thus the "God" of Alexander is that state necessarily superior to yours, just ahead of you in time, the next step up, or the next *plane* up, in the evolutionary Progress. All that *is*, is not, and cannot, indeed, be God. God can only be when *He temporally is not*: and (since evolutionary doctrine postulates the "Progress of the Species") when He is *ahead of* the evolutionary present. Tomorrow we, men, shall be what today is God: but *then* we shall not be God, for He will have moved farther on, and higher up: and so by our translation to another and higher sphere, whatever else we shall have gained, we shall not have become "God." So Alexander's "emergent"-evolutionary picture is for us, who move, a series of antechambers, with the Deity as one who never *is*, but always *to be.*

The problems of "God" and of "Intelligence" are one, according to Dr. Sheen:

As men lost faith in the intelligence, they acquired faith in the God of becoming. The modern God was born the day the "beast of intellectualism" was killed. The day the intelligence is reborn, the modern God will die. They cannot exist together: for one is the annihilation of the other.

This last passage indicates the ground, the solid ground, upon which the thomist doctrine and the one adumbrated here must necessarily meet: but we subsequently quit it at different points and for very different supernal destinations.

The intellectual [scholastic, catholic] approach began with the *world* — not the world of internal experience, but the external world of movement, contingency, varied perfections, efficient causality and finality. Its point of departure was extra-mental. The source of its proofs was in the open air. In reacting against this so-called indirect method, the modern approach placed itself not in the external world but in *self* — the world of internal experience. It goes to God, not through the world, but through the ego.

It will be clear, perhaps, at once, to the reader, how such a statement as that allies us here to the position taken up by the catholic, and also the way in which it separates us. For us no road can be too far round to Nirvana, to use the phrasing of Professor Santayana. The "source" of *our* proofs, too, is "in the open air": our "subjectivity" is of an objective order. Nothing can be too "indirect" for us.

Scholastic rationalism was (and is) bound up with the pagan "materialism": with "the concrete," and its objective, external ordinance. *Matter*, for it, was the path to God, that *between* God and the individual. And that, piously, it trod. There is a great deal of popular misunderstanding about the catholic, or thomist, position, and one point may be cleared up for the reader not at all acquainted with these theologies. The dispute between the thomist and the average "Idealist" or Absolutist, is not at all a dispute between, on the one hand, a "religious" man, and, upon the other, an "irreligious" man. In a sense it is quite the opposite. As things stand today, it is not a paradox to say that the catholic is much the less "religious" of the two. Indeed, it would not be at all a paradox to say that the catholic position (making abstraction of such extremist and mystical converts as those of the Cocteau variety) is that of the *irreligious*, or *non-religious* mind, in contrast to the God-hungry mysticism of the James type.

"[Empiricism] hitherto, through some strange misunderstanding . . . has been associated with *irreligion*," James writes (*Pluralistic Universe*) in discussing the new "religious" rôle of philosophy. The catholic philosopher, in the same way almost, could complain that hitherto what he taught, "through some strange misunderstanding," had been associated with *religion.* It would not be quite true, even in the popular meaning of "religious," but it would be more nearly so than the mistake involved in the anti-"religious" prejudice he has to overcome.

So, according to a swarm of philosophers more or less inspired by James, the way to attain God is the *direct* one of personal "religious experience" possessed of "a certitude stronger than that attaching to religious truth." It is the manner of the protestant Reformation, of course, the direct plunge to God, not only without mediation or by means of reason (with all the dangers of that confusing exercise), but with a debased reliance upon some kind of semi-philosophical, half-rational image: for clearly no plunge of that sort is entirely "direct," unless a great heat of mystical emotion is called into play, which is not usual with philosophers. How much cleaner, and in the end more efficacious, is the method of the catholic, the inventions of Reason rather than the irresponsible and lonely gushings of "intuitive" heat. About the wish to seize and mingle with the supreme Reality in a passionate attack there is something lunatic and egotistic. To maintain this supreme divinity in isolation from our imperfection, instead of exacting jealously its democratic descent to where we are, to approach it only circuitously and with a measured step, at the risk of appearing unfervid, is, it would seem, to the human reason and to human taste, the better way.

"Modern religion bases its knowledge of God entirely upon experience: it has encountered God," one of the "progressists," quoted by Dr. Sheen, exclaims. But even if it were possible, as many semi-mystical sensationalists claim, to *encounter* God, then it would be necessary for any rational being to avoid such an occurrence, and confine himself to an approach to Deity only by the intellectual road. The intellect has been given us as the appointed and natural path on which to make our approach to God. The emotional is too indiscriminate, and it is in any case unlikely that then God would be encountered. Rather our hungry Self would waylay us.

But if you read carefully the account of the religious experiences of the "progressists" of our great european "decadence," you will see that it is not really God in any high and significant sense of which they are thinking, or rather *feeling.* How indeed could it be? For there is no God already *there.* "As the world progresses,

He progresses; as the world acquires perfection, He acquires perfection." This evolutionist God in-the-making, who *is* not, but who is a non-existent progressive potential Something that is pushed along and "upwards" (it is noisily hoped) by the advance of evolving mankind, is evidently nothing but the Subject experiencing Him in his "religious" moment.

But Western theological mysticism has been as fervid as any: we are now considering only the position taken up by contemporary thomistic philosophers within the catholic church, in their dispute with the anti-intellectualist tendencies of the present time, and behind that a well-defined background of classical rationalism, which has been the most valuable contribution of the Church to intellectual life. With that position we are in sympathy here. That characteristic traditional health of the catholic mind is an island in the midst of our "decadence" and "decline," whose airs it is invigorating sometimes to breathe.

The "dark night of the Soul," the tragic asceticism that is one of the phases of dogmatic belief, is not the necessary accompaniment of the presence of God, though it has often been a very beautiful one. When driven to these dark expedients, there is always some chance that the devout are entertaining the dramatic Antagonist instead of the authentic Deity. So it is the "materialism," the pagan health, of the classical inheritance that I am thinking of when I invite you to fraternize with the catholic thinkers, in their high and nobly-ordered pagan universe.

The recrudescence of superstitious emotion (envisaged as "religious experience") engineered by the contemporary philosophic thought that we are here analysing, is part of the great pseudo-revolutionary movement *back* to the primitive world; and that is another reason why, in preference to such a movement, we would turn to the catholic side in the religious dispute. "Religion" is primitivism; and as practised by the neo-mystical philosophers following upon James and Bergson, it is part of the cult of the "primitive," as illustrated by the child-cult (the exploiting of infancy and its "naïf" reactions), or the exotic romance of such a painter as Gauguin, or the Black Bottom of the Swanee River — which is merely another phase of the "Moon and Sixpence" — or the sex-primitivism initiated by Freud. At the moment all our interests are identified with the characteristic resistance of that church, and some support can be found in it. But to rely upon St. Thomas Aquinas entirely at such a juncture, or some synod at Rome open to every imaginable influence, would prove in you a meagre sense of the reality, and of the forces that are driving in the other direction. We should support the catholic church perhaps more than any other visible institution: but we should make a new world of Reason for ourselves, more elastic than the roman cult is in a position to supply, and employing all the resources of the new world to build with. Outside we can actually assist that church more than we could within it, if we were, otherwise, inclined to such a communion.

The discursive, the rational, approach to Reality is discarded by contemporary thought for the emotional, direct, intuitive. Dr. Sheen quotes Professor Wildon Carr as follows: an "intuition," he says, is "a direct apprehension of a reality which is non-intellectual, and *non-intellectual means that it is neither a perception, nor a conception, nor an object of reason.*" Just as in philosophical theorizing the attack is upon the "perception" in favour of a primitivist, dynamical, group of fluctuating sensa, so in the matter of the supreme Reality, again, the same methods are applied. Instead of remaining over against a rigorously conceived, independent, objective, conceptional God, these philosophers prefer to disintegrate this solitary image; although that conceptual detachment is the natural form that the idea of Deity has for our minds; just as it is more natural for us to conceive of a tree conceptually, than to visualize it as a fluctuating mass of sensa: to which argument may be added that already employed, namely that it is *natural* for man to wish to keep Deity intact, and, in suitable humility, not to wish to mingle it with his imperfection.

What is this "faith-state," however, William James inquires (in a passage quoted by Dr. Sheen), and how, exactly, do we feel when we get in touch directly with Deity? How do we register this contact? His answer is exceedingly characteristic and illuminating: for, in order to reach this condition, we have to "primitivize" ourselves to the extent of reaching the mineral world — we do not even stop at the animal. We become a bar-of-iron, without touch or sight, which, "without any *representative* faculty whatever, might nevertheless be strongly endowed with an inner capacity for magnetic feeling; and as if, through various arousals of its magnetism by magnets coming and going in its neighbourhood, it might be consciously determined to different attitudes and tendencies. Such a bar-of-iron could never give you an outward description of the agencies that had the power of stirring it so strongly, yet of their presence and of their significance for life it would be intensely aware through every fibre of its being."

We are not bars-of-iron, or course; and if we were we should probably resent very much the disturbance occasioned us by "forces" prowling in our neighbourhood, and should be as likely to assume them to be diabolic as the reverse. And a thinking bar-of-iron, electrically disturbed, does very well illustrate the sort of "religious experience" preconized by James. The "cheerful and expansive" disturbances he elsewhere indicates give us a further enlightenment as to what would no doubt be the ultimate seat of such experiences, of the "bar-of-iron" order: for the "expansive and searching" movements of sex (the organism seen as an electrified bar-of-iron) indicate where we should get to in our intimate and personal attack upon Deity. It would be very much *sans façon*, in the end, that we should "experience" our God. In James' highly-stimulated bar-of-iron we have the link between his later mystical philosophy and the sexual character of most mystical religiosity.

> The religious impulse which gives us God . . . is to be identified [according to contemporary philosophy] with an impulse of life; it is *biological* and belongs to all the orders. Even the animals have a religious sense. [I am still quoting from *God and Intelligence* of Dr. Sheen.]

Let us substitute for the bar-of-iron of James the impulsive, tail-wagging, sentimental dog. There we certainly have a *religious animal*—the dog of Anatole France's *Monsieur Bergeret*, for instance.

But is not the dog's worship of his master "religion" of a more absolute order than any of which man is capable? In the first place, the dog does not require to *imagine* his God (in the fashion of Mr. Fawcett's "Imaginist" doctrine), as we do. His god is there in the flesh before him, sitting in the armchair, filling his pipe, devouring a turkey or what-not.

Whether as bars-of-iron or as dogs, the God that results must be corporeal: and that is why so often the mystic is a voluptuary, unconscious or otherwise. But men are degrading what should be their God by returning to those elementary conditions in search, at one and the same time, of Sensation and of Deity. We say a dog's God is his stomach, and that is a just description of it: the God of your "cheerful and expansive" feelings would be a God of the same order. The human imagination, even, is too carnal for that high Object. The reason alone seems to satisfy the requirements of the highest possible human Deity.

But the fundamental implication of William James, and the school that has come after him, is that the human intellect should be dispensed with, in this supreme investigation; that it is in some way inadequate (because not "immediate," that is sensuous, enough), and that it is not an instrument of adoration. And that seems to us to involve the deepest misunderstanding of our destiny and faculties. Where James exults at the death-blow given by Bergson to the "beast," *Intellectualism*, he is rejoicing in reality at the birth of another "beast" — namely, his sort of God. Indeed, if you listen to his ecstatic letter to Bergson, you will understand better what description of intelligence you have to deal with. "I am so enthusiastic as to have said only two days ago . . . I thank heaven that I have lived to this date . . . that I have witnessed the Russo-Japanese War, and seen Bergson's new book appear . . . the two great modern turning-points in history and thought." The Russo-Japanese War no longer appears to us a colossal, heaven-sent blessing — nor any other war: and Monsieur Bergson's *Evolution Créatice*, as a great world-event of the same order, can scarcely have so overwhelming a charm to anyone today as was experienced (religiously) by James at that time. "Intellectualism" is not, at all events, the "beast" of *our* Apocalypse.

"Religious experience of the lutheran type brings all our naturalistic standards to bankruptcy," James writes (*A Pluralistic Universe*). It has done so, but it need not, is what is here advanced. And in that we are at one with the catholic.

But catholic and "absolutist" alike, in their admirable plan for divine exclusiveness, have for one of their capital dogmas something to which we are unable to subscribe. Without going at all in the direction of the pantheist, or believing in an immanent deity in Time, it is possible still to leave God to His necessary solitude, and yet to believe in a first-hand experience of the divine in human life, or at least so it seems to us. The angels of St. Thomas (like the playful "angel" introduced by Alexander for the purposes of illustration) do not help that view, but interfere with it. Indeed it is easy to see why Alexander introduced the angel, for the thomistic hierarchy does contain a similar idea to his evolutionary picture of ascending layers of truth or "deity." Even

Aristotle's God towards which all Nature strives, which, like food held just out of reach of a hungry animal, keeps it hopping up and down, in a state of ferment, vaguely suggests the flying Deity of the emergent evolutionist. But the thomistic angel-world seems a tawdry and irrelevant interloper in the greek physical world of Aristotle; and Aristotle's contemplative God is a far cry from the evolutionist God of Time and Action. It is the classical background that gives thomism its health. Aristotle is more important in it than St. Thomas.

As an epigraph to this book, I have used a passage from the *Metaphysics* of Aristotle. In it he says that if all we had to make up our idea of God with were what we possess in our experience (what we could take from the highest reaches of our own contemplative states), then that God would "be worthy of our admiration." What we are suggesting here is that that is exactly all that we have, indeed, with which to construct our God; and that, further than that, it is completely adequate. To at once be perfectly concrete, we can assert that a God that swam in such an atmosphere as is produced by the music of a Bach fugue, or the stormy grandeur of the genii in the Sistine Ceiling, or the scene of the Judgment of Signorelli at Orvieto, who moved with the grace of Mozart — anyone may for himself accumulate such comparisons from the greatest forms of art — such a God would be the highest we could imagine; that God would be so perfect in power and beauty that, however much people may assert they find it possible to experience a greater God (to whom all human experience would be relatively imperfect) or analogically to posit one, we are entirely justified in not believing them. Such people, indeed, are usually those who are proved to be congenitally incapable of experiencing the things from which we draw our analogies. And so, for them, no doubt, it is quite sensible to fix the "divine" upon some plane inaccessible to their senses. But we may without immodesty conclude that they are referring precisely to that plane that we have experienced in our enjoyment of our intellectual and artistic faculties.

Having considered the relation of our position on this question with that of the Latin theologians, I will proceed to a very brief consideration of how the views of the absolutist would accommodate themselves to what we have to say. And I will take

Bradley as the most representative and original of the philosophers of the Absolute.

The notion of feeling or sensation as a bastard experience of an immediate absolute Wholeness, or the further idea that sensation is the Whole, *feeling* through us, is useful to convey a sense of the intensity of the individual life; but we claim for the intellect an equal part in this immediacy; and our "individual" is not the individual of Time, or a creature of the nisus of the progressist system. For why should not the Whole think as well as feel? The idea of a merely *feeling Whole* is repugnant. And that in thinking we are poorer than we are in feeling is not the view taken here, but, on the contrary, that feeling and thinking are equal deliverances of Reality, under whatever figure you suppose that these things occur.

So when we are told that "This Whole [Reality] must be immediate, like feeling, but not, like feeling, immediate at a level below distinction and relation . . . because it . . . does not suffer a division of idea from existence, it has therefore a balance of pleasure over pain"—we do not agree to that. First of all, the sort of superior type of "feeling" suggested does not seem to us real. Our sensation, as sensation, and as far as it goes, at its best, seems the best sort of sensation possible.

But let us consider the possibility of Reality in the gross, as a pure lump of perfection. Bradley is an ideal guide to the Absolute; him we will still use. "Reality," he says, "is being in which there is no division of content from existence, no loosening of 'what' from 'that.' So Reality, the full and whole Reality, does not" (which means would not) "suffer a division of idea from existence." That is to say, that what it thought and willed (as we think and will and carry on as gods, or a kind of finite-Absolute, in our personal image-world) would be *true* or *real*. What it *imagined* would be as real as what we externally *enjoy*. The trouble here is that it would only have a "balance" of pleasure over pain. For it would be impossible to imagine it *nothing but pleasure*. That would be in the end uninteresting or without significance. And how else would the "pain" be supplied but by something outside itself?

Bradley's "balance of pleasure and pain" is to say that Reality cannot be "perfect," it would appear: just as indeed, with us, he affirms that no truth can be entirely true. And yet this designer of the Absolute ends by saying, "In every sense it is perfect." Yet for him it is *ens perfectissimum*; it is a perfect and immaculate God, owning a substantial balance, when all his contretemps, reverses and disappointments are totted up, of pleasure over pain. So it is a God that comes out on top, but is hardly an "Absolute." It is, for us, too realistic a God.

Human individuality is best regarded as a kind of artificial godhood. When most intensely separated from our neighbour and from all other things—most "ourselves," as we say—we are farthest away, clearly, from an Absolute, or any kind of Unity. Yet, in another sense, we are nearest to it. This is the great problem that has wrecked so many metaphysics: it is this that has divided stoic from epicurean, nominalist from realist, and indeed every varying genus of philosopher. For such an infinitely disputed difficulty of thought, all that can be done is to give the solution that is imposed upon us individually by all the rest of the complex of belief in which we build our personal system.

Everything analogically indicates God as a great Unity. We, when most individual (least automatic, and least religiously or otherwise entranced), possess most a similar unity to that we must attribute to God. When we "expand" most (to use a favourite word of James)—reach out towards Deity and melt ourselves in a "cosmic" orgasm of feeling—we are least *ourselves* and possess least centre and organic unity. What, then, is the conclusion, as far as the practice of religion is concerned? If there is a God, we can say, we have, for this life, our backs turned to each other. This must be so for things to be bearable at all for us as creatures: for such unrelieved intimacy as would otherwise exist, such perpetual society—of such a pervasive, psychic, overwhelming kind—would not be socially possible. We at least must *pretend* not to notice each other's presence, God and ourselves to be *alone*. So when the other of us two was not attending, did we steal a glance round at what was behind us, then we should always see a blank wall, a *back* view. To confront or "encounter" God is for us physically impossible, we can conclude; *we can only see God, if at all, from behind.* As we determine ourselves, we negate Perfection, understood as an absolute Unity; it is written, we cannot avoid this cancellation. Whatever happens, we are bound to shut the door upon Mr. Bradley's Absolute, or upon Spinoza's God. "An immediate experience is not exclusive," says the guardian of the Absolute. We assert, on the contrary, that it *is* exclusive.

As it is, then, our sense of personal reality is so great that we are not able, at the same time, to entertain the *sensation* of the existence of a God. On the other hand, we may quite well, rationally, entertain the idea of His existence. God is for us something to *think*, not *feel*. All mystical sacrifices of the self to any absolutist creature whatever, we do not understand. We are against a mystical "belief," then (in the special sense of Belief in a Divinity), though not against rational belief; we consider it incompatible with "belief" in the more universal sense of experiencing and holding in ourself the sensation of reality. It is as thieves only — a thief of the real — that we can exist, or as parasites upon God. The Absolute, we think, crushes, and is meant by its hierophants to crush, the personal life.

If you say that it is "connection with the central fire which produces in the element this burning sense of selfness," we say that we do not believe in a central fire feeding finite centres; we do not, simply, experience that *central* attraction. If there is such a thing, we are convinced that somehow we are there already, for we feel that we are entirely free, or more exactly, we can say we "*believe*" that we are entirely free, within our own borders. When William James was asked if he had ever had direct experience of God, he replied simply, "No": a strange reply for a mystical theorist — who happened to be honest — to have to make. The truth probably is that James did not understand himself very well when he adopted mystical interpretations. That was probably a romantic gesture. In reality, I should say that James was a rationalist in religion, and that the attitude most in consonance with the native character of his mind would have been that which is being outlined here. It is at least a contradictory spectacle to see him (after his theatrical denial of "consciousness," and his many onslaughts upon the "mind" and "psyche") fling himself effusively at the feet of another entity, whose existence it is easier to question than that of "consciousness." It was *too* easy, perhaps, for James.

The two following statements appear to us true or untrue, according to the way in which they are understood. (1) "Every sphere or level of the world is a necessary factor in the Absolute. Each in its own way satisfies, until compared with that which is more than itself." (2) "One appearance is more real than another. In short, the doctrine of degrees of reality and truth is the fundamental answer to our problem." Bradley, who was a great metaphysician, appears nevertheless to us discouraged and crushed, himself, by the contradictory, invisible weight of his monotonous Absolute. *Nothing* "satisfies" in his world; for he lives incessantly beneath the oppression of Something which is "more than itself." There is no point at all in being more "real" than another "appearance." For, measured with the Absolute, this advantage is derisory. So the "fundamental" answer I have just quoted, cannot really be called the core of this doctrine.

Weighed down by too great a discouragement, the power to translate these valuable principles into fact seems wanting in some way to Bradley. His Absolute *appears*: but it shows a perplexed and dismal face, and, it must be added, a rather narquois tendency to ape the gestures of its creator's german master, which are gestures of almost comic power. While introducing his Absolute, Bradley exhibits what seems a lack of belief, and so fails to inspire it: belief, that is, quite simply in reality — "belief" in the sense of steady conviction of objective reality. That "vivid, lively, forcible, firm, steady conception" of the object, as Hume puts it when defining "belief," is required as much in handling the Absolute as in dealing with a three-penny-bit. A philosopher at least as much as anybody else requires "belief" of that sort, if he is to put the "reality" before us, and make us say: "Yes. That is *true.*" For it is only by "belief" in this sense, that supremely concrete thing, that we reach truth, which is simply reality. But in Bradley's world "no truth is *entirely true.*" That is it.

"We should . . . find a paradox in the assertion," Bradley says, "that everything alike has existence to precisely the same extent." But he did not accompany those statements by such further ones, nor did he weave them together in such a way, that we immediately feel that he has achieved *truth.* Another thing about his Absolute is that he does not succeed in relieving it of a certain oppressive scale and impending weight. Had he succeeded in doing that, his philosophy would have no doubt worked out differently. We think so naturally in quantitative terms — of stellar universes, of *battalions* of stellar universes, of immense Meat Trusts, of constellations of monstrous Trusts, of great Wars and still greater ones, of various Napoleons — it is well to bear in mind, as we have pointed out elsewhere in this book, that inevitably, when we are engaged in constructing a conception of the Absolute, or of any Perfection, it turns out invariably to be very very *large.*

It is more and more, and then still more, of the same stuff. It is the *enlarged*, in the "enlarged non-natural man" of Arnold, which provides the distinction. I have already quoted a passage in which Bradley exposes this mistake, but he seems to have succumbed to it himself in some way.

It is by reason of its "concord" that Bradley's particular Perfect can gain nothing he tells us by swelling itself out to vast proportions. For the more it determined and swelled and complicated itself, the more self-contradictory it would, in his view, become. And when we consider that in the mathematical sense "small" means merely constant, there is perhaps no limit to the littleness that any being would be compelled to aim at, in order to avoid inconstancy of change, discord and struggle. The flea is thus, of familiar animals, the true symbol of "perfection," much more than the mammoth. But so, too, on that absolutist, quantitative scale, you arrive at *nothing* which is the only safe and stable thing to be! Nevertheless, the fallacious tendency to identify perfection with quantitative scale does not gain from these qualifications.

Again, for the idea of the consummate Perfection — "a being at the same time fully possessed of all hostile distinctions and the richer for their strife" — the idea that discord and negation, the opposition and oppugnancy of one thing against another, or of the Many against the One — always *against*, always a murderous conflict — can contribute to Perfection, and is its condition, is what we deny. It is the old darwinian, evolutionary nightmare, in whose clutches we are at present all of us more than ever wallowing.

The personality that we each possess we are apt to despise, certainly, because it has so little material power; but still without conceit at all or even blasphemy, we have a god-like experience in that only. Or rather the usually ill-defined term "God" can only justify itself therein: since material power, like scale, is irrelevant. If we consider that the analogy expires in the abjectness of that concept, "man," of which we hear so much disparagement, then we surely should discard it altogether. Let us attempt now to express the most sanguine belief we can have on this subject, such as would be most hospitable to the notion of God. The rapprochement is not so absurd as it at first sounds, especially to our ears, so accustomed to disobliging descriptions of the human state, in the service of levelling mass-doctrines. It is only blasphemy or absurdity, rather, for those who have long grown accustomed to blaspheme and heap ridicule on mankind, or to listen credulously to those engaged in that cheerful occupation, not to us. We are not at all disposed to ridicule or despise men because they are materially insignificant, because they are not as big as the earth, or the solar system, or as powerful as the forces of an earthquake. Those are the habits of a world that is not our world. We regard it as a similar vulgarity to ridiculing or despising a man because he is poor. Worldly or material power is not the standard used here. But if people could for a moment be persuaded to neglect that aspect of the affair, by which they are obsessed, we are sure that the matter would at once appear in another light. Meanwhile we can say that no Absolute need be ashamed of the feelings or thoughts of what we call a great artist or a great poet. Let us repeat this argument. Any God could put His name to the *Oedipus* or to *King Lear*. Anything communicating, not in a mechanically-perfect way, but still directly, more "greatness," we cannot imagine; and hence, scale apart, any other material of deity for the construction of God is meaningless, to us. And the vulgar delusions connected with quantity, scale or duration, delusions largely fostered by the gross subject-matter of positive science, are the only things that could be an obstacle to the embracing of this view. The Sistine Chapel Ceiling is worthy of the hand of any God which we can infer, dream of, or postulate. We may certainly say that God's hand is visible in it.

When at some moment or another in the process of evolution we were introduced to that extraordinary Aladdin's Cave, that paradise (which the behaviourist and many other people regard with such fanatical displeasure, belief in which will soon, it is very likely, be taxed, or definitely put out of bounds, with angels of a jealous God of Science sweeping fiery swords hither and thither in front of it), *our minds*: or when the magnificent private picture-gallery of its stretched-out imagery was thrown open, and we were allowed to wander in it in any direction, and to any private ends we pleased; that was certainly, if it is the gift of a God, a highly democratic proceeding on His part: especially when you consider that this is not *one* picture-gallery, thronged by a swarming public, but is *one-apiece* for any number of individuals — the conception of so democratic a God that He became aristocratic again, as it were, for the sake of others — each individual, however small, made into an "aristocrat" at once where His mind's eye is concerned. It is indeed evident that thereby in a sense God abdicated. He apparently no longer *wished* to be "the Absolute." So He introduced us to, and made us free of, His heavenly pictures. What it was that brought about this change of heart, or mental crisis, in the Absolute — if that should be by chance the true account of what occurred — it is otiose to speculate upon. But it must be remarked at the same time that, alongside of this *absolute* and princely gift, the "iron-round of necessity" was maintained outside the magical circle of mind, or at least so it appears.

If the contrast is between a conception of the world as an ultimate Unity on the one hand, or a Plurality on the other; if you have, dogmatic and clear-cut, or rather if you could have, on the one side a picture of a multiplicity of wave-like surface changes only, while all the time the deep bed of Oneness reposes unbroken underneath: on the other side the idea of an *absolute* plurality, every midget existence, every speck and grain, unique (for what such "uniqueness" was worth) and equally *real*, irrespective of any hierarchy of truth at all: then can there be any question that the hypothesis of Oneness is the profounder hypothesis, and must, if it lay thus barely between those two, be the real? But we are surface-creatures only, and by nature are meant to be only that, if there is any meaning in nature. No metaphysician goes the whole length of departure from the surface-condition of mind — that fact is not generally noticed. For such departures result in self-destruction, just as though we hurled ourself into space — into "mental-space," if you like, in this case. We are surface-creatures, and the "truths" from beneath the surface contradict our values. It is among the flowers and leaves that our lot is cast, and the roots, however "interesting," are not so ultimate for us. For us the ultimate thing is the surface, the last-comer, and that is committed to a plurality of being. So what in a sense we have arrived at, is, for practical reasons, the opposite to the conclusions of Kant's "practical reason." For the same reason we think it is most true and better to *say* there is *no* God. To us the practical requirements seem to indicate the contrary of Kant's pragmatical solution — to require the conception of a Many instead of a One. On the other hand, if anything, the speculative reason seems to us to point to a One. But on the One we must turn our back in order to exist. Evidences of a oneness seem everywhere apparent. But we *need*, for practical purposes, the illusion of a plurality. So in one sense we are more near to the conception of a God than Kant: in another — the official and practical — we are farther from it. The illusion must in short be our "real." And our reason is not the pragmatical member among our faculties at all, but for us the ultimate truth-bearing vehicle. Yet it is only in league with our sensuous machinery of illusion that it is able to convey the "real," which machinery is pluralistic. We feel that we have to ignore the possibility of a God emotionally, as positive Science must, for the purposes of its empirical activity, ignore the unknown — to pretend, in order to be able to act at all, that it is omniscient. And perhaps we are more fundamentally religious than the kantian, with his chilling pragmatical deity; and if there is such a Reality, closer in touch with it than he. For Kant pleased all the positivists who came after him too well not to be too positive himself for us. In any case, we come to this contrary conclusion: that it is *we* who have to pretend to be real, if anyone has to, not to pretend that God is. For if He is real, He is so much realler than we that there is no need for Him to be bolstered up by our "practical reasons": and if He does not exist, then there is no need at all to invent Him, with a voltairean gesture.

Philosophy, in the end, will always probably find the idea of God essential, as did Aristotle, with no incentive except the passion for truth to come to some such notion. But whether that idea is either necessary or suitable for the majority of people is open to question. (The opposite of this is generally supposed to be true: "the majority cannot dispense with religion," it is said, "as can the philosopher.") The true religionist is such a scourge that his God is always an engine of destruction, and bears no resemblance to any Absolute with which metaphysics deals: "I should rather like to extend my empire over the plains of Damascus," said Mahomet in the fable, "chiefly because this empire must be extended by the sword, which is tempered nowhere in such perfection as by the waters of Abana and Pharpar."

In another european fable Melanchthon says:

It is sorrowful to dream that we are scourges of God's hand, and that he appoints for us no better work than lacerating one another. . . . There is scarcely a text in the Holy Scriptures to which there is not an opposite text written in characters equally large and legible; and there has usually been a sword laid upon each. Even the weakest disputant is made so conceited by what he calls religion, as to think himself wiser than the wisest who thinks differently from him; and he becomes so ferocious by what he calls holding it fast, that he appears to me as if he held it fast much in the same manner as a terrier holds a rat, and you have about as much trouble in getting it from between his incisors. When at last it does come out, it is mangled, distorted, and extinct.

All-Fathers have always been Battle-Fathers, used by us to exterminate our "enemies," that is people whose prosperity we envied and whose goods we coveted: the practical difficulty of a "God" among savages — as we more or less are — lies there. That is the most practical of all the so-called pragmatical tests.

Earlier in this chapter the assertion has been made that the catholic thinker is, if anything, the *irreligious* one of the two ("irreligious" used in the popular sense), if he is contrasted with such a thinker as William James or Fechner. So we have been moved to choose the catholic thinker as a confederate on account of his non-religious bias — because, in short, of the secular, common-sense basis of his thought. This would no doubt seem an extravagance to some people; for on one side is the professional religionist — the Roman Catholic — and on the other the layman, the scientific intelligence, the sceptical philosopher. As it has occurred to me that this remark might not have been completely understood by the general reader, I will for a moment revert to it.

Let us take a definition of "the secular" — a very clear and excellent one, to be found in a book of Edward Caird's — and see if that throws any light on what we are discussing.

The secular consciousness [he says], *i.e.*, our ordinary unreflective consciousness of ourselves and the world, starts from the division and separation of things; it takes them all, so to speak, as independent substances which might exist by themselves, and whose relations to each other are external and accidental. . . . If it (the secular consciousness) rises to the eternal and infinite, it is only as to something beyond and far away — something that is not present in experience. . . . The religious consciousness is the direct antithesis of this way of thinking.

Is not this excellent description of "the secular consciousness" also a very good description of the average and characteristic consciousness of the catholic theologian? At the basis of the thomistic philosophy is the "common-sense" of everyday perception, "our ordinary unreflective consciousness" of things. It was this "unreflective," direct, everyday consciousness that scholasticism sought to organize: just as it was of that consciousness that greek philosophy also, in its day, and for the first time in the world, achieved the organization. And it must always be remembered that the best in scholasticism was greek thought: and that, again to quote Caird, "the beginning of theology is to be found in Greek Philosophy."

The *secular mind of common-sense starts from the division and separation of things*, taking them all to be what to the eye of common-sense they appear, "independent substances which might exist by themselves, and whose relations to each other are external." The religious view, on the other hand, proceeds very soon to merge and melt all these seemingly isolated and distinct "things" or substances into one another. Beyond that, the "religious" consciousness attacks the distinctiveness of that other, supreme Object, God, and soon fuses it with the rest — the tables, the chairs, the garden-hose, the bath-salts, looking-glass and chimney-pots. Soon everything — to the religious consciousness — is possessed of a jazz-like, dogmatical movement, and is pulsing with life, working itself to a higher and higher pitch of communion and ecstasy. God has become merged in everything, the Kingdom of Heaven is running about inside every individual thing in a fluid ubiquity. Whatever arrangements are made for the separate existence of God (such as St. Thomas made), they go down once the religious drums begin to beat. That is, I think, a just account of how the "religious" consciousness realizes itself in most cases — when it is a first-rate, high-powered, religious consciousness. It is that kind of consciousness that we are here combating: and the catholic consciousness is also engaged, from its side, and with its different interests, in a similar attempt. As the catholic consciousness is in reality secular and non-religious, we can, as we have said, fraternize with it where we meet upon this controversial field. And we both can claim, with a considerable show of reason, to be engaged in the defence of God, in whose interest it is that we should be in this sense *secular* — that we should retain our objective hardness, and not be constantly melting and hotly overflowing, that we should find our salvation in being simply what we are, without wishing to disintegrate and invade the Infinite or the mind of Deity.

CHAPTER FOUR

THE OBJECT CONCEIVED AS KING OF
THE PHYSICAL WORLD

THE SUBJECT, IN ITS CAPACITY of soul, ego, or psyche, was dealt with in an earlier chapter, and we will now undertake to do for the *Object* what we have done for the Subject. Strangely enough, its fate has been a similar one; indeed it has turned out to be (in the minds of its critics) a kind of Subject. Mr. Russell accuses Bergson of confusing the Subject and the Object: but Bergson is not the only culprit. Mr. Russell himself is not entirely guiltless of such a confusion, if confusion it be.

We have shown the attack upon the Subject to be one of the ultimate phases of that universal attack upon "Substance," and upon the common-sense of the Schoolmen, or, behind that rationalist body of dogma, upon the beliefs of the Classical World. Indeed with Spengler we have seen this attack developing in the most open and naïf way. He crosses all the t's for us and dots all the i's. We see him arraigning Classical Man in his capacity of *Objective Man* or Plastic Man, and pitting against that sensuous and "popular" figure (with his common-sense, "popular" view) the *Subjective Man* of the Faustian or present period (though that, too, is in its "decline"). We have seen the subjectivism of the "faustian," or modern Western Man, associated fanatically with a deep sense for the reality of *Time* — as against "Space." And the Classical Man was so shallow and "popular," we have been told by Spengler, not only because he based his conception of things upon the immediate and sensuous — the "spatial" — but because he entirely neglected, and seemed to have no sense, indeed, of *Time*. His love of immediate "things" found its counterpart in his love of the "immediate" in "time." He was that creature of the Pure Present so admired by Goethe. The "timelessness" of Classical Man, then, his *objectivity*, his *sensuousness*, his *popular* and *common-sense* view of things, were what pre-eminently distinguished him. This, Spengler further says, was symbolized by his plastic and pictorial pre-eminence. (This "plastic" pre-eminence seems to some extent a superstition of Spengler's, we have said: but there is enough truth in his contrast to make it worthwhile treating it as the entire fact that it actually is not.) Classical Man — that inveterate "spatializer" — was in love with *Plastic*. Modern, Western, "Faustian" man, on the other hand, is pre-eminently interested in *Music*: he spurns and abandons *Plastic*, and all its ways. It is in music that he supremely expresses himself. The Renaissance was a little aberration of his — quite artificial, in any case: "Plastic" got its foot in for a moment quite by accident: Gothic, Western, European, "Faustian" man soon drove it out, and reinstated Music and the gothic yearning for the infinite, the vague, that which has no outline and is innocent of either sense of locality or of any concrete value at all. This spenglerian background is extremely useful to bear in mind if you wish to understand better the far more seemingly abstract notions of the philosophers with whom we now will have to deal.

We say of things or of persons that they are "substantial." Substance in that sense means a quite different thing from "substance" or "substantival" in the philosophic sense. But what we now must understand is that really "substantial" in the physical sense has at present come to be also "substantival." After the destruction of the "thinking Subject," the Object became a "substance" of sorts, and as such is still being attacked: for the Object is not quite extinct yet; we are at present assisting at its demise. That this should come about was inevitable; the "mind" being so entangled with the body, it was difficult to destroy one without impairing the other.

We have shown how extremely easy it would be to assert that the attack upon the Subject was of political origin. Indeed, we have agreed that politics has played an important part in it. But instead of leaving it at that relatively simple and obvious stage of enlightenment, we have attempted to get behind that over-simple statement, and show something of the intricate interplay of politics and science, and to see how really science, in the end, rather than politics, must be regarded as the main revolutionary factor.

Now that we come to the Object, we have to ask ourselves again: Is the attack upon the Object a political disturbance, or is it a movement of the pure intelligence (if such a thing exist)? But here the situation is reversed. Whereas with the Subject it is difficult *not* to believe that we are in the presence of a purely

political phenomenon, in the case of the Object it would be equally hard, at first sight, to see how any *politics* could enter into
the destruction of a *table* or a *chair*. Yet, paradoxical as that must
seem, I believe there is as much political emotion engaged in one
as in the other. So in this case we shall have rather to insist upon
the political element, whereas with the Subject we had to
deprecate that too obvious generalization.

In recent theoretic thought it has been found that ultimately
a *table*, a *chair* or a *handkerchief* becomes as troublesome and
suspect as a "soul" or "psyche."

The traditional belief of common-sense, embodied in the "naïf"
view of the physical world, is really a *picture*. We believe that
we *see* a certain objective reality. This contains stable and substantial objects. When we look at these objects we believe that what
we are perceiving is what we are *seeing*. In reality, of course,
we are conscious of much more than we immediately *see*. For
in looking at an orange lying before us on the table, we are more
or less conscious of its contents, we apprehend it as though we
could see all round it, since from experience we know it is round,
of the same colour and texture, from whatever position it is examined, and so forth. In short, every time we open our eyes we
envelop the world before us, and give it *body*, or its quality of
consisting of *objects*, with our memory. It is memory that gives
that depth and fullness to our present, and makes our abstract,
ideal world of objects for us.

This belief, as I started by saying is, in fact, a picture. And
it is this picture for which the cinematograph of the physics of
"events" is to be substituted. It is to be "taught in schools" (according to Mr. Russell and other enthusiasts); therefore people
are to be trained from infancy to regard the world as a *moving*
picture. In this no "object" would appear, but only the states of
an object. It is sought already to cut down the picture of the
physical world to what we *see*. What we *know* should be excluded. If we want to approximate to the discarded view of the
percipient of common-sense, we must move round the object,
and as far as possible get inside it. With the thousand *successive*
pictures we thus obtain we shall have—only *successively*, nothing
all at once, except a punctual picture and momentary sensation—
the perceptual picture of common-sense. Having walked all
round, picked up, smelt, cut into as many pieces as possible, and
then eaten, the orange, we shall have *successively* reached the

discarded all-at-once *perceptive* (but platonic) picture of common-sense. But thought, perception, and indeed all the *stationary acts* of the observer of "common-sense" or of "naïf" realism, must be turned into movement. We must *move* and *act*, if we wish to apprehend anything, or to have *a thing*, at all. Through having said that all thought is "a movement," this type of professor-of-action will in future exact that we shall move and physically function before we can say that we have "thought" or "seen." And there will, of course, be no need to think at all, or even to see. For the action will *be* the thought, or the vision: just as a thing *is* its successive "effects."

What we are discussing is the philosophy — much more, the fanatical dogma — of *movement*, it is well to remember. The complex that it at present rests upon would be better described as Time-space than Space-time, since Time (in the bergsonian sense) is of its essence, whereas Space is not. It is a world according to the crude or elementary optic sense, and therefore *a picture*. But it is a flat world: it is one of successive, flat, images or impressions. And, further, these images or impressions are, as far as possible, naked and simple, direct, sensations, unassociated with any component of memory.

Now you will be in a position to approach more nearly to the contrast that it is essential to seize. It is a *flat* world, it is almost also a world of looking-glass images. In this connection I will repeat the significant words of the distinguished Professor of Movement already cited: they are in his conclusion to a long argument setting forth the pros and cons of this *central* or *systematic* point of view. For all his labours he finds nothing more decisive than this to say against even such a disreputable thing as the Pure Ego.

I think that it (the theory of the "mental event") would have no particular advantage over the Pure Ego theory if we were confined to the psychology of normal human minds. But it does seem to have great advantages over the Pure Ego theory where we are concerned with the facts of abnormal and supernormal psychology: just as the corresponding theory about material substances has very great advantages where we are concerned with abnormal physical facts, such as mirror-images.

The ego or "mind" has been displaced in favour of a movement group, largely on account of data peculiar to the demented: and parallel to that the perceptual object has given place to a mirror-image. This very honest professor is full of such illuminating things as this rapprochement of the facts of dual personality, freudian neuroses, with the reality of sensa — that is to say, of the psychologically deluded with the physically delusive.

Virtually a visual (but a flat) world of successive *images* of the type seen in a mirror is to be substituted as the ideal equivalent (if there were to be an equivalent it would be that) of the static mnemo-sensational contemplation of the "object." Whether you moved round the object or the object round you would be immaterial, and indeed meaningless: but movement there must be. This insistence upon succession does, although the field is a visual one, approach this theory much more to the art of music, for instance, than to the art of painting, or the pictorial, visual, arts. A world of motion is a world of music, if anything. No visual artist would ever have imagined (or had he imagined, he would have turned in horror from) such a world as the bergsonian, relativist world. The fact that Einstein comes from the country of music may not be without significance, though it is well to be on your guard against racial interpretations, as we have said.

By means of that *series* of direct, flat (or not-memory-inflated) impressions, you arrive at reality in the following manner: *each* impression, or visual sensum, fragment as it is, and unassisted by "thought" — little temporal *tabula rasa* — is more *real* in one sense than the ideal rounded perceptual object. It gains in sensational and temporal intensity what it loses in completeness. Out of the whole *movement* or *series* blossoms "the thing": but it is in no *one* movement, it is spread out time-wise, and is *seen* as it were as time-movement, rather than as a spatial and static "thing." In space *alone* it is no longer allowed at all to exist except on a very degraded and naïf plane, or at best as Time pretending to be Space.

Taking the object as *cause*, the same process is illustrated in causation. A thing's appearances, not itself, are the reality: so the effect, not the cause, *is* the reality. We call an effect an "event," of course, to square with Time's rôle in the transaction. "A piece of matter . . . is the collection of all those correlated particulars which would normally be regarded as its appearances or effects in different places." That is Mr. Russell. Then, as far as causation is concerned, in the latest philosophy of the subject (Whitehead, for instance) there is the fatal intrusion of *Everything*, at any moment and at any point. Every *possibility* competes as a "cause" with what we consider the proximate cause;

so that no cause can ever really claim an effect. That is the doctrine of *"event"*-fact, as it could be called. It is the effect that matters: the cause is immaterial. Any possible cause will do. What trips up the cause and effect of common-sense is that fatal intrusion of the *Everything*. Without it it is impossible to calculate, except approximately. The existence of this new myth, the Everything, everywhere, is a significant arrival. Alexander is directly responsible for it in its contemporary philosophic incarnation.

For Alexander there is "No thing so concrete as you, a person, except the universe itself: between you and that are all the categories, less real than you." So it is not to be wondered at that you and the Universe should "get together" fairly often, or even that you should be said to be "inseparable."

The object, the "perceptual object of common-sense," is *in practice* what this universal Immanence, à la Alexander, is in theory. The following passage will further establish, I hope, what I wish to make clear:

> . . . An ordinary perceptual object, like a penny, as understood by common-sense, is really a *compositum* consisting of a number of correlated constituent objects of various kinds, all occupying a place in the movement-continuum. . . . The compositeness of a perceptual object infects the notion of "its" duration with an incurable vagueness. We can make accurate statements about the durations of its constituents, and we can make accurate statements about the durations of the correlated scientific objects, but the perceptual object of common-sense is too much a mixture of non-homogeneous constituents to be worth treating very seriously as a whole.

From this passage you will be able to obtain some idea of the position of the *object* — or as described here, the "perceptual object of common-sense," in the orthodox philosophical system ensuing from Relativity. What is the matter with it from the point of view of that system, as you see in the statement I have just quoted, is that it possesses a certain timelessness, which it shares with the percipient. Perception, indeed, has no "date," only *sensation* has that. Thus, for accurate dating, perception has in a sense to be abandoned in favour of sensation; or this at least must, schematically, be the tendency. Perception, with its element of timelessness, has, in conjunction with that, a detestable *repose*. Perception, in short, smacks of contemplation, it suggests leisure: only *sensation* guarantees *action*, and a full consciousness that "time is money" and that leisure is made for masters, not for men, or for the old bad world of Authority, not the good new world of alleged mass-rule (to give this concept its political affiliations).

That we can no more ever *see* a "perceptual object" (that is what we habitually suppose that we are looking at) than we can see a mathematical point, is true enough. But the system of the "percept" has been for unnumbered years the material of our life. We have overridden time to the extent of bestowing upon objects a certain timelessness. We and they have existed in a, to some extent, timeless world, in which we possessed these objects, in our fastness of memory, like gods. That is perhaps our, and their, offence. While we were looking at the front of a house, if we had ever seen its back we saw that back along with the front, as though we were in two places at once, and hence two times. And our infinite temporal and spatial reduplication of ourselves, this long-stretched-out chain existing all-at-once, was our *perceptual self*, which to some extent was a timeless self. It is by way of the mystery of memory, of course, that we reached this timelessness.

Appearances, in the philosophic theory of the physics of "events," are held to be a peculiar kind of objects. That is Broad's description: and his view of the value of the sensum is general among the systematic thinkers working in agreement with Relativity, and translating its results into philosophic formulae. It is purely a "sensationalist" thought: it transports "reality" away from the central object, which it reduces to the status of a discredited and unknowable thing-in-itself, and bestows it upon its immediate sensational appearances: the succession of which, in its spatio-temporal history, is *it*.

I will take the exposition of these doctrines a step further, still using the excellently lucid text of Mr. Broad. "Whenever a penny looks to me elliptical, what really happens is that I am aware of an object which is, in fact, elliptical. . . . When I look at a penny from the side, what happens is this: I have a sensation, whose object is an elliptical, brown sensum: and this sensum is related in some specially intimate way to a certain round physical object, viz. the penny." The elliptical "sensum," that is the appearance of the penny from the side, is as real as the round "sensum" of the penny, its appearance if we are looking down on it. Common-sense supposes that a penny keeps its shape and size as we move about, while the "sensa," or complex of appearances, of the penny alters. But the believer in the "reality" of the sensum is not of that way of thinking: for he says one and the same thing cannot, at the same time, and in the same sense, be round and elliptical.

This theory again is put forward in the form of three stages in exactitude, in this sensing of the side of the penny. The *first* stage would be the *perceptual* stage. *We see a penny.* The *second* is the stricter sense in which we see one side of a penny. The *third* stage, and presumably the best, is that in which *we see only a brown elliptical sensum.* That is the stage that blossoms, for this theory, in the Theory of Sensa. It is of the nature of the cartesian return to *naked, direct,* vision. It implies to some extent the *tabula rasa.* It is temperamentally, and in time, still more nearly affiliated with Bergson's plunge into the sensational flux, or with Alexander's more recent bergsonist doctrine of "emergence."

For the example that is put forward to illustrate the difference between the *sensing of the sensum* and the perceiving *of a physical object,* is this. In reading a book what we notice is the *meaning of the printed words: not* the peculiarities of the print or paper. We "perceive," that is; we do not "sense." With all of the external world it is the same. Objects, for us, in the course of our daily perceptual abstraction of them, are never really looked at at all, never *directly sensed.* The "sensa" that comes out to us from physical objects — or which represent to us what we believe to be a physical object — we never really *see* at all: they are signs that come and go, assuring us that all is well with our drove of "objects," or warning us that all is not well with them, as the case may be.

The sensa-world is a world of the Unconscious or automatic in the sense, and to the extent, indicated above. It is the world of things that, in the usual way, we do not explicitly notice, which we *repress* and push down and away, out of sight, and yet which throng our sense-field. They are the stream of sensations that pour in (*the stream of unconsciousness* would be a better way of putting James' *stream of consciousness*). For we are not conscious of this inrush, but only of its accommodation to the waiting forms of cognition, the "physical objects" that is feeds — our static drove within.

As much as Bergson's, because it *is* Bergson in the sense of being an integral part of the peculiar and clearly hall-marked movement of which he is the most typical, now the classical, ornament — that is a philosophy of sensation, we will again point out. It is this *stream of the Unconscious* — which is the stream of incoming sensa — which is so nearly the incoming stream of what are usually called "sensations" that we can use it in spite of any fine quibbling that may go on about it — into which we are once more invited to plunge.

Both Einstein and Bergson are river officials of the great River Flux, of its conservancy staff: they both, in different ways, administer it.

The intensity, nakedness, *reality* of the immediate sensation, even though it gives you no ideal *whole*, though it is dogmatically a creature of the moment, even though it gives you the "objects" of life only as strictly experienced *in Time*; evanescent, flashing and momentary; not even existing outside of their proper time, ideally having no prolongations in memory, confined to the "continuous present" of their temporal appearance: consumed (and immediately evacuated) as "events": one with *action*, incompatible with reflection, impossible of contemplation — the *sensation* (in spite of these peculiarities) is nevertheless, is it not? *the real thing.*

We have now, with all necessary insistence, established, I think, the natural applications of this cult. But there is still the very interesting testimony afforded by the detailed working-out of the Theory of Sensa to be dealt with. To that we will now address ourselves.

That theory admits that all its assumptions are based on optical illusions, the phenomena of distorting media, and the "physically" abnormal or seldom experienced; just as psychoanalysis is founded upon the curiosities of the clinic. Physically these philosophic theories are the exact counterpart of the psychology of the freudian. But imported into the centre of them are also a set of astronomical curiosities. For instance, one of the key-illustrations to show the credibility of "sensa" — the new specifically optical "object" — is the fact that, owing to the immense distances separating us from many of the stars, the star's light that reaches us today may be the light of a world now dead. Hence the point of light that we see is a sort of apparition. The nearest thing that we have to this in our daily experience is provided by sound. We could no doubt arrange an experiment by which we could hear a distant event *after* we had seen the actors in it blown up. It is out of these phenomena that a kind of world of apparitions is being constructed.

Returning to the penny, the philosophical penny we have been considering, we find that we are asked to believe that there is brownness without shape in "me," and round shape without colour out there where the penny is, and yet that in some mysterious way the shapeless brownness "in me" is projected into the round contour of the penny "out there." To solve this difficulty we have the theory of the "sensum." The "brownness," the colour, of the mind, on the one side, and the "shape of the object," on the other, are given to a third hypothetic unit: namely, the "sensum." Neither "object" nor "mind" can exist any longer so fully or independently as before, of course, although they still remain in the background, as subordinate, but rather neglected, "problems." They both impoverish themselves for their strange child, the "sensum." But if they both lose, the "object" loses most. So a *mental* world of some sort, however mixed and degenerate a one, is indicated from the start.

What is not said, this philosopher sometimes claims, is that the perceptual object is "unreal." It is only an "unsuitable unit for scientific purposes." However, let us see what ultimately happens with him, to the "object." Now first of all solidity has somehow to be got into the "sensum-object"; and it *must*, for that purpose, be got off the retina, and back into the brain: which indeed is what happens in this theory. But once in the brain, it is in touch with "tactual traces." But these traces of other "objects," of the other senses of touch or of smell, merely co-operate with the visual matter thrown back from the retinal stimulus. So disunity is saved! We have not dropped into a unity of the combined senses, though we seemed perilously near it. *The visual ascendancy is saved* — only by a few words, on a piece of paper. "Merely co-operates" — that is all that is required.

The perceptual object of common-sense, then, is divided up into (1) itself, the perceptual object; (2) the "scientific object" (Professor Whitehead's "object"), that is the "object" as conceived by science, a multitude of colourless particles, moving about at extreme velocities; (3) the "optical object" or "sensum." Now, for this theory, none of these objects are, ultimately, and by themselves, real. Each is a separate, and often contradictory, reality. Science says that a "penny" is an electronic mass of colourless particles, moving about at very high speeds. If all the inhabitants of a substantial town, such as Nottingham, said that a penny was a brown balloon, the size of the moon, then there would be a "nottingham object" as well, provided there were a respectable amount of agreement. Both science and common-sense, however, believe certainly, at the moment, that there is a penny that is a perceptible brown penny, and that the colourless particles are a part of that brown penny, just as the King's head is a part of it. This is absurd. No: the perceptual penny is not one homogeneous object, but is a complex of connected constituent objects, all occupying a place in the movement-continuum. There is the *scientific penny*, the *perceptual penny*, the *optical penny*, or any other penny believed in by a certain number of people. The penny of common-sense is, however, a very sophisticated affair indeed compared with the optical penny. The latter is a slice of life, cut off by the most innocent possible eye, a child's for preference. The penny of science is the most original of all of them; it is equally real, though not more so: and very different indeed from the others. But there is no central absolute round, brown, penny. Sometimes it is colourless, sometimes brown, or another colour, sometimes round, sometimes elliptical. *Altogether*, acting in unison, as in "common-sense" (which term describes just that sense-unity), our senses could and do agree on *one* penny. But isolate them, and you at once get a half-dozen different sorts. None of these various sorts pretend to the reality and completeness of the "perceptual" penny. Each is only true at a certain moment, in a certain place. It is not really a "penny" at all: but then there is no penny in reality: for the nearest effort at a "penny," the "perceptual" penny, is "too vague for it to be worth while to take any notice of."

The retinal *flatness* has certainly not been got out of his "optical object" or "sensum" by this philosopher. And movement has been substituted for the missing dimension. The "object" in short is as broken up or distorted in the medium of Time as by movement. The most characteristic part of the theory is where the "sensum" is a stick seen partly in water, and so appearing *bent*. According to this theory it, of course, *is* bent. Similar to this is the appearance of the houses on the other side of the road to the time-philosopher, gazing out of his window, but through a very imperfect pane of glass; they appear, as he slowly turns his head, *to be moving about*. Well, for him they *are* moving about. There are no real houses that are still: there are only at that moment moving houses in the world. His "sensum" is as good an object as "they" (whatever they may be) any day of the week. So the houses not only appear to move, but they do in fact move. The medium imparts *movement*. What these illustrations reach is *the moving thing*, which is what is required. For the *bent stick* is an example of a sort of frozen *movement*. The appearance of the movement in the houses produced by the glass is the old Relativity illustration of the two trains — "which is moving?" — in another connection. A Maskelyne and Devant illusion (duly explained beforehand and everyone knowing exactly how he came to be fooled) would be a more complicated example of the same sort of thing. For it would be real — since it appeared real. As most of Maskelyne's illusions are effected by arrangements of looking-glasses, they would very well illustrate this theory, which is almost entirely based on the experiences of a looking-glass world. It is a world in which the *image* comes to life, and the picture, under suitable conditions, moves and lives inside its frame.

I now come to one of the most critical points in any argument raised against the philosophy of Time-space or of the Flux. It will be recalled that at the start I intimated that this essay was to be an attempt to provide something in the nature of a *philosophy of the eye*. That description of it in the present connection, however, it could be claimed, is the opposite of the truth. Or rather, *it would be the opposite of the truth if you wish to isolate the Eye*. For it is against that isolation that we contend. On the other hand, if by "philosophy of the eye" is meant that we wish to repose, and materially to repose, in the crowning human sense, the visual sense; and if it meant that we *refuse* (closing ourselves in with our images and sensa) to retire into the abstraction and darkness of an aural and tactile world, then it is true that our philosophy attaches itself to that concrete and radiant reality of the optic sense. That sensation of overwhelming *reality* which vision alone gives is the reality of "common-sense," as it is the reality we inherit from pagan antiquity. And it is indeed on that "reality" that I am basing all I say. But "a philosophy of the eye" would be a description diametrically opposed to the truth, if it were to be the expression of our technical position in this phase of the argument. Again, let me quote from the same misguided but scrupulous investigator. "Nearly all," he says, "the *general concepts* that we use in dealing with space, *e.g.* distance, direction, place, shape, etc. come from *Sight*: whilst the notion of *one* Space and the *particular quantitative values* which these general concepts assume in special cases are due mainly to touch and to movement." Or, quoting Mr. Russell: "As physics has advanced, it has appeared more and more that sight is less misleading than touch as a source of fundamental notions about matter."

This capital point has to be seized hold of very firmly by the student of the time-doctrine. For the theories supported by these philosophers — both Mr. Broad and Mr. Russell offer us varieties of the one great philosophy of the time-school — *for them touch is the enemy, not sight.* It is in every instance, to substantiate their claims, *touch* that has to be got around — and they tend more and more to attribute a less conditioned reality to sight.

Why this should be is not far to seek. The apparitions of the *visual* sense — such as your image in a concave mirror, or the distortions produced by any medium, such as water or glass — can only be exorcized by *touch.* If you *touch* the thing you *see* in the mirror, you at once find it to be "unreal." Or if you do what we all do in our everyday perceptive experiences, associate the experiences of sensations of touch with those of sight (making *one* corrected picture of these, in some cases, contradictory, senses), you can no longer attribute the "reality" that is required by these philosophers to all the images of sight. So *their* truth is entirely built upon the facts of the visual sense, but that sense in isolation; and in that special and narrow way their doctrine could claim, no doubt, to be a visual philosophy more technically than the body of criticism that is being brought against it here.

It may be useful, in this place, as well, to add that the idea of *force* derives from the sense of touch, it is generally supposed. This idea astronomical mathematics, being visual, was naturally led to abandon. Again, the eye is, in the sense in which we are considering it, the *private* organ: the hand the *public* one. The eye estranges and particularizes more than the sense of touch. Its images are of a confusing vivacity, and its renderings are readily more subjective. The notion of *one* Space, they say, is due to the sense of "touch": and space is the "timeless" idea. Space is the "public" idea. And in order to be "timeless," and to be "public," it must be *one.*

It is our contention here that *it is because of the subjective disunity due to the separation, or separate treatment, of the senses, principally of sight and of touch, that the external disunity has been achieved.* It is but another case of the *morcellement* of the *one* personality, in this case into a tactile-observer on the one hand and a visual-observer on the other, giving different

renderings of the same thing. Its results must be the disintegration, finally, of any "public" thing at all. Mr. Russell is quite correct when he says that from Relativity some form of berkeleyan
idealism must ensue. It has already ensued. Those who, committed to that theory, argue against this, or seek to give it another
direction, like Broad, are providing arguments against their own
principles all the time. However true it may be that the einsteinian
"Observer" might just as well be a photographic plate as a human
brain, nevertheless the cutting up of the ideal, public, *one*, exterior, reality of human tradition, into manifold spaces and times,
leads to a fundamental "subjectivity" of one sort or the other.
And we would emphasize that our ideal, objective, world, which
was wrought into a unity — the common ground of imaginative
reality on which we all meet — is being destroyed in favour of
a fastidious egoism, based on a disintegration of the complex unit
of the senses, and a granting of unique privileges to vision, in
its raw, immediate and sensational sense.

The conceding of "reality" to appearances is a thing that, if accepted, must lead to results very different from what the authors
of that procedure intend. For once you begin conceding "reality"
to physical appearances, where do you propose to stop? There
is one overwhelming impression of reality that many of us receive,
for instance: that is the impression of the reality of our personal
life. When you analyse the notion of the "self," it is true, it falls
to pieces. But the means you use to effect this disintegration are
of the same nature as those you would employ to demonstrate
the unreality of an optical illusion.

The impression of reality you receive from within has this
peculiarity — namely, that the illusion in this case is yourself. If
this is an illusion it is certainly the arch-illusion, the ground and
condition of all others. And it is an indestructible one so long
as you live, is intact and untroubled at the termination of any
analysis: for it is *it* that has been employed in this curious occupation all the while, of necessity. So as a rival to the optical
apparitions we have so far been considering, it is well placed to
make its particular "reality" felt, at least. These regions, I am
aware, are guarded over by the hideous problem of self-evidence
and subjective truth: but if we stopped to settle accounts with
every traditional dragon that we encountered, we should pro-
long this essay indefinitely.

In the case of the personality, if you consider the exterior world as a mirror world, you are *inside the image in the mirror*: you do not have to touch it; it is a thing, obviously, that can be far more potently verified than by touch or by physical displacement. The "objects" that are its originals exist merely for it. It is *they* that are the apparitions. It is their spatio-temporal reality that are the solid projections as it were of this *one*, immaterial thing. Looked at in that way, to be coloured and to be extended is, conversely in this connection, to be unreal. Messrs. Maskelyne and Devant, or many other competent illusionists, are able to provide you with an *appearance*, which your eyes swear to you is true. No illusionist, however, is able to provide anyone with the illusion of a self: or rather, since everyone possesses a self, it would in that case be *a disappearing trick*: and no illusionist, of the bluff "behaviour" type or of any other, is able to convince the self who is so much behind the scenes when that particular trick is staged, that it is not there, or to lock it into any of the spatio-temporal, infinitely-divided compartments provided for "selves" in the contemporary psychologic laboratories. The only truly magical thing would be if the "self" could really be given to the psycho-conjuror to cut up. Then if each piece were put into a separate glass receptacle, not only the same self, but the whole self, would be found staring at the spectator out of each of its prisons.

As an epigraph for this part of my essay I have used a passage from a book by Mr. Russell. This is it:

Then there are other things, which seem material, and yet present almost no permanence or rigidity. Breath, smoke, clouds are examples of such things — and so, in a lesser degree, are ice and snow; rivers and seas, though fairly permanent, are not in any degree rigid. Breath, smoke, clouds, and generally things that can be seen but not touched, were thought to be hardly real; to this day the usual mark of a ghost is that it can be seen but not touched. (*Our Knowledge of the External World*. Lecture iv.)

That, and the lecture from which it is taken, I will now examine, and so conclude this part of my argument.

This book of Mr. Russell's presents what I have called the time-view in all its pristine brilliance and naïveté. It is the fruit of the early impact of the full time-thought upon Mr. Russell's highly receptive and interesting mind. At present the novelty has worn off a little, I think, and Mr. Russell is a man who depends a great deal upon that: political considerations are creeping in, very naturally confusing and discouraging. But this book, written in 1914 and since then revised (I have been using the 1926 edition), is one of the best of his books, I should say, and no one who reads it can help admiring the vigour, integrity and charm of this fine philosophic intelligence. (As to Mr. Russell's political thought, of course, the less said the better: and here we can ignore that altogether.)

In the chapter from which I have quoted Mr. Russell is considering the "apparent difference between matter as it appears in physics, and things as they appear in sensation." The world of "common-sense," and its "things," and the abstract world of physical theory, *appear* to contradict each other, he says. Like Professor Whitehead, Mr. Russell sets out to reconcile and rationally marry these two disparate conceptions. The "materialist" of Professor Whitehead is also the villain of this piece. "Men of science, for the most part, are willing to condemn immediate data as merely 'subjective,' while yet maintaining the truth of the physics inferred from those data." That will not do, Mr. Russell says. To justify such an attitude "matter" would have to be shown as "a logical construction from sense-data." Hence it is necessary "to find some way of bridging the gulf between the world of physics and the world of sense." That is the problem with which Mr. Russell is here dealing.

Like Professor Whitehead he is, of course, a convert from "materialism," which merely means that he is a convert from a very barren, romantically-"scientific," matter-of-fact attitude, to something or other, which we must define. So the point is, a convert to *what*? In my view the old romance and, for these philosophers, inspiration of the hard-as-nuts, matter-of-fact, straight-Jane-and-no-nonsense, weakest-go-to-the-wall, "impersonal" attitude of the old-fashioned materialist attitude is still theirs. They are converts to a "new materialism," worse than the last: an idealo-materialism. The bridge that we here witness Mr. Russell building (as he tells us, indeed, by means of the "mathematical knowledge required" for such an engineering feat) over the gulf that separates the world of physics from the world of sense, is a very *material* bridge indeed. When you stand back and examine it from a distance, it looks like a business-like iron structure built between two clouds, with its girders thrust into the waves of an exceedingly deep ocean. In his *Analysis of Mind* he writes (as quoted elsewhere):

> When we are speaking of matter, it will seem as if we were inclining to idealism; when we are speaking of mind, it will seem as if we were inclining to materialism. Neither is the truth. Our world is to be constructed out of . . . "neutral" entities.

This "neutral" stuff of Mr. Russell's world is effectively the same as that of Professor Alexander and Professor Whitehead. It is a more "primitive" thing, like "a common ancestor": this *one* primeval stuff from which "mind" and "matter" emerge, and are then separated out. We are in the presence, that is, of pure evolutionist theory. Having, once more, made sure of our bearings, we can proceed to an examination of the text. I will follow his argument for a little in the order he gives it in his lecture, commenting *pari passu*.

Let us begin, he says, with a description of the two contrasted worlds. First, we take the world of physics. ("The world of pure sense [has] become strange and difficult to rediscover": that is why.) But the world of physics started from the "common-sense" world—that of "belief in fairly permanent and rigid bodies—tables and chairs, stones, mountains, etc."

The common-sense world of objects was, however, "a piece of audacious metaphysical theorizing." The table that was there, whether we looked at it or not, we owe to a "savage ancestor in some very remote prehistoric epoch." This wild person, dreaming in his cave, constructed the "world of common-sense" we inherit and currently use. He imagined a mountain and a tree that *were always there.*

"Matter" must be, if anything, we have been told, "a logical construction from sense-data." This primitive metaphysician evolved for us the logical world of common-sense, and that first immense theoretic structure which resulted ultimately *in the belief in the existence of objects without the mind*, a capital "error" for Berkeley.

Before proceeding, I may say at once that I regard this picture of the antediluvian metaphysician—of the "savage ancestor" in the "very remote prehistoric epoch"—as a "fake antique."

Mr. Russell goes on to say that even tables, chairs, stones and mountains, "are not *quite* permanent and rigid." They are all, however solid, susceptible of change—by accident, frost, earthquake, etc. Then comes the passage I started by quoting. "Breath, smoke, clouds, and generally things that can be *seen* but *not touched*, were thought to be hardly real; to this day *the usual mark of a ghost is that it can be seen but not touched.*"

No one will dispute that we do not call the policeman in the street, or the statue of Shakespeare in Leicester Square, a *ghost*; and that is among other things because we can, if necessary, *touch* as well as *see* them. If the police-constable, or the statue, were composed of smoke, and we could see things through him, we should then, "to this day," describe him as a phantom. (The "to this day," is one of the revelatory signs to be noted in the language of this exposition.) The only question is whether we are wrong in this discrimination between "the ghost" and "the reality," in our notion as what (for us — for whom else should we be discriminating?) is *intangible* and so "hardly real," and what is *tangible*, and so "real." Further, whether the primitive intelligence was being quite idiotic or not in providing us with these categories; whether that intelligence was being highly "metaphysical," or quite natural. (And, of course, whichever is your "natural," then the opposite is likely to appear highly metaphysical and unnecessarily ingenious. It resolves itself, from that side, into what is your "natural," what your norm or standard is.)

The post-relativist (for me highly "metaphysical") standpoint, that makes "the world of pure sense . . . strange and difficult to rediscover," that regards "common-sense" as an "audacious" theoretic system, is the type of thinking that Berkeley described as the sign of "a mind . . . debauched by learning." For me that is not natural; the natural view for me is that (according to Mr. Russell) "audacious metaphysical theory" of the cave-man.

My main accusation against Mr. Russell is not that he is an ill-disposed man in any way, on the contrary, but that his mind is that of an excited and rather sentimental amateur, bursting for mild "sensations," for things that are "amusing" and that will surprise his intelligence into activity. The things he supports are always in the nature of what Berkeley called *difficiles nugae*. He is a sort of born entertainer: and his entertainer's instinct has always led him to take the "entertaining" or "exciting" side in the debate.

Berkeley, in his attack upon the mathematician and his dupes, made that criticism (in favour of common-sense, of the *concrete*, and against the idea-mongers of an *intensive abstraction* of his time) in such a masterly way, that, even if it is only a few lines, it is always worth quoting him:

The opinion of the pure and intellectual nature of numbers in abstract, hath . . . set a price on the most trifling numerical speculations, which in practice are of no use, but serve only for amusement; and hath therefore so far infected the minds of some, that they have dreamt of mighty mysteries involved in numbers, and attempted the explication of natural things by them. But if we inquire into our own thoughts, and consider what hath been premised, we may perhaps entertain a low opinion of those high flights and abstractions, and look on all inquiries about numbers, only as so many *difficiles nugae* so far as they are not subservient to practice, and promote the benefit of life.

Or again (in discussing the problem of the Infinite) Berkeley refers to "all those amusing geometrical paradoxes, which have such a direct repugnancy to the plain common-sense of mankind, and are admitted with so much reluctance into a mind not yet debauched by learning." . . . "Of those unnatural notions," he says, "it is impossible [that such a notion] should ever gain the assent of any reasonable creature, who is not brought to it by gentle and slow degrees, as a converted gentile to the belief of trans-substantiation."

That Berkeley discerned the main principle working on behalf of the "amusing geometrical" paradoxicality at which he struck, is shown by his constant use of the word "amusing" and "amusement." And "amusement" is also the word that must come most often into any analysis of the springs of such an intelligence as that of Mr. Russell.

I think that no reader able to free his mind of certain prejudices can fail to detect in reading these chapters of Mr. Russell's book an abnormal irritability where "the entity" is concerned. At last he must, I think, say to himself that this "austere," "scientific," dislike of the entity conceals some fanatical impulse much less truly "scientific" than it is something else, which has introduced itself into the author's mind perhaps without his knowledge.

The disintegration of the world-picture of "common-sense" effected by the introduction of private and subjective time-systems, by the breaking up of the composite space of the assembled senses into an independent space of touch, a space of sight, a visceral space, and so forth: the conversion of "the thing" into a series of discrete apparitions — all this comprehensive and meticulous attack upon the very basis of "common-sense" (the term used in philosophy for the ordered picture of the classic world, and equally the instinctive picture we inherit from untold generations of men) is as a spectacle impressive at first, no doubt, but it does not seem to bear the mark of a truth-telling or veridical passion, so much as a romantic and fanatical impulse of some description.

I will take a few of the statements that suggest these conclusions, though it is impossible here to go in great detail into the arguments.

Why should we suppose that, when ice melts, the water which replaces it is the same thing in a new form? . . . What we really know is that, under certain conditions of temperature, the appearance we call ice is replaced by the appearance we call water. We can give laws according to which the one appearance will be succeeded by the other, but there is no reason except prejudice for regarding both as appearances of the same substance.

But what does common-sense mean when it refers to the water as *one* substance, or one "thing," an "entity"; a pond of water, for example? Nothing, surely, so very much more than Mr. Russell's or Professor Whitehead's reformed man-of-science would mean with his "appearances." A "thing," says common-sense, that occupies a certain place, is contained in a certain fashion and prevented from breaking up or running away; it becomes frozen when it is "water," that is, becomes "ice," when the temperature falls below a certain point. There is no particular "entity" here.

To make a pond of ice a quite *different* thing (for an 'appearance" is still in popular language a "thing") from the pond of water, seems more complicated and elaborate, and so hardly more "scientific."

The "conception of matter" (that is the non-organic theory of a constant *dead* environment for the processes of organic life) gives in all important respects identical results to those of "revolutionary modern physics." From that point of view the whole argument is much ado about nothing. Where the great change occurs, or where it is sought to make it occur, is in our heads, only. It is our attitude to the external world that it is proposed to modify, not the external world itself, of "materialist" practice, for that is impossible. *It is art or metaphysics that is in question, rather than fact or natural science.* In the external world itself there is no change.

The external world has been for several centuries of the modern era ordered and investigated upon the basis of the "material" conception: it is upon calculations based upon that conception that we have arrived at all our verifiable knowledge of the external world. Far from blaming the men engaged in that work for not being metaphysicians, there is every reason to be thankful that they were not.

Water freezes just the same, and the "matter" involved remains of constant volume, whether you call it water and frozen-water, or whether you call it two separate apparitions, named "water" and "ice" respectively (where "ice" is one thing and "water" quite another). This Mr. Russell naturally admits. "It is only necessary," he says, "to take our ordinary common-sense statements and reword them without the assumption of *permanent* substance." It is a "word" merely that is being attacked: but behind that word, or system of words, there is a whole conception of things that is largely misinterpreted by the organic theorists. Above I have shown how the supposed "entity" of common-sense where the water is concerned is made much more formidable and precise than in fact it is. So with most of the "entities" that come up for execution.

Mr. Russell employs another illustration:

. . . given any sensible appearance, there will usually be . . . a continuous series of appearances . . . leading on . . . to the new appearances which common-sense regards as those of the same thing. Thus a thing may be defined as a certain series of appearances . . . Consider, say, a wall-paper which fades in the course of years. It is an effort not to conceive of it as one "thing" whose colour is slightly different at one time from what it is at another. But what do we really *know* about it? . . . the assumption that there is a constant entity, the wall-paper, which "has" these various colours at various times, is a piece of gratuitous metaphysics.

The "what do we *know*" introduces the principle of "verifiability" and of "truth." It is on the distinction between "verifiability" and "truth" that all relativist or phenomenalist philosophy is constructed. At all events, the "wall-paper" must cease to be a "constant entity"; it becomes "a series of its aspects" (though the "its" in this definition of Mr. Russell's leaves all the "entity" of the wall-paper intact, I am afraid.) Having, however, eliminated this hated "entity" — the wall-paper — Mr. Russell tells us that *everything will then proceed as before:* whatever was verifiable is unchanged": only our "language" has been changed, that is all, and the "metaphysical assumption of *permanence*" has been guarded against. For working purposes nothing has been altered. We then "proceed as before."

But what is this supposed metaphysical construction of common-sense, after all, that is supposed to have made the wall-paper into an "entity" of detestable "permanence"? All people know that the wall-paper on their wall will fade: they all know it is a piece of paper stamped with various coloured patterns at a factory: and that the paper itself comes from another factory where it is made out of rags or pulp, and so forth. It has just as much "permanence" ascribed to it by common-sense as indeed it is likely to have. There it is, after all, day after day, and for a considerable time, although gradually becoming a little less sharp and full-blooded. It *is* "permanent" in the sense in which we metaphysicians of the mere world of "common-sense" mean permanent. Mr. Russell ascribes meanings to us, however, that have never entered our heads. Our "things" are by no means so absolutist or time-defying as they are supposed to be by the "entity"-destroyer.

Mr. Russell admits, of course, that the relativist picture is apt to be much more complicated than that of common-sense or of materialist science. "Very often the resulting statement," he says, "is much more complicated and difficult than one which, like common-sense and most philosophy, assumes hypothetical entities there is no good reason to believe in." My reply has been that the loss in simplicity is not compensated in any way by the novelty of the relativist system: and, also, that the "hypothetical entities" assumed are usually no more than can be verified, and that there is every reason to believe in them on the basis of the general apprehension of common-sense.

But let us go with Mr. Russell a step further in his elucidation of his *serial* picture of "the thing." The wall-paper fixed upon the wall in January is *one* "appearance"; the wall-paper next December (however imperceptible the change) is *another* and an absolutely distinct "appearance"; causally related to the first, but otherwise independent. But an "appearance" is, it must be remembered, an "event" in space-time doctrine. It is a sort of flock of spatial apparitions made up of pure instantaneous sensations, enclosed in a temporal pen or corral.

Now, actually as an *object* directly experienced, in isolation, the two wall-papers (of January and of December) are almost identical: so nearly so that it would be symptomatic of an almost demented anti-absolutist fussiness to wish to suppress this identity. What, then, is the actual rationale behind this insistence upon a rigid differentiation between these various "aspects" of the wall-paper? It is this. *What really is at stake is the time-picture.* Only by this insistence upon an absolute dissociation of the wall-paper of January from the wall-paper of the following December, can the full significance of its time-relations be got out of it or got into it. Its "integrity" as a thing would make that impossible. It is because it is now to be regarded not as a spatial object, but as a *temporal succession of objects.* It is the time-obsession in Space-time that exacts a "plurality of things" in place of one "thing." To common-sense, looking at it "spatially," it looks just the same wall-paper. But the relativist (in this case Mr. Russell) whose office it is to "take Time seriously," and see that the full dignity of Time is upheld and ceremoniously guarded, bounds forward with an inquisitorial fury, a time-serving zeal, and pointing at the piece of wall-paper exclaims: "Can't you see how *different* it is? Can't you see that it is no longer the same wall-paper at all?" The eyes of that "sense" we have inherited from our savage Past, metaphysical or otherwise, refuse to conform to this view of the wall-paper. No, for common-sense it is the *same* wall-paper. It is a simple sense that knows nothing about time-series, temporal-"enclosures," "event"-groups, and so on. It is not a sense that, as Berkeley would say, has been "debauched with learning." Else, like Mr. Russell, it would *see* anything it was *told to see.* As it is, it sees, quite simply, what is there. The relativist, however, now turns on it passionately, and overwhelms it with a disobliging scorn.

It should not be difficult for anyone to grasp what has happened in this instance: and it is an exceedingly important point. The wall-paper of common-sense is being treated "organically" in this doctrine of "organic mechanism." It becomes a wall-paper with a soul, when made into an organic thing. For in an important respect the *Time* at stake is psychological. Beyond that, it is really the integrity of a "soul," or of a "mind," that is being envisaged. The objection to the "entity" in the wall-paper of common-sense is an irritable reflection of the disputes of Psychology that have resulted in the elimination of the "mind," "soul," or "psyche." So the "object" is suffering for the sins of the "subject."

Time does not lay its hand on wall-papers to the extent that could be wished, sometimes for a couple of years, if the wall-paper is a good one. You would not know, looking at it with the unaided senses, that the wall-paper was in *Time* at all. Here is the secret spring of this whole theory. If the wall-paper is allowed to be just the wall-paper of "common-sense," the conditions of Time-theory are not satisfied. That is why this simple object hanging on our walls has to be turned into a very complex temporal "event"-series of discrete and rigidly dissociated "appearances."

I have said that I regard Mr. Russell's notion of the antediluvian, cave-man, metaphysician, as a "fake antique." The truth is much more that Mr. Russell is himself a susceptible individual who became a victim of the fashionable "primitivism" or "infantilism" that he found all round him when he first began expounding the time-doctrine. The doctrine that he expounds of serial "appearances" (in conformity with the time-law of relativist physics) is a form of primitivism, and so, at one remove, related to the child-cult. Take the water and ice illustration. We are in the presence, with that argument, of a description of the savage or primitive mind, surely, or an attempt (unconscious or otherwise) to approximate to it. For that is precisely how the primitive mind would, *naïvely*, as we say, regard those "appearances." Much less than for a civilized man would the water be *one thing* that "froze." It would be, discretely, a deep-green fluid apparition — water: or suddenly for no reason, a glassy white apparition — ice. From that point of view einsteinian physics is the physics of the primitive mind, the physics of the *naïf*. And Relativity Theory as interpreted by Mr. Russell is just as much a manifestation of "primitiveness" as was Paul Gauguin, and probably just as ephemeral.

Indeed, in all *exposés* of Relativity Theory it is quite evident that the *naïf* (the dissociated, intermittent, discrete, wide-eyed "primitivist") point of view is what we are being fed with. The spoon of Mr. Slosson or of Mr. Russell (in his "A.B.C." for little Relativists), held out invitingly, but firmly, towards the Public's little astonished mouths, is full of *that* particular treacle. Einstein-physics, too, are "tremendous fun." But the sort of nursery atmosphere that develops in the popular *exposé* of Relativity, the "*shut your eyes* and Open-Your-Mouth!" ("you'll feel giddy at first! you'll soon get over that!") sort of attitude of the Relativity nurses and governesses, is due to this side of the matter, which I think has not, so far, been put in evidence. What the Relativity handbook is saying the whole time is: Now try and feel about all these things *just like a little child.* Look at all these things *primitively!* Look at that big star up there, or at that duck-pond over there, or at the image in that great big mirror of that funny little girl or boy (and much play is made with the concave or the convex mirror, too) *as though you saw it for the first time!* And all the stalest political revolutionary machinery is used (of suggestion, snobbery, intimidation) to ensure its success.

How far this criticism of the *effect* of Relativity-physics could be brought home to its cause, Einstein, it is the business of the mathematical expert to decide, ultimately. Such critics as Maritain attack the metaphysical position of Einstein with a considerable show of reason. But I, for my part, prefer to deal with what is directly in front of all our eyes — the resultant philosophy, and confine myself to stimulating the mathematicians to seeing if they cannot discover the parallels in the mathematical theory of what all of us must eventually come to see in the philosophy — namely, that it is romantic, "primitivist," and open to the same objections as other sensational, over-coloured, marvellous and too exclusively emotional things.

More important for us here even than the multiplication of everything by time, is the fantastic readjustments which the treatment of the time-problem in Relativity-physics requires, in the disintegration of normal views into an isolated space of sight, one of touch, etc.: and especially is this divorce of *sight* from *touch* of critical importance.

In the world of "common-sense," Mr. Russell has told us, "things that can be seen but not touched [are] thought to be hardly real: to this day the usual mark of a ghost is that it can be seen but not touched." There are no "ghosts" in Mr. Russell's world, of course. A thing that endures for an hour (kept going in a constant "causal" cinematograph, or pattern-group causally connected, and supplied with an abstract soul by Time) has no privileged place from the point of view of reality over a thing that endures only for a few moments.

But what results from the isolation of the space-world of touch and that of sight, is that the pure non-tactile visual world introduces a variety of things to us, on a footing of equality as existing things, which in the world of common-sense (where the tactile sense is fused with the visual) do not possess that equality. Thus it is that the mirror-image draws level with the "thing" it reflects. And so you arrive at the non-plastic, illusory, Alice-in-Wonderland world of post-einsteinian philosophy.

It may still be objected that this is only a mathematician's technical device, necessitated by the present march of knowledge: as a technical device it interferes with nobody, it is the business only of the physicist or mathematician. The material world continues to be dealt with in a masterly fashion on the assumption of the "material" postulates of "common-sense," and that is the end of it. This would be ignoring, however, the fact that these conceptions of the external world are intended to supersede those of the classical intelligence and of the picture of the plain-man: that it is proposed to teach Relativity-physics and the relativist world-view everywhere in our schools: and that vast propaganda is carried on by popular treatises and articles to impose this picture upon the plain-man and the simple common-sense intelligence. In other words, the "common-sense" of tomorrow, it is proposed—the one general *sense* of things that we all hold in *common*—is to be transformed into the terms of this highly-complex disintegrated world, of private "times" and specific amputated "spaces," of serial-groups and "events" (in conformity with the dominance of the time-factor) in place of "things."

Mr. Russell stresses the impossibility of effecting this transformation without the cooperation of the powerful influence of habit, of "familiarity." And, of course, there is nothing at all that once people are familiarized with it and taught to take it as a matter of course, does not seem natural, and that would not therefore assume the authority of a "common-sense." But a thing that has to appeal to this special discipline can hardly claim that it is its intention to "free" the mind from prejudice. It is evidently introducing the mind only to another orthodoxy, which appears to have every practical interest of the average life against it, to go no further than that.

This whole theory, as is obvious [Mr. Russell writes], depends upon the nature of compact series, and *demands, for its full comprehension, that compact series should have become familiar and easy to the imagination as well as deliberate thought.*

I am quite familiar, and my imagination is quite at home, with "compact series," but they do not appeal to my imagination as does the classical "thing," so hated by Spengler, and upon which everyone from Bergson onwards has made incessant war. I have attempted to lay bare the motives for this animosity of the time-mind. And in this Part, dealing with the "Object," I have given sufficient prominence to the theory of apparitions and of optical illusions to have impressed it on the mind, I hope, of the general reader, whether I have succeeded or not in convincing him upon which side truth and his personal interests alike are to be found.

CHAPTER FIVE

SPACE AND TIME

IT IS BERGSON WHO put the hyphen between Space and Time. The at that time unborn hyphen is suggested by him when he is insisting on *continuity*, as against, in Descartes, the conceptualizing of time. "Evolution," he writes, "implies a real persistence of the past in the present, a *duration which is, as it were, a hyphen, a connecting link.*" It is out of the bergsonian "durée" that the hyphenated "space-time," in philosophy, was born. His doctrine of *durée* is the hyphen. Since Bergson has played this supreme part in the launching of "Time" as we have it today in philosophy, it is necessary, for the benefit of those not conversant with his time-theory, to give some idea of what it is.

First of all "Time," for Bergson, is *mental* as opposed to *physical*. Before him the mental character of Time had not been stressed in philosophy. The physical is "real" for him, in the sense that it is *dead mind*, as it were — the result of the great reverse movement in the heraclitean see-saw of his flux. As the opposite of life, however, it is no more "unreal" than Nothing is nothing. Space and Time become for Bergson personified; and he has an ecstatic feeling of veneration at the thought of the latter. But at the thought of Space he has nothing but a sensation of disdain and hatred. So to all the pagan, "spatializing," instincts he is hostile, in the manner of Spengler. The unfolding of the fan is the *spatial* image. The closing of it is the time image. They are, respectively, extension and intensity.

In philosophy the problem of Space (not its "Reality," but whether it is isolable, as Kant thought, or not) is somewhat the same as the problem of Nothingness. For Alexander the "unextended blank" that Space would be without time to break it up into fragments, is very like the Nothing, on the face of it. The things that are contrasted in the traditional conception of Space are precisely what we mean by "something" and "nothing." Space is a paradigm, a Tussaud's, of Something and Nothing. It is Time that makes reality.

Kant's conception of Space is about identical with the popular or "common-sense" view: it is a datum we cannot get behind, installed in the very centre of our perceptive faculty. It is independent of its content. The homogeneous, empty, isolable space of Kant, is as instinctive to us as the supposed ineradicably qualitied, full, differentiated space of animals. The manner in which birds and insects find their way to their destination, sometimes covering great distances, is apparently owing to the fact that for them there is no space, as we apprehend it, but an infinitely varied, thick, highly magnetized and coloured, medium, instead. *Their world is not a world of distinct objects. It is an interpenetrating world of direct sensation.* It is, in short, Mr. Bergson's world. It is not our hated geometric world, of *one space.* It is a *mental,* as it were an *interior* world, of palpitating movement, visually indistinct, electrical; not all arranged on the principles of surfaces and lines; and it is without a "void" at all. What we have to grasp in the Bergson world of "durée," is that it is an *interior* world. And the world of animals or insects is also a mental, interior, world. The exterior world is where "Space" is, or the mere conception "external," which is the prime "spatial" one, is enough: to that concept Bergson, as Alexander, is extremely and temperamentally hostile.

Memory, again, is a thing Bergson does not like to think about very much, as memory, for the simple reason that, with it *stretched out behind us,* we have a sort of *Space.* When we cease to act, and turn to reflect or dream, immediately we "degrade duration" into a bastard Space. We make it into an old-fashioned "Time," in short. The living principle, which we illustrate and enjoy, makes us one-way machines, essentially forward-moving — "go-ahead." But our consciousness, "though it does indeed move in the same direction as its principle, is continually drawn the opposite way; obliged, though it goes forward, to look behind." But what we see when we "look behind" is the artificial landscape cut out for us by the mere intellect; the "tout-fait," the already-made, the completed. We have turned away from what is *in-the-making,* from the "becoming," the world of *action,* to idle away our time in this private space of ours, provided by the machinery of memory, with its mass of images, which we can arrange at will. "Suppose we let ourselves go and instead of acting, dream . . . our past, which till then was gathered together into the indivisible impulsion it communicated to us, is broken up into a thousand recollections made external to one another. They give up interpenetrating in the degree that they become fixed. Our personality thus descends in the direction of space." This "dreaming" is to be very much reprehended. We do not *live* when we behave in this way. When we "look back" in this fashion we turn everything into a stone, as it were, in a trice, ourselves included. Everything in our minds takes on the qualities of matter and of the extended. But matter, for Bergson, is relaxation of the same sort, only *outside* our minds instead of *inside*. And since we have these deplorable habits *inside*, it is no wonder we have them *outside* as well. We feel quite *chez nous* when we open our eyes, look around, and notice the sleepy drove of twisted "objects," stretched untidily in front of us on a summer morning, as devoid of pep as a herd of cattle. But that might have been expected of us, by anyone acquainted with our mental habits. He says: "We shall now understand why the mind feels at its ease, moves . . . naturally in space, when matter suggests the more distinct idea of it. This space it already possessed as an implicit idea of its own eventual *detention*, that is to say, of its own possible *extension*." Since "physics is simply psychics inverted," physics comes naturally to man. That is it: man is a physical animal, his whole life one long, almost scandalous, *detention*.

How this disparaging view of Space affects Science, whose "domain is inert matter," is as follows. "For a scientific theory to be final, the mind would have to embrace the totality of things in block, and place each thing in its exact relation to every other thing. But in reality we are obliged to consider problems one by one, in terms which are, for that very reason, provisional . . . Science as a whole is relative to the particular order in which the problems happen to have been put." Science bears "on reality itself," but it works with intellect only. Mind, however, "overflows" the intellect. This overflowing of the intellect by the mind is "at bottom the same thing" as to say that *duration* has an absolute existence. So the business of metaphysics is clear: it is to place itself in the "mind" overflowing the intellect, or in other words in "duration"; and from that central vantage-spot it will occasionally catch very brief glimpses of the Whole. These difficult and semi-mystical exercises will give it an immediate superiority over Science.

Bergson's "main concern is with motion": but his fanatical objection to the static is satisfied once Time is radically installed in the heart of everything that otherwise might momentarily flout

Time, or set up Space against it by offering to men that illusion of security and repose necessary for human creativeness, and belonging to contemplation, but which Time, with its "becoming" and never "finishing," its fidgeting or flowing away, its inability to remain in one place, is unable to provide.

Having acquainted ourselves with Bergson's "space," let us turn to "durée." "Duration" is what occurs when we completely telescope the past into the present, and make our life a fiery point "eating" like an acetylene flame into the future. "Duration" is *inside us*, not outside. There is nothing but "mathematical Time" outside us. "Duration" is the *succession* of our conscious states, but *all felt at once* and somehow caught in the act of generating the "new," as "free" as Rousseau's natural man released from conventional constraints, but with much more élan; never, at least, *dreaming*, as that personage was in the habit of doing. It is the organization of the past into a moving and changing present, into an incessantly renewed intensive quantity, which produces what Alexander calls, following the same line of thought, the "emergent quality" — also, like Bergson's, both absolutely "new" and peculiarly "free." Memory, on the other hand, unorganized, with its succession of extended units, is that degraded *spatial-time*, as it might be called, regarded with so much hostility by the inventor of "duration." "Duration" is all the past of an individual crammed into the present; and yet this present is not the bare present that forgets its past and is unconscious of its future. This mystical condition of "pure duration" is a kind of ecstatic fishing for the Whole; the past is hauled in like a rope, and concentrated upon the present spot, gathered into unity by action. The present pervades the past, and so the past is renewed: for, for some reason, the present, concentrated in this way, and swelled out to bursting with *all* the past, is both "free" and "new." It is never *quite* free, or absolutely "new," we are told, even for the fraction of a moment. But it is quite free and new enough to provoke a great deal of rejoicing and enthusiasm, we are assured; though the delicate subject of *how* new and free is invariably dropped at the moment that our enthusiasm is supposed to be reaching boiling point, and that a discreet withdrawal seems necessary. But the main condition to be borne in mind for the achieving of "duration," is the complete *interpenetration* of all the parts of the past. The sign that it is *not* a "duration," is when you find these parts *separating* and *lying side by side*. That shows that you are not in the presence of "duration," but of its degraded, spatial counter-part. On that you must immediately turn your back.

Musical analogy is frequently indulged in by Bergson. The separate notes or isolated sounds composing a piece of music are by themselves without meaning. Organized into a *whole*, they have meaning. This whole is like the living being. Time, as it is generally understood, is nothing but space and simultaneity — it is an exterior succession of impenetrabilities, and not an organized whole. "To say that an event will occur at the end of a time *t*, is to say that our consciousness will note meanwhile a number *t* of simultaneities of a certain order." And we must not be taken in by the term "meanwhile" (*d'ici là*), since the interval of *duration* only exists for us, because of the mutual penetration of our states of consciousness. Outside ourselves, we should find nothing but *Space*, and, consequently, *simultaneities*, of which one cannot even say that they are objectively successive, since all "succession" is arrived at by a comparison of past and present. Concrete consciousness *lives* these intervals: but, on the other hand, outside us nothing *lives*. When we surrender ourselves to Space we, too, cease to live. We convert our sort of *lived* time, or "duration," into space: or, on the other hand, we interpret our concrete, qualitied time by analogy with spatial simultaneity. We keep the past alive for Space, and hold the image in veneration of its past, and so provide it with a succession which it does not possess itself. On the other hand, we divide up our interior indivisible concreteness into mathematically-intervalled conceptual units, by reference to Space. In short, it is we who supply Space with a past, a duration. We in that sense break it up, just as it breaks us up into parts: and that is Alexander's explanation of what happens, as it is that of Bergson.

The clock is the central object of Bergson's time-philosophy, naturally, as it is the central object in einsteinian physics. It is not a clock that says, "Esto Memor! Souviens-toi!" but a metal object whose pendulum cuts up "mathematical time" into neat little parcels. It is quite an objective instrument; the romantic timepiece of poetry is *inside us*. The poor metal machine does not even remember its last oscillation: it possesses (without our assistance) nothing but simultaneities, and is irretrievably spatial. In watching a clock, and following its movements, you are counting simultaneities, merely. "Outside of me, in space, there is never any more than *one* position of the hand of the clock, since the past positions of the hand do not any longer exist." *Inside me,* however, a process of organization and penetration is going on, which is "durée." "It is because I endure in this fashion that I represent to myself what I call the past oscillation of the clock." Once more, then, according to Bergson, in watching the oscillations of the pendulum of the clock, I reduce my own qualitied, "concrete," heterogeneous, psychological states to a series of simultaneities, with intervals not filled with "life" or "lived-time," but lifeless mathematical intervals. The way to interpret Time, to make it into "durée," is, holding the memory of all the past oscillations of the clock, to conceive them all as "penetrating and organizing each other like the notes of a melody, in such a way as to form what we will call *an indistinct or qualitative multiplicity*, without any resemblance at all to number." That, as far as we need pursue it, is the heart of the bergsonian time-philosophy. Listen for a moment to Alexander, and see if you can even distinguish it from the doctrine we have just been examining.

The distinctive character of Time . . . is to be a succession within duration; it conceives of Time as given all at once as if it were a line. In other words, it conceives of Time as if it were precisely the same as Space. But Time in the abstract is distinct from Space in the abstract. The one is in the abstract mere coexistence; the other mere succession. Since the instants of abstract Time are homogeneous, the conclusion is drawn that in an infinite Time everything which can happen has happened. But this overlooks what is essential to Time, that it is creative: that something comes into being which before was not.

It is Bergson word for word and term for term. That "something that comes into being which before was not" is Bergson's novelty, for which we are indebted to Time; and for Alexander, too, the essential thing about Time, or as he, too, calls it, "duration," is that it is "creative." As to the conceiving of Time "as if it were a line," or as, generally, spatial, these words, too, are Bergson's where he is busy dissociating Time from spatial interpretations. He imagines "a straight line, and on that line a material point A which displaces itself." "If this point," he goes on, "became conscious of itself . . . it would perceive a succession, but would that succession take first the form of a line? Yes, no doubt, if it were able in some way to raise itself above the line, and simultaneously perceive several juxtaposed points." But let us follow Alexander into his conversion of objects into movements. (We have nothing to do here with a *thing,* but with a progress, says Bergson. "Move-ment, regarded as a passage from one point to another, is a mental synthesis [etc.]")

In every individual instance the whole in a sense abolishes the parts. "Everything is a piece of Space-Time and breaks up therefore into *parts,* of which it is the *whole,*" Alexander tells us. This small whole is a "finite" as understood by the space-timer: but it is difficult to fix this new sort of object down, or to see quite where it begins or ends, since it is regarded always as a prolongation and as interpenetrating other things on all sides. This sort of isolation of a *movement* is manifestly much more difficult than that of the traditional "thing," and seems indeed im-possible. Yet to obtain its necessary, "intensive," "emergent" mean-ing it is essential somehow to close it. So we have to suppose these groupings within space-time or "complexes of pure events or motions" as "pure" and distinct. And we have to imagine them as engendering, in the finite unity, something *new.* Alexander gets his "novelty" or "newness" in the same way as Bergson did; but he calls it an "emergent quality" (the word "emergent" com-ing through Lloyd Morgan from G. H. Lewes). It is produced by the same manipulation of Kant's idea of "intensive quality," which is at the bottom of Bergson's conception of time — a use, it is hardly necessary to say, to which Kant did not anticipate its being put.

In an empirical philosophy, according to Alexander, "space-time" is at the bottom of everything; space-time *possesses no quality at all, except motion.* Throughout this partnership of Space and Time, "Time plays the directer rôle and takes the lead." Time is "the soul of Space." Indeed, the more you consider the ascendancy of what is understood by "Time" in the Bergson or Alexander systems of thought, the less use you can discover for Space at all. It is true you are constantly told that Time requires Space as a handy subordinate to "cut it up." But it seems a very small step to arrange for Time to be able to cut itself up, and to dispense with Space — which is such an unpopular figure in that philosophy — altogether. At all events, we are told, and to that we must attach ourselves for the moment, that "Time disintegrates Space directly by distinguishing it into successive spaces; Space disintegrates Time indirectly" (it cannot do anything, even *directly,* Space) "by making it a whole of times, without which whole there would be no separate times either." It is these "times" that are the subordinate final *wholes*, which engender a *new quality*, the new "emergent" quality, in short. This new, intensive, quality, is the "meaning," however, of that of which it is *not* a quantitative summation, but from which it has mysteriously "emerged" into a higher plane of things, leaving a group behind it on the lower level, in what seems a rather undemocratic way. So, going from one complexity on to a still higher one, the mysterious bare original "pure motion" which is plain and unadorned "space-time," and which is so completely meaningless that we can call it a sort of nothing, has "emerged" in more and more complex "quality," and more and more intense meaning. That *we* mean as much as it is possible for anything to mean — that is, that we are as real as anything can be — seems, on the whole, unlikely. Therefore, according to this system, things will probably go on "emerging" and "evolving." If God were reached, no doubt the process would begin all over again, for it is a circular system, a moving system: and "God" is a helpless part of it. But luckily for that God, it seems unlikely that He can ever be reached.

There is, of course, no explanation possible of this "emergent" happening. "The existence of emergent qualities . . . is something to be noted," Alexander says, "to be accepted with the *natural piety* of the investigator. It admits no explanation." This means that you must accept it *from* the "investigator" with "natural piety" — the more piety, the better. "The new quality, life, emerges from physical and chemical processes," but life is *not* adequately accounted for by those processes: "life *is* at once a physico-chemical complex and *is not* merely physical and chemical: for these terms do not sufficiently characterize the new complex." We know that ourselves, of course — before we are informed of it in this roundabout way. "Such is the account to be given of the meaning of quality as such." Well, we are no nearer the meaning. But "it admits of no explanation." So that is the end of it. What we are all familiar with has a new name "emergent"; that is all that has happened, except that in return for this name we are asked to accept at the same time a group of very dubious doctrines that similarly explain nothing, but imply a variety of things that strike us as fundamentally untrue. So it is as well not to be instantly misled on account of a few pretty words, as has been the case with many people. But we will proceed for a short distance yet with the text of Alexander.

"Time and Space, being indissolubly interwoven, do not remain

extended blanks, but break each other up into differences," says
Alexander: but he cannot see "why these finites should exhibit
actual repetition in their kinds." There are two alternatives to
this problem: one is that molecules of carbon and gold, for instance, contain the essence in some way of all other classes, as
that of oaks and of men: or it may be that all these multitudes
derive from solitary prototypes, as in the hebrew or babylonian
creation, men issue from the "first parents." If the former were
true — and it is to that solution that Alexander and his friends
naturally incline — anywhere in the world, or perhaps anywhere
in the universe — men or oaks, for instance, might spontaneously
appear. The molecule of carbon or gold ideally posits the man
and the oak: and anywhere that you have one you are extremely
liable to have the other. This is the theory of the whole universe
in some way existing, or being in some sense involved in any
particular existent whatever: and the judgment that one thing
passes on another, or its *meaning*, for it, is as it were the temporal judgment of the whole universe concentrated at the moment of judgement in that point-instant, and contemplating itself
laid out in front of it, equally in spatio-temporal fancy-dress.

All these descriptions, it is essential to note, do to some extent masquerade as solutions. The "empirical method," it will be
observed, is to announce solemnly that there is "no explanation,"
and then to explain. The "modesty" of the scientific investigator
is an admirable cloak for the conveying of dogmatic beliefs. These
habits of the universe, then, are taken as an ultimate datum; and
why a universe should contract the habit of oaks or of men, rather
than any other, is, of course, a question outside the picture.

But the Time conception of Bergson seems to us entirely to
misrepresent the rôle of Space, and, as it were, shuffle and
transpose their respective "realities." So what we seek to stimulate,
and what we give the critical outline of, is a philosophy that will
be as much a *spatial-philosophy* as Bergson's is a *time-philosophy*.
As much as he enjoys the sight of things "penetrating" and "merging," do we enjoy the opposite picture of them standing apart — the
wind blowing between them, and the air circulating freely in and
out of them: much as he enjoys the "indistinct," the "qualitative,"
the misty, sensational and ecstatic, very much more do we
value the distinct, the geometric, the universal, non-qualitied —
the clear and the light, the unsensational. To the trance of
music, with its obsession of *Time*, with its inalienable emotional

urgency and visceral agitation, we prefer what Bergson calls "obsession of Space." If the painter's heaven of exterior forms is what above all delights you, then the philosophy of Time, with its declared enmity for "spatializing" mankind, will, if you understand it, please you as little as it does me. You will prefer the world of greek philosophy, the pagan exteriority, to the world of music, or to the time-mathematics, or mathematics of events or "durations," the mathematics of *motion*, which is temperamentally associated with that.

The interpretation of the ancient problems of space and time that consists in amalgamating them into space-time is for us, then, no solution. For, to start with, space-time is no more real, but if anything a little less real, in our view, than Space and Time separately. The wedding of these two abstractions results, we believe (as a triumphant feminism would result not in equality but in feminine ascendancy), in the ascendancy of Time (which also happens to be the feminine principle in this partnership) over Space: and of the two, if we have any preference, it is for Space; for Space keeps still, at least is not (ideally) occupied in incessantly slipping away, melting into the next thing, and repudiating its integrity. Regarding mind as Timeless, it is more at home, we find, with Space. And as stability is the manifest goal of all organic life, and the thing from which we all of us have most to gain, we see no use, in the first place, and in the second see no theoretic advantage, in this fusion. For the objective world most useful to us, and what may be the same thing, most "beautiful," and therefore with most *meaning*, and that is further to say in a word with most *reality*, we require a Space distinct from Time.

If then, in recapitulation, Space and Time are mere appearances, as we believe, riddled with contradictions that bar them from anything but a relative reality, they are, from that standpoint, in the same case when joined to each other by a hyphen, as when standing distinct and unhyphenated. That Alexander goes further, in a sense, in his Time obsession, than Bergson, can be shown by his attitude to the statement of Minkowski, which he criticizes as not giving enough place, even, to Time. I will quote what he says, and let him speak for himself.

. . . to think of Time as a fourth dimension in a world in which the other three dimensions are spatial, is a legitimate and the only possible way of representing mathematically the nature of the world or Space-Time.

(You will remember that this was also Bergson's criticism of the mathematical use of Time as a fourth dimension, describing it as a necessary mathematical device.)

But if the empirical analysis is correct, the representation cannot be regarded as other than a means of mathematical manipulation. For it seems to treat Time as an additional dimension, not of course a spatial one, much in the same way as the third spatial dimension is additional to the other two, that is, as a further order in which three-dimensional Spaces are arranged. But the relation between Space and Time which we have found empirically appears to be of a much more intimate kind than is thus suggested. For not only are Space and Time indispensable to one another (as in the conception of Minkowski), *but Time with its distinctive features corresponds to the three dimensions of Space, and in a manner of speech Time does with its one-dimensional order cover and embrace the three dimensions of Space, and is not additional to them*. . . . Metaphysically (though perhaps mathematically) it is not therefore a fourth dimension in the universe, but repeats the other three. Space, even to be Space, must be temporal. . . . It follows that the three dimensions of Space, just because they correspond to the characters of Time, are not in reality independent of each other.

This certainly out-bergsons Bergson. Time must not be considered as *additional* to the other three dimensions of Space, since spatial dimension has its "time," and all the three together are "covered and embraced" by Time; and, even to be spatial at all, must first be *Time*. With this we will take leave of the main stream of Alexander's rag-time philosophy.

Space seems to us by far the greater reality of the two, and Time meaningless without it. Time as change was the "Nothing" of the Greek, and it is ours. *Space* is rapidly, under the guidance of a series of Bergsons, each Time-obsessed, becoming the "Nothing" of the modern European.

CONCLUSION

". . . l'absolu d'aujourd'hui . . . n'est plus quiétude, mais agitation; l'Éternel est devenu passion."

Belphégor, J. Benda

". . . to show how and why the universe is so that finite existence belongs to it, is utterly impossible. That would imply an understanding of the whole not practicable for a mere part. It would mean a view by the finite from the Absolute's point of view, and in that consummation the finite would have been transmuted and destroyed."

Appearance and Reality, F. H. Bradley

"For what is there on our part, or what do we perceive amongst all the ideas, sensations, notions, which are imprinted on our minds, either by sense or reflexion, from whence may be inferred the existence of an inert, thoughtless, unperceived occasion?"

Principles of Human Knowledge, Berkeley

CONCLUSION

IT IS NOW OUR BUSINESS to draw the arguments of our critical survey to a head, and to state briefly our conclusions. Throughout the progress of the argument I have everywhere associated the conclusions towards which I was leading with the actual scrutiny of the adverse position. But there is still a final summation to be made. I propose to organize this "Conclusion" under numbered sections: to retrace in them, extremely briefly, the ground we have covered, chapter by chapter; and then to state in longer sections the final argument of this book.

1. In contemporary philosophy — which has its roots in the doctrines of Bergson and James — an orthodoxy has grown up around the conception of Time-as-real. Whether "realist" or "idealist," it makes no difference when it comes to the treatment of this central doctrine. In that, all are at one.

2. The Time-doctrine, first promulgated in the philosophy of Bergson, is in its essence, to put it as simply as possible, anti-physical and pro-mental. A great deal of partisan feeling is engendered in the course of its exposition: and all that feeling is directed to belittling and discrediting the "spatializing instinct" of man. In opposition to that is placed a belief in the *organic* character of everything. Dead, physical, nature comes to life. Chairs and tables, mountains and stars, are animated into a magnetic restlessness and sensitiveness, and exist on the same vital terms as men. They are as it were the lowest grade, the most sluggish, of animals. All is alive: and, in that sense, all is mental.

3. "Realist" or "idealist" are, as a consequence, terms that have very little meaning. The "realist" of the Alexander type is, as Bosanquet points out, more often than not far more "idealistic"

421

(in the traditional sense of the word) than the "idealist" of the Gentile type. Let me recall Bosanquet's description of this paradox.

> It is a strange experience in the cases before us to turn from the idealist to the realist. With the idealist . . . everything was passionately human. . . . With the realist — extraordinary reversal! — we move in a larger air. We are with Meredith, the poet of the stars, of motion, of colour.

But even apart from the special confusions to which these terms are exposed, in the merging that has occurred today, they had at no time the fixity that popularly they are assumed to have. Professor Alexander expresses this as follows:

> No sane philosophy has ever been exclusively the one or the other [realist or idealist], and where the modern antithesis has hardly arisen, as with Plato, it is extraordinarily difficult to say under which head the philosophy should be classed.

Mr. Bertrand Russell, where he is announcing, in his *Analysis of Mind,* under what heading his doctrine should come, writes as follows: "When we are speaking of matter, it will seem as if we were inclining to idealism; when we are speaking of mind, it will seem as if we were inclining to materialism." This is indeed what generally happens with these philosophers; especially with a professor with the absolutist manners of Alexander is this illusion readily generated.

4. What is the cause of this unanimity, so that "realists" and "idealists" merge in the common worship of Time and Change? Is it a political impulse that has brought this about (since implicit in the doctrine of Time and Change is the revolutionary doctrine of the "Progress of the Species")? Often the liaison is so apparent that it is impossible to doubt that, once engaged, from whatever motive, in that way of thinking, the Time-philosopher does also tend to become a "Progress" enthusiast of the most obvious political sort. Further, no doctrine, so much as the Time-doctrine, lends itself to the purpose of the millennial politics of revolutionary human change, and endless "Progress." Nevertheless we believe that the impulse to this doctrine is the outcome mainly of Science: that it is really the philosophy of the instruments of research. It is the inevitable child of positivist and phenomenalist thought. The politics come afterwards, when they are found in it. Possibly their officious assistance may help

to harden it into an orthodoxy, and to turn the honest "pessimism" of Schopenhauer into the insincere optimism of Bergson and his followers.

5. The chronological doctrine of Spengler insists upon this *political* character of all thought. "Each 'Culture' is an *organism*, very fierce and warlike, struggling, in true darwinian fashion, for survival. Pictures, fugues, cathedrals, physical theories, cosmologies — the differential calculus as much as Darwin, herzian waves as much as indian zeros — are the weapons of the Cultures to which they belong. They have no absolute validity, or meaning at all, apart from their practical use, any more than has poison-gas or a submarine." We showed the hollowness of this belief: and gave the reasons that make the "world-as-history" or the "world-as-politics," unacceptable.

6. So we did not deny that many philosophers or men-of-science may act — think and prosecute their "discoveries" — under the chronological influence of politics and of "Time." The researches directed to eliminating the absolute certainly have borne a great deal the character of a *war*. Such men as William James rejoice at the "victories" of Bergson in the same breath as they exult at the result of the russo-japanese war. They *do* perform war-dances to celebrate the extinction of the "Consciousness." They *do* assume a festive tone when they inaugurate the reign of the "Unconscious." Man, unless a very unusually fine specimen, *is* a "political animal." And such a man as James, whom Whitehead describes as the supreme philosopher of the present age, was not a person who ever attained to the maturity of mind of a greek sage; he was surrounded by, and belonged to, a raw and unsatisfactory life: he saw things in the crude terms of aggression, of tit-for-tat, of "fun" and high-jinks, with the eyes of the "eternal child" that the American is supposed to be. But still that does not prove that even all *his* thought was engendered upon that level. And it certainly proves nothing of greater civilizations than ours. The human reason is not eternally discredited because some barbarian of genius (growing in a bleak and violent atmosphere of radicalism and dissent) mixes his science with the politics of his traditionally-rebellious tribe: for in the youth of

James, America was much more provincial than it is today, and a belligerent unorthodoxy was no doubt lapped up with the mother's milk.

7. The later chapters, those dealing with the problems of reality and belief, were intended partly to introduce the reader who had not made a special study of philosophy to a few of the capital problems which have most application today, and with which it is essential to have some familiarity in order to understand the full implications of the philosophy of Time. Those there is no occasion to resume: for the remainder of this conclusion will deal with the same problems, taking the argument a step further, although still dealing with them mainly from a critical standpoint, and so terminating my book.

In these pages the "spatializing" instinct of man is celebrated, in place of the universally advertised alternative, that attitude of mind that seeks to glorify Time, and mix that "restlessness" that is Time's, as Alexander describes it, into everything.

Do those arguments point to ours being a "sensationalist" philosophy? since the spatializing faculty that builds up and enjoys the material and solid world might, superficially, be interpreted as more "sensationalist" than that mentalizing of things, which is the result of mixing them with Time? Alexander we consider a pure sensationalist philosopher. Yet he says: "A philosophy which pursues an empirical method is not necessarily a sensationalistic one" (vol. i, p. 5, *Space Time and Deity*). So it would seem that he does not regard himself as one, or does not wish to be so regarded. But how can that statement be reconciled, for instance, with the following: ". . . since we have no enjoyment of ourselves which is not the contemplation of a non-mental object, all our experience, whether enjoyed or contemplated, is provoked through the sense-organs. The most complicated objects or enjoyments are resoluble into elements of sense, or its derivative idea, and their groupings in some empirical plan, and from beginning to end these experiences are qualified by categorical as well as empirical features." *Prima facie*, that sounds sensationalist enough to satisfy all general requirements. Actually, his philosophy when carefully examined proves to be of the purest sensationalism that it is possible to imagine. The literary embellishments of a meredithian order that took in Bosanquet (making him say that with this "realist" we were among the stars and clouds) can be quite disregarded. That is only part of the machinery with which he disguises his too vulgarly "materialist" dispositions.

The whole question of "sensationalism" or something else, of "materialism" or its opposite, turns upon the value you attach to the sensational reality. "The sting of absolute idealism," says Alexander, "lies in its assertion that the parts of the world are not ultimately real or *true*, but only the whole is *true*." That is it: and to say that "all philosophies are concerned with experience as a whole," and therefore all equally should be called "idealistic" (if anything is to be named in that rather silly and today quite meaningless way), introduces a second qualification: namely, it will depend upon what value you attach to *the whole*.

The most "solid" object in the world is never, for us, so solid as it is for Alexander: it could not be, however hard we tried. He, it is true, disintegrates all objects into a fluid, futuristic mass in his system. But that is merely to make them still more piping hot, and vividly "real." Surely our ideal *static* perceptual object (of "common-sense," as it is termed) is far more unreal, if that is what you want. The *more* static, the more solid, the more fixed, the *more* unreal; as compared with the vivacious, hot, mercurial broth of an object, that results in the alexandrian or bergsonian realism. Surely the famous "spatializing" instinct produces a more "unreal" world (from the exactest physical standards) than does the *temporalizing*, chronological instinct of a Bergson or an Alexander. On a still day consider the trees in a forest or in a park, or an immobile castle reflected in a glassy river: they are perfect illustrations of our static dream; and what in a sense could be more "unreal" than they? That is the external, objective, physical, material world (made by our "spatializing" sense), to which we are referring. It is to that world that the hellenic sculpture (which is the *bête-noir* of Spengler) belongs, and all the Pharaohs and Buddhas as well, and even more.

That is *our* world of "matter," which we place against the einsteinian, bergsonian, or alexandrian world of Time and "restless" interpenetration.

8. The hypothesis of Alexander and of Whitehead leads to the assumption of an equal reality in everything, a democratically

distributed reality, as it were. There is no supreme reality already in existence. Time is *real*, and owing to this reality of Time and Change, it is we who are in the process of making a superior reality to ourselves: we are *improving ourselves*, in short. That is the evolutionary doctrine of Time.

If that is the arch-progressist doctrine, or when it becomes that, there are two contradictions in it from a practical standpoint which it is worth pointing out. What it pretends to do is to supply man with new causes of self-congratulation, since it shows him (in his evolutionary capacity) participating at the very making and perfecting of things. Just as he looks down upon the monkey or the fish — the latter of which he eats, the former of which he puts in a cage — so future men will look back at him with disdain and pity. Presumably if they could they would either eat him or put him in a cage. Even the strange barbarian of today is solemnly taught — we have seen it occurring with Spengler and Alexander — to look down on the Hellene as a creature without his advantages of enlightenment and in every way inferior.

But what must be the practical effect of this teaching upon the general sensibility? First of all, though it is flattering to think that you are a finer fellow than your forebears, it is none the less psychologically discouraging to reflect that as they do not live upon equal terms with you, so you, in your turn, will not live upon equal terms with those who follow you. You, in imagination, are already cancelled by those who will "perfect" you in the mechanical time-scale that stretches out, always ascending, before us. What you do and how you live has no worth in itself. You are an *inferior*, fatally, to all the future. You are — once your eyes are unsealed, in the evolutionist sense, to this time-reality — in the position of a man who is building a house that he knows to be a bad house, fit only for a low-down-in-the-scale individual like himself to live in, which will be recognized in the sequel as a thing not, in itself, worth building, for a creature whose life, in itself, was not worth living. This may or may not be true, but it is only at the cost of sincerity that it can be twisted into an "optimistic" value, as a version of our destiny.

In this eternal manufacturing of a God — which is really the God of Comte, "Humanity" — you cooperate, but in such a negligible way that you would be a great fool indeed to take much notice of that privilege. Looked at from the simplest human level, as a semi-religious faith, the Time-cult seems far less effective, when properly understood, than those cults which posit a Perfection already existing, eternally there, of which we are humble shadows. It would be a very irrational conceit which, if it were given the choice, would decide for the "emergent" Time-god, it seems to me, in place, for instance, of the God of the Roman faith. With the latter you have an achieved co-existent supremacy of perfection, impending over all your life, not part of you in any imperfect physical sense, and touching you at moments with its inspiration. With the other you have a kind of Nothing, which it is your task, perspiring and mechanical — weaver of the wind that you are, architect of nothingness — to bolster up and somehow assist into life and time, in a region just out of your own reach. But the moment that eventually your strenuous creation, the embryo-god, was brought out into the daylight, it would no longer be anything more than a somewhat less idiotic *you*. Could you penetrate that distant future where what is God to you (as you are god to your dog) is to exist, you would behold the same world, but one storey up, still perspiring, fighting and fuming to give actuality to the existence of the next-storey-up. A more unsatisfying, as well as foolish and misbegotten, advertisement of divinity could scarcely have been found to stimulate the tired businessman or the unhappy person born to the dullest mechanical labour, sorely in need of comfort. The vociferous priests of this God of Progress seem almost to be mocking us: for they are at great pains to elucidate their pretensions, and yet any child that gave itself the trouble would at once perceive how hollow they were.

Or let us take another feature of this philosophy, the hostile attitude to "mind." That from the practical standpoint of a saving religious, or semi-religious, faith, is wanting in the same manner. However much you stress the "democratic" nature of your proposed reform, still you will be unable in the end to disguise the fact that you have, for practical purposes, left man poorer than you found him. And he is certain in the end to find out how he has been robbed. This is Alexander's statement when he comes to the question of "the mind," in the early part of his essay, *Space Time and Deity*.

The empirical method in metaphysics is seriously and persistently to treat finite minds as one among the many forms of finite existence, having no privilege above them except such as it derives from its greater perfection of development . . . *prima facie* there is no warrant for the dogma that, because all experience implies a mind, that which is experienced owes its being and its qualities to mind. Minds are but the most gifted members known to us in a democracy of things. In respect of being or reality all existences are on an equal footing.

The language of progressist politics breaks out at once. It is indeed almost impossible for any of the philosophers engaged in the task of putting the mind in its place, to express themselves without political analogy and phrasing. Mr. Russell, with his altruistic bias, seldom fails to try and make us feel ashamed that when we sit in a chair, in our lordly way, we conclude that the chair is dead matter and without feeling: only *we*, forsooth, can *feel!* If he could he would lead a revolt of the upholstery and all the humble, put-upon springs, to teach us a little sense at the same time that our arrogance suffered a sharp rebuff. So morals and physics go hand in hand, altruism — after everything else — uses solar energy for its purposes. But there is no difficulty at all in showing that this altruism is against and not for us — mankind as a whole. For, by its very nature, altruism penetrates lower and lower in the scale. It has long ago passed the line of the humblest human being. To be completely humane you have to legislate in favour of the sub-human. Even the most miserable beggar is already in the position of an insolent king, who lords it over cabbages, grass, tinned tomatoes; and, when he gets a chance, sits heavily upon an inoffensive chair, or takes a knife and murderously attacks a tree, to provide himself with a crutch. But there are other things besides physical objects that benefit by this universal sensitiveness: a host of abstractions (words, or ideas) are given more than your superfluity of life; they are taught to feed upon us, rather than let us use them.

Let us return to Alexander and again quote from him:

. . . though we do not assume in mind any prerogative being or reality which should make other reality in some way dependent for its existence upon mind, it by no means follows that the study of mind may not be of special importance and value for philosophy.

In other words, though he dismisses mind from its "privileged" position, it by no means follows that we cannot still *use* it — for further destructive enterprises; just as, in fact, we used it to overthrow itself, ironically enough.

An illustration (of the uses to which our minds can be put) is found in the notion of causality. After naïvely describing how the behaviour of the sun towards a piece of wax enables us to collect the idea of a power in the sun to melt the wax, Locke says that this power may be most easily discovered in the operations of our wills, or in the power of our mind over its ideas.

Let us interpret this. In order to get causal meaning into the sun, we must hand it over our will, so to speak. The sun becomes to some degree, by means of that transaction, an animal devouring the wax: and we and our will become to some degree what the sun was *before* it had had our will bestowed upon it — a "thing." That it is a large, hot and powerful "thing," the sun, and that it may be of more "importance" than a human "person," is beside the point. If you asked the humblest of men if he would allow you to chop his head off, provided he received the assurance that his head would instantly become the sun, even if he believed that you had the ability to procure him this advantage, he would certainly refuse with indignation. Such is human conceit! The thought of it saddens Mr. Russell. His reality is the sun (let us state it that way), and our reality is the man's head.

Professor Alexander, following on the passage just quoted, observes:

With this analysis in our mind we may ask ourselves whether causality in the physical world is not in turn the continuous transition of one physical event into another. To do so is not to impute minds to physical things, as if the only things which could be active must, on the strength of the experience referred to, be minds.

Let us follow that for a moment, and interpret it.

Why it is not necessary, in the view of Professor Alexander, "to impute minds to physical things" (to the sun, for instance), is because man (the introspective pattern for this experience of *activity*) himself has become a "physical thing": and his "mind" has become a thing almost exactly similar to the activity of the sun, only on a small and, as it were, intimate and personal scale. The will of the sun in devouring the piece of wax, or the will of man in devouring a piece of fish, is the same thing: man picks and chooses, whereas the sun devours everything indiscriminately, that is the only difference; and the selection is in his "consciousness" or "mind." Our personalities become, in this doctrine, "the continuous transition of one physical event into another." The sun, on the other hand, or any other agent whatever, gets a certain amount of our will. But — that is the point of this argument — *it is not what happens to the sun (ideally) that interests us. It is what has happened to us at the end of the transaction.* And what I think is beyond question is that, as a consequence of the analysis of mind, of the universal attack upon "mind," we lose, in practice, and in the aggregate (and we are now discussing the practical bearing of those matters, the political), to an overwhelming degree.

What I have been trying to show by this argument and these illustrations is that *pragmatically* we are the losers by certain operations that are said to be, with much optimistic advertisement, all undertaken for ourselves. It is in the interests of "equality," it is in conformity with the "democratic" principle, that "mind" is to be suppressed or annihilated. On the same principle we are to be converted into machines or into "events" in place of persons (the "person," the free-man of antiquity, is not for the likes of us), and we are to accustom ourselves to regard our personalities as "the continuous transition of one physical event into another." In this way we get rid of that embarrassing thing, the "mind," which gives us (compared to mere tables, chairs or even vegetables and dogs) a rather unfortunately aristocratic colour. Bearing "minds" about with us is all very well: but is it not a little "conceited": that is, would it not appear rather conceited, as swagger or swank, from the point of view of an observant tea-pot? It is *not* a "democratic" possession, a "mind" — come, own up, Mr. Everyman and Mr. Philosopher: what can "Redman Labour" do with a fancy thing like that? Hands, arms and legs and two good sharp eyes and two rows of honest teeth: but a *mind!* No. The mass-democracy can find little use for a mind, except, of course, its *group-mind.* So far as your individual life is concerned, take yourself as a "reaction-mass": or you can call yourself an "event" — not a very important one, still we're all a part of history, and history is enormously important; indeed it is God. When we are *all together,* for some reason, we are really a serious proposition — we have a "mind" then, of sorts. Even objective truth is merely an effect of our *collectivity.*

In our better mind about the same reality we represent the collective mind. . . . The rose is red whether we see it or not. . . . But the redness of the rose is judged true . . . only through the clashing and confirmation of our judgments. . . . Values then or tertiary qualities of things involve relation to the collective mind, and what is true, good, or beautiful is not true, good, or beautiful except as so combined with the collective mind. (*Space Time and Deity.*)

The unfortunate thing, of course, is (to interpret the above statement) that we all know that the rose is red (quite as we all know that we have a mind): when we "get together," and clash and fuss, scrutinize and sift, we frequently arrive at a point at which *collectively* we become convinced that the rose is *not* red. That is usually, indeed, what happens. It may be our private belief, again, that a certain person is beautiful: but when we go to the "clash and confirmation" of collective opinion we more often than not discover that for *us* they were beautiful, but that as true cells of our collectivity we must abandon this false belief. So, too, with the "good." The surrender of our private mind, of our "independence," in a similar way to our admission that we have no mind at all, is not—that is what we are stressing—an unmixed blessing. But if that practical side of the matter were resolved in our favour, there still would remain the *truth*. It may be to our *advantage* to believe that the rose is red: but supposing, in fact, many things lead us to believe, on closer inspection, that it is not red? Before deciding even then to embrace any destructive paradox, we must have a great deal more confidence in our intellectual processes than men customarily exhibit, one would have thought.

9. The conception of the real, or of God, advanced by Alexander is an expanding (or contracting) one; it is not constant. His God is a variable one, that is. "Deity is an empirical quality like mind or life. Before there was mind the universe was straining towards infinite mind. But there is no existent infinite mind, but only many finite minds." The many finite minds, then, are God: or, which is the same thing, there is no God. For if God existed, he would be finite, and then not God. So he is—if he can be said to *be* at all—what all the fuss is about: he *is* the fuss; but he has not yet been born. He is always, *what is not* at a higher level: though as to what "higher" may be, we are left in doubt. *"High" and "low," like "beautiful" or "true," are values of the collectivity*, it is to be assumed. What Alexander thought a higher form of beauty I should almost fatally consider a lower. What would decide would be what the majority or "collectivity" thought. And we know by experience what they generally decide. In this case they are

provided with the supreme function of deciding what God shall be, and of then proceeding to produce him.

"God" is a value of better and worse, higher-and-lower (he being its "highest" and "best") — a value analogous to "beauty" or "truth." But, since these values, "beauty" and "truth," are not absolute, but are questions for the collectivity, so is "God." "Deity is subject to the same law as other empirical qualities."

. . . in the lapse of time the quality (God) comes to actual existence, animates a new race of creatures, and is succeeded by a still higher quality. God as an actual existent is always becoming deity, but never attains it. He is the ideal God in embryo. The ideal when fulfilled ceases to be God. . . .

As to the variability of this God, Alexander meets all objections as follows:

Since God's deity is different . . . and varies with the lapse of time, how can we declare him to be the whole universe? Must not God be different at each level?

The answer to that is quite simple:

The variation lies in the empirical development within the universe, and therefore not in God's totality. . . . *It is still one Space-Time, within which grows up deity.*

God-the-child, "growing up," or God-"the-embryo," as Alexander puts it, will be a fine big God one day (oh, ever so many years hence!). At present he's still in the nursery — that is to say *we* are — the same thing. He's just a kid like us, bless his little perspiring face, "straining to the infinite."

It is thus always the universe of Space-Time which is God's body, but it varies in its empirical constitution and its deity.

The quantity of God is, however, always the same. It is only the quality that changes. And when I said "expanding" it was the quality to which I referred. *Quality* is the thing that changes. *Quantity* is the universal and fundamental thing.

Alexander's objection to a pagan plurality of gods is that it is an attempt to "secure deity in finite forms." But is not his the same? The only difference is that he is a little bit more cunningly anthropomorphic, and a trifle more speculative. It is exactly the same endeavour. It is forcing Deity into finite existence, and identifying it with change and time. The only difference is that the polytheist gives us a concrete God, however ridiculous, whereas Alexander gives us an abstract God which is the concrete-of-tomorrow, or any concrete that has not yet existed in Time — for he never suggests that evolution is reversible, and that we may be retrograding from, say, the hellenic principle of "deity."

Bosanquet comments as follows:

The unity is space-time. This is the absolute for (Alexander). It is the lowest expression of the universe, not, as the absolute for absolutist, the highest.

And he then continues:

There is no universal mind; no common mind either in family, society, State, or the religious experience, such as the facts of a general will, or a will shared in religion by God and man, seem to most of us to affirm. . . . Every mind is, for this attitude, a thing among things; a complex of qualities, including consciousness, carried by a special complex of space-time, within the pattern which constitutes an organism.

And later he remarks:

It is not an infinite or individual unity, one in which the whole inspires every member. If infinite in a sense, it is an infinite of a low order.

"Does infinite deity exist?" asks Alexander. "Infinite deity does not exist," he replies. The only "infinite" that exists is his peculiar spatio-temporal infinite "of a low order," as Bosanquet says. For him there is only the restless, evolutionist mud, or space-time stuff, out of which life springs, "tending towards infinite deity," which is, however, not existent. *It has not had time yet to come into existence.* So bottomless is the naïf belief in the reality of Time of this philosopher. But to that further position an acceptance of the reality of Time and Change must lead any person thinking at all consistently.

Finally, with regard to the God of Alexander, this practical deity that is a carrot held before the donkey's nose, it is essentially a *God of action* with which we are dealing. "When Faust rejects the words 'in the beginning was the word' and substitutes 'in the beginning was the act,' he marks the passage from transcendence to immanence, from theism to pantheism" (Professor Alexander writing in the *Hibbert Journal*, January 1927). So for us for whom the greek Logos, rather than the principle of futurism and *action*, is the true God, Faust's correction was one of the turning-points, in the bad sense, of the modern world, the opening of our decadence of sensationalism and "action."

In an earlier chapter we have enumerated a few of the most obvious advantages of a transcendent over an immanent God, and need not repeat them here. Professor Alexander's theory of deity might, perhaps, masquerade as an attempt to provide the religious sensibility with a God possessing the advantages both of immanence and transcendence — both of which needs are felt, so he says, by the average man possessed of a religious consciousness. This account of what he has done we should certainly repudiate; for his theory is a particularly muddy form of pantheism, leaving the minimum of individuality to the finite mind involved in it. Indeed, dependence upon that lowest type of Infinite on record, as the God of Alexander's doctrine may safely be described, would exert an immense retrogressive influence upon any mind submitting itself to it. Only with a transcendent God is it possible to secure a true individualism: and the limited transcendence of such a principle as Bradley's Absolute withdraws all individuality from us more even than does a pantheistic system, as must be felt immediately by any attentive reader of his famous book.

It is in connection with our definition of reality that we are turning to those pictures of God. Is it not possible to define reality without considering the notion of deity at all? it might be asked. That question has already been answered. The sense of personality, of being a person, is, according to us, the most vivid and fundamental sense that we possess: sharper and more complete than sight, built up like sight with reminiscence, though belonging to an infinite rather than a finite memory, so much so indeed that some philosophers have thought that this sense was memory only: and it is also essentially one of *separation*. In our approaches to God, in consequence, we do not need to "magnify" a human body, but only to intensify that consciousness of a separated and transcendent life. So God becomes the supreme symbol of our separation and of our limited transcendence. He is also our memory, as it were, and when we refer to God it is as though we were bringing memory to life. It is, then, because the sense of personality is posited as our greatest "real," that we require a "God," a something that is nothing but a *person*, secure in its absolute egoism, to be the rationale of this sense. On the other hand, the God of pantheism is the *impersonal* God (and that for us is no god), as ours is the *personal* God. Also, whenever natural science constructs a deity, it is invariably an *impersonal* one: a certain form of pantheism is the true religion of science. Perhaps an easy way to give definition to this notion is to suppose us as being the natural material of God's isolation. But whatever the figure you employ to bring before you the nature of God may be, we suggest that it cannot be by appeals to our human desire to be cherished or watched over or bathed in a maternal warmth, that you should inspire yourself. God must be a sexless image, not the "matrix" of Alexander, but a head and its mind; so the body goes, a better way than into the matrix of space-time. And so we shall be considered as originating in a *mind*, too, rather than in a *matrix*. Also God must be imagined as indifferent. We do not want a God that is a kindly uncle, nor do we wish to see a God "in love." Any interest taken in us can be nothing but an intellectual passion: and surely we should be satisfied to be "thoughts," rather than "children."

Is God, according to your notion, the reality, then? you may inquire. That could be answered in several ways. It could be answered that we were the only "reality," that it would be ridiculous to imagine God as "real," which is our term to describe the actualities of our life. Professor Alexander would say the opposite to that; he would say that everything is real, and that God is real, too, when we imagine him, or where we experience the want to become something *more* than we are. And we should then say that Professor Alexander is only capable of imagining a "real" God, that he has not the sense for what is unreal. That is what he means, of course, when he says with a satisfied consciousness of being certain of popular approval, that he is a "realist."

William James (in defending the idea of growth, or of our expanding and contracting reality, as against the reality of an unchanging amount of what is real) expresses the difficulty as follows:

The world seems, on the concrete and proximate level at least, really to grow. So the question recurs: how do our finite experiences come into being from moment to moment? By inertia? By perpetual creation? Do the new ones come at the call of the old ones? Why do not they all go out like a candle? . . . Who can tell offhand? The question of being is the darkest in all philosophy. All of us are beggars here, and no school can speak disdainfully of another. . . . Fact forms a datum, gift, or Vorgefundenes, which we cannot burrow under, explain or get behind. It makes itself somehow, and our business is far more with its What than with its Whence or Why.

The type of "realism" that we have been considering might affect to agree with that statement; but it would immediately proceed to "burrow under, explain and get behind," to weigh divinity in its balance, and establish the status of the "real." If, then, in one sense you wished to know what the "real" was, you could not do better than go to Alexander. With him you get the "real," in one sense, right enough, intelligently organized and ready for use. It is an expanding "real": "the world seems," as James says, "on the concrete and proximate level at least, really *to grow.*" So it does. But what Bosanquet says of Croce and Gentile is very applicable also to the philosophy of Alexander, and to a less degree of James.

. . . there is no question that in their minds this is what they intend to affirm — viz., that in its very basis and meaning, reality is a history or an unending dialectical progression. And the narrowness of their conception of progress is quite typical of the views which belong to Progress of the Species theories. It is the progress *ad infinitum* of the human species on the surface of the earth. They speak of the whole, but in practice the universe either disappears altogether or is entirely secondary to terrestrial history. Immanence is to be absolute. . . . Though it is strikingly argued that "all history is contemporary," this can only refer to the nexus of events as seen by finite minds from their position as a centre in time at any moment.

It is some combination of the immense vistas opened up by science on the one hand, and this parochial progressiveness of time-philosophy on the other, that is so disconcerting in the world of contemporary thought. The physical vastness of the scientific picture, and the emotional or intellectual narrowness of the philosophical generalization accompanying it, is very striking. The phenomenalist assurance and neatness of the "realist" in philosophy is sometimes staggering.

But if there is to be any "real," it may be contended, it must be the "real" that we can immediately know and of which we have some experience: and so to narrow our view to the progress, or retrogression, of the human species upon the surface of the earth is necessary. Otherwise we simply lose ourselves in the vague and inane. Practically, and in certain connections, that is no doubt the case. But the "real" cannot be considered as residing either in the "narrowness" on the one hand or in the vastness on the other — both regions for which science is responsible.

For Alexander actually the question of "reality" would present no difficulties. He knows quite well what reality is. "The real is Space-Time." There is no hesitation at all as far as he is concerned. "Our consciousness of reality," he affirms, "is the consciousness that anything we apprehend belongs to Space-Time."

This "reality" of Alexander's, however, is not the same thing as truth. Everything is real, but not everything is appropriate. ". . . in being aware of a real proposition as true we add nothing to its reality." The reality is quite independent of us. We merely establish a system of orthodox perspectives.

The mind which has truth has it so far as various minds collectively contribute their part to the whole system of true beliefs; the mind which has error is so far an outcast from the intellectual community. . . . Error is detected . . . on its subjective side [when] it fails to cohere with the social believings . . . truth means the settling down of individual believings into a social whole and the condemnation of the heretical or unscientific believing. . . . True knowledge therefore owes its truth to the collective mind, but its reality to the proposition which is judged. The divergences of standard minds from the isolated minds of the victims of error are the mode by which we come to apprehend propositions as true.

There is no absolute truth, then, for Alexander, or unity of truth, but only a majority-judgment or belief. Any other truth would be equally true, which some other majority decided upon. If the majority decided that the sun was black, the heretical and exceptional minds who regarded it as usually a sort of yellow, would be in error. In contradiction to this theory of a collective truth, our experience shows us that it is always an "heretical" minority that imposes its truth upon the majority. In the Copernican Revolution or the Relativity Revolution, or in any other, we know that some "truth" that seemed quite mad at first to the common-sense of the majority gets itself accepted. Whether ultimately truer or not is immaterial, for what it superseded equally might be false. Again, what is "unscientific" believing today is "scientific" believing tomorrow. So it does appear that "truth," like Alexander's God, *is variable.* It expands and contracts. "Truth" is only what is within our temporal purview. But it comes about in the opposite manner to that involved in the "collective" doctrine of Alexander. It is always "heretical": and it is always the truth of a minority, or of an "isolated mind," that today is regarded as "a victim of error," and is found tomorrow to have been possessed, against the general belief, of the purest truth. For, like the space-time God, the truth-bearing individual is always ahead of the rest of the world, although no one could claim that they willed him, and strained towards him, in order to reach his higher level. Rather he *drags them up* by the scruff of the neck.

Truth for Alexander, then, and equally for Whitehead, is merely a coherence. "Reality" is quite incoherent. What we call truth is a perspective of the incoherent reality; which gives it, for us, a meaning, a quite arbitrary, chronological meaning. This, too, is Spengler's view of the matter. The same "reality," from another point of view, with another "perspective," would be totally different, and our "truth" would be then, under those differing circumstances, the most consummate error.

But what is this mysterious "incoherent" reality, that may assume any form, and that is amenable to a million different "truths"? For it has an objective settled "truth" of its own, in spite of all its variability. Variously combined, it produces different "truths": but there is something about it that is invariable, and therefore objectively "true." In other words, what is "true" in the "real"?

What is true in the real, the *only* fundamental objective truth, is Space-time, says Alexander. Time and change are *true* — nothing else. All the other "truths" in the world are, like our human "tertiary qualities" ("beauty," "truth," etc.), infinitely variable. The intuitional basis of space-time is, however, constant and real. *It* is real in its own right, and related to nothing. For Kant, for instance, that was real only as related to us. For the contemporary time-philosopher space-time is fundamental: and it is also an *objective* reality, upon which a house of cards of emergent qualitied relata are constructed. Constructed what by? By themselves? By inertia? By perpetual creation? Alexander is not so modest as James, though he retains all the attitudes of diffidence. "Space-time" becomes distinctly personal even from time to time, and in his system we can perceive it at work in the days of its earliest perplexities. We can almost see it scratching its head.

If it is asked . . . by what steps it is that *mere motion under the guiding hand of time* leads to the emergence of the material complexes of motion which we find in the world of things; how a specific motion like that of light is generated, with constant and maximal velocity, and how atoms come into existence as combinations of electrons . . . with relatively constant constitutions: I can only reply that *I do not know . . . in the absence of indications from the physicist*. . . . Yet it is difficult to refrain from hazarding conjecture by way of asking a question.

And so I dare to ask if there may not be in these ages of simpler existence something corresponding to the method pursued by nature in its higher stages. . . . *Whether . . . nature or Space-time did not try various complexes of simple motions and out of the chaos of motion preserve certain types.* The ground which justifies us in asking this question is . . . for instance, in the organization of the atoms; in the law that the physical and chemical elements observe certain periods or cycles which are connected with the number of the atomic weights . . . in the observed transformation of atoms into atoms of other properties; all phenomena which suggest *growth* of a certain kind.

I have italicized what I want to draw attention to in this passage. "In the absence of the physicist" and his theory, Professor Alexander can say nothing on this point. But he can, of course, suggest that probably evolution plays its part inside the atom as outside. He goes back to the "ages of simpler existence," when the "intuitive" chaos of the original Space-time of his imagination was in its first undiscriminated flux. What its quantity then was, how long it lasted, down to *what* simplicity it should be supposed to reduce itself if you go far enough back (for we must not suppose a time when it did not exist), he does not say. But he tentatively shows us "nature or Space-time" trying this and trying that, "preserving" certain types, rejecting others. Or he shows us "mere motion" being benevolently "guided," or led by the hand, by Time, already bent upon producing, somehow or other, Sir Isaac Newton, Abraham Lincoln, a line of Mikados, Pola Negri and Pirandello, Chaplin and Chaliapin, and so forth. Space-time in "nature" is very clearly personified for the occasion—for it is difficult, in such elementary conditions, to keep some personality out: but having got so far in "hazarding conjecture," the writer thinks that he has gone far enough. It is already much!

So for some reason our low-grade, spatio-temporal, evolutionary first-stuff was resolved to complicate itself at all cost; or some kind of spirit ("nature") was there imbued with that resolve. But really no primitive story of the creation, however naïf, is more clumsy and irrational than the myth into which we are led by this philosopher, that that he finds it "difficult to refrain" from imagining.

Something in the dark backwood of the simplest ages was very busy and intelligent, though "empirically" there is no clue to the motive of this urgent selective activity, and the "absence of the physicist" complicates matters: and again, on the face of the picture given us, it seems highly improbable that any such thing should have occurred. But it *did* occur. I suggest that the fact that it *did* occur is Professor Alexander's trump card, and that he has no other at all. It is all of the nature of a *miracle.* Elsewhere he writes:

. . . quality is carried by particular complexities of the *a priori* foundation of all things, Space-time, whose fundamental features the categories are. *Miraculous we may call the existence of quality if we choose.* But it is at least a miracle which pervades the world of things. The relation of the secondary qualities to matter is not stranger than the relation of life or mind to that which carries them.

It is not "if we choose," however, that we call these things miraculous. We have no choice, and Professor Alexander displays very fully indeed that he has no choice either in the matter. In attempting to rationalize the miracle he can hardly have expected to succeed.

So there is a reality, that is Alexander's version, more real than "truth," a very simple one, and it is called Space-time. It is an objective reality. It is related to nothing, it does not get its being by way of relation. But how or why this ultimate reality should be objective, why it should be unrelated to anything, any more than anything else, or why it should be peculiarly "real," is difficult to understand, and we are given no clue. Surely, if you go far enough back to the sources of this *real* dialectical progression, the "Unmoved Mover" of Aristotle is at the least no more difficult to accept than is "Space-time"? No "realist should go so far back.

So for Alexander "truth is different from reality"; whereas for us truth is reality, and there is only one truth. The various appearances of it are in no sense "true," though certain combinations of empirical things are able, like a magical word or a countersign, to reveal the truth for a moment.

. . . truth is indeed what works [he says]. Reality is indeed no fixed thing, but being temporal is evolving fresh types of existence.

Again:

. . . truth is . . . *progressive* . . . truth *varies* and grows obsolete or

even turns to falsehood. Hence a theory may be true for one generation and false for the next.

These quotations should be enlightening. *Truth is what works.*
But that is why the truth of one time is not the truth of another:
the truths in question are merely *working* truths or formulae.
A theory is true today: tomorrow it will be false, says Alexander.
But would it not be better to say that *neither* was ever *true*: that
no truth of ours can ever be comprehensive enough to be true:
and that to put ourselves at the point of view of the Absolute,
would be so to "transmute" our finite life, as Bradley puts it, or
to destroy it altogether. Both the "theories" in question were working hypotheses. One may have improved upon the other, or it
may not. At all events, another is tried in the place of the first.
First we stress one side, then the other. But no first-rate man-of-
science today pretends that his theory is *true*. "True" is a word
that does not exist in his vocabulary. And in this connection it
should not exist in ours, as far as our working hypotheses are
concerned.

In what sense can "reality," that consuming fire, be said to be
usable by us? It is certainly not a deliverance of the "collectivity,"
or the possession of a "standard mind": neither truth nor reality
are that. Alexander carefully separates the "real" from the "true";
and we have given an outline of our reasons for repudiating that
separation. Once they are together again, touching and warm-
ing us from their distant sphere, we have to ask ourselves what,
in the language of common-sense, is the "realest" thing of which
we have experience. This reality would certainly lie in the region
of the "secondary" or "tertiary" qualities, and not in the region
of mere punctual and instantaneous entities, or in the hypothetic
atom, or in any of the *simpler* conditions, nor in a nature
"saturated with Time" sufficiently to satisfy Alexander. Truth is
found rather by the individual than by the collectivity, to commence with: the standard mind and variable truth of Alexander
is a practical truth, and he has every justification for separating
it from reality, if only he would not call it "truth."

In Bradley's account of the degrees of reality the amount that
an individual possesses can be tested by the amount of strain
beneath which he is able to retain the individuality, or the point
at which that breaks down. The Absolute would be the individual
of individuals, the self that has never broken down but has

maintained its isolation. So according to that view, and according to ours, reality is to be sought in the self or the person.

To take the things of our common world, the chairs and tables, as the most obvious examples of "reality," it is often believed that a philosophy that denies a full reality to these things volatilizes them in some way. That is what "idealism," for instance, is supposed to do. But science could with more truth be said to do that: and yet science does not deny the appearance; it merely asserts that, using eyes of a different magnitude, the appearance would be a different one.

The problem can be illustrated best, perhaps, by reverting to the question of the "beautiful." In looking at Helen of Troy the average man would no doubt assert that Helen was "beautiful." If all that he had ever seen of Helen of Troy were a section of her cheek under a microscope, he would have a different view of Helen. The velvet surface of the peach would become a pitted, scarred and hairy surface. Taking a contemporary Helen, and imagining a man first observing her with the "naked eye," and after that observing a section of her cheek considerably magnified, were this observer possessed of a martial mind, insensibly his emotion would pass from that stimulated by a "beautiful" cheek to that belonging to a battlefield covered with shell holes. That might have its beauty too: so it would be a passage from one sort of "beauty" to another, from the beauty of sex to the beauty of war. But plainly there is an element of unreality or artificiality in this "beauty" of ours that is only "beautiful" according to one scale and standard pair of eyes: and equally the section seen under the microscope would convey nothing of the virtues or meaning of the whole.

In every separate and familiar object you get contrasted several forms of reality or truth, after the manner of Alexander's exposition. In any armchair, for instance, there is to be found side by side, (1) the "truth" about it belonging to the artist who observes it as a factor in some picture he is painting: (2) the "truth" of the upholsterer: there is (3) the practical "truth" appreciated by its possessor: and then there is (4) the "truth" of the electronic mass of science. These four examples will suffice.

This last truth, that of science, is precisely the picture of the early chaos, the "simplest ages" of Alexander — only, as it were, in the form of an armchair: and here it swarms, domesticated, with us, we are assured, transfixed in this shape and that, in our rooms, for our daily use and comfort. And according to science, we carry up that ultra simple material, too, concentrated into lumps, and given, magically, the diagram of our organism.

Nothing could be more different than these various armchairs as seen by the artist, the upholsterer, by the imagination of science, etc. What we assert is that the armchair of science — the simplest armchair — is the least "real," that it has, indeed, almost no reality. The armchair of the artist is the most "real." But the armchair of the artist is scarcely any longer an armchair, if the artist is a good enough one. It then goes out of reality at the other side, the opposite to that of science. What science has done for us is to restore the primitive chaos and "bring it into the home," as it were. There it is installed in the midst of our daily life. We know now, or think we know, that the pipe we hold is a lump of "the simplest ages," or implicitly is that. Our bed is a volcano, potentially, as far as power goes and incalculability, and if we had powerful enough instruments to observe it, it would be a seething ocean of movement, or would disappear altogether.

The scientific object, the simplest aspect of any given object, "exists" in the same sense and on the same level of reality as the image. It is a world of hypothesis: it is what *should* be there if the empirical systems of fact could lead us to some absolute. It would be an absolute of a very low and very dull order; but there it would be, and our reality would be held by grace of it. It is in that sense the material of such a sign-world as that of Berkeley, who said of the external world of objects, that they were not actual, but that that is what they would be like and how they would behave, if they *were* real: that if there could be such a thing as an actual fire, that then it would *burn* us when we touched it, just as we now imagine that it burns. And in this sense it is argued here that the entire physical world is strictly unreal; and the unrealest part of it we believe is that part or aspect supplied us by science. So with bridle and bit we ride the phantoms of sense, as though to the manner born. Or rather it would be more descriptive of our actual experience to say that, camped somnolently, in a relative repose of a god-like sort, upon the surface of this nihilism, we regard ourselves as at rest, with our droves of objects — trees, houses, hills — grouped round us. Berkeley is a popular hero of many relativists today: and he is the greatest exponent of an extreme "idealism." The characteristic essence of the doctrine of Berkeley is to be found in the following words of his (*Principles of Human Knowledge*):

As to what is said of the absolute existence of *unthinking things* without any relation to their being perceived, that seems perfectly unintelligible. Their *esse* is *percipi*, nor is it possible they should have any existence, out of the minds or *thinking things*, which perceive them.

And the essence of that is that for that doctrine, or any resembling it, the objects of the external world shall be *unthinking things*. All the arguments of such a philosophy as Alexander's are directed to distributing mind or feeling of some sort ("Time" is his word for the mental principle that is so distributed) throughout the external universe. For those philosophers there is no especially *thinking thing*, called a "mind." All is mind to some extent. Whereas for Berkeley there are "unthinking things." For him all is mental too, but in a different and opposite manner.

When you look at a red-brick house, with its windows and chimney-pots, in one of two directions you must go. If you go with Berkeley in the direction of common-sense, it will be for you a collection of "unthinking things." But what is so *unreal* as a collection of "unthinking things," of dead, inanimate matter? If you stick to that direct deliverance of common-sense, the moment you begin reflecting about it, you will be compelled to admit that that cannot be "real." It is a thing that our minds, *in cold-blood, as it were, and reflectively*, are unable to imagine. This conclusion is generally labelled "idealism."

The other direction you can take is to repudiate altogether this view of common-sense. You then attempt to rationalize the picture of common-sense. You bring the external world to life, you animate it with some degree of mental existence. The philosophies grouped under that attitude are known as "realism." Realism, thus interpreted, Berkeley attributes to the ascendancy of "abstract ideas."

It is indeed an opinion strangely prevailing amongst men, that houses, mountains, rivers, and in a word all sensible objects, have an existence natural or real, distinct from their being perceived by the understanding. . . . If we thoroughly examine this tenet, it will, perhaps, be found at bottom to depend on the doctrine of *abstract ideas*. For can there be a nicer strain of abstraction than to distinguish the existence of sensible objects from their being perceived, so as to conceive them existing unperceived.

Berkeley quite rightly up to a point claims to have common-sense on his side. Yet of course the plain man would scarcely recognize himself in the shape Berkeley attributes to him. There is no doubt, also, some little confusion in detail in his manipulation of this delicate point. He opens his discourse (in the treatise from which I am quoting) with eloquent advances to the plain man and his common-sense, as against the "verbalism" and "abstractions" of the philosophers. It might be thought, he says, that the pursuit of philosophy would bring "calm and serenity of mind." But this is not the case: whereas "the illiterate bulk of mankind, that walk the highroad of plain, common-sense . . . [are] for the most part easy and undisturbed." It is the illusion of the abstract that makes thought a curse to the philosopher. Yet above we see him attributing the view he is attacking to the prevalence of a "strain of abstraction" in the majority. But he clings, and I think successfully, to his paradox: thus "a man need only *open his eyes* to see" that there is nothing there except what his mind puts there; and so forth. This last scrap of quotation will serve to show the reader, I think, how berkeleyan idealism is by no means incompatible with the kind of vivid realism that is being advocated in these pages. For he implores you merely to "open your eyes" and to *see* that the world is not real in the sense you had thought: the wider you open them the more you will perceive that this is the case. And yet in another sense for that very reason the more real it will be.

This may at first seem puzzling: for although the real of a "realist" like Alexander is certainly very different from the real of the man in the street, all the same what is alleged by him is that his "real" is nearer that direct and naïf reality than is the real of Berkeley or of Bradley. But Berkeley claims, as we have seen, the same support for his real, too.

He, too, is never tired of appealing to common-sense. What I suggest is that both are so far from the normal real that neither has strictly any right to lay claim to the confirmation of the naïf vision. Yet in a very important sense Berkeley's doctrine derives from it more truly than that of a critical or neo-realist.

What is not sometimes quite understood is that equally for the most fanatical "idealist" and the most dogmatic "realist" the picture of the external world is precisely the same. For both the tables and chairs are there just the same, when we are looking at them, at least. Bosanquet quotes Bradley in this connection as follows:

If the reader believes that a steam-engine, after it is made, is nothing but a state of mind of the person or persons who made it, or who are looking at it, we do not hold what we feel tempted to call such a silly doctrine, and would point out to those who do hold it that, at all events, the engine is a very different state of mind, after it is made, to what it is before.

That will settle that difficulty, I hope. There should really be no confusion at all here. It is not the objective reality, but the value to be attached to what is "objective," that the argument is about. Even if you, in the Berkeleyan sense, *put* the chair and the table there, it is natural to assume that you should experience these images more intensely than if they merely exist there in the naïvest sense, independent of your consciousness. Again, "the effect of the empirical method in metaphysics," says Alexander, "is seriously and persistently *to treat finite minds as one among the many forms of finite existence, having no privilege above them*," etc. And this, as we have shown, must involve some degree of "mentalism" (and the other fine things that human minds have arrogated to themselves as contrasted with saucepans and chimney-pots) being bestowed upon all material objects. They cease to be the "unthinking objects" they still remain, from the legacy of common-sense, for Berkeley. They change more under the "realist" régime than they do under the "idealist." The latter leaves them more like what they are in common-sense. It says of them that *all* that they are is what they *appear*: and, in consequence, indeed unlikely and unreal, although orderly and persistent.

But having got so far, it is necessary to point out that the contrast of these two points of view has been assuming a uniformity in "idealism" and in "realism" that does not at all exist: and what would be true of one of the time-philosophers would not be true of another in detail. Messrs. Russell, Alexander, Broad and Whitehead, for instance, are all zealous supporters of Relativity. But Russell is very hostile to Bergson, and inclines to berkeleyan idealism, and believes that Relativity will result in a merger with another idealism of that type. Professor Alexander would not be of that opinion at all — his is another view. Broad is less "realist" than Alexander, and so on.

If there were such things today as pure berkeleyans, you would find them interpret objective fact very differently. One would give the concrete images of things more substantiality than another. Cardinal features of Berkeley's doctrine they would most likely dissent from. And so it would not be any use to expect something hard and fast either in one place or the other: and I have been using this hard and fast contrast for the purposes of demonstration only.

But there is a further complication, I regret to say, and that is that not everybody would consent to this view of the matter. Indeed, Professor Moore, in his famous *Refutation of Idealism* (reprinted in *Philosophical Studies* [Harcourt, Brace & Company]), gives a quite contrary view to the one I have just enunciated. For the benefit of those not acquainted with that essay, I will quote from its opening:

Modern Idealism, if it asserts any general conclusion about the universe at all, asserts that it is *spiritual* . . . whatever be its meaning [that of the above assertion] it is certainly meant to assert (1) that the universe is very different indeed from what it seems, and (2) that it has quite a large number of properties which it does not seem to have. Chairs and tables and mountains *seem* to be very different from us; but when the whole universe is declared to be spiritual, it is certainly meant to assert that they are far more like us than we think. The idealist means to assert that they are *in some sense* neither lifeless nor unconscious, as they certainly seem to be. . . . When the whole universe is declared to be spiritual, it is meant that not only is it in some sense *conscious*, but that it has what we recognize in ourselves as the *higher* forms of consciousness. That it is intelligent; that it is purposeful; that it is not mechanical. . . . In general, it may be said, this phrase "reality is spiritual" excites and expresses the belief that the *whole* universe possesses *all the qualities* the possession of which is held to make us so superior to things which seem to be inanimate: at least, if it does not possess exactly those which we possess, it possesses not one only, but several others, which, by the same ethical standard, would be judged equal to or better than our own.

It will be noted that Professor Moore is describing "Modern Idealism," and he is referring no doubt to such philosophers as Croce and Gentile. But I feel sure that since the days when he wrote that, Professor Moore has had reason to change his opinion on the respective merits of "realism" and "idealism"; or, rather, that he would express himself very differently today in "refuting" the latter.

First of all, the "Modern Idealism" he envisaged was the pantheistic *Progress of the Species* variety which is *toto caelo* different from anything imagined by Berkeley. Professor Moore had not at that time the enlightening experience that since he must have had of seeing a certain brand of cleverly-adulterated idealism drawing ever nearer to a highly-mentalized type of "realism," that was a very different doctrine to anything that Professor Moore would expect to see appearing under either of those generic terms, until the present merger was effected.

What I venture to suggest is that Professor Moore is very much nearer to Berkeley (on the showing, for instance, of the above passage) than he is either to Samuel Alexander, the "realist," or Giovanni Gentile, the "idealist." And so I do not think that the above statement, in such extreme contradiction to all I have just said, need be taken, if properly understood, as contradicting me at all. It can even be regarded as a confirmation. For the organic conception of nature, that makes the universe into an absolutist intuitive animal, is at an equal distance from the mode of thought of Bishop Berkeley and of what is apparently Professor Moore's way of reacting to the mundane spectacle.

It is, to begin with, extremely just as a description of the italian "idealism" which, under the one composite banner of "Time," marches together in perfect fundamental unison with Alexander, with Bergson or with James. But it would be totally untrue of Berkeley, if I understand his doctrine at all.

Berkeley could not, I am sure, be interpreted as wishing to say that "chairs and tables and mountains . . . are far more like us than we think." For him they are "unthinking objects" essentially. Or rather, in proving that "unthinking objects" or a "materia prima" is a mistaken belief or even an absurdity, was he not indirectly showing that we *think* it since it cannot *be*? "The general idea of being," he writes, "appeareth to me the most abstract and incomprehensible of all other." And "the general idea of being," he says, is identical, for the materialist, with "matter." We could further say that by the idea of being is meant *absolute being*. ("It is on this therefore that I insist, to wit, the *absolute* existence of unthinking things are words without a meaning." — *Principles of Human Knowledge*, xxiv. It is the *absolute* that is stressed by him.) *Anything short of that* is imagination.

And so the material world must, from that standpoint, be imaginary: and the very effrontery of its superb solidness and the bland assurance with which it is camped before us, should actually help us to realize that. That air of being so perfectly *at home*, at rest and serenely unconcerned (of being "unthinking," in short, and without feeling) should be the greatest proof of its unreality. It seems almost to know, if it could be said to realize anything, that it is playing at *being*. And the more *solid* it is the more unearthly, in that sense.

Professor Moore, as I have said, was not referring to Berkeley: for Berkeley that would be as untrue an account as it is a true one of the "idealists" whom he had in mind. For Berkeley the world would certainly be "mechanical" — our sign-world in his system would be beneath a strict system of laws. It would not be "purposeful," except for *our* purposefulness, for it would have no impulse of its own, it would depend upon us entirely, itself in reality non-existent. But the point need not be laboured. I may add that as regards the general temper of Professor Moore, I am far more in sympathy with it than with that of the "idealists" he was refuting in that early essay of his, or with his "realistic" colleague, Alexander. Professor Moore's desire to have matter *dead* (which at once makes it palpably unreal) appears to me to mark him down as possessing one of the most important components of an "idealist" disposition of mind, if that term must be employed. Even the reasons he implies in the passage quoted above are all of them "idealist" reasons. I vie with Professor Moore in wanting things *solid* and wanting them *dead.* The only difference is that he believes them to be "real," and I do not. But that separates us far less radically than do those differences of a more fundamental order that divide me from the doctrines of Alexander, Whitehead, Bergson or Croce.

The difficulty where the philosophy of Berkeley is concerned is to arrive at the exact value attaching to his imaginary world. For instance, he says that you can believe if you like that bodies exist without the mind, but that it must at the best be "a precarious opinion": and the reason he gives is that that would be to suppose that "God had created innumerable beings *that are entirely useless, and serve to no manner of purpose."* Now it is impossible that it should not have occurred to him that the *ideas* of these innumerable beings, likewise, that do exist and that God has equally created, represented just as strictly *useless* an activity, as if he had actually created them "naïvely" in the flesh. What is there to choose, from the point of view of "uselessness," between one world and the other? So it is evident, surely, that that was not the point that interested him. We have before us, to every detail, the appearance of a world run with the sweat of the brow and in a hot and living travail. The point of the argument is therefore the mere technical one, as it were, that the "real" is an illusion; that the external material world does not even belong to what Hegel referred to as "so poor a category as *being*, the very poorest and most abstract of all." And the more you penetrate into it, of course, as a result of "taking it seriously," the more it reveals itself as an abstraction, the more abstract it becomes, until it loses every semblance of reality even.

What would be the likely practical outcome of such a view as I have just been outlining? What perhaps has most interest for us here, is that one of the various attempts to impart reality to the world of appearance has the curious result of making it, in effect, less real — in fact, of converting it into a sort of mirror-world, as we have elsewhere conveniently described it. The result of "taking it" too "seriously" has invariably been to make it almost disappear altogether. In a sense, of course, that could be described just as *not* taking it seriously. It is scepticism, in the first place, that leads to such results. To accept it at its face-value is to "take it seriously," if you like, though scepticism is the more "serious" of the two approaches. Nothing, in a certain sense, more flippant has ever been invented than the gimcrack world of façades of Berkeley — that of tables and chairs that come and go, of hollow and one-sided mountains, like theatrical structures of stucco, of bodies into which food passes, but that have no insides, since no insides are, after all, *perceived*; and "*esse* is *percipi*" forbids all entrails. It is an extremist philosophy for *surface-creatures*: and it is as that, essentially, as I have remarked in an earlier part of this book, that we should, I believe, regard ourselves.

Without adhering to the detail of the world of Berkeley — it is too dim in its mentalism, and dark, definitely, sometimes — and the disproportion of his theologic bias is a great obstacle ultimately — it is one of the best of all possible philosophic worlds. But using again, to make myself clear, the word employed above, it is not quite "serious" enough. We think, for instance, that the mind, in its unconscious part, could be said to maintain the mountains, tables and chairs in imaginative sub-existence, when not directly objects of perception: and I think we should be justified in saying that by some analogical process the inside of an elm or a cedar, for example, could be said to be there, although it has never been perceived. When the food goes into the body we can *feel* it, of course, so that gives us back our own insides, even on the berkeleyan basis.

It has not been with a view to promoting any theory of my own, however, that I undertook the writing of this essay, but only to supply a fairly detailed analysis of the prevalent time-doctrine. To specify further or even to outline the particular beliefs that are explicit in my criticism would require another book. That I propose soon to publish. But, as far as this particular critical task is concerned, I now have completed it. So I leave this critical essay in the hands of the reader, without further comment, in the belief that it will serve to throw into immediate relief the origins and implications of time-doctrine, in a form accessible to the general educated person.

EDITORIAL SECTION

AFTERWORD

I

1. *Structure and argument*

Time and Western Man is Wyndham Lewis's chief work of
criticism, and it is probably cited more frequently than any of his other
critical books. This is because of its notorious attacks on the work of
Lewis's friends, James Joyce and Ezra Pound, and its less well-known
attack on the work of Gertrude Stein. Because Joyce incorporated his
response to Lewis in *Finnegans Wake*, the chapter on him is often consulted by students of that work. But what tends to be overlooked is
that Lewis's critiques, fascinating though they are as individual essays,
are part of a more general critique of modern culture which is the subject of the book as a whole. Lewis himself is partly to blame for this.
Time and Western Man was not carefully planned and executed, but
grew out of a scheme of publications that developed and altered over
several years. This development is described in Part II of the Afterword. The consequence of the process of revision, expansion and
reorganization is that the structure of ideas that Lewis unfolds does not
fully determine the structure of the book as a whole. Many readers,
however dazzled they may have been by the critical attacks in Book
One, "The Revolutionary Simpleton," must have been baffled by the
references to the "Time-philosophy" which Lewis opposes. Each reference to it in Book One seems provisional; all will become clear when
Book Two is reached, the reader hopes. But for many readers it
never really does, since Lewis does not explain, systematically and
step by step, first, what "Time-philosophy" is, exactly how it is related
to the work of the writers he criticizes in Book One, why he considers
its effects to be pernicious, and finally in what respects he considers
it to be untrue. It is not that Lewis fails to treat these matters; the problem is that he does not discuss them in a systematic way, and a reader
is left to draw the threads together himself. A sometimes confusing structure leads to a confused response, and even the sympathetic reader
is tempted to ask if the book is held together by much more than Lewis's
apparently paranoiac belief that everything he opposes is a symptom
of an all-pervasive but unidentifiable "Time-philosophy." Why, anyway,
oppose the incorporation of time into art or philosophical systems? Our
world is marked by both time and space, so to oppose with such fer-
vor one of its dimensions must be the result of a hobby-horsical
eccentricity amounting almost to lunacy. But *Time and Western Man*

455

has its own coherence, and Lewis's claim for it as a critique based on consistent principles is largely justified.

Lewis himself was a little surprised at such criticisms of his books. In a draft opening of what became Chapter 3 of Book One of *Time and Western Man*, Lewis wrote that critics had complained about the lack of connection among the thirteen parts of *The Art of Being Ruled*:

This criticism, I came to the conclusion, was the result of the inability on the part of the critics to grasp the connection between things so superficially dissimilar as those occupying the place of honour in the respective main divisions of the book . . . rather than any omission on my part to make clear this connection.[1]

Lewis, although better read and more learned than most academics, was not academically trained, and he took his ideas for the organization of books from such favorites of his youth as Nietzsche and Georges Sorel, neither of whom systematically expound their ideas. Something of a skimmer and skip-reader himself, Lewis expected readers to dip in here and there until they had grasped the argument of a book, then to read more extensively in the light of their preliminary conclusions — which is what he did himself, as can be seen by the pattern of annotations in that portion of his personal library that is preserved in the Harry Ransom Humanities Research Center at the University of Texas. His editor at Chatto and Windus, Charles Prentice, seems not to have advised Lewis on these matters.[2] But for the American edition (the text of which is followed here) Lewis included instructions for the reader on what he thought was the best order to proceed with the preliminary dipping and skimming.[3]

The merit of a book is not dependent solely on its organization, and there is at least one precedent for a great work of criticism to be thoroughly disorganized: Coleridge's *Biographia Literaria*. The precedent is a happy one, for, leaving aside the comparative merits of the two works, there are also other, more important, similarities between them. *Biographia Literaria*, the work of one of the great initiators of the Romantic movement in England, enunciates a set of philosophical principles by which poetry is to be judged, and subjects the work of Coleridge's old associate, William Wordsworth, to a penetrating critique in the light of these principles. In the process it sorts those aspects both of Wordsworth's practice and of his theory (expounded in the 1801 Preface to *Lyrical Ballads*) which accord with the principles from those that do not. *Biographia Literaria* contains a lot of "hostile" criticism (nowhere near as much as *Time and Western Man*, though) but its philosophical standpoint has become a major component of our idea of Romanticism.

In *Time and Western Man*, Wyndham Lewis attempted to do something similar for what is now (but was not then) called Modernism:

to expound the philosophical presuppositions of truly "revolutionary" art, and assess the achievements of the major Modernists in the light of these.

2. *"Kill John Bull with Art"*

As an advanced painter, and as a writer, before the First World War in London, Lewis had been associated with Ezra Pound in organizing a militant avant-garde movement (Vorticism) which constituted the first determined effort in England to establish a culture of Modernism. Vorticism was the counterpart of similar movements in Europe (Futurism providing the archetype), Russia and the United States. Lewis and Pound were easily the two most important "Vorticists." But, partly because they came to the movement from different directions, and diverged in their later careers, historians have found it difficult to describe a coherent Vorticist aesthetic. Vorticism looks like one thing if seen as part of the development of the poet of *The Cantos*, but looks different as part of Lewis's development.[4] But their association, and the association of the other Vorticists, was not fortuitous; there was a shared purpose, perhaps best summed up in Lewis's battle-cry, "Kill John Bull with Art!"[5] John Bull was England's national symbol, a beefy British yeoman who, despite his straightforward good humor, would brook no "nonsense" from intellectuals or foreigners. Depending on the nature of the political emergency, his figure was deployed in alternation with that of the more passive Britannia (a lady in Grecian draperies with trident and shield) in the cartoons of the middlebrow "humorous" magazine *Punch*. So he was (for Lewis) a symbol of a peculiarly British thick-witted complacency and philistinism. Each nation, as Lewis wrote, had its own national symbol to slay, and Ezra Pound, with his feeling that London was the cultural capital of the English-speaking world, shared the common cause.

Vorticism, then, was a movement aimed at replacing an old culture with a new one. Pound saw it in terms of a renaissance, Lewis more in terms of a revolution. They shared the belief, however, that the art and literature prized by the cultural powers of the time was second- or third-rate (suitable for John Bull or his more sensitive and pure-minded consort), and that it needed to be replaced by the sort of thing that Pound and Lewis themselves were producing. A society that understood itself and saw its values and its potential in the terms pioneered in the new arts would be better than one which believed it and its aspirations were mirrored in dreary realism, half-hearted impressionism, celebration of boy-scout decency and open-air manliness, or the ethereal evocation of diaphanous feminine loveliness. A certain kind of classicism was demanded.[6]

When Lewis wrote *Time and Western Man*, this revolutionary ambition was still alive in him. Avant-garde culture seemed to be making headway, but how well did it measure up to its revolutionary pretensions? It seemed to Lewis that the time had arrived to make a critical discrimination between those aspects of Modernist culture which served the function intended for it by Vorticism and those which belonged with a view of the world that Modernism should be superseding:

> A rigorous restatement is required, I have felt for some years, of the whole "revolutionary" position; nowhere more than in my peculiar province — art and literature. For me to undertake that statement must involve me also in a restatement of my personal position.[7]

Just as Coleridge, who called himself the "Friend," felt it necessary to dissociate himself from his old collaborator, William Wordworth, as a part of redefining his own position, so Wyndham Lewis, the self-styled "Enemy," found that his own restatement "must bring me into conflict with the interests of several people with whose names my own has been fairly closely associated."[8] Primarily this was Pound, but Lewis was also associated with Joyce, both personally and through Pound's promotion of *Tarr* and *A Portrait of the Artist as a Young Man* as the two most important novels of the new movement. And of course Lewis goes beyond, to attack the whole fashionable avant-garde movement, especially that part of it domiciled in Paris. It is a whole culture, though, that is under examination in *Time and Western Man*, and the avant garde is only a part of it. Philosophy, psychology, the cinema, advertisement and historiography are all part of Lewis's subject, since he is attempting to trace a pervasive ideology, as well as to show its deleterious effects in " 'advanced' — that is the only significant — contemporary literature."

The kind of ambition that Lewis's Vorticism had for the arts as providing the meaning, values and aspirations of a society presupposes assumptions about the relationship between the artist and society, about the nature of the work of art and its relationship to values, and about politics and progress. It is doubtful that Lewis had made these assumptions explicit even to himself during the short period before the First World War when Vorticist ambitions seemed most realizable. That war, in which Lewis served as an artilleryman at one of the most dreadful battles, the third battle of Ypres, seemed to be the negation of all that Vorticism hoped for, yet at the same time the consequence of precisely those forces and technologies that Vorticism had celebrated. After the war, with the avant garde in a seemingly discouraged state, Lewis decided that he needed to go more deeply into the assumptions underlying his ambition for the arts.

He originally intended to treat these subjects (and many others), in a vast treatise called *The Man of the World*, which was never published in its intended form.[9] *The Lion and the Fox*, the first major offshoot of it, studies the relationship between Lewis's ideal artist and society, taking Shakespeare as the main instance. Next, *The Art of Being Ruled* canvassed the possibilities of politically restructuring society, and provided an anatomy of the kind of modern consumer society for which this politics must be devised—one which, shocked by the First World War, has lapsed into passive enjoyment of the novelties supplied to it by science and industry. *Time and Western Man* returns to the arts and shows where modern culture, influenced partly unconsciously by the ideologies of this society, fails to perform the function of independent creative valuation that *The Lion and the Fox* showed Shakespeare accomplishing.

3. *The artist and the promised land*

Rather than attempt to summarize the positions expounded in these books solely, I shall range more widely, and try to summarize from Lewis's earlier work as much as is necessary for an understanding of *Time and Western Man*. First of all, the nature of Lewis's "classicism" needs explanation. It consists primarily in a belief that, to fulfil a social function, art should take its material from the here and now. Lewis's Vorticist paintings emulated the surfaces of modern cheap mass-produced materials and deployed the forms of modern architecture and machinery to express a changing consciousness of life in a technological environment. The esoteric practices by which this everyday material was re-presented as art have tended to obscure the fact that Vorticism and its magazine, *Blast*, were firmly embedded in the common experience of all city-dwellers of 1914. *Blast* made a kind of poetry out of the style and typography of the banner-headline of popular newspapers. In the manner of the sports-fan it celebrated heroes and jeered at "villains" who were taken impartially from the worlds of art, music-hall, patent medicine, boxing, the gossip column and popular nationalism. Lewis's "play," *Enemy of the Stars*, with its abrupt cutting and sudden shifts of scale and perspective, is influenced by the new, popular art of film, and the wind that blows in it, causing the actors' clothes to flap and their voices to blare up, is compared with that which is commonly met in the Tube (the new underground railway in London). Though Lewis never gave the Italian Futurist leader credit for it, it was F. T. Marinetti whose influence was responsible for this.

The work of art makes from this contemporary material something to be contemplated or more actively explored by the imagination of the spectator or reader.[10] Things are changed when they appear in a work of art, since (Lewis quotes Schopenhauer), art "plucks the object of its contemplation out of the stream of the world's course."[11] For

Schopenhauer, art is concerned with a pure, Platonic realm. But Lewis differs from Schopenhauer in regarding this pure, disinterested realm of the aesthetic as not the concern of humanity, since our own lives are too imperfect for its perfection to have meaning for us in itself.

Perfection, therefore, from this standpoint, appears as a platonic ideal, and is a thing with which we have not much to do on our present road. With perfect snowballs or lightning conductors, we have some commerce; but not with "perfect" works of art or human beings.[12]

The point is made more graphically, in relation to the "imperfection" of Shakespeare's tragedies:

The contests of pure art would be like the battles of the norse heroes in heaven. They would ride back after the battle to Valhalla or some more congenial Elysium, the wounds and deaths abolished by magic at the termination of each day. Only heroes would participate; and no reality would mar their vigorous joys.[13]

The work of art does not belong entirely to that congenial Elysium, but neither does it belong to this world, and in another place Lewis suggests that it might be seen as a form of currency making possible some form of trade between them:

It is a half-way house, the speech, life, and adornment of a half-way house. Or it is a coin that is used on a frontier, but in neither of the adjoining countries, perhaps. As we know nothing about these or any other countries, it is impossible for us to say. Art is a coin, if you like, that has no aesthetic value, only an historic one.[14]

By re-presenting and projecting our world into a new, quasi-platonic model, the artist reveals the potential inherent in our actual world. His imagination projects us into a larger air: a realm of imagined possibility rather than one whose perfection mocks man's enterprise.

The artist's urge to make things different comes from personal interests and needs. But if the work of art is to be more than individually interesting, these must be needs also felt (unconsciously, perhaps) by society.[15] In such large aggregations as modern societies this can be difficult, and Lewis can certainly be tempted (in *The Art of Being Ruled*, for instance) by the idea that life would be made more pleasing by forcing society into a rigid mold. But such a "utopia" is envisaged only in order to increase efficiency and release creative forces that modern society wastes. A fascist-type political organization of society is not, for Lewis, itself an expression of some "spirit" of a culture or people (though Lewis knows that political power is certainly exercised on behalf of ideas).[16] For Lewis does not propose, as the Romantics did, that the artist's "needs" give him access to an eternal, unitary principle from which modern societies have unfortunately alienated all but a few uncontaminated spirits, nor that it is the business of politics to ensure that that principle finds expression in the state. More characteristic of Lewis (and certainly more attractive) is the idea suggested in "Inferior Religions," that the variety of the artist's and society's needs should instead be reconciled by a social pluralism:

> Beauty is an icy douche of ease and happiness at something *suggesting* perfect conditions for an organism: it remains suggestion. . . .
> Beauty is an immense predilection, a perfect conviction of the desirability of a certain thing, whatever that thing may be. It is a universe for one organism. To a man with long and consumptive fingers, a sturdy hand may be heaven. We can aim at no universality of form, for what we see is not the reality. . . .
> —It is quite obvious though, to fulfil the conditions of successful art, that we should live in relatively small communities.[17]

But his (in terms of aesthetics, at least) more radical proposal is that the necessary pluralism of society should find an answering pluralism in the artist as well (and consequently also in the work of art).[18] The artist is a "crowd," as Lewis sometimes describes him, made up of warring impulses and contradictory possibilities and values, some of them springing from some pure, uncontaminated self, some from the necessary traffic of that self with the world. Lewis is again anti-romantic, since, just as he does not locate the work of art in a pure aesthetic realm, neither does he believe that what it expresses can be the pure "platonic" essence of the artist's self—though that self, impossible though it is to define, is the origin of what is most valuable to the artist.[19]

4. *Ideology and the critical construction of the self*

In allowing a multiple personality to put itself forth into the largest possible field of interests, the artist is in danger of losing his personality altogether, Lewis acknowledges. The danger is increased because this "putting forth" is, in the case of the truest artists, a mystical identification with what his world offers:

> In art we are in a sense playing at being what we designate as matter. We are entering the forms of the mighty phenomena around us, and seeing how near we can get to being a river or a star, without actually *becoming* that. Or we are placing ourselves somewhere behind the contradictions of matter and mind, where an identity (such as the school of American realists, William James, for example, has fancied) may more primitively exist. . . .
> The game consists in seeing how near you can get, without the sudden extinction that awaits you as matter, or as the machine.[20]

This is reiterated in *Time and Western Man*, though with the emphasis more on the artist's shamanistic contact with a non-material "supernatural" world: "The production of a work of art is, I believe, strictly the work of a visionary. . . . That the artist uses and manipulates a supernatural power seems very likely."[21] The material that is collected in the artist's forays is synthesized into a work of art partly under some form of compulsion, as in dreams:

Dreams are an example of sensations evolved, with great complexity, in a new order, and with new emotional stresses and juxtapositions. The work of the dramatist or novelist is in this category, and that of most painters whose work is remembered.[22]

But, Lewis emphasized, the synthesis is also a critical activity, since, he continues, "the work of art does the re-ordering in the interests of the intellect as well as the emotions." Indeed, "the best creation, further, is only the most highly developed selection and criticism."[23] So, although the artist allows his personality to identify with all the forms of nature, he still must find himself again and synthesize that material in favor of some fundamental interests:

For our only terra firma in a boiling and shifting world is, after all, our "self." That must cohere for us to be capable at all of behaving in any way but as mirror images of alien realities, or as the most helpless and lowest organisms, as worms or as sponges.[24]

We come here to the great dilemma of Lewis's thought about the personality: the purest self is uncontaminated with external accretions, but in fact we are all "contaminated" by our commerce with the world. The artist, that "sacred prostitute," by identifying himself with matter, contaminates himself more than most. How, then, can he be anything more than a reflection of those "contaminating" alien realities? Lewis's answer is at first sight simplistic, and disconcertingly close to a darwinism that, elsewhere in *Time and Western Man*, he denounces as a "nightmare." The personality or self of the artist cannot simply be known to himself; Lewis subscribed to the Upanishadic belief that one cannot go behind oneself, as it were, and "know the knower of the known." So—

I have allowed these contradictory things to struggle together, and the group that has proved the most powerful I have fixed on as my most essential ME.[25]

This may seem a haphazard procedure, but if we look at Lewis's actual practice, we can see that at this point he is eliding a full description of the struggle. It is not simply a matter of an immediately recognized preference, but an active, intellectual, and critical process involving reason. In the modern world the artist needs to analyze and understand the implications of all the ideologies that now, almost unnoticed, saturate the world. Until he does this, he cannot hope to know who he is, or what his preferences are, since these ideologies saturate him, too. It is Lewis's complaint that too many modern writers (Joyce and Pound among them) have simply allowed themselves and their work to be invaded by ideologies of which they have no real understanding:

To receive blindly, or at best confusedly, from regions outside his own, all kinds of notions and formulae, is what the "creative artist" generally does.

Without knowing it, he receives into the central tissue of his work political or scientific notions which he proceeds to embody, if he is a novelist, in his characters, if he is a painter, or a poet, in his technique or emotional material, without in the least knowing what he is doing or why he is doing it. But my conception of the rôle of the creative artist is not merely to be a medium for ideas supplied him wholesale from elsewhere, which he incarnates automatically in a technique which (alone) it is his business to perfect. It is equally his business to know enough of the sources of his ideas, and ideology, to take steps to keep these ideas out, except such as he may require for his work.[26]

It would be hard to overstate the importance of this description of the artist's role. The recognizable features of a standard "Modernist" aesthetic are present in the ideas I have sketched, but transformed by the inclusion of this element of ideological awareness. T. S. Eliot proved unable to graft such an element onto his own theory,[27] while I. A. Richards suggested that it was not necessary: art would "save" us by saving us from the necessity of taking ideologies seriously, at least when we were reading literature. One reason for the lack of recognition of Lewis's Modernist aesthetic is that the idea of the creation of a work of art as (at least partly) a self-conscious ideological critique of society is one that has a place in Marxist aesthetics, but not, until recently, in the Modernist tradition. And Lewis's ideological critique does not follow a Marxist model, nor is it mobilized in the service of the emergent consciousness of either the proletariat or the classless society towards which the dictatorship of the proletariat is supposed to progress.[28]

5. "Progressive" ideology versus progress

If the only art that Lewis considers worth taking seriously at the time of writing *Time and Western Man* is advanced (that is, "revolutionary"), and if works of art present the valuations that are made concrete in revolutions,[29] what are revolutions, and what is the nature of the progress they bring? Lewis scorns the fashionable propaganda of revolution, used as a spice to warm up ideas or art-works that are cold and stale in themselves, but he has no doubt that there is such a thing as true revolution, and that it is stimulated by the advances of science and resulting changes in technology. So much is clear from the Appendix to Book One of *Time and Western Man*. What is not clear from there is that Lewis takes a Sorelian definition of revolution as a change of ideas rather than as any accompanying social upheaval (though social upheavals are usually the consequence).[30] Lewis affirms the necessity for such a stimulus to new life and thought as the atmosphere of revolution provides.[31] For him there are new things under the sun, even if the material at man's disposal at almost any period of history has provided scope for a life and civilization as satisfying and fulfilling as any

other, on an absolute scale, as Lewis argues in the essay "Creatures of
Habit and Creatures of Change." Some societies, being ill-organized
or otherwise stultified and jaded, so that their best ideas remain
neglected, their creative figures unacknowledged, fail to live up to
their possibilities; progress, in any society, would be the fulfilling
of the potential for life revealed by the most creative of its members,
even though there is no absolute progress from the highest that has so
far been envisaged by the greatest creators: "There is no 'progress'
from Sophocles to Shakespeare."[32] But these high achievements do
not render all subsequent art redundant in advance. Quite the contrary; the rate of change of modern society means, according to Lewis,
that "There is nothing for it today, if you have an appetite for the
beautiful, but *to create new beauty.* You can no longer nourish yourself upon the Past; its stock is exhausted, the Past is nowhere a
reality."[33]

Politics, in this framework of ideas, becomes not much more than
a series of techniques to bring about the kind of society where true
revolution (the will to spiritual change and progress) is not impeded
by the conservative majority (creatures of habit), nor corrupted by those
men of the world who flourish as parasites on the genuinely creative.
The Art of Being Ruled describes the existing society that will need re-
organizing, and the techniques available; and shows how contemporary
ideologies and social forms do in fact serve to corrupt and impede genuine revolution by disguising themselves as what they betray. Western
Society has lost its nerve and handed itself over to the machine which
it has created. Lewis is not a democrat. The majority of people, Lewis
thinks, are happy with the goods that science gives them, would in-
itiate no great change in life if given the chance, and are anyway passive
consumers of what society gives them. Their "vote" they simply cast
in the way the mass-media instruct them. An egalitarian political revolution would do no more than privilege (or pretend to privilege) this conservative mass and validate their dislike of creative change, while those
with real power continued to reap the profits. Such, at any rate, is
Lewis's position in *The Art of Being Ruled,* where he tentatively proposes some form of division in society, so that the majority can benefit
from the inventions of the creative "creatures of change," and these inventions can be placed in the service of something other than a selfish
or commercial spirit.[34] Lewis did not write much about the equal
distribution of society's goods among all people, or about equality of
opportunity, which has led people to believe that he did not favor
them, whereas he did. Nevertheless, his views about the conformism
of the majority (irrespective of mere "class") did not please, as Lewis
recognized, and in *Time and Western Man* he announces that he has
modified them in an "enlightened" direction, but mischievously states
his new view in a way that he knows will be as offensive as the old:

I now believe, for instance, that people should be compelled to be freer and more "individualistic" than they naturally desire to be, rather than that their native unfreedom and instinct towards slavery should be encouraged and organized.[35]

Lewis's politics had always been directed towards securing freedom and individualism for those who wanted them — but he was sceptical that everyone would know how to benefit from them. There is no doubt then, that in the twenties, Lewis was not a democrat; he was an authoritarian, though he was to develop an enthusiasm for democracy while living in the United States during the Second World War. Wise after the event, no doubt; but his authoritarianism had on the whole been opposed to totalitarianism (despite the endorsement of Soviet and Fascist regimes in *The Art of Being Ruled*), and in favor of pluralism and the values of the Enlightenment. Strong central authority would guarantee those pluralistic values, not enregiment a population into a massive structure expressing the will of an inhuman state. I am not judging whether this is a viable political position (it was not one that Lewis was able to sustain in the face of political reality), but merely stating that it was the position held by Lewis in the twenties.

Briefly, then, Lewis believed in the ability of human beings to detach themselves sufficiently from the ideologies of their time and to project, by an act of visionary (and critical) imagination, from the materials that their time presented to them, an ideal and values that could lead to a fuller and more meaningful life for their society. This was the function of artists. History, in the sense of real change, occurs, and nobody but human beings is responsible for history. Inspired by the values and techniques of artists, philosophers and other inventors, human beings could consciously change their circumstances and thereby make progress. Progress, in this sense, means "to increase gusto and belief in . . . life," and to disseminate a "state of mind of relish, fullness and exultation."[36] The present time, with its new standards in the arts and its unparalleled production of inventions, should be highly favorable to this. But it is not, and people treat the world that has been created for them by exceptional creators as if it were simply a normal growth of nature, over which they have no control. So the inventions that could benefit humanity are simply used to exploit it in commerce or destroy it in wars. There are a number of reasons for this.

One set of reasons is ideological, and these are the subject of *Time and Western Man*. Lewis is concerned with groupings of ideas that deny creative power to man, or hand creativity over to a larger power of which man is only an instrument; or similarly deny that history results from men's conscious decisions, attributing a fatality to it instead; that disparage the reality and individuality of consciousness by depicting it as a peripheral surface-effect of a more real, undifferentiated and irrational unconscious; that exalt those forms of social life which have not traditionally exercised conscious, willed and decisive behavior (associated in Western cultures with masculine gender) but have traditionally been characterized by passivity and irresponsibility, such as children and the insane;[37] that deny power to the human intellect by claiming that the material world it perceives is a false construction of reality, so that the intellect's deliverances have only a relative, inferior validity; that assert that the freeing of "deeper" unconscious forces in ourselves will put us in touch with a life-force perceived only dimly, at best, by the intellect; that deny the capacity of the intellect to formulate any truth or vision that is not predetermined by ideology — groups of ideas that yet present this vision of life as if it represented for the human race a liberation from the oppression of outmoded systems of thought that had enslaved humanity in the chains of a dead, mechanical rationalism. No single thinker subscribes to all these ideas, for this is a general ideology, a series of ideas with family resemblances, not a single, logically coherent system. This ideology is what Lewis christens "Time-philosophy." *Time and Western Man* is devoted to charting its history, showing the pervasiveness of its various forms, and denying both its validity and its supposed liberating effects.

6. *Time and free will*

By suggesting that this ideology was closely connected with an attitude to time, Lewis chose to emphasize only one (though an important one) of the links between the ideas thus grouped together. This gave him a magnificent title for his book (he was an excellent inventor of titles), but has also led to the bewilderment I have already mentioned: what is so offensive about time, and why shouldn't it have its rights as well as space? Readers are tempted to conclude that Lewis merely has an irrational and overdeveloped hatred of one of the dimensions of the universe and snaps at the heels of anyone who includes it as a component of their art or philosophy. But while Lewis has an understandable apprehension of this dimension in which we all grow old and die (without being as consoled as many are that in the same dimension others are born, grow, and perhaps carry on our work), his objection is not to time itself, but the use made of it by philosophers to subvert the Kantian world of common sense that his own theory of art and society took for granted. Lewis fixed on time because it was the key element in the philosophy of Henri Bergson, the philosopher who had inspired a whole generation (Lewis among them) with his visions of a liberating *élan vital* (life force) before the First World War in Paris. When Lewis, in *Time and Western Man*, denounces Bergson as "the perfect philosophic ruffian, of the darkest and most forbidding description," he does so with the resentment of an apostate who has seen through what once deceived him.

Lewis never acknowledges that Bergson's philosophy set out to overcome real problems with the common-sense scientific view of the world. This may be because of the force of his rejection, but the more likely explanation is that Lewis simply takes Bergson's problematic for granted, having inherited it from him. In a nutshell, that problematic centers on a fear of the mechanization of mankind. This is a fear that particularly affected thinkers at the end of the Nineteenth Century. The Newtonian system had been a victory for the scientific enterprise, showing how the interactions of physical objects and forces could be calculated and predicted. The prestige of this achievement was such that it led Enlightenment thinkers to try to systematize other phenomena according to the Newtonian model, including human behavior. For these thinkers, achievements of this sort would have a liberating effect: a positive, rational picture of the universe, and of man's place in it, would be attained. Perhaps the most optimistic expression of this ambition in English is Alexander Pope's *An Essay on Man.*[38] With the effective application of scientific principles in technological invention during the Nineteenth Century, the prestige of scientific rationalism was further raised, though there was also, in the Romantic movement, a reaction against it. Industrialization seemed to alienate us from our true nature, which can only be recovered by turning elsewhere (to nature, children or peasants, for example). The culmination of the rationalist-scientific model applied to humanity is the Positivism of Auguste Comte and the Utilitarianism developing from the idea of Jeremy Bentham that there is a simple calculus for all human behavior. This is the application of the laws of cause and effect according to the principle, "Nature has placed mankind under the governance of two sovereign masters, *pain* and *pleasure.*"[39] Since pleasure is good and pain is bad, actions are to be adjudged good or bad insofar as they increase or decrease the total stock of happiness (pleasure). Modern Behaviorism is an elaboration of this thesis, backed up by experiments. Given knowledge of the forces (or motives) affecting a person, the resulting behavior is predictable, just as a knowledge of the physical forces affecting an object enables us to predict with certainty the behavior of the object. This is the nightmare of determinism, in which we are no more than passive respondents to the network of stimuli presented to us by our environment directly through our senses and indirectly through our memories; we are bound to the same law of cause and effect that inexorably governs the Newtonian cosmos.

It was Immanuel Kant who was chiefly responsible for confirming this picture of our condition. Taking it for granted that the Newtonian model was correct, he sought to explain why, therefore, features of the world that are an essential presupposition of Newton (of science in general, in fact) cannot be accounted for in any thoroughly empirical investigation of the evidence of our senses. David Hume had shown how causality, in particular, could not be thus accounted for, and so undermined the foundation of science. Kant's answer was that we do not need to look for proof of the existence of categories such as causality (or space and time) in the external world. For these and other categories were simply built into the mind (rather than the world) as conditions of experience from the first (they are *a priori*), and automatically structure our experience of reality. This reality (the thing-in-itself) we cannot know except as it is presented through these *a priori* categories. Any thinker, therefore, who wishes to protest against the "Newtonian" scientific picture of man is likely to find himself quarreling in some way with Kant.[40] This is what Lewis's "time-philosophers" tend to do.

Bergson, for example, denies that we need to be restricted to the cut-and-dried scientific world of common sense, where objects and humans simply obey mechanical rules. That common-sense world is a product of the intellect, which is not a truth-telling faculty, but an instrumental one, that enables us to do biologically useful things like make tools. Another faculty that nature has also provided us with (but which is more perfectly manifested in insects) is a kind of intuition. We can get behind the Kantian categories of our intellect, and through intuition become one with a normally unperceived vital force, bursting the bounds of space and time. Matter, space and time, are the product of our relaxation and inertia: the deadest part of us, in Lewis's paraphrase. Bergson associates the intellect and the deterministic common-sense world with space, and the creative freedom of the vital force (*élan vital*) with time. Not ordinary time, however, but *durée*, which is apprehended through the intense effort of the intuition, while ordinary time is simply the degraded product of the intellect, a sequence laid out in our minds much like space. Ordinary time has been "spatialized"— that is, it can be divided up mathematically into separate instants; it is homogeneous. *Durée* is qualitatively heterogeneous, is continuous and flowing, and cannot be divided; it is not bound by the laws of physics (inventions of our relaxed intellect) but ceaselessly creates unpredictable novelty. And, did we but realize it, we are part of this life-force. Hence we too can be free, and our behavior need not be determined by an inevitable chain of cause and effect.

Much of Wyndham Lewis's satire, in his novels, mocks mankind for its tendency to reduce itself to pure, determinate mechanism. Otto Kreisler, in *Tarr*, is in this respect typical:

He compared himself to one of those little steam toys that go straight ahead without stopping; that anyone can take up and send puffing away in the opposite direction.[41]

Valuing freedom and creativity, Lewis yet came to feel that Bergson's claim to restore them to man was a cheat. We cannot simply transcend the Kantian limitations of common sense, and the end-result of Bergsonism is exactly the opposite of what Bergson claimed. What happens is that we surrender what control we have over our lives by consigning ourselves passively to the flux of events. We become simply creatures of time. If we use our reason, on the other hand, at least we can critically assess our options, and choose which course will best lead to a desired goal.

7. The comfortable cosmos of A. N. Whitehead

Lewis, in *Time and Western Man*, therefore remained broadly loyal to the Kantian solution that space and time are categories of experience given by the mind. What he opposes is any variety of philosophy that would claim that they are "real" independently of mind. But the reality of space is not really his concern. It is those who argue for the reality of time, and argue for it as the medium through which the universe improves itself and works towards a meaningful goal, that he opposes most vigorously.

Thus, though he lays far less emphasis on "time" as a force in his philosophy than Bergson does, Alfred North Whitehead is indicted by Lewis as a "Time-philosopher" because of his destruction of the Kantian world of common sense and his belief in the reality of time and process (Whitehead's fully worked out metaphysical system was published two years after the appearance of *Time and Western Man*, under the title *Process and Reality*). Although Whitehead does not disparage man's "spatializing" intellect, he mistrusts as much as Bergson the picture of the common-sense world it gives us. One of the aims of *Science and the Modern World* is to go back to Hume's criticism of causality and draw from it different conclusions to those of Kant. In doing so he also rescues elements of "science" that do not conform to the Newtonian–Kantian picture, such as that in the passage by Bacon, noted by Lewis on page 309 of *Time and Western Man*, attributing a quasimental "perception" to inanimate material objects.

Whitehead is concerned to overcome several undesirables, and frames his philosophy accordingly. First, he finds the traditional post-cartesian division of nature into dead, mechanically determined matter and live mind unsatisfactory. Starting from Hume, he finds a problem within the concept of matter itself, related to scientific method, with its reliance on causality and causality's methodological correlative, induction. Traditional conceptions of matter assume that a current state determines the future state, and is itself determined by a preceding state. This is a way of describing the chain of cause and effect that seems to abolish man's freedom. But this assumption (true though it must be, if nature behaves according to recognizable patterns) cannot be justified, as Hume showed. No "causes" can be identified in nature, only customary conjunctions of events. It was this observation of Hume's that led Kant in an "idealist" direction. Rejecting Kant's solution (as Bergson did), Whitehead substitutes for the "matter" of traditional science a substance[42] of which any momentary state (any "event") contains information about (or reflects) the past that has determined it and information about the future it will lead to. Further, in place of the traditional linear chain of cause and effect of mechanics, he desires a network of influence or relationship that will not be spatially limited, so at any point and instant his substance must reflect the states of all other points in the universe. (Whitehead does not deny, of course, that certain points and moments are more influential on a particular state than other points and moments, but asserts that all are nevertheless reflected).

Lewis would not object to this reform of concepts if it is helpful to the scientist. But Whitehead also redefines the matter–mind relationship so that cognition is simply a particularly sophisticated example of such a state reflecting other states in space and time. Mind is not, as traditionally, a separate order of being from matter, but simply a very high order of it. Thus, to say that an object is simply located at a certain time (the view of "common sense"), while the mind that perceives it is located elsewhere, is a fallacy, for Whitehead (it is the fallacy of misplaced concreteness, arrived at by attributing an exhaustive reality to abstractions derived from no more than a portion of experience). Whitehead is happy to back up his case with "idealist" arguments, since in a left-handed way he is in accord with the idealist goal of arguing a certain kind of homogeneity between mind and matter. So Whitehead uses an argument of George Berkeley, the great idealist philosopher, in which the separateness of remote objects from the mind that perceives them is denied. Lewis quotes Whitehead's discussion on page 192.

Whitehead thus heals the split between mind and matter, and according to his own account heals the wound that this split has inflicted on our culture. This was the split against which the Romantics had protested. They found meaning and value in the life of the mind, and protested when science depicted the external world of matter as dead, alien and devoid of the value the mind finds in it. So Whitehead arranges his metaphysic so that the "external" world has in itself the same kind of meaning that the mind of Romanticism found in it. It is probably because Whitehead believes that this performs a valuable service, in helping to "end the divorce of science from the affirmations of our aesthetic and ethical experiences"[43] that Lewis characterizes him as an "honest sentimentalist" (while Bergson is a "philosophic ruffian"). For only if the alternative substance that Whitehead has described (partaking of aspects of what are traditionally assigned to the separate substances, mind and matter) retains for mind the freedom, creativity and value traditionally desired for it could that claim be made. Whitehead would argue that it does, while it also allows a measure of these "mental" characteristics to the less "conscious" manifestations of his substance as well. Yet the whole thrust of Whitehead's argument is away from a concern to retain privileges for man's perceptions, emotions and values. Indeed his later terminology, in which "emotion" and "feeling" are substituted for such neutral terms as "prehension" (used in *Science and the Modern World*) for the "perception" of one event in another, is specially calculated to reduce the mind's privileges, by sharing them out amongst a fundamentally democratic set of "events." Even a sympathetic commentator, Dorothy Emmet, finds this difficult to take:

Are we to take seriously the statement that wave-lengths and vibrations are simply terms, under the abstractions of physics, for "pulses of emotion"? The only answer is that we must take our choice. We may agree with Whitehead, Bergson, Bradley, that philosophy must approach as near as possible to an expression of the concrete, and that concrete reality is meaningless except as some form of sentient experience, and in this case some view like this, which describes the organic connections between things in terms of something like feeling, is inevitable. [But] if we can find a general term which is less suggestive of pathetic fallacies, so much the better.[44]

"We must take our choice"; Lewis is convinced that concrete reality is meaningless except *in* some form of sentient experience, but disputes the idea that we are really any better off if we describe concrete reality *as* some form of sentient experience of itself. Lewis does not agree with Whitehead that regarding reality as sentient solves the problem of determinism or provides meaning and value to the universe. For how do the meaning and value of the universe relate to our own meaning and value? The means Whitehead employs to make such a relationship are not such as Lewis can take seriously.

Whitehead postulates a realm of quasi-platonic essences (the "eternal objects"), which he first calls on to account for the fact that nature keeps turning up according to its customary templates (such things as colours are eternal objects: a particular shade of green, for example, can always be drawn from the library of possibilities in appropriate circumstances). Without these eternal objects his underlying substance would presumably not manifest itself except as chaos. But what Whitehead postulates for these purely physical ends he also proposes as his realm of value. His "eternal objects" have those values that are found in the nature poems of the great romantics: "Shelley brings vividly before us the elusiveness of the eternal objects of sense as they haunt the change which infects underlying organisms."[45] In assigning values to this transcendent realm, Whitehead is in a sense doing nothing different from what Lewis, with his more traditional metaphysical position, does, except that Lewis reserved the valuing process for man, and pre-eminently for artists. The difference is crucial, and Lewis took no notice of any similarity, seeing the eternal objects as no more than a sort of pattern book, inadequate for the aesthetic and ethical role that Whitehead claims for them. To decide whether ultimately the conditions that Lewis demands for mind can be satisfied by Whitehead's metaphysics would require at least a close study of *Process and Reality*. But it is certainly the case that, although Whitehead uses the word "value" in relation to any actualization of an eternal object or actualization of a synthesis of eternal objects, he could easily be taken to be referring to no more than the determination of the "values" of variables. These are not the kind of "values" that will console an alienated poet.[46]

The realm of eternal objects might also be criticized (as it was by R. G. Collingwood in *The Idea of Nature*) on the grounds that, impressive though it is in Whitehead's technical descriptions of its hierarchies of complexity and abstraction, it could be interpreted as no more than a repetition on an "ideal" plane of the phenomena that are already given in nature. An infinite regress is threatened, with yet another realm necessitated to perform the functions for the eternal objects that the realm of eternal objects performs for Whitehead's part-mental, part-physical substance. Although, then, Lewis should strictly take Whitehead's eternal objects more seriously, the result of his not doing so may not be unfair. Fusing mind with matter into an undifferentiated stuff certainly robs mind of the privileges which give it value, and Whitehead's complacency at the cosmic togetherness that results is a legitimate target for Lewis's scorn. It is, as Lewis states, the desire to harmonize or synthesize the abstractions that man makes for his various purposes with regard to nature that leads Whitehead, great thinker though he was, into such complacency.

8. *"Alexander's rag-time philosophy"*

It is not the purpose of this Afterword to re-survey the whole range of thinkers that Lewis discusses, but to try to clarify his notion of "Time-philosophy" in the hope that the underlying argument of *Time and Western Man* may be made more easily accessible. Oswald Spengler requires no commentary, since Lewis makes admirably clear the similarity between his mystical notion of Destiny and Bergson's *durée*, and shows how, operating in the realm of history, this philosophy robs mankind of any prospect of altering history by any conscious efforts. But a few words need to be devoted to Samuel Alexander,[47] since his ideas provide a link by contrast to Lewis's own positive ideas of the theological basis of our freedom. Large-scale metaphysical systems are now out of fashion, perhaps because of the obscurity and complexity of modern physics (since metaphysics tends to call for aid on physics), because of the scepticism of modern philosophy of science (expressed most anarchically in Paul Feyerabend's "anything goes" philosophy), and because philosophy itself has not recovered the pretensions it had before the assaults of Wittgenstein and the logical positivists. And the solemn earnestness of the metaphysical system-builder is anyway out of style with the philosophical dandyism of our fin-de-siècle Humanities departments. Lewis was certainly aware of the reduced truth-claims made for natural science in the work of such philosophers and historians of science as Pierre Duhem and Henri Poincaré, as *Time and Western Man* makes clear,[48] and he has little time for the full-scale "metaphysical fustian" of Alexander's big two-volume work, *Space, Time and Deity*. But his contemporaries thought highly of Alexander, and the neglect of his work is out of proportion with its merits and rewards.

Like Whitehead, Alexander is a difficult philosopher, yet difficulty subsists alongside a fundamental child-like simplicity — "natural piety," in the phrase Alexander borrowed from Wordsworth. Whether this simplicity makes him, as Lewis calls him, "something like a fool," or is the simplicity of the truly wise must be decided by readers of his work. Alexander takes the mind–body relationship and extends it by analogy to the whole of what exists. In other words, like Whitehead, he attributes something like consciousness and "mind" to entities normally considered too low in the scale of things to be endowed with them. What the mind does for the body in living things, "time" does for the substance of Alexander's universe; it directs it towards some goal (*nisus*). This substance is space-time itself. From space-time, Alexander describes the evolution of progressively higher forms of organization, in each of which a quantitative change results in a qualitative novelty, rising to man and beyond him angels and God. Alexander is a "realist" and, though the mind–body relationship provides his model for the rest of the universe, mind has no privilege and is not different in kind from other substance. What is thought is *real*, like the chairs we sit on, not a fiction; the space and time (or space-time) in our minds is the same space and time in which real events occur. This homogeneity of the single substance, space-time, and its manifestations is almost impossible to imagine; like Whitehead's, Alexander's philosophy is a "realism" behaving very much like an "idealism," as Lewis, taking his cue from Bernard Bosanquet's study of *The Meeting of Extremes in Contemporary Philosophy*, explains.

Whitehead used "eternal objects" for the twin purposes of explaining how his undifferentiated substance takes on the shape of the world and providing the whole process with "value." Notoriously, Alexander could not account for the evolution of differentiated forms from space-time:

The existence of emergent qualities thus described is something to be noted, as some would say, under the compulsion of brute empirical fact, or, as I should prefer to say in less harsh terms, to be accepted with the "natural piety" of the investigator. It admits no explanation.[49]

Lewis's comment is scathing: "This means that you must accept it *from* the 'investigator' with 'natural piety'—the more piety, the better." As far as value is concerned, Alexander's concept of God is important. The whole process of evolution is an evolution of value, as is symbolized in Alexander's concept of Deity as the next stage in evolution (in our present condition, the stage beyond mind), always about to be, but always the unaccomplished *nisus*.[50] The final value (deity) is both transcendent (by being un-realized) yet immanent in the process. Only if it is immanent can it be both "real" and actually directing the process, which would otherwise be a meaningless flux, for Alexander's deity is not a "first cause," but a hoped-for result. For Alexander, then, reality is by definition a striving for value, and man is simply a part of that process. But for Lewis, who sees no reason to accept this account of God or value, Alexander's reality is indeed a meaningless flux, and his criticism of it, as of all these Time-philosophies, recalls Coleridge's "Scholium" in *Biographia Literaria*:

A chain without a staple, from which all the links derived their stability, or a series without a first, has been not inaptly allegorized, as a string of blind men, each holding the skirt of the man before him, reaching far out of sight, but all moving in one strait line. It would be naturally taken for granted, that there was a guide at the head of the file: what if it were answered, No! Sir, the men are without number, and infinite blindness supplies the place of sight?[51]

This brings us happily back to the comparison with which we began. In an important sense, Lewis is in a direct line of descent from Coleridge in protesting against philosophies of meaningless mechanism (as he takes the Time-philosophies, despite their claims to oppose mechanism) to be, even though he does not share Coleridge's persistent temptation to backslide into pantheism.[52]

9. *O felix culpa! The value of imperfection*

For Lewis, situating man as part of a cosmically meaningful process can be scarcely any more satisfying than to situate him as part of a cosmically meaningless one. In both cases his autonomy is undermined, and the purpose or purposelessness he fulfills is determined elsewhere. The world of common sense, in which objects are radically different from minds, in which, the "other" is distinguished from the self (that is, the object is distinguished from the subject) is, as it were, the badge of what autonomy we have; autonomy, that is, to interpret nature in accordance with the values that we invent (which implies the autonomy to make a botch of things, too).[53] Lewis constantly emphasizes the limitations of our condition. The aesthetic realm where all is reconciled in truth and beauty is, it will be remembered, only skirted in works of art, according to Lewis's theory. Art is "une promesse de bonheur," a promise of happiness (to quote the Stendhalian formula used by Nietzsche); but it "remains suggestion," as Lewis put it. The price of this is that we never achieve perfection, and must remain "shadows" of it, as Lewis says,[54] but with at least the opportunity to imitate the creativity and freedom of God, even though "alongside of this *absolute* and princely gift, the 'iron-round of necessity' was maintained outside the magical circle of mind."[55] As Lewis expressed it in his 1922 "Essay on the Objective of Plastic Art in Our Time":

The art impulse reposes upon a conviction that the state of limitation of the human being is more desirable than the state of the automaton; or a feeling of the gain and significance residing in this human fallibility for us. To feel that our consciousness is bound up with this non-mechanical phenomenon of life; that, although helpless in the face of the material world, we are in some way superior to and independent of it; and that our mechanical imperfection is a symbol of that.[56]

Even to the reader who has followed so far, several questions are likely to remain. First, what of the problem of free will versus determinism? It is clear that Lewis considered that Bergson's claim that by plunging into *durée* we could free ourselves from determinism is false, and that such a plunge would reduce even further our power to act like autonomous beings. Lewis does not present his own solution to this perennial philosophical problem, yet the passages just cited indicate that he believed man to be "in some way . . . independent" of the empirical world of cause and effect. It is likely, bearing in mind how much Lewis leans on Kant for his philosophical views, that he would have adopted some form of Kant's solution, but without Kant's moralistic bias. Kant wished to secure both the Newtonian world of empirical science, as I have explained, but also the truths of Christianity. One of those truths is that we are free moral agents. Kant proposed that from one point of view all our actions are determined (because subject to cause and effect), but from another point of view (that of the noumenon, or thing-in-itself) they are free. Hence we can consider ourselves responsible for our acts, and (at least according to Kant and his God) are obliged to act morally. Lewis wishes to secure the same freedom, not in order to chain humanity to a particular moral code, but to account for the capacity for autonomous artistic creation that he felt in himself and found in the works of the greatest artists and thinkers. (Lewis, of course, opposes Spengler's notion of cultures as total "organisms," in which any work of art or thought is virtually a pre-programmed component.) In a sense this point of view is not something Lewis feels the need to argue, precisely because the conviction of his own intellectual and imaginative freedom was so powerful within him.[57] It is, as he says, a limited freedom, but it is the "state of limitation" that makes our condition interesting to us.

Second, assuming for the moment that Lewis's picture of things may be desirable, must it not yield before the superior evidence of scientific investigation? Is not Whitehead's metaphysics based on the truths made available by modern science, while Lewis's is no more than the wishful thinking of a presumptuous painter? Such an assumption rests on a false notion of the nature of the "truths" of science, which are no more than working hypotheses directed in particular, specialized, directions.[58] Ultimately these "truths" are still abstracted from the common-sense world. Whitehead objects that the range of abstractions that science has customarily worked with are incomplete, given the direction science is now taking (thanks mainly to relativity). Fair enough. But to claim that we need a metaphysic reinterpreting the common-sense world in the light of a more comprehensive or logical set of such abstractions in order to make sense of our lives (and "scientifically" validate the insights of the poets) is altogether more dubious. The common-sense world is the thing itself, the world where we live, and abstractions from it, however comprehensive, have no valid claim to encompass an ultimate truth prior to that common-sense world:

No metaphysician goes the whole length of departure from the surface condition of mind—that fact is not generally noticed. For such departures result in self-destruction, just as though we hurled ourself into space—"mental-space," if you like, in this case. We are surface-creatures, and the "truths" from beneath the surface contradict our values.[59]

It is from the common-sense world that the artist constructs possible paradises. And, says Lewis, these re-presentations of the world are sufficient not only for our purposes, but as a sign of the transcendent. In his draft statement of this belief, Lewis cited the "natural magic" of Celtic art as the material of this paradise:

It is not the moment to forget that spring of imagination and miraculous fable, pouring everywhere from the valleys of the "Celtic fringe," which dominated with its beauty Europe in its most characteristic age . . . We worship, if we worship, still the virgin-goddess, the stars on the ocean, the break-of-day: the natural magic that inspired our earliest beliefs. We worship things, or emblems of nature, before the swarming of Time; Chance rather than a God of Law or a God of Science.[60]

With the allusion to Callicles' song from Matthew Arnold's *Empedocles on Etna*[61] and to his *The Study of Celtic Literature*, Lewis perhaps feared that this passage anchored his affirmation too closely to Arnold's individual crusade against philistinism on behalf of culture, and more particularly to a descent from aspects of Romanticism, which were out of place in the argument he was developing.[62] The fear is understandable, and the passage which replaces this draft in the finished text is to that extent more appropriate, but the alignment with Arnold reminds us that Lewis was Arnold's most complete successor.

There are tensions in Lewis's philosophy of art that should briefly be mentioned. The desire to take the common-sense world at face value (common, Lewis believes, to visual artists, who work with appearances) is to some extent in conflict with the realization that social reality is ideologically constructed, and is thus not quite what it looks. This tension is the source of the "metaphysical" aura of many of Lewis's paintings and drawings, which are all surface, yet possess a heraldic significance that cannot be consistently retrieved. In Lewis's fiction, on the other hand, an urge to translate into the verbal medium the "outside of things" is also in tension with the desire to reveal the ideological underpinning of social reality. Lewis's characters do not have "no inside" as he sometimes claimed. We expect, in a novel, the characters to have an "inside" consisting of "natural" emotions and feelings with which we can empathize. But Lewis's characters are physical bodies inside which the "natural" is displayed as a man-made ideological system.

10. *Lewis unfair to Modernism*

Like Arnold, Lewis was prepared to use resources of language not normally employed in a sober treatise, and *Time and Western Man* is shot through with irony, sarcasm, metaphor, wild fantasy and memorable eloquence. Throughout it is a person speaking, sometimes, as in his criticisms of people who thought of him as their friend — James Joyce and Ezra Pound — too unguardedly perhaps. Yet the magnificent eloquence of some parts of "God as Reality" shows that, whatever personal disloyalty his exasperation with his friends led him into, the basis of his criticisms was a belief in the supremacy of the human imagination and human creativity.

Two questions remain. First, is Lewis right to collect together those he attacks in "The Revolutionary Simpleton" under the heading of "Time-philosophy"? Only, surely, in a very loose and general way. Certainly he points to aspects of the work of some of them that can be directly related to the tendencies he goes on to discuss in his "Analysis of the Philosophy of Time," in Book Two, such as the similarity of the historicism of Pound and Joyce to that of Spengler, or the obsession of Gertrude Stein with "time" in composition. And, given the philosophy of art and the metaphysical principles that I have tried to outline, it is clear why he needed to dissociate himself from this Paris-based Bohemia, even though his friends were prominent members of it. And the value of the purely literary criticism that resulted (right or wrong — but what meaning attaches to such terms in a discipline so closely allied to the interests of those who pursue it?) is beyond doubt. As William Pritchard has pointed out, the victims of Lewis's criticism are not diminished in that criticism, but are vividly re-created.[63] His Stein and Joyce may seem monstrous, but they are nevertheless members of a "gyant race." Given the claims that were being made about the kind of masterpiece that *Ulysses* was (making it appear as if it exactly fulfilled Lewis's criteria for art, and projected out of a concern with contemporary society and ideas a "revolution" of the word), Lewis needed to make his own disagreement clear — to himself as well as to the public. Of course the result is unfair, but it is certainly valuable.[64] Lewis's evident belief that Joyce's "silence, exile and cunning" were the typical strategies of the man of the world, and that by seeking the advantages of associating with a fashionable avant garde, Joyce was tempted into producing work (*Finnegans Wake*) that was inferior to his best has something to be said for it, too. And Lewis's case against Pound is also a strong one. There is nothing dismissive in Lewis's attitude to Stein, Joyce or Pound, however. The writing of *Ulysses* has merited "eternal glory" for Joyce, Lewis says, and, although Lewis's Pound is an unreliable guide to the present, he is still, when he gets under the skin of one of the great creators of the past, a "lion or a lynx."

But if *Time and Western Man* were to be held to stand or fall by Lewis's success in proving that all the members of the artistic Bohemia he analyzes exemplify in their work the particular doctrines of Alexander, Bergson and Whitehead, then it would probably fall — even if such a case might be made, following Lewis's inspiration, by a more ploddingly systematic analyst. But the value of the book does not depend on such a narrow interpretation of its success. What Lewis does succeed in doing is showing how, according to his ideals for the function of art in society, which he takes to be the proper ideals for truly "revolutionary" art, the products of this artistic Bohemia are in various ways flawed and contaminated by ideology inimical to these ideals. He also, in Book Two, shows how an ideology similar in many ways is expressed in other contemporary thought, traces its growth, and shows how a different kind of metaphysics would suit his ideals, leaving man free (within limits) to create values and control his own history. That is a great achievement, well-meriting Hugh Kenner's 1954 praise of *Time and Western Man* as one of the dozen most important books of the century.

The second question concerns the book's continuing life and relevance. Its continuing life as the most ambitious purely theoretical work of one of the great English prose-writers of the century should not be in doubt. It will always attract readers. Its importance as almost the only non-Marxist and non-moralist contribution to the tradition of cultural criticism initiated in England by Matthew Arnold should surely receive increasing recognition. Its specific criticisms of such masters as Joyce and Pound will always be important in the history of the reputations of those writers, and are likely to continue to provoke readings attempting to circumvent the criticisms; so it should have a continuing contribution to the meaning of *The Cantos, Ulysses* and *Finnegans Wake*. As a key to understanding Wyndham Lewis, *Time and Western Man* will, of course, always remain important, and it should be seen to be important by critics concerned with the nature and history of Modernism. As I have hinted, it may be judged to perform in relation to Modernism something like the function that *Biographia Literaria* is now seen to perform for Romanticism. The book's faults of garrulity, slapdashness, disorganization and an unphilosophically vehement temper are simply complements of the tremendous energy that created it as part of a series of about seven massive works published in a space of four years. Without the "faults" there would simply not have been the books. The faults are the excesses of an intellectual and creative (and destructive) vitality that is unsurpassed in our time, though there will always be critics, especially in England, who attribute them to a paranoiac, misanthropic personality with bad manners and delusions of grandeur.

11. *Has time overtaken* Time and Western Man?

Finally we must ask whether the purely philosophical discussions can still have relevance when philosophy has moved so far from where it was in 1927. To answer this at all adequately is impossible here. In 1947, Lewis himself, though no longer interested in "Western Man," was prepared to affirm a "timeless" value for his philosophical standpoint:

> The group of thinkers upon which I delivered an assault — "Time-philosophers" I named them — represent a type of thinking common to all ages. They increase in numbers and influence in such a period as this. In all times and places, however, they should be answered in the manner used in this book. It should be a permanent armoury for the reduction of their pretensions.[65]

Certainly, although "mind" has been replaced by "sign systems" as a focus of speculation, the basic problems and concerns of philosophy since Kant have changed their appearance, not disappeared. Such "solutions" to the oppressive order of rational ("phallocentric") language as the invitation to plunge into a pre-logical non-system of signification belonging to a stage in development before the separation of the subject and the object in a child's psychological growth (the basis of much French feminist thought) are in a direct line of succession from Bergson's invitation to bypass oppressive determinism by plunging into *la durée*. The "Post-modernist" picture of the substance of reality as signs, and the experience of the Post-modern self as the locus of transitory but for some reason exciting interlocking and patterning of such signs is simply a translation into a new vocabulary of William James's explanation of the nature of consciousness and external reality as "experience."[66] Equally, within philosophy that concentrates on the operation of sign systems there is a Kantian opposition. Paul Grice's "ordinary language" theories of Conversational Implicature (from which much of that branch of linguistics known as "Pragmatics" stems) posit certain categories of "maxims" for the interpretation of all utterances, and these maxims are consciously modelled on the Kantian categories that guaranteed the stability of the common-sense world.[67]

The point I wish to make is simply that the issues that are discussed with so much heat (and light) in *Time and Western Man* have not passed away, and that *Time and Western Man* is still a useful guide for those who wish to understand them. It is of course, open to readers then to take a point of view opposite to Lewis's: "I, of course, admit that the principle I advocate is not for everybody."[68] But, whether one accepts or rejects the position that Lewis states so forcefully, it remains as true now as it was in 1952 that "in that bleak fortress there is still much loot."[69]

II

1. *The Man of the World*

The Man of the World was the title Lewis gave to a long "treatise" (Lewis's word[70]) that he began writing in the early twenties (probably around 1922) and that he submitted to the London publisher Chapman and Hall on 2 February 1925. It was, claimed Lewis, 500,000 words long, and, perhaps not surprisingly, Chapman and Hall regarded it as unpublishable in that form. Lewis immediately began breaking it up into separate sections, which he worked up into self-contained volumes. It has long been known that *Time and Western Man* derived from *The Man of the World*, and I hope to show how it did so. It was not a matter of simply filling out the structure or developing the thesis of *The Man of the World*. Lewis's own necessary engagement with the "material" culture of his time as he attempted to get his work to its potential audience was crucial to the conception of *Time and Western Man*, which was the last substantial offshoot of the original project. Lewis was known as an avant-garde painter and polemicist, and he turned naturally to the avant garde in order to secure (by extracts from his new work) the audience he felt himself to be addressing. "I have quarrelled with almost everybody in order to get the money and time to write this and other books," Lewis wrote to T. S. Eliot, just when *The Man of the World* was virtually finished and apparently on the verge of publication, in January 1925. Much of what was to become *Time and Western Man* was not yet written, but would emerge out of the "quarrels" that Lewis would shortly carry on with the avant-garde "counter-culture" as he attempted to get extracts from what became *The Lion and the Fox* and *The Art of Being Ruled* published in small magazines.

Lewis's notion that avant-garde culture should be based on critical engagement with the ideologies shaping "mainstream" culture was sharpened by his realization that the actual avant garde (based mainly in Paris) was quite indifferent to the critical engagement with culture, ideology, and politics in Lewis's own new work. Lewis's old associate Pound was deeply implicated in this indifference. And Lewis could hardly help noticing James Joyce's position as the almost archetypal "avant-garde" writer, publishing sections of *Work in Progress* (as *Finnegans Wake* was then known) in little magazines based mainly in Paris. Lewis's "quarrel" with T. S. Eliot, on the other hand, did not involve a difference of principle: *The Criterion* was interested in precisely the kind of work that Lewis was producing, but Eliot found it difficult to print extracts of the length Lewis desired. When, in 1926, Lewis secured the patronage to set up his own little magazine, he solicited contributions from both Joyce and Eliot. Eliot's was published, but Joyce's was not; reading Joyce's typescript may well have precipitated Lewis's decision to break with the avant garde and compose *Time and Western Man*. "The Revolutionary Simpleton," published in the first issue of Lewis's magazine, *The Enemy*, in early 1927, and later absorbed into *Time and Western Man*, actually constitutes the act of breaking, and must be understood as such. Because of this break, Lewis has never benefited in his reputation from the romance that still attaches to the "Lost Generation" avant garde domiciled in Paris during the twenties, even though, ironically, his own intellectual and artistic preoccupations had been decisively shaped by Parisian culture during the years leading up to the First World War.

Much of what Lewis was writing during the early twenties could hardly be considered to be material for a "treatise." First, there was the "life of a Tyro," or *Hoodopip*, a work of fiction for which Lewis was contracted to the publisher Constable; secondly, there were the beginnings of *The Apes of God*, at least four sections of which were sent to T. S. Eliot, who published two of them in his magazine, *The Criterion*. The *Apes* was related to *Hoodopip*, but was more fundamentally an offshoot of another fiction, *Joint* (an account of a schoolmaster in which Lewis attempted to absorb but transform some of the Rabelaisian techniques of *Ulysses*). There was also an account of a pupil at Joint's school, Archie Hetman, in *Archie*. Archie may be considered a prototype of Archie Margolin in *The Apes*. A section of *Joint* ("The Infernal Fair") describes a visit to an afterworld where major philosophers and other writers continue their lives in ways that make concrete their earthly ideas. So *Joint* is a precursor, also, of Lewis's major fantasy of life after death, *The Childermass* (probably started about 1926). About forty years after Lewis began dismembering *The Man of the World*, Froanna, his wife, told Hugh Kenner that sections of the book had gone into both fictional and non-fictional works.[71] *Time and Western Man* and *The Apes of God* were both mentioned by her. Kenner, having examined the surviving manuscripts of *Joint* and other fragments at Cornell, observed that all of Lewis's work at this period were "parts of one vision," sharing a theme of "the quality of life after the 1914 War."[72] Not surprisingly, given Lewis's creative disrespect for the boundaries of genres, Kenner went on to conclude that *The Man of the World* would have been a "huge fusion of genres," "a sort of prose Sistine Ceiling, though a Sistine Ceiling on which Goya has collaborated with Cézanne."

Since Kenner's original study, more information has come to light, and his idea of *The Man of the World* as a multi-genre work must be revised. Two letters are important here. First, a draft of a covering letter sent with the virtually complete manuscript of *The Man of the World* to Alec Waugh, of Chapman and Hall; and, second, a letter to Ezra

Pound sent a few weeks later, when Lewis had already begun dismembering the by now rejected book.

Lewis wrote to Waugh:

61. Palace Gardens Terrace   Feb. 2 /
Kensington <u>W. 8</u>.   / 25

Dear Mr. Waugh. Here is the complete Mss. of the book, <u>The Man of the World</u>: except for ① 3 pages at the opening (introducing M. of the W. theme) these[?] I have mislaid, but shall post them you tomorrow. And there are still a few pages, four or five, to come quite at the end, which I will also forward you.

I suggest if you [*sic*] reading it tomorrow, that you should start at page 13 ("There at any rate the problem" etc.) & read to p. 19. inclusive. After that the part numbered XVII & called The Shaman. It deals principally with sexual inversion, & explains the term shamanizing [used *del.*] fully, used frequently elsewhere.

[Parts IX–X & XI (all called <u>THE LION & The FOX</u>) you might glance at next. *del.*]

Part VIII (pp. 225–231): & Parts IX, X & XI (these three parts principally about Shakespeare) you might glance at next.

Next p. 510 to p. 514. from Politics & Personality, Part XV.

The Conclusion (p. 496 to 506) next.

Reading these fragments first you may find useful.[73]

Writing to Pound on 29 April 1925, Lewis mentions the following sections that will be publishable now that the work has been split up: (i) a section on class that was intended for publication by Robert McAlmon; (ii) a 100,000 word volume, *The Lion and the Fox*; (iii) *Sub Persona Infantis*; (iv) *The Shaman*; (v) *The Politics of the Personality* (which Lewis explains is principally the evidence of philosophy and is 100,000 words long; (vi) *The Politics of Philistia* (also 100,000 words); and, finally, (vii) a 40,000 word volume on *The Strategy of Defeat*. Two parts, he says, are already out. Lewis also states that *The Apes of God* is "not of course part of the Man of the World," and lists some of his other projects.[74] In the light of this detailed letter, there is no need to assume that Lewis's *magnum opus* was anything other than the "treatise" he set out to write.

It is now difficult to track down all of this material, and we can only speculate about the precise contents of the work and the order in which it was originally arranged. But through Lewis's correspondence, his published works of the twenties, and his unpublished manuscripts, it is possible to make informed guesses about the identity and fate of most of *The Man of the World*.

Some of the earliest material written seems, in fact, to have been about philosophy, and was thus the origin of *Time and Western Man*. Lewis sent a batch of manuscript to Eliot in February 1924, explaining:

I need not tell you that it is still rough. For instance, to establish the full relationship of the monad to God (in the Leibnizian sense) I shall require at least three or four pages. And I wish to give a small chart of the vicissitudes of the ego, through Kant down to the "Critical Realists."[75]

Soon afterwards he sent more material, which he advised Eliot to read first. This was in two parts, the first of which Lewis did not describe beyond saying that he had not sent Eliot some pages of it that summarized some of Kant's theories for a popular audience, and the second of which, he says, "deals with evolution, the usual teleology of the biologist (his interpretation of Form), and the evolution of 'forms' into civilized life." "After Part II," Lewis writes (and Part II is presumably the portion of the manuscript that Eliot already had) "comes (with all the resources of inductive vividness at my command) a part burrowing, on more personal lines, into the 'problem of knowledge' and so forth."[76] This section found its way into the projected volume mentioned to Pound, *The Politics of the Personality*, which Lewis submitted to Macmillan perhaps in March 1925. In a letter to Charles Whibley, he describes it as tracing "the systematic crushing of the notion of the Subject in favour of the propaganda of collectivism" and as "showing philosophy obediently harnessed to physics and psychology, circumscribed to a fashionable and purely political role."[77] But Macmillan rejected the book, and, as we shall see, Lewis cannibalized its contents for another project before using them finally in *Time and Western Man*.

Eliot was keen to publish work by Lewis in *The Criterion*, and, shortly before submitting the complete manuscript of *The Man of the World* to Chapman and Hall, Lewis gave him a 20,000 word article called "The Perfect Action." Lewis argued for the publication of this article uncut, urging that a long extract from the book would help both Eliot and himself. "The Perfect Action" must have been extracted from *The Man of the World*, since Lewis told Eliot that he had no time to write independent articles.[78] It was not published in *The Criterion* because Lewis withdrew it after it failed to appear in the issue for which it had been advertised. Eliot explained that he had announced its forthcoming publication in order to keep Lewis's association with his magazine before the public mind.[79] Dissatisfied with this, Lewis sold the extract to *The Calendar of Modern Letters*, where it was published in a revised version as "The Dithyrambic Spectator" in the issues of April and May, 1925. It is this publication Lewis refers to when telling Pound that "two of them are out."

Lewis hoped that sections of *The Man of the World* might be published in Paris. In the first number of *This Quarter* (1925) a contribution from Lewis had been promised for the next issue. *This Quarter* was edited by Ernest Walsh and Ethel Moorhead, both associated with Ezra Pound (to whom the first issue was dedicated). Lewis believed that there was substantial financial backing for the magazine. The American

writer, Robert McAlmon, who had married Bryher, the daughter of
the wealthy shipping magnate Sir John Ellerman, was also associated
with *This Quarter*. With the benefit of Ellerman money, he ran a
publishing outfit from Paris, producing "Contact Editions" of avant-
garde writers. McAlmon had been friendly with Lewis for some years,
and had helped him by introducing him to Ellerman and securing com-
missions for drawings of "society beauties" for reproduction in the
magazine *The Sketch*. McAlmon apparently told Lewis that *This
Quarter* had the financial backing of the Ford Motor Company.

Lewis hoped to sell an extract from *The Man of the World* to *This
Quarter*, and believed he also had McAlmon's agreement to publish
a section as a Contact Edition. He wrote to McAlmon on 1 April 1925
hoping to finalize business arrangements for a 70,000 word book tentatively called *The Politics of the Primitive*. It was to be in three parts,
"named respectively the Cliché-Personality, the Patria Potestas and
Primitive Communism."[80] But four weeks later, in his 29 April letter
to Pound, Lewis stated that the book of *The Man of the World* that
McAlmon was to publish would be on the subject of Class, and that
it would be ready "next week." Yet "next week," on 7 May, Lewis wrote
again to Pound updating him on publication plans, and told him that
he now had a contract with Methuen to publish the *Critique of Class*.
These changes of plans caused (or perhaps were caused by) McAlmon's
less than whole-hearted commitment to the kind of material that Lewis
was sending him. An undated letter from McAlmon seems to be a reaction to yet another section that he had been offered. McAlmon writes
that he is concerned that his press should not get a reputation for "pro-
poganding [sic] for inversion," and suggesting that he publish a different
part. So it seems that Lewis had also offered him a section on "The
Shaman," though it is difficult to think that this, or any of Lewis's
writing, could be construed as propaganda for sexual inversion. Lewis
was simultaneously negotiating with *This Quarter*, and probably offered
them this section on "The Shaman." Lewis became annoyed with
McAlmon for suggesting to Pound that the authorities that Lewis cited
were not up to date. Ernest Walsh, the editor of *This Quarter*, had
offered to print a 40–50,000 word section of *The Man of the World*,
but Lewis suspected Pound of passing on McAlmon's criticisms to
Walsh. Walsh effectively rejected the manuscript by offering a mere
£30 for it.[81] Pound was, in fact, markedly unenthusiastic about the kind
of work Lewis was producing, and advised him that the only use for
controversial or critical works was to advertise one's friends or their
work. On 24 July 1925, Lewis wrote a sarcastic letter to McAlmon telling him that *This Quarter* had offered him £30 ("oddly enough, the price
you advanced for the other mss."), and that his relations with the
magazine seemed to have terminated.[82] In his reply, McAlmon dis-
claimed directly influencing *This Quarter*, and reiterated his view that

"on matters so controversial one had best show complete awareness of all data at least to the last moment of the contemporary."[83] Despite the lack of enthusiasm emanating from Paris, Lewis still did not abandon the idea of McAlmon publishing some of his work, though he now devoted most of his efforts to planning larger volumes for mainstream publishers.

The first to be accepted and brought to a finished condition was *The Lion and the Fox: The Rôle of the Hero in the Plays of Shakespeare*, accepted by Grant Richards early in May 1925. Lewis promised Richards the finished manuscript apart from a rehandling of the historical portion at the end of that month.[84] But on 23 July Lewis visited the London office of a New York publisher, Harper, and, after consultation with Professor Vincent Canby there, decided to rearrange and shorten the text somewhat (mainly abridging the original Part One, on Race, and moving it into an Appendix) in order to secure a beneficial agreement with them for simultaneous publication in the U.S. Lewis completed the revisions by early September,[85] and thus became free to work on his next project, *The Art of Being Ruled*. But first, in line with his view that the publication of extracts in magazines enhanced the prospects of books, Lewis submitted "The Foxes' Case" to *The Calendar of Modern Letters*, where it appeared in October 1925.[86]

The next portion of *The Man of the World* published was in fact *The Art of Being Ruled*, issued, according to Bradford Morrow, on 11 March 1926, but certainly seen (perhaps in an advance copy) by Robert McAlmon at least a week earlier.[87] This book used the material of *Sub Persona Infantis*, *The Politics of Philistia*, *The Shaman*, and most of the material on class. It is impossible to assign the contents of *The Art of Being Ruled* to their original sections in *The Man of the World*. Lewis would have revised and reorganized this material when assembling the new book, but he probably did not greatly expand it "from the inside" (in the usual way that Lewis's work grew), or extend it much with completely new material.[88]

Immediately on publication of *The Art of Being Ruled*, McAlmon wrote to Lewis that he didn't now want to print a volume of his large treatise because so much of what Lewis had shown him was now in print in the new book.[89] But Lewis evidently still believed that he could get his hands on some of the fabulous wealth of the Ellerman family through McAlmon, and, seemingly ignoring this letter, wrote on 27 March 1926 telling McAlmon that *Critique of Class* would soon be ready for him, and that it would not be a large volume. Of the three parts Lewis had promised in April 1925, probably much of the "Patria Potestas" and perhaps some of the "Cliché-Personality" had been included in Parts V and VII of *The Art of Being Ruled*. The section on "Primitive Communism" seems impossible to trace. But a few pages of manuscript inscribed by Lewis "from 'Art of Being Ruled'.?" are in the

Lewis collection at Buffalo. One of them is headed "*Primitive Communism.*" They refer to W. H. R. Rivers's study *The Todas*, the Laws of Manu, Lewis Morgan's *Ancient Society*, Sir Henry Maine's *Ancient Law*, Bogoras and Czaplicka on Siberian ethnology and Howitt on Australian Aborigines. This material is indeed related to some of *The Art of Being Ruled*, but was not included there, and it is also related to some of the passages of "The Perfect Action" that Lewis cut out in altering it for publication as "The Dithyrambic Spectator." The fragment is only a few pages long, and the section of which it is a part seems to have been lost. McAlmon published nothing by Lewis.

Lewis's dealings with McAlmon, *This Quarter*, and Pound were, I have suggested, crucial in determining him to reassess (and dissociate himself from) the Paris-based "avant garde."[90] He understood from McAlmon that *This Quarter* was backed by Ford money, and he knew that McAlmon himself had money. When he saw the first issue of *This Quarter* in May 1925, he must have been contemptuous of it (though still prepared to accept a fee, if sufficiently high, from it). The next issue was to be the target of his scorn in "The Revolutionary Simpleton." Here were, in Lewis's view, a group of wealthy amateurs playing at being painters and writers. His annoyance with them spilled over into annoyance with Ezra Pound, both for being so naïve and foolish as to inform them that Lewis was poor (thereby effectively telling them that he would have to accept low payment) and for conveying to Walsh his own lack of interest in *The Man of the World* and McAlmon's criticisms of Lewis's scholarship. Lewis was convinced that his work was important, and Pound's reaction must have reminded him of what he saw as the poet's intellectual limitations. Pound, generous as always, wanted to "sell" Lewis to *This Quarter* as an avant-garde painter, but this would be for Lewis only a distraction from his new career as a writer. He did not welcome such a revival of his earlier role, in which he had been thwarted in England, he believed, by the machinations of Bloomsbury. Besides, Pound's attitude to painting at this time showed both blindness to the crucial role of the artist's transforming imagination, and the naïve enthusiasm for machines that Lewis was to charge him with in "The Revolutionary Simpleton":

I have also told [*This Quarter*] that rather than use bad art they ought to do a number simply 50 photos of machines and parts.[91]

Some of *The Man of the World* remains unpublished. There is a large amount of material bound with the *Lion and the Fox* typescript at Buffalo, and a separate section entitled "The Critical Realists." Lewis did publish one further section, however: "Creatures of Habit and Creatures of Change," in *The Calendar of Modern Letters* in April 1926. Its criticism of conventional social classes links it closely with *The Art of Being Ruled*, and its discussion of the philosopher

F. H. Bradley seems to connect with what Lewis called in his letter to
Pound *The Politics of the Personality*. But there was clearly much
more of this section still unused, including the philosophical discussion that Lewis had sent to Eliot in 1924. It had been submitted to
Macmillan in 1925 when *The Man of the World* was originally dis-
membered. After it was rejected, it was the most substantial portion
of *The Man of the World* to find a place (if only temporarily) in one
of Lewis's fiction projects, in the way Mrs. Lewis later described to Hugh
Kenner. It included the section he originally mentioned to Eliot in 1924,
on "the vicissitudes of the ego." Eventually, this was to become the basis
of *Time and Western Man's* "The Subject Conceived as King of the
Psychological World." A typescript of passages not included in the
published *Childermass* (now at Buffalo) contains, almost verbatim,
several pages now found in this (and another) *Time and Western Man*
chapter. This means that Lewis must have turned *The Politics of the
Personality*, or some of it, into "fiction" in 1926 when he drafted *The
Childermass*.[92]

2. The Enemy *and* The Childermass

The Childermass was, in 1926, the fiction-project that Lewis believed
he could complete first. In a draft version of the "Preliminary Note to
the Public," for the first issue of his magazine, *The Enemy*, Lewis promised that a "large book of, roughly, two hundred thousand words,
The Childermas [*sic*], a book of fiction, will be ready in the early spring"
of 1927.[93] Lewis had evidently decided to make this book the main vehicle of his criticism of tendencies in philosophy of which he disapproved
and of an exposition of an alternative metaphysics. The opening scenes
with Pullman and Satters were originally very much shorter than
in the published text, so that the debate in the court of the Bailiff
was more prominent. Three Hyperideans (Terpsion, Hippias and
Sumerledes) held forth on philosophical topics at great length. This
threatened to be more a series of monologues than the Platonic dialogue
that Lewis was partly imitating. Lewis inserted the word "pause" in
parentheses every few paragraphs in these monologues (where one might
expect replies from the Bailiff if this were a real debate). The draft never
reached the point of being invigorated by Lewis's dramatic imagination. Lewis used most of the typescript of the "fictionalized" version
of this material when he revised it for inclusion in *Time and Western
Man* in 1927, which would explain why only some of it now remains
among the *Childermass* typescripts. The "Preliminary Note to the
Public," as actually printed in *The Enemy*, is less definite about *The
Childermass* than the draft had been, probably because Lewis had now
decided to cannibalize his draft in order to complete the non-fiction

project he was planning. The title and word-count are no longer given, and Lewis simply refers to *The Childermass* as "a large book, coming under the head of what is technically known as fiction."[94] By the time the main essay in *The Enemy* was finished, Lewis was probably less sure about how to develop his fiction of life after death than he had been at an earlier stage of composing it, because of the transformation that "The Revolutionary Simpleton" went through as he wrote it.

When Lewis became the beneficiary of patronage from Sir Nicholas and Lady Waterhouse in 1926, he was suddenly in the position of being able to start his own magazine and publish his own books. At last he had the opportunity to put his work into the marketplace without dependence on people who, being practising artists or writers themselves, would give him "advice" about his work. The freedom that this represented for Lewis after his years of dependence on wealthy "colleagues" like Richard Wyndham, Edward Wadsworth and Sidney Schiff, must have been enormous. There was no longer any need, either, to solicit the moneyed Parisian avant garde. Lewis initially decided to call his press "Free West Publications," and planned to produce a magazine called *The Enemy*, plus a series of "Enemy" pamphlets. The manuscript title page of the first projected pamphlet is at Buffalo, embellished with a fine ink design: *ENEMY PAMPHLETS* | No. 1. *The Revolutionary Simpleton.*[95] A deletion in the manuscript of what is now Chapter 5 confirms that the magazine was originally a separate project, since it announces that Lewis's "paper," *The Enemy*, is shortly to appear.[96] Even after Lewis decided to devote the first issue of his new magazine to "The Revolutionary Simpleton," he still initially thought of the essay as a self-contained work, and intended to reissue it as "the first of a series, under the title of '_____ Publications' " (Lewis filled in the dash left in the printed proof portion of this note in ink: "Free West"; evidently he had had second thoughts about the word "Enemy" in this context).[97]

Lewis could now incorporate in this new work whatever was left (or completed) of the "Politics of the Primitive" volume that McAlmon had decided not to publish. This was probably some of the material on the cliché-personality, since "The Revolutionary Simpleton" centered on the analysis of a particular type of conventional romantic and enthusiastic personality. But the clear break with the American avant garde in Paris also left Lewis free to introduce a critique of these people into his study, for their work was, in his view, an expression of precisely the "cliché-personality" that was his subject. He went to work with a will, until what he had written burst the bounds of his original plan.

This original plan is given on a handwritten Contents page following the embellished title page for Enemy Pamphlet No. 1. Three sections were envisaged: (1) "Revolution"; (2) "Romance"; (3) "Art, revolution and romance." The typescripts of all of section one and the beginning of section two for this arrangement of the pamphlet can be pulled together from various files of the collection at Buffalo.[98] Lewis was evidently dissatisfied with the public response to *The Art of Being Ruled*, which he felt had not been fully understood, so he attempted in his new pamphlet to clarify the distinctions between the various meanings of the word "revolution." True revolution is based on a permanent impulse in man for improvement and social advance. Lewis associates it particularly with the Enlightenment ideals of individual liberty. The various mechanisms of revolution in the West are characteristically those suggested by the techniques resulting from the development of science.

Lewis was writing not long after the unsuccessful 1926 General Strike in England, and, although he does not mention the strike itself, he instances the Miners' leader, A. J. Cook, as an agent of Moscow, drearily fomenting a political revolution that has lost all romantic appeal. Marxist Communism is based on an "unreal" economics that will turn out to be "disguised" capitalism. The only political movements with the romantic appeal of the traditional "red" are the extreme right-wing Action Française and the "german 'aryan' bands," whose "hackenkreuzler" gunmen Lewis likens to "Sinnfeiners." The "Hackenkreuz" is the swastika emblem of Hitler's National Socialist movement. They represent, Lewis says, impoverished minorities, and they defend "with a devoted piety the bare, bankrupt and deserted traditions of our race." Yet according to Lewis their appeal is solely romantic, and their romanticism would lead to the "deadliest impasse," for "They have no programme . . . for absorbing what is novel and technically alive in the modern world." On the other hand, it is the "revolutionary rich," the uncreative bourgeois-bohemians, who are primarily responsible for stifling the genuinely revolutionary thought of the creative minority. Following this discussion of "Revolution" is a section on Romance that does not differ significantly from the opening chapters of *Time and Western Man*.

Lewis next decided to break his essay into smaller chapters, eliminating the tripartite division. Handwritten and typescript contents pages at Buffalo show the new plan. What had been Part One, on revolution, now took up the first six chapters:

1. Plato legislated for perfection only
2. What is revolution
3. The very small number of individuals responsible for the revolutionary ferment
4. The instalment of the Millennium presented to us by the high-Bohemia
5. How "revolution" has become estranged from romance
6. The criticism of the *Action Française* type of revolution
7. An analysis of the romantic[99]

Because of yet another reorganization that I shall shortly outline, Chapter 7 is the equivalent of what is, in both *Time and Western Man* and *The Enemy*, No. 1, now Chapter 1. The remainder of the list follows closely the order of chapters as eventually published in *The Enemy* (apart from 11 and 12, which become a single chapter there — "Chapter 5") up to Chapter 23, "The most gentlemanly parasite I know" (that is "A Man in Love with the Past," Chapter 15 in *The Enemy* and *Time and Western Man*). The handwritten contents page leaves blanks for Chapters 24 and 25.

On 26 September 1926, James Joyce wrote to his patron Harriet Shaw Weaver from Brussels, where he was holidaying with his family, "Lewis, it seems, has been to Paris and asked for the MS and is coming here as he wants to see me."[100] Lewis and Joyce had been good, though not close, personal friends since meeting in 1920 — both great drinkers, they were probably the best personally matched pair of the "Men of 1914" — and Lewis wanted a sample of Joyce's latest work for his projected magazine, *The Enemy*. He was probably dismayed by the sample of "Work in Progress" that he was given. This was the draft of "The Muddest Thick that was ever Heard Dump" now in the Lewis collection at Cornell.[101] Whether he discussed the matter with Joyce in Brussels is not known, but Joyce apparently expected the piece to appear in the first issue of *The Enemy*.[102] Instead, the chapter on Pound was there followed by the long, destructive analysis of the "mind" of James Joyce.

It seems that, in writing "The Revolutionary Simpleton," Lewis began to see that his critique of the pseudo-revolutionary aspects of modern culture would connect with a critique of modern metaphysics. In both there was, as he saw it, an abandonment of common-sense attitudes to time. Such writers as Pound and Proust presented a reality which was "historical" rather than one that dealt with the salient features of the present. Lewis believed that there was a connection between this and recently published works like Oswald Spengler's *Decline of the West* and A. N. Whitehead's *Science and the Modern World*, which presented reality as a temporal process. In this context, the work of Joyce was even more important to him than the work of Pound or the clumsy amateurs published in *This Quarter*, since, as well as representing what Lewis considered a remote and provincial past (Dublin, 1904), *Ulysses*, in the forms of representation it pioneered, such as stream of consciousness, appeared to embody the elements of the philosophies Lewis had decided to attack. Joyce's latest writings, which Lewis knew were structured on the cyclical theory of history constructed by Giambattista Vico, certainly did not alter this image of the significance of his work.

Lewis therefore added to his typescript contents page "James Joyce" in ink, in the space left vacant for the title of Chapter 24. The blank for Chapter 25 he filled with "Conclusion." "The Revolutionary

Simpleton" would now be the first part of a longer study of "Time-doctrines." It would therefore no longer be published as a self-contained pamphlet, and could form the main contents of the first issue of the magazine, *The Enemy*. So it is as "the first part of a longer and more comprehensive study of the 'time'-notions which have now . . . gained ascendancy in the intellectual world," that "The Revolutionary Simpleton" is announced in *The Enemy*.[103] Some reorganization was now necessary. So Lewis scrapped the original Preface and adapted a small section of it for the close of section 2 of the Joyce chapter. He wrote some new material linking Joyce, in particular, with the "time" doctrines he was now criticizing.[104] At around the time Lewis was making these adjustments he issued a prospectus for *The Enemy*, describing its contents:

> The first number of THE ENEMY contains a fifty-thousand-word essay by Mr. Wyndham Lewis. In this he examines in detail the condition of contemporary literature. He directs an attack on the grand scale against all that body of fiction, poetry, and sociology which he assembles under the head of "time-philosophy," or as deriving from that. — In the earlier part of this essay he discusses the meaning of Revolution, which he identifies with the technique of Science; he reviews the various aspects of the contemporary revolutionary betrayal, as he regards it [sic] the assimiliation of the revolutionary impulse in the West to the standards of the gilded Bohemia that has come in the wake of the War. . . .
>
> Not since the appearance of BLAST ten years ago has such a demonstration of revolutionary zeal in the service of the arts been launched upon the English world.[105]

Lewis's emphasis, then, is still upon "revolution," and he attributes to himself "revolutionary zeal."

But now that "Time" was to be the central subject of the study, Lewis wrote more chapters. The first was in six sections and contained an outline of his criticism of the "Time" school, discussing a book he had studied when working on the "critical realists," Samuel Alexander's *Space, Time and Deity*, and another book that had become available in March 1926 — A. N. Whitehead's *Science and the Modern World*. Other chapters on *La Poésie pure* and *The Decline of the West* were then written, but given no chapter numbers, for the new focus of "The Revolutionary Simpleton" evidently demanded a more radical reorganization. So Lewis drastically shortened the material on revolution in what had been the first six chapters and relegated it to an Appendix, renumbering other chapters accordingly. He also cut up and expanded his "Chapter 25" on the time-philosophers, to make what are now Chapters 17, 18, 19, 21 and 22 in "The Revolutionary Simpleton" as published in *The Enemy*.[106] These changes were still being made, it seems, after *The Enemy* was actually scheduled to appear (one of the revised pages is dated "Jan. 25.").

This remodelling of "The Revolutionary Simpleton" had several consequences. In that the political element was now reduced, making the work less subsidiary to *The Art of Being Ruled*, the change of focus was undoubtedly to its benefit. But insofar as this change made the work take on the appearance of a reaction, rather than a manifestation of "revolutionary zeal," it led to a misunderstanding of the nature of Lewis's critique of his fellow-Modernists that has persisted to this day. The avant garde persistently presented Lewis's critique as no more than the revenge of an embittered and reactionary turncoat. Middlebrow critics, on the other hand, welcomed Lewis as a convert who exposed the pretensions of "modern" art and literature. But Lewis remained a Modernist, as his drawings in *The Enemy* showed. The immediate consequence of his changed plan for Lewis himself, however, was a need to complete his work, expanding and amplifying the critique of "Time-philosophies." He would find himself raiding drafts of *The Childermass* in order to do this, and that work itself would no longer suffer the burden of being the vehicle for his philosophical speculation.

3. Time and Western Man

C. H. Prentice of Chatto and Windus, who had published *The Art of Being Ruled*, agreed to consider the proposed new work. On 24 February he wrote to Lewis that he had read "The Revolutionary Simpleton" and had no doubt that the firm would take the book on, and also assured Lewis that, for the first part of the book, the type that had been set up for publication in *The Enemy* could probably be used.[107] Two months later Prentice reported that he had now read "Book II of 'Time and Western Man,'" and that Chatto would like to publish it. Prentice judged the book to be much longer than *The Art of Being Ruled*, adding that this would mean that "The Dithyrambic Spectator" could not be used as an Appendix (which Lewis had presumably suggested). Prentice commented on his enjoyment of passages on "Schopenhauer, Bergson, the Subject and the Object, God and the Thomists." He liked "the excursus on the Tester," but felt that there might be "too much about Spengler at the end of Chapter 3." He concurs with Lewis's suggestion that the Introduction to Book Two might profitably be moved to the beginning of the work.[108] This letter, then, confirms that much of the book's final contents were in the first version submitted to the publisher. Lewis must have been able to produce such a large amount of "new" material in such a short time because a great deal of it came over directly, with minimal revision, from the draft *Childermass*.

Nevertheless, *Time and Western Man* went through much reorganization and revision before it was published. Large sections were discarded and others entirely rewritten. When rewriting, Lewis would re-use some pages from a previous draft, sometimes cutting them up, pasting them in a different order and interpolating handwritten material or passages from other pages. He would be left with a batch of unused sheets or carbons from the previous version. Some of these "leftover" sheets of typescript survive in the Wyndham Lewis Collection at Buffalo, along with two of the complete sections Lewis decided to remove from the book.[109] From these and from the final manuscript copy used by the printer, now in Cornell, a picture of the development of the text can be deduced. Lewis at first envisaged reprinting the *Enemy* version of "The Revolutionary Simpleton" straight off as Book One, including in it all eight chapters that follow the Joyce chapter there. Book Two would begin at what is now Book Two, Part I, Chapter 7, " 'Time' upon the Social Plane and in Philosophy," which fills in the outline of "Time-philosophy" found at the end of Book One, and then moves on to an elaboration of the critique of Spengler started earlier in Book One.

Book Two was at first divided, not into "chapters" but "parts." From surviving title-pages, some of these can be identified:

Part V   God as Reality
Part VI   Reality and Non-Being
Part VII   Space and Time
Part VIII   The Pragmatical Test of the Doctrines of Relativity
            and of Time

Typescripts for Parts VI and VIII survive and are printed in the Appendix to this edition. Part VII probably contained roughly what the chapter "Space and Time" now contains (Book Two, Part III, Chapter 5).[110] Whether Part V contained what is now "Belief and Reality" within it cannot be shown; but this seems likely. We know from Prentice's letter that "the Subject and the Object" were discussed in the early draft, so they, perhaps in a single part, preceded Part V and most probably came later than the new Spengler material.[111] A leaf left over from revising Book Two into chapters begins "In the last part of this book we reviewed the effects of the great doctrines growing out of positive science: and after that the great contemporary snobberies, respectively of *speed, light and scale*, belonging integrally now in the physics of events."[112] Neither in the published text, nor in any remaining typescripts, is there any material readily identifiable as dealing with speed, light, and scale in relation to modern physics. But the material on "the effects of the great doctrines growing out of positive science" could well be what is now in the two chapters on the Subject and the Object, where the two "Kings" are shown as being undermined by the effects of science.

"Part IV" would in that case have been primarily on "Subject and Object." Using the chapter titles finally chosen as a guide to the contents of the "parts," the draft organization of the last section of the book would have looked something like this (though it must be remembered that final versions of chapters cannot simply be projected back into an earlier structure, since with reorganization came revision):

The Subject conceived as King . . . } "Part IV" {	Two, II, 3
viii The Object conceived as King . . . }	Two, III, 4
iv Science and Scepticism . . . }	Two, III, 1
v Belief and Reality } "Part V" {	Two, III, 2
vi God as Reality }	Two, III, 3
vii Reality and Non-Being "Part VI"	[deleted]
Space and Time "Part VII"	Two, III, 5
The Pragmatical Test . . . "Part VIII"	[deleted]

The left-hand column should be ignored for the moment. The right-hand column gives the place of the chapters in the text as finally published. It can be seen that, once "Reality and Non-Being" and "The Pragmatical Test . . ." had been deleted, Lewis only needed to move the "Object" portion of Part IV into the place of Part VI to achieve the organization of this section of the volume as published. But there was an intervening stage or series of stages which complicate the picture and cannot be definitely reconstructed, because it cannot be established when Lewis decided to delete the two parts. Before he did so, he renumbered the "Parts" of Book Two as "Chapters." As can be seen in revisions on the printer's copy, "Time, upon the Social Plane and in Philosophy" became Chapter 1, "The Fusion of Idealism and Realism" became Chapter 2, the Spengler material became Chapter 3 (or Chapter III), while what can be traced of the further numbering can be seen in the left-hand column of the list of chapters, above. These numbers are taken from manuscript title pages. Some chapters, it will be noticed, are unnumbered. No trace of whatever numbering they may have been given remains on surviving manuscripts. The "Object" chapter, at this stage, therefore, did not simply replace "Reality and Non-Being," but was first moved down the order to follow it: indeed the draft of "Reality and Non-Being" as "Chapter vii" announces that the next chapter will treat the "Object." Yet the printer's copy of the "Object" chapter (bearing a deleted title, "Chapter viii" — or what looks like "viii" over-written by a larger "vii" — on the title page and headed "Chapter 8" in ink, deleted, on its first page) states in a deleted passage that the preceding chapter had been about the "Subject." Perhaps when "Reality and Non-Being" was deleted (some time during or after changing "parts" to chapters), Lewis at first substituted the "Subject" chapter for it (numbering it "vii" on a title-page now lost) only to move the "Subject" chapter back up to its "original" position before "Science and Scepticism" in a further reorganization, necessitating the change from "viii" to "vii" in the numbering of the "Object" chapter. (Where Lewis had placed the "Subject" material before he discarded "Reality and Non-Being" cannot be known.) After these operations, all these chapters would be in their final positions.

Since Prentice's letter of 26 April 1927 suggests that Lewis had devoted too much space to Spengler "at the end of Chapter 3," it is clear that the text Lewis submitted to Chatto was an intermediate one, with Book Two not yet divided into three parts. It also lacked a conclusion (Prentice states that he is "anxious to see the end"). Prentice notes that the book is much longer than *The Art of Being Ruled*, so the version he saw probably still contained "Reality and Non-Being" and "The Pragmatical Test . . ."[113] On 11 May, Prentice commented on the "last two chapters" of the book, which he had just read, welcoming "the promise, at the end, of a new and constructive work."[114] When Lewis deleted two chapters, despite (presumably) expanding the chapters he retained, there was space for him to make additions. Prentice welcomed the receipt of additional material for the end of the "Object" chapter on 1 July and assured Lewis that if he wished to, he could still add to the conclusion.[115]

When Lewis decided to alter the *Enemy* version of "The Revolutionary Simpleton" is not clear. The disadvantage of leaving it as it stood was that it contained, in Chapters 17–24, discussions of Spengler and Time-philosophy, topics which Lewis returned to at the opening of Book Two. Lewis will have wanted to avoid giving the impression that Book Two was simply another shy at the same targets, so he at first put some of his new material on Whitehead into Book One, Chapter 19. More went into a "new" Chapter 21 ("Romantic Art Called in . . ."), necessitating a revised numbering for the remaining four chapters of "The Revolutionary Simpleton." But Spengler and Time-Philosophy were each still discussed twice—first in Book One, then in Book Two—and Lewis evidently decided that this arrangement reflected the chronological growth of his book rather than the structure of the critique he wished to make. He therefore redrew the boundary between the two Books, concluding Book One with the Joyce chapter and turning *The Enemy*'s Chapter 22 ("A Final Word about the Time-School") into a conclusion to Book One. The original Appendix to "The Revolutionary Simpleton" remained as an Appendix to Book One. This book now concentrated on the concrete manifestations in high and popular culture of thinking typical of the "Time-school," while Book Two analyzed the Time-philosophy itself.

By this time Lewis had decided to delete the two chapters from Book Two, and he divided up the remaining chapters of the Book into the three parts it now comprises. Part I contains those late chapters of "The Revolutionary Simpleton" that Lewis wrote when he decided that that essay would form a part of a longer study of Time-philosophy, amplified with new material absorbed into them or placed in three additional chapters. In Part II all the material on history and Spengler is now collected, together with the long analysis of the history of the decline of the "Subject," functioning here both formally as a counter-example to Spengler's fatalistic cultural history and substantively as an account of a development within philosophy that Lewis opposes. It is with this material on the "Subject" that the oldest portions of *Time and Western Man* are reached: those that had originally formed part of *The Man of the World* and had been fictionalized for *The Childermass*. Part III is devoted principally to the concept of "Reality," divided more or less equally between criticism of the concept of reality that has been developed by philosophers out of the materials provided by Natural Science (both past and present), and hints towards a construction of Lewis's own philosophical account of "Reality." It was presumably because Lewis intended to write the work of "positive" metaphysics promised in his conclusion that he felt the two chapters on "Reality and Non-Being" and "The Pragmatical Test of the Doctrines . . ." would be best withheld. But that book, like the battle for the idea of reality promised at the end of Section I of *The Childermass*, was never written. All that remains of both or either is a collection of notes in the *Childermass* file at Cornell.

Time and Western Man was published in England on 29 September 1927.[116] When Montgomery Belgion, of the U.S. publisher Harcourt Brace, accepted *Time and Western Man* for publication, he evidently suggested that Lewis should write a new Preface to make the book a little more accessible to the general reader. Lewis moved the English edition's Preface, making it the Preface to the American edition's Book Two (this was what it had originally been intended for). A new Preface was then provided for the book as a whole, incorporating the original Preface to "The Revolutionary Simpleton" as its conclusion. Belgion suggested a few further changes of wording, and the American edition appeared, probably with no further oversight by Lewis, on 19 January 1928.[117] This edition was reissued as a paperback in a photographic reprint by Beacon Press of Boston in 1957. Lewis began writing a new preface[118] for it, regretting the space given to Samuel Alexander, but he was too ill to complete it, and he died shortly before the Beacon Press edition was published.

All editions of *Time and Western Man* have had Lewis's striking ink design on their title pages. The drawing seems to have originally been intended for *The Art of Being Ruled*, and to have appeared in an earlier version on the title page of the manuscript of that book. Lewis's publisher, C. H. Prentice, asked him to redraw it to fit the space available on the printed title page. Lewis did so, but neither he nor Prentice were satisfied with the result. Lewis evidently promised to try again, but on 1 February 1926 Prentice wrote to him "No drawing this morning, alas! The title page will, therefore, be bare." What is represented in the design can plausibly be interpreted as an act of fellatio (certainly a phallic protuberance is unmistakable). Lewis was a little unsure of the wisdom of using the drawing, as he had explained to Prentice on 10 December 1925:

One thing I meant to emphasise more; if you think the presence of this small squatting figure will draw attention to things of a controversial nature and nothing to do with the writing or selling of a book, and prejudice at all events the sale, I do not at all mind omitting it. I have very little vanity and certainly none where my pictorial experiments are concerned, or in such a connection.[119]

Whatever his doubts, he used the redrawn design for the title page of "The Revolutionary Simpleton" when it appeared in *The Enemy*, and later placed it on the title page of the complete book. Hence *Time and Western Man* is adorned with the most "controversial" (if ambiguous) drawing ever to grace a book of philosophy.

NOTES TO AFTERWORD

1. Buffalo, B14 F15.

2. That Lewis was prepared to take such advice is shown by his willingness to reorganize and cut *The Lion and the Fox* on the advice of Vincent Canby of Harper.

3. See also the letter quoted on page 483, in which Lewis instructs a potential publisher as to the best order to skip-read his manuscript.

4. See, for example, Walter Michel, *Wyndham Lewis: Paintings and Drawings* (London: Thames and Hudson, 1971), Hugh Kenner, *The Pound Era* (London: Faber, 1972), W. C. Wees, *Vorticism and the English Avant Garde* (Manchester: University of Manchester Press, 1972), Richard Cork, *Vorticism and Abstract Art in the First Machine Age* (London: Gordon Fraser, 1976 and 1977), Timothy Materer, *Vortex: Pound, Eliot and Lewis* (Ithaca: Cornell University Press, 1979), Michael Durman and Alan Munton, "Wyndham Lewis and the Nature of Vorticism," in G. Cianci, ed., *Wyndham Lewis: Letteratura/Pittura* (Palermo: Sellerio Editore, 1982). The most determined attempt to describe a coherent Vorticist aesthetic that will embrace painting and writing, the practices of Wyndham Lewis (as painter and writer), Ezra Pound and Gaudier-Brzeska (the sculptor) is Reed Way Dasenbrock, *The Literary Vorticism of Ezra Pound and Wyndham Lewis: Towards the Condition of Painting* (Baltimore: Johns Hopkins University Press, 1985).

5. "Kill John Bull with Art" (1914) rpt., *Creatures of Habit and Creatures of Change*, pp. 37–40.

6. In the sense of attention to the here and now. This was something with which Pound had difficulty. Pound's best strategy for dealing with the present was to approach it through what was remote: "the classics in paraphrase." *Homage to Sextus Propertius* is a successful poem because it dramatizes an unwillingness to do otherwise — a reluctance, in fact, to assume the epic ambition that Pound had prescribed for himself.

7. Page 22.

8. Ibid.

9. See Part II of this Afterword, for an outline of the composition and contents of *The Man of the World*.

10. Here is the crucial difference with Marinetti, who is interested in turning art into life, and experiencing the aesthetic thrills of sublimity in life itself. The culmination of this would be (as Walter Benjamin famously pointed out) to dedicate the productive forces of industry to the creation of the biggest possible sensation, in other words, to war. This merging of art and life was something Lewis denounced throughout his life.

11. "Essay on the Objective of Plastic Art in our Time" (*The Tyro*, No. 2) rpt. *Wyndham Lewis on Art*, p. 208.

12. Ibid.

13. *The Lion and the Fox*, p. 198.

14. "The Credentials of the Painter" (1922) rpt. *Creatures of Habit and Creatures of Change*, p. 76.

15. Lewis does not deny that good art can be made out of "needs" that are not related to current social circumstances, nor that some of our needs are timeless, such as those that seek satisfaction in a relationship with nature. These forms of art he sometimes calls Romantic. "Romantic" becomes a word of abuse for him when it signifies an attempt to evade the here and now, however (as in the never-never land of Romance analysed at the beginning of *Time and Western Man*). It is also a term of abuse when Lewis uses it to refer to bogus art which only pretends to deal with the here and now. Lewis also values the art of the past, which can at the least perform the function of great Romantic art, and at the best speak as fully to our own condition as contemporary "classical" art.

16. Compare the following passage, from f. 176 of the *Childermass* file (Cornell): "Every theory whatever means dialectical, [words indecipherable] another, & every technical invention even, must be regarded as the *invention* of certain types of mind. Every thing that offers, directly or indirectly, a picture of the universe or suggests implies or necessitates a certain response to it, its author must be held *personally* responsible for; or it must at least be interpreted as an experience of that type of mind to which he belongs. There is no possible exception to this. Even an inventor of motor-car bodies or engines *sees* the world driving about in motor-cars *to start with*, hopes[?] he invents, or wants to ride about himself. Ruskin, even had he been a mechanical genius, would not have invented a locomotive. Or if you like, he was not a mechanical genius because he was not interested in locomotives. All beauty, all ideas are the expression of a peculiar need. Their acceptance & popularization in no way depends on their general desire for what they imply — generally the contrary — but on the will of the people who at the moment are the real powers in the community."

17. "Inferior Religions" (probably written 1914–16, revised 1927) rpt. *The Complete Wild Body*, pp. 153–54. The idea of "small communities" motivated by particular sets of needs may have been suggested to Lewis by Fourier's Phalanstery and by some of Proudhon's ideas. Both Fourier and Proudhon are critically discussed in *The Art of Being Ruled*.

18. In this respect Lewis's aesthetic ideas bear a resemblance to the theories of I. A. Richards and of the New Critics who developed them, but only a faint resemblance to the other, intolerant wing of Richards's succession — that expressed in the thought and behavior of F. R. Leavis. But, for Richards, pluralism finds its satisfaction in the reconciliation and ordering of various psychological "drives" within the reader, making him a more contented citizen. The Leavisite school is always concerned to show that the finest works of art order their "plurality" in accordance with a monistic moral schema that is immanent in literature as a whole (and hence available only to students of literature — who are accordingly the growing point of civilization, and should be recognized as such). Lewis always opposed the "interference" of morals and was contemptuous of the claims of psychology as it existed to account for aesthetic values. Whatever the social function of art, aesthetic values needed no ulterior justification: "A picture either is or it is not."

19. This concept of the pure self is one of the main themes of Lewis's 1914 "play," *Enemy of the Stars*. Lewis discusses it explicitly in "The Meaning of the Wild Body," where he uses it as part of his exposition of laughter. See *The Complete Wild Body*, p. 157. A similarity with, and distinction from, the theory of T. S. Eliot can be noticed at this point. Like Lewis (and this seems to be

one of the presuppositions of Modernism), Eliot denies that the poet simply expresses his personality (what I have called in Lewis's case the "pure" self). But while Lewis suggests that the work of art expresses the mixed "personality" of the artist, with all the at times disagreeable tics and foibles that result from its passionate engagement in the world, Eliot rather dissociates artistic production from any merely personal needs, and represents the exclusion of the personality from the work of art as a form of martyrdom: "What happens is a continual surrender of himself as he is at the moment to something which is more valuable. The progress of an artist is a continual self-sacrifice, a continual extinction of personality" ("Tradition and the Individual Talent"). Besides having doubts about the importance for us of a quasi-Bradleyan Absolute to which one should sacrifice oneself, Lewis felt that his own theory fitted the facts (even of Eliot's practice) better, and that there was an element of self-deception or hypocrisy in Eliot's theory of impersonality.

20. "The Objective of Plastic Art in our Time," *Wyndham Lewis on Art*, pp. 204–05. Given Lewis's criticism in *Time and Western Man* of William James's fusion of matter and mind in a single substance, "experience," his attitude here may be surprising. But Lewis saw the artist's role as specialized; his criticism of the "time-philosophers" was that they appeared to lend support to a tendency to value a quasi-mystical immersion into the flux for its own sake.

21. Page 187.

22. "Essay on the Objective of Plastic Art," *Wyndham Lewis on Art*, p. 215.

23. "A Review of Contemporary Art," *Blast*, No. 2, p. 46.

24. Page 132.

25. Ibid.

26. Pages 135–36.

27. Hence Lewis's mockery of the conflict between Eliot's desire to retain his theory of "impersonality" and his desire for the work of art to be evaluated in terms of the belief-system it expresses. Eliot's only way out of the dilemma was a compromise proposal that the least "personal" belief systems (that is, those which were most grounded in tradition, such as that of the Anglican church) produced the best (because least "personal") art. See Lewis's criticism of Eliot's critical theory in *Men Without Art* (1934), Chapter III.

28. For the Marxist, although Lewis's critiques of his society are useful, they are the expression of Lewis's class-position as a member of an alienated petit-bourgeoisie in a period of financial instability. Unable (because blinkered by the false consciousness generated by bourgeois ideology) or unwilling to admit the true motives for his actually conservative preferences, Lewis locates them instead in an arbitrary and merely personal preference for the eye over the ear. See Fredric Jameson, *Fables of Aggression: Wyndham Lewis, the Modernist as Fascist* (Berkeley: University of California Press, 1979), pp. 123–30.

29. "Life as interpreted by the poet or philosopher is the objective of Revolutions, they are the substance of its Promised Land." (Page 24.)

30. See *The Art of Being Ruled* (1926), Part I, Chapter I, where Lewis notes Sorel's idea that it is "a change of ideas that constitutes a revolution" (p. 19). And note "Creatures of Habit and Creatures of Change": "Social revolution is the old (and it must be admitted ill-favoured) expedient." (*Creatures of Habit and Creatures of Change*, p. 161.)

31. "Without this *technical* dissolvent that has come to the assistance of philosophy and religion, men would have ceased to criticize life, perhaps, and a sad stagnation would have been the result." (*The Art of Being Ruled*, p. 23.)

32. *Creatures of Habit and Creatures of Change*, p. 147.

33. Page 81.

34. This summary does little justice to the complexity and richness of *The Art of Being Ruled*. But in that book Lewis notoriously suggests that a "modified form of fascism" might be the way to secure these ends. Yet Lewis considered himself a socialist, though one in the anarcho-syndicalist rather than Marxist tradition. His later qualified support of Hitler's "National Socialism" is not directly related to the political views of *The Art of Being Ruled*, however. Lewis had by 1931 despaired of Western societies instituting "revolutionary" values, engulfed in slumps as they were. Communism he opposed, and he also felt that a humiliated Germany was ultimately a danger to Europe (the novel *Tarr* allegorises the danger of a German inferiority complex). Lewis's critical 1926 views of Nazism are discussed in Part II of the Afterword, page 490. But, in 1931, "under compulsion of such emergency conditions, values change, and we are forced to admit arguments which, in other circumstances, we might regard as unsound" (*Hitler*, p. 129). Lewis is fair to himself when he writes, in his perceptive and witty attack on Hitler, *The Hitler Cult*, that he had never been a Nazi: "Such books as *The Lion and the Fox: The Rôle of the Hero in the Plays of Shakespeare*, or *The Art of Being Ruled*, are records of my tendency to aspire to a classless society and a world in which barbaric social values have no part. Though favouring always Proudhon rather than Marx, as a political thinker, some species of authoritarian control, it seemed to me, some 'planning' from a creative centre, were imposed upon us." (*The Hitler Cult*, p. 21.)

35. Page 118.

36. *The Caliph's Design*, p. 30.

37. And women, bohemian artists and male homosexuals; but these topics are more the concern of *The Art of Being Ruled* than of *Time and Western Man*.

38. It is an affirmation of rationality rather than a fully-worked out rational system itself, however. A measure of the amount that values have shifted is the fact that Pope's pessimistic counterpart to *An Essay on Man*, *The Dunciad*, which argues that civilization is under terminal threat from "Dulness," means by that a zany, fanciful irrationality that is closer to modern Surrealism than it is to anything else. It is now reason that seems dull.

39. Jeremy Bentham, *An Introduction to the Principles of Morals and Legislation* (1789), Chapter I.

40. Lewis suggests that the thought of Arthur Schopenhauer is the best guide to the "Time-philosophy." Certainly Schopenhauer's *On the Fourfold Root of the Principle of Sufficient Reason*, *On the Freedom of the Will*, and portions at least of *The World as Will and Representation* are immensely helpful in understanding the philosophical arguments sketched here. The first of these works in particular explains the complementarity of the law of cause and effect and the concept of matter. Schopenhauer thought of himself as a disciple of Kant, yet went beyond the limits Kant prescribed for metaphysics by claiming to describe the thing-in-itself. It is Will.

41. *Tarr*, p. 117.

42. "Substance" does not mean "matter," just any fundamental "stuff" of which reality is made. As John Locke put it, it is a word that covers "an uncertain supposition of we know not what."

43. *Science and the Modern World*, p. 218.

44. Dorothy Emmet, *Whitehead's Philosophy of Organism* (1932), 2nd ed. (London: Macmillan, 1966), p. 143.

45. *Science and the Modern World*, p. 108.

46. This is noticed by Dorothy Emmet: "Is there an ambiguity here in [Whitehead's use of the term] 'values,' which covers both the ethically and aesthetically neutral logical notion of supplying values to variables, and the teleological notion of value as something which for some reason it is good to achieve?" Op. cit., pp. xxx–xxxi.

47. Samuel Alexander was an Australian, and John Passmore, in *One Hundred Years of Philosophy*, reports that his influence on Australian philosophy was substantial. Passmore also states that some admirers of *Space, Time and Deity* consider it "the most important contribution to philosophy our century has known." Op. cit., (Harmondsworth: Penguin, 1972), p. 266.

48. "But of course the 'facts' of science turn out usually not to be facts, except in a limited sense. And it is far more the breakdown of *scientific* beliefs than that of religious beliefs which has precipitated the present *crisis of belief*, as I suppose it would be called . . ." *Men Without Art*, p. 71.

49. *Space, Time and Deity*, Vol. II, pp. 46–47.

50. Alexander distinguishes between deity and God: "God is the being which possesses deity" (ibid., p. 343). God remains undefined, but Alexander's system is fundamentally pantheistic, and God can be identified with the whole process of Space-Time.

51. S. T. Coleridge, *Biographia Literaria* (1818) ed. J. Engell and W. J. Bate (Princeton: Princeton University Press, 1984), [Vol. I], p. 266.

52. Like Samuel Alexander, Coleridge loved the philosophy of Benedict Spinoza.

53. This is implied by Lewis's celebration of the "abdication" of God (page 377), but is most explicitly stated on a scrap of paper in the *Childermass* file at Cornell (f. 143) quoted in the note on this passage.

54. Page 427.

55. Page 377. To pursue the connection between the idea of man as imitating God and the meaning of Lewis's satire, *The Apes of God*, would take us beyond our subject here.

56. *Wyndham Lewis on Art*, p. 204.

57. Compare Lewis's comments on Nietzsche in *The Art of Being Ruled*: "Nietzsche saw the surplus — because, of course, he *felt* it in his own organism — left over from the darwinian 'struggle for existence' " (p. 117). Lewis's pragmatic solution to the problem of free will and determinism is summed up in *Rude Assignment*: "From the start I have behaved *as if I were free*" (p. 113).

58. A note in the *Childermass* file (f. 118) at Cornell establishes Lewis's attitude on this point: "Science should be regarded very strictly indeed as a pure technique. It is and should be steadily & constantly recognized as an activity (requiring a high order of skill and power of attention) of a purely practical nature. What it does and what it *thinks*, when it thinks apart from its specialized

activity, — should be shown to be not only as having no connection with truth or reality, but to be on the whole hostile to them." In his copy of René Guénon's *Introduction aux doctrines hindoues*, Lewis marked a similar assertion on p. 24, annotating: "*Scientific* or practical minds discoveries impossible for metaphysical use[?]."

59. Page 377.

60. The passage is quoted at greater length in the Textual Appendix, note to page 375.

61. The allusion is to Arnold's verses describing the procession of the muses, led by Apollo:

> —Whose praise do they mention?
> Of what is it told? —
> What will be forever;
> What was from of old.
>
> First hymn they the Father
> Of all things; and then,
> The rest of immortals,
> The action of men.
>
> The day in his hotness,
> The strife with the palm;
> The night in her silence,
> The stars in their calm.

In a draft (holograph) "Conclusion," probably to a version of the discussion now in "The Subject Conceived as King of the Psychological World," Lewis instances those who desire to enjoy "the beauty of the morning, 'the stars in their calm,' a moonbeam, a mountain peak of metaphysics or of plastic art," along with the poor, who enjoy themselves with *"nothing at all,"* such as walking down the road or buying a packet of cheap cigarettes, as particular objects of the animosity of the rich (Cornell). In his 1954 review of a selection of Matthew Arnold's writing, Lewis affirmed his belief that "no greater poetry was ever written than the concluding song of Callicles in *Empedocles on Etna.*" (*Creatures of Habit and Creatures of Change*, p. 375)

The reference to "Chance" as the object of worship is illuminated by a fragment in the *Childermass* file at Cornell (f. 145): " 'Our god if we have one is Chance.' (p. 56. Hume)." The citation is of Hume's *Enquiry Concerning Human Understanding*, Section VI, "Of Probability": "Though there be no such thing as *Chance* in the world; our ignorance of the real cause of any event has the same influence on the understanding [as if there were] and begets a like species of belief or opinion." Lewis, by asserting that the world must be, from our perspective, at least, contingent in the sense suggested by Hume, is reinforcing the dissociation of his "abdicated" God from the moralistic God of Law of Judaeo-Christian and Kantian tradition, and the evolutionary God of science and the Time-philosophy.

62. No doubt Lewis also had Yeats in mind, particularly early Yeats. Lewis would not have wished to suggest that Romantic beauty was his main concern, nor that "Naturalism" should be the way to achieve it; *Time and Western Man* is written on behalf of Lewis's individual version of Modernism, which, like other Modernisms, including Yeats's, evolved out of late Romanticism.

63. See William Pritchard, "Literary Criticism as Satire," Jeffrey Meyers, ed., *Wyndham Lewis: A Revaluation* (London: Athlone Press, 1980), pp. 196–210.

64. One tradition of criticism of Joyce crucially depends on Lewis's chapter on Joyce, developing through Hugh Kenner's *Dublin's Joyce* and S. L. Goldberg's *The Classical Temper*. Insofar as these works are also the necessary predecessors of Arnold Goldman's *The Joyce Paradox* and other works that synthesize opposed critical traditions, Lewis's criticism is also ultimately an important ingredient in those approaches, such as Stephen Heath's ("Ambiviolances") that see Joyce's writing as a constant deferral of closure or definitive "meaning." But *Time and Western Man* provides a vantage point from which this approach (in which meaning resembles Alexander's deity) can be criticized.

65. *Rude Assignment*, pp. 208–09.

66. William James, "Does 'Consciousness' Exist?" (1904). The essay is of exceptional importance in the "family" of ideas that make up Lewis's "Time-philosophy," because of its consonance with Bergson, its favourable citation by Whitehead, and its importance as one of the presuppositions of Behaviorism. See pages 337–40 for Lewis's discussion of James. For Post-modernism as a modern version of the delirium of Futurism, see Peter Nicholls, "Futurism, Gender and Theories of Postmodernity," *Critical Practice*, Vol. III, No. 2 (Summer 1989), pp. 202–21.

67. See Paul Grice, "Logic and Conversation," *Studies in the Way of Words* (Cambridge: Harvard University Press, 1989), p. 26. The paper was first delivered in 1967 as part of the William James lectures at Harvard.

68. Page 341.

69. *Rude Assignment*, p. 209.

70. Lewis to Eliot, c. October 1923, *The Letters of Wyndham Lewis*, ed. W. K. Rose (London: Methuen Ltd, 1963), p. 136.

71. Letter from Hugh Kenner to the editor, 14 March 1992.

72. Hugh Kenner, "Excerpts from 'The Man of the World,' " *Agenda: Wyndham Lewis Special Issue*, Vol. 7, No. 3 –Vol. 8, No. 1 (Autumn–Winter 1969–70), p. 182.

73. Wyndham Lewis Collection, Cornell University Library. The "page 13" at which Lewis advises Waugh to begin reading is at Buffalo, bound with the manuscripts of *The Lion and the Fox*, along with much other unpublished material from *The Man of the World* (most notably a section on race and one on the idea of "goodness" — from which part of "The Physics of the Not-self" was excerpted). The first two paragraphs on the page were used in *The Art of Being Ruled*, Part V, Chapter V (15th and 16th paragraphs, beginning "Men and women . . ." and "When you are dealing . . ." [pp. 144–45]). The first 12 pages of the manuscript (about 8,000 words) are missing, but may be assumed to have contained earlier versions of material now comprising Chapters II and III of Part V of *The Art of Being Ruled*. The passage Lewis advised Waugh to read (ff. 13–19 of the typescript) was revised slightly and included in "The Foxes' Case," where it forms the final two-and-a-half paragraphs of Section 4, and Sections 5 through 7 (*Creatures of Habit and Creatures of Change*, pp. 129–36).

74. Lewis to Pound, 2 February 1925, T. Materer, ed., *Pound/Lewis: The Letters of Ezra Pound and Wyndham Lewis* (New York: New Directions, 1985), pp. 144–45. See also Materer's informative introduction to this letter, pp. 142–44.

75. Lewis to Eliot, February 1924, *Letters*, p. 193.

76. Lewis to Eliot, c. March 1924, ibid., p. 140.

77. Lewis to Whibley, c. March 1925, ibid., p. 155.

78. Lewis to Eliot, c. January 1925, ibid., p. 147.

79. Eliot to Lewis, 31 January 1925, ibid., p. 150.

80. Lewis to McAlmon, 1 April 1925, ibid., p. 156.

81. Pound reports McAlmon's criticisms in a letter of 12 May 1925 (*Pound/Lewis*, p. 148), and on 1 October reports Walsh's denial that McAlmon had any part in the rejection. Evidently Walsh told Pound that he had only been able to afford to offer Lewis £10 (ibid., pp. 154–55).

82. Lewis to McAlmon, 24 July 1925, *Letters*, p. 161.

83. McAlmon to Lewis, 1 August 1925, Wyndham Lewis Collection, Cornell.

84. Lewis to Grant Richards, 20 May and 26 May 1925 (Harry Ransom Humanities Research Center, University of Texas).

85. Lewis to Grant Richards, 24 July and 16 September 1925 (Texas). It was probably due to Richards's wish to sabotage Lewis's hoped-for deal with Harper (under which Richards would not have been able to sell them printed sheets of the book) that publication of *The Lion and the Fox* was first delayed (later delays resulted from the firm's financial problems). The book finally appeared under the imprint of The Richards Press.

86. *The Calendar of Modern Letters*, II, No. 8 (October 1925), pp. 73–90, rpt. Wyndham Lewis, *Creatures of Habit and Creatures of Change*, pp. 120–36.

87. Bradford Morrow and Bernard Lafourcade, *A Bibliography of the Writings of Wyndham Lewis* (Santa Barbara: Black Sparrow Press, 1978), p. 40; see note 89.

88. But (for example) the first three chapters of Part VI of *The Art of Being Ruled*, "Sub Persona Infantis," each contain references to newspaper articles published after the "completion" of *The Man of the World*. So some reorganization and expansion certainly occurred.

89. McAlmon to Lewis, 6 March 1926, Cornell.

90. For a sarcastic account of these dealings, combined with a rejoinder to Lewis's criticisms of McAlmon and *This Quarter*, see "Unrecommended Pages: Alex's Journal: Re *The Pekker*— Edited by Winnie Jewit" (probably written by McAlmon), *This Quarter* (Spring 1929), Vol. 4, pp. 281–91. Julian Symons, in *Makers of the New: The Revolution in Literature, 1912–1939* (London: André Deutsch, 1987), p. 211, also gives an account of the affair.

91. Pound to Lewis, 6 June 1925 (*Pound/Lewis*, p. 149).

92. Confirmation that it was in 1926, rather than earlier, that Lewis was working on the book is supplied by a note on the back of a letter from Edgell Rickword to Lewis of 29 April 1926 (Cornell). This is a memo of an inventive obscene remark which was incorporated into a draft of *The Childermass*.

93. Buffalo, B15 F8.

94. Among the *Childermass* typescripts are materials that were revised for "The Subject Conceived as King of the Psychological World" and "Science and Scepticism" (Buffalo, B6 F6 and 7; also elsewhere in the collection: B16 F4), while some drafts of *Time and Western Man* show evidence in their deletions of having been converted from use in *The Childermass*: "God as Reality" (B16 F1), and the deleted chapter, "The Pragmatical Test of the Doctrines of Relativity and of Time" (B16 F7).

95. Buffalo, B15 F4.

96. Buffalo, B14 F8.

97. Draft "Preliminary Note to the Public," Buffalo, B15 F8, and typescript in B14 F9, where "Enemy" is deleted.

98. In the following order: B15 F4, B15 F7, B15 F3, B14 F11. One leaf in B15 F7 belongs at the end of B14 F11. A Preface, most probably for this version of the pamphlet, is in B14 F3, wrongly identified in Lewis's hand as a Preface for *Time and Western Man*.

99. Buffalo, B14 F9.

100. R. Ellmann, ed., *The Letters of James Joyce* (London: Faber, 1966), Vol. III, p. 142.

101. Revised and expanded into *Finnegans Wake*, pp. 282–304. Joyce wrote this section over the summer of 1926. Lewis parodied and quoted from it ("Anny liffle mud which cometh out of Mam will doob, I guess") in additions made to *The Childermass* in March 1928, though the Joyce passage was not published till 1929. (*Finnegans Wake*, p. 287; *The Childermass*, p. 171.) Lewis was at least tactful enough not to quote in *The Enemy* from the section Joyce had expected him to publish, only resorting to this after being lampooned as Professor Jones by Joyce in *transition*, No. 6 (September 1927).

102. According to Sylvia Beach's account. Beach reports that it was the "Anna Livia Plurabelle" chapter that Joyce gave to Lewis — but this had been published the previous year in *Le Navire d'Argent* (*Shakespeare and Co.*, [London: Faber, 1966], p. 173). *The Childermass* and *The Apes of God* can be read as containing critiques of Joyce and Ezra Pound respectively. In expanding the opening (pre-Bailiff) scenes of *The Childermass*, Lewis modelled the character Pullman, an intellectual who is a dupe, and purveyor, of the Bailiff's "Time" ideology, on Joyce, and included a parody of "Work in Progress." For the presence of Pound in *The Apes of God*, see Antonio M. Feijo, "Wyndham Lewis's Knotty Relationship with Ezra Pound," *Enemy News*, No. 32 (Summer 1991), pp. 4–10, and Peter L. Caracciolo, " 'Like a Mexith's renowned statue bristling with emblems': Masquerade, Anthropology, Yeats and Pound among Wyndham Lewis's 'Apes of God,' " *Pound in Multiple Perspective*, ed. A. Gibson (London: Macmillan, 1993), pp. 126–57.

103. "Preface," *The Enemy*, No. 1, p. 27.

104. *Time and Western Man* pages 81–93 originate in a series of insertions in the manuscript: Lewis used the pages of a duplicate account book in drafting them, which was not the case for the rest of the chapter. The manuscripts are at Buffalo, B15 F1, B14 F16, B15 F16, B14 F17. In the printed text this material follows immediately the material adapted from the earlier Preface.

105. Quoted from a copy of the prospectus at Cornell.

106. In *The Enemy*, Chapter 16 is devoted to James Joyce. The remaining chapters are:

17 Professor Alexander and the Age of Time or Motion
18 The Philosophy of the Instruments of Research
19 Professor Whitehead: Spatialisation and Concreteness
20 Pure Poetry and Pure Magic
21 The Counter, "Life"
22 A Final Word about the Time-School
23 History as the Natural Art of the Time-School
24 The "Chronological" Philosophy of Spengler.

107. Prentice to Lewis, 24 February 1927. Chatto and Windus Archive, Reading, Letterbook No. 116, 574.

108. Chatto and Windus Archive, Letterbook No. 117, 92–93.

109. B14 F4, B16 Fs 1, 4, 6, 7, 9, 13, and 14.

110. In the printer's copy at Cornell, the last leaf of "Space and Time" has a supplementary pencilled number (69), and matches in typewriter, paper type, ribbon-colour (purple) and spacing a batch of typescript at Buffalo (B16 F14). That batch is similarly numbered in pencil, and sheet 70 begins a revised version of "The Pragmatical Test . . ."; the previous sheet in the batch, numbered 58, comes from near the end of a version of "Reality and Non-Being" that lacks about two leaves of what is probably its conclusion, and announces a discussion of Space and Time to follow. "Space and Time" is therefore almost certainly a revision of sheets 61 (approximately) to 69 of this batch of typescript.

111. But the possibility that this part or parts may not have immediately preceded the material on belief, reality and God cannot definitely be ruled out.

112. Buffalo, B16 F14. The leaf is unnumbered, but it initiates a discussion of issues raised in passages from Kant and Bergson (on science as a "doctrine of motion" and on nature as seeking to constitute "naturally closed" systems; now quoted on pages 348 and 351, in Chapters 1 and 2 of Book Two, Part III) which is concluded on two leaves, one numbered 43 and the next unnumbered (also in the file of "leftovers," B16 F14). The passage on these leaves reverts to discussion of the same quotations and summarizes the purpose of the section. This "conclusion" is preceded by other (numbered) leaves containing draft versions of passages of "God as Reality." Leaf number 44 begins a new chapter (untitled) based on "Reality and Non-Being." This suggests that what are now the first three chapters of Book Two, Part III, were at one time conceived as a unit: perhaps "Part V: God as Reality."

113. The typescript contains some corrections (of "Mr. Moore" to "Prof. Moore") in what looks like Prentice's hand. "The Pragmatical Test . . ." was also revised as a "chapter" (large portions are in the file of "leftovers" at Buffalo, B16 F14, but are not identified by a title).

114. Chatto and Windus Letterbook No. 117, 223.

115. Ibid., 725. The addition to "The Object Conceived as King of the Physical World" forms the conclusion of the chapter, and begins after the three-line break on page 395.

116. *A Bibliography of the Writings of Wyndham Lewis*, p. 46.

117. Ibid; proofs of new Preface at Buffalo: B16 F5.

118. Typescript at Cornell.

119. Prentice to Lewis, 2, 9 and 23 December 1925 (Cornell) and Lewis to Prentice, 10 and 20 December 1925 (Chatto and Windus Archive, University of Reading).

THE CRITICAL RECEPTION OF *TIME AND WESTERN MAN*

Time and Western Man was extensively and, on the whole, favorably, reviewed in England. Most critics commented on the undisciplined gusto with which Lewis went about his work. Catholics welcomed, with reservations, Lewis's limited endorsement of Thomism (and James Joyce believed that Lewis was about to make a "clamorous conversion"). Lewis's closest intellectual affinities were thought to be with the international "classical anti-humanist" reaction, whose chief representatives were T. S. Eliot and the late T. E. Hulme in England, Henri Massis, Julien Benda and Charles Maurras in France, and Irving Babbitt in America. The most extended reading of *Time and Western Man* and of Lewis's career as a whole as a distasteful outgrowth of this movement is Geoffrey Wagner's 1957 study, *Wyndham Lewis: A Portrait of the Artist as the Enemy*. A similar alignment of Lewis with classicism occurs in the U.S. reception of the book.

Most later full-length general studies of Lewis (not listed below) devote space to discussing *Time and Western Man*, and there have been two specialized studies, by SueEllen Campbell and Pamela Bracewell, that focus on *Time and Western Man* as a key to understanding Lewis's critical strategies and his aesthetic. *Time and Western Man* is not part of the academic canon of Modernist criticism, and, in keeping with the omission of Lewis's other writing from the major "teaching" anthologies of literature, it is not represented in, for example, David Lodge's vast anthology of Twentieth Century Literary Criticism; nor is it mentioned in Malcolm Bradbury and James McFarlane, eds., *Modernism: 1890 – 1927* (Harmondsworth: Penguin, 1976).

The following bibliography is selective; a fuller list can be found in Bradford Morrow and Bernard Lafourcade, *A Bibliography of the Writings of Wyndham Lewis* (Santa Barbara: Black Sparrow Press, 1978).

1. Early reactions

Anon., *"Time and Western Man," Times Literary Supplement* (27 October 1927): respectfully summarizes Lewis's philosophical argument, and praises the book for bringing the whole of an intelligence into play.

Anon., " 'Time-Philosophy' and the Artist," *The Saturday Review*, Vol. CXLIV, No. 3757 (29 October 1927): a knowledgeable discussion, suggesting Lewis's affinity with Eighteenth Century Deism — "it is evident already that nothing in the nature of traditional theism will be his alternative to the prevalent pantheism."

Roy Campbell, "The Emotional Cyclops," *The New Statesman*, Vol. XXX, No. 762, Supplement, X–XII: "though one would like to believe him when he says his outlook is classical and intellectual, his methods, his style and his excitability betray him as the emotional romantic."

M. C. D'Arcy, "A Critic among the Philosophers," *The Month*, Vol. CL, No. 76 (December 1927): highly favorable review, but "if God exists, by what right does Mr. Lewis say God must not love . . . ?" " 'Time and Western Man' is one of the most significant books of the age, and the Catholic philosopher very readily accepts the offer of an alliance which Mr. Lewis makes in these pages."

William Empson, "Ask a Policeman," *Granta*, 21 October 1927: "There is no doubt that he has collected with breadth and acuteness a body of valuable critical material to which a critique may yet be applied, and it is possible that his next book, which he has assured us will make his own position more clear, may do what these important and very readable essays do not."

"Fr. Gr.," "*Time and Western Man*," *Laudate* (March 1928): compares Lewis with Léon Daudet and associates him with European Catholic reaction against Modernism in religion and philosophy, noting his reliance on Aquinas, but conceding that Lewis is defending a classical rather than a Catholic position.

I. Levine, "*Time and Western Man*," *The Sociological Review*, Vol. XX, April 1928: "I refuse to take the so-called philosophical arguments and sections seriously. . . . The book as a whole . . . has nothing but its extraordinary literary criticism of the First Part to recommend it."

Herbert Read, "*Time and Western Man*," *The Nation and Athenaeum*, Vol. XLII, No. 7 (19 November 1927): sees Lewis as part of an international "anti-humanist" movement — "by far the most active force among us," but a "blind force." Lewis's criticism is "not philosophical," but a "painter's criticism of a world which has no place for his art."

I. A. Richards, "*Time and Western Man*," *The Cambridge Review* (9 March 1928): an enthusiastic review, suggesting nevertheless that Lewis should not spend his energies on attacking "Time-philosophy," since it "only threatens people . . . whose feelings, mode of perception, and capacity for response are welded (by accident or education) to their opinions about the world picture."

W. A. Thorpe, "*Time and Western Man,*" *The Monthly Criterion,* Vol. VII, No. 1 (pp. 70–73): "Underneath his critical brilliance [Lewis's Aristotelianism] is both sentimental and pragmatical. . . . His book is a yearn working itself off as a grouse." Lewis "misunderstands" Whitehead, missing his Platonism.

Humbert Wolfe, "*Time and Western Man,*" *The Observer* (9 October 1927): "Mr. Lewis is concerned with the real thing. He sees that right and wrong are the shadows of truth and error, and that until the cognitive problems are faced and in part solved the ethical and artistic do not, in fact, arise."

W. B. Yeats, *W. B. Yeats and T. Sturge Moore: Their Correspondence 1901–1937,* ed. Ursula Bridge (London: Routledge and Kegan Paul, 1953): letters to Moore, December 1927–February 1928 – "he has intellectual passion, and of that there has been very little these thirty years. His last book is among other things Plotinus or some Buddhist answering the astrologers [who think that nothing is real but space-time] . . . I do not always hate what he hates and yet I am glad that he hates" (p. 117).

Conrad Aiken, "Mr. Lewis and the Time-Beast," *The Dial,* Vol. LXXXV, No. 20 (August 1928): "Here is no Platonic serenity, but the gesticulatory vehemence of the dynamists whom he would depose; he is tainted, and deeply, with the excitements, the fashions and fads, of his age . . ."

R. P. Blackmur, "The Enemy," *The Hound and Horn,* Vol. I, No. 3 (March 1928): Lewis associated with the classic anti-humanism of Babbitt, Massis, Fernandez and neo-Thomists: "As to Mr. Lewis' judgments on James Joyce, Ezra Pound and company, they are valid only from Mr. Lewis' attitude. But that is no matter. . . . What the reader has to decide is whether he can accept the total attitude which makes these criticisms possible; when [*sic*] he will make his own minor corrections."

Joseph Wood Krutch, "Plastic and Temporal in Art," *The Nation,* Vol. CXXV, No. 3257: praises Lewis as the proponent of a classicizing formalism that results from "a longing for something outside of time which is closed and complete in itself — for something with a pattern in which each part is so joined to every other part that it returns upon itself . . ."

Lewis Mumford, "The Case against Time," *New Republic*, Vol. LIV, No. 692 (7 March 1928): finds the book indigestible — "if Mr. Lewis had not been so upset by reading Bergson, or so impervious to all ideas of historic sequence, he might have performed a valuable service by working out the development of our time-consciousness, and showing how our great spatialising activities, painting, architecture, sculpture, city-building, have been weakened or undermined by it."

John Cowper Powys, "The God of Time," *The Dial*, Vol. LXXVI, No. 5 (November 1928): "Two diametrically different ways of responding to the universal spectacle are here brought into a dramatic opposition such as would provoke Hegel to cold fury. *Being*, in fact, is here confronted with *Becoming* and subjected to a degree of antithesis such as these mystic ultimates have rarely known."

2. Later Studies

P. J. Bracewell, *Space, Time and the Artist: The Philosophy and Aesthetics of Wyndham Lewis* (Thesis presented for the degree of Doctor of Philosophy, University of Sheffield, July 1990): the clearest and most comprehensive exposition of Lewis's philosophical standpoint in *Time and Western Man*.

SueEllen Campbell, *The Enemy Opposite: The Outlaw Criticism of Wyndham Lewis* (Athens: Ohio University Press, 1988): excellent and sympathetic guide to Lewis's critical strategies; also traces the hidden influence of Lewis's criticism of Joyce on subsequent critics.

Timothy Materer, *Vortex: Pound, Eliot and Lewis* (Ithaca: Cornell University Press, 1979): sets Lewis's philosophical ideas in the context of his fellow-"Men of 1914."

Daniel Schenker, "Homo Ex Machina: Wyndham Lewis on the Definitions of Man," Seamus Cooney, ed., *Blast 3* (Santa Barbara: Black Sparrow Press, 1984), pp. 96–108: perhaps the best single essay on *Time and Western Man*.

E. W. F. Tomlin, "Reflections on 'Time and Western Man,' " *Agenda* (Wyndham Lewis Special Issue) Vol. VII, No. 3–Vol. VIII, No. 1 (Autumn–Winter 1969–70), pp. 97–108.

————, "The Philosophical Influences," Jeffrey Meyers, ed., *Wyndham Lewis: a Revaluation* (London: Athlone Press, 1980), pp. 29–46.

René Wellek, *A History of Modern Criticism, 1750–1950: English Criticism, 1900–1950* (London: Jonathan Cape, 1986), pp. 169–75: "Lewis's critical principles are very simple: independence, freedom of the artist, distaste for the contemporary scene. . . . sharp formulations are drowned in dreary polemics and often nit-picking verbal disputes. To this one must add Lewis's bad reputation for his political opinions . . ."

TEXTUAL APPENDIX

The copy-text for this edition is the first U.S. edition, published by Harcourt Brace in 1928, which principally derived from the first (and only) English edition (published by Chatto and Windus the previous year). The principal difference between the U.S. and English editions is the new Preface added to the U.S. edition, which necessitated the movement and alteration of the original English Preface. The printer's copy from which the English edition was set is in the Lewis collection at Cornell. The proofs of the U.S. Preface are in the Lewis collection at Buffalo. The present text varies from the copy-text partly on account of adoption of more modern printing conventions, partly on account of correction of spelling mistakes and misquotations, and partly as a result of a collation of the printer's copy with the English and American texts. No proofs for the English edition have been preserved, so far as is known. The printer's copy cannot therefore be assumed to represent Lewis's final intentions in all places where it differs from the printed editions, though in one or two places it has been followed, where the editor has assumed that printers' errors were overlooked.

Physically, the printer's copy provides valuable evidence for a study of Lewis's methods of composition. Most of Book One comprises loose pages from the first issue of *The Enemy*, with occasional alterations in Lewis's hand. Book Two is mostly typescript, again with corrections and additions in Lewis's hand. Lewis appears to have been very much a "scissors and paste" author, and some pages of the typescript are made up from paragraphs rescued from earlier drafts, pasted down and linked by handwritten passages. Four main paper-types are used, and four different typewriters, sometimes single-spaced, sometimes double. Some pages appear to be carbons. *Time and Western Man* is organized in a confusing manner at times; but anyone who examines the palimpsest typescript is likely to be struck more by the surprising coherence of the final product than by its disorder.

For Lewis, the process of composition often did not cease until the final proof stage of the book. This was especially the case with his fiction, as the proofs of *The Childermass* and *The Apes of God*, both at Buffalo, testify. But comparatively few changes were introduced to *Time and Western Man* at the proof stage, and the text as published follows the printer's copy quite closely. The main changes were to capitalization, punctuation, and presentation of quotations. Lewis preferred a capitalization system that left adjectives of religion, race or nation uncapitalized, and many (though not all) words of this type were "corrected" to this from the conventional form in the typescript. Some were overlooked, but no attempt has been made to alter the present text to conform more closely to Lewis's declared principles. Likewise, Lewis's curious negligence in the matter of subject–verb agreements has (or *have*, as he might put it) not been rectified; the U.S. edition corrects many of them.

The most extensive alteration of Lewis's typescript in the original publication process was to punctuation. Lewis used punctuation more as a form of pointing, to indicate the intonation and rhythm of a sentence imagined as spoken, than as a system of marking the grammatical relationships between groups of words. Commas are omitted where normal conventions require them (round parenthetical *of courses* or *therefores*, for example), or are illogically interpolated between a subject and its (perhaps delayed) verb. Dashes abound. Much of this was brought into conformity with normal practice, and though one may sometimes regret the loss of idiosyncrasy, rather than attempt to restore the original punctuation, the editor has thought it best to reproduce the text in the form that Lewis himself was contented with. His publishers were indulgent of many of his eccentricities, and, had he really objected, he would have put up a fight (as he did with Grant Richards over capitalization in *The Lion and the Fox*). Quotations, in the printer's copy, tend not to be indented, and all are enclosed in quotation marks. Lewis's editor, C. H. Prentice, marked these up for indentation.

The following changes have been made silently to the text. Double quotation marks have been substituted for single. The first few words of every chapter have been set in small capitals. The copy text's "to-morrow" and "to-day" have been changed to "tomorrow" and "today." "Any one" and "every one" have been changed to "anyone" and "everyone." The editorial alterations to quotations Lewis placed inside curved brackets have been placed within square brackets. The etceteras that sometimes follow quotations (and which in typescript are usually outside the quotation marks) have been placed in square brackets. Colons are used where the copy text has a colon followed by a dash. Ligatured vowels have been silently expanded to "ae" and "oe" as appropriate. Periods have been removed after Roman numerals ("V." becomes "V"), or replaced by commas where appropriate. Titles of books identifying epigraphs have been changed from italic to roman, and the periods after them have been replaced by commas; periods have also been removed after the authors' names. *Time and Western Man* is divided into two Books; the copy text's Roman Books I and II have been changed to Books One and Two. Of course, all internal page references have been adjusted silently to suit the present edition.

All other changes to the copy text are recorded, and their justification supplied, in the following Table of Variants. The most important set of changes has been to Lewis's quotations. The editor has assumed that

Lewis wished to quote accurately, but was not pedantic. So all verbal errors have been corrected and ellipses indicated. But no attempt has been made to restore punctuation where it has been transcribed inaccurately. Sometimes a "quotation" is virtually a paraphrase, and in such cases it has not been "corrected," but the correct version has usually been provided in the Explanatory Notes.

TABLE OF VARIANTS

All variants between the U.S. and English edition are recorded. Only significant variants (usually verbal) from the printer's copy are recorded. Significant deletions from the printer's copy are given, along with passages from draft versions from other material in Buffalo. The most important and interesting details not given in the following table are the alterations Lewis made to "The Revolutionary Simpleton" from its first publication. A broad picture of these is given in Part II of the Afterword. The details can readily be discovered by straightforward comparison of the texts.

Note that, in the following table, all closely-spaced ellipses (...) indicate an editorial ellipsis from the text of *Time and Western Man*, and simply facilitate citation (except in the case of page 71, line 36), while broadly spaced ellipses (. . .) have substantive significance. Note also that each entry gives the text first as printed in this edition, then *as printed and punctuated* in the cited source. Basically, this means that the text from this edition will usually have double quotation marks, while citations from the U.S. and English editions will have single ones.

> A = Buffalo manuscripts
> B = Buffalo proofs (of *The Enemy*)
> C = Printer's copy at Cornell
> E = English (first, Chatto and Windus) edition
> U = U.S. (second, Harcourt Brace) edition

page	*line*	
xi 1–xix	25	Author's Preface ... *The Enemy*: [Not in E or C; in U, the title is "Preface." The remainder of the Preface from "This essay" to "this book" comprises the first three paragraphs of E, "Preface to Book I." The English Preface continues at the passage found in this edition on page 130, line 19: "The position from which this essay ..." and concludes where this edition's Preface to Book Two finishes, on page 144: further detailed variants between the Prefaces of E and U are given in the order of the appearance of these passages in the present edition.]
xvi	10 & 25	p. U: page
xvi	26	Mr. U: Professor [source]

xvi	32–35	At the . . . Prof. Bergson . . . U: 'At the . . . Professor Bergson.' [normal punctuation conventions for longer quotations, and source]
xvii	5	*action—* U: *action, —* [redundant comma omitted]
1		[In E this epigraph precedes the "Preface to Book I"]
3	8	these C: those
6	25–26	'beauty' . . ." E: "beauty" . . ."
6	40	apparent . . . E, U: apparent. [words omitted from source]
7	20–21	might . . . describe E, U: might describe [words omitted from source]
9	5 & 21	"classic–romantic" E, U: "classic-romantic" [preferable punctuation]
9	29	classic–romantic E: Classic-Romantic U: classic-romantic
25	26	But in art . . . all revolutionary impulse B [*del.*]:

In connection with the communal principles applied to artistic production, there is no more zealous authority in England than Mr. Roger Fry. He has been very explicit on the subject of individual effort; the drawback of being "creative" in any way is a favourite topic with him. The very word "creative" is rather disgusting, from his standpoint, suggesting the throes of parturition: *c.f. Nation,* 1924.

Mr. Roger Fry has been a conspicuous organiser of revolutionary guilds and societies, and the ecstatic phalansteries imagined by him are where the soviet system is best seen joining hands, in a cultural backwater, with the utopianism of Morris, rather as Trotsky leans, in his propaganda, upon Fourier. Further parallels might no doubt be drawn between the regime of the soviets, and such as obtains in these small art-families, often autocracies, in fact, and as far from an egalitarian reality as their larger political correlates.

To-day the sovietist, or collectivist, has a monopoly of what is called "revolution." He has the objectionable habits of other monopolists. All impulse to revolution, or to change, is not necessarily sovietic, communist, or collectivist, at all: that is a superstition. You may ardently desire a change in any of a million directions. To-day you are restricted sternly to one. All revolutionary impulse [B14 F12]

25	34	*Ruled* (1925) C: *Ruled* last year (1925)
26	24	sleep of the dance. B [*del.*]: sleep of the dance — the Dance of Death, it is to-day. [B14 F12]
27	2	of Book One of this C: of this E, U: of Book I. of
27	5	plane C, E: plane U: place [printer's error]
30	9	That Marcel C: Marcel
30	27	As to . . . B [*del.*]: The outlook on life, or the philosophy, of such

a man as Sigmund Freud, his particular, and, for us, original way of interpreting his experience, the report he gives of human existence as he has observed it, is very much that of Proust, and the Dadaists, for instance, pouring out behind him, or the Surréalistes into which the latter become very slightly transformed.

Whether the millionaire-revolutionary society is destined to have any stability or suite is not our concern. We are dealing only with what is actual and there before us, the most powerful thing in sight; only adding the pious hope that it may suffocate itself with itself before it entirely overwhelms all art and meaning in the world whatever; for no one else (in sight) can do that for us, short of a miraculous intervention.

As to . . . [B14 F12]

31	2	forth [your] own E, U: forth your own [emendation of source]
38	7–8	about twelve C: ten or twelve
40	32	two summers ago C: this summer

43	10	and there she E, U: and then she [source]
44	1	dull. . . . He E, U: dull. He [source]
44	17	Ring W. E: Ring. W.
44	18	english E: English
44	35–36	wouldn't of allowed it after she seen E, U: wouldn't have allowed it after she had seen [source]
45	5	Wush's E: Wishes
55	23	Ring W. E: Ring. W.
59	5	*became* U: became [reverting to E]
60	5	are undoubtedly E: is undoubtedly
69	27	wits' E: wits' U: wit's [reverting to E's more usual plural]
71	14	salt bright . . . E, U: salt bright. [source]
71	36	money . . . E, U: money . . . [source; to distinguish from editorial ellipses]
71	37	I ain't had E, U: I had [source]
73	18	poets"— E, U: poets,'— [redundant comma omitted]
83	34	goethean E: göethean
84	37	darwinian theory E: Darwinian Theory U: darwinian Theory [inconsistent capitalization]
87	19–20	*A la Recherche du Temps perdu* E: *A La Recherche du Temps Perdu*
87	23	Bergson–Einstein, Stein–Proust E, U: Bergson-Einstein, Stein-Proust [preferable punctuation]
91	4	left it E: left them
91	6	*his* present E: *his* present U: his present [printing error in U]
94	39	Stephen's E, U: Stephan's [misspelling]
95	7 (and all subsequent appearances of this name) Stephen E, U: Stephan
95	37	down. . . . E: down. . . .'
95	40	*halfway* E: *half way*
96	34	impatiently. . . . E, U: impatiently. [source]
100	18	Cézanne's E: Cezanne's
103	3	vacuum. . . . E, U: vacuum. [omission from source (*Ulysses*)]
103	5	person," E, U: person, [close quotes because the "etc." is not part of the speech]
103	10	ain't it? . . . E, U: ain't it? [omission from source (*Pickwick Papers*)]
103	14	Come— . . . stopping E, U: Come—stopping [omission from source (*Pickwick Papers*)]
104	32	years. E, U: years . . . [source]
106	6	lodging houses, and E: lodging houses and
108	2	Flower of E, U: Flower girl of [source]
111	26	halfway E: half-way
113	26	at its ease E: at its ease U: at ease [probable printing error in U]
114	28	of a Hunnish E, U: of Hunnish [source]
118	26	engaged in E: engaged
119	27–33	Will-to-change . . . one confusing mass B [*del.*]: This analysis and "sorting out" was what my other treatise, from which I quote, was directed to achieve; not to advertise mere Revolution, of which boost there is a glut.

        The ultimate definition of the revolutionary impulse is that it is some human interest or other exploiting a casual material technique. The human interests in question are two in number; there is the distinctive philosophic interest, and, on the other side, the practical one: — (1) the intellect, and (2) the pocket or the "power-complex." The philosophic intelligence hastening to utilise a technique for its finer purposes, usually discovers some predatory figure already on the spot who has had the same idea, only whose motives are simple loot. All science is in fact pillaged almost as soon as it comes into existence, and most art gets degraded as soon as it is well out of its cradle.

The extreme antiquity of the revolutionary impulse must always be borne in mind. Whenever a technical revolution (such as that from stone to bronze) has occurred, this impulse has asserted itself. In the West it has shown a certain duality. Western science is all that Europe has to boast of. Always weak in mystery — with no sacred books or mastery in religion — weak in art, positive science alone redeems the picture. Perhaps this is the reason why Europe is inclined to reach through science what has been facultatively denied her elsewhere. And, as a professional of science, and in that an initiator, it is perhaps also natural that the techniques should not interest the European as much as they do other people, who have learnt their secrets from us. In that respect the European has, no doubt, the cynicism of the creator where his "shop" is concerned.

However this may be, the Western revolutionary impulse, arising in technical power and material mastery, takes a religious or philosophic form. *Technique does not interest the Western Genius*, that is my paradox, if you will. Its revolutionary impulse is in conflict, even, with what is only its occasion. This pretext, the eruption of a new technical system (in response to its special genius) is as much its enemy usually, slugging it from behind, as the corrupt, long-undisturbed social system confronting all creative thought. Then the facile professional of "revolution" with whom it is compelled to associate itself, is apt to be merely a fanatic of new technique, with different purposes to it; or with no purposes, beyond technical expertness.

The technique of the engineer, the method, and temper, of positive science, is magic, philosophy, religion and art for the European. And, it could be added, his religion has been his literature and philosophy, into which his magic passes. That is the meaning of the "natural magic" said to be found in his literature. Through technique, and the magic of natural discovery, the European began to attempt (when interrupted by the financier) to reach the same heaven as the Asiatic did on other roads. It is doubtful now whether he will be allowed to go on, his god may remain in the rough. He omitted to protect himself against mystical, political and other attacks in the rear. His political technique has been faulty. But there, in those activities, you have the seat of the impulse we call "revolutionary." Revolution was the great attempt of the european genius, rising at last, in its science, to maturity and spiritual power.

But its Revolution is very surely being betrayed. It is that new and creative impulse that, as Westerners, we should do our utmost to protect; not spend our time in the unimaginative manner of the present "patriotic" minority sects, of Austria, Germany and France, in attempts to shelter and revive the remnants of Christendom, which science (not any organised political power) overthrew. Viking and Valois emblems have their romantic uses; but to-day we require deeper and more compelling ones to represent our cause — less *historical* ones. And we have to absorb those of our antagonists or they will absorb us. It is White Science, in short, not White Religion (which in any case was not european), or White political systems, which have no relation to our present circumstances, and were in themselves barbarous, that should claim our attention. And beyond that, for all such things are not, unfortunately, simple, but very complex, it is not science-for-science sake, or mere technique, that is ultimately in question. That would only open the road to perversion, or inversion, of science. If these tasks, in their complexity, cannot be grasped by the modern European or American, and if they are not grasped extremely soon, then the West will have been cheated of its chance of self-expression.

Revolution, then, is *will to change*, as I define it, technique. But what we are attempting here ... [Bound proofs]

122	28	that is, E: that is
122	40–41	English people E: English-people
127	18	hería E, U: heriá [source]
127	19	suspendía E, U: suspendiá [source]
129	1–10	Everywhere ... The finest E:

At the opening of this second book, it will be as well to state what I am setting out to do, and what I am not setting out to do, more or less, before plunging into the work of argument and exposition. The complete essay, *Time and Western Man*, is divided into two books for the following reason. In the first (named The Revolutionary Simpleton) the reader will find, upon the more concrete plane of general literature (as indicated in the preface) the *time-idea* in full, unconscious operation; or at least he will find what was originally a philosophic theory used currently in the practice of the arts of expression, and become a second-nature for the practitioners. But everywhere in the earlier part of my essay this liaison has been stressed; at each stage of the literary criticism in Book I. the metaphysical cable connecting the practice of time-thought with its origin in philosophic theory was laid bare; and how such a theory came to combine with, and of course often to be disfigured by, the living material of concrete experience and expression was shown.

In the second half of my essay it is my intention to provide the general educated reader with some account of the main doctrine of the time-school. I hope to lay bare, and offer for general inspection (in as much detail as is possible for a treatise intended to secure the interest of the largest possible educated public) the very fountain-head of those notions which, in their popular and immediate form, and transformed into living experience, have had an overwhelming effect upon contemporary life. This book, certainly, cannot be so easy to read as the first, as some familiarity with philosophic thought is necessary. But I very much hope that I shall have contributed to expose the true nature of those ideas underlying the artistic ferment of this time, and have indicated, however summarily, the various positions involved in those activities. For to understand the time he lives in at all, and to take his place as anything but a lay-figure or infinitely hypnotizable cipher, in that world, he must make the effort required to reach some understanding of the notions behind the events occurring upon the surface.

The finest

129	7	fountain-head E: fountain-head U: fountain head [probable printer's error in U]
130	16–18	For the remainder ... Time-doctrine E: This brief foreword will no doubt suffice to effect the transition from my first concrete method of investigation to this second more abstract one, in which the values of the ideas themselves are examined, before they have clothed themselves in this or that working uniform or fancy-dress. [E's "Preface to Book II" concludes here; the remainder of U's and the present edition's Preface having already appeared in E's "Preface to Book I."]

134	12	have been scrutinizing E: are scrutinizing
134	23	upaniṣadic E: upanaṣadic U: upanasadic [reverting to Lewis's preferred spelling and to spelling on page 234]
140	23	among [us] E, U: among us [Lewis's emendation of source]
140	37	mark in E, U: mark on [source]
140	41	which would E, U: which could [source]
141	32	our day E, U: the present day [source]
141	38	of time E, U: of the time [source]
158	22	Bergson–Whitehead E, U: Bergson-Whitehead [preferable punctuation]
161	38	philosopher's E: philosophers'
161	40	perception has E: perception have
163	6	them E: them U: *them* [U's italics irrational]
163	37	metaphysical (today E: metaphysical: (to-day
164	1	[illustrate this] E, U: illustrate this [emendation of source]
167	8, 10	*naïveté* C: naïveté E: naiveté
167	25	where it E, U: when it [source]
168	16	concept of matter E, U: concept matter [source]
168	35	shape (or formation) occurs E, U: shape occurs [source]
173	3	[*Science ... World.*) [not in E.]
173	22	side, E: side
175	19	inert, . . . they E, U: inert, they [words omitted from source]
175	20	image E, U: images [source]
175	33	*inertness . . .* E, U: *inertness.* [words omitted from source]
176	40	Montessori E: Montefiori
176	41	Émile E, U: Emile [misspelling]
180	41	induced. (*Op.* E, U: induced. −(*Op.* [redundant dash]
181	28	first. It E, U: first. −It [redundant dash]
182	12	cent E, U: cent.
183	37	are E: is
190	13	human conceit E, U: human sense [source]
191	6	will . . . be E, U: will be [word omitted from source]
191	10	bergsonian E: Bergsonian
192	16	away−the ... seen− E: away (the ... seen) U: away, the ... seen, [restoring Lewis's parenthetic force]
193	1	Ouspensky E, U: Ousspensky [normal spelling in 1927]
193	35	meaninglessly. E, U: meaninglessly. − [redundant dash not in source]
195	11	recommend E: recommends
196	15	their survival E, U: their revival [source]
196	19	special objects E, U: special object [source]
197	29	duality E: duality U: quality [printer's error in U]
198	6	disintegrate E: disentegrate
198	31–32	transformations E, U: transformation [source]
201	5	évangile E: evangile
202	3	imperialism or E, U: imperialism and [source]
202	36	safety has E, U: safety and order has [source]
204	18	that, E: that

205	1	C: (epigraph) "The epoch which marks the birth of our culture . . . marks also the discovery of the wheel-clock. Without exact time-measurements, without a *chronology of becoming* to correspond with his imperative need of archaeology . . . Western Man is unthinkable." (Spengler. *Decline of the West* Chap. IV)
205	11	speculative E: speculative U: spectacular [printer's error in U]
207	10	an endless E, U: one endless [source]
207	20	*Prof.* E, U: *Professor* [source]
207	23	on philosophy E, U: in philosophy [source]
207	32	Mr. E, U: Professor [source]
207	36	writes . . . "The E, U: writes: 'The [source]
208	2	and to E, U: and that to [source]
209	14	Whitehead, to the E: Whitehead, the
209	17	Macmillan, 1921 E: Methuen, 1924
209	21–22	accommodating. It is C: [*del.*]: Did he not understand that in accepting (with however many reservations) Alexander's pretended reconcilement of the contending views, for instance, that he had lost, in the course of the bargain, everything that gave his own characteristic position any meaning? It is
210	32–33	position of today E, U: position to-day [source]
211	27	so far E, U: as far [source]
211	30	Arguments E, U: Agreements [source]
211 43–212 1		Six — the six american . . . Spaulding — (with E: Six (with [explanatory addition by Montgomery Belgion of Harcourt, Brace]
213	32–33	merely the personal E, U: merely personal [source]
213	37	ourselves. . . . E, U: ourselves. [words omitted from source]
214	16	perspective . . . E, U: perspective. [words omitted from source]
214	19	of their E, U: of this [source]
218	41	[Time] E, U: Time [emendation of source]
219	40–41	*one definite direction* E, U: *one direction* [source]
222	10	with flowers E: in flowers
223	4	use; all E: use, all
223	16–17	as types of C: as types of E: or types of U: or type as [printer's error in E; reverting to C]
223	37	ukulele E: ukelele
224	8	intellectual E: Intellectual
224	17	[Bergson's philosophy] E, U: Bergson's philosophy [emendation of source]
226	21	the more E: and more
230	1	C: (epigraph) "Everyone knows that there is time & change in the universe. It is the first lesson of experience, and the question for philosophy is whether it is also the last. . . .The latter conviction (that time and change is the last) has come upon the modern philosophical world like a flood, and in the regions prima facie most removed from each other." *Bernard Bosanquet. Meeting of Extremes in Contemp. Phil.*
230	29	suppose (for E: suppose; (for
231	7	common sense E: common-sense
234	19	upaniṣadic E: upaniṣadic U: upanisadic [Lewis's preferred spelling]
238	9	them. Note E, U: them. — Note [redundant dash]
238	14	probability E, U: philosophy [source]

238	32	the essays ... Peirce (...). E. the english edition of the writing ... Peirce.
240	12	fine and dissolvent E, U: fine dissolvent [source]
240	23	interpenetrations C, E, U: interpretations [demanded by context; cf. page 242, line 9]
247	12	cent E, U: cent.
247	39	exam E, U: exam.
248	29	Mathilde E, U: Matilda [misspelling]
249	5	meeds E: meeds U: needs [U's "correction" nonsensical]
252	28	all these E, U: all those [source]
252	28	*Chronology* . . . E, U: *Chronology* [words omitted from source]
253	7	philosophies use E: philosophies are U: philosophers are [source]
253	9	*name* . . . something E, U: *name* something [words omitted from source]
253	10	overpowered . . ." E, U: overpowered.' [words omitted from source]
256	3	Become. . . . E, U: Become. [words omitted from source]
256	5	-quality . . . that E, U: -quality, that [word omitted from source]
256	6–7	"motion" . . . of E, U: 'motion' of [word omitted from source]
256	43	with flowers E: in flowers
258	28	in our sense E, U: in one sense [source]
258	33	because it pleases God so E, U: because so it pleases God [source]
258	35	Pythagoreans. E, U: Pythagoreans. . . . [source (no omission from final sentence of quote)]
259	13	not arguing E, U: not saying [source]
259	31	. . . [is] E, U: . . . is [emendation of source]
259	39	-experience . . . , E, U: -experience, [words omitted from source]
260	19	A. A. E, U: A. N. [source]
260	20	Lorentz E, U: Lorenz [source]
261	41	urging E, U: urgent [source]
262	17	inertia . . . , least action . . . , E, U: inertia, least action, [words omitted from source]
262	18	energy . . . E, U: energy. [words omitted from source]
264	3	from the E: rom the
266	37	The rise and fall C [*del.*]:

Slightly changed, changed into very slightly different people, we are, for the "historic" mind, always passing again, in our periodic and cyclic course, the same objects, and historic features, and experiencing, with slight modifications, the same passions. "I have been here before: How long ago I may not know: But when your head turned so" etc. — And these things are as *true*, and obvious, to us to-day at all events, as the rising of the sun or the disintegrating property of fire. These other selves, at other places in what we call Time, advancing on such and such "world lines", in their eternal course, like generations of a new Cartophilus, are the strictest realities. They have the sun, the life, and the reality, as much as we. Having pondered on these things a little, people often write, or say to you, "I don't know if I am alive or dead. If you asked me to say truthfully which I was, I could not tell you. I am a factor of time: whether I live or not I find it impossible to say." Naturally in that case you may safely assume that they are *practically* dead. — The problem of *reality* immediately awakes, and asserts its function;

it exists for such work as this crossroad suggests.

The distant and immensely extended materials of the periodic picture are true and obvious as we said: but if we did not "know" about them, would they then be equally true? Were they true for Cromagnon Man? Would they be true for men who "knew" much more than we do? Is all this immense *Unconscious* that has recently brought to life (for the periodic, "historical", picture is very definitely a description of the "Unconscious", just as much as is Freud's or Von Hartmann's) — the Unconscious which yesterday was what we call "Nothing", and to-day is "Something" — in any sense real or true? Is it *real* in its own right, or is it we who endow it with reality? — On the threshold of such a discussion it is appropriate to point out that those are the sort of questions that we are brought to consider by any investigation at all upon these lines.

The rise and fall

267	10	habit-picture. Life is quite exactly for it E, U: habit-picture, for it [in deleting the original conclusion of the sentence beginning 'It wishes ... ,' in C, Lewis deleted the beginning of the following sentence, probably by mistake (since he appears to have altered the comma following "-picture" to a period). Restoring the deleted opening of the second sentence restores sense to the passage]
267	30	Arts [are] E, U: Arts are [emendation of source]
269	23	or states E, U: states [source]
270	19	-statue . . . and E, U: -statue and [words omitted from source]
272	9	artists E, U: artist [source]
272	34	drawing . . . E, U: drawing. [words omitted from source]
272	37	*and soul* E, U: *and the soul* [source]
273	8–9	[account of . . . "Faustian"] E, U: account (of . . . 'Faustian') [emendation of source]
273	11	even E, U: ever [source]
275	29	Arabian . . . the E, U: Arabian the [omissions from source]
275	31	Alchemy . . . E, U: Alchemy [words omitted from source]
275	39	individuals . . . E, U: individuals [words omitted from source]
275	40	influence . . . E, U: influence. [words omitted from source]
276	9	Faustian . . . E, U: Faustian. [words omitted from source]
277	24	of sweeping E, U: sweeping [source]
279	9	despecialized E: despecialized U: despicialized [misprint in U]
279	10–11	chinese, tuscan, arabian or mayan . . . tuscan E: Chinese, Tuscan, Arabian or Mayan . . . Tuscan
279	20–21	never to return E: *never to return*
281	9	[gothic] E, U: gothic [emendation of source]
281	9–10	new-born soul E, U: new-born culture [source]
281	15	roots of life E, U: mode of life [source]
281	20	gothic-musical E, U: gothic — musical [source]
283	15	*senses* . . . E, U: *senses.* [words omitted from source]
284	23	high creator E, U: high creation [source]
285	31	Nietzsche . . . E, U: Nietzsche [words omitted from source]
285	32	this "dionysiac" E, U: the 'dionysiac' [source]
290	12–13	with regard to him. We C [*del.*]: with regard to him, one burdened, as he was, that is with the contending[?] policies and enthusiasms of dogmatic faith. And, beyond that, his humane nature corrupted him

intellectually, into selling his genius to the democracy of the Enlightenment.

The paradox and the tragedy here are that this great intelligence would have been freed for a far greater service to mankind if he had not exhibited such a generous regard for it. We

290	38	a similar distraction. So C [*del.*]: There is no need to accumulate [words illegible] philosophic frailty, either cynically under-hand[?], or inspired by the loftiest motives. It will be enough to say that most powerful conceptions of the modern age in Europe can be shown to have been put to some fanatically dogmatic or humanitarian (or with the prophet of the Will-to-Power, to an anti-humanitarian, sentimentally diabolic) use, by their authors, or else by the populariser: or to have been accommodated to the requirements of political fashion, and so have foregone their purer speculative destiny. So
293	4	in his E: in his U: on his [printer's error in U]
296	18	Louis E, U: Lewis [misspelling]
299	18, 25 & 26	Émile E, U: Emile [misspelling]
301	27–29	*Unconscious* (. . .). E: *Unconscious.* [advertisement inserted by Montgomery Belgion]
302	26	age only E, U: age early [source]
302	28	up into E, U: up to [source]
302	35	the silently creative E, U: the creative [source]
302	36–37	seed-grain E, U: seed-germ [source]
303	8	Regius E, U: Regis [misspelling]
304	30, 40	Leibnitz E, U: Leibniz [source]
304	32	I can find E, U: I find [source]
304	34	That Monads E, U: That the Monads [source]
307	2	objectivation." E: objectivation." U: objectivation. [printer's error in U]
307	29	caesarian E: Caesarian
308	29	must . . . E, U: must [words omitted from source]
308	35	*élan vital* E, U: élan vital
310	24–25	to man . . . knowledge, [or] the E, U: to men . . . knowledge, or the [source]
311	34	of this book. So C [*del.*]: of this book. I for instance am far too much "the plastic artist" to be a philosopher. So I am merely a correction to the man who is too much a man of science to be Philosophy as it were, all that the man of science is not. What is left, when we have struggled for some time, should be Philosophy. So
313	29	Frauenstaedt E, U: Francenstaedt [misspelling]
316	20	propagate . . . E, U: propagate [words omitted from source]
316	21	of the will E, U: of will [source]
316	24	the unmistakable influence of the passion of anger . . . E, U: the influence of passion or anger [source]
316	31	approaches . . . the . . . God only knows E, U: approaches the . . . God knows [source]
317	7	Schopenhauer–von-Hartmann E, U: Schopenhauer-von-Hartmann [preferable punctuation]
319	23	"our consciousness" C: "the consciousness"
321	9	american E: American

322	5	mind: the E, U: mind: — The [redundant dash and incorrect capital]
322	8	Sorel–Péguy E, U: Sorel-Péguy [preferable punctuation]
322	15	Yerkes–Yoakum E, U: Yerkes-Yoakum [preferable punctuation]
322	33	Tests E: Texts
323	36–37	dance. . . . [A new . . . constructed] . . . interrupted electric circuit E, U: dance. A new . . . constructed . . . interrupted circuit [source]
325	10	Pavlov's E: Pawlow's
328	1	firing in another E, U: firing another [source]
329	40	takes on refinement E, U: takes a refinement [source]
331	9	connect E: connects
335	12	of the voice E, U: of our voice [source]
336	12	current superstition E, U: current of superstition [source]
336	23	. . . We E: . . . we
340	30–31	On the other hand . . . 'mind.' C: It becomes a bastard "mind", its personal character as "Matter" is lost. It is, in short, a fusion of the same kind as all the other fusions and minings occurring in this time, of which the sex-fusion is its most obvious physiological and social counterpart.
347	1	[Nature] E, U: Nature [emendation of source]
347	6	Bradley: *Appearance* E: *Appearance*
356	1–2	[of an object . . . belief,] E, U: (of an object) . . . belief, [source]
356	3	senses, [that . . . habit]. E, U: sense, that . . . habit. [source]
359	37	percurrent E: percurrent, U: precurrent [printer's error in U]
360	1	conception . . ." E, U: conception.' [words omitted from source]
361	1	C (epigraphs): "Contemplation is thus the best and happiest of activities, and if all we could say were that God's life is like our life in the highest moments of contemplative thought, it would be worthy of our admiration." *Aristotle. Metaphysics XII.*

"In spite of rationalism's disdain for the particular, the personal, and the unwholesome, the drift of the evidence we have seems to me to sway us very strongly towards the belief in some form of supernatural life with with which we may, unknown to ourselves, be co-conscious. We may be in the universe as dogs and cats are in our libraries, seeing the books and hearing the conversation, but having no inkling of the meaning of it all." *William James. A Pluralistic Universe*, viii.

"Recent political and social developments, which make men increasingly impatient of masters, prepare them also to reject God who rules also by Divine right." *D. W. Fawcett. Divine Imagining.*

361	3–4	time-doctrine, although C [*del.*]: time-doctrine, and to offer nothing formally in the place of what I attacked, although
364	38	["Empiricism] E, U: 'Empiricism [emendation of source]
366	37	by Freud. At C [*del.*]: by Freud. Against such powerful engines as these it seems highly unlikely that the dogma of the catholic church can stand. Yet at
370	9	St. Thomas. C [*del.*]: St. Thomas. And above the summit of the human world we can and need imagine nothing but Deity.
371	2	Absolute. C [*del.*]: Absolute. For us there must be a hierarchy of reality among appearances. That we are occupied in ordering. "There will be no truth which is entirely true — it will be a question of amount". To that we cannot agree: our

highest truth is entirely true—as it is to the Thomiste in contrast to Bradley. And we discover that in all cases our "reality" is nearer to the composite perceptual reality of common-sense than it is to the more pedantically "direct" sensationalist, material of the reformed reality of Time, or of Space-time.

The notion

371	17	and relation ... it . . . does E, U: or relation ... it does [source]
373	22	"No": E: 'No': U: 'No':— [redundant dash in U]
374	27	should . . . find E, U: should find [words omitted from source]
375	25–28	darwinian, evolutionary ... The personality A: darwinian, neitzschean, nightmare, in whose clutches we are at present all of us more than ever wallowing. It is the brutal mindlessness of the capitalist industrial world, with its deadly array of gigantic machines to destroy us, with its ideologies marshalled to infect us with its soulless will. The Moloch of Modern Ideas and its hierophants are a far greater destructive force for *us* than the peaceful courses of the stars and the occasional disquietude of volcanoes or hurricanes. It is not Nature, but they, that is our enemy. Nature is indeed our friend. And Time has brought us round, through its revenges and adjustments, to the point at which we look to Nature, that great, though uncertain, power, for help but to that issue the tradition of our race if nothing else, invite us. It is not the moment to forget that spring of imagination and miraculous fable, pouring everywhere from the valleys of the "Celtic fringe", which dominated with its beauty and with its noble myths Europe in its most characteristic age since greek antiquity, the post-roman, and catholic, age. So if we have a God, it is not any Absolute, but is still our particular Unknown, what industrial civilisation have not policed, or compressed for its purposes into a monstrous and inhuman Absolute. We worship, if we worship, still the virgin-goddess, the stars on the ocean, the break-of-day: the natural magic that inspired our earliest beliefs. We worship things, or emblems of nature, before the swarming of Time; Chance rather than a God of Law or a God of Science. Our self is our only Absolute, finally. We are our own version of God. The personality [B16 F14 (f.37)]
379	31	as to something E, U: as something [source]
385	35	is the E, U: is . . . the [source]
386	23–25	of its constituents, and we can make accurate statements about the durations of the correlated E, U: of the correlated [words omitted from source; probably through eyeskip]
393	37–38	*senses, principally* E: *senses principally*
396	20	those data E, U: that data [source]
397	6	of . . . "neutral" E, U: of 'neutral' [words omitted from source]
404	38	-Your-Mouth!" E: -Your-Mouth!' U: -Your Mouth!' [printer's error in U]
405	32	causally E: causally U: casually [printer's error in U]
406	33	as is E, U: it is [source]
408	1	C (epigraph): "There is nothing given which is sacred. Metaphysics can respect no element of experience except on compulsion. It can reverence nothing but what by criticism and denial the more unmistakably asserts itself." (*F. H. Bradley. Appearance and Reality.*)
409	27	makes us E: makes us U: make us [U ungrammatical]
410	14–15	moves . . . naturally E, U: moves naturally [words omitted from source]

410	18	Since "physics E, U: 'Since physics [source]
410	26–27	provisional . . . Science E, U: provisional. Science [words omitted from source]
410	36–37	[3-line space inserted, following E; not present in U owing to page division at this point]
413	19	The distinctive . . . [in E and U this quotation is placed two sentences earlier, immediately after ". . . resemblance at all to number." This edition reverts to the order of C, restoring sense and Lewis's apparent intention]
415	20	qualities . . . is E, U: qualities is [words omitted from source]
415	22	admits no E, U: admits of no [source]
416	28	the picture. C [del.]: the picture. Such whys are rigidly banished from empirical systems; and yet we can observe them being surreptitiously reintroduced, and everywhere suggested. In a primitive creation-myth men and trees are taken for granted, but we are unable to do that: and yet we must. So neither the myth of the first parents, of prototypes, of classes produced by fiats, nor the other solution just outlined, can satisfy us. The result of these happenings is to make one think that if the Why is to be excluded, all science and philosophy should be under a much stricter discipline than is at present the case, and the mass of imagery, assumption and speculation that pervades the material of such texts as those of Bergson or Alexander, should be disallowed and in their place something much more tentative and verifiable be substituted. James states the situation as follows: [quotes passage now on pages 435–36.] That is the statement of the empirical position. But is it adhered to?
418	8	three-dimensional E, U: the dimensional [source]
418	18	temporal. . . . It E, U: temporal. It [words omitted from source]
419	2	l'Éternel E: l'Éternel U: l'Eternel [printer's error in U]
424	30–31	provoked E, U: provided [source]
427	20	unsatisfying C: dissatisfying E: satisfying [correction made by Montgomery Belgion, probably on Lewis's instructions]
430	37	the same reality E, U: the sense of reality [source]
431	28	existent E, U: existing [source]
432	27	is thus always E, U: is always [source]
436	1	datum, gift E, U: datum, a gift [source]
437	10	true we add E, U: true you add [source]
439	5	these ages E, U: those ages [source]
441	1	a theory may E, U: a thing may [source]
444	6	minds or E, U: minds of [source]
447	8–10	Idealism (reprinted . . . Company]), gives E: Idealism, gives [publisher's advertisement added by Belgion]
447	40	toto caelo E, U: toto coelo [misspelling]

The place of the following two chapters in Lewis's schemes for *Time and Western Man* is discussed in Part II of the Afterword. The texts are taken from typescripts in the Lewis collection at Buffalo. "Reality and Non-Being" is filed as B16 F13. It contains deletions and revisions in Lewis's hand. B16 F14 contains another typescript of most of this chapter (ff. 44–58) in a version very close to that of B16 F13 before revision. "The Pragmatical Test of the doctrines of Relativity and of Time" is filed as B16 F7. It also contains deletions and revisions in Lewis's hand, indicating that it was revised from material intended for *The Childermass*. The chapter was retyped, incorporating the revisions, and most of this version is also in B16 F14 (ff. 70–80; ff. 61–69, as explained in note 110 of the Afterword, were used in composing "Space and Time" for the printer's copy).

B16 F14 has been consulted in establishing a text for both of these chapters, but has not been used as the copy text. Longer quotations have been set in smaller type, in conformity with the practice in the rest of the book, and some minor editing of punctuation and some correcting have been carried out. No notes have been provided. Bergson and Alexander are quoted from *Creative Evolution* and *Space, Time and Deity*. C. S. Peirce is quoted on pages 533 and 559, and the William James quotation on page 549 is from "Does 'Consciousness' Exist?"

BOOK II   CHAPTER vii

Reality and Non-Being (in which is included an analysis of the optimism of Bergson)

HAVING ESTABLISHED our perspective for the arch-Reality, I will take up once more our way of defining the "reality" that we associated with our most concrete "belief." And first, another of those capital terms around which most speculation settles and masses itself can be introduced: namely, "meaning." Meaning can be used in many senses: but it can be said assuredly that without meaning, in the sense in which we use it, there can be no "reality."

Meaning may be employed in the extensive sense to signify the reference of the "this" to the "that"; that is its most technical meaning. It is there the external relation of a sign to its symbol. But here it is rather its most complex and symbolical use that we are taking up: its

use, for instance, when we say "New York means very little to me,"
or "Doris means a great deal to me," or "Communism means more to
me every day." Or, again, as the meaning of a judge's wig, a ribbon
used by a Knight of the Garter, or the hat of Napoleon, or the nose
of the Duke of Wellington, the thing would by itself pass unnoticed,
except as an object of a certain shape and colour. It is as a symbol of
honour or power that it has meaning. But it is more than a symbolism,
too, in the sense that I have in mind. For when a greasy fragrance rises
from the lower part of the house and attacks your nose, that olfactory
stimulus *means* a joint of beef or a nice leg of mutton. It is one of the
characters of a complex thing broken away from the rest, and yet meaning to you all that it has not been able to carry with it, mere smell-of-
a-joint that it is, unillustrated. Or rather your memory seizes on it and
rapidly supplies the picture of the smoking meat — the salivary glands
engage in a preliminary discharge, your mouth waters, you already
feel the hot plate in fancy beneath your fingers. Yet what has meant
all this to you is nothing but a little movement in the olfactory cells.
This sort of "meaning" is reference only. "Meaning" can simply mean
that any part of a whole suggests and summons, either by recalling or
by some rational process ensuing from a new fact, the *whole* to which
it belongs. And always it must signify *reference* of some sort to
something else.

The appearance of a thing means to us, however, its function,
first: as a *nose* means that of sniffing, and that which the noses sniffs;
or a hand the things which it is meant to grasp and manipulate.
But such a thing as the celebrated nose of the Duke of Wellington
ceases to have that purely functional meaning, and may lose it
altogether. The nose of the person on whom you have set your affections, though in fact nothing but an organ of sense, is more than a
sniffing apparatus. It "means" more, that is, to you. A "roman nose"
means empire, and a "grecian nose" means art. The nose in these instances ceases almost entirely to be an organ, or to be just a nose, only
that. It becomes a symbol of something very different from itself. So
a thing ceases in one sense to be a direct sensational object at all when
it acquires "meaning." It has transcended its functions almost entirely.
And for a thing to have "meaning" in this sense it must be alienated
from its function: if it lapses into function, again, at once its meaning
evaporates.

All meaning in art is of that nature. It must have no functional, or
practical, meaning, otherwise it can have no meaning as art. All artistic meaning flourishes only when all function has, to start with, been
killed or suppressed. The moment an object of beauty, a picture or
statue, affects you as a *living person* would — to anger, concupiscence
or what not, its appeal, as art, has ceased. Before the work of art you
must forget, as the philosopher in the *Theaetetus* was described as doing,

you must cease to be aware at all of "what description of creature you are." All such "meanings" involve the transcending of the human condition. Those not inclined to this sort of self-abstraction will not experience the delights of art or indeed be able to guess at what those can be.

The hegelian *infinity* achieved in art is a thing that imposes itself on us as complete — that does not refer itself away in self-transcendence, to a series that seemingly has no end: so it is a thing that exists on its own terms. When you say that a person "means the world to you," you convey that all your world is made out of the stuff of that person. Though not infinite, it is individual, a "world," with, it is hoped, a certain respectable duration. And it is *all one thing* or *all one person*. It is "individual."

Next let us examine the idea of Not-being or of Nothing: and as our argument here is circumscribed by the systems of our immediate contemporary antagonists, we will go to the arch-prophet of the Time-philosophy, Bergson (especially as he has much to say on that subject). "Bergson repudiates the notion of nothing except as something different from the something which constitutes the circle of our experience," Alexander writes. The Nothing becomes for time-thought another time-thing, temporally removed or chronologically absent.

But Bergson gives to *Nothing* a solely temporal interpretation, as you would expect. His real objection to *Nothing* was because it was of nothing (or nothing in particular) that all *interval* consisted, as he saw, for the champions of conceptual thought. That *interval* was of course motion or time, as well, with which all its operations were conducted.

The *forms* picked out by the platonist from the flux, and alone conceded "reality," were originally surrounded by something or other, as islands in a stream are by the flowing water. This flux, that composed their *intervals*, was the material of which the traditional Nothing was really made. This must be revived and reinstated before the "forms," or conceptual entities, could be once more plunged back into the stream.

Greek philosophy, which Bergson describes as "the natural metaphysic of the human intellect" (just as Spengler described it, you will remember, as "the popular," the elaboration of the thought of the "natural man"), is the great *conceptualising, spatialising,* antagonist for him.

The "conceptualist" manner of thought, the thought that results in such a thing as a platonic form or idea, Bergson describes as *cinematographical*. This sort of thought begins "by substituting for the continuity of evolutionary change a series of unchangeable forms which are, turn by turn, caught 'on the wing.' . . . As the stable forms have been obtained by extracting from change everything that is definite, there is nothing left," Bergson protests: "nothing to characterize the instability on which forms are laid, but the *negative attribute*, which must be indetermination itself." This indetermination, this Nothing, is "Change in general" (Change that, in other words, is Time). So in "Nothing," considered from this point of view, we arrive once more at *Time*, with which it is found to be identical.

The "conceptualist" philosophy will in the end, then, construct its real, with one hand, by means of "definite Forms or immutable elements"; and with the other, by means of "a principle of mobility which, being the negation of form, will escape all definition and be purely indeterminate." This reducing of mobility to *nothing* it is not in Bergson's nature to allow. For his nature is in its deepest springs vowed to this ceaseless mechanical mobility (this "restlessness" that is, as Alexander says, peculiar to Time): and in its essence it is hostile to those "forms," to the noble and supreme hellenic exemplars. "The more [this philosophy] directs its attention to the forms delineated by thought and expressed by language, the more it will see them rise above the sensible and become subtilised into pure concepts, capable of entering one within the other, and even being at last massed together into a single concept, the synthesis of all reality, the achievement of all perfection." That God, meaning itself, as it were, within the platonic thought, and *almost* created, would perhaps have been a difficult God to overthrow. At all events, the very thought of such a contingency mobilises all Bergson's resources to destroy even retrospectively this splendid embryo.

Nature requires for its "closed systems" the *blankest* kind of interval obtainable, not an interval full of the swarming concreteness of "duration." Nature needs, it can be said, a *true Nothing* for its success.

It is round the questions of continuity and discontinuity, "forms" and intervals, that all controversy in the future will centre, if any controversy is countenanced. The Theory of Quanta for instance at the present day seems to be attributing to Nature the power to suppress interval which formerly was said to be the peculiarity, in contrast to Nature, of the Human intellect. Primitive science and modern science are divided, and offer the spectacle actually of methods representing *opposite* principles. "Science" can no longer be used as though it signified in any sense one thing. Bergson is extremely scientific, and yet he attacked "Science." In this the tendency has been everywhere to follow Bergson's lead: and all the most advanced scientific and mathematical thinkers attack "Science" much as Bergson did. That is why, of course, we hear so much about mere artists and romantic poets in Professor Whitehead's *Science and the Modern World*. The overtures to the neighbouring province of aesthetics that is such a feature of that book is highly symptomatic of this cleavage in Science, of which Bergson was the pioneer.

One of the keys to this reversal of method is to be sought in the opposition of the two processes, one of which consists in marking the *difference*, the other the *resemblance*, in things. How the observation of a sufficiently small and unimportant difference can lead to the establishment of a close resemblance is well brought out in the following passage from an american philosopher. It will be seen that this sort of "difference" has a different sense, and an opposite result, to difference on another scale. The smaller "difference," and then the yet smaller, within that, results, in short, in the filling-up of the *interval*.

When a naturalist wishes to study a species, he collects a considerable number of specimens more or less similar to one another. He observes certain ones more or less alike in some particular respect. They all have, for instance, a certain S-shaped marking. He observes that they are not *precisely* alike, in this respect: the S has not precisely the same shape, but the differences are such as to lead him to believe that forms could be found intermediate between any two of those he possesses. He now finds other forms apparently quite dissimilar — say a marking in the form of a C — and the question is whether he can find intermediate ones which will connect them better with the others. This method he applies to one character, then to another, and finally obtains a notion of a species of animals. . . . It is by taking advantage of the *idea of continuity, or the passage from one form to another by insensible degrees*, that the naturalist builds his conception. . . . By means of the idea of continuity the greatest differences are broken down and resolved into differences of degree.

This idea of continuity as it applies to the *filling up of the gaps* between individuals and the making of species in the method of the naturalist — so that in the result you get *one* continuous, subtly-woven, stream of life, in which all individual difference melts into its neighbour — is matched by the mathematical processes superseding number, and dealing in continuous quantities. Now we have already said, how, automatically, the more exact research becomes, the more it inevitably reaches the Bergsonian ideal of "following all the sinuosities of nature." Primitive Science and full-blown Science are the difference between an archaic mannikin, carved stiffly and making itself into a few simple shapes, and a fourth-century athenian statue, almost suaver and more *flowing* than Nature itself. It approximates, inevitably, in its closer and closer application to the physical truth, to the plasticity, sinuosity and vanishing contours of life. How this applies to the ideal of "forms," in contrast to the ideal of merging and continuity, can be best seen by a few quotations at this point from Bergson, the arch-champion of the continuous flux where he is actually engaged in an onslaught upon the platonic "form."

With definite forms and immutable elements on the one hand, and on the other the aristotelian "matter" or the platonic "non-being" — the principle of mobility and change, the region where Time is — the Greeks constructed their world. But then, says Bergson, you have to make your "reality" by means of the symbolism of a sort of metaphysical necessity, which substitutes for all the *real* degrees and grades composing, in fact, the unreal *interval*, the two affirmations of an absolute *Real* and an absolute Zero. By exalting the perfect element into an Everything you have to provide yourself with a Nothing to match it. But if Bergson refuses any validity to this conception of things, he is not ready either to fall in with the procedure of the Science contemporary with his treatise, which, although much nearer to Nature than the Hellenic, still was cinematographic. It, too, substituted, in its practical operations, static entities and intervals "for the moving continuity of things." Science "may consider re-arrangements that come closer and closer to each other; it may thus increase the number of moments that it isolates: but it always isolates moments. As to what happens in the interval between the moments, science is no more concerned with that than are our common intelligence, senses and language: *it does not bear on the interval, but only the extremities.*" So "modern science" up to date was still not "scientific" enough for Bergson. But since that time much has happened: the man-of-science is to-day much less unbending. Bergson has beaten "Science," or of him more than of anybody else that can be said. The man-of-science of the early days of bergsonism was certainly much less intelligent than his critic. To-day he finds it impossible any longer to behave as though the metaphysician were dead. He will soon be more "artistic" than any artist to-day can afford to be. So the criticism directed against Positive Science by Bergson was generally misunderstood at the time. It was not because it was "Science" that he disliked it, but because it was not Science enough.

Returning to Bergson's criticism of the forms or ideas of Plato or Aristotle, the metaphor of his language becomes very instructive for one aspect of our present research. For with Bergson you are never free of the feeling that you are in the presence of a political intelligence to whom Spengler could point in triumph as testifying to the truth of his theory. But luckily you also never escape from the conviction that he is a thinker of anything but the highest order. He refers to these as representing "*privileged* or *salient* moments in the history of things." The platonic "form," in short, was *the individual* rising proudly above the herd-level of *the group*, and, drawing all eyes to itself, abolishing the group from which it rose and in which it grew, which then became "nothing," or "non-being." Not to be a "form" was to be *nothing*, as not to be [a] free-man with the Romans was not to be "a person." These "forms" were the "quintessence," the summation, of a period, like Napoleon or for that matter Plato himself: "all the rest of this period being filled by the passage, of no interest in itself, from one form to another form." It is this dull uninteresting *passage* (a favourite word in the post-einsteinian philosophy), this *interval*, that is the object of all Bergson's solicitude: just as, had he been a politician instead of a philosopher, it would have been Mr. Everyman that he would have been busy with (much more to take the conceit out of somebody who was "somebody" it is unnecessary to say and perhaps surreptitiously slip into his place, than to waste his mental-time and his valuable breath on Nobody-in-particular, for the beaux yeux of a Nothing-at-all).

So much for those tyrants the Greeks, as far as Bergson goes! But Galileo, now, was already in the democratic, bergsonian, age. For Galileo, unlike the typical Greek, "there was no *essential* moment, no *privileged* instant." Time (dear old democratic "Time") is "any moment of time whatever." It is not exceptional or *privileged*; not *Time!* (it is important to remember that bergsonian Time is a very personal and peculiar Time). Again: "our physics differ from that of the Ancients chiefly in the indefinite breaking up of time. For the Ancients, time comprises as many undivided periods as our natural perception and our language cut out in its successive facts, each representing a kind of *individuality*." It is that *individuality* that sticks in Bergson's throat: for his God, Time, is a jealous God, and is offended at these beautiful hellenic fortresses rising, in white marble, all along the course of his stream. For a Kepler or Galileo, on the contrary, time is not divided objectively in one way or another by the matter that fills it. It has no natural articulations. We can, we ought, to divide it as we please. "All moments count. *None of them has the right to set itself up as a moment that represents or dominates the others.* . . . The difference is profound. In fact, in a certain aspect, it is radical." And Galileo and Kepler are made into a sort of champions of the mass democracy for the occasion. With them no "moment has the right to set itself up as a moment that dominates others!" No, one moment is as good as another moment in the true bergsonian Time-world. Each, in its way, is "unique": and each is fulsomely told by its profound, benevolent, father, or perhaps sage old uncle, that it is "creative": though what possible satisfaction it can be to a little obedient moment of bergsonian time, or a little "point-instant" of Alexandrine Space-Time, to be told beamingly that it is "creative," it is difficult to see. It is in the nature, I suppose, of a pewter cup or medal. And the passage from this base kind of greek knowledge to the more perfect and desirable european knowledge of our own illustrious age, has been effected simply (Oh miracle!) "simply by seeking a higher precision." How remarkable: yet how *simple*. Even the process of perfection is simple and most ordinary. Take the attitude to movement of the sculpture of the Parthenon. Consider the gallop of a horse as it would be viewed by a greek sculptor and by instantaneous photography.

Instantaneous photography isolates any moment [good, honest, humble instantaneous photography!]. It puts them all in the same rank [no favouritism: three cheers for the camera, the camera for ever!]: and thus the gallop of a horse spreads out for it into as many successive attitudes as it wishes, instead of massing itself into a single attitude, which is supposed to flash out in a *privileged* moment and to illuminate a whole period.

No summation, no completion: only the impassible deliverance of incorruptible Time, which, *being* all its moments together is placed above our human predilections and values, for, all moments are equally good.

It may seem exaggeration to some readers that we should attach ourselves to this phraseology. But it is necessary to remember that we are in the world of ideas: and ideas are very real things for the speculative mind. Indeed, this world of ideas is the world that influences fact constantly: and so however much we live in fact, it is yet unwise to ignore or underestimate the reality of this ideal world. And it is at least interesting to observe the politics of that abstract world, as it were—since what is its politics to-day will be ours to-morrow, and vice versa and that entirely aside from the question of whether the master of ideas is himself politically-minded or not. But where he is, obviously, not a disinterested and "scientific" intelligence, it is doubly important to take note of such a thing as his language. So these constant applications of such terms as "privilege," "domination," etc. to mere instants and points (as at first sight they seem) in their proposed theoretic readjustments, have at least some slight significance.

*   *   *

Our Alexander is a vaguer figure, shrouded in much more of the stuff of traditional philosophy, less clearly cut out of the pure flux-stuff, than is Bergson. But his heart is in the same place, that is to say the wrong one. He should be taken as a sub-Bergson, and used to show bergsonianism-beyond-Einstein in its most authoritative transformation.

We have already surprised him in the congenial task of getting a little life into "universals," and protesting that, because they owe nothing to thought, there is no reason for calling them lifeless, or "petrified." In the conceptual world, as in the perceptual, all must be flux, all alive and kicking, no platonic statues, but living people. Universals do not move or act; it is their particulars which do this. But they are the plans of motion and action, to which all action conforms. Like the cockles and mussels of the fishergirl's song they are "Alive, alive O!" A plan that never stops still is not an easy thing to imagine: but perhaps the universals perform a slightly more sedate and restricted measure in the background, slightly more diagrammatic and simple, while the horde of little particulars frantically gyrate in the foreground, in confused emulation.

No, the "spatio-temporal vitality" of universals must never be doubted! "In the end the character of all action, physical or mental, depends on universals; and in the end all universals, mental as well as physical, are spatio-temporal habits," installed in the centre of our organic suggestibility. Habit resolves itself into repetition, due to the constant curvature of Space-time. To get your circle there must be a balance of the repetitive. This balance is the pull in to a centre, is the material of universality. But the passage that I have already quoted

in my first book gives the gist of the matter, and really, as I understand it, gives it away.

Rodin, the Bergson of sculpture, was, you will remember, dragged
in by Alexander as a witness: and Rodin certainly did in his practice
follow nature in *all* her sinuosities, in his flowing, emasculated, waved-
lined marble, where the full abysses of the impressionist dogma was
at last revealed. Canova in his way was not more debased. Every tradition of the intellect was betrayed in Rodin to the pointing machine and
to the camera. And worse than all, these exercises were not confined
to a disarticulate, cheaply-softened, saponaceous surface of imitative
exactitude, but he freely passed into a plastic lyricism of the most unexampled sort, into pure "Music," in fact, as that term is understood by
Spengler. Many of his figures and groups, the gelatinous marble of the
lips sticking together in embraces reminiscent of the cinema close-ups
with which films end, were veritable illustrations of M. Bergson's *élan
vital.* He was Bergson in stone — if you can call "stone" what, when he
had finished with it, had none of the character of stone.

Alexander dismisses the problem with the following words: "The
whole controversy as to whether forms are beside particulars or in them
loses its importance when both form and particulars are spatio-
temporal." With that we are in the most thorough agreement.

I will now return to Bergson's account of Non-being, having touched
on that aspect of it which involves the ideas of interval and continuity.
There is in reality, independent of us, everything, so to speak. And
we merely mean, by our notion of "nothing" or "nonentity," something that does not interest us: or else something that does interest
us, and which for the moment is *absent,* and whose *place* (where we
desire that it should be, or have expected to find it) we imagine a "void."
So volition and the idea of free-will plays a great part in his idea of
Non-being.

All action aims at getting something that we feel the want of. In this
sense it fills a void — goes from the empty to the full, from an absence
to a presence, from the unreal to the real. The reality which is here
in question is purely relative to the direction in which our attention
is engaged. "So it is that we express what we *have,* or have *not,* as a
function of what we *want.* Just as we pass through the immobile to
go to the moving, so we make use of the *void* in order to think the
full." In a sense the "void" is merely a useful concept or diagrammatic
fiction arising in connection with our personal action upon things. More
generally, this influential school of thought would describe the order
or uniformity of nature as that which we pick out of it, and stabilise
because we are interested in it, as recurrences and systems of recurrences of vital use to our organism. The "nothing" is the new that we
wish (in the future) to include in this personal system, or what "no longer
is" — something in the past, which we regret; or, thirdly, something

which we have never paid attention to, because it has not interested us. The opposite of what we either *want* or *expect* we describe by a negative idea.

So Bergson's hegelian account of the concept Nothing, which he wishes to see abolished, is that it is a hypostasis merely of *want*: that negation and affirmation are two sides of the same coin, one implying the other, and that in the absence of one or the other we introduce a third entity: namely, "Nothing." This is bound up with the problem of order and disorder: our "disorder" being a similar sort of hypothetic phantom. For suppose that there are two species of order beneath the same genus, he says; and supposing we go to look for one and unfortunately do not find it, but find instead its contrary. Then very likely the idea of *disorder* would arise in our minds. "The idea of disorder would objectify, for the convenience of language, the disappointment of a mind that finds before it an order, different from what it wants, an order with which it is not concerned at the moment, and which, in this sense, *does not exist for it*." It will be seen from this brief statement the road he takes to arrive at his final analysis of Nothing: it is the road essentially of sensation — of wish, disappointment, indifference — the personal and psychic, in short, and one from which the absolute order of the rational mind is completely banished.

Bergson's universe is, with a heraclitian compensating *up* and *down*, an incline which is ascended by mind at the same time that it is descended by matter (which in its turn is a relaxation of mind). What we call "Nothing" is the inverse of our actual ascent. It is the unpicking or destructive operation which we are overcoming, the chaos or nonentity out of which we are climbing; only, of course, after a little, to fall back and perish. The paradoxical sugarplum of this system is the *assurance* (on the part of Bergson) that our little ephemeral desperate *reascent* of the current flowing downward steadily towards perdition (and which progressively beats down the store of energy we have cleverly accumulated for this puny feat) is really *new* and, if a small thing, *our own*.

Thus does this strange individual overestimate, or so we think, the human love of novelty for its own sweet sake, and thinks to win our hearts, almost comically, by this testimonial that every time we sneeze, or open the morning paper, we are doing something *quite new!* Take the trouble to look into his system (at this time of day it is a burdensome retrospective task, but will repay you) and you will find that everything is removed from human life that gives it any value at all except this word "creation" (so that *everything* becomes "creative") and that queer testimonial of "novelty." But the words "creation" and "novelty" (without an accompanying scrutiny of what that entailed) have generally sufficed for most of those people who made the success of his time doctrine, in this country all the Wildon Carrs, T. E. Hulmes and so forth, and of those who follow in his footsteps to-day, only with the readjustments required by space-time. So it is that this little superficial coating of ecstatic optimism, a few silly words repeated over and over again, have concealed the annihilating pessimism of his thought. For beneath this smiling appearance of "vitality" with its "élans" of sugary "creativeness," is the deepest and most absolute exhaustion of soul, expressed in a system of the most poisonous, because most disguised, mechanism that the modern world has to show.

It is strange that this bergsonian nonentity can have passed itself off for so long as "life" with a capital L. It is so vitally important that it should do so no longer, and that we should not have the unhappy experience of assisting at a recrudescence of it in the forms of the Alexanders, Whiteheads and those who certainly will follow them, that it is worth penetrating a little more thoroughly into the heart of these ideas. First of all, then, the arch pretence in Bergson's philosophy is that it is an attack, or a reaction against, the mechanistic view of things, in favour of a "vital" and "creative" view. It is in reality nothing at all of the sort, but a more subtle darwinism, of more absolute negation. It calls itself "life," merely, in order to advertise death. As a "life" doctrine it is of the same order of "vitality" as a broadly advertised drug to retard or momentarily resuscitate the impotent. It is an ecstatic advertiser's scream of "Be young again" to the decrepit. His *flux* into which you are to *plunge*, is an invitation, by a hotel-proprietor, or a hotel-tout, to visit a Spa. "Our waters will cure you," it says. It is a parallel to the primitive christian invitation to *baptism*, to immersion in the "laver," addressed to a tired and distracted, too complex, civilisation. It is even associated with miracles, but with miracles of natural science, as it were. "When we *put back our being into our will*" (that is, when we get down into the sparkling, life-giving, medicinal, gasping, health-laden, etc., etc. flux) "we feel that reality is a perpetual growth, a creation pursued without end. Our *will* already performs this *miracle*. Every voluntary act in which there is *freedom* . . . brings something new into the world!" But then, after such lyrical promises and pats-on-the-back, comes discreetly muted, the obverse of this picture, the brief reminder that, of course, we must not expect too much even of "freedom," or of the perfectly "new," and that "creative" as undoubtedly even the least among us is, what is created is "only a creation of form." This means, as has been fully explained before by him, that it is only a rearrangement of things already existing, as a child rearranging its box of letters, and spelling "cat" instead of spelling "dog." "Bravo! well done! you see! He's spelt "cat," he has, *all by himself*, no one to help him! Oh, I do think you're a little *marvel!* You are a little walking miracle! Really and truly you are!" We seem to hear the conventional encouragement of the sage old bourgeois uncle, bending over the "creative" exercise of the child. For Bergson is the first famous european

philosopher to write, to *think*, for *children*. He is a person to whom
in the very form of his writing, if nothing else, an aggravated form
of insincerity can be brought home. The poorly and carelessly articulated, deliberately unsevere, the profusely imagined, text, was an
insult in itself to the European World. Such books as Spengler's *Decline
of the West* could simply never have been written if Bergson had not
prepared the way for them with his affective, "intuitive," dissolvents.

"Consider the letters of the alphabet," he writes, "we do not think
that *new letters* spring up and come to join themselves to the others
in order to make a new poem." No, they are the same old letters, my
little lad: but Tommy puts them together differently: clever little chap,
"creative" little Tommy! Uncle Henry will give him a penny for his birth-
day! But little *Tommy himself* is really the perfectly *new* poem. There
have been many many Tommies before this particular Tommy, and
there will be many many Tommies after him. But never exactly *this*
Tommy. Tommy is the new poem, the material atoms that compose
Tommy form themselves, in their multitudes into T-O-M-M-Y and—*if
you mix Time into the composition*; that is the important thing where
Tommies are concerned. If you don't mix Time you get the same old
Tommy over and over again: a platonic Tommy in short, instead of
a brand new one. That we don't want at all at all—do we now, little
man?—we want to be our own little selves, and bother all the other
Tommies! That's right, isn't it? And Berg smiles and pats the good, obedient, little fellow on the head.

So let us hear Uncle Alexander on the same subject. He is hanging
back a little bit coyly where his views with regard to "motion" are
concerned—he does not wish to go *too* far.

. . . [I]n describing universals as patterns of motion I do not go to the length
of the later Pythagorean, Eurytas, of whom Mr. Burnet tells us that he
represented the form of man (supposed identical with the number 250) by sticking pebbles to that number into wet plaster along the outlines of a human shape.
Exaggerated as the procedure is, the spirit of it is sound, and I delight in Eurytas.

Bergson would not have admitted at the time he was building his evolutionary system that he delighted in Eurytas. Yet his "letters of the
alphabet," with which the weakened, degraded, European of Industrial
Democracy was told that he "created" the something "new" that was
his "unique" self, is the same thing as the numbers of the "exaggerated"
Eurytas, only far more so, for the pythagoreans were not priests of the
flux.

To give a net conception of the true meaning of bergsonism to
anybody unacquainted with his doctrine is not easy without extensive
quotation. One quotation of some length I will give, from a part labelled
"Ideal genesis of Matter." That part I specially recommend as containing (with a little scraping of the sugar-coating of "creative" matter) the
core of his pessimistic belief—though "pessimism" is not the word, for

that implies some saving grace of despair; whereas Bergson is smug, opportunist, slick and untruthful. There is a "God" at the bottom of his "creation." This God he describes as "unceasing life, action, freedom." At the mere sound of the words, mingling with "creation," "liberty," "free-will," "the absolutely new," and so forth, the audience should wildly applaud, of course, if it had not removed its caps it must surely be compelled to fling them up into the air, and then light-heartedly catch them. "Creation, so conceived, is not a mystery" (there is nothing up my sleeve): "we experience it in ourselves when we act freely." But do not run away with the idea that it is anything stable or durable that is being "created." No, it is the *doing* that is the "creation" — there is nothing there at the end of it — not even *yourself*. You have been "creating" a self, it seems, that is, however, daily losing ground, in the incessant struggle against the Styx which is the bergsonian flux. So you must not imagine, in your first eagerness, "new things" joining themselves to things already existing. That would be "absurd": since the *thing* results from a solidification performed by our understanding, and there are never any things other than those that the understanding has thus constituted.

To be the Never-completed, that is the idea: like the "emergent" God, who is made by Time, but never completed, and which in reality can be said never to exist. So in this magnificent way *you* will never exist. And it is the *making*, the *action*, that matters. Disraeli remarked, "I only live when I act: and then I feel a God." That is exactly the assertion of Bergson. His God, too, is *action*. And he would impose it, of course, upon us. It is not difficult for us to focus, under these attributes, what is certainly an extremely mournful and destructive being. He only calls himself "creative" to recommend himself to us. But it would be easy to turn upon this God, and his priests, and ask them what it is that he *creates*? We surely do not live in "an age of advertisement" for nothing! Surrounded as we are, at all hours of the day, with competing announcements of the *absolute novelty* and *absolute perfection*, of this brand of goods and that, surely we are not going to take these other fine words, because we find them issuing from the Temple of Philosophic Truth, on trust? So let us examine still more closely the composition of this bergsonian-alexandrine God.

Life is a *movement* (a dual contradictory movement, simultaneously anabolic and catabolic, each of these opposed movements simple). The matter which forms a world is an undivided flux, and undivided also the life that runs through it, cutting out in it living beings all counter to the first, but the first obtains, all the same, something from the second. There results between them a *modus-vivendi*, which is "organization."

We now have a definition, at least, of what this "creativeness" amounts to. It is a pact with death and destruction — a *modus-vivendi* between the great force that is sweeping everything to destruction at every minute of Time, and the "life force" entrenched momentarily in our organism, playing its losing game, or its self-cancelling game, or the game of its pyrrhic victory, of compensating, or providing the other side of the medal, for death. Now, it is strange, as I have said, that the pessimism, as it would be called, of Bergson, has never been noted. The flamboyant advertisement for the "life force" pasted all over his sinister system has really served to conceal its ultimate meaning even from its opponents, it seems. The vulgarity of the advertisement, its effect on the life of the society contemporary with it, what sort of *person* in the everyday world it stood for, and whose gospel it naturally was, all have received considerable attention. But I believe that the heart of his doctrine of "mental time" has never been properly examined. We will do so more fully presently, and in connection with the ideas of Space and Time. But first we will endeavour to find out a little more about this first draught of the Time-God.

The God of Bergson turns out to be on the closest attention, a steam-engine. Men have made gods of everything, from old shoes to mountains. Bergson has been attracted, apparently, by the locomotive. Perhaps at an early date his infant-intelligence was overawed at the power and speed of the "puff-puff," as later one of his successors, Marinetti, made a god of the motor car or aeroplane. So machine-worship punctually takes the place of animal worship. His boiler with the crack may be some other industrial monster, of course. But let us examine it.

"If the same kind of action is going on everywhere (as the dispersal and assemblage of worlds and nebulae)" he says "whether it is that which is making itself or whether it is that which is striving to remake itself, I simply express this probable similitude when I speak of a centre from which worlds shoot out like rockets in a fire-work display." This "centre" he says, is the definition of God. And it has first been visualised by him — just prior to his admitting that this was a *God* that he was defining — as a steam-engine — rather a dilapidated one I am afraid.

Let us imagine [he says, as he stealthily approaches his *God* — which he springs on us rather unexpectedly —] a vessel full of steam at a high pressure, and here and there, in its sides, a crack through which the steam is escaping in a jet. The steam thrown off into the air is nearly all condensed into little drops which fall back, and this condensation and this fall represent simply the loss of something, an interruption, a deficit. But a small part of the jet of steam subsists, uncondensed, for some seconds; it is making an effort to raise the drops which are falling; it succeeds at most in retarding their fall. So, from an immense reservoir of life, jets must be gushing out unceasingly, of which each falling back is a world.

Having, however, drawn his unequivocal picture, he realises that it is perhaps a little too near the bone of his thought: its mechanistic imagery and affiliations are too obvious, his *libre arbitre*, his *élan vital*, and all the rest of the bag of tricks, will hardly tally with this iron cylinder blowing off steam. So he withdraws a little.

But let us not carry too far this comparison [he remarks]. It gives us but a feeble and even deceptive image of reality; for the crack, the jet of steam, the forming of the drops, are determined, *necessarily*, whereas the creation of a world is a *free act*, and the life within the material world participates in this liberty.

So he whisks back his "free-will," "liberty," and so on, covering up his picture of the machine quickly with these pretty words. So more generally, a *storing-up* — whatever the receptacle — is the first process: and this is succeeded by a *discharge*, or orgasm, which is life. So we are a result of a defect, a blemish, an untidiness, in Bergson's God.

A *falling* drop — that is what life is, *retarded* in its fall by the "creative" impulse, though still it, fatally, *falls*. All the emphasis in his philosophy really is on the *fall* of these drops. His *élan vital*, his *ascent* undertaken by the vital, works out much more as a *fall*, if you look at it at all closely. If our "consciousness" (or life) were pure, it would be "pure creative activity." This unfortunately it is not. It can only become "pure" with the assistance of Bergson, for a few instants at a time, when of course it becomes (or should according to the prescription) pure orgasm. All the rest of the time it is still, inevitably, fall and dejection. But "in fact, it is riveted to an organism that subjects it to the general laws of inert matter." So most of its time is necessarily spent in a gravitational *drop*. The life force, "incapable of *stopping* the course of material changes downwards, succeeds in *retarding* it." As the gland-specialist might say in his advertisement: "We cannot put off decay indefinitely: but what we can do is we can retard it." Bergson's "creative" *élan vital* turns out to be, in the end, a sort of [brake] only upon a very severe and inevitable *chute*. It is, in short, in the nature of a *parachute*. That is what, when all the flourishing and shouting is over, his famous, universally-advertised, life-force, turns out to be. Very much ado about — yes — *Nothing*.

The *fall*, the descent, or at best (thanks to the very ineffective interference of the life-force — the jet of steam) the *decline*, is what his philosophy is really about. From the very start it is obsessed with the motif of destruction or change — for his Time obsession is really, were its psychologic impulses analysed, an obsession of destruction. Everywhere it is essentially mournful and discouraged, though frantically inventing *brakes* and *restoratives* to put off its doom. His *vital impulse* is the constant reaction against this sensation of decline and corruption — the instinctive reaction, evidently, with this philosopher; which (it is true) no doubt noticing with his quick eye, he puts to good account. He early grasped the excellent effect that this rather cheerless and hollow piece of behaviouristic, or couéistic, machinery, would have on a sensational public. The Kruschen-feeling, and its accompanying momentary alertness, was probably not a source of self-congratulation to him, or a thing that he felt there was anything much to brag about. But still it would enable him to misrepresent himself to the public, and come before it smiling. So he made it the cornerstone of his system.

He knew, no doubt, perfectly well, himself, all along, how soft and unsubstantial this material was; a stone that would be despised and rejected by any sane and competent builder. So this little sad and febrile insect imposed his private prescription for stimulating the effete upon the great and apparently flourishing european world. But he was not able, indeed he made no serious attempt, to banish from his system the sufficient cause, the mournful obsessing consciousness of decay and age — or to hide from us the true face of that soul into which he showed his great rat, Time, "gnawing incessantly," "biting into," devouring. What was this personal bent, or "sport," that imposed on this depressed, mournful, though ambitious and nervously-active, nature, this "gnawing" obsession, so that actually in his philosophy you got a sensation like the presence of Poe's raven, of the ticking of some pervasive, sinister, sometimes frantic, time-piece? That is impossible to say: but its optimism-to-order is in curious contrast with the robust suicidal pessimism of such a figure as Schopenhauer, who enjoyed, we are told, every minute of his life, and probably possessed a digestion, as a will, of iron.

As we have already remarked, if Bergson's classical prototype is Heraclitus, how is it that men have not called Bergson "the weeping philosopher," as the Greeks called Heraclitus? The answer is plain: because, having the same unhappy picture of the world at the bottom of his mind, Bergson gave it a smear of optimism, and behaviourised himself into an affirmative ecstasy, a more composed nietzschean "Yea!"; partly, perhaps, I have suggested, to cheer himself up; and partly to win attention for his system. It is quite impossible, once you are familiar with the tone, or colour, of his mind, not to associate this conception of Time, his insistence upon Time, as a reflection of that obsessing strain that is like some Old Testament lamentation echoing in his pages. "Wherever anything lives there is open *somewhere* a register in which time is being inscribed . . . *something* ages," etc. This is not it seems a personal lament, but some predisposition to a certain type of emotional melancholy, some set of values [adhered] to quite beyond his personal world. It is as it were the heart-cry of an ineradicable materialism, that no reflection can root out, rather than the expression of a certain metaphysical consciousness. Speaking of a book, of which he approves, which is apparently written to oppose to Evolution the conception of Dissolution and decay as the main fact of life, "M. André Lalande," he writes, "shows us everything going towards death, the tide setting towards destruction." So it is really a dance of death that his ballet of "Creative Evolution" performs. A preoccupation of that sort, a being "much possessed with death," seeing "the skull beneath the skin," etc., is unobjectionable, and would make the proper material for a dirge or threnody. It is the despairing refrain of many beautiful lyrical expressions. But that is not what we ask of philosophy: rather its contrary is the popular requirement — seeing things in their due proportion, "objectively," rather than exploiting the prompting of some personal mood, however beautiful. Just as there is a great deal in Henry James that enables us to understand his brother the philosopher, William, so there is much in Proust that enlightens us as to Bergson, and vice versa. Wherever we can we should always go to the expression of some kindred mind in another material to give us a fuller understanding. Certainly, where what is so *personal*, so *felt*, so *mental* as Bergson's doctrine, thrusts its way into philosophy, it is apt to cause both a great deal of surprise at first (on the score of its originality), and, for the duration of its vogue, considerable confusion.

It is "life," it must always be recalled, that is put forward as the capital advertisement and central rationale of this and similar systems. As opposed to "pessimism," which also claims to exhibit the authentic, if very melancholy, reality, *they* claim to show that really everything in the garden is lovely and that the goose hangs high. If they fail in that claim they fail in everything. The *pragmatism* of the american psychologists is of the same order: they ask not *what is truth*, but does it "work," does it "answer": they say that they provide only truths such as are wholesome and useful for life. And of course all positive science stands or falls by the same claim. Science is *useful*, it says, to human beings, in their supposed struggle with "forces of nature" (though in reality, as we all know, they are engaged in struggles with other human beings all the time, so when "struggle with nature" is said, "struggle with other men" is understood): its advertisement lies entirely in its *pragmatical* claim, too. That Bergson's system does *not* irradiate "life," or altogether abound in comfort, or that on the facts displayed, or implied there, that it does not justify his ecstatic optimism, has now been shown, I think. Scrutinized at all closely, it is not gay or full-of-hope, whatever else it may be. But with it, in Bergson's case, go other things which it will be instructive to glance at before passing on.

If we said that Bergson was at once too personal and too inert — too interested and too uninterested — that contradiction would I think be true. Putting his picture of the universe into plastic terms, the *line* he uses is not that resolute, certain, and "classical" line which we prefer, but a thin, wavering, tentative one, such as children use in their drawings, or like the line of the "automatic" hand. We have said that in his picture of the descending and ascending lines of (1) the inert and (2) the vital, that it is not, in reality, the elation and power of the ascending line that predominates, but the dead *drop* of the inert, that of matter. It is the *material* that in every case wins the struggle in Bergson: for as we have said, he is in the clearest sense a "materialist." If we plunge into Bergson, if, following his advice for things in general, we identify ourselves with his being, get inside and to the centre of this mind, we shall become conscious of the gravitational pull, and have more the sensation of an automatic and fatal descent and *drop*, than of a movement of *ascent*. And yet he *personalizes* everything: that is what we have to reconcile with this depressing sensation: for if we were inside a stone that was falling, and sharing the sensation of its fall, we should not be conscious of this *personal* factor traversing its automatism. His Time, again, is *mental* Time, and yet it is terribly mechanical, and, wrapt into the soul of its periodic measure, certainly no "free" thing could exist. Where most he shouts "freedom" and "liberty," "spontaneity," "individual creation," he is making it ideally impossible either to be "free" or to "create." That is why, having described or defined something in mechanistic terms, as we have seen him doing (which is the true illustration of his thought, which *is mechanistic*, for all his criticism of mechanistic systems and of mathematical time), he then has to step aside, to reassume his life-prophet's robe, and protest that *all the same* this mechanical image does not give us any idea of the "freedom," "life," "incalculability," etc., etc. of the thing in question, when it is a vital process he has been defining.

His analysis of the concept, Nothing, is an ideal example of his manner of personalising everything, and attributing to some purely human action the concept to which he objects.

The full always succeeds the full [he says] and an intelligence that was only intelligence, that had neither regret nor desire, whose movement was governed by the movement of its object, could not even conceive an absence or a void. The conception of a void is only a comparison between what is and what could or ought to be, between the full and the full.

The representation of the void is the positive thing. We are "immersed in realities," absent or present. And we call the *present* the *real*, and everything else the *void*: that is all.

Yet all this piping-hot "reality" we have a regrettable tendency to deny, and to say it is not "real," perhaps. Why is this? It is because he says we have this notion of the Nothing, against which we match this flimsy, scurrying, quickly-forgotten "reality" of our finite life, and we feel that that sort of reality is not strong and stable enough to vanquish the Nothingness — for the mere existence of bodies and minds suggests a primitive victory at some time over Nothing. But a logical principle, such as A = A, or the concept, or "logical essence," of the circle, *that* is not easily snuffed out. If the principle on which all things rest and which all things manifest, is of that substantial order, then the being which is at the base of everything "posits itself in eternity as logic itself does." Then indeed we see how it is that there is all this strange "becoming," instead of Nothing: for otherwise even Nothing would most likely be more viable than it. But for Bergson these logical principles are the dead and skeletal portion of the whole, the mere habit or pattern which serves to support the minute variety of living matter, the pulp, the filling-in. "Life" for him is the proximate confused seething and not the structure or form presiding at this or that accidental event. He does not want to go back behind this appearance to something relatively stable, and he refuses this "petrified" substructure a background or opposite, a Nothing.

For Alexander what is at the base of everything is *Space-Time*, which is *bare movement*, without meaning. For Bergson at the basis of everything would be *Time*. But the more you enquire as to what "Space-Time" really may be, the more you realize that Bergson's "Time," and it, bear a very strong family resemblance, and can for all practical purposes be regarded as one. Again, memory, for Bergson is indispensable for the idea of Nothing. For memory is where the *absent* subsists for our mind's eye: and if we did not look *before*, we should also hardly look *after*. And memory, when it means in his language "detension," is as much hated as is "Space." It is in his insistence upon Memory that is to be sought his great contribution to the Image-world, or Mirror-world of illusion, that has now, in philosophy, taken definite shape.

This chapter, and the two chapters preceding it, have been occupied with the question of reality — with what we mean when we say "real." I will now point to a few of the conclusions that my analysis should suggest, starting with the considerations of the association of "reality" and "belief" with which we began.

Reality (to state what I have intended to arrive at in a sentence) is simply the sense of a *creation*; and that is the sensation of a *cause*. The uncaused world of Hume — in which things merely lay side by side, without any reason to suppose, except the suggestions of experience and habit, that they were particularly connected — was a visual world: it was the world not of all the senses, but essentially of the visual sense. And that is what the world of contemporary philosophy is also almost entirely become. It is a world of images — the illustration often used to elucidate its theories is of mirror-images — and it has the same standards of reality as that.

But in such an opium-world, the standard of reality is very low, as it was effectively in Hume's. Just as art — the sphere in which illusion has usually been concentrated — has been broken down, and everyone has sought in one way or another to participate in it (the spectators swarming on to the stage, as I described it in the *Dithyrambic Spectator*): so the concrete reality of "classical" common-sense has everywhere been fused with the picture-world or image-world, of our mental states. The cinema is a silent world like that seen in a looking-glass: and the mental-world of our dream-states is also a silent world, in which sight, not touch, is paramount: and a world of this sort is also in process of being made for us within the everyday reality itself. All the influences that flow in on us from philosophy and physics are directed to the formation of such a world.

In a dream we are in the most dynamic of our mental or memory-states. We have little sense of causation; since it is the world of our ultimate volition that is natural. This may not at first sight seem to follow. But it is the consciousness of the exercise of our *will* in waking life from which we derive our keenest sensation of a causative principle, that is evident. There, you would perhaps say, in the very domain of our volition — our dream-world in which we can exercise our will to the top of our bent — we should be more, not less, conscious of "power." This is however not the case; for it is always against some opposition, such as we have in waking life, that we get the keenest sense of our causative ability.

Again, our sense of touch is a far keener sense than that of sight: we get from it much more sense of causative power — as manifested in ourselves or another — by way of touch, than by way of sight. But it is exactly *touch* that is characteristically suppressed in the space-timeist or Time system, or it is diminished in favour of sight. To the further implications of this we shall arrive in the next chapter. All we need say here is that the world of pure sight (of sight in isolation) is the most *unreal* world of all those provided by the senses. The world of sound, even, is far more immediate and *real.* The evidence of this is the very much greater *physical* effect of a piece of music than of a picture or than of architecture.

In words already quoted Hume says: "All belief of matter of fact or real existence is derived merely from some object, and a customary conjunction between that and some other object." This "object" of Hume's is a *visual* object, that is what essentially he has in mind. The reason that "things rattle dryly together like dice in a box in Hume's philosophy," as James noticed, is because his world is a visual external one.

But the "Plastic" of Spengler — the term he opposes to "Music" — must of necessity be a plastic of touch as much as of sight, or the touch is implicit in the sight. The visual external world of his "Classical" man was not a world of Alice-through-the-Looking-Glass. Hence the object seen, or the famous "objective" consciousness of the sensuous Antiquity, so often contrasted with our abstract habits, was not *seen* purely. Just as it was a *perceptive* unit, the perceptual factor giving it depth, "spatialising" it; so the sense of touch, co-operating fully with the eye, gave it depth, and a concrete *reality.*

Until we come to consider the Object (in the next Chapter) it is difficult to make this more explicit: so all I will say here is this: that the object of perception is the *real* object, never the object of sensation. When Hume says that "Belief is nothing but a more vivid, lively, forcible, firm, steady conception of an object, than what the imagination alone is ever able to attain," he is pointing to the *perceptual* experience, composed of the direct stimulus of sensation on the one hand, and memory on the other, with all its host of conjunct images. "The conception accompanied by *belief*," he says, "arises from a *customary conjunction* of the object with something present to the memory or sense." This "customary conjunction" is the memory or habit-factor. The single, isolated, direct sensation, however "real" (as we should describe a sensation) in one way, and perhaps violent, would yet not bear with it the consciousness of *reality* or of *belief*. Take any sudden, violent sensation. Imagine yourself walking along a platform waiting for a train, and that suddenly a "crashing" aeroplane dropped on top of you. For an instant, before you were killed, you would be aware of the aeroplane. But that instantaneous sensation, without anything preceding or following it, would lack *reality*. Such an event (for the brief moment of your awareness) would have a dream-quality.

It is on such grounds as these that the sensationalism of Bergson, for instance, is to be rejected. On examination, his naked, direct sensation (an "impression" in the language of Hume, which gives the clue better to the word "Impressionism," of which Bergson is the great philosophic exponent) would be found not to contain as much reality as the perceptual, or in his case conceptual, unit it sought to displace.

Let us return to the statement with which we started: namely that reality is the sense of a *creation*, or of a thing caused. There is no possibility of reality (of the sensation of belief that is) without the sense of certainty of *truth being the same everywhere*, of a universal law of nature (that will always make the fire burn your hand if you touch it, or the stone drop). This we call cause-and-effect. "Mental fire is what won't burn real sticks," James wrote. If you take the direction, philosophically, that leads you to bring into frequent contact imaginary flames and "real sticks," "real" doors and imaginary winds, and compose amusing hypotheses of marvellous Natures where anything that exists, mentally or otherwise, may familiarly mingle, you may inhabit a delightful world, such as hashish, with a lucky "kip," may procure for you: but "reality" in any sense you have abandoned, and at the same time "life." It would be an oppressive régime that forbade you so to fade away into a delightful world in which Cheshire Cats, or the smiles of Cheshire Cats, appeared and disappeared with a curious and happy unexpectedness. Thus you would be of less use to anybody else (that is why legislation is directed to discourage extreme forms of intoxication) but that in the abstract might be all the better. In time, however, you of course would become impotent in the matter of "belief" — much more so than "that notorious sceptic," Hume — in a too hedonistic pursuit, that is, of the delights of "scepticism." Dementia is of course a violent and chronic form of "scepticism." What is a madman but a person with a weakened sense of belief; who, unable to keep at the necessary tension his artificial system of public habit, retires in his private "system of reality," abandoning "common-sense"? And what is Nihilism, with its joys, but a prolonged association with the notion of Nothing — all that is not "reality"? It is a very foolish man who pities the lunatic: still Nature shows a universal obstinacy to deter us from retreating into that organised "scepticism" that is very impressive; an obstinacy, indeed, that, when you come to think of it, is absolutely lunatic, if it is possible to suppose Nature to be mad. So in the end even these opposite terms "sane" or "demented" have to be carefully held down to this or that meaning: and of course "the sane" man, full of an insane "belief-feeling" (and so, we say, possessed of the sense of the "reality") is madder, if you care to look at it in that way, than is the certified lunatic who has retired into the pleasant retreat of the most thorough-going "scepticism" available. These few remarks will have served to show, I hope, that it is in no spirit of irrational (or of rationalist) pride, that we have undertaken the scrutiny of "reality."

The sensation of causation is essential, we said in Chapter _____, for the sensation of reality (for what that sensation is worth, it is now understood: though here it is highly valued, certainly). This seems to us fundamental. Further we believe that the issue of the elimination of "power" with regard to the immediate empirical world, and that of the elimination of "power" in our conception of the Everything, is *one* question. In short, to sustain any sensation of reality, "power" (which is implicit in the notion of a cause) is essential. And it is in consequence of this, in our view, that the conception of Deity, of a God or Supreme Reality, is essential, not only to our intellectual life, but to life itself. For it is upon this, to-day, more fragile sensation of "reality," that life depends. Only that seems to keep us where "belief" is sane, for "scepticism" at its intensest too often is a violent form of belief; there are many other beliefs than that of "Nature." The insane must always have a different God from us — different to our "natural" one, that is. Then there are what are called "borderline cases" where the God of the sane is seen distorted, as it is observed passing into a foreign medium, becoming a kind of a caricature of our "true": we can see the Reality transforming itself into what we call the "untrue." This leads us to the full significance of the remark of Bradley already quoted: "No truth shall be entirely true." Bradley was a "border-line case." It is a splendid spectacle to observe, in *Appearance and Reality*, his powerful Absolute in the first throes of self-repudiation, dying with great difficulty, in a, for it, suffocating region where "no truth is *entirely* true," in a world of fragments, turning to an alien, unnatural hegemony.

The sceptical extremism of Hume has suggested to Prof. G. E. Moore a very interesting idea, to be found in his *Philosophical Studies.* It seems of such very great importance for what we are discussing here that I will give it more prominence than I think it has elsewhere received. In his essay upon the Philosophy of Hume, face to face with the utmost scepticism, Prof. Moore, who has always been engaged in a very strict and rigorous examination of philosophic ideas, borders on a revelation which it is a pity he did not elaborate, and which no one, really, has ever thoroughly broached in Western thought. For *strictly* speaking, he was brought to confess, the most extreme of the three alternative positions that Hume's *Treatise* and *Enquiry* provide, is as unobjectionable, from the point of view of reality, as any other position, more moderate and more in conformity with common-sense. Out of this very interesting essay of Prof. Moore's emerges the cleavage between our thought as living beings, and our thought as philosophical minds, with an exemplary clarity.

The main questions asked by Hume are: What can we *know*, of what can we be certain that we possess really something we can call truth? Do the objects we perceive really exist? and so on — in the heroic attempt to exhaust the problem of knowledge. If the sceptical inquirer is only rigorous enough, and adheres with sufficient strictness to his arguments, and if the results of his arguments were adhered to consistently by him and by us, *in life, as well as in philosophy* (and it is for his emphasis upon this point that Prof. Moore's account recommends itself so much) — then we should be in a world, according to standards imposed upon us by Nature for our existence in Time and Space, quite foreign to our "reality," and all our "intuitive," causal beliefs. But let me quote a passage from his essay. Of Hume's three (inconsistent) positions, as marshalled by Prof. Moore, the *second* implies "that we cannot have any basis in experience for asserting any *external* fact whatever": and "the third view is still more sceptical, since it suggests that we cannot really know any fact whatever, beyond the reach of our present observation." And this is Prof. Moore's next comment:

As regards the last two views [he says] it may perhaps be thought that they are too absurd to deserve any serious consideration. . . . And Hume himself, it might seem, does not seriously expect or wish us to accept these views. He points out, with regard to all such excessively sceptical opinions, that we cannot continue to believe them for very long together — that, at least, we cannot, for long together, avoid believing things flatly inconsistent with them. The philosopher may believe, when he is philosophising, that no man knows of the existence of any other man or of any material object; but at other times he will inevitably believe, as we all do, that he does know of the existence of this man and of that, and even of this and that material object. There can, therefore, be no question of making all our beliefs consistent with such views as this, of never believing anything that is inconsistent with them. And it may, therefore, seem useless to discuss them. But in fact, it by no means follows that, because we are not able to adhere consistently to a given view, therefore that view is false; nor does it follow that we may not sincerely believe it, whenever we are philosophizing, even though the moment we cease to philosophize, or even before, we may be forced to contradict it. And philosophers do, in fact, sincerely believe such things as this — things which flatly contradict the vast majority of the things which they believe at other times. Even Hume, I think, does sincerely wish to persuade us that we cannot know of the existence of external material objects — that this is a philosophic truth, which we ought, if we can, so long as we are philosophizing, to believe.

So according to this version of the nature of extreme philosophic thought, there are, for it, two visions of the world, or two realities. One is a kind of state we pass into when we are "philosophizing." What we believe when we are in that condition flatly contradicts what we believe when we come out of it, and pass back again into every-day life, integrating once more our common-sense self. When this contemplative state, this fit of abstraction, or whatever you like to call it, is intense (or "extreme") enough, "we cannot continue" wrapt in its world of contradictory beliefs "for long together." This fit of abstraction, in which we *believe* things that at other times we are unable to believe, this belief-state so opposite to the wonted "reality" of our life, is then a sort of trance. But like the "trance" experienced by all creative artists (to which we referred in Chapter _____, Book I) it is not accompanied by the inanition and stoppage of the senses of the hypnotic condition. The patient still is aware of the external world much as usual: and this in a sense makes it a more peculiar and more significant event. For it is as though in those moments he integrated another personality altogether, which, however, was in "full possession of his faculties," and which (Personality No. 2) remained in the midst of the same external nature as the other (Personality No. 1). But there are certainly great differences between the two personalities: one (No. 2) is a terrible "voyant" and his intenser reactions entirely transfigure the visible world. He is really to some extent No. 1 disembodied.

So, in fact, this reduplication of the natural man and the philosophic man is more like a phenomenon of double personality than anything else. The question that next arises is which is the "true" world — that of the most fully entranced extremist-sceptic — of the Hume who *disbelieved in everything* — for very short periods at a time: or the world of the natural observer, *believing in everything* — the one vividly "disbelieving," or believing differently, therefore "believing" (as we say) equally vividly? That question I for my part have already answered. But this I can add: these two states of mind are, properly considered, equally "intense," and even equally "extreme." There is nothing so extraordinary as our public world of "classical" common-sense. It is only very ancient habit indeed, and the most immemorial custom, that enables us to support it so lightly and easily as we do, and to *take it so much as a matter of course.* Were it a novelty we should be able

to occupy it for very brief intervals only. It is in breaking this down
that we reach the other state. Actually, with the collapse of health, or
as a consequence of any violent shock or disorder, we are disposed immediately to plunge back into the completest "scepticism" — which we
call madness, because really that is the easier of the two to support:
our normal condition is what we should describe in another connection as too "artificial."

Before closing this part of our argument dealing specifically with the
idea "reality," it may be as well to say something on the subject of the
more popular uses to which the word reality is put, with especial
reference to what is currently meant by the word "realist."

The author of this essay for instance (to go right into the heart of
the "literary" circus) has been styled "our greatest anti-realist." That is
a description, seeing the sort of individual who used it, which seems
to me in the nature of a significant flattery.

In practice, we know, a person will describe another as a "realist"
if the other play his game, and manifest an interest in the same things
as himself. A stockbroker would say that so-and-so was a "realist" who
displayed an interest in stockbroking: that such-and-such a man was
not a "realist" who was indifferent to those arts of the exchange. For
a society hostess, a person interested in society (that is to say, mainly,
the private life of the stockbroker) and in social functions, would be
a "realist": a person not manifesting those interests would have no sense
of "reality." If you had neglected to pay your respects to a society hostess
for a couple of years, the next time your name was mentioned — in connection perhaps with some whimsical extravagance — she would say
"That is because he is so out of touch with reality." Whatever the realities
you had been *in touch* with in the meantime, there would be one all-
important "reality" with which you had been *out of touch*. Then a
Mayfair novelist would call a "realist" a man the centre of whose world
was Curzon Street: a freudian enthusiast would call "realist" a person
who saw everything in terms of sex or in terms of the mind or psyche
as a sex-centre: a great newspaper proprietor would consider anybody
very "realistic" who was preoccupied with world-politics, and an
amateur of the mass-adjustments of the "New Era." An interest in
philosophy or in art on the other hand, would earn you the title "realist"
from few people: and this in spite of the fact of the immense influence
of the world of ideas, the theoretic world, upon stocks and shares, the
salon and dance-hall, world-politics, and even upon Mayfair novels.

It is perhaps unnecessary for us to say that all modes of "reality" even
upon this ultra-popular, social plane, do not appear to us equally real.
Any form of "belief" has its quantum of reality. And just as we hold
that, as a fact of observation that anyone can verify for themselves,
the great world of "realists" is entirely run by the small world of
"idealists," theoretic men, dreamers, "fous disinteressés," as Poincaré

called them: so we hold that the spring-head from which the ideas, and subsequent ideologies, crazes, fashions — all the swarm of minor, diluted "beliefs" in short, start, has a far better title to the word "real" than the inferior, receptive layers that it feeds. Also it literally feeds those legions with *life* — not merely with fads and toys. It is even, as has already been shown, the prime source of all "revolution." So much for the pragmatical side of the "real."

BOOK II   PART VIII

The Pragmatical Test of the Doctrines of Relativity and of Time

THE DIFFERENCE BETWEEN "truth" and "reality," from our standpoint, will now be canvassed, in the light of the analysis already provided. "Truth follows in the wake of reality," Alexander says. Nothing is added to the reality by our awareness. Truth is the passing-over into knowledge or awareness, from its original ignorance, of some mind or minds. It is the discovery of the pre-existing or the already, and always, existing, the unmasking of the *Nothing* of Bergson. This works very well, and is intended for the physical, for that sort of reasoning. But it would be a difficult matter to fix down that "reality," or set limits to it — to say *here* you are "real," beyond that you cease to be real — if you introduce values other than physical values — such as the yellowness of the yellow rose, or the hotness of the sun — into it. Meanings other than physical meanings upset at once your "reality" of that sort; or rather, when you are using "reality" in that connection, you are confining yourself to the non-organic abstract of the physical order, and that is not "real" except by courtesy, and in relation to the reality of minds. "The reality owes to mind its being known, but it would be what it is without being known." And further, "its reality, being independent of its being-known, is independent of its being known truly."

Now all these statements of Alexander, are, from our standpoint, mistaken. Human life is interpreted by him as an eternal, *progressive* matter of finding-out, of discovery. It is, that is to say, as incurably physical, quantitative and mechanical as the notion of exploring and discovering on an imperfectly known and uncharted globe, the subject-matter of the eternal schoolboy-tale of moving accidents — which are Alexander's "errors" — the planting of the Union Jack — which is his "truth." The reality is lying there, flourishing and boundless, like a physical America. Slowly it is "discovered," the "savages" are killed, it is charted, towns are built. *Truth* has been achieved. He quotes

Bacon's image of the "mirror of Reality," to describe the mind, with approval: or rather he says were the mirrors only *completely flat*, then there would be *nothing but truth*, there would be no longer any error. Without "inequalities of the surface," minds would mirror the physical external world in perfect truth.

That sounds, on the face of it, too perfect to be true, or rather too exact to have any meaning. It also transfers the meaning, the inequality, away from the mind, which it reduces to an absolute flatness and emptiness, and gives it to physical nature. This transaction is wholly in the interest of physical nature, of course. Let us return to the other statements: so "the reality would be what it is without being known." The undiscovered, unknown America, the "reality," is there waiting to be discovered, quite indifferent as to whether it is discovered or not, its waterfalls and large rivers all in full working order, its prairies flourishing with abundant grass, "real" storms breaking out when they should break out, and so forth. Its "discovery" affects it in no way. It merely affects the discoverer. Its discoverer, however, reaches, looks at, and possesses America. He then *knows* America. Whenever anyone speaks to him about America, he knows the *truth* about it. That would seem at first to be the end of the matter. Or, if I take Alexander's namesake, and catch him up at that point in his mortal career when, having conquered the world, he will be found in the act of sighing for fresh worlds to conquer. As there are for the Alexanders of this world, unlimited worlds, presumably, to conquer, discover, possess, *know* – so all there is to do when the "reality" we have considered under the name of "America" is known, is to start off for some other globe; and so on. There is nothing else for us to do. (This analysis will also serve to indicate the *kind* of mentalism that the Time-philosophy implies. I have shown in my first book how a Time-trotter could be as dull a person as a globe-trotter; and have pointed out that *all* [that] happens inside "a mind" – that is "mental" – is not necessarily better than what happens *outside* it; just as some of the greatest achievements of the mind require the physical and not-mental. So this mentalism à la Alexander is as it were of a physical order).

That, then, is the view of "reality" which these particular remarks of Alexander imply. And that is the view that for the most part his philosophy suggests. But a little further on we come to a complication that changes the whole face of things.

It is only within the sphere of reality [we then learn] as revealed (the only meaning which minds can attach to any department of reality, for example life) that the true propositions are real. As knowledge grows, life may be revealed more fully. . . . The once true proposition may even turn out to be erroneous for the newer knowledge, while it remains true and real as such within the narrower range. Truth is at once eternal and progressive. . . . Truth varies and grows obsolete and even turns to falsehood. A theory . . . remains true for the range of facts open to the minds of the earlier generations. This is possible because truth is different from reality and implies possession by a standard mind.

These remarks make that infinite reservoir of possibilities, "reality," a very shadowy thing, and our "reality" (what our standardized believers call "truth" at the moment) a very absurd and meaningless affair. For (now looking back) — what exactly is the America that we have discovered? For other creatures, rediscovering it at some remote date, it would bear no resemblance, at all, to *our* America. What is "true" to-day, would be "false" then: and *they* would say that we had not even seen it or been in it at all. And others would say the same of theirs.

Truth is not "reality" at all then. It is merely a synthesis of the small fragment of Reality covered by our temporal existence. Its only title to reality is that it is accepted that in every judgment there is an awareness that what is judged is a part of Space-Time as a whole. The various "truths" of the differing "times" contradict each other, so that what is true for one is *false* for the other. But these blacks and whites, truths and falsehoods, are mysteriously reconciled within the Absolute, or by reason of that invariable reference to the Whole; so that, wherever it is, always, side by side with any finite centre, with its eye to its slit, peering at the temporal cross-section, is *the compendious Whole*, peering too. (It is of those notions of Alexander that Whitehead and others especially make use.)

All judgments are ultimately about the whole Reality. Between themselves they contradict each other flatly. That does not matter at all. The Absolute has a broad back, and carries them all, and makes sense of all of them. Now we find it very difficult to understand, as has been already remarked in the case of the hegelian artifice of negation, how this reconcilement is effected. It is easy to talk of hypothetical spheres and planes of knowledge, on which our blacks will appear whites; but those airy suggestions make no claim to truth, at best, and in any case leave us where we were, sunk in the blackest "error," surrounded by the most unrelieved unreality. This Alexander's (the philosopher's) "progress," and his bergsonian Time-obsession (with which he in reality operates everywhere) produces. Where Bradley is thoroughly depressed, Alexander, much more of a religionist, is full of equanimity, and a kind of bergsonian optimism, reminiscent of that of some more conventional secondary school-master or slumming clergyman, shared by Whitehead and others, when they are treating of the mysteries of "emergence." Your definition of "reality" will ultimately depend, first, on whether you believe that *everything* is "real" or not; and secondly, whether you think that the "real" can be reached or touched in human life. Alexander will say: "the real is Space-Time as a whole, and every complex or part within it." We do not consider that everything (or everybody) is equally "real." To have "In Space-Time" posted upon it, is not only not necessarily a recommendation but does not satisfy us of a thing's reality. There appears to be both the superiority and the lack of candour of ultra-democratic (that is devotionally — "Mass") thought in this labelling. And as "reality" is what interests us, and to be real is all that interests us, we consider what is more "real" cancels what is less so. Only, as to the second condition, we believe that the "real" can be *touched*, and has often been touched and even handled, in human life, and is indeed a fairly common substance within it; so we do not believe in the superior, "evolutionary," picture of "higher" and "higher" truth, like a schemata for exams, existing in a superior indulgent security on a plane above some "lower one" from which it has "emerged." This appears to us the conception natural to some pedagogic judge or examiner: that of some knowledge-snob or power-snob, that is dressed in a little brief authority, or immersed in the delight of some particular "knowingness." It would not occur to an artist, whose intuition was of the true pierean spring (not merely the intuition-to-order of Bergson) for instance.

The philosopher of the *Theaetetus*, who does not, in his contemplative trance, "know what manner of man he is," is actually, we think, not pinned down to any form, but is free. In such moments he is at the heart of the "real." Either there is no higher reality possible than that: *or* everything we are acquainted with is completely meaningless, and worth strictly nothing at all. This "reality," or this capacity of self-transcendence, is not the preserve of the philosopher or artist, but is shared by everybody able to step out of their machine, to one degree or another.

New *facts*, then, do not make new "reality," but merely new "truth." One "reality" is "as good as" another. That is not the case with truth, in the sense of scientific truth, for that is *quantitative*. The more facts, the more "truth." That is why it is so meaningless. Truth is even the enemy of reality, in the sense that its facts continually limit it. To put the matter in an abrupt formula: the truth about a thing is its *reality*, and not its truth (or the "truth about it"): so that "hard fact" is in this sense often as soft as wax, and easily moulded when it comes in contact with immaterial reality. The matter can be put in another way by saying that *Illusion is our truth*. We can only reach reality indirectly; but if there is a God, he, it seems, is in the same case. However that may be, our life is fundamentally symbolical and indirect.

As I have used Alexander so frequently, and in order to do so have been compelled to read him fairly thoroughly, I will make another sort of use of him now — taking that part where he is discussing art quite unobjectionably — a subject on which a philosopher is not able to go far wrong. Beauty, he says, is strictly an illusion.

Considered from the point of view of cognition, the beautiful object is illusory, for it does not as an external reality contain the characters it possesses for the aesthetic sense. . . . The more perfect the artistry the more definitely does the work of art present in suggestion features which as a cognised object it has not.

And he also remarks that observing a man with a face as majestic as that of the Zeus of Otricoli, we may, on learning that he "is really as fine a character as he looks," have our aesthetic pleasure spoilt for us by that inopportune discovery. It will immediately turn, as though by wicked enchantment, into *moral* admiration, probably; which will spoil everything. This can be applied, in our view, throughout the whole field of our experience, and is not merely an explanation to be kept in reserve for some brief analysis of artistic expression. All through everything, what we know has not the same *meaning* for us as what we do not: though we may be experiencing at the contact of an unknown thing something that is appropriate to a known thing, but which knowledge and a variety of *facts* prevent us from feeling. What we said earlier on the subject of the Deity, namely that if there is a God, we should never be able to see anything but his *back*, is what is meant here. We cannot apprehend reality "front on," but only with an awkward obliquity, or in its contrary; via something else; by surprise, when asleep; or *when we do not desire it.* So what can we say of reality in definition? Hardly anything except what it is *not*; as to which we are most fully documented, indeed more so every day.

A thing that has constantly to be insisted upon is that *artifice* is of the very essence of our existence. Further, this applies to everything; and of this fundamental condition art is merely the most explicit illustration. All realization, of a high intensity, must be analogical: we cannot twist *entirely* round upon ourselves: we cannot experience reality "front on," we must make use of the external to experience what is ultimate — having no "outside" or "inside." And always more externality, not less, and a finer and finer externality is required: and the more we part company with that, and go *inside* — into the emotional, visceral, interior — the farther we are from the Real, not the nearer. The definite, externalised, and concrete is the only reality for us, the spatial dream.

All that is "scientific" in the propaganda of the Industrial Age is a challenge to this profound law of our nature. In everything we are told to dispense with "pretence," to be naked and not ashamed, aggressively "rational" in every way. The disasters that ensue are all the proximate result of this literalness. What pushes us to this literalness, and advances the "scientific" truth as the panacea and only system is another matter: it is not pure science, whatever else it may be. The propaganda against the "artificial," taking the practical form of an invitation to dispense with all formalities, all rules of the game, to put *all one's cards on the table*; or an invitation for a general communal pooling of everything so that all that it is possible to know about any individual shall be available at any moment (in the interests of "truth," or of law, of the community) to anybody, is a proposition which, if it were made by one tradesman to another, would be met with becoming ridicule. Yet it is accepted as a general creed (wherever and by whomsoever propagated) by our society at large, which is, however, a society of traders and their employees. These practical, political reformers are not our immediate concern here: but it is important always to bear in mind what on the pragmatical plane is the shadow of this philosophy, or its political counterpart. For, with the best will in the world, how, in all common sense, can we entirely separate them?

It is by means of artifice, then, and by way of illusion, that alone we can arrive at knowledge: and it is "truth," in the sense of the positivist truth of science and pseudo-science when applied interpretatively as philosophy, that is the supreme humbug and delusion. To return to the technique of our argument, every mind is a sort of artificial eternity. Reality or belief are in this sense demonstrably rank illusions, bred in habit. Habit can be described as the illusion of permanence and endlessness, or, if you like, of substance. The newborn baby cannot *believe* anything, because it has not had the time to form habits; that is, beliefs which are so strong that they enable us to take no notice of them, and to build them into an automatism. Our attention is aroused only by what fails to convince us—when, that is, we *doubt*. So our active life is spent in doubt, among the untried factors outside our experience.

"The feeling of believing is a more or less sure indication of there being established in our nature some habit which will determine our actions." Belief could in this sense be described as the mass of satisfied equations, satisfied expectations, the multitude of instinctive predictions that have come true, behind us. The quality of our belief would be the quality, density and impressiveness of that mass. Thus the man who is able to believe most is he whose unconscious base is firmest, whose crust over the flux is deepest and hardest. Crack it, and there is still the flux all the time. Belief can therefore be further defined as our *acquired unconscious*. It is within that that we receive the impression of *fact*, the sense of "reality." What fundamentally we mean by reality is *what does not change*. Or reality is the law that holds a thing or group of things in place. So it is the region of repose, not that of action: it is everyone's personal, earthly nirvana. It is really as much a blank as the figure of our ultimate Absolute, or the bosom of God, tends to be.

The "clearness" at the bottom of the "distinct idea" of the [XVII] century philosopher reduces itself to the *individual*: that would be the conceptual shorthand that would cover most of it. The thing that will never be mistaken for another thing, that is the "clear," or the "distinct." But a plurality of the most highly individualised entities is necessary for this conception of clearness. And, conversely, wherever you do not get *distinctness*, or clearness, or wherever you find a tendency to break up that conception or go counter to it (as in Bergson, Alexander, Whitehead, etc.), you get a straining (probably mystical, and instinct with renunciation of self) towards "the Whole," there is the movement to merge the individual in the Oneness. So in Professor Whitehead's *Science and the Modern World* what we are really getting (under the appearance of a scientific account of the world) is a doctrine of philosophic communism. The war on the "clear idea" is a war on the *individual*. That is why his statement was so popular — whether he knew the true meaning of his doctrine or not, and whether those who were so pleased knew what they were really applauding or not. I have no quarrel with communism, but find that it makes bad art and bad philosophy.

So *externalised* living, concrete living, in the pagan, classical, european sense, demands plurality, thrives on an individualism both in the person and in the thing. There are many different sorts of individualism, however, it is as well to note — even the flux-song of the cosmic ecstasy, and of the bath in the Infinite, can be advertised as an *augmentation of the personality*. When the spider is preparing to swallow the fly he could likewise explain to it that this operation would *augment* its personality — its personality, that is, would be absorbed into that of the spider, and in that sense — only — *augment* itself. The "individualism" we are speaking about refers to a different standard from that of personal development, and regards the "group" — that little simulacra of the "Whole" — as equally subversive of the self. It regards "personality" as expressed through, or at the instigation of, the social group (with its intolerant, unstable, fashions) as rather a merged personality than an emergent one.

All mysticism, then, whether it be religious mysticism or social mass-mysticism, plunges the subject into a mood which is designed to melt all separate, refractory, isolated parts of him, into a mystical unity. The individual man, within himself, has to be as completely merged and mixed, as he has to be merged and mixed outside himself with other creatures. This is what is ultimately meant by Alexander when he says: "Our consciousness *belongs to Space-Time* (i.e., the Whole) . . . we are aware of our own reality so far as we enjoy ourselves as part of the Whole"; not *as ourselves*, that is; and thus we shall get our allotted "consciousness of reality" — such as the timespacer wishes us to have, it is understood. The old merger, and professional baptiser, is assuring us, before he plunges our heads under the waves, that all will be well; and that we shall certainly become one with the Whole of things, and in every sense better citizens, and be much, much happier! But we, strangely enough, take the opposite view to this. By some strange, and possibly hereditary, predilection, we prefer the immediate opposite of all that these people profess and promise. When confronted with these doctrines (we say to you) apply at once, if in doubt, the famous pragmatical test: namely, *"Who would benefit if this were true?"* The form taken here, specifically, by this test, would be to ask yourself: "What kind of people, individuals or races, would naturally incline to doctrines of merging and mixing? In the interest of what kind of man is it to *mix* himself indiscriminately, in a pantheistic brotherhood, or to see all other people mixing?" Not certainly the successful type who is conscious of a *personal* destiny. It is always the inferior or the slave, the unsuccessful, ill-equipped, weak, or strong but twisted, senile or inveterately dependent or parasitic, who, from revenge or ambition, or desire of mechanical self-betterment, would be attracted by such a doctrine, or who would launch it. Even interest in the personal or ubiquitously vital (Browning's "Need of a world of men for me") is not the sign of a noble or secure intelligence. An interest in *things* is more its sign than an interest in *persons.*

To resume this portion of our argument then; the "vivid, lively, forcible, firm, steady conception" of *the object,* of Hume, is still, although transparent illusion, the nearest we can get to reality. It is the analogical reality (one of many alternatives) best suited to us; that in which we can best repose — that is — get on with our work! It is the master-sham which we have all practised for so long that it is second-nature. But were it not, it would be impossible to imagine another as good. And so we return to the hotly-contested material of our object-world (our *artist-world*) with which we started. We will now recapitulate, placing our spatial or material doctrine against the mental doctrine of Time.

We as men have kept, as long as we can remember, the objects, as we called the tables, chairs, houses, trees and hills by which we are surrounded, as slaves; or as an innumerable drove of more or less stationary "things." We still label physical life in most philosophy to-day as a "lower order" of existents. (And, as we have repeatedly suggested, it is not a lucky thing to enter the sub-conscious of the contemporary industrial-man — whether man of science, philosopher or labour-leader — marked "member of a higher order." These social spheres all *interpenetrate,* about that there is at least no question.) Over these inferior, "dead," *things,* we rule, by ancient right. The physical universe around us is an automatic universe, analogous, in our own organism, to the basis of automatism and habit upon which our "conscious" life depends, and thanks to the obscure labours and constant stalwart attentiveness of which it flourishes and enjoys itself. We have not yet arrived at the stage at which this inequality of rank between a man and his table breaks out into a domestic feud. Indeed, although there is a strongly marked tendency to proclaim animals — horses, dogs, cats — as superior to man, yet, if a man were observed kicking a dog to-day, he would certainly nowhere escape a disobliging comparison with the animal, as a response to his uncorroborated human arrogance;

and no racehorse owner could compete in our sympathy with his beautiful horse — yet in practice it is still possible for a man to walk down the street without getting off the pavement on the approach of a dog; and he can still for all practical purposes ignore cats, and behave to them as if they were creatures inferior in privilege to himself, though everybody knows they are not. (We owe these concessions to the fact that other people — in their off-times — are "people" too.)

But the pantheistic tide is in full movement towards a time when these conditions will no longer obtain. And there is already in philosophy a premonitory, revolutionary sensitiveness on the subject of tables and chairs. (Plato's "mob of the senses" has long established itself as a constant challenge to our everyday-more-precarious little band of "thoughts," or "ideas".) Is it not with a certain humanitarian pointedness that the liberalism of Mr. Russell (passing over into his philosophy) points out to the slothful, self-satisfied occupant of a *chair* (the "aristocrat-in-the-chair," it could be called on the principle of the "god-in-the-car") that his unawareness of this humble "object" (for so he refers to it, just as Alice called Time "it," and was rebuked) this powerful and put-upon group of molecules, individually and in every way as good as *him* (as "he" calls "himself" — for he calls himself a "self") abjectly offering itself (we still have to use "it" in describing this painful scene, for otherwise, owing to the degraded verbal conservatism of man, we should not be understood) in its primeval innocence, to his hind-quarters, that his air of taking-for-granted all this persistent, unobtrusive support — not to mention the thoughtful domestic touch exhibited in the tactful, yielding, springs, is on a par with his other inconsiderateness, and all the long toll of his "unimaginative" life. The treatment of his chair (this colony of entelechies, as Leibniz would describe it) — the way he sits brutally upon it, kicks it and pushes it, never asks it if it is tired or bored, or would like a chair to sit in itself, is on a par with his treatment of black races, and his own servants, relatives and friends. Man is incorrigibly brutal is the reflection that must come to the philosopher as he watches a man sitting upon his chair.

Against these philosophic tendencies, then, we raise ourselves. We demand that these worlds should remain "distinct." We wish to force apart the agglutinating, or interpenetrating, subject and object, or object and object; just as, whether Time is the mind or soul of Space, as Alexander tells us that it is, or not, we do not wish to see it sink into Space entirely, like a ferment, and fill our object-world with an unrelieved temporal instability and unrest. Further, in the life of everyday we draw boldly an impassable line between Black and White, the Negro and ourselves, yes, even that: between all that is not us, and us. We do not want a *grey* mixture. We *like* strong Whites and Blacks: we like blacks, and, strangely enough, whites, too. We — in marked but unavoidable contrast to all fashionable philosophic doctrine — want *distinctness* in everything. If the "individual" is indeed the "real," as well; then we do not see how you are going to achieve that reality if you mix and mix and still further mix: although it is difficult to believe that the uniformity rapidly spreading all over the world in response to the spirit of industrial technique, and the standardizing of life, can be held up by any purely intellectual force. Ours is not, however, a purely intellectual force. Although we do not talk so much about it as Bergson, it too is rather an intuitional, a life-force, than one of pure intelligence. Indeed, the "intellectuality" of the bergsonian anti-intellectualism, is patent: it is the intellect selling itself to sensation, and corrupting even the most sensational of things with its own corruption. We, on the other hand, if anything, affect to be much more "intellectualist" than we are; for the upholding of the intellect at all costs we know to be essential to our life.

How should we apply the pragmatical test of our pragmatist opponents to the einsteinian physics of events? We should go about it as follows. We should say: "Is this theory anything more than a hypothetic formula to account for this phenomenon as that of the empirical reality, a working technique for elucidating a mechanism? Is a metaphysic implicit in this particular theory of movement — is it really a *doctrine* of movement, and is a wider doctrine implied in it, to be taken along with it, calculated to affect our view on every object of experience? If so, our answer is this. On reflection we find that we want the wind to blow once more in between the objects of our world, to feel it upon our faces, and remark it flapping, distinctly and chillily, our clothes: we wish to feel ourselves *separated* from other things and people (not, except at certain moments, penetrating, amalgamating, clinging and sticking) by fresh air, by some indifferent medium. The Earth, we say, is a *dead* paradise. We are *alive*; and we are in a dead paradise of *things*. And that is how we want it to be.

If there were no *place* for the Son of Man to lay his head, there would be no Son of Man. Is life good? Answer, optimists! — Yes! Very well: then it is good because it is composed of *dead things*. Is this paradise, this breathing-space, precarious, unnecessary, artificial, accidental, unreal? Yes, or so it seems. But you have not long to live and enjoy it: so its unreality is not a reason for committing suicide. Oh what a lucky accident! you should exclaim as you survey the fairly immobile objects around you. And the great *use* of the popularisation of Einstein — which we are told is shortly to be taught to little children as part of their education — the very practical advantage — and the only advantage — should be to show people what a lucky escape they have had from chaos — it is true, not without some effort and mental manipulation at the start. If there is some religious advantage again, to be found in Relativity, it must be that it would constantly move people to lift up their hearts in prayer, and thank God for his infinite mercy in not having them born in the midst of the primitive, mercurial chaos, [of] the picture of which Einstein and his followers make us a present. And at the same time all people separately and together should offer up an earnest prayer, morning and night, that, in some weakminded imitative frenzy, the mass-mind should not precipitate itself backwards, and that people should not begin to try to imagine (as they will certainly be told by their thousands of little, earnest, horn-rimmed-spectacled, cross, superior and fanatical teachers to do) that the houses across the way are really restlessly moving about like frightened and fidgetty men; that the express train, par contre, is *really* standing still: and obsessed with such exercises of the "imagination" (as it will be emphatically called in order to encourage the little acrobats) really end where Saint Vitus long ago began. If that is really the mercurial ocean in the midst of which, on our volcanic island of "matter," we live; if that is what is around or under us, let us take advantage of our stroke of luck. Do not let us, for the beaux yeux of any predicating, scientific prophet, make ourselves into fishes for *that* laver. That would be the first result of the application of the pragmatical test to Relativity and other widely-advertised super-doctrines of movement and of flux.

There is nothing in the world as firm or "real" then, as what we believe the ground under our feet to be, as solid as we suppose a lead-pencil to be, or in short as "real" as any of our beliefs, except our self: and it is the reality of that, entirely, which provides us with all this array of convictions, assumptions and beliefs. Immaterial itself, all the concreteness, the "spatialising," comes from it. When, however, we get up after having been ill in bed for some time, the very sensation of firmness again beneath our feet appears highly unreal, and unconcrete, for a time. This "concreteness," at normal times, is the result of the push and resistance in our muscles, which sensation in ourselves we bestow upon the ground beneath. If you imagine, for a moment, that you had never *touched* anything in your life, and then that an elephant appeared before you for the first time, that great and solid animal would seem a phantom: and indeed, without first the experience of touch, or secondly with all things met with only once, no sensation of "concreteness" would ever occur, or rather become organised at all. So the "reality," derived from our sensation of solidity in the external world, is built on very sandy and uncertain ground. But the "real" world of common-sense is nevertheless the most "real" available to us, because it is the world of our ego. It, and not the image-world of our dreams and hallucinations, is the *self's-world*, opposite as that may seem at first to the truth. It is the world of our *personality*, which is bound up with, and is dependent on, that "concreteness." It is *that* world that we personally make — the external world — much more than those other worlds of our automatic fancy.

The obvious criticism of Berkeley would be in connection with the interpretation of his term "real": for its mere use by him presupposes, on his part, a much harder and more absolute notion of "reality" than bears any examination at all. It is such a *very* common-sense "reality" that he evidently has in his mind that it is difficult to deal with his reaction against it at all. He uses "real" too much as though we knew what we meant, or could know, possibly, what we meant, by that. There was such a thing as the real, he said. But what we thought was "real" was a degraded shadow of the "real," a mere appearance. For this conception an absolute was essential to *stand for* the term "real." Without Berkeley's God his system was pointless. But, with it, it still is infected with the limitation of our senses, our knowledge, and the vagueness of the words we use to convey their sense. This is proved by his own description of our world. For his sign-world, although dimmed down, and devitalized, was still, except for the certain languor and dimness (which, in any case, was quite unnecessary, and only the result of his dramatic desire to take the stuffing out of it for his own purposes), exactly the same as our common, generally perceived, world of common sense. Everything happened in it just the same as it happens in ours. It was merely the *meaning* he gave to it that differed. He said it was *not* real: common sense says it *is* real. But it was all the time just the same world, differently interpreted. It was no more different than a tea-cup would be looked at by Berkeley and by Dr. Johnson, respectively: the one, the good bishop, saying: "that tea-cup that you and I see, is *not real*": the other, the doctor, saying "Sir, that tea-cup is perfectly 'real.' " It resolved itself into a question of standards of reality only: or at the most of the technique of the construction of our images.

In sum, our only criticism, or symbol, of reality, is the physical, and that it must remain. But it is the reality that makes it physical, as it were; and it is not the physical, but our immaterial ego, that is responsible for the "real" at all. So however much we think we are identifying "real" and "physical-concrete," it is a manifest delusion due to the mode of our receptivity. We can see this best by reflecting on *when* the external world is most "real" to us: and we at once recognise that it is most unreal at those moments when it is otherwise most real. For instance, when our vitality is low and discouraged, the world is "flat, stale and unprofitable": and in that sense not very "real." On the other hand it is then quite concrete, even more so, perhaps; like a mass of dough. When, on the other hand, we are in a state of extreme elation — supposing we have just won a motor-race, or received a medal, and a great deal of congratulation, for saving a drowning woman's life — then we are said "to walk on air." Nothing at such moments, of otherwise supreme "reality," is quite so *solid* as normally it is. So it is not a question really of the absolute concreteness and solidity of the external world that constitutes "the real." Our truest "real" lies somewhere between these two extremes of ecstasy and matter of fact (or *matter*). But our type of "real" is more in the latter extremity than the former, though it is not because it is more "real" in any very vivid or sensational sense. We should, we claim, *will* the concrete and the solid; not will it away, as the tendency of the doctrines we have been examining is to do. And it is not so much a question that the criticism directed against the concrete-objective-real is wrong, as that the *other* real offered to us, that of science, that is that of *movement*, is not "real" either; but is, as we insist, far less real from any point of view. The concrete or physical is not a *degradation* of some intense, "creative" condition, but is simply one way of apprehending reality. There is no other way, if you are consistent and entirely rational in your pursuit of the opposite "cosmic" course, except death.

So the reality of the spatialising faculty is not *dead*, because it is not *itself at all* that is there, but *us*; and we are never so much ourselves as when we most firmly possess the external material, spatialised reality. If Individuality is the very essence of Reality, as Bradley thinks, it is then, in the interplay of the so-called "dead" objective not-self, and of our self, these *opposites*, that we are most real; and there is in that the maximum of reality for us. So even the moment of extreme elation is less real, because in each moment of transport we are *less ourself*: we begin already *to merge* a little too much in such feverish moments.

EXPLANATORY NOTES

The following notes are keyed by catchwords to the text. Where the editor has been unable to identify a quotation, there is no note. A certain amount of general knowledge has been assumed, but some readers will find some of the notes superfluous.

page

xiii   **Sacco and Vanzetti:** Nicola Sacco and Bartolomeo Vanzetti, two anarchists, were executed in the U.S. in 1927 for the murder of a guard and paymaster at a factory in South Braintree, Massachusetts, in 1920. Considerable doubt surrounded the case, and they were generally felt to have been executed for political reasons.

xiv   **Chigi Palace:** Villa Farnesina in Rome, built for Agostino Chigi (1465–1520). Lewis's reference is presumably to the speeches of Benito Mussolini, the Fascist dictator of Italy.

        Bonnot: Jules Bonnot (1876–1912), the leader of a particularly violent band of anarchists who carried out bank robberies in France.

        Miss Stein writes: See note to page 55.

xv   **"mind of space":** See note to page 149.

1   **"It is in literature . . .":** A. N. Whitehead (1861–1947), *Science and the Modern World* (Cambridge: Cambridge University Press, 1926), p 106. Lewis's annotated copy of the March 1926 printing (a reset edition that appears to be something of a bibliographical rarity) is at Texas; where Lewis gives page references to *Science and the Modern World*, it is to this reprint that he refers. All references in these notes are to the first edition, however. See Afterword, pages 469–72, for a discussion of Whitehead's ideas.

3   **John Bright:** (1811–1889) British liberal politician. The conference was held in Edinburgh, 13 September 1853. G. B. Smith, *The Life and Speeches of the Right Honourable John Bright, M.P.* (London: Hodder and Stoughton, 1882), Vol. I, p. 210.

4   **Fourier:** Charles Fourier (1772–1837), French utopian socialist thinker. The passage quoted is on p. 331 of *The Art of Being Ruled.* The quotation from Fourier is a translation of a variant of Fourier's *Théorie des quatres mouvements et des destinées générales* (3rd ed.), *Oeuvres Complètes* (1846, rpt. Paris: Editions Anthropos, 1966), Vol. I, p. 274.

6   ***The Spirit of Romance:*** *The Spirit of Romance: An Attempt to Define Somewhat the Charm of the Pre-Renaissance Literature of Latin Europe* (London: J. M. Dent, n.d. [1910]).

        "There is one sense . . .": Ibid., p. 1. Lewis is paraphrasing.

        "When England had . . .": Ibid., p. 5.

        It is dawn at Jerusalem: Ibid., p. vi.

567

7   **The application of the "homology" principle:** Oswald Spengler, *The Decline of the West: Form and Actuality*, tr. C. F. Atkinson (London: G. Allen and Unwin, [1926]), p. 112. Lewis's annotated copy is at Texas.

8   **Bergsonian durée:** Time conceived as a continuum rather than (as it appears to the intellect) divisible into standard units. See Lewis's discussion on pages 411–13.

        an imperfect belief in their existence: Compare Ker-Orr, narrator of Lewis's *Wild Body* stories: "I admit that I am disposed to forget that people are real . . ." (*The Complete Wild Body*, p. 17).

9   **the Unities:** Neoclassical rules of dramatic construction deriving from Aristotle. Racine observed them; Shakespeare generally ignored them.

10   *Literature and Dogma:* (London: Macmillan, 1903), p. 30 (Section 3 of Chapter I).

11   **jamesian psychology . . . couéism:** William James's *Principles of Psychology* is discussed on pages 337–40. E. Coué (1857–1926) founded "Couéism," a form of auto-suggestion employing the expression "Every day in every way, I am getting better and better."

        pragmatical test: "Test every concept by the question 'What sensible difference to anybody will its truth make!' and you are in the best possible position for understanding what it means and for discussing its importance." William James, *Some Problems of Philosophy: A Beginning of an Introduction to Philosophy* (London: Longmans, Green, 1911), p. 60.

12   **Professor Alexander:** Samuel Alexander (1859–1938) was professor of philosophy at the University of Manchester. A brief outline of his views is given in the Afterword, pages 472–74.

14   **"ancient order of the aryan world":** "Civilization is nothing more than a name for the old order of the Aryan world, dissolved, but perpetually reconstituting itself under a vast variety of solvent influences, of which infinitely the most powerful have been those which have slowly . . . substituted 'several property' for collective ownership." Sir Henry Sumner Maine (1822–1897), *The Effects of Observation of India upon Modern Thought: The Rede Lecture Delivered in the Senate House, Cambridge, 22nd May, 1875* (Calcutta: Thacker, Spink and Co., 1875), pp. 20–21.

16   **Pater:** Walter Pater (1839–1894), author of *Studies in the History of the Renaissance* (1873), the Conclusion of which, with its exaltation of aesthetic pleasure, was taken by some as support for a cult of "Greek Love."

17   **the genevan Bible:** The Geneva Bible of 1560 was an English translation accompanied by anti-Catholic, Calvinist glosses, produced by Protestant exiles in Geneva. It had run to about 140 editions by 1644.

18   **Bunthorne poet:** Gilbert and Sullivan's opera *Patience* (1881) made fun of the "aesthetic" movement, and caricatured Oscar Wilde in the character Bunthorne.

20   **superman, or super-Dreadnought:** Nietzsche's *Übermensch* and a type of battleship, respectively.

21   **what Nietzsche called the dionysiac:** In *The Birth of Tragedy*; see note to page 284.

26   **fourierist fancy:** Fourier's utopianism was based on a concept of an absolute cosmic order.

27   **Tories:** Members or supporters of the Conservative Party.

28   **mammock a butterfly:** See Shakespeare's *Coriolanus*, Act I, Scene 3, and Lewis's comments in *The Lion and the Fox*, p. 238.

theophrastian booby: Theophrastus (4th century BC) wrote a set of sketches (*Characters*) portraying disagreeable aspects of the human character. It appears from a leaf of typescript at Buffalo (B14 F15) that Lewis thought of citing the "socialist" Oliver Baldwin, son of the conservative Prime Minister. An article in the *Daily Express* (4 November 1926) describes his attempt at "practical socialism": living off an income provided by his father and running a chicken farm with his partner, "a typical public [i.e. private] school man."

"carried towards the East": Lewis reverses the directions of John Donne's "Good Friday, 1613. Riding Westward."

30   **the Black Man sees one tree:** Compare William Blake, *The Marriage of Heaven and Hell*: "A fool sees not the same tree that a wise man sees."

31   **If it be necessary:** Jonathan Swift (attr.), "A Letter of Advice to a Young Poet" (1721), *Prose Works*, ed. Davis: *Irish Tracts 1720-1723 and Sermons* (Oxford: Basil Blackwell, 1948), p. 333.

Ballet created by Diaghileff: A company run by Serge Diaghilev (1872-1929), that had tremendous influence in Europe before the First World War, especially with the *Rite of Spring* (1913). Diaghilev employed many advanced painters and composers, but his 1917 *Parade* (music by Satie, design by Picasso) has been seen by some as showing the decadence of an originally innovative cultural force.

Les Précieuses Ridicules, **or** *Le Misanthrope*: Satirical plays by Molière.

as Benda also immediately noticed: In *Belphégor*. See page 274 and note.

32   **Ritzes and Rivieras:** Compare *The Apes of God* rpt. (Santa Barbara: Black Sparrow, 1981), p. 262.

Gentlemen Prefer Blondes: Novel by Anita Loos. See pages 53-54.

33   **Petroushka:** Ballet from 1911.

34   **"culture" gospel of Arnold:** In, for example, *Culture and Anarchy* (1867).

Symons: Oscar Wilde (1854-1900), Aubrey Beardsley (1872-1898) and Arthur Symons (1865-1945).

the Yellow Book: 1894-1897. A quarterly edited by Henry Harland, it was a famous "decadent" production, reproducing drawings by Aubrey Beardsley.

The Fascist Revolution: Of 1922, in Italy.

axes of the lictors: Axes tied up with other rods, to signify the strength of collective unity.

futurism: Art movement launched in 1909 by F. T. Marinetti (1876-1944). The Vorticist movement of Wyndham Lewis launched in 1914 was influenced by, but strongly critical of, it.

35   **the primitive Matriarchate:** See the discussion of M. and M. Vaerting's *The Dominant Sex* in *The Art of Being Ruled*, Part VII, Chapter 10.

37   **death, under tragic circumstances:** Ernest Walsh (1895-1926), who edited *This Quarter*, died in Monte Carlo on 16 October from tuberculosis.

an old associate of mine, Ezra Pound: Pound was an early and consistently enthusiastic public supporter of Lewis both as a writer and painter. The two men were closely associated in the Vorticist movement, which was named by Pound.

Mr. Hueffer . . . Edward Fitzgerald: The novelist Ford Madox Ford, who changed his surname from Hueffer, had a great influence on Pound's critical ideas. His grandfather, Ford Madox Brown, was associated with the Pre-Raphaelites, whom Pound admired. Pound also admired Edward FitzGerald's *Rubáiyát of Omar Khayyám*.

Blast: The Vorticists' magazine; edited by Lewis.

38   **Royal Academy tradition:** *Creatures of Habit and Creatures of Change* reprints several of Lewis's attacks on this institution, intended to be the guardian of academic tradition in painting. According to Lewis it had no interest in this role, but was dedicated to making money for its members out of inferior art.

Chinese Crackers: The reference is to Pound's interest in Chinese poetry.

39   **He was taking to music:** Pound had left London for Paris in 1921. During the early twenties he composed an opera, *Le Testament*, with the assistance of his and Lewis's friend Agnes Bedford.

M. Paul Valéry: See page 179.

"sense of the Past": The phrase is Henry James's. The concept of tradition, and the "presence" of the past is important in the aesthetics of Pound and T. S. Eliot.

Antheil: George Antheil (1900–1959). Avant-garde U.S. composer living in Paris in the twenties. Pound befriended him and publicized his work.

40   *romance sans paroles:* Alluding to *Romances sans paroles*, poems by Paul Verlaine.

"Lips, cheeks . . .": "Eyes, dreams, lips, and the night goes." Ezra Pound, "Cino."

"It is possible . . .": "Vision of a Musical Factory" (an interview with Pound), *Christian Science Monitor* (21 August 1926), p. 8.

41   **Villon:** The subject of Pound's opera is the life of the French poet François Villon.

the *Q. Review*: *This Quarter*. The first number (1925) was dedicated to Pound, and announced that Lewis would contribute to future issues (p. 265).

42   **"Tradition is an unimportant fact . . .":** This cento of quotations is derived from the first two pages of Ernest Walsh's Editorial in *This Quarter*, Vol. 1, No. 2 (Autumn/Winter 1925–26), pp. 283–84.

43   **The protestant pastor:** Ethel Moorhead, "Incendiaries," ibid., pp. 243 and 247.

"I'll be American and try anything . . .": Robert McAlmon, "Transcontinental," ibid., pp. 131 and 132.

Bud Macsalmon: Robert McAlmon (1896–1956). See Afterword pages 484–87 for his relations with Lewis.

I can't wait: Ernest Walsh, "A New Book by Robert McAlmon," *This Quarter*, Vol. I, No. 2, p. 331 (name changed by Lewis, and Walsh's "writes," at the end of the passage, primitivized to "write").

44   **"the school that writes by instinct":** Ibid., p. 334.

Before we started: Ring W. Lardner (1885–1933), "The Golden Honeymoon," *Round Up: The Stories of Ring W. Lardner* (1924) rpt.

(London: Williams and Norgate, 1935); 1st paragraph, p. 232; 2nd paragraph p. 233.

45   **He never told me his thoughts:** Ernest Walsh, "A Young Living Genius" (review of Emanuel Carnevali's *A Hurried Man*), *This Quarter*, Vol. I, No. 2, p. 326 (Lewis's italics).

     The Hasty Bunch: McAlmon's first book of stories (1921). The title (properly *A Hasty Bunch*) was suggested by James Joyce.

     I received from a friend: Final verse of E. Carnevali, "A Girl—D," *This Quarter*, Vol. I, No. 2. (Autumn/Winter 1925-26), p. 23.

46   **Hemingway is the shyest and proudest:** Ernest Walsh, "Mr. Hemingway's Prose" (review of *In Our Time*), ibid., p. 321.

     The genius of: Ibid., p. 320.

     Mencken: H. L. Mencken (1880–1956) was well known for his satire of provincialism and stupidity.

47   **Minkowski:** H. Minkowski (1880–1956) showed how Einstein's theory of special relativity necessitated the fusion of space and time, with time treated as a fourth dimension of space.

     "In the beginning there was the time . . .": Gertrude Stein, *Composition as Explanation* (London: The Hogarth Press, 1926), p. 29.

     "The time of the composition . . .": Ibid., p. 28.

48   **Relativity . . . has:** See note to page 84.

49   **sting Miss Stein into a rejoinder:** They did not; and Gertrude Stein treated Lewis kindly (though briefly) in *The Autobiography of Alice B. Toklas* (1933).

50   **Mr. Joyce even has caught it:** Lewis is referring to the sections of *Finnegans Wake* that had begun to appear during the early twenties under the title *Work in Progress*.

51   **analysed by me elsewhere:** In *The Art of Being Ruled*, especially Part VI.

53   **Melanctha Herbert had not:** Gertrude Stein, *Three Lives: Stories of the Good Anna, Melanctha and the Gentle Lena* (London: John Lane, The Bodley Head, 1920), p. 89.

     There is singularly nothing: *Composition as Explanation*, p. 5.

54   **Paris is devine:** Anita Loos, *"Gentlemen Prefer Blondes": The Illuminating Diary of a Professional Lady* (London: Brentano's, n.d. [1926]), p. 93.

     If you hear her snore: This is not a complete poem, but a part of the first section ("A History of Giving Bundles") of "Bundles for them," *The Little Review* (Spring 1923), p. 8. Lewis had previously quoted the passage in his discussion of Stein and Joyce in *The Art of Being Ruled*, p. 347.

     So while we: *"Gentlemen Prefer Blondes,"* p. 122.

     In my beginning: *Composition as Explanation*, p. 28.

55   **There must be *time*:** Ibid., p. 30.

     "In this way at present . . .": Ibid.

     Dear Miss Gillespie: "Some Like them Cold," *Round Up*, p. 357.

56   **the *Young Visiters*** : A bestseller by a nine-year-old, Daisy Ashford, first published in 1919 and frequently reprinted ever since. It is briefly discussed in *The Caliph's Design* (p. 53).

In beginning writing: *Composition as Explanation*, pp. 16–17 and 18–19.

57   **a sort of Epstein in words**: Sir Jacob Epstein (1880–1959) was a sculptor associated with the Vorticists who turned to more naturalistic work in bronze after the First World War. Lewis admired his work.

Arlen and Huxley: Michael Arlen (Dikran Kuyumjian, 1895–1956), author of the bestseller, *The Green Hat* (1924), and Aldous Huxley (1894–1963), author of *Crome Yellow* and *Antic Hay* (1921 and 1923). The aspect of Proust Lewis has in mind is indicated by a discussion in *The Apes of God*, where Zagreus calls him "the high-priest of Gossip" (p. 265). Arlen and Huxley based their characters on the famous.

60   **Sir James Barrie**: (1860–1937), the author of *Peter Pan* (1904).

Her latest book: *The Making of Americans* (1926).

Patience sitting on: "And with a green and yellow melancholy, / She sat like patience on a monument, / Smiling at grief." William Shakespeare, *Twelfth Night*, II, iv.

61   **Picasso's pneumatic giantesses**: The large, "classical" female figures often found in Picasso's work of the early twenties.

Romance: A collaboration of 1903.

In *The Caliph's Design*: See *The Caliph's Design*, pp. 108 and 120–21. *Nature-morte* (dead nature) is the French term for still life.

62   **fashion for child-art**: See ibid., "Child Art and the Naïf," pp. 51–55.

64   **the heroes of Ossian**: The Celtic epic poet "translated" (that is, largely fabricated) by James MacPherson (1736–1796) and published in the 1760s. Lewis quotes from Matthew Arnold's epigraph to *The Study of Celtic Literature*: "They went forth to the war, but they always fell," which slightly adapts Duan II of "Ossian's" "Cath-Loda."

The Keystone giants: Keystone Kops — authority-figures frequently outwitted by Chaplin in his early films.

the small man: Part III, and Chapter 1 of Part IV of *The Art of Being Ruled* are devoted to an analysis of the "small man."

It is Pippa: "God's in his Heaven— / All's right with the world!" Robert Browning, *Pippa Passes*.

65   **Drake against the Armada**: Sir Francis Drake (1540?–1596). English naval hero, especially famous for finishing a game of bowls before going out to engage the vastly superior force of the invading Spanish Armada.

I think it is an age: Lewis is quoting himself; a version of the poem is at Cornell: "I [think *del.*] this is an age for eunuchs, said an intelligent flea / But I will see. / I'm sure at all events it's a good age for the tiniest thing, / As I am, on foot or wing." (Stanza 2).

67   **Sophocles to Cavalcanti**: Pound published no translations of Sophocles until 1956 (*Women of Trachis*); his translation of Guido Cavalcanti's *Sonnets and Ballate* appeared in 1912.

68   **"museum official"**: See Pound's poem "Pagani's, November 8."

a Propertius or an Arnaut Daniel: Latin and Provençal poets imitated and translated by Pound, the first in "Homage to Sextus Propertius" (1917), the second in *Instigations* (1920).

69 **the *Seafarer***: Anglo-Saxon poem; Pound's translation appeared in *Ripostes* (1912).

70 **Cave of Nerea**: "Canto XVII," *This Quarter*, Vol. I, No. 2, p. 5.

71 **Now supine**: Ibid., p. 7.

Cantos XVIII–XIX: Actually Cantos XVII– XIX.

And the answer: "Canto XIX," ibid., p. 13.

73 **about six or seven years ago**: *A Portrait of the Artist as a Young Man* was serialized in *The Egoist* immediately before Lewis's novel, *Tarr*, beginning in 1914.

"among the english poets": Keats's famous phrase, expressing his aspiration for a place in what is now called "the canon" after his death. *Chamber Music* dates from 1907.

74 **not a homologue of Swift**: These comparisons with Swift and Flaubert were made by Pound in "James Joyce et Pécuchet," *Mercure de France*, Vol. CLVI, No. 575 (1 June 1922) rpt. Forrest Read, ed., *Pound/Joyce: The Letters of Ezra Pound to James Joyce, with Pound's Essays on Joyce* (New York: New Directions, 1970), pp. 200–11. For the importance of Pound's view of *Ulysses* in this chapter, see Paul Edwards, " 'Clodoveo' and 'Belcanto,' " *Blast 3*, ed. Seamus Cooney (Santa Barbara: Black Sparrow Press, 1984), pp. 126–33. *Terribilità* (awesome power) is traditionally attributed to the work of Michelangelo.

the "sedulous ape": "I have thus played the sedulous ape to Hazlitt, to Lamb, to Wordsworth, to Sir Thomas Browne, to Defoe, to Hawthorne, to Montaigne, to Baudelaire and to Obermann," Robert Louis Stevenson (1850–1896), *Memories and Portraits*, Chapter 4.

75 ***The Dead***: "The Dead" is the final story in Joyce's *Dubliners* (1914).

Mister-this and Mister-that: Lewis enlarges on these personal remarks in *Blasting and Bombardiering*, Chapter 7.

76 **the Rebellion**: The "Easter Rising" of 1916 against British rule.

"My ancestors threw . . .": James Joyce, *A Portrait of the Artist as a Young Man* (London: Jonathan Cape, 1924), p. 231.

"You talk to me . . .": Ibid.

78 **A thousand naked women**: George Borrow (1803–1881), *The Bible in Spain* (1843, rpt. London: Constable, 1923), Vol. II, p. 297.

79 **the syndicalist doctrine**: Lewis discusses this doctrine in *The Art of Being Ruled*, Part I, Chapter 4.

William Blake foresaw that development: Blake held that in the highest level of existence (Eden), sexual differentiation will be overcome.

Modesty among primitive people: David Corbett suggests Lewis is referring to "The Evolution of Modesty," *Studies in the Psychology of Sex* (Philadelphia: F. A. Davies, 1910), Vol. I.

81 **doctrinally . . . the material of the Past**: *Ulysses* depicts a single day in Dublin, 1904.

82   **a broomstick on the Brocken**: A Mountain in the Hartz range famous for its "spectre"; Goethe set the Witches' Sabbath in his *Faust* on the Brocken.

83   **"mental climate"**: See note to page 259.

        politics would be goethean: Lewis frequently praises Goethe's universalism; for example, *Paleface*, p. 67.

84   **Péguy**: Charles Péguy (1873–1914). Poet and editor of *Cahiers de la quinzaine*. See *The Art of Being Ruled*, Part XII, Chapter 1.

        enthusiastic reception given by Bergson: Bergson's 1922 *Durée et simultanéité* contains his discussion of Einstein.

        "Emergent" principle of Lloyd Morgan: Lloyd Morgan's Gifford Lectures, *Emergent Evolution*, were published in 1923. He was in some respects critical of Bergson's unscientific approach.

        "Creative Evolution": The subject of Bergson's book of that name, first published in 1907.

85   **as Napoleon called it**: See the *Oxford English Dictionary*, under "Ideology," 2.

87   **notion of periodicity**: Lewis refers to Joyce's use of Vico's cyclical model of history (a major structural element of *Finnegans Wake*).

89   **moeotic**: This word is in no English dictionary, but is carefully spelled out thus in the manuscript. It may relate to the rhetorical term "meiosis" (a form of understatement), but Lewis hardly seems to be charging Joyce with understatement. Richard Ellmann in his biography of Joyce silently alters it to "noetic" (pertaining to the intellect), which is possibly what Lewis intended.

        that at least is the idea: The example is Lewis's invention, however.

92   **motif of the house-drain**: Bloom defecates in the outside lavatory of his house at the end of the fourth chapter of *Ulysses*.

        the reply of Antigonus: Antigonus (d. 301 BC) was a general of Alexander the Great. His response to Hermodorus's flattery was to ask the poet to find out from his (Antigonus's) servants whether it was justified. Lewis means that it is foolish to be scandalized by Bloom's doing what everyone does.

        Lady Bolingbroke's remark about Pope: This and the following phrases quoted concerning Alexander Pope come from Samuel Johnson's *Life of Pope* in his *Lives of the English Poets*.

        When Joyce was about twenty: The same story is garbled in conversation in *The Apes of God*, p. 281.

93   **Mr. Shaw has affirmed**: "Every man over forty is a scoundrel." One of George Bernard Shaw's "Maxims for Revolutionists" in *Man and Superman* (1903).

94   *John Bull's Other Island*: Play by Shaw (1907).

        "pale eyes like the ocean . . .": "Eyes, pale as the sea. . . . the seas' ruler," *Ulysses* (New York: Vintage Books, 1966), p. 18. Just over 400 pages of Lewis's slightly annotated copy of *Ulysses* (Paris: the 2nd, 3rd or 7th issue) are at Texas.

        "the cracked looking-glass": "— It is a symbol of Irish art. The cracked lookingglass of a servant." Ibid., p. 6.

95 **Stephen Dedalus stepped**: Ibid., p. 3 (Lewis's italics).

96 **". . . Tell me, Mulligan"**: Ibid., p. 4. Lewis annotated his copy of *Ulysses* on p. 129 (134 in the edition cited in these notes) against "J. J. O'Molloy said in quiet mockery," observing that if a character in the novel speaks quietly, he is intended by Joyce to be "sympathetic."

 "the real Oxford manner": Ibid., p. 4.

 "Stephen *suffered* him . . .": Ibid. (Lewis's italics).

 Mulligan "turned abruptly . . .": Ibid., p. 5 (Lewis's italics).

 "He [Haines] thinks . . .": Ibid., p. 4.

 " 'Then what is it?' . . .": Ibid., p. 7.

 "We oughtn't to laugh . . .": Ibid., p. 19.

99 **he is more feminine**: "DR. DIXON: . . . Professor Bloom is a finished example of the new womanly man" (ibid., p. 493); "BLOOM: O, I so want to be a mother" (ibid., p. 494).

 computing with glee: "How much would that tot to off the porter in the month?" Ibid., p. 58.

101 **that is Joyce**: Lewis's annotations on pp. 151–52 of his copy (ed. cit., 158–59) show him attempting to sort out Joyce's narrative practice, with its shifting boundary between omniscient third-person narration, free indirect narration and direct "first-person" presentation of stream of consciousness. On p. 158, "Flakes of pastry on the gusset of her dress," he questions whether Bloom or the author uses "gusset," and whether Bloom would know the word.

 All the rest is literature: "Et tout le reste est littérature," Paul Verlaine, "Jadis et Naguère." *Literature and Dogma* is the title of one of Matthew Arnold's books.

102 **Goya-like fantasia**: The 15th chapter of *Ulysses*, known as "Circe."

 the *Tentation*: Gustave Flaubert, *La Tentation de Saint Antoine* (1874).

 homeric framework: The events and characters of *Ulysses* are modern "equivalents" of those in the *Odyssey* of Homer.

 . . . the repetition [used by Miss Stein]: *The Art of Being Ruled*, pp. 346–48, with omissions following the second paragraph.

103 **"Provost's house. . . ."**: The first paragraph is from *Ulysses*, pp. 164–65; the second from p. 179.

 "Rather short in the waist . . .": The first paragraph is from *The Posthumous Papers of the Pickwick Club* (1836–37, rpt. Harmondsworth: Penguin, 1975), p. 86; the second from p. 163.

 Urquhart's translations: Sir Thomas Urquhart (1611–1660) translated the first three books of Rabelais's *Gargantua and Pantagruel*.

104 **There was a herring**: Thomas Nashe (1567?–1601), *Nashe's Lenten Stuff* (1599), rpt. in *The Unfortunate Traveller and Other Works*, ed. J. B. Steane (Harmondsworth: Penguin, 1972), pp. 446–47.

 The posterior Italian: Ibid., p. 403.

105 **Shem is as short**: "Extract from Work in Progress," *This Quarter*, Vol. I, No. 2, p. 108. Revised version printed in *Finnegans Wake*, p. 169.

 . . . a ladies tryon hosiery: *This Quarter*, pp. 114–15. Revised in *Finnegans Wake*, pp. 179–80.

he is not writing about himself: He is.

106   **Every morning, therefore**: *A Portrait of the Artist as a Young Man*, p. 67 (Lewis's italics).

107   **scene on the seashore**: The conclusion of Chapter 4.

The Enemy of the Stars : Published in *Blast*, No. 1. Lewis marked p. 209 of his copy of *Ulysses* (ed. cit., pp. 217–18) as being a mixture of *Enemy of the Stars* and Yeats (presumably "Aengus of the Birds"). "Day. Wheelbarrow sun over arch of bridge" is reminiscent of Lewis's "play," but one would have expected Lewis to have singled out the "Circe" chapter, which resembles his work in its simultaneous use, and transcendence, of the conventions of textual presentation of drama.

"What are they always rooting . . .": "theyre all mad to get in there where they come out of youd think they could never get far enough up," *Ulysses*, p. 760.

108   **the jessamine and geraniums**: Ibid., pp. 782–83.

He comes again: "A Saint in Seven," *Composition as Explanation*, p. 44.

Stephanos Dedalos: *A Portrait of the Artist as a Young Man*, p. 192.

110   **Nietzsche and then Bergson**: Nietzsche preached in *Thus Spake Zarathustra* that man is something to be "overcome" and replaced by the "superman," while Bergson, in *Creative Evolution*, suggests that man might develop powers that will enable him to overcome death itself. See also *The Art of Being Ruled*, p. 24.

112   *Matière et Mémoire* : By Henri Bergson; published in 1896.

114   **"greatest happiness of the greatest number"** : Jeremy Bentham's standard for judging the morality of any act.

I might defend: The passage is in the fourth paragraph of *Areopagitica*.

117   **an essay by Mr. Haldane**: *Callinicus: A Defence of Chemical Warfare* (London: Kegan Paul, Trench, Trubner, 1925).

119   **Modern industry**: Quoted from *The Art of Being Ruled*, p. 22.

There are two kinds: Ibid, p. 25.

120   **It is only necessary**: Henri Poincaré, *Science et méthode* (Paris: Flammarion, 1918), p. 9. Annotated fragments of Lewis's 1920 copy are at Texas.

121   **In an attempt to get**: *The Calendar of Modern Letters*, Vol. III, No. 1 (April 1926), rpt. *Creatures of Habit and Creatures of Change: Essays on Art, Literature and Society 1914–1956*, pp. 151–52, with minor variants.

122   **It is quite true**: Sir Henry Sumner Maine, *Popular Government* (1885, rpt. London: John Murray, 1909), p. 145 and (final sentence) p. 146.

123   **the very detailed analysis**: In *The Art of Being Ruled*, Part V, Chapters 3 and 4, and in "The Apes of God" (a draft of *The Apes of God*, Part III), *The Criterion*, Vol. II, No. 7 (April 1924), pp. 300–10.

124   **Trianon existence**: The Trianon is a chateau built by Louis XIV in the park of Versailles. Lewis is evoking the frivolous life of luxury led by the aristocracy before the French Revolution.

Mürger's sub-world of art : The reference is to Henri Mürger's *Scènes de la vie de bohème* (1848). The spuriousness of modern "artistic" bohemias is one of the subjects of Lewis's first novel, *Tarr* (on the first page of which

Mürger is also mentioned), and is the principal subject of *The Apes of God*, which Lewis was composing at the same time as *Time and Western Man*.

William Morris . . . utopist dream: William Morris, *News from Nowhere* (1890). Compare *The Apes of God*, pp. 118–19.

127 *"But I marvel . . ."*: *Leonardo da Vinci's Note-Books*, ed. and tr. Edward McCurdy (London: Duckworth and Co., 1906), pp. 85–86.

"Then overcome . . .": Eunapius, *Lives of the Philosophers and Sophists*, tr. Wright, Loeb Classics Library (London: Heinemann, 1921), pp. 355–57. The passage refers to Porphyry.

"The same taunt . . .": *The Theaetetus of Plato* with translation and notes by B. H. Kennedy (Cambridge: Cambridge University Press, 1881), p. 158. Lewis's 1894 edition is at Texas.

"Con su mano serena . . .": "Canciones del Alma," verse 8: "With his gentle hand / He wounded me in the neck / And suspended all my senses." The poem concerns the stages through which the soul passes in achieving divine union with God. See the note to page 366.

". . . time is the medium . . .": Thomas Mann, *The Magic Mountain* (London: Secker, 1927), Vol. II, p. 683.

130 **The Cynic philosophy**: Edward Caird, *The Evolution of Theology in the Greek Philosophers: The Gifford Lectures delivered in the University of Glasgow in Session 1900–1 and 1901–2* (Glasgow: MacLehose and Sons, 1904), Vol. II, pp. 56–57. Caird describes Antisthenes as a "narrow, passionate soul" in comparison with the "temperate and almost ascetic" Socrates. The Megarians "maintained the exclusive reality of the abstract universal." In this they "became the opposite counterpart of" the Cynics, who "maintained the exclusive reality of the abstract individual" (ibid., p. 70). Compare Lewis's dealings with the problem of the one and the many in Book Two, Part III, Chapter 3.

132 **heraclitean "injustice . . ."**: But Heraclitus considered that the "strife" of opposites was only superficially "unjust": " 'We must know,' he says, 'that war is common to all, and strife is justice, and that all things come into being and pass away through strife.' " B. D. Alexander, *A Short History of Philosophy* (2nd ed., Glasgow: MacLehose and Sons, 1908), p. 31. Lewis's annotated copy is at Texas.

134 **upaniṣadic thought**: Lewis's knowledge of Indian philosophy was extensive. Just over 100 pages of his annotated copy of René Guénon's *Introduction générale à l'étude des doctrines hindoues* (Paris: M. Rivière, 1921) are at Texas. Lewis particularly marked passages in Chapter 5 separating metaphysics from science, evolution and progress. Guénon's exposition was important in encouraging Lewis to reject the notion that metaphysical truth can be approached by the empirical and scientific methods of A. N. Whitehead and Samuel Alexander. Metaphysics, according to Guénon, has no use for scientific or practical discoveries.

alexandrian mystical doctrine: The reference is to the Jewish-Hellenistic philosophy of Philo of Alexandria (25 BC– 40 AD) and his successors. Philo held that God was inaccessible through reason, and, being above thought, was attainable through ecstasy or intuition. Plotinus (*c*.204–*c*.270 AD) (see following note) is generally classified as Alexandrian.

"the flight of the Alone to the Alone" : Plotinus's description of the ecstatic union with God, in which all dualities of subject and object are transcended: "This is the life of gods and of the godlike and happy among men; a quittance from things alien and earthly, a life beyond earthly pleasure, a flight of the alone to the Alone" (*Enneads* 6, 9, 11 [771 b]).

135   **famous imperial ballad** : "Oh East is East, and West is West, and never the twain shall meet," Rudyard Kipling, "The Ballad of East and West."

first and already published part of this essay : "The Revolutionary Simpleton" was first published in the first issue of Lewis's magazine, *The Enemy*, early in 1927.

137   **criticism of the newtonian system** : In his *Philosophical Commentaries* (not published till 1871).

138   **identifying Einstein with Bergson** : Criticisms of this sort were made in a letter to Lewis from J. W. N. Sullivan, a contributor to *The Enemy*, No. 1. Sullivan warned Lewis against taking on Einstein, whose theories were supported by the Michelson–Morley experiments. He pointed out that Lewis's general case did not depend on the supposed falsity of Einstein's theory, and warned him against accounting for that theory by reference to the "time-spirit." This letter may also have encouraged Lewis to be more subtle in distinguishing his own account of the relationship between ideas and their historical setting from that of Spengler, who believes that all thought is a product of the Zeitgeist. Sullivan's letter (23 February 1927) is at Cornell.

"It is not . . . metaphysical concepts . . ." : Lewis summarizes Sullivan's point.

139   **Bosanquet or Benda** : See notes to pages 210 and 274.

Minkowski : See note to page 47.

Sorel : Georges Sorel (1847–1922), French political thinker frequently cited by Lewis (in *The Art of Being Ruled* and *The Lion and the Fox*, for instance). The links between Sorel and Bergson (and Bergson and Marcel Proust) have often been noticed.

***Enchiridion* of More** : Henry More (1614–1687), one of the Cambridge Platonists. His *Enchiridion Metaphysicum* was published in 1671. Newton is supposed to have formulated the main features of his system in the mid-1660s. But Lewis's general point about More's influence stands.

Philipon : Jean Philipon, called by Pierre Duhem (1861–1916) Jean d'Alexandre. His influence is discussed in Duhem's "Nicholas de Cues et Léonard de Vinci," *Études sur Léonard de Vinci: Ceux qu'il a lus et ceux qui l'ont lu*, Première Série (Paris: Librairie Scientifique A. Hermann, 1906).

140   **"We are precluded . . ."** : Alexander Moszkowski, *Einstein the Searcher: His Work Explained from Dialogues with Einstein* (London: Methuen, 1921), p. 88.

It seemed to me : Ibid., p. 89.

141   **rather as Heine regarded Kant** : See the opening of Part Third of Heinrich Heine, *Religion and Philosophy in Germany*, tr. J. Snodgrass (1882, rpt. Boston: Beacon Press, 1959), pp. 107–09.

History does not : *Einstein the Searcher*, pp. 90–91.

deep down : Ibid., pp. 91–92.

142   **Bergson's "intuition"**: An intensive, inward knowledge, as opposed to the extensive knowledge of the intellect: "But it is to the very inwardness of life that *intuition* leads us, — by intuition I mean instinct that has become disinterested, self-conscious, capable of reflecting on its object." Henri Bergson, *Creative Evolution*, tr. Arthur Mitchell (London: Macmillan, 1911), p. 186.

        Duhem's law of reversal: The theory of Pierre Duhem that no "crucial" experiment can prove a scientific theory is discussed and rejected by Moszkowski on pp. 105–07. He believes that the "sum-total of experiments in the realm of spectral analysis" prove Einstein's theory correct.

        "In Newton's theory . . .": Bertrand Russell, *The A.B.C. of Relativity* (London: Kegan Paul, Trench, Trubner, 1926), p. 196. More of the passage is quoted on page 264.

        Sorel gives an analogous account: Georges Sorel, *Les Illusions du progrès* (3rd ed., Paris: Rivière, 1921), pp. 33–34. The subject is discussed on pp. 28–29 of *The Art of Being Ruled*.

145   **"But, let the consequences . . ."**: C. S. Peirce, "The Order of Nature," *Chance, Love and Logic: Philosophical Essays*, ed. Morris L. Cohen (London: Kegan Paul, Trench, Trubner, 1923), pp. 129–30. Lewis's annotated copy of this book is at Texas.

        "Classical man . . .": *The Decline of the West*, p. 392.

        "The pilgrim fathers . . .": *Science and the Modern World*, p. 14.

147   **It is in fact the cardinal defect**: *Space, Time and Deity: The Gifford Lectures at Glasgow 1916–1918* (London: Macmillan, 1920), Vol. I, p. 226 (Lewis's italics).

        Auguste Rodin: Alexander's footnote refers to Rodin's observation that Greek statues secure the impression of repose "by the opposite inclinations of the lines of the shoulders and the hips."

148   *élan vital*: Vital Force; discussed in Bergson's *Creative Evolution*.

        Pujol or Canova: Abel-Alexandre-Denis de Pujol (1787–1861), French painter and sculptor, and Antonio Canova (1757–1822), neo-classicist sculptor.

149   πάντα ῥεῖ: "All things" (Greek); presumably referring to Heraclitus's statement that all things are flowing.

        "make anything of anything": "Your wit is of the true Pierean spring, / That can make anything of anything." George Chapman, *The Conspiracy of Charles, Duke of Byron*, Act II, *George Chapman*, ed. W. L. Phelps (London: Fisher Unwin, 1895), p. 349.

        chap. ii of book ii: Actually Chapter 2 of Book III of *Space, Time and Deity*.

        "mind of Space": "Time is the mind of Space and Space the body of Time," ibid., Vol. II, p. 38.

150   **conshie**: Conscientious objector (derogatory slang for those whose consciences prevented them serving in the armed forces during wartime).

152   **Professor Whitehead's definition**: "The reason why we are on a higher level [than the 19th Century] is not because we have finer imagination, but because we have better instruments. . . . These instruments have put thought onto a new level." *Science and the Modern World*, pp. 161–62.

those employed by Michelson: A. N. Michelson's apparatus for measuring the effect of the "ether wind" on light. This was crucial in the development of Relativity theory, and is discussed by Whitehead on pp. 162–65.

154   **"Whatever I may say . . ."**: William James, *A Pluralistic Universe* (London: Longmans, Green and Co., 1909), pp. 328–29.

als ob **behaviour**: "As if" behavior. Lewis's annotated copy of Hans Vaihinger's *The Philosophy of As If* is at Texas.

Aristotle as the last great: *Science and the Modern World*, p. 242.

alexandrian hellenizers: See note to page 134.

155   **"But all the same it moves!"**: The famous words of Galileo after signing for the church a recantation of his belief that the earth moves around the sun.

157   **"problems left over"**: William James states that those problems that philosophy solves become part of the domain of scientific knowledge, so that "Philosophy has become a collective name for questions that have not yet been answered to the satisfaction of all by whom they have been asked." *Some Problems of Philosophy*, p. 23.

"World-as-history": A concept Spengler opposes to "World-as-nature," which has been the traditional field of philosophy. *The Decline of the West*, pp. 5–7.

158   **"Bergson . . . introduced . . ."**: *Science and the Modern World*, p. 206.

"In many ways . . .": Ibid., p. 205.

"Descartes," Whitehead says: Ibid., pp. 201–02.

159   **I knew him very little**: As an art student in Paris before the First World War, Lewis attended Bergson's lectures at the Collège de France, and became enthusiastic about Bergson's ideas. No doubt, after Lewis had thought critically about Bergson, he considered that he had previously known him "very little."

For the ancients: *Creative Evolution*, p. 363.

160   **the intellect "spatialized" things**: "This simple location of instantaneous material configurations is what Bergson has protested against . . . He calls it a distortion of nature due to the intellectual 'spatialisation' of things. I agree with Bergson in his protest: but I do not agree that such distortion is a vice necessary to the [intellect]." *Science and the Modern World*, p. 72.

"Fallacy of Misplaced Concreteness": See Afterword, page 470.

161   **Berkeley, Bradley or Bosanquet**: The point is that traditional (Berkeleyan) idealism denies the existence of a substance like "matter," underlying all things, but accepts the world of common sense fairly uncritically. But modern realists, in teasing out the ultimate ingredients of the common-sense world, finish up with concepts so remote from it that they seem far more abstract than the idealist who claims that the world is simply an idea in the mind of God. As Lewis acknowledges, the contrast cannot so easily be drawn with absolute idealism (such as that of F. H. Bradley) stemming from the notoriously "abstract" Hegelian tradition.

a new race of *things-in-themselves*: Whitehead's "Eternal Objects." See Afterword, pages 471–72.

162   **The kind of objection**: By J. W. N. Sullivan, for example. See page 138 and note.

163   **"The more comprehensive . . ."**: *Space, Time and Deity*, Vol. I, pp. 2–3.

164   **The point-instants of relativist philosophy**: The smallest analytic unit of the "substance," space-time, which the world comprises, according to Alexander. In Whitehead's philosophy these are "events."

    "points métaphysiques": "Système nouveau de la nature . . . ," Gottfried Leibniz, *Nouveaux Essais sur l'entendement humain* (Paris: Flammarion, 1921), p. 513. Fragments of Lewis's annotated copy are at Texas. Leibniz denies that simple atoms of "matter" could account for the vital unity of life: "It is only *atoms of substance*, that is to say unities which are real and absolutely without parts, which can be the sources of actions, and the absolute first principles of the composition of things, and as it were the ultimate elements into which substantial things can be analysed. They might be called *metaphysical points*; there is about them *something vital . . .*" (Translation, G. H. R. Parkinson, ed., Leibniz, *Philosophical Writings* [London: Dent, 1984], p. 121).

    I proceed to examine: George Berkeley (1685–1753), *A Treatise Concerning the Principles of Human Knowledge* (1710), "Introduction," paragraph 11. Berkeley's reference at the end of this quotation is to John Locke's *An Essay Concerning Human Understanding*.

165   **Abstract ideas are not**: Ibid., paragraph 13.

    "all knowledge and demonstration . . .": Ibid., paragraph 15.

    Universality, he says: Ibid.

166   **"the things experienced . . ."**: *Science and the Modern World*, p. 124.

167   **the *naïveté* of the romantic nature-poet**: Whitehead stresses the value of naïve experience as the court of ultimate appeal on p. 125 of *Science and the Modern World*.

    There is yet a third fact: Ibid., p. 121 (Lewis's italics).

    "eternal forms": Lewis refers to the fact that Whitehead's "eternal objects" are similar to Platonic forms or ideas. See Afterword, page 471.

    "The doctrine I am maintaining,": *Science and the Modern World*, p. 111.

168   **"The question is . . ."**: Ibid., p. 144.

    "Value," we have been told: " 'Value' is the word I use for the intrinsic reality of an event. Value is an element which permeates through and through the poetic view of nature." Ibid., p. 131.

    "real togetherness": Ibid., p. 147.

    Empirical observation shows: Ibid., p. 147. "Thing-for-its-own-sake" is italicized by Lewis.

169   **"I would term the doctrine . . ."**: Ibid., p. 112.

172   **a "futurist" picture**: Lewis no doubt has in mind Giacomo Balla's famous picture, *Dynamism of a Dog on a Leash*.

    a *reiteration*: See page 168.

    We find in the eighteenth century: Ibid., p. 107.

173   **"It is the problem . . ."**: Ibid., p. 109.

    "the electron blindly runs . . .": Ibid., p. 111.

174   **"In the present lecture,"**: Ibid., p. 106.

Now the poet [Shelley]: Ibid., p. 119 (Lewis's italics).

as Alexander says: E.g., *Space, Time and Deity*, Vol. I, p. 197.

175   **the "century of genius"**: The title of Whitehead's third chapter.

There can be no idea formed: *The Principles of Human Knowledge*, Part I, paragraph 27.

All our ideas: Ibid., paragraph 25.

176   **Montessori . . . Émile**: Maria Montessori (1870–1952) was an educationalist who based her system on the child's creative potential and drive to learn. *Émile*, a philosophical romance (1762) by Jean-Jacques Rousseau, concerns the natural upbringing of a child.

178   *La Poésie Pure*: Henri Brémond, *La Poésie pure: avec un débat sur la poésie par Robert de Souza* (Paris: Bernard Grasset, 1926).

179   **M. Brémond, with his academic position**: Brémond was a member of the Académie Française.

Studies in the Genesis of Romantic Theory in the Eighteenth Century, **by J. G. Robertson**: *La Poésie pure*, p. 15.

"this confused, massive experience . . .": Ibid., p. 27.

Enveloping magic: Ibid., p. 27 (Lewis's italics).

According to Walter Pater: Ibid.

Paul Valéry comes in: Valéry is the subject of Chapter IV. Brémond registers his disagreement with Valéry's conception of poetry in a footnote on p. 62.

180   **"I have been sent a quantity . . ."**: Ibid., p. 107 (Lewis's italics).

The word which is: Ibid., pp. 107–08.

[The object of art]: Ibid., p. 109.

183   **M. Souday**: Paul Souday's objections are discussed on pp. 31–49.

It is always the same: Ibid., p. 94.

184   **"the poetic experience . . ."**: Ibid., p. 99.

"Today," exclaims M. Brémond: Ibid., p. 16.

185   **"There is reason . . ."**: Ibid., p. 136.

186   **M. Brémond contrasts two lines**: Ibid., p. 45. The second line and the following example are from Villon's *Testament*.

187   **"If all poetry . . ."**: Ibid., p. 24.

There is no poetry: Ibid., p. 25.

188   **Pirandello**: Luigi Pirandello, author of *Six Characters in Search of an Author*. Lewis alludes to this play in the chapter "Chez Lionel Kein, Esq.," in *The Apes of God*.

Widow Wadman: Character in Laurence Sterne's *Tristram Shandy*, in which she shows a delicate curiosity concerning the effects of the war wound that Uncle Toby sustained in his groin.

190   **Evolutionism**: Bertrand Russell, *Our Knowledge of the External World: As a Field for Scientific Method in Philosophy* (1914, revised and reset, London: George Allen and Unwin, 1926), p. 21.

The difference between man: Ibid., p. 22.

M. Bergson's form: Ibid., p. 25.

191   **"the motives and interests . . ."**: Ibid., pp. 25–26.

"it will . . . be admitted that . . .": Ibid., p. 29.

I have been made aware: Ibid., p. 8.

"The universe . . .": Ibid., p. 18.

"By this it means . . .": Ibid.

192   The concrete enduring entities: *Science and the Modern World*, p. 111.

The things which are grasped: Ibid., pp. 98–99.

192 &   J. W. Dunne . . . Hinton . . . Ouspensky: J. W. Dunne, author of *An*
193   *Experiment with Time* (London: A. and C. Black, 1927), which provides techniques of telling the future through dreams (Lewis mocks the book in "You Broke my Dream," in *The Wild Body*); C. H. Hinton, "Author of What is the Fourth Dimension" and other "Scientific Romances"—his *A New Era of Thought* (London: Swann Sonnenschein, 1900) shows how the manipulation of cubes and tesserae can lead to an apprehension of the fourth dimension of space; P. D. Ouspensky, annotated fragments of Lewis's copy of whose *Tertium Organum (the Third Organ of Thought): a Key to the Enigmas of the World* (London: Kegan Paul, Trench, Trubner, 1920) are at Texas.

193   "Relativity is a . . .": *An Experiment with Time*, p. 108.

Nature is a dull affair: *Science and the Modern World*, pp. 77–78.

195   Now the poet: Ibid., p. 119.

196   I hold that philosophy: Ibid., p. 122.

197   they were told by James: "My thesis is that if we start with the supposition that there is only one primal stuff or material in the world . . . and if we call that stuff 'pure experience,' then knowing can easily be explained as a particular sort of relation . . . into which portions of pure experience may enter." William James, "Does 'Consciousness' Exist?" *Essays in Radical Empiricism* (London: Longmans, Green and Co., 1912), p. 4.

198   "Thus we gain . . .": *Science and the Modern World*, p. 123.

Shelley thinks of nature: Ibid., pp. 120–21.

Wordsworth, we are told: Ibid., p. 121.

201   Marinetti, their prophet: Marinetti was the leader of the Futurists, and wrote the "Founding and Manifesto of Futurism" in 1909. Marinetti was an early and staunch supporter of Mussolini's fascism, which borrowed much from Futurism.

Sorel: Sorel's *Réflexions sur la violence* was published in 1908 and appeared in T. E. Hulme's translation in 1915.

Thus we shall have philosophies: Bertrand Russell, *The Philosophy of Bergson: with a Reply by Mr. H. Wildon Carr, Secretary of the Aristotelian Society, and a Rejoinder by Mr. Russell* (Cambridge: for "The Heretics" by Bowes and Bowes, 1914), pp. 1–2.

202   To the schoolmen: Ibid., pp. 20–21.

203   Turati: Filippo Turati (1857–1932), Italian socialist leader—actually a gradualist rather than a revolutionary.

the futurists: Lewis's opposition to the aspects of Futurism that he discusses here is also expounded in *Blast*, Nos. 1 and 2.

204 **the late Lord Leverhulme**: W. H. Lever, Viscount Leverhulme (1851–1924), a soap magnate, philanthropist and art collector, was displeased with a 1920 portrait of him commissioned from Lewis's friend Augustus John. Since the painting was a large one, Leverhulme cut out a square containing the head and hid it in his safe. The remainder of the mutilated canvas was returned (inadvertently, Leverhulme claimed) to the artist. The incident occasioned much publicity.

Severini: Gino Severini (1883–1966) turned to a kind of "classical" cubism after about 1915, having been one of the most prominent of the Futurist painters. Lewis discusses his earlier work in "The Melodrama of Modernity," *Blast*, No. 1, pp. 143–44.

An immense snobbery: See " 'Life' is the Important Thing," *Blast*, No. 1, pp. 129–31.

205 **Swann**: The reference is to Marcel Proust, via *Du Côté de chez Swann*.

207 **In a famous passage Kant**: The italics are Lewis's.

The most important requirement: Lewis's italics.

209 **Whatever philosophical criticism**: Fulton J. Sheen, *God and Intelligence in Modern Philosophy* (London: Longmans, Green and Co.), p. 13. Lewis's annotated copy of this book, signed by Henry John, the Jesuit son of Lewis's friend Augustus John, is at Texas. Henry John contributed an essay to the second issue of *The Enemy*.

Time as a whole: *Space, Time and Deity*, Vol. II, p. 32.

210 **I will not begin my discussion**: *The Meeting of Extremes in Contemporary Philosophy* (London: Macmillan, 1921), p. 1. Bernard Bosanquet (1848–1923) was a philosopher of absolute idealist persuasion who has tended to be overshadowed by F. H. Bradley. Like Bradley, he was a successor to the Oxford idealist tradition of T. H. Green.

211 **I said in the Preface**: Ibid., pp. 117–19.

the Six: New Realists, who, following William James, posited a neutral "stuff" underlying both the material and the mental. They published a collaborative volume: *The New Realism: Coöperative Studies in Philosophy* (New York: Macmillan, 1912). The Critical Realists (D. Drake, A. O. Lovejoy and others) published *Essays in Critical Realism: A Cooperative Study of the Problem of Knowledge* (London: Macmillan, 1920) in reaction against New Realism's tendency to undermine the "things" of common sense.

212 **"It is the assertion . . ."**: Lewis's italics.

"The distinction at stake . . .": Ibid., p. 129 (Lewis's italics).

213 **It makes a great difference**: *The Decline of the West*, pp. 8–10.

214 **In the Indian Culture**: Ibid., pp. 11–12 (Lewis's italics).

the "poor Indian" of the english verse: "Lo! the poor Indian, whose untutor'd mind / Sees God in clouds or hears him in the wind . . . ," Alexander Pope, *An Essay on Man*, Epistle I, lines 99 *et seq.*

217 **Weyl's physical system**: Hermann Weyl (1885–1955).

218 **as Alexander asserts**: Untraced; it is possible that Lewis is misremembering Bergson's statement that *"the world the mathematician deals with is a world that dies and is reborn at every instant . . ."* (*Creative Evolution*, p. 23).

"We create [Time] . . .": *The Decline of the West*, p. 122.

219   **There is every indication**: H. Wildon Carr, " 'Time' and 'History' in Contemporary Philosophy; with Special Reference to Bergson and Croce," *Proceedings of the British Academy* (1917- 1918), p. 348. The paper was read on 20 March 1918.

220   **The comparison I wish**: Ibid., p. 334.

        First, the theory of Bergson: Ibid.

        It will be seen that: Ibid., p. 348.

        The concept of history: Ibid. (Lewis's italics).

221   **History is not something**: Ibid. (Lewis's italics).

222   **"Poetical metaphors . . ."**: R. F. A. Hoernlé, "A Note on Bergson and the Origin of Life," *Studies in Contemporary Metaphysics* (London: Kegan Paul, Trench, Trubner and Co., 1920), p. 198.

224   **Among animals**: Bertrand Russell, *The Philosophy of Bergson*, p. 3.

225   **Science has given us back**: Jane Harrison, *Ancient Art and Ritual* (London: Williams and Norgate, n.d.), pp. 246–47 (Lewis's italics).

226   **We are keenly interested**: Ibid. (Lewis's italics). The reference is to Arnold Bennett's *Clayhanger* (1910) and its sequel, *Hilda Lessways* (1911). They depict the lives of characters from a pottery-manufacturing district of the midlands of England: the "Five Towns."

227   **Berkeley simply could not find**: Paragraphs 6 to 17 of Berkeley's *The Principles of Human Knowledge* argue that the existence of "abstract ideas" is an unwarranted inference encouraged by misuse of language: "I cannot by any effort of thought conceive the *abstract* idea above described."

        The memory of the Classical: Spengler, *The Decline of the West*, previously quoted on pages 213–14.

228   **Quantity is often introduced**: F. H. Bradley, *Appearance and Reality: A Metaphysical Essay* (2nd ed., London: Swann Sonnenschein, 1902), p. 245.

        too much of a ponderous abstraction: See Lewis's remarks on Bradley's Absolute in Part III of "Creatures of Habit and Creatures of Change," *The Calendar of Modern Letters*, Vol. III, No. 1 (April 1926), rpt. *Creatures of Habit and Creatures of Change*, pp. 157–61.

230   **Idealism [he writes]**: Jacques Maritain, *Réflexions sur l'intelligence* (1924) (Paris: Nouvelle Librairie National, 1926), p. 27. (Lewis's translation).

231   **Did not Descartes**: Ibid., pp. 29–30.

232   **once a bergsonian**: Jacques Maritain (1882–1973) was a Thomist philosopher who had been influenced by Bergson in his youth, and lectured on Bergson's philosophy in 1913.

        "ces petits-neveux de Kant": *Réflexions sur l'intelligence*, p. 215.

        "docteur brutal": Ibid., p. 24.

233   **"Où sont les neiges d'antan?"**: "Where are the snows of yester-year?" Refrain in François Villon's ballad beginning "Dictes moy où, n'en quel pays," from *Le Testament*.

        the "moving image of Eternity,": *Timaeus*, 37 d.

        shadows upon the wall: *The Republic*, Book 7, 514 ff.

235   **the Academy and the Lyceum**: Parts of Athens where Plato and Aristotle respectively pursued their philosophical teaching.

Elliot Smith and his school: Sir Grafton Elliot Smith (1871–1931) was an anthropologist prominent in the "diffusionist" school. His theory about the origin of art is discussed in Lewis's "The Dithyrambic Spectator" (originally called "The Perfect Action"), published in *The Calendar of Modern Letters*, Vol. I, Nos. 2 and 3 (April and May, 1925), rpt. *The Diabolical Principle and the Dithyrambic Spectator* (1931). Lewis's argument there connects with the present discussion. See also "Books of the Quarter" (*The Criterion*, Vol. II, No. 10 [January 1925], rpt. *Creatures of Habit and Creatures of Change*, pp. 108–13).

236   **assailed by William James**: See *A Pluralistic Universe*, p. 16.

      Russell's rule: Enunciated in *The Philosophy of Bergson*, p. 1.

237   **"critical realists"**: See note to page 211.

238   **It has been noticed**: Edward Caird, *The Critical Philosophy of Immanuel Kant* (Glasgow: James MacLehose, 1889), Vol. I, pp. 161–62. The last part of the passage (beginning "Note, however,") is a footnote. Lewis's extensively annotated copy of the second (1909) edition is at Texas.

      Not only the pragmatism: *Chance, Love and Logic*, p. xxv.

239   **"Nominalism" and "Realism"**: Two schools of medieval philosophy; nominalism held that universals had no reality except as generalizations from particulars; realism held that they were real. Realism is thus in some respects the ancestor of idealism (James's "rationalism"), while nominalism (confusingly) is the equivalent of modern realism ("empiricism," for James). Roscellinus was the foremost advocate of nominalism, while Anselm was a realist.

      "to do justice . . .": *The Meeting of Extremes in Contemporary Philosophy*, p. vii.

      It is certain [Bosanquet writes]: Ibid., pp. vi–[vii].

240   **What first attracted my attention**: Ibid., p. viii (Lewis's italics).

242   **"No sane philosophy . . ."**: *Space, Time and Deity*, Vol. I, p. 8.

243   **"It is only by such external . . ."**: *The Mind and the Face of Bolshevism* (New York and London: Putnam, 1927), p. 2.

245   **"There are progressists . . ."**: *The Meeting of Extremes*, p. 113.

248   **Professor Perry . . . H. J. Massingham**: W. J. Perry, author of *The Growth of Civilization* (London: Methuen, 1924). Perry adhered to the "diffusionist" anthropological ideas of Sir Grafton Elliot Smith (whose writings influenced Lewis). Smith wrote the Preface to Massingham's *Downland Man* (London: Jonathan Cape, 1926).

      Spencer and Gillen: Sir W. B. Spencer and F. J. Gillen published *Across Australia* in 1912, and a study of *The Arunta* (a "stone age people") in 1927.

      Mathilde and Mathias Vaerting: Authors of *The Dominant Sex: A Study in the Sociology of Sex Differentiation* (New York: G. H. Doran, 1923), discussed by Lewis in *The Art of Being Ruled*, pp. 199–200.

250   **Low-like**: David Low (1891–1963) newspaper cartoonist much admired by Lewis.

251   **"mental climate"**: See the note to page 259.

252   **"We ourselves are Time"**: *The Decline of the West*, p. 122.

      "Time is a counter-conception . . .": Ibid., p. 126.

      "Between Becoming . . .": Ibid.

      Mathematics as a whole: Ibid.

253 **"Understanding loses . . ."**: Ibid., p. 124.

"All systematic philosophies . . .": Ibid., p. 123.

What is not experienced: Ibid., p. 124.

In the beginning: See note to page 47.

255 **All that has been said**: *The Decline of the West*, p. 124.

The way to the problem: Ibid., pp. 121–22.

256 ***"Forlorn! . . ."***: Quoted from the final stanza of Keats's "To a Nightingale": "Forlorn! the very word is like a bell / To toll me back from thee to my sole self."

257 **Every higher language**: *The Decline of the West*, p. 117.

258 **We see then**: Ibid., pp. 392–93.

259 **General climates of opinion**: *Science and the Modern World*, p. 24.

"The inexpugnable belief . . .": Ibid., p. 17.

I am not arguing: Ibid., p. 18.

When we compare: Ibid., p. 17.

Faith in reason: Ibid., p. 26.

The appeal to "experience": *The Decline of the West*, pp. 393–94 (Lewis's italics in sentence beginning "The contrast . . .").

260 **. . . the ruthlessly cynical**: Ibid., pp. 419–20.

261 ***There is a Stoicism***: Ibid., p. 385–86.

It is tension: Ibid., p. 386.

262 ***Every atomic theory***: Ibid., p. 387.

Goethe once remarked: Ibid., pp. 411–12 (the second set of italics are Lewis's).

263 **Boro-Budur**: Borobudur is a Buddhist monument in Java, Indonesia, dating from the 7th to 8th centuries AD.

We can indeed: *The Decline of the West*, pp. 413–14.

264 **If people were to learn**: Bertrand Russell, *The A.B.C. of Relativity*, p. 196.

266 **von Hartmann**: See the discussion of Eduard von Hartmann's *The Philosophy of the Unconscious* on pages 314–18.

The rise and fall: a deleted passage (see Table of Variants in the Textual Appendix) links this discussion with *The Childermass* by alluding to the Wandering Jew, Cartaphilus (spelt "Cartophilus" by Lewis; see *The Childermass*, p. 2).

267 **"Arts [are] *organisms* . . ."**: *The Decline of the West*, p. 281.

268 **. . . the more we know**: *Science and the Modern World*, p. 7.

269 **It is *tension***: see note to page 261.

270 **"The Faustian building . . ."**: *The Decline of the West*, p. 224.

"a cathedral of voices": Ibid., p. 225.

The seated Buddha-statue: Ibid., p. 347 (Lewis's italics).

271 **Perhaps the man who**: *Science and the Modern World*, p. 60 (Lewis's italics).

272   **Duhem believes that we have in Cardan**: "His vanity, as well as his mediocre moral sense, virtually condemned Cardan to plagiarize the discoveries of Leonardo da Vinci, provided only that he knew them; which he did, as his own testimony guarantees." (Pierre Duhem, "Léonard de Vinci, Cardan et Bernard Palissy," *Études sur Léonard de Vinci: Ceux qu'il a lus et ceux qui l'ont lu*, Première Série, p. 226.

       Oil-painting: *The Decline of the West*, p. 279 (Lewis's italics).

273   **In the light of this**: Ibid., pp. 279–80.

       In Fra Bartolommeo: Ibid., p. 280.

274   **Consider, now, Western painting**: Ibid., pp. 329–30.

       In the *Dithyrambic Spectator*: See note to page 235.

       We speak of the bad taste: Julien Benda, *Belphégor* (London: Faber and Faber, 1929), pp. [xxi–xxii]. Lewis translates from the French text. The same passage is quoted in *The Art of Being Ruled*, p. 219.

275   **Art (in contemporary doctrine)**: Ibid., pp. 6–8; Lewis's translation (with elisions).

       (1) The "Nature": Passage (1), *The Decline of the West*, p. 382; passage (2), p. 329; passage (3), p. 278; passage (4), p. 224; passage (5), pp. 224–25 (Lewis's italics); passage (6), p. 404; and passage (7), p. 403.

276   **"the beholder's sphere . . ."**: Ibid., p. 329.

277   **"the Faustian music . . ."**: Ibid., p. 231.

       A whole world of soul: Ibid., p. 292.

       "The Arts of Form": Part I of Chapter VII.

278   **"the technical form-language . . ."**: Ibid., p. 221.

       "a mysterious *must* . . .": Ibid.

       "determined by perfectly . . .": Ibid.

       "to a timeless . . .": Ibid., p. 220.

279   **"If an art has boundaries . . ."**: Ibid., p. 221.

       "every individual art . . .": Ibid., p. 222 (Lewis's italics).

280   **Michelangelo— was in reality a "Gothic"**: Spengler discusses Michelangelo on pp. 274–77.

       With the eighteenth century: Ibid., p. 285 (Lewis's italics).

281   **We have only to think**: Ibid., pp. 233–34.

282   **"What Darwin originated . . ."**: Ibid., p. 369.

       the same principle as Nietzsche: See Lewis's discussion of "Nietzsche as a Vulgariser" in *The Art of Being Ruled*, pp. 113–18.

283   **The Classical Culture is**: *The Decline of the West*, p. 326.

       A creation is "popular": Ibid.

284   *dionysiac*: Nietzsche's term for the principle of orgiastic intoxication that penetrates through the veil of māyā to a primordial unity (identified with Schopenhauer's *Will*), discussed in *The Birth of Tragedy*.

       Every high creator: *The Decline of the West*, pp. 327–28.

285   **Wagner's Nibelung poetry**: First paragraph, ibid., p. 372; second paragraph, ibid., p. 370; third paragraph, ibid., p. 371.

       The great mass of Socialists: Ibid., p. 328 (footnote).

289   **under the battery of William James**: In "Does 'Consciousness' Exist?" See
        note to page 197.

290   **Averroes . . . Maïmonides**: Averroes (1126–1198), a Muslim, was op-
        posed by both Muslim and Christian theologians. Moses Maïmonides
        (1135–1204) was a Jewish philosopher in Muslim Spain.

        The leibnizian monad: Gottfried Leibniz (1646–1716) expounded his theory
        of monads in *The Monadology* (1714): "these monads are the true atoms
        of nature and, in a word, the elements of things" (paragraph 3). For "con-
        fused" perceptions, see paragraph 49. Lewis also has Leibniz's "Système
        Nouveau de la Nature . . ." in mind: "in comparison with [other forms
        or souls,] minds or rational souls are little gods, made in the image of
        God, and having in them some glimmering of Divine Light" (*Nouveaux
        Essais*, p. 510; *Philosophical Writings*, p. 117).

        Swedenborg: Emanuel Swedenborg (1688–1772).

291   *Sic et non* : (*Yes and No*), 1122: a work in which some of the theological
        orthodoxies of Abélard's time were questioned.

292   **Marcion**: *c.85–c.165*. Marcion's vengeful "God of Justice" was the
        Demiurge, who cursed mankind for failing to keep his law. When the
        higher "God of Mercy" sent his son to redeem mankind, the Demiurge
        had him crucified, but had to acknowledge the efficacy of Christ's redemp-
        tive mission. Lewis discusses the marcionite heresy again in *Left Wings
        over Europe*.

296   **dynamical concept first undermined by Hume**: The reference is to Hume's
        analysis of causality.

        Kant, in his reinstatement of God: Having "killed" God (in Heine's
        phrase — see note to page 141), Kant reinstates the Christian ethic through
        a categorical imperative that is an inner principle felt without the aid of
        understanding and irrespective of our personal or practical desires. The
        "Reason" (the highest synthetic power) goes beyond the Understanding
        (which had seemingly disposed of God), and reinstates God, freedom and
        immortality.

297   **It cannot however be ignored**: Hermann Lotze, *Metaphysic: In Three
        Books; Ontology, Cosmology and Psychology*, 2nd. ed. (Oxford: Claren-
        don Press, 1887), p. 138. In this chapter Lotze denies the existence of a
        mysterious non-mechanical "Life-force," but maintains that an unprejudiced
        person must recognize that life is shaped by a higher power, working
        towards an end, even if this recognition "has too often intruded itself rashly
        and confusingly into the treatment of special cases . . ." Lewis's copy is
        at Texas, annotated by another reader.

        behaviourism of Watson: Discussed on pages 324–31, and in *The Art of
        Being Ruled*, pp. 339–42.

298   **Flourens**: This and other experiments are described in Eduard von Hart-
        mann, *Philosophy of the Unconscious: Speculative Results According to
        the Inductive Method of Physical Science* (London: Trubner and Co.,
        1884), Vol. I, p. 67.

        not a *person*, but a *res* or *thing*: "Thus, the Res Mancipi of Roman Law
        included not only land, but slaves, horses and oxen." Sir Henry Sumner
        Maine, *Ancient Law* (London: John Murray, 1861), p. 274.

299   **Lotze (in his *Microcosmos*)** : Hermann Lotze, *Microcosmos: An Essay Concerning Man and His Relation to the World* (Edinburgh: T. and T. Clark, 1885), Book III, Chapter III (Vol. I) is concerned with the forms of reciprocal action between body and soul, presenting the soul as throughout bound to reciprocal action with the body. The precise passage Lewis intended to quote has not been traced.

Mr. Yerkes: See the discussion of Yerkes on pages 321–24.

Froebel and Maria Montessori: Friedrich Froebel (1782–1852) was the founder of the kindergarten movement, stressing the importance of education in early childhood. For Montessori and *Émile*, see the note to page 176.

301   **Dr. Caligari**: *The Cabinet of Dr. Caligari*, film directed by Robert Wiene (1919).

He [Leibniz] declares: *Philosophy of the Unconscious*, Vol. I, p. 18.

the seat of sexual love: Quoted, ibid., p. 22.

302   **"That only a few spots on . . ."**: Quoted, ibid., p. 20.

All great creations of popular force: Quoted, ibid., p. 41 (Lewis's italics in sentence beginning "All that is free . . .").

303   **When I am asked [he says]**: Gottfried Leibniz, "Considerations on Vital Principles and Plastic Natures," rpt. in *Philosophical Papers and Letters*, tr. and ed. L. E. Loember (Dordrecht, 1969), p. 586.

Descartes called animals *machines* : "they have no reason at all, and . . . nature . . . acts in them according to the disposition of their organs, just as a clock, which is only composed of wheels and weights . . ." René Descartes, *Discourse on the Method of Rightly Conducting the Reason . . .* , *The Philosophical Works of Descartes*, tr. Haldane and Ross (1911, rpt. Cambridge: Cambridge University Press, 1970), Vol. I, p. 117.

"Socrates awake": See the discussion in Plato's *Theaetetus* (159) and Locke's *An Essay Concerning Human Understanding*, Book II, Chapter 1, paragraph 11.

304   **In laying down the principle**: *Metaphysic*, Vol. I, pp. 150–51.

305   **Voltaire's caricature of Leibniz**: In *Candide*, the character Pangloss, with his reiterated optimism ("Everything is for the best in the best of all possible worlds") is a caricature of Leibniz.

"*Enthusiasm* signifies that . . .": *Nouveaux Essais sur l'entendement humain*, Book 4, Chapter XIX, p. 453. In the English translation by P. Remnant and J. Bennett (Cambridge: Cambridge University Press, 1985), the passage is on p. 504.

Schopenhauer's great book: *Die Welt als Wille und Vorstellung*, translated as *The World as Will and Idea* by Haldane and Kemp (London: Trubner, 1883).

306   **"Ding an sich."**: "Thing-in-itself"; that is, the "substance" prior to the phenomenal world, to which Kant denied that we have access.

"As such it is throughout . . .": *The World as Will and Idea*, Vol. I (II, 19), p. 133.

307   **"free from all multiplicity . . ."**: Ibid., p. 146 (II, 23).

Although the Will: The passage can be found in E. J. Payne's edition of the *Parerga and Paralipomena* (Oxford: Clarendon Press, 1974), Vol. I, p. 223.

A sort of *roman genius* : This discussion is based on that part of the essay found ibid., p. 223.

308   **"The whole body . . . must be . . ."**: *The World as Will and Idea*, Vol. I, p. 139 (II, 20).

"every impression . . .": "Every impresson upon the body is also . . . immediately an impression upon the will." (Ibid., pp. 130–31; II, 18).

The parts of the body: Ibid., p. 141 (II, 20).

"Si l'homme *pouvait* . . .": Parodying the French proverb, "If youth only knew; if old age were only able."

309   **He quotes Bacon and Kepler**: In a footnote on p. 137 of *The World as Will and Idea* (II, 19). See the note to page 340.

If there is one thing: *The Analysis of Mind* (London: George Allen and Unwin, 1921), p. 11.

310   **"a very low type of infinity**: See note to page 433.

"Only those changes . . .": *The World as Will and Idea*, Vol. I, p. 147 (II, 23).

The bird of a year: Examples given ibid., p. 148.

312   **'Those that level . . .'**: Shakespeare, Sonnet 121: "they that level / At my abuses, reckon up their own."

313   **"strange fact that everyone believes . . ."**: *The World as Will and Idea*, Vol. I, p. 147.

Frauenstaedt: Julius Frauenstaedt, friend of Schopenhauer, and his literary executor.

314   **"I cheerfully confess . . ."**: *Philosophy of the Unconscious*, Vol. I, p. 18.

"It does not follow . . .": Quoted, ibid., p. 17.

"instantly perceiving . . .": Ibid.

315   **"the soul, as a thinking being . . ."**: Quoted, ibid.

"To ask at what time . . .": Quoted, ibid., p. 16.

Hume does not dispute: This and the following sentence are quoted from ibid., p. 19; and all but the first seven words of the next sentence ("But in his . . .") are quoted from pp. 19–20: hence Lewis's ellipses.

The Feminine is identified: "Woman namely is related to man, as instinctive or unconscious to rational or conscious action; therefore the genuine woman is a piece of Nature, on whose bosom the man estranged from the Unconscious may refresh and recruit himself . . ." (ibid., Vo. II, p. 43).

316   **no brain at all is required**: "From this example of the decapitated frog . . . it follows that *no brain at all* is requisite for the exercise of will." (Ibid., Vol. I, p. 62).

But we cannot confine the will: Ibid.

Let anyone take a glass of water: Ibid., pp. 63–64.

317   **The *praying cricket***: Discussed ibid., p. 62.

Hartmann says that christian: Hartmann expresses this view, and praises the "unerring wisdom of the Unconscious in creating the world" in Chapter xii of Section C of *Philosophy of the Unconscious*.

319   **"that absolute bird" . . . that *ka***: *A Pluralistic Universe*, p. 192; see "The Dithyrambic Spectator," *The Diabolical Principle*, pp. 190–95.

Professor Watson: J. B. Watson (1878–1958), the prime exponent of Behaviourism.

321   **Binet**: Alfred Binet (1857–1911) devised the first "intelligence" tests.

"Our war department" : C. S. Yoakum and R. M. Yerkes (eds.), *Mental Tests in the American Army* (published in America as *Army Mental Tests*) (London: Sidgwick and Jackson, 1922), p. viii (italics Lewis's).

322   **"The purposes of psychological testing,"** : Quoted in *Mental Tests in the American Army*, p. xi.

"These pictures . . ." : Ibid., p. 115.

323   **The four labyrinths** : R. M. Yerkes, *The Dancing Mouse: A Study in Animal Behavior* (New York: The Macmillan Co., 1907), pp. 210–11.

There was no motive : Ibid., p. 212.

"Its passages are so large . . ." : The "quotation" is a cento and partial paraphrase of several sentences, ibid., p. 214 and 218.

324   **Mr. Bertrand Russell** : See *The Analysis of Mind* for Russell's acceptance of Behaviorism. On Watson's rejection of visual imagery in the "mind," Russell writes: "This view seems to me flatly to contradict experience," though he acknowledges that "Professor Watson is a very learned man" (pp. 153–54).

325   **Pavlov's apparatus** : Watson discusses this on pp. 65–68 of *Behavior: An Introduction to Comparative Psychology* (New York: Henry Holt and Co., 1914). Watson concludes that "negative results" are not likely to satisfy "behavior students" because of the imperfections of the technique.

"substitution" : "Certainly many objects (non-affective stimuli, stimuli distantly or not at all connected with the sex-stimuli) do not, in the beginning, arouse these groups, but through the ordinary mechanism of habit come later to arouse the one or the other [i.e. sexual activity or avoidance] (substitution . . .)" (ibid., pp. 24–25). Watson suggests that all aesthetic, artistic and religious forms of response (or "preferences," in common language) are "at bottom sexual."

the "centric part" : "So we her ayres contemplate, words and heart, / And virtues; but we love the Centrique part" (speaking of the one thing men should prefer in a woman they love); John Donne, "Elegy XVIII: Love's Progress," lines 35–36.

"expansive or seeking movements" : *Behavior*, p. 22; Watson is discussing the sex response.

327   **We see in passing** : J. B. Watson, *Psychology: From the Standpoint of a Behaviorist* (Philadelphia: J. B. Lippincott Co., 1919), p. 5.

328   **"The more constantly . . ."** : Ibid., p. 2.

"An equally important result . . ." : Ibid.

329   **"The larynx and tongue . . ."** : Ibid., p. 20.

"Now it is admitted by all . . ." : Ibid., p. 21.

"As language habits become . . ." : Ibid., p. 19.

333   *The Glands and Human Personality* : Louis Berman, M.D., *The Glands Regulating Personality: A Study of the Glands of Internal Secretion in Relation to the Types of Human Nature* (1921, 2nd ed., 1928, rpt. New York: Macmillan and Co., 1930).

"The religion of science . . ." : Ibid., p. 16.

334   **Rozanov** : Vasily Vasilyevich Rozanov (1856–1919), Russian writer who advocated a naturalistic religion of sex and procreation.

"If at all," he says: *The Glands Regulating Personality*, p. 17.

"Darwin changed Fate . . .": Ibid., p. 12.

Bolivar Berman: That is, champion of liberty.

"The chemistry of the soul!": Ibid., p. 22.

335   **More and more**: Quoted, ibid., pp. 22–23.

Brown-Séquard: His experiments are discussed on pp. 42–43. On rejuvenation, Berman writes that, apart from "persistence of early glandular predominances . . . Nature's only other mode of securing perpetual youth seems to be by prolonging the time allotted to the sex-gland crescendo" (ibid., p. 299).

"All the glands, in fact . . .": Ibid., p. 138.

336   **"The Kinetic Chain . . ."**: Ibid., p. 139.

". . . modern thought does not regard . . .": Ibid.

"oldest part of the Mind": Ibid., p. 140.

"There is indeed room for rhetoric . . .": Ibid.

". . . We think and feel,": Ibid.

". . . There is the fascinating story . . .": Ibid.

337   **"Events rattle . . ."**: "Events rattle against their neighbours as drily as if they were dice in a box [in Hume's philosophy]," William James, *Some Problems of Philosophy: A Beginning of an Introduction to Philosophy* (London: Longmans, Green and Co., 1911), p. 198.

"The worst a psychology . . .": William James, *The Principles of Psychology* (London: Macmillan and Co., 1890), Vol. I, p. 226 (Lewis's italics).

338   **"a mere subjective phenomenon"**: Ibid., p. 331. The force of James's "mere" is to restrict his discussion to the "subjective" side of the "consciousness of personal sameness" — that is, "as a feeling" (ignoring the "objective" side of it) — he is not at this point presenting his conclusions.

"it thinks here": Compare *Principles of Psychology*, Vol. I, p. 224: "If we could say in English 'it thinks,' as we say 'it rains' or 'it blows,' we should be stating the fact most simply and with the minimum of assumptions."

339   **"pulverizes perception . . ."**: *Some Problems of Philosophy*, p. 200.

340   **"It is certain that all bodies . . ."**: Quoted in *Science and the Modern World*, p. 58.

345   *"By space the universe encompasses . . ."*: Blaise Pascal, *Pensées*, No. 348.

"But the chief advantage . . .": Part I, paragraph 117.

"To be plain, we suspect . . .": Part I, paragraph 118.

347   **[Nature] is the aspect**: F. H. Bradley, *Appearance and Reality: A Metaphysical Essay* (2nd ed., London: Swann Sonnenschein and Co., 1902), pp. 293–94.

More: See note to page 139.

348   **Agrippa**: Most probably Cornelius Agrippa of Nettesheim (1486–1535), occult philosopher and controversialist who eventually rejected all attempts at knowledge, preferring faith and charity; but possibly the equally sceptical (but hardly "disreputable") Greek philosopher Agrippa.

"**natural science is nothing but . . .**" : Immanuel Kant, *Metaphysical Foundations of Natural Science*, tr. Ellington (Indianapolis: Bobbs-Merrill Co., 1970), p. 14. A note in Cornell indicates that Lewis found the passage in Caird's study of Kant.

metis : That is, *métis*, hybrid.

350   "**In order to supply . . .**" : Quoted in Caird, *The Critical Philosophy of Immanuel Kant* (1st ed.), Vol. I, p. 629. The passage is found on p. 291 of the 2nd ed. of Kant's *Critique of Pure Reason*.

"**frozen music**" : By Goethe, in conversation with Eckermann; quoted in Schopenhauer's *The World as Will and Idea*, Supplement to Book III, 39.

351   "**undermine the reasonings . . .**" : David Hume, *An Enquiry Concerning Human Understanding*, [*and An Enquiry Concerning the Principles of Morals*], ed. Selby-Bigge (Oxford: Clarendon Press, 1894), Sect. V., Part I, paragraph 34.

Nietzsche remarks somewhere : *The Genealogy of Morals*, Essay III, Section 9. Lewis's annotated copies of the Oscar Levy editions of Nietzsche (Vols. 2, 10 and 13 — *The Genealogy of Morals*, *The Joyful Wisdom* and *Early Greek Philosophy and Other Essays* (Edinburgh and London: T. N. Foulis, 1909-13) are at Texas.

"**a necessity of the first order . . .**" : Ibid., Section 11. Page 150 of Lewis's copy of *The Genealogy of Morals*, with the quoted passage, Lewis's annotation and a commentary, is reproduced in facsimile in Paul Edwards, ''Wyndham Lewis and Nietzsche : 'How Much Truth does a Man Require?' '' G. Cianci, ed., *Wyndham Lewis: Letteratura/Pittura* (Palermo: Sellerio, 1982), pp. 214-17.

the remark of Bergson : "We may conclude, then, that individuality is never perfect, and that it is often difficult, sometimes impossible, to tell what is an individual and what is not, but that life nevertheless manifests a search for individuality, as if it strove to constitute systems naturally isolated, naturally closed" (*Creative Evolution*, p. 15).

352   "**In that they side against** *appearance*,**"** : *Beyond Good and Evil*, Section 10.

353   **For Hume, habit is** : *Enquiry Concerning Human Understanding*, Section V, Part I, paragraph 36.

354   **that Poincaré calls "beauty"** : "I speak of that beauty . . . which comes from the harmonious order of parts, which a pure intelligence can group. That is what provides a body, a skeleton, so to speak, to the scintillating appearances that please our senses; and without this support the beauty of these fleeting dreams could only be imperfect" (*Science et méthode*, p. 15).

355   "**If I ask you why . . .**" : *Enquiry Concerning Human Understanding*, Section V, Part I, paragraph 37.

not-self of pure sensation : The first section of "Creatures of Habit and Creatures of Change" discusses "The Not-Self of Communism" (*Creatures of Habit and Creatures of Change*, p. 137).

"**Nothing is more free . . .**" : *Enquiry Concerning Human Understanding*, Section V, Part I, paragraph 39.

Belief is nothing : Ibid., Part II, paragraph 40.

Belief is something : Ibid.

356   **This manner of conception**: Ibid.

        "on the view we take of *belief . . ."*: *Analysis of Mind*, p. 231.

358   *Specimen Days*: Published in 1882, *Specimen Days* presents "specimen"
        events from Whitman's life, and the life of nineteenth century America.

359   **"since the idea of a power . . ."**: *Space, Time and Deity*, Vol. I, pp.
        290–91.

360   *"inducement* **to stir it into activity"**: In fact Alexander is at this point
        answering the metaphysical claim that causality is "unreal," and criticis-
        ing it for regarding a "cause" as something separate from the activity of
        causing: "Thus when causation appears to be obnoxious to [that is, logical-
        ly implying, and vulnerable to] the infinite regress, for that A should cause
        B there must be a third thing C which moves A to its work, it is assumed
        that a cause itself is not causative. It is waiting for an inducement.
        Something, as Mr. Broad so well puts the point, is wanted to stir it into
        activity. But its real activity consists in passing over into its effect" (ibid.,
        p. 298).

361   *Varieties of Religious Experience*: Published in 1904.

        "thomist": That is, follower of the scholastic (realist) philosophy of St.
        Thomas Aquinas.

363   **Chesterton**: G. K. Chesterton (1874–1936), a Catholic apologist with an
        agrarian vision of England, provided a Preface for Dr. Sheen's book.

        "though coming from the past . . .": This and the other phrases quoted
        in this paragraph are from *God and Intelligence*, p. 1.

        As men lost faith: Ibid., p. 2.

364   **The intellectual [scholastic, catholic]**: Ibid., p. 31.

        "[Empiricism] hitherto . . .": *A Pluralistic Universe*, p. 314.

365   *"Modern religion bases . . ."*: H. G. Wells, *God the Invisible King*, quoted
        ibid., p. 25. Lewis's copy of Sheen is annotated with his draft of the two
        sentences of comment on the quotation ("But even if . . . our approach
        to God.").

366   **"dark night of the Soul"**: The phrase used as a title for the English transla-
        tion of St. John of the Cross's *Noche Oscura* published in 1908. The work
        is a commentary on the poem quoted as an epigraph on page 127. "Souls
        begin to enter this dark night when God is drawing them from the state
        of novice (which is that of those who are considering the spiritual path)
        and is beginning to set them in the state of contemplation; so that, pass-
        ing through it, they may arrive at that state of perfection which is divine
        union of the soul with God." *Obras de San Juan de la Cruz, Doctor de
        la Iglesia*, ed. P. Silverio de Santa Teresa, C.D. (Burgos: Biblioteca Mistica
        Carmelitana, 1929), Vol. II, p. 365.

        "Moon and Sixpence": *The Moon and Sixpence*, a novel by Somerset
        Maugham based on the life of Gauguin, published 1919.

367   **"a direct apprehension . . ."**: H. Wildon Carr, *Theory of Monads*, quoted,
        God and Intelligence, p. 35 (Lewis's italics).

        "without any *representative* **faculty . . ."**: William James, *The Varieties
        of Religious Experience*, quoted, ibid., p. 35.

368   **"cheerful and expansive"**: From James's description of a "faith-state,"
        quoted, ibid.

        The religious impulse: Ibid., p. 36 (Lewis's italics).

Anatole France's *Monsieur Bergeret* : *Monsieur Bergeret à Paris* (1901).

Mr. Fawcett's "Imaginist" doctrine : Douglas Fawcett's theory of reality as an evolving expression of "Divine Imagining," of which a sentient God is also the product, is discussed, *God and Intelligence*, pp. 57–59.

369   **Where James exults at the death-blow** : "It seems to me that nothing is important in comparison with that divine apparition [*Creative Evolution*]; all our positions . . . asserted magisterially, and the beast intellectualism killed absolutely dead" (letter to Schiller, *Letters*, Vol. II, p. 290), quoted, ibid., p. 12.

"I am so enthusiastic . . ." : *Letters*, Vol. II, pp. 290–94, quoted, ibid.

"Religious experience . . ." : William James, *A Pluralistic Universe*, p. 304.

"angel" introduced by Alexander : The point of view of a hypothetical "angel" is used to illuminate his theory of mind as simply compresent with what it perceives. Alexander reverts fairly frequently to the angel's point of view. Later he suggests that were deity finite it would be this hypothetical angel.

370   **a passage from the** *Metaphysics* : See Textual Appendix, note to page 361.

371   **"This Whole [Reality] . . ."** : *Appearance and Reality*, p. 242.

"Reality," he says : Ibid., p. 225.

no truth can : "There will be no truth which is entirely true . . ." Ibid., p. 362.

"In every sense . . ." : Ibid., p. 242.

372   **"An immediate experience . . ."** : "An immediate experience, viewed as positive, is so far not exclusive," ibid., p. 228. Bradley is arguing that particular experiences are not to be considered as incompatible with the unitary "experience" of the Absolute on which they depend.

373   **William James was asked** : See *God and Intelligence*, p. 217.

"Every sphere . . ." : *Appearance and Reality*, p. 487.

"One appearance . . ." : Ibid.

374   **its creator's german master** : G. W. R. Hegel.

"We should . . . find a paradox . . ." : *Appearance and Reality*, p. 360.

375   **"enlarged non-natural man"** : "A magnified and non-natural man," Matthew Arnold, *Literature and Dogma*, p. 23.

"a being at the same time . . ." : *Appearance and Reality*, p. 244.

377   **God abdicated** : Compare the following fragment from the *Childermass* file at Cornell, f. 143: "The problem of an absolute God can it seems, be put in this way. Without such a God we cannot be real, and yet with him we cannot be either: for if we postulate an Absolute there is no end for us. A plurality of powers seems the only possibility for conferring of any sense at all on life."

ultimate Unity : Compare ibid., f. 132: "Diversity is the essence of individuality. The more diversity nature can contrive, the intenser the individualism promised. Every [word] from that exclusiveness is a step towards a Unity that is strictly Nothing. . . ."

conclusions of Kant's "practical reason" : One of the three postulates of the practical reason is the existence of God. See the note to page 296.

379   **Fechner**: G. T. Fechner (1801–1887), about whom James wrote in Lecture IV of *A Pluralistic Universe*, had a concept of an evolutionary God and believed in a "world-soul."

      The secular consciousness: *The Evolution of Theology in the Greek Philosophers*, Vol. I, p. 34.

380   **"the beginning of theology . . ."**: Ibid., p. 29.

381   **Mr. Russell accuses Bergson**: "The distinction between subject and object, between the mind which thinks and remembers and has images on the one hand, and the objects thought about, remembered or imaged — this distinction, so far as I can see, is wholly absent from his philosophy." *The Philosophy of Bergson*, p. 23.

385   **"A piece of matter . . ."**: *The Analysis of Mind*, p. 101.

386   **. . . An ordinary perceptual**: C. D. Broad, *Scientific Thought* (London: Kegan Paul, Trench, Trubner, 1923), pp. 398–99.

387   **Broad's description**: "The Theory of Sensa, and the Critical Scientific Theory," Chapter 8 of *Scientific Thought*, opens with an announcement that its subject will be a full statement of the "theory that appearances are a peculiar kind of objects" (p. 39).

      "Whenever a penny looks . . .": Ibid., pp. 239–40.

388   **In reading a book**: See ibid., p. 247.

390   **"unsuitable unit . . ."**: Ibid., p. 331.

      "Merely co-operates": "Among [the conditions in the brain independent of the present stimulus on the retina] are traces left on the brain by past experiences of sight, touch and movement. These do not generally show themselves in consciousness at all. . . . Generally these traces merely co-operate with the brain-states which are due to the retinal sensation to produce a visual sensation . . ." (ibid., p. 294).

      Science says that a "penny": Lewis's discussion follows and comments on Broad's, ibid., p. 331.

391   **"too vague for it to be . . ."**: Paraphrase of the passage from Broad quoted on page 386.

      stick seen partly in water: "When we judge that a straight stick [half in water] *looks* bent, we are aware of an object which really *is* bent . . ." (ibid., p. 241). Of course, Broad includes appearances within his category of "objects."

      appearance of the houses: An example discussed by Broad on pp. 286–87.

392   **Maskelyne and Devant**: Popular conjurors and illusionists of the period.

      "Nearly all," he says: Ibid., pp. 299–300; *"sight"* is italicized by Lewis.

395   **Then there are other things**: Bertrand Russell, *Our Knowledge of the External World*, p. 107.

396   **"apparent difference between matter . . ."**: Ibid., p. 106.

      "Men of science . . .": Ibid.

      "mathematical knowledge required": Ibid.

397   **When we are speaking of matter**: *The Analysis of Mind*, p. 36.

      I will follow his argument: In "The World of Physics and the World of Sense," ibid., from which the following quotations are taken.

398   **"a mind . . . debauched with learning"**: *The Principles of Human Knowledge*, Part I, paragraph 123.

399   **The opinion of**: Ibid., paragraph 119.

      "all those amusing geometrical . . .": Ibid., paragraph 123.

      "Of those unnatural notions,": Ibid., paragraph 124.

400   **Why should we suppose**: *Our Knowledge of the External World*, p. 110.

401   **"It is only necessary,"**: Ibid., p. 111.

      . . . given any sensible: Ibid., pp. 111–12.

      "everything will then . . .": Ibid., p. 112 (Lewis's italics).

402   **"Very often . . ."**: Ibid.

404   **Mr. Slosson**: E. E. Slosson's *Chats on Science* and *Keeping up with Science* were both published in 1924.

      his "A.B.C.": Bertrand Russell, *The A.B.C. of Relativity*; see note to page 142.

405   **Maritain**: Jacques Maritain, *Réflexions sur l'intelligence*, Chapter vii, "On the Metaphysics of the Physicists or Simultaneity according to Einstein."

406   **This whole theory**: *Our Knowledge of the External World*, p. 142 (Lewis's italics).

408   **"Evolution . . . implies . . ."**: Henri Bergson, *Creative Evolution*, p. 24 (Lewis's italics).

409   **we "degrade duration"**: Ibid., p. 218.

      "Suppose we let ourselves go . . .": Ibid., p. 212.

410   **matter, for Bergson**: "Matter is a relaxation of the inextensive into the extensive and, thereby, of liberty into necessity . . . ," Ibid., p. 230.

      "We shall now understand . . .": Ibid., p. 213.

      Since "physics is simply psychics . . .": Ibid.

      "For a scientific theory . . .": Ibid., p. 218.

      "main concern is with motion": *Space, Time and Deity*, Vol. I, p. 149.

411   **It is never *quite* free**: "Let us seek, in the depths of our experience, the point where we feel ourselves most intimately within our own life. It is into pure duration that we then plunge back, a duration in which the past, always moving on, is swelling unceasingly with a present which is absolutely new. But, at the same time, we feel the spring of our will strained to the utmost limit. We must, by a strong recoil of our personality on itself, gather up our past which is slipping away, in order to thrust it, compact and undivided into a present which it will create by entering. Rare indeed are the moments when we are self-possessed to this extent: it is then that we are truly free. And even at these moments we do not completely possess ourselves. Our feeling of duration . . . admits of degrees." (*Creative Evolution*, pp. 210–11).

412   **Musical analogy**: For example, "Could we not say that, though these [musical] notes follow each other, we nevertheless perceive them within each other, and that together they are comparable to a living being, whose parts, though distinct, penetrate each other by the effect of togetherness itself?" R. Gillouin, ed., *Henri Bergson: Choix de texte avec étude du système philosophique* (Paris: Louis-Michaud, 1910), p. 44. Lewis's (undated) annotated copy of this anthology is at Texas. The Section on *durée*

is selected mainly from Bergson's *Essai sur les données immédiates de la conscience* (translated as *Time and Free Will*). Lewis quotes another example on page 413.

"To say that an event will occur . . ." : Ibid., p. 55. The two sentences following the quotation are a continuation of this passage of Bergson's.

"Esto Memor! Souviens-toi!" : Sundial mottoes warning of passing time: "Remember this!"

"Outside of me . . ." : *Choix de texte*, p. 50.

413   **"It is because I endure . . ."** : Ibid.

"penetrating and organizing . . ." : Ibid., p. 47 (Lewis's italics).

The distinctive character : *Space, Time and Deity*, Vol. II, p. 337. Alexander is answering the theory that, "since Time is infinite . . . every form of existence must have existed in the past."

"a straight line, . . . : *Choix de texte*, p. 46.

414   **"Movement, regarded as a passage . . ."** : Ibid., p. 52, where the preceding sentence can also be found.

"Everything is a piece . . ." : *Space, Time and Deity*, Vol. I, p. 312.

Lloyd Morgan . . . G. H. Lewes : See ibid., Vol. II, p. 14.

Kant's idea of "intensive quality" : That is, intensive quantity or magnitude. See Immanuel Kant, *Critique of Pure Reason*, part 2 of Section 3 of Chapter II of Book II of the "Transcendental Analytic," on "Anticipations of Perception," tr. Kemp Smith (1929, rpt. London: Macmillan, 1982); "But since . . . apprehension [of the real] by means of mere sensation takes place in an instant and not through successive synthesis of different [empirical] sensations, and therefore does not proceed from the parts to the whole, the magnitude is to be met with only in the apprehension. The real has therefore [intensive] magnitude, but not extensive magnitude" (p. 203). Alexander denies that Kant's "anticipations" must be referred to the mind: "From our point of view, the non-empirical element in experience is not referrable to the mind but to Space-Time itself" (*Space, Time and Deity*, Vol. I, p. 310). Bergson turns Kant's analysis of sensation to his own purpose at the opening of *Time and Free Will*, and alludes to Kant's concept in a passage included in *Choix de texte*: "True *durée*, that perceived by consciousness, therefore ought to be grouped among the so-called intensive magnitudes; in truth, it is not a quantity, and as soon as we start to measure it we unconsciously replace it with space" (p. 48).

space-time *possesses no quality* : See *Space, Time and Deity*, Vol. II, p. 45.

"Time plays the director rôle . . ." : Ibid., Vol. I, p. 312.

"Time disintegrates Space . . ." : Ibid.

415   **"The existence of emergent qualities . . ."** : Ibid., Vol. II, pp. 46–47 (Lewis's italics).

"The new quality, life . . ." : Ibid., p. 46 (Lewis's italics).

"Time and Space, being . . ." : Ibid., p. 316.

416   **The "empirical method,"** : See note to page 427.

417   **. . . to think of Time** : Ibid., Vol. I, p. 59.

418   **But if the empirical** : Ibid. (Lewis's italics); the final sentence of the quotation is a footnote.

438   **"Reality" is quite incoherent**: "There is no property of coherence in reality itself. Coherence is a property of the perspectives which we have ourselves selected . . ." (ibid., pp. 258–59). Alexander's coherence-view of truth, like the philosophy of science propounded by Thomas Kuhn, holds that truth and falsity are judged by the coherence of any particular statement with a larger system of beliefs; but his stress on the "majority-vote" elides the problem of "scientific revolutions"—those moments when the larger system collapses under the strain of assimilating particular anomalies.

        If it is asked: Ibid., pp. 54–55 (Lewis's italics).

440   **. . . quality is carried by particular**: Ibid., p. 142 (Lewis's italics).

        "Unmoved Mover" of Aristotle: That is, a God who sets nature in motion.

        "truth is different from reality": *Space, Time and Deity*, Vol. II, p. 263.

        . . . truth is indeed what works: Ibid., p. 265. Alexander is discussing the Pragmatist view of truth rather than expounding his own, and he finds it wanting precisely because it lacks an objective element: "Truth is indeed what works. But it works because truth is determined by the nature of reality. Reality is indeed no fixed thing . . ."

        . . . truth is . . . *progressive*: Ibid., p. 263. Lewis elides: "Thus truth is at once eternal and progressive. 'Once true always true,' so long as the range of facts is restricted as before. But truth varies . . ."

441   **as Bradley puts it**: See note to page 419.

        Bradley's account: *Appearance and Reality*, Chapter xxiv.

444   **As to what is said**: Part One, paragraph 3.

        It is indeed an opinion: Ibid., paragraphs 4–5.

445   **It might be thought**: Ibid., Introduction, paragraph 1.

        "a man need only . . .": Ibid., Part One, paragraph 6.

446   **If the reader believes**: Quoted from Bradley's *Ethical Studies* by Bosanquet, *The Meeting of Extremes*, p. 4.

        "the effect of the empirical method . . .": See note to page 427.

447   **Modern Idealism**: G. E. Moore, "The Refutation of Idealism," *Philosophical Studies* (1913, rpt. London: Kegan Paul, Trench, Trubner, 1922), pp. 1–2.

448   **"The general idea of being,"**: *The Principles of Human Knowledge*, Part I, paragraph 17.

        "It is on this, therefore . . .": Part I, paragraph 24.

449   **"God had created . . ."**: Ibid., Part I, paragraph 19.

450   **"so poor a category as *being* . . ."**: "It would be strange if God were not rich enough to embrace so poor a category as Being, the poorest and most abstract of all." Hegel, cited by William James in *Some Problems of Philosophy*, p. 43 and *A Pluralistic Universe*, p. 87.

BOOKS BY WYNDHAM LEWIS

References in the Editorial Section to Lewis's books are to Black Sparrow editions where such have been issued. In other cases first editions have been used.

1914   *Blast*, 1. (Magazine edited by Lewis: facsimile of issues 1 and 2 by Black Sparrow Press, 1981.)

1915   *Blast*, 2.

1918   *Tarr*. London: The Egoist Ltd. (Reissued by Black Sparrow Press, edited by Paul O'Keeffe, 1990.)

1919   *The Caliph's Design: Architects! Where Is Your Vortex?* London: The Egoist Ltd. (Reissued by Black Sparrow Press, edited by Paul Edwards, 1986.)

1921   *The Tyro*, 1. (Magazine edited by Lewis.)

1922   *The Tyro*, 2.

1926   *The Art of Being Ruled*. London: Chatto and Windus. (Reissued by Black Sparrow Press, edited by Reed Way Dasenbrock, 1989.)

1927   *The Lion and the Fox: The Rôle of the Hero in the Plays of Shakespeare*. London: Grant Richards Ltd.

The Enemy, Vol. 1. (Magazine edited by Lewis.)

The Enemy, 2.

Time and Western Man. London: Chatto and Windus. (Reissued by Black Sparrow Press, edited by Paul Edwards, 1993.)

The Wild Body: A Soldier of Humour and Other Stories. London: Chatto and Windus. (Incorporated in *The Complete Wild Body*, edited by Bernard Lafourcade. Black Sparrow Press, 1982.)

1928   *The Childermass: Section I*. London: Chatto and Windus.

Tarr [Revised edition]. London: Chatto and Windus.

1929   *Paleface: The Philosophy of the "Melting-Pot."* London: Chatto and Windus.

The Enemy, 3.

1930   *The Apes of God*. London: The Arthur Press. (Reissued by Black Sparrow Press, 1981.)

1930   *Satire and Fiction.* London: The Arthur Press.

1931   *Hitler.* London: Chatto and Windus.

1931   *The Diabolical Principle and the Dithyrambic Spectator.* London: Chatto and Windus.

1932   *Doom of Youth.* London: Chatto and Windus.

Filibusters in Barbary: Record of a Visit to the Sous. London: Grayson. (Partly incorporated in *Journey into Barbary*, edited by C. J. Fox, Black Sparrow Press, 1983.)

Enemy of the Stars. London: Desmond Harmsworth.

Snooty Baronet. London: Cassell. (Reissued by Black Sparrow Press, edited by Bernard Lafourcade, 1984.)

1933   *The Old Gang and the New Gang.* London: Desmond Harmsworth.

One-Way Song. London: Faber and Faber.

1934   *Men Without Art.* London: Cassell. (Reissued by Black Sparrow Press, edited by Seamus Cooney, 1987.)

1936   *Left Wings over Europe: or, How to Make a War about Nothing.* London: Jonathan Cape.

1937   *Count Your Dead: They Are Alive!* London: Lovat Dickson.

The Revenge for Love. London: Cassell. (Reissued by Black Sparrow Press, edited by Reed Way Dasenbrock, 1991.)

Blasting and Bombardiering. London: Eyre and Spottiswoode.

1938   *The Mysterious Mr. Bull.* London: Robert Hale.

1939   *The Jews: Are They Human?* London: George Allen and Unwin Ltd.

Wyndham Lewis the Artist, from Blast *to Burlington House.* London: Laidlaw and Laidlaw.

The Hitler Cult. London: Dent.

1940   *America, I Presume.* New York: Howell, Soskin and Co.

1941   *Anglosaxony: A League That Works.* Toronto: The Ryerson Press.

The Vulgar Streak. London: Robert Hale Ltd. (Reissued by Black Sparrow Press, edited by Paul Edwards, 1985.)

1948   *America and Cosmic Man.* London: Nicholson and Watson Ltd.

1950   *Rude Assignment: a Narrative of My Career Up-To-Date.* London: Hutchinson. (Reissued by Black Sparrow Press, edited by Toby Foshay, 1984.)

1951   *Rotting Hill.* London: Methuen. (Reissued by Black Sparrow Press, edited by Paul Edwards, 1986.)

1952   *The Writer and the Absolute.* London: Methuen and Co.

1954   *Self Condemned.* London: Methuen. (Reissued by Black Sparrow Press, edited by Rowland Smith, 1983.)

1954   *The Demon of Progress in the Arts.* London: Methuen.

1955   *The Human Age: Book Two: Monstre Gai; Book Three: Malign Fiesta.* London: Methuen.

1956   *The Red Priest.* London: Methuen.

1963   *The Letters of Wyndham Lewis.* Edited by W. K. Rose. London: Methuen.

1969   *Wyndham Lewis on Art: Collected Writings 1913–1956.* Edited by Walter Michel and C. J. Fox. London: Thames and Hudson.

1985   *Pound/Lewis: The Letters of Ezra Pound and Wyndham Lewis.* Edited by Timothy Materer. London: Faber and Faber.

1989   *Creatures of Habit and Creatures of Change: Essays on Art, Literature and Society 1914–1956.* Edited by Paul Edwards. Santa Rosa: Black Sparrow Press.

INDEX

The following conventions have been used: "n" refers to an entry in the Explanatory Notes for the specified page number. When printed in boldface (thus: **n**), the note contains bibliographical details. Notes to the Afterword are cited by the number of the page on which they are printed. In general, Explanatory Notes and notes to the Afterword are only indexed where they contain bibliographical references or references that are not predictable from the context of the passages to which they are keyed. Quotations are indicated by "q" (or "qq" for more than one quotation) following the page number. References to the Table of Variants in the Textual Appendix are indicated by the page number of the entry in the Table, followed by "v." Epigraphs are indicated by "e."

Abélard, P., 291
Action Française, 119v, 490
Agrippa, Cornelius, 348
Aiken, Conrad, 511
    "Mr. Lewis and the Time
      Beast," 511q
Alexander, B. D.
    A Short History of
      Philosophy, 132n
Alexander, Samuel, xv–xvii, 12,
    15, 47, 82, 84, 109, 138,
    147–51, 152, 158, 163–65, 169,
    174, 176, 179, 182, 190, 197,
    198, 199, 207–15, 209v, 218,
    221, 224, 236, 240, 242, 245,
    307, 310, 347, 359, 361, 363,
    369, 386, 388, 397, 408–09,
    411–18, 416v, 421–22,
    424–42, 445–46, 448–49,
    472–74, 478, 492, 497, 531,
    532, 535, 536–37, 539–40, 547,
    554–56, 557–58, 560, 562
    Space, Time and Deity, xv,
      xviqq, 84, 147q & n, 152,
      163–64q, 207–08q, 209–10q,
      215q, 242q, 359–60qq,
      386q, 410q, 413–18qq,
      422q, 424–25qq, 427–33qq,
      437–41qq, 446q, 492, 531q,

      536q, 540q, 554–56qq,
      558q, 560q
    "Theism and Pantheism,"
      433q & **n**
Alexandrians, 134, 154
Amenhotep, 24
Anaxagoras, 258, 261
Anderson, Sherwood, xiv
Anselm, St., 239
Antheil, George, 39, 41, 42, 59
Antigonus, 92
Antisthenes, 130
Aquinas, St. Thomas, 158,
    231–32, 291, 362, 366, 370, 380
Archimedes, 7
Archytas, 7
Aristides, 114
Aristotle, 154, 174, 257, 258, 261,
    270, 289, 319, 370, 378, 440,
    511, 534
    Metaphysics, 361v, 370
Arlen, Michael, 57
Arnold, Matthew, 10, 34, 375,
    476–77, 478, 504
    Culture and Anarchy, 34n
    Empedocles on Etna, 476,
      504q
    Literature and Dogma, 10 &
      n, 375n

Printed August 1993 in Santa Barbara &
Ann Arbor for the Black Sparrow Press
by Mackintosh Typography & Edwards
Brothers Inc. Text set in Palatino by
Words Worth. Design by Barbara Martin.
This edition is published in paper
wrappers; there are 250 hardcover trade
copies; & 126 deluxe copies have been
handbound in boards by Earle Gray.

WYNDHAM LEWIS (1882–1957) was a novelist, painter, essayist, poet, critic, polemicist and one of the truly dynamic forces in literature and art in the twentieth century. He was the founder of Vorticism, the only original movement in twentieth-century English painting. The author of *Tarr* (1918), *The Lion and the Fox* (1927), *Time and Western Man* (1927, 1993), *The Apes of God* (1930), *The Revenge for Love* (1937), and *Self Condemned* (1954), Lewis was ranked highly by his important contemporaries: "the most fascinating personality of our time . . . the most distinguished living novelist" (T. S. Eliot), "the only English writer who can be compared to Dostoevsky" (Ezra Pound).

PAUL EDWARDS lives in Cambridge, England. He works as an occasional part-time lecturer and supervisor at Cambridge and London Universities, and as a tutor for the Open University. He has edited several of Wyndham Lewis's books for Black Sparrow Press. He was a member of the organizing committee for the exhibition "Wyndham Lewis: Art and War" held at the Imperial War Museum in London by the Wyndham Lewis Memorial Trust in 1992, and is the author of the accompanying book, *Wyndham Lewis: Art and War* (London: Lund Humphries, 1992).